GW00459249

INTRODUCTION SIMON DIFFORD

Sauce Guide to Cocktails is published once every six months, thus allowing the inclusion of newly discovered cocktails and constant updating of established recipes. This is our fourth volume with some 150 new drinks, bringing the total up to over 1,500. Once again I'd like to thank the many amateur cocktail makers and professional bartenders who've emailed me their recipes and suggestions. Please keep them coming - with your help the updating of this guide every six months ensures a vitality that sets it apart from more traditional, staid cocktail tomes.

There are often different versions of drinks that share the same name; I've used the version(s) I believe to be the best. Some drinks may have originally been created using brands other than those stated, or with slightly differing proportions. Occasionally recipes have been 'interpreted' in order to make them simpler and to avoid obscure ingredients. I have endeavoured to credit drink inventors even where recipes vary slightly from their original creation.

Originally for my own benefit, I recently started grading recipes one to five as I tried them. However, I thought you may be interested to see what I consider outstanding (five) or acceptable (three), including my own creations, so these grades now feature above those recipes. I've also graded the bars within our new bar section. As with the cocktails, these grades reflect my own tastes – yours may be very different. Please let me know.

Cheers

Simon Difford
simon@SauceGuides.com

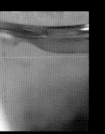

 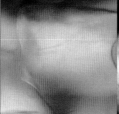 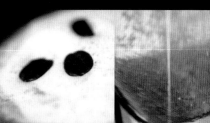

sauceguides would like to thank
ARCH 635, Clapham for the
venue used for this cover.

Please note
- This guide is intended for adults of legal drinking age.
- Please enjoy alcohol and cocktails in a responsible manner.
- Consumption of alcohol in excess can be harmful to your health.
- The high sugar levels in some cocktails may mask their alcohol content.
- Please do not consume cocktails and drive or operate machinery.
- Great care should be exercised when combining flames and alcohol.
- Consumption of raw and unpasteurised eggs may be harmful to health.
- Please follow the alcohol content guidelines included in this guide where a shot is equal to 25ml or 1 US fluid ounce (29.6ml) at most. A 25ml measure of spirit at 40% alc./vol. is equal to 1 unit of alcohol. Most men can drink up to three to four units of alcohol a day and most women can drink up to two to three units of alcohol a day with out significant risks to their health.
- Women who are trying to conceive or who are pregnant should avoid getting drunk and are advised to consume no more than one to two units of alcohol once or twice a week.

sauceguides® are:
CEO Valerie Steele-Colton, **Author & Publisher** Simon Difford, **Art Director** Dan Malpass, **Cover Photography** Naki **Cocktail Photography** Rob Lawson.
Published by Sauce Guides Limited, 11 Plough Yard, Shoreditch, London, EC2A 3LP. **Email:** simon@SauceGuides.com SAUCEGUIDE is a registered trademark in UK, Europe, USA, Australia and other countries and may not be used without written permission. All other trademarks are the property of their respective owners and are used in this publication under licence. All material ©Sauce Guides Limited 2003 all rights reserved. The views expressed in SAUCEGUIDE TO COCKTAILS are not necessarily the view of Sauce Guides Limited. While every effort is made to ensure the accuracy of information contained in this publication at the time of going to press, no responsibility can be accepted for errors or omissions and Sauce Guides Limited specifically disclaim any implied warranties of merchantability or fitness for a particular purpose. The advice and strategies contained herein may not be suitable for your situation. Softback magazine
Soft back: ISSN 1475 6560, Hard back: ISBN 0-9546174-0-1

BRITAIN'S TOP TEN COCKTAILS

1
BLOODY MARY

2
SEA BREEZE

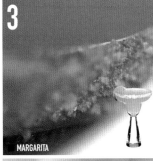

3
MARGARITA

4
LONG ISLAND ICED TEA

5
CAIPIRINHA

COCKTAIL CULTURED
WHAT'S IN AND WHAT'S GOING OUT

THE TOP FIFTY RETRO COCKTAILS

The old classics that have survived the test of time - I've not included many of the simplest mixed drinks such as the G&T and Screwdriver as many would argue they're not cocktails as they contain only two ingredients.

✪ Drinks that transcend fashion – safe bar calls ▲ Drinks becoming fashionable – show you're in the know
★ Popular drinks of the moment – high street fashionable cocktails ● Famous but seldom drunk - everyone knows the name but...
▼ Drinks becoming / already unfashionable – order discreetly

● **Americano** – a new generation is discovering Campari, will they also take to this classic?

● **Aviation** – akin to a gin based Daiquiri, hopefully this will ride gin's newfound popularity.

★ **Batida** – first we discovered the Caipirinha, now it's the Batida's turn.

★ **Bellini** – traditionally made with peach but now flavoured with all manner of fruits.

● **Between the Sheets** – silly name but a great drink all the same.

★ **Blood & Sand** – even people who don't like Scotch love this cocktail.

▲ **Bloody Mary** – even tastes like it should cure a hangover, sadly it rarely does.

● **Bobby Burns** – so few young people in the UK like Scotch, I fear this drink is doomed.

▼ **Brandy Alexander** – a nice, spicy, creamy drink but not a particularly cool bar call.

● **Bronx** – said to be the first cocktail to use fruit juice. Now, sadly, all but forgotten.

▼ **Bucks Fizz (& Grand Mimosa)** – served flat and warm once too often at weddings.

▲ **Caipirinha** – this South American classic has taken Europe by storm.

★ **Champagne Cocktail** – potentially a great way to ruin good Champagne.

▲ **Collins (John & Joe)** – Wonderfully refreshing whatever the base spirit.

● **Clover Leaf (& Club)** – This Philadelphia classic should appeal to modern palates.

▲ **Cuba Libre** – More often ordered as a rum and cola. There are better things to do with rum.

✪ **Daiquirí (Natural & On-the-rocks)** – one my own favourites (try in place of above).

▼ **Daiquirí (Frozen or Fruit)** – suffering from connotations of 70s fluffiness.

● **Dark & Stormy** – a dark rum based Mule with masses of flavour.

● **Fish House Punch** – another great drink to come out of Philadelphia – sadly forgotten.

● **Gibson** – the Martini with cleavage, may leave you with bad breath.

● **Gimlet** – the kind of drink Bond would order if off his usual Martini.

● **Gin Fizz** – a smoothed gin Collins with a frothy head.

▼ **Irish Coffee** – a cream moustache suits Melanie Sykes but few others.

▼ **Kir & Kir Royale** – suffering from being badly served at receptions.

▲ **Long Island Iced Tea** – this multi-spirit based drink is still as popular as ever.

▲ **Mai Tai** - Trader Vic's fruity rum concoction has found wide appeal.

✪ **Manhattan (Dry, Perfect & Sweet)** – growing on the back of Bourbon's UK growth.

✪ **Margarita (Straight-up & On-the-rocks)** – Tequila meets mass market sophistication.

▼ **Margarita (Frozen)** – has suffered at the hands of many a Tex-Mex.

✪ **Martini (Dry, Traditional & Vodkatini)** – benefits from James Bond promotion.

✪ **Mint Julep** – this drink has come a long way since reaching Britain in 1837.

▼ **Moscow Mule** – not the same since the Smirnoff alcopop in the copper coloured bottle.

▲ **Mojito** – when made well this is a great summer's drink.

✪ **Old Fashioned** – a manly way to drink diluted, sweetened and spiced Bourbon.

▼ **Pimms Classic** – too jolly hockey sticks and croquet for its own good.

★ **Pisco Punch** – benefiting from promotion by Dale DeGroff both here and in the US.

★ **Pisco Sour** – this traditional South American drink has at last travelled to the UK.

● **Planter's Punch** – this dark rum punch patiently waits to be the next big thing.

● **Rickey (Gin & Vodka)** - basically a short Collins. People seem to prefer the tall version.

● **Rob Roy (Affinity)** – a Scotch based Manhattan, suffers from being more challenging.

★ **Rum Punch** – promising Caribbean laid back fun and sun.

● **Rusty Nail** - everybody knows the name but few have tried what is a great drink.

▼ **Sangria** – another casualty of the Tex-Mex chainsaw massacre.

★ **Sazerac** - people are discovering this sophisticated old-fashioned sipper.

★ **Sidecar** – cognac may once again become fashionable - it's expensive enough.

▼ **Singapore Sling** – many recipes, sadly mostly badly made.

✪ **Sour (Amaretto, Brandy, Vodka & Whiskey)** – a poor imitation without fresh egg white.

▼ **Spritzer** – akin to ordering "a reduced fat white wine".

▼ **Zombie** – few risk ordering this heady mix of rums.

BRITAIN'S FIFTY GREATEST CONTEMPORARY COCKTAILS

Modern day drinks which appear most often on UK cocktail lists. Interestingly at least seven of these are credited to one man, the UK's cocktail guru, Mr Dick Bradsell.

✪ Drinks that transcend fashion – safe bar calls   ▲ Drinks becoming fashionable – show you're in the know
★ Popular drinks of the moment – high street fashionable cocktails   ● Famous but seldom drunk - everyone knows the name but...
▼ Drinks becoming / already unfashionable – order discreetly

▲ **Apple Martini** – one of New York's most popular cocktails hits the UK.

▲ **B-52** – order a round and watch the bartender cringe.

★ **B-55** – make your mates as well as the bartender cringe.

▲ **Berry Caipirinha (& other fruits)** – fruity vodka variation on the Caipirinha.

▲ **Black 'N' Blue Caipirovska** – vodka based berry version of a Caipirinha.

▲ **Bramble** – Dick Bradsell's contemporary classic has found mass appeal.

★ **Breakfast Martini** – Martinis flavoured with conserves are now all the rage.

▲ **Caipirovska** – appeals to those after a bland Caipirinha.

▼ **Cape Codder** – few realise this is simply a vodka & cranberry with a squeeze of lime.

▲ **Carol Channing** – Dick Bradsell's answer to the Kir Royale.

▲ **Chimayo** – this simple to make Tequila drink is widely listed and by default ordered.

▼ **Chocolate Martini** – the first of the neo-martinis to fall from favour.

▲ **Cosmopolitan** - Carrie Bradshaw may have moved on but her fans are still catching up.

▲ **El Diablo** – translates to 'devilishly good' - very popular although not quite that good.

★ **Elderflower Collins** – many cool bars claim the invention of this newly hip drink.

★ **Espresso Martini** – for drinkers who like stimulation with their alcohol. Forget vodka Red Bull.

▲ **French Martini** – the sweet, fruity neo-martini that appeals to Martini beginners.

★ **Frisky Bison** – a great, well balanced cocktail that's finding new friends.

▲ **Fruit Margarita (various fresh fruit flavours)** – just as long as it's not served frozen.

▼ **Harvey Wallbanger** – a tad 70s but this spruced up vodka and orange could come back.

▲ **Hedgerow Sling** – long fruity and refreshing with a great name – much copied.

★ **Honey Berry Sour** – the name says it all and ensures it flies off of bar menus.

▲ **Jamaican Mule** – has kicked the Moscow Mule and is reason enough to buy spiced rum

★ **Ja-Mora** – much promoted by friends of the two influential bartenders that created it.

▲ **Killer Punch** – a long and fruity innocuous drink that sounds hard, is actually a wimp.

▲ **Lychee Martini** – thought to have heralded from New York, now popular here.

▲ **Lynchburg Lemonade** – the thinking man's alternative to Jack & cola.

▼ **Madras** – this dry version of a Seabreeze lacks the spice its name promises.

▲ **Melon Martini (& Watermelon)** – bar owners love the G.P., drinkers love the fruity taste.

▲ **Metropolitan** – this currant flavoured Cosmo is popular both sides of the Atlantic.

▲ **Mitch Martini** – created in the first Match Bar, this wonderful drink is now even in TGIs.

▲ **Mocha Martini** – Starbucks popularised the coffee which drives this great cocktail.

▼ **Piña Colada** – struggling with a fluffy 70s 'Del Boy' image but still a great drink.

★ **Polish Martini** – tangy balance of flavours by Dick Bradsell – increasing in popularity.

▲ **Raspberry Collins** – the Collins and indeed flavoured Collins' are the hit of the noughties.

▲ **Raspberry Martini** – another of the many popular fruit driven modern Martinis.

▲ **Raspberry Mule** – fruity with a hint of ginger spice offers wide appeal.

★ **Rude Cosmopolitan** – Tequila based Cosmo offers a popular alternative to the original.

▲ **Russian Spring Punch** - yet another of Dick Bradsell's fashionable concoctions.

▲ **Sake'tini** – this cocktail is riding the Asian-fusion wave.

▼ **Seabreeze** – this simple drink is simply overexposed and now a tad naff.

▼ **Sex on the Beach** – better to get sand in your privates than be overheard ordering one.

★ **Tetanka** – wonderfully simple and yet complex tasting. Sure to grow in popularity.

★ **Treacle** – it's hard to cram more flavour into an Old-Fashioned glass. Great drink.

▼ **TVR** – Tequila, vodka and Redbull – need I say more?

▲ **Uncle Vanya** – sweet and sour blackcurrant – popular across the UK.

★ **Vanilla Daiquiri** – my absolute favourite drink. Others are now joining me.

★ **White Russian (& Black Russian)** – young drinkers are discovering this 70s classic.

★ **Wibble** – this gin and sloe gin combo is finding its way onto more menus.

▼ **Woo Woo** – like ordering a Babycham but without the irony.

6   ■ COSMOPOLITAN

7   KIR ROYALE

8   ■ DAIQUIRI

9   IRISH COFFEE

10   MOJITO

PRECISE FIGURES ON THE UK'S BESTSELLING COCKTAILS SIMPLY AREN'T AVAILABLE, SO THE FOLLOWING LIST REFLECTS THE ACTUAL SALES OF A NUMBER OF OUTLETS AND THE OPINIONS OF BAR AND RESTAURANT MANAGERS ACROSS THE COUNTRY. IGNORING SIMPLE MIXED DRINKS SUCH AS THE GIN & TONIC, THE BLOODY MARY WINS THE AWARD MAINLY DUE TO ITS WIDESPREAD AVAILABILITY IN OUTLETS FROM OLD BOOZERS TO MODERN COCKTAIL LOUNGES. IF YOU RUN A BAR OR RESTAURANT I'D LOVE TO KNOW YOUR TOP TEN SELLERS. SIMON@SAUCEGUIDE.COM

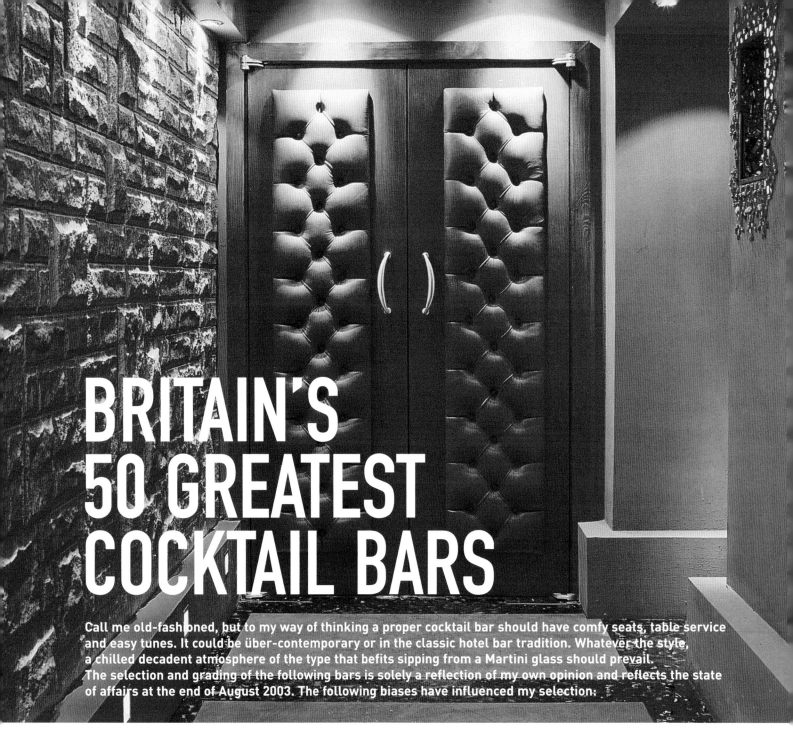

BRITAIN'S 50 GREATEST COCKTAIL BARS

Call me old-fashioned, but to my way of thinking a proper cocktail bar should have comfy seats, table service and easy tunes. It could be über-contemporary or in the classic hotel bar tradition. Whatever the style, a chilled decadent atmosphere of the type that befits sipping from a Martini glass should prevail. The selection and grading of the following bars is solely a reflection of my own opinion and reflects the state of affairs at the end of August 2003. The following biases have influenced my selection:

LOUNGES

The fifty cocktail bars I've picked over the following pages are mostly of the upscale lounge genre but there are a few very notable exceptions – for instance Mojo in Leeds.

CLUBS

The average club struggles to serve a cold beer or a simple G&T with a decent amount of ice, let alone a cocktail to die for. However, there are some exceptions which survive my lounge bar favouritism.

RESTAURANT LICENCES

I've avoided listing bars with restaurant licences where the service of alcohol is dependent upon on dining. That said, I love snacking while drinking and have favoured bars that offer at least tapas-style snacks.

CHAIN BARS

Chains of anything struggle to match the standards and style of one-off enterprises and although there are many chains of bars where reasonable cocktails are available, it is rare to find even small chains offering consistently great drinks made from fresh quality ingredients. The few I've selected here have a style of their own and tend to staffed by career bartenders that care.

MEMBERS CLUBS

I make no apologies for including a number of members only bars. The best of these keep their membership happy and usually fee paying by offering excellent drinks and service. Your bank manager and their membership committee may bar your (and my) entry, but that doesn't stop them being places of excellence.

PRICE

By their nature most of the bars selected serve drinks that can hardly be described as cheap. The old adage is true, "you get what you pay for" – especially in London. If you want superb cocktails served in homely surroundings at bargain prices, I suggest you buy the ingredients, follow the recipes in this guide and enjoy them in the comfort of your own home.

YOUR FEEDBACK PLEASE

I make more than a thousand bar visits a year in my quest to find new recipes, cocktail trends and great bars. You, the readers of this guide visit, and indeed work in, many times that number and I greatly value your feedback. Has a bar that I've selected recently gone down hill? Has one improved? Do you agree with my selection, review and grading? Have I missed a truly great bar? Your feedback and any new bars that have opened since going to press will be considered for Sauceguide to Cocktails vol. 5 (published in March 2004).
Please reply to: simon@sauceguides.com

AKBAR

●●●●○

The Red Fort, 77 Dean Street, Soho, London, W1D 3SH

Tel: 020 7437 2525, **www.**redfort.co.uk/akbar
Hours: Mon-Fri 12:00-01:00, Sat 17:30-01:00

Entry:	Arrive early late in the week
Dress code:	Designer jeans and T-shirts
Clientele:	Style set, media, music
Cocktails:	31 priced: £6.00 - £7.50
Must try:	Perfect Alibi
Bar snacks:	Mughal court food (posh Indian)

Soho's famous Red Fort first opened in 1983 and became instantly renowned for its stylish design and a quality of food and service aeons beyond that of your average Tandoori. A serious fire in the kitchen one night closed the place down and a smart new look was evident when it reopened in October 2001 after a complete refurbishment.

With this phoenix-like reincarnation came 'Akbar', the superb lounge bar in the basement, which takes its name from the greatest of the Mughal emperors. The small (70 capacity) room has simple but lush décor with two intimate booths tunnelled under Dean Street.

Tasty bar snacks should be washed down with one of the sublime cocktails which exploit typical Indian flavours such as date, jasmine, ginger, rosewater, mango and sweet spices.

Akbar's clientele are predominantly the young Soho set drawn from local media companies. The bijou space can get packed and the atmosphere DJ charged, but I prefer the quieter early week Red Fort.

APARTMENT 195

●●●●○

195 King's Road (above Henry J Beans), London, SW3 5ED

Tel: 020 7351 5195
Hours: Mon-Sat 16:00-23:00, Sun 16:00-22:30

Entry:	Members & guests only
Dress code:	Smart casual (no trainers)
Clientele:	Well dressed & affluent
Cocktails:	27, priced £15.00-£26.00
Must try:	Pineapple Mojito
Bar snacks:	Served all hours

Above and partly owned by Henry J Beans, this three roomed 'apartment' in its listed building houses a very homely den to which members gain access by swiping their membership card, so releasing the door.

I could get very used to living here. The lounge is full of leather sofas and an open fire burns in winter. The salon is ideal for hosting a dinner party while the TV room shows old movies and sport. Best of all, this apartment comes with its own all-female staff dressed in very sexy uniforms and serving amazing cocktails. Altogether a man's dream - home from home.

Centre stage in the lounge is the burnished copper, star encrusted bar salvaged from Criterion in Piccadilly Circus. Here the girls, led by manager Charlotte Voisey, mix an interesting array of classic and bespoke cocktails delivered by attentive table service. Being predominantly locals, the thirty-something clientele are both well-heeled and well-dressed.

THE APARTMENT

●●●○○

2 Donegal Square, West Belfast, County Antrim, N.I., BT1 6JA

Tel: 028 9050 9777, **www.**apartmentbelfast.com
Hours: Mon-Fri 08:00-01:00, Sat 09:00-01:00, Sun 12:00-00:00

Entry:	Over 21, no tattoos, no vests
Dress code:	Mixed but urban cool
Clientele:	Partying 25-45 year olds
Cocktails:	40, priced £3.75-£5.50
Must try:	Rhubarb Daiquiri
Bar snacks:	Cajun spiced wedges, cod goujons, cheesy nachos etc.

Set within a grand building opposite the even grander City Hall, The Apartment is entered via a continental style café. During the day this serves shoppers with coffee, pastries and the like which can be taken upstairs to The Apartment proper where you can sit on one of the comfy sofas and watch the people of Belfast through the floor to ceiling windows.

The bar is split into two distinct rooms. The first, with its light box illuminated Belfast skyline and open kitchen, has a restaurant feel. The second room features a curtained wall, comfy seating and a true lounge vibe.

A friendly, skilled bar team use fresh ingredients to make a good selection of cocktails including well executed classics. The bar's own creations, mostly named after desirable addresses, are tasty if a tad on the sweet side. Unfortunately, the skills of the barstaff are generally unappreciated by the young, upwardly mobile crowd who appear to favour beer.

ATLANTIC BAR & GRILL

●●●○○

20 Glasshouse Street, Piccadilly, London, W1B 5DJ

Tel: 020 7734 4888, **www.**gruppo.co.uk
Hours: Mon-Fri 12:00-03:00, Sat 17:00-03:00, Sun 17:00-22:30

Entry:	Few turned away these days
Dress code:	Smart with funky exceptions
Clientele:	Mixed – but not poor
C-tails:	40 priced: £6.90 - £14.00
Must try:	Thai Lady
Bar snacks:	Platters and snacks

This splendid art deco ballroom beneath the Regent Palace Hotel dates back to 1919, the height of the ocean liner era. Its high coffered ceiling and gridded network of columns, mouldings and friezes were for years covered during its incarnation as the Cactus discotheque. In April 1994, Oliver Peyton restored the room to its former glory and opened London's foremost lounge bar. To the side of the main bar is the smaller Dick's Bar, named after London's cocktail guru Dick Bradsell, its first manager.

Years later, lesser ventures have come and gone, but the Atlantic rolls on. Although drinks aren't quite what they were in yesteryear, this impressive venue still boasts some talented bar staff and an interesting cocktail list.

In its heyday few bars could compete with the Atlantic. Its door staff had a reputation for being choosy and the place was packed with A-listers. Today the door policy is more relaxed and business and city types replace the celebs.

AURA KITCHEN & BAR

●●●●○

48-49 St James' Street (corner of Piccadilly), London, SW1A 1JT

Tel: 020 7499 9999
Hours: Mon-Tue 17:00-00:30, Wed-Sat 17:00-03:00 (non-members must leave after 11pm)

Entry:	Members have priority
Dress code:	Glamorous
Clientele:	City boys, Essex girls and gorgeous models
Cocktails:	63, priced £5.00 - £9.00
Must try:	Pornstar
Bar snacks:	Oysters, pâté, steak sandwich, fries etc.

Hidden in a basement beneath Caviar House lies a one room restaurant and bar lined with deep plum leather banquettes and mirrors. Other design features include two chandeliers that previously hung in Claridge's Ballroom, a sea mural complete with cruising luxury yacht and projected films over the bar.

The concept behind Aura echoes that of Amsterdam's famous Supper Club - once diners have finished their dessert, the lights are dimmed, the music turned up and the restaurant transformed into a club. Even the tables here are lowered by hydraulics to a height befitting that of a club rather than a dining room.

If drinking at the bar early evening rather than dining you're bound to feel like you're missing out. However, the drinks are good, as is the friendly service and once the lights are dimmed and the non-members ushered out, the party kicks off.

BALTIC

●●●●○

74 Blackfriars Road (corner The Cut), Waterloo, SE1 8HA

Tel: 020 7928 1111, **www.**balticrestaurant.co.uk
Hours: Mon-Fri 12:00-23:00, Sat 18:00-23:00, Sun 12:00-22:30

Entry:	No door policy
Dress code:	Office attire to hip
Clientele:	Locals & those in the know
Cocktails:	24 priced £4.50 - £6.50
Must try:	B.S.P. (Baltic Spring Punch)
Bar snacks:	Blinis & other Polish snacks

Lying behind the narrow frontage of Baltic is a deceptively large modern Polish bar and a vast barn-like restaurant. Baltic is noted for its extensive list of Polish vodkas and beers; the huge glass demi-johns behind the bar are home to their in-house flavoured vodkas. The Karamalowka (caramel) and Wisniówka (cherry) are particularly worth a try, whether neat or as part of one of the many outstanding cocktails on the list.

Poland is bar snack heaven and it's surprising that blinis haven't found their way onto more menus. The Slavs seem to have an obsession with beetroot, the purple tuber the UK forgot. They manage to turn beetroot broth into a delicacy, so be sure to try the Ukranian barszcz yourself.

Baltic draws a friendly crowd of locals and after work drinkers who are joined by travelling foodies and fun seekers in the know.

BLANCH HOUSE

●●●●○

17 Atlingworth Street, Kemp Town, Brighton, BN2 1PL

Tel: 01273 603 504, www.blanchhouse.co.uk
Hours: Mon-Sat 19:00-23:00

Entry:	Subject to space and your looking friendly
Dress code:	Funky casual
Clientele:	Funky thirty-somethings
Cocktails:	46, priced £5.50 - £8.00
Must try:	George Edward Martini
Bar snacks:	Tapas

Maybe it's just my romantic notion of speakeasies during Prohibition, but there's something special about a bar that's hidden to all but a few in the know. Lying a pebble's throw from Brighton's seafront, hidden behind the façade of an ordinary looking townhouse, is just such a bar.

Back in 2001 husband and wife, Chris Edwardes and Amanda Blanch, mortgaged their lives to buy what was a shabby B&B and turn it into the dream that is Blanch House – a very funky hotel with twelve individually themed bedrooms, a noted restaurant and a tiny bar.

A mere forty drinkers are enough to fill the intimate bar with its warm, cosy atmosphere complete with Tom the cat curled up in the corner. Superb classic and contemporary cocktails are consumed by a decadent crowd of hotel residents, locals and visitors to the restaurant.

Staying at Blanch House is like sleeping at a pop star's seaside retreat. Drinking in the bar is like being at a mate's house party.

BLOODY MARY'S

●●●●○

28 Vinicombe Street, West End, Glasgow, G12 8BE

Tel: 0141 560 8004, www.bloodymarys.co.uk
Hours: Sun-Thur 11:00-23:00, Fri-Sat 11:00-00:00

Entry:	No door policy
Dress code:	Hip casual
Clientele:	Arty West End crowd
Cocktails:	52, priced £3.00 - £5.00
Must try:	Bloody Mary
Bar snacks:	Modern British Dishes

As the name suggests, Bloody Mary's is a cocktail bar in the West End of Glasgow. It is the one bar in this part of town in which I can sip a Martini without feeling like a southern Jessie.

The awnings, white walls, large windows and outside chairs and tables give this bright airy bar the feel of a continental café. The use of wood throughout and the stone back bar help create a warm cosy atmosphere.

The glass shelves of the back bar heave with premium spirits and liqueurs, the quality of which continues to the house pouring brands. The extensive cocktail list includes many classics but also has a number of good drinks specific to Mary's. Local savvy thirty-somethings are the main clientele and it's good to see a staggeringly high proportion drinking cocktails rather than the more predictable beer.

BLUE BAR

●●●●◐

The Berkeley Hotel, Wilton Place, Knightsbridge, SW1X 7RL

Tel: 020 7201 1680, www.savoy-group.co.uk
Hours: Mon-Sat 11:00-01:00

Entry:	Past uniformed doormen
Dress code:	Can be casual, must be expensive
Clientele:	Media, business & celebs of all ages
Cocktails:	20 priced: £10.00 - £12.50
Must try:	Wilton Martini
Bar snacks:	Modern tapas - bite sized (but gorgeous)

Be careful to turn left as you enter the Berkeley Hotel lobby - turn right and you'll hit another bar altogether and probably be disappointed. The Blue Bar is aptly named with its beach hut blue walls. Cherubs and floral woodcarvings drip from the ceiling and surround the fish-eye mirrors, while the black leather floor adds a further touch of loucheness.

Among the exquisite décor highly skilled bartenders in white jackets serve some excellent classic cocktails and some of their own creations. Should the tasty nibbles provided with each drink not hit the spot, there's slightly more substantial 'modern tapas' available.

This five star venue attracts five star money, so expect cosmetically challenged ladies of leisure perusing the impressive Champagne list which includes magnums of Dom Pérignon 73 at a heady £975 a pop. There are also a good few young professionals who heard that Madge dropped by once.

DETROIT

●●●●○

35 Earlham Street, Covent Garden, London, WC2 9LD

Tel: 020 7240 2662, www.detroit-bar.com
Hours: Mon-Fri 17:00-00.00, Sat 18:00-00:00

Entry:	Open to all subject to space
Dress code:	Casual and relaxed
Clientele:	Everyone
Cocktails:	40 priced: £4.90 - £10.00
Must try:	Robin Hood
Bar snacks:	Spring rolls, fried calamari, bruschetta

Detroit is housed in a cavernous rabbit warren of rooms in a basement close to Covent Garden's Seven Dials. The interior, and come to that some of the drinkers, look like something out of a Star Wars movie. Detroit attracts a very esoteric and interesting crowd.

In its time Detroit has been home to some of London's best-known bartenders and has a justified reputation for outstanding cocktails. The ever-evolving list bears evidence of those bartenders who have passed through its portals and left their mark. The narrow shelves of the back bar groan with a truly superb range of bottles, the palette from which talented bartenders work their magic. The food is also surprisingly good.

Detroit is best midweek when it has a relaxed lounge atmosphere. Weekends can be hectic with a DJ driven buzz. Find yourself a dark corner in one of the tunnel like rooms, a cocktail menu and try something new.

ECLIPSE

●●●●○

111 Walton St, SW3 2PH; 108 New Kings Rd, SW6 4LY; 186 Kensington Pk Rd, W11 2ES; 158 Old Brompton Rd, SW5 0BA & 57 High St, SW19 5EE.

Tel: 020 7581 0123, www.eclipse-ventures.com
Hours: Vary by branch

Entry:	No discernible door policy
Dress code:	Stylishly relaxed
Clientele:	Varies greatly by branch
Cocktails:	33 priced: £5.00 - £9.00 (varies by branch)
Must try:	Honey Bee
Bar snacks:	Vary by branch

The Chelsea branch was the original version of what is now a chain of five. This cosy little lounge bar used to be not much bigger than a large cupboard, but since a knock through to next door its capacity has doubled. Part of the charm of Eclipse was enforced intimacy due to its meagre proportions and the extension has not destroyed this. Indeed, the second room with its cosy corners is perhaps more snug than the original.

The other Eclipse bars can be found in Fulham, Wimbledon Village, South Kensington and Notting Hill. The clientele found in each varies greatly according to its location - Chelsea has more than its fair share of hooray Henrys, Notting Hill attracts the style set while Wimbledon has an older crowd. All are rarely empty and all have a fun atmosphere watered with some great drinks, the Passion Fruit Martini and Watermelon Martini being two of the most popular. This chain quietly continues to grow, taking its own translation of the lounge experience to other London neighbourhoods and even Cape Town.

G.E. CLUB

●●●●◐

Great Eastern Hotel, Liverpool Street, City of London, EC2M 7QN

Tel: 020 7618 7076, www.geclub.co.uk
Hours: Mon-Fri 11:00-02:00, Sat 20:00-02:00

Entry:	Members & hotel guests (membership free – if you fit)
Dress code:	Funky casual (suits not encouraged)
Clientele:	Shoreditch posse, music types, funky city crowd
Cocktails:	35 priced £4.00-£8.50
Must try:	Stairs Martini
Bar snacks:	Served all hours

Conran's beautiful Great Eastern Hotel near Liverpool Street station houses this elegant members bar which is hidden at the top of an unlikely looking staircase and behind a heavy wooden door. Leather armchairs, dark wood panelling and intimate table lamps are conducive to fat cigars, fine wines and good conversation. Late week brings DJs and a more clubby atmosphere with as many dancing as chilling. Party nights are legendary.

A good selection of both classic cocktails and new creations are all expertly produced. If the drinks menu doesn't appeal, then the daunting wine list from Aurora restaurant below is available. Food also comes from the kitchens of Aurora, so quality and choice is far better than offered by the average bar, while efficient table service means you don't even have to leave your seat. To gain membership and one of the coveted key tags schmooze an existing member.

CIRCUS

●●●●○

1 Upper James Street (corner Beak St), Soho, London, W1R 4BP

Tel: 020 7534 4000, **www.**circusbar.co.uk
Hours: Mon-Wed 12:00-01:30, Thu-Sat 12:30-03:00

Entry:	**Possible entry charge after 11pm**
Dress code:	**Magazine style pages**
Clientele:	**Media, PRs and wannabes**
Cocktails:	**32 priced: £6.00 - £8.50**
Must try:	**Eden or Threesome**
Bar snacks:	**Spring rolls to caviar & blinis**

Circus lies underneath the successful restaurant of the same name which occupies the ground floor of what was the Granada TV building on the corner of Beak Street and Golden Square. This split-level, basement, minimalist bar is a sociable and refined affair in media Soho. Black leather seating is scattered along the lengthy lower lounge which looks out onto an illuminated Japanese style garden of gravel and bamboo.

The well-stocked bar, complete with goldfish swimming in two giant test tubes, knocks out classic cocktails as well as some interesting original concoctions. The food menu is short but every bit as good as that on offer in the restaurant above.

The clientele ranges from magazine styled local media darlings to the unstylish after office crowd.

Circus enjoys a late licence Thursday through to Saturday, but I'd advise arriving early as non-members have to pay an entry charge after 11pm.

HAKKASAN

●●●●○

8 Hanway Place, Fitzrovia, London, W1T 9HD

Tel: 020 7927 7000, **www.**hakkasan.com
Hours: Mon-Wed 12:00-00:30, Thu-Sat 12:00-02:30,
Sun 12:00-00:00

Entry:	**Dinner bookings take preference**
Dress code:	**Suits to mag style pages**
Clientele:	**Business, style set & wannabes**
Cocktails:	**40 priced: all £8.00**
Must try:	**Strawberry & Basil Martini**
Bar snacks:	**Modern Oriental**

The grime of Hanway Place does little to prepare the virgin visitor for the elegance of Hakkasan with its dramatic staircase leading down to a basement lobby bathed in a baby blue neon glow. The main room's architecture is amongst the most impressive of any London restaurant with the large space divided into restaurant, lounge and bar by cage-like dark wooden latticework screens. These and the slate wall of the 16 metre bar are much copied by architectural counterfeiters who always fail to achieve Hakkasan's wow factor.

The name? 'Hakka' is a Chinese dialect and 'san' is the Japanese form of addressing someone. Hakkasan is the vision of Alan Yau, the man who also bought us Wagamama.

Hakkasan buzzes with a business led clientele enhanced by some very beautiful women and successfully cool men. They are served dim sum to die for and some highly imaginative cocktails by waitresses who look like they have been squeezed into Chinese lanterns.

HALO

●●●●○

3 Melvile Place, Edinburgh, EH3 7PR

Tel: 0131 539 8500
Hours: Mon-Fri 11:00-01:00, Sat-Sun 10:00-01:00

Entry:	**No door policy**
Dress code:	**Urban trendy**
Clientele:	**Local moneyed 30-somethings**
Cocktails:	**21 priced: £3.00 - £8.95**
Must try:	**The Diamond**
Bar snacks:	**Lunch only – try the haddock & chips.**

Football fans may be interested to know that Halo is owned by Keith Murray, son of David Murray - the owner of Murray International & Rangers Football Club. Keith likes his bar to be known as a "residential style bar" - appropriate considering its position in domesticity just outside the heart of Edinburgh's night scene. In fact Halo is something of a modern cocktail bar crossed with a local pub. The décor and drinks offering may be cocktail bar but the atmosphere is pub, enhanced by the warm welcome and the impression that the clientele and staff all known each other.

Laid out in an L-shape, Halo is tiny but homely. Design features include padded walls, distinctive modern chandeliers and a marble topped bar.

Although the cocktail list was about to be revamped when I visited, the bartenders are passionate about their trade and took positive delight in recommending some of their new concoctions. Judging from my night's sampling the new list shouldn't disappoint.

HOTEL DU VIN
●●●●○

Birmingham, Brighton, Bristol, Harrogate, Tunbridge Wells & Winchester

Tel. 01962 850 676 **www.**hotelduvin.com
Hours: Vary by branch

Entry:	Priority to residents and diners
Dress code:	Smart casual
Clientele:	Mature, civilized and wealthy
Cocktails:	67 priced: £6.50 - £9.50
Must try:	Apple Tree, Palermo
Bar snacks:	Vary - modern British

In 1994 Robin Hutson and Gerard Basset opened the first Hotel du Vin & Bistro in Winchester. Its warm welcome, individual style and acclaimed restaurant and bar ensured its overnight success. This successful formula has been replicated in the other five Hotel du Vins that have since followed.

Each hotel is designed to complement the architecture of the historic or landmark buildings in which they are housed. All the bars have a homely feel with comfy sofas, subdued warm lighting and even billiards. Extensive wine lists with both predictable and quirky bins befit the wine theme at the heart of these hotels, but the cocktails are also worthy of note and delivered to your table with attentive service.

If you find yourself in a town with a Hotel du Vin, it's a good bet that it will not only be the friendliest, warmest and most civilised bar in the locality but also have the best cocktail menu and certainly the finest wine list in town.

THE KINGLY CLUB
●●●●○

4 Kingly Court, Soho, London, W1B 5PW

Tel: 020 7287 9100, **www.**kinglyclub.co.uk
Hours: Mon-Sat 18:00-02:00, Sun 18:00-00:30

Entry:	Members & guests
Dress code:	Anything but a tie
Clientele:	Soho set
Cocktails:	51, priced £7.50 - £9.00
Must try:	Charlie's Angel
Bar snacks:	Sushi

This visually stunning bar sits in a subterranean tunnel that was once home to the legendary Pinstripe Club. This 1960s club attracted famous revellers and is claimed to be where John Profumo met Christine Keeler. However, popular history has them first meeting by the pool at Lord Astor's Cliveden country residence in Berkshire. Wherever they met, the demise of both Profumo and the Pinstripe Club followed the scandal and the site was forgotten until the opening of The Kingly Club in August 2003.

With a capacity of just 125, the small space is made to feel bigger by the use of mirrors and a white burnished, almost wet ice finish to the tunnel walls. A row of cats-eye style lights leads from the bar down the tunnel to two intimate antechambers with booth seating. At the time of going to press this club with its space age look and fish tanks was only a matter of weeks old. However, it had already forged a reputation for itself, hence its inclusion.

KU DE TA BAR
●●●○○

9 Glasshouse Street, Piccadilly, London, W1R 5RL

Tel: 020 7439 7771, **www.**elysiumlounge.co.uk
Hours: (Ku De Ta Bar) Mon-Tue 11:00-23:00,
Wed-Sat 11:00-03:00

Entry:	Bar is easy, club is hard
Dress code:	To impress
Clientele:	Moneyed and beautiful
Cocktails:	64, priced £7.50 - £8.00
Must try:	Apple & Sage Martini
Bar snacks:	Choice of platters

By day and early evening this ground floor bar under the Café Royal is entered through a dedicated door on Glasshouse Street and attracts a mixed crowd of office escapees. After 11pm both the entrance and clientele change and the bar becomes a lobby for the grandly titled Elysium club, serving as a kind of compression chamber to acclimatise the moneyed and beautiful for the club below. When Elysium is open, it and Ku De Ta must be entered via the scarlet ropes and clipboard autocrats who protect the main entrance to the Café Royal on Regent Street.

Enjoy the superb cocktails and attentive staff at Ku De Ta or reserve a table (subject to a minimum spend of £300) at Elysium where drinks are also sold by the bottle. This Indo-Persian styled club challenges the likes of Chinawhite in the fashion stakes, attracting capacity crowds of model types and city boys wanting to meet them.

LAB
●●●●◐

12 Old Compton Street, Soho, London, W1D 4TQ

Tel: 020 7437 7820, **www.**lab-bar.com
Hours: Mon-Sat 12:00-24:00, Sun 15:00-22:30

Entry:	Open to all subject to capacity
Dress code:	Practically anything goes
Clientele:	Soho set and drinks industry
Cocktails:	100+ priced: £5.50 - £15.50
Must try:	Daiquiri Noir
Bar snacks:	Food is not always available

A big name on the bar circuit and rightly so, Lab has been and continues to be home to some of the best bartenders in London. The name is a throwback to the long defunct London Academy of Bartenders, but it could be argued that this bar itself has been something of an academy of bartending excellence, even if they do insist on using granulated sugar instead of sugar syrup.

The distinctive 70s retro décor sees rounded corners far outnumbering sharp ones. Set over two floors, some describe the two long narrow bars (ground floor and basement) as intimate, others as claustrophobic. The beer and wine lists are also bijou, but if you drink anything other than a cocktail here you're missing out. If the extensive list leaves you undecided, the bartenders will helpfully oblige with a recommendation.

Lab is busy pretty much nightly and even if there is no DJ expect loud music and a pumped up atmosphere.

HUSH

●●●●○

8 Lancashire Court (off Brook Street), Mayfair, London, W1S 1EY

Tel: 020 7659 1500, www.hush.co.uk
Hours: Mon-Sat 11:00-23:00

Entry:	No door policy
Dress code:	Suits, glamour, designer jeans
Clientele:	City types & Mayfair set
Cocktails:	65 priced: £7.25 - £15.00
Must try:	Strictly Hush
Bar snacks:	Potato wedges to caviar

Hush is owned by Jamie Barber and Geoffrey Moore (son of Roger) and sits serenely in its Georgian townhouse in a cobbled courtyard that lies off Mayfair's Brook Street. Clement weather sees diners from the popular ground floor brasserie spill out onto the courtyard in a continental style.

The lounge bar and a second more upmarket restaurant known as 'Hush Up' lie at the top of a wood and Perspex staircase. The Hush lounge is a cosy den of soft furnishings, with velour banquettes and lush satin cushions. But the place to blag is the cosy wood-lined intimate boudoir that seats ten and is filled with deep cushions.

Being close to Bond Street and next to the Versace store, Hush caters for ladies who lunch and suited young gentry who gather to enjoy an array of superbly conceived cocktails mixed by a very able bar crew. All in all, a very civilised experience which can also be great fun.

ISOLA BAR

●●●○○

145 Knightsbridge, Knightsbridge, London, SW1X 7PA

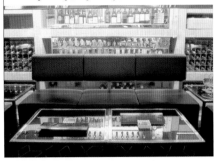

Tel: 020 7838 1044
Hours: Mon-Sat 17:00-00:00, Sun 17:00-22:30

Entry:	Can be closed for private parties
Dress code:	Office suits to glitz
Clientele:	PR/media types, locals, business
Cocktails:	42 priced: all £7.00
Must try:	Rapaska
Bar snacks:	Pizzette (small pizzas) & other Italian specialities

Above Isola, Oliver Peyton's contemporary Italian restaurant, three vast wall-to-wall, floor-to-ceiling windows form the backdrop to this bar. The contemporary design includes stainless steel columns rising to a high white ceiling, red leather bar stools and banquettes and a curiously unItalian painting of a cowboy on a rearing horse.

Cocktails are mostly original, interesting and superb. Most corners of Italy are represented in the extensive wine list and if your knowledge is lacking a range of 'tasters' provide a sample of five different wines to try.

I am something of a fan of this bar but judging by the number of people who frequent it, I'm in a minority to have even discovered it. Fortunately the large high ceilinged room is broken up by the comfy red furnishings so even when empty it doesn't appear so. Those other souls who do frequent Isola tend to be the Knightsbridge mix of business, PRs, models and those whose career is simply socialising.

KEMIA BAR

●●●●○

Momo, 25 Heddon Street (off Regent St.), W1B 4BH

Tel: 020 7434 2011
Hours: Mon-Tue: 19:00-01:00, Wed 19:00-02:00,
Thu-Sat 19:00-03:00

Entry:	Mon-Wed: invited guests, Thurs-Sat: members only
Dress code:	Expensive & gorgeous but casual
Clientele:	Elegant, classy, models
Cocktails:	37 priced: £6.50 - £7.50
Must try:	Momo Special
Bar snacks:	Mezze-style, served 7pm-11.30pm

At the end of a tiny cul-de-sac just off Regent Street, a doorway nestles alongside the fashionable Momo restaurant. Beyond a narrow, medieval, castle-like staircase leads down to a tiny basement club. Walking in for the first time is like stepping into a Bedouin's tent which has been erected in a cave where a visiting North African band and their entourage are celebrating their first number one hit.

Authentically decorated in an Algerian/Moroccan style, this low vaulted, incense burning den is lined with leather, organza and luxurious silk drapes. With its celebrated music policy the Kemia Bar is a gem for the sophisticated party-goer.

Drinks and food are in keeping with the theme, so mint is delivered by the truck load to supply cocktails such as the refreshing Momo Special or the Pepe.

The ethos behind Momo's is fun and the place is full of sophisticated, beautiful, stylish people having lots of it.

LIBRARY BAR

●●●●◐

Lanesborough Hotel, Hyde Park Corner, Mayfair, SW1X 7TA

Tel: 020 7259 5599 www.rosewoodhotels.com
Hours: 11:00-23:00 everyday (residents only after 11pm)

Entry:	Subject to space and management
Dress code:	Smart (jacket not required)
Clientele:	Rich Americans, couples, celebs
Cocktails:	102 priced: £7.00 - £13.00
Must try:	Breakfast Martini
Bar snacks:	Served all hours

This swanky bar is housed in a room that might well once have been an operating theatre. For the building that's now the Lanesborough Hotel dates back to 1719 and was formerly St George's Hospital (closed in 1980). The Lanesborough, which opened in 1991, is named after a country house that once stood on the site.

As the name suggests, this intimate and atmospheric mahogany lined bar is in the style of an old library. It is a classic hotel bar in the tradition of London's crusty private clubs, only with some young and beautiful people amongst the fat old bankers.

The refined clientele soak up the atmosphere and sip Martinis from frozen cut crystal glasses while the pianist plays in the corner. Skilled bartenders wear suits to rival those of the guests on their way to or from black-tie dinners.

If you visit be sure to say hello to the bar's celebrated manager and Inspector Cleuso lookalike, Salvatore Calabrese. Be warned - he's written a lot of cocktail books.

LIGHT BAR

●●●●○

St. Martins Hotel, St. Martins Lane, Covent Garden, WC2N 4HX

Tel: 020 7300 5599, www.ianschragerhotels.com
Hours: Mon-Sat 17:30-03:00,
Sun 17:30-22:30 (00:00 hotel residents)

Entry:	Members & hotel guests only
Dress code:	High fashion
Clientele:	Media, music, fashion
Cocktails:	53 priced: £8.05 - £10.93
Must try:	Sangria Martini
Bar snacks:	Sushi served Tuesday to Saturday

When Ian Schrager's St. Martins Hotel opened in October 1999, the original Light Bar that lay at the end of the Starck designed lobby was noted for being full of celebs, being impossible for mere mortals to access and for not having a bar. It was a bar without a bar! Waitresses took your order and a hidden bartender created your drink.

The new look Light Bar still sits at the end of the hotel's lobby, between Asia de Cuba and Tuscan restaurants. And, yes, it still has the waitress service and the hidden bar screened from view by a cabinet of antique glassware, but there's now also a very visible second bar in the middle of the room. Sofas replace the uncomfortable, wobbly high chairs that used to line the room. The bar's eponymous light filled ceiling shafts are also still there, as are the celebs, great cocktails and the door policy.

LOBBY BAR

●●●●◐

One Aldwych Hotel, 1 Aldwych, London, WC2B 4RH

Tel: 020 7300 1070, www.onealdwych.com
Hours: Mon-Sat 09:30-23:00, Sun 10:00-22:30

Entry:	No door policy
Dress code:	Suited business to extremely casual
Clientele:	Hotel guests, pre-theatre
Cocktails:	72 priced: £8.50 - £10.75
Must try:	Sujin or Tamirillo Martini
Bar snacks:	Flavoured sausages, dim sum, sushi etc.

The lobby of the boutique hotel One Aldwych is no ordinary foyer and its bar is no ordinary lobby bar. This airy grand hall with its double-height ceiling and tall arched windows on both sides oozes class. Centre stage on the polished floor is a vast sculpture by André Wallace of a hunched man rowing what looks like a bathtub with long oars. Around this are well-spaced chairs, low tables and impressive flower arrangements.

This opulence is nothing compared to the delights contained within the extensive but simply presented drinks list. Wonderfully unique cocktails using ingredients such as saffron infused gin, wine, port and fresh fruits are mixed and served to your table by friendly professional staff.

Situated in central theatreland, the Lobby Bar attracts the pre and after show crowd, local business types and glamorously wealthy hotel guests. All in all a bar with the service and grandeur that befit a hotel of this quality.

LONSDALE

● ● ● ● ●

44-48 Lonsdale Road, Notting Hill, London, W11 2DE

Tel: 020 7227 4080
Hours: Mon-Fri 18:00-00:00, Sat 12:00-00:00, Sun 12:00-23:00

Entry:	**Subject to space & management**
Dress code:	**Casual but expensive**
Clientele:	**Gorgeous, affluent locals & celebs**
Cocktails:	**46,** priced **£5.50-£8.50**
Must try:	**Basil Bramble Sling**
Bar snacks:	**Small dishes - order 1 or 2 for a snack 3 or 4 for a meal**

Originally a Truman's pub and more recently Jac's Bar this place, situated on a residential road in deepest Notting Hill, remained closed for the best part of a year. That was until brothers Charles and Adam Breeden opened one of the best lounge bars in London late in 2002.

It's not just the cocktails that have a wow factor. The interior, inspired by a photograph Charles saw of Lenny Kravitz's Miami residence, is also worthy of description. Hemispherical bubbles line the walls - bronze in the downstairs bar and chromed spun aluminium upstairs in 'Genevieve', a space named in deference to the Breedens' mother.

The sartorially elegant Henry Besant keeps an eye on both floors and on the local beautiful and stylish folk of Notting Hill who flock here. Lonsdale is hard to fault – it's full of beautiful people, drinking balanced imaginative cocktails whilst nibbling on tasty bar snacks, all served by skilled, attentive staff. Just wish I lived nearer.

LOUNGELOVER

● ● ● ● ○

1 Whitby Street (off Club Row), Shoreditch, London, E2 7DP

Tel: 020 7012 1234
Hours: Tue-Sat 18:00-00:00

Entry:	**Subject to space**
Dress code:	Casual, way-out, hip
Clientele:	Arty, music & media
Cocktails:	37 priced: £8.50 - £9.50
Must try:	Bour-berry
Bar snacks:	Served all hours

Loungelover's location in a former butcher's warehouse on a grungy, cobbled Shoreditch back street sets the scene for what resembles a designer Steptoe & Sons' yard filled with the hoard of a kleptomaniac. In fact the multitude of chandeliers and light fittings which illuminate the taxidermy, antiques and eclectic bric-a-brac was assembled by the trio of antique dealers who also own Les Trois Garçons, a highly respected and equally unique nearby restaurant.

The drinkers are as diverse and unusual as the décor, ranging from arty, media types to young bankers and solicitors who have moved into the area due to its proximity to the City. The cocktail list bound in mock-crocodile leather with its many original concoctions is also inimitable.

Loungelover would be an unusual venue to find in any location, but in London's East End, a short walk from the curry houses of Brick Lane, it is bizarre and truly superb.

THE MET BAR

● ● ● ● ○

18-19 Old Park Lane, Mayfair, London, W1K 1LB

Tel: 020 7447 5757, www.metropolitan.co.uk
Hours: Mon-Sat 10:00-03:00, Sun 10:00-22:30

Entry:	Members & hotel guests only (membership can't be bought)
Dress code:	Gorgeously casual
Clientele:	Celebs, hotel guests, media
Cocktails:	75 priced: £7.00 - £11.50
Must try:	Watermelon Martini
Bar snacks:	Nibbles from Nobu

This is the bar that changed the mould for London hotel bars and paved the way for a new scene in members clubs. When The Met first opened it was consistently rammed with A list celebs while hordes of paparazzi froze their nuts off outside.

Unfortunately, most of the celebs moved on to the next place to be seen and some of the magic was lost. While lesser bars would have relaxed their door policy, The Met stuck strictly to its members and guests only policy, a strategy that's paid off, for the celebs and that famous Met atmosphere have returned. On a good night it's like being at a friend's house party only with great DJs, bartenders and the odd TV presenter.

The décor remains unchanged with the original black and red American diner-style booths and tables still crammed into a surprisingly small space. But The Met is about the music, the cocktails and the atmosphere, all of which can be fantastic.

MANDARIN BAR

●●●◐○

Mandarin Oriental Hotel, 66 Knightsbridge, Knightsbridge, SW1X 7LA

Tel: 020 7235 2000, **www.mandarinoriental.com**
Hours: Daily 11:00-02:00

Entry:	No obvious door policy
Dress code:	Business suits & Prada darlings
Clientele:	Guests, City types & wealthy set
Cocktails:	49 priced: £10.00 - £11.00
Must try:	Nutty Kentucky
Bar snacks:	Oriental platters

The Mandarin Oriental was built in 1889 but was only recently restored to its former grandeur. With this refurbishment came the opulent Mandarin Bar which lies at the back left side of the grand marble-lined lobby.

You can lounge in the elegant, comfortable chairs or sit at the stools around the central bar. This is, however, no ordinary bar. All the bottles are stored behind frosted glass so when you order a drink your bartender disappears into a futuristic pharmacy, reappearing minutes later with your prescription in hand – usually well mixed and beautifully presented. It's strange being at a bar that hasn't got a parade of bottles to tempt your fancy and some might miss the theatre of watching a bartender mix a drink.

Occasional jazz duos play to wealthy hotel guests who are joined at this bar by young successful city types and gorgeous socialites. The clientele's decorum and flaunting tends for a demure, refined atmosphere regardless of the efforts of the band.

MILK & HONEY

●●●●●

(Full address withheld) Soho, London, W1

Tel: 07000 655 469, **www.mlkhny.com**
Hours: Mon-Fri 19:00-03:00, Sat 20:00-03:00

Entry:	Members only after 11pm (membership £250 p/a)
Dress code:	Smart casual
Clientele:	Media & fashion kids
Cocktails:	43, priced £4.00 - £20.00
Must try:	Honeysuckle Cocktail
Bar snacks:	Land & sea platters, oysters, caviar, venison etc.

Jonathan Downey, the man behind the Match bar chain, has teamed up with Sasha Petraske, owner of Milk & Honey in New York, to turn what was Papa Gaio into a larger copy of the famously secretive Manhattan club. The austere exterior and lobby confer a satisfying feeling of entering a seedy den. Beyond are three dimly lit floors, all sharing the same 30s speakeasy décor. The two main bars are on the ground floor and basement with the smaller VIP 'Red Room' on the first floor. The comfortable moody surroundings and superb cocktails make this a great addition to London's 3am bar circuit.

Members are requested to ring prior to visiting. Non-members can visit until 11pm provided a telephone reservation is made well in advance. So what's the address? That's meant to be a secret and I'd hate to blow a good urban myth.

MATCH BARS

●●●●◐

45 Clerkenwell Rd, EC1; 37 Margaret St, W1; 2 Tabernacle St, EC2, London

Tel: 020 7250 4002, **www.matchbar.com**
Hours: Mon-Sat: hours vary by venue, Sun: closed

Entry:	Subject to space rather than dress
Dress code:	Anything goes – suits to jeans
Clientele:	City, pre-club, media & plain nice people
Cocktails:	49 priced: £5.75 - £6.50
Must try:	Grapefruit Julep
Bar snacks:	Cumberland sausage, tortillas, wraps, tapas, burgers etc.

Some years ago I spent a night barhopping with a former lawyer called Jonathan Downey who told me of his plans to open a lounge bar in Clerkenwell. Well, he did. Such a good thing was Jonathan on to that he now has a chain of such bars and a list of 'best bar' awards tucked under his belt.

The original Clerkenwell Road branch has a sunken, stone-floored 'pit', which houses the bar. When it's busy, it's not dissimilar to feeding time at the zoo and best watched from the sofas on the mezzanine floor. Details of the stylish décor such as the railings and sofas from the original are repeated in the newer Match Bars, which are bigger and possibly better than the original.

The superb cocktail list is filled with original creations now much copied by other bars, which unfortunately usually fail to mimic the quality of service and ingredients found at Match.

MOJO

●●●●○

18 Merrion Street, Leeds, LS1 6PQ

Tel: 0113 244 6387
Hours: Mon-Thurs 17:00-23:00, Fri-Sat 17:00-01:00

Entry:	**Subject to space**
Dress code:	**Clothing should be worn**
Clientele:	**Friendly, fun loving folk**
Cocktails:	**70ish,** priced **£3.50 - £5.50**
Must try:	**Rum Punch**
Bar snacks:	**None**

Mojo was here years before Austin Powers lost his. It is a legendary rock & roll bar, a place to get downright dirty. Outwardly unassuming, the bar runs along one wall of a room plastered in black & white prints of rock stars. An extremely mixed crowd pack in to enjoy the holiday atmosphere, driven by loud eclectic music and shots.

Mojo is unsophisticated in the extreme. It is simply a fun place and the drinks reflect this. Although Mally and the boys are extremely proficient mixologists, delicate Martinis just don't fit Mojo's image. Instead chunky glasses of fruity cocktails generously charged with liquor vie with some excellent bottled beers between rounds of shots.

There are many bars that serve better cocktails, but Mojo makes my shortlist due to having the best atmosphere of any cocktail bar I know in the world.

OLOROSO

●●●●○○

33 Castle Street, Edinburgh, EH2 3DN

Tel: 0131 226 7614, www.oloroso.co.uk
Hours: Daily 12:00-23:00

Entry:	**Priority to diners, subject to space**
Dress code:	**Conservative smart casual**
Clientele:	**Friendly, 30-somethings & the more mature**
Cocktails:	**22,** priced **£5.50 - £10.00**
Must try:	**Pear & Cardamom Sidecar**
Bar snacks:	**Fab fries to fish cakes all day & night**

Location, location, location – the three best attributes of Oloroso, which incidentally is Spanish for aromatic and is also a style of sherry. Housed in what resembles a modern houseboat perched on top of a contemporary building, this restaurant and bar boasts panoramic views across Edinburgh with the Castle in one direction and the Firth of Forth in the other.

Oloroso is accessed via a sterile office-like foyer and elevator. Its interior is clean and minimalist with the bar area akin to a modern department store café, but with views like this, who cares?

Oloroso is primarily a restaurant and so popular is it that if you want a table I'd recommend booking at least a fortnight before you intend visiting. If it's liquid sustenance you're after, then climate permitting Oloroso's roof terrace must be the best spot in Edinburgh to sip Martinis alfresco. The mixed but mature clientele enjoy a range of well executed cocktails delivered by friendly and efficient table service.

OPAL LOUNGE

●●●●○○

51a George Street, New Town, Edinburgh, EH2 2HT

Tel: 0131 226 2275, www.opallounge.co.uk
Hours: Daily 12:00-03:00

Entry:	**Priority to members, expect to queue**
Dress code:	**Fashionably casual**
Clientele:	**Extremely mixed but mature**
Cocktails:	**48,** priced **£5.25 - £6.95**
Must try:	**Raspberry Mojito**
Bar snacks:	**Sushi, spring rolls, fishcakes, platters etc.**

This hybrid club, bar and restaurant lies in a labyrinth of basement rooms bang opposite the famous Assembly Rooms, the heart of the annual festival. Minimalist design and bare concrete floors are softened with walls and furnishings of various shades of brown. The sunken lounge is the main restaurant area but bottles of soy and oyster sauce even on the tables in the bar hint that the cuisine here is heavily Asian influenced and that a good range of snacks are available.

Three levels of membership (£50 to £400 per year) buy you varying privileges including free entry, use of the express lane to avoid the worst of the queue and access to the VIP area known as the Den.

Opal Lounge is operated by Montpeliers, who among other bars in Edinburgh also own nearby Rick's (also in my greatest fifty). An in-house 'mixologist' and company policy in both these bars ensure high cocktail standards.

OPIUM BAR

●●●●◐

3 Skipper Street, Cathedral Quarter, Belfast, N.I. BT1 2DZ

Tel: 028 9023 2448, www.opiumbar.co.uk
Hours: Tue-Sat 17:00-01:00

Entry:	**Subject to appearance & space**
Dress code:	**Cool casual and posh frocks**
Clientele:	**Mid twenty, early thirty-somethings**
Cocktails:	**38,** priced **£4.50 - £5.25**
Must try:	**Opium Martini**
Bar snacks:	**Oriental – served till 9pm**

Set in a townhouse down a narrow back street, this is no opium den or even a den of iniquity, but its two tiny floors are a lounge haven for discerning Belfast drinkers. Although one of the newer bars in town, Opium has already won a string of industry awards and is setting the standards for the town's other bars to follow.

The dimly lit intimate ground floor bar with its dark wood and bamboo walls has an unmistakable oriental theme. Early evening the upstairs lounge is reserved for diners. However, after 11pm this padded lounge filled with comfy leather seats is open to all and the place to be.

Opium attracts a young professional crowd who appear very receptive to exploring the Lab (London) influenced cocktail list. Classic cocktails are lovingly made and in-house drinks such as the signature Opium Martini (a Vodkatini flavoured with root ginger and coriander syrup) are also sublime.

THE PLAYER LOUNGE BAR & KITCHEN

●●●●◐

8 Broadwick Street, Soho, London, W1F 8HN

Tel: 020 7494 9125, www.theplyr.com
Hours: Mon-Wed 17:30-00:00, Thur-Fri 17:30-01:00
Sat 19:00-01:00

Entry:	**£3 door charge may apply (Members only after 11pm)**
Dress code:	**Soho**
Clientele:	**Young Soho set**
Cocktails:	**40+** priced **£5.75 - £6.50**
Must try:	**Prestige Cocktail**
Bar snacks:	**Spare ribs, crab fritters, cheese fondue**

A simple doorway in the heart of Soho, the entrance to The Player would look complete if it had a sign saying 'model downstairs', a feel which is further enhanced by the lingerie in the window of Agent Provocateur next door. At the bottom of the narrow staircase, you are greeted by a well stocked bar overlooking a single room with black leather banquette seating, red walls and a scattering of tables and chairs.

When The Player first opened in September 1998, it enjoyed immediate success, partly due to the presence of bar guru Dick Bradsell. However, he left, there were 'licensing difficulties' and eventually. The Player closed. It was reopened by the Match group in October 2001, looking and feeling even better than it did before, with Dale DeGroff (another legendary guru) overseeing the excellent cocktails.

The Player attracts a young crowd partly drawn from nearby media and film companies.

THE RESTAURANT BAR & GRILL

●●●○○

14 John Dalton Street, Manchester, M2 6JR

Tel: 0161 839 1999
Hours: Bar: mon-Sat 12:00-23:00, Sun 12:00-22:30

Entry:	**If you look the part**
Dress code:	**Designer smart**
Clientele:	**Thirty plus style set, footballers & wives**
Cocktails:	**18,** priced **£4.95 - £6.95**
Must try:	**Tatanka Breeze**
Bar snacks:	**Mezze to spring rolls (served until 5pm)**

The Restaurants super clean modern design features magnolia walls, dark wood and black leather banquette booth seats with tea lights. Black and white photographs, louvre blinds and potted palms lend this place something of a colonial feel.

The 'Grill' part of the name refers to the restaurant, accessed by stairs that sit over a nifty water feature. This appears to attract the middle aged and wealthy who graze in the bar while waiting for their table. The bar also draws Manchester celebs with Gary Neville and mates on the next table when I visited. There are some amazing hair dos using copious amounts of gel, and that's just the guys. The girls show legs, lots of them. Much time is spent in front of the mirror before setting off for this particular Restaurant Bar & Grill.

The cocktail list is somewhat staid, but what's offered is well executed.

OPIUM

●●●◐○

1a Dean Street, Soho, London, W1D 3RB

Tel: 020 7287 9608, www.thebreakfastgroup.co.uk
Hours: Mon-Fri 18:00-03:00, Sat 19:30-03:00
(members only after 22:30)

Entry:	**Members have priority**
Dress code:	**Bling bling**
Clientele:	**Young glamour seekers**
Cocktails:	**43** priced **£6.50 - £29.00**
Must try:	**Chan Crush**
Bar snacks:	**French-Vietnamese snacks**

As you walk down the steps into the basement the smell of incense prepares you for the theme. Designed by Paris'-based Miguel Cancio Martins (famous for Paris's Buddha Bar), this dimly lit louche bar has the feel of a French-Vietnamese opium den with silky gold banquettes, hand-carved screens, lanterns and figurines. A carved wood pagoda covers opulent seating in the middle of the space, which is often reserved, leaving the 'non vogue' crowd standing at the bar looking longingly at the comfy chairs and silky cushions. A club-like atmosphere prevails with the young and upwardly mobile pulling and being pulled.

The small bar tucked into the corner as you enter offers an ambitious cocktail list that's beautifully presented and handily indexed. The menu also features a brief history of Vietnam's decades of struggle, written in English, French and of course Vietnamese.

Depending when you visit, you may encounter an entry charge – members have priority.

SANDERSON HOTEL

●●●●○

Long Bar & Purple Bar, 50 Berners Street, Fitzrovia, London, W1P 3AD

Tel: 020 7300 1400, **www.**sandersonhotel.com
Hours: Mon-Sat 09:00-00:30, Sun 09:00-22:30

Entry:	Hotel guests only in Purple bar
Dress code:	To the hilt
Clientele:	City boys, jet set, models
Cocktails:	36 priced: £9.00 – £11.00
Must try:	Sanderson Martini
Bar snacks:	Finger food – foie gras, smoked salmon

Walking into Sanderson's Purple bar is like travelling celebrity class to Wonderland. It's snug and dimly lit, with miniature tables and chairs, decoratively cut mirror work and opulent deep purple furnishings in front of a solid stone bar. Best book a room as the Purple bar is designed for VVIPs and hotel residents only.

The Long Bar, Sanderson's slightly less exclusive second bar, is, well, long. The island bar sits in the middle of this white room, allowing the banker/fashion clientele, who ooze cash from every orifice, to check each other out from opposite sides.

Outside, a wooden decked courtyard of bamboo, candles, slate and running water is welcome relief from star-hungry rubberneckers. Grab yourself a seat outside and ask one of the waitresses who slink about in black dresses for the oversized cocktail list. Whatever you choose will be eminently drinkable.

SKETCH

●●●●○

9 Conduit Street, Mayfair, London, W1S 2XG

Tel: 08707 774 488
Hours: Mon-Sat 09:00-00:30, Sun 09:00-22:30

Entry:	Members and diners only
Dress code:	To the hilt
Clientele:	Business types & the glamorous
Cocktails:	36 priced: £9.00 – £11.00
Must try:	Atheist Falls
Bar snacks:	Finger food – foie gras, smoked salmon

The interior of Sketch sets clinical 70s futurism against a backdrop of high ceilings and grandeur original to the Georgian Grade II-listed building in which it's housed.

Along with The Lecture Room, noted for being London's most expensive restaurant, Sketch also boasts a 150-seat brasserie-style restaurant with moving wallpaper called the Gallery and two bars: The East Bar and, yup you guessed it, the West Bar – both with original 1970s furniture. The East Bar is better known as the capsule due to its design and on either side of this are stairs leading to the much talked about toilets, each housed in its own egg shaped white pod.

Sketch attracts a glamorous well-heeled crowd, admitted because they have paid the £350 annual membership or have previously reserved a table at one of the two restaurants. Thanks to wonderfully polite staff the whole experience is far more approachable than it sounds – that's if your credit card is up to it.

SUGAR LOUNGE

●●●●◐

Arch 12, Deansgate Locks, Manchester, M1 5LH

Tel: 0161 834 1600
Hours: Daily 14:00-02:00

Entry:	Members & beautiful people only
Dress code:	Designer glamorous
Clientele:	Attractive, moneyed & wannabes
Cocktails:	70ish, priced £6.00-£22.00
Must try:	Old-fashioned variations
Bar snacks:	Not available

Lying at the end of a row of bars housed in refurbished railway arches, Sugar Lounge is not only the slickest of the line-up, it's also the best bar in Manchester.

Intimate in its proportions, Sugar Lounge is THE place to be seen in Manchester, so the management can afford to be very choosy about who passes the velvet rope. To be certain of entry you need to have been interviewed and paid £350 for elite membership, turn up early evening or early in the week, or be both stunningly dressed and gorgeous looking.

Downstairs padded cell walls surround a black tarmac floor with a white Roman laurel pattern on which sit tan leather sofas and a beech wood bar. It is only when this area fills to capacity that the super fashionable mezzanine bar is opened.

Both upstairs and down you'll find skilled bartenders working with a superb selection of premium spirits to make great drinks. Very pretentious, but justifiably so.

RICK'S BAR & CAFÉ
●●●○○

55a Frederick Street, Edinburgh, EH2 1LH

Tel: 0131 622 7800, www.ricksedinburgh.co.uk
Hours: Daily 07:00-03:00

Entry:	No door policy
Dress code:	Business to glam
Clientele:	Hip thirty somethings
Cocktails:	55, priced £3.00 - £6.95
Must try:	Vanilla Car
Bar snacks:	Far Eastern fusion cuisine

This small basement bar and restaurant sits under an attached and equally bijou hotel with just ten rooms. Unlike many basement bars which are approached via narrow dingy steps, Rick's has a grand, welcoming, wide stone staired entrance. The width of the bar's semi-subterranean frontage is windowed onto the street with a narrow terrace. Beyond the bar and its secluded booths lies the restaurant area proper. Formerly an open courtyard, its originally exterior stonework contrasts with the modern décor of the rest of the bar.

During the day (it opens for breakfast at 7am) and early evening, Rick's is predominantly a restaurant, but as the night goes on the tables are cleared and a bar environment prevails.

Rick's attracts a hip thirty-something crowd drawn by the Far Eastern fusion cuisine and a drinks offering that includes a formidable cocktail list. Rick's is operated by Montpeliers, who also own The Opal Lounge nearby, also in my greatest fifty.

ROCKWELL
●●●●○

Trafalgar Hotel, 2 Spring Gardens, Trafalgar Square, London, SW1A 2TS

Tel: 020 7870 2900, www.thetrafalgar.hilton.com
Hours: Mon-Sat 09:00-01:00, Sun 09:00-22:30

Entry:	Fairly relaxed door policy
Dress code:	Jeans to suits
Clientele:	Hotel guests, funksters & after workers
Cocktails:	45 priced £8.00 - £10.00
Must try:	Apple Toddy
Bar snacks:	Fish and chips to pastrami and buffalo mozzarella

Walk through the doors off Trafalgar Square and you're straight into this high-ceilinged, airy, modern bar housed in the lobby of Hilton's Trafalgar Hotel. Polished concrete pillars rise from a dark wooden floor, scattered with sofas and chaise longues.

There's only one choice of brand across most of the spirit categories, but they're all super premium. The only category where the bartender will offer you a choice of spirits is Bourbon, which could prove daunting as there are over eighty of them. Cocktail wise, the Bourbon-led list is full of delights.

Considering that Rockwell operates within the corporate limitations of a Hilton Hotel lobby area this is a stylish bar. Sadly Rockwell struggles to be consistently busy and on quiet nights can lack atmosphere and soul.

In clement weather a few special guests are invited up to the roof terrace bar to enjoy views of Trafalgar Square and London.

RAOUL'S
●●●●○

32 Walton Street, Jericho, Oxford, OX2 6AA

Tel: 01865 553 732, www.raoulsbar.com
Hours: Sun-Thurs 16:00-00:00, Fri-Sat 16:00-01:00

Entry:	Welcome subject to space
Dress code:	Comfortably casual
Clientele:	Students and mature students
Cocktails:	90+, priced £5.10 - £9.00
Must try:	Pear Essential
Bar snacks:	Nachos, cheese plate & excellent cold tapas

Hardly sophisticated and certainly not pretentious, Raoul's is something of an Oxford institution, noted for great drinks and its friendly atmosphere.

Those of you familiar with London's LAB bar will spot similarities in both the menu and interior design. Curved edges, bold wallpaper and subdued lighting come together in a seventies lounge that sprawls over three levels. Conveniently there's a bar as you walk in and another in the basement. However, the cosiest place is the room that lies between, where attentive table service makes visits to either bar unnecessary.

While many of Oxford's bars are filled with students, Raoul's attracts a mixed crowd with any students being of the mature variety. They pack in to enjoy the relaxed vibe, excellent cocktails and occasional bottle of wine. The menu not only boasts a bewildering array of classic and contemporary cocktails (many of which were created by Raoul's own bartenders), but also a fine spirits selection with 33 different vodkas.

TOWNHOUSE
●●●●◐

31 Beauchamp Place, Knightsbridge, London, SW3 1NU

Tel: 020 7589 5080, www.lab-townhouse.com
Hours: Mon-Fri 12:00-00:00, Sat 11:00-00:00, Sun 11:00-23:00

Entry:	Subject to appearance & space
Dress code:	Designer casual
Clientele:	Wealthy Knightsbridge youth
Cocktails:	100+ priced £6.50 - £9.00
Must try:	Date Bourbon Sour or Lemongrass Collins
Bar snacks:	Platters & tapas through to burgers

Formerly a vaguely Moroccan themed bar called Min's, this ivy-covered Georgian townhouse is now owned by the team from Lab bar in Soho. They've poshed their act up somewhat to suit the locality but naturally there's an extensive cocktail list and a DJ booth.

Townhouse is set over three floors. Dark hardwood flooring, refined décor and tall leather banquettes appear throughout. The largest space is at street level and dominated by a seven metre purple, lava rock topped bar with front panels which gradually change colour – there are comfortable lounge areas at either end. Downstairs is an intimate space designed for private parties, while upstairs is a second bar and a very cosy lounge.

Townhouse's cocktail list is one of the most impressive in Britain, but sadly some of the Sloanes and It-girls who frequent the bar have yet to progress beyond Kir Royales and Seebreezes. Help educate them - be adventurous at Townhouse.

TOWNHOUSE
●●●◐○

Assembly Street, Leeds, LS2 7DA

Tel: 0113 219 4004
Hours: Tue-Sat 11:30-02:00

Entry:	No large groups
Dress code:	Casual
Clientele:	Young party loving crowd
Cocktails:	46 priced £4.50 - £6.00
Must try:	Vanilla Laika
Bar snacks:	Downstairs in coffee shop

Duplex in its layout, Townhouse has a couple of bars and a coffee shop. The cocktail bar is up sauna-like timber-clad stairs. If you arrive early and the place is quiet, the large single room appears soulless and sparsely furnished with only a couple of sofas against the windowed wall backed by floor to ceiling radiators. Come back late in the week or a bit later in the evening and you won't even be able to see those features for revellers enjoying cocktails and the DJ driven music.

Jake Burger and his team have put together the best cocktail list in Leeds. This includes outstanding classics, a few modern drinks borrowed from other bars and a host of their own creations, with names like Daisy Duke and Love Potion No.9. Visitors from London will also be blown away by what great value the cocktails are.

TRADER VIC'S
●●●●○

Hilton Hotel (basement), 22 Park Lane, Mayfair, London, W1Y 4BE

Tel: 020 7208 4113, www.tradervics.com
Hours: Mon-Thu 11:30-15:30 & 17:00-01:00, Fri 11:30-15:30 & 17:00-03:00, Sat 17:00-03:00, Sun 17:00-22:30

Entry:	No door policy
Dress code:	Smart (but not strictly)
Clientele:	Tourists, businessmen
Cocktails:	72 priced £5.00 - £15.00
Must try:	Mai Tai
Bar snacks:	'Tidbits' & 'bar bites' (try the Piri Piri Prawns)

In 1934, Victor Jules Bergeron or Trader Vic as he became known, opened his first restaurant 'Hinky Dink's' in Oakland, San Francisco. Here he served Polynesian food with a mix of Chinese, French and American dishes cooked in Chinese wood-fired ovens. As well as his then exotic menu, Vic became famous for the rum based cocktails he created, particularly the Mai Tai.

He acquired the 'Trader' nickname due to offering free food and drinks to customers who brought him aged rums (then hard to obtain). After a trip to Tahiti in 1937 he changed the bar's name to Trader Vic's and the Tiki theme was born.

Vic died in 1984, but his bars live on with branches around the world. At this one under the London Hilton you'll find his take on Polynesian food, great rum cocktails and South Pacific themed décor including shark's teeth, puffa fish and hand carved Tiki poles.

ZANDER

●●●●○

Bank Restaurant, 45 Buckingham Gate (opp. Vandon St),Westminster, London, SW1E 6BS

Tel: 020 7379 9797 www.bankrestaurants.com
Hours: Mon-Wed 11:00-23:00, Thu-Sat 11:00-01:00, Sun 12:00-22:00

Entry:	Relaxed door policy
Dress code:	Smart casual / suits
Clientele:	Business, young trendy
Cocktails:	75, priced £5.50-£15.00
Must try:	Berry Breeze
Bar snacks: Mon-Tue 17:30-22:45, Wed-Sat 17:30-23:30

Beyond Zander's fairly bland exterior is a contemporary designed interior which is both maze-like and long - very long. In fact the bar appears to go on for ever and is one of a few claiming to be the longest in Europe. Anyway it's long enough to house a good few bar stools and is the best place from which to enjoy Zander. Unless that is, you're on a romantic rendezvous, in which case you should head for one of the intimate alcoves, which is where the labyrinth kicks in. There is something disorientating about the number of pillars and mirrors which divide this large space and create those cosy alcoves.

This destination venue (who goes drinking in Westminster?) boasts a slick and well-run bar, with a friendly and personal approach to service. Cocktails from the list of classics and Zander originals are usually faultless. As in the rear restaurant, the bar food is both interesting and good, although pricey.

ZETA

●●●●○

35 Hertford Street, Mayfair, London, W1Y 7TG

Tel: 020 7208 4067, www.zeta-bar.com
Hours: Mon-Tue 18:00-01:00, Wed-Fri 18:00-03:00, Sat 17:00-03:00

Entry:	**Cardholders take precedence**
Dress code:	**Casually couture**
Clientele:	**City crowd & the style set**
Cocktails:	**80 priced: £7.50 - £12.50**
Must try:	**Jineeto**
Bar snacks: **Oriental influence**

Zeta is one of London's funkiest hotel bars, so with that in mind, you'll be surprised to hear that the name was inspired not by the sixth letter of the Greek alphabet, but by the brand name of a fire bell Robbie Bargh (the inspiration behind this bar) spotted in another bar's toilets. (Those who know Robbie won't be.)

The interior has a subtly Oriental theme with delicate looking illuminated walls that appear to be made from brown packing paper.

Apart from the odd out of place Hilton guest and businessmen celebrating winning or losing an award in another Park Lane hotel, Zeta is packed with model types enjoying sublime drinks from the recently much improved cocktail list.

Fridays and Saturday nights here are huge, with DJs spinning chilled vibes, subdued lighting, comfy chairs and superbly attentive staff combining to make this one of the hottest bars in town.

ZUMA

●●●●○

5 Raphael Street, Knightsbridge, London, SW7 1DL

Tel: 020 7584 1010
Hours: Mon-Sat 12:00-23:00, Sun 12:00-16:00

Entry:	**Dress well or book table**
Dress code:	**Designer glamorous**
Clientele:	**Rich & pretty or just pretty rich**
Cocktails:	**30** priced: **£7.00 - £9.50**
Must try:	**Rubabu or Big Appleberry**
Bar snacks: **Sushi and other oriental nibbles**

This modern pan-Asian restaurant and bar attracts more rich and pretty people in one night than were assembled in a whole series of Dallas. Zuma occupies the former site of the Chicago Rib Shack and it's not just the clientele that has changed. 108 tonnes of Italian granite was specially quarried and imported to add a cave-like feel to the clean designer interior (the largest piece forms one corner of the bar and required special lifting gear).

The front area of the large open-plan restaurant houses the island bar and surrounding lounge. Here you'll find a range of sakes and sake based cocktails along with other imaginative, contemporary and well-executed classic drinks. Sushi and other bar snacks such as the spicy beef are also superb.

This is fashionable Knightsbridge so expect some very glamorous looking It-girls, well-heeled business types and a few visiting stars of stage and screen. Zuma is one of London's places to see and be seen. ∎

Glassware should always be handled by the base or stem to avoid leaving finger marks on the glass. Check your glassware is clean and free from chips and marks such as lipstick.

Ideally glassware (particularly Martini glasses) should be chilled in a freezer prior to use. This gives the glass an icy coating. When this is not possible, chilling can be achieved by filling the glass with ice and topping up with water. Leave the glass to cool while you assemble the drink, then discard ice and water when you are ready to pour the drink.

Conversely, to warm a glass ready for a hot cocktail, place a bar spoon in the glass and fill it with hot water. Then discard the water and pour in the drink, before removing the spoon, which is there to help disperse the 'shock' of the heat.

Using a jigger helps ensure that the proportions of ingredients are correct.

By definition any drink that is described as a cocktail is a mixed drink. So if you are going to make cocktails you have to know how to combine the various liquids that will ultimately compose your drink. Cocktails may be mixed in four different ways. The method used depends on the ingredients used and the type of cocktail you are making.

1. **Shake**
2. **Stir**
3. **Blend**
4. **Build (combine in glass)**

At the heart of every cocktail lies at least one of these four methods. Understanding these terms and other techniques such as layering, floating and muddling is fundamental. Without this knowledge you will not be able to translate the written recipe into a finished cocktail – just as you would not be able to cook a food recipe if you were not familiar with the techniques of baking, frying and grilling.

MIXING METHODS EXPLAINED

PLEASE READ THE FOLLOWING INSTRUCTIONS BEFORE ATTEMPTING TO FOLLOW THE RECIPES IN THIS GUIDE.

Shaking a drink using a standard shaker.

When you see the phrase "shake with ice and strain", you should place all the necessary ingredients with cubed ice in a cocktail shaker and shake briskly. Then strain the liquid into the glass, leaving the ice behind in the shaker.

Mixing a drink by shaking also chills the drink and dilutes it. The dilution is as important to the resulting cocktail as using the right proportions of each ingredient. If you use too little ice it will quickly melt in the shaker and the result will be an over-diluted cocktail - so always fill your shaker at least two-thirds full of fresh ice.

Note that care should be taken as to how you hold your shaker. Losing your grip while shaking will make a mess, be embarrassing and could cause injury to those close by. Always hold the shaker with two hands and never shake fizzy ingredients. There are two types of shaker available, which should be used as follows:

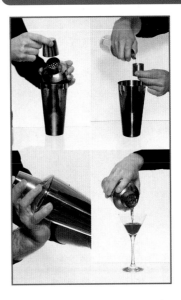

Making a drink using a standard shaker.

A standard shaker is one that consists of three parts and hence is sometimes referred to as a 'three-piece shaker'. The three pieces are 1) a flat-bot-tomed, conical base or 'can', 2) a top with a built-in strainer and 3) a cap. I strongly recommend this style of shaker for the amateur or inexperienced bartender due to its ease of use. Be sure to purchase a large shaker as this will allow the mixing of two short drinks at once and also ensures space for the liquid and ice to move inside and so aid mixing.

TO USE:
1/ Combine ingredients with plenty of ice in the base of the shaker.
2/ Place the top and cap firmly on the base.
3/ With one hand on the top and one on the bottom, shake vigorously. The cap should always be on the top when shaking and should point away from guests.
4/ After shaking for a count of around 20 seconds, simply lift off the cap, secure the top with one finger and pour through the built-in strainer.

SHAKER - BOSTON

■ Pouring into a Boston glass.

■ Sealing the shaker.

■ Shaking a Boston shaker.

A Boston shaker comprises two flat-bottomed cones, one made of glass and the other of stainless steel. The can should be flexible, which enables the metal to make a watertight seal with the glass. Avoid Boston shakers which rely on a rubber ring to seal. Boston shakers demand an element of skill and a practice period is usually required for a new user to be proficient in their use.

TO USE:

1/ Combine ingredients with plenty of ice in the glass part of the shaker or 'Boston glass'.

2/ Place the metal half over the top of the glass half and lightly tap the top with the heel of your hand to create a seal. Closing the shaker too tightly will make it difficult to open.

3/ With one hand on the top and one on the bottom, shake vigorously. The glass part should always be on the top when shaking and should point away from guests.

4/ After shaking for a count of around 20 seconds, hold the metal part of the shaker and tap the side of it close to where you estimate the glass rim sits. This will break the seal between the glass and the metal, allowing you to lift off the glass. If you fail to break the seal on your first attempt, turn the shaker one quarter turn and repeat the process.

5/ Place a Hawthorne strainer (the device in the photo with the spring) over the top of the metal half and strain the mixture into glass.

■ Breaking the seal between glass and can.

■ Using a Hawthorne strainer.

FINE STRAIN

'Standard shakers' have a built in strainer and Boston shakers are used with a Hawthorne strainer – as explained above. Some drinks, like the Natural Daiquiri, benefit from an additional finer strainer to remove small fragments of fruit and/or flecks of ice. A small (tea) strainer held between the shaker and the glass is perfect for this task. Some bartenders refer to this as 'double straining'.

◄

'Fine straining' or 'double straining'

STIR

The two methods of stirring with a bar spoon. ▲

If a cocktail recipe calls for you to 'stir with ice and strain', use a bar spoon with a twisted stem and a mixing glass. (Although a special lipped mixing glass is preferable, the glass half of a Boston shaker will suffice.) Place ice and the ingredients into the mixing glass (or base of shaker if you do not have a mixing glass). Slide the back of the spoon down the inside of the mixing glass and twirl gently between thumb and finger. The spoon will rotate inside the mixing glass, gently stirring the drink. Strain the drink into a glass using a Hawthorne strainer – or the top of a standard shaker if you are using a standard shaker.

Some bartenders (and I'm one) prefer to use the flat end of a bar spoon to stir a drink. Simply place the flat end on top of the ice in the mixing glass and start to stir, working the spoon down the drink as you go.

BLEND

When a cocktail recipe calls for you to 'blend with ice', place ingredients and ice into a blender and blend until a smooth, even consistency is achieved. Ideally you should use crushed ice, as this lessens wear on the blender's blades. You should place liquid ingredients in the blender first, adding ice and/or ice-cream last. If you have a variable speed blender, always start on a slow speed and build up.

BUILD

The term 'build drink' refers to making a cocktail by combining the ingredients in the glass in which the cocktail will be served. For simplicity, recipes in this guide where the drink is to be 'built' include the instruction "pour ingredients into glass and stir" or similar. You only need to stir built drinks for a couple of seconds.

Layering is a particular way of building a drink in a glass. Each ingredient is carefully poured into the glass so that it floats on the previous layer.

The success of this technique is dependent on the density (specific gravity) of the liquids used. As a rule of thumb, the less alcohol and the more sugar an ingredient contains, the heavier it is. The heaviest ingredients should be poured first and the lightest last. Syrups are non-alcoholic and contain a lot of sugar so are usually the heaviest ingredient. Liqueurs, which are high in sugar and lower in alcohol than spirits, are generally the next heaviest ingredient. The exception to this rule is cream or cream liqueurs, which can float, especially when whipped.

One brand of a particular liqueur may be heavier or lighter than another. The relative temperatures of ingredients may also affect their ability to float or sink, hence a degree of experimentation is inevitable when creating layered drinks.

Layering can be achieved in one of two ways. The first is pouring down the twisting handle of a bar spoon, keeping the flat, disc-shaped end of the spoon over the surface of the previous layer so that the liquid disperses over the surface of the drink. Alternatively you can hold the bowl end of a bar spoon (or a large teaspoon) in contact with the side of the glass and over the surface of the drink and pour over it.

▲
The two methods of layering a drink with a bar spoon.

This refers to the crushing of fruits with a muddler or a blunt tool similar to a pestle. (You can also use a rolling pin.) As when using a pestle and mortar, push down on the muddler with a twisting action. Only attempt to muddle in the base of a shaker or a suitably sturdy glass and always exercise extreme caution when doing so. Never attempt to muddle hard unripe fruits in a glass as the pressure required could break the glass and cause injury.

This means floating the final ingredient on top of a cocktail by slowly pouring it over a spoon (see 'Layering').

Some use this term to describe the frosted effect on glasses stored in a freezer or refrigerator. 'Frosting' can also describe coating the rim of a glass with salt or sugar. In this guide I use the terms 'rim glass' for coating the rim of a glass with salt or sugar (see Salt / Sugar Rim) and 'chill glass' for freezing glasses.

The balancing of each ingredient within a cocktail is key to making a great drink. Therefore the accuracy with which ingredients are measured is critical to the finished cocktail.

In this guide I've expressed the measurements of ingredients in 'shots'. Ideally a shot is a 25ml measure (UK) or a 1oz measure (US). Alternatively, use a clean medicine measure or even 'half an egg cup' to measure a 'shot'. Whatever the measure you use as a shot, be sure to use the same measure for all the ingredients so that the proportions of one ingredient to the other remain as the recipe intended. Please follow the alcohol content guidelines included in this guide and choose a measure equal to 25ml or one US fluid ounce (29.6ml) at most. When using a thimble measure fill to the rim for a 'shot'.

SPOON

The term 'spoon' as used in this guide means a bar spoon, which is slightly larger than a standard tea-spoon. If you are using a 25ml or 1oz thimble measure an eighth of a shot is equal to a bar spoon: if you are using a smaller or larger measure, you will need to use an eighth of that measure where the recipe calls for a spoon. You'll probably find it easier to measure using a spoon than to judge at what point your measure is one eighth full. The odd recipe in this guide which calls for half a spoon, is equal to one sixteenth of a shot.

FREEPOURING

This term refers to pouring measures of drink without using a physical measure. In well trained, experienced hands, fairly accurate pouring is achievable by counting time and estimating the amount of liquid flowing through a bottle's spout while pouring. In the wrong hands this is a terribly inaccurate method of pouring measures and I strongly recommend the use of a thimble measure.

INGREDIENTS - ICE

A plentiful supply of fresh ice is essential to making good cocktails. Fortunately most supermarkets and liquor stores now sell bags of ice (avoid hollow tubular shaped ice). Alternatively, if you're making your own in ice cube trays, use bottled or filtered water to avoid the taste of chlorine often apparent in municipal water supplies. Your ice should be dry, almost sticky to the touch. Never use 'wet' ice that has started thaw.

Whenever using ice in a drink, always fill the glass with ice, rather than just adding a few cubes. The greater quantity of ice makes the drink much colder, the ice lasts longer and so melting ice does not dilute the drink. Unfortunately, many drinkers perceive this as a way of reducing the quantity of liquid in a glass so that bars can make more profit. Such customers who ask for some ice to be removed and their drink topped up are merely showing their ignorance.

Never use ice in a cocktail shaker twice, even if it's to mix the same drink. You should always throw away ice after straining the drink and use fresh ice to fill the glass if so required. Unless otherwise stated, all references to ice in this guide mean cubed ice.

If crushed ice is required for a particular recipe, the recipe will state 'crushed ice'. This is available commercially. Alternatively you can crush cubed ice in an ice-crusher or simply bash a bag of cubed ice with a heavy rolling pin.

If a glass is broken in the vicinity of your ice stocks, melt the ice with warm water, clean the container and re-stock with fresh ice.

INFUSIONS

Some recipes call for an infused spirit. An example of this is vanilla infused rum, which is made by putting three split vanilla pods in a bottle of rum and leaving for a fortnight. Warming the bottle and turning it frequently can speed up this process. Other herbs, spices and even fruits can be infused in a similar manner in vodka, gin, rum, whiskey and Tequila. Whatever spirit you decide to use, pick a brand that has an alcohol content of 40% alc./vol. or more.

Be aware that when the level of spirit in a bottle drops below the level of the flavouring, the alcohol loses its preservative effect and the flavouring can go off.

WATER

The dilution of a cocktail is key to achieving the right balance. Whether your ice is fresh or beginning to melt, how hard you shake your drink and how much ice you use can all affect this dilution. Even if a recipe doesn't call for a splash of water, don't be scared to add a shot next time you make it if you feel it needs it. As with making ice, use bottled or filtered water to avoid the taste of chlorine often apparent in municipal water sup-plies. Always keep a bottle of still water in your refrigerator next to the bottle of sugar syrup. Both are equally useful for adjusting the bal-ance of a drink.

EGGS

Raw eggs can be hazardous to health so you may decide it is safer to use commercially produced pasteurised egg white in place of fresh egg white. If, like me, you prefer to use fresh eggs, I recommend you use small free range eggs. Always store your eggs in a refrigerator and use well before the sell-by-date.

CREAM OF COCONUT

This is a non-alcoholic sticky blend of coconut juice, sugar, emulsifier, cellulose, thickeners, citric acid and salt. Fortunately it tastes better than it sounds and is an essential ingredient of a good Piña Colada. One 15oz/425ml can will make approximately 25 drinks. Once it has been opened the contents should be transferred to a plastic container and stored in a refrigerator. This may thicken the product, so gentle warming may be required prior to use. Coconut milk is a very different product and cannot be substituted.

FRUIT JUICE

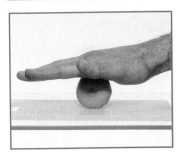

In an ideal world fruit would always come from a tree and not a bottle or carton, so (with the exception of cranberry juice) the best way to obtain your juices is to squeeze, press or use a juice extractor on fresh fruit. If you buy packaged juice don't use products made from concentrate - look for terms such as 'freshly squeezed', 'pressed' and 'not from concentrate' on the label and look in supermarket chill cabinets not on the ambient shelf. Poorer quality, heavily pasteurised juices tend to be sweeter and less flavoursome than fresh or 'not from concentrate' packaged juices. This difference in flavour can ruin a drink formulated to be made with fresh juices.

▲
Rolling citrus fruits before cutting them means they produce more juice.

Before cutting fruit such as limes or lemons to juice, roll the fruit on a surface under the palm of your hand. Surprisingly, this will enable you to squeeze more juice from it. When using an electric spinning juicer, be careful not to grind the pith as this can make the juice bitter. Fruits such as pears, pineapples and kiwis are best juiced in an electric centrifugal juice extractor. The juice of soft berries can usually be released by simply muddling in the base of the shaker or glass.

PURÉES

Fruit purées are fresh fruit which have been chopped up and liquidized. Bars tend to use commercially available frozen purées which often have added sugar. If using such a product you may have to adjust the balance of your drink to allow for the extra sweetness.

SOUR MIX

(Sweet 'n' Sour or Margarita mix) Sour mix is a term for a blend of lemon juice or lime juice mixed with sugar syrup. Commercial pre-mixed sour mix is available in a dried crystal or powdered form. Margarita mix is a similar pre-mix, but with the addition of orange flavours. Many bartenders rightly frown on the use of such pre-mixes. Fresh citrus juice makes a much better drink. I strongly advocate the use of freshly squeezed juice and sugar syrup.

SUGAR SYRUP

Many cocktails benefit from sweetening but granulated sugar does not dissolve easily in cold drinks. Hence pre-dissolved 'sugar syrup' (also known as 'simple syrup') is used.

Similar, commercially made 'gomme sirop' (gum syrup) is sugar syrup with the addition of gum arabic, the crystallised sap of the acacia tree. Some brands of gomme sirop also include orange blossom or other flavourings. In taste, sirop de gomme is very clearly distinguishable from sugar syrup. Many top bartenders don't like using gomme syrup but prefer to use simple or sugar syrup. Others prefer gomme as it adds mouth-feel and smoothness to some drinks.

Buy sugar syrup commercially or mix it yourself as follows: gradually pour in and stir two cups of granulated sugar (I use unrefined cane sugar) into a saucepan containing one cup of hot water and simmer until the sugar is dissolved. (Note that the longer you boil the water and sugar, the stronger the syrup will be and that if you boil it for too long your syrup will be too strong and liable to crystallise.) Allow to cool and place in an empty bottle - if kept in a refrigerator this mixture will last for a couple of months. A wide range of flavoured sugar syrups are commercially available. Orgeat (almond), grenadine, passion fruit and vanilla are amongst the most popular.

HALF AND HALF

A blend of 50% milk and 50% cream pre-mixed by some bartenders for use in cocktails. Where used in this guide I've listed these ingredients separately.

GRENADINE

A sweet red pomegranate flavoured sugar syrup, with little or no alcoholic content. It is usually made from red berries such as cherries, strawberries and raspberries, with added flavour from vanilla essence.

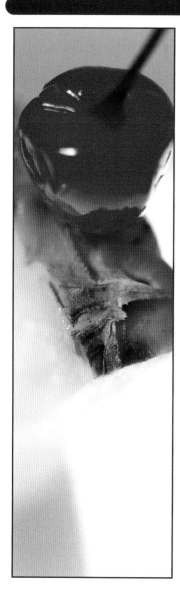

Garnishes are used to decorate cocktails and are usually anchored to the rim of the glass. Strictly speaking, garnishes should be edible so please forget about paper parasols. Fruit should be unblemished and washed prior to use.

Cut citrus fruits have a maximum shelf life of 24 hours when refrigerated. Cherries and olives should be stored refrigerated and left in their own juices. Olives should be washed before use to prevent an oily appearance to the drink.

Anything from banana chunks, strawberries or redcurrants to coffee beans, confectionery, basil leaves and slices of fresh ginger can be used as a garnish. The correct garnish will often enhance the aroma and flavour as well as the look of a drink.

The term 'split' refers to the cut in a piece of fruit used to fix it to the rim of a glass: a 'wheel' is a circular slice of citrus fruit. For wedges see under Lemon / Lime Wedges.

Garnishes such as olives, cherries or pickled onions are sometimes served on cocktail sticks. A 'sail' is a whole slice of citrus fruit served on a cocktail stick mast, often accompanied by a cherry.

Celery sticks may be placed in drinks as a stirring rod; cinnamon sticks are often served in hot drinks and toddies.

To sprinkle chocolate on the surface of a drink you can either shave chocolate using a vegetable peeler or crumble a Cadbury's Flake bar. 'Dust with chocolate' refers to the use of chocolate or cocoa powder.

Citrus peels are often used as a garnish (see 'Flamed Zest'). A 'Horse's Neck' is the entire peel of either an orange, a lemon or a lime, cut in a continuous spiral and placed so as to overhang the rim of the glass. A 'twist' is a narrow sliver of fruit zest twisted over the drink and then dropped in. Thin, narrow lengths of citrus peel may also be tied in a knot.

Mint sprigs are often used to garnish cups and juleps.

DUST

You 'dust' a drink by sprinkling ground nutmeg, chocolate powder etc. on top of it. When dusting with nutmeg it is always best to grate fresh nutmeg over the drink, although the powdered product may be used if fresh is not available.

◀

Dusting with nutmeg.

The term ignite, flame or flambé means that the drink should be set alight. Please exercise extreme care when setting fire to drinks. Be particularly careful not to knock over a lit drink and never attempt to carry a drink which is still alight. Before drinking cover the glass so as to suffocate the flame and be aware that the rim of the glass may be hot.

FLAMED ZEST

This is a very dramatic garnish which involves burning the aromatic oils emitted from citrus fruit zest over the surface of a drink. Lemons and limes are sometimes treated in this way but oranges are most popular - ideally firm, thick-skinned navel oranges, like Washington Navels. First cut a 25mm (1 inch) wide strip of zest. Holding the cut zest, peel side down, between the thumb and fore-finger about four inches above the drink, gently warm the zest with a lighter flame. Then pinch the peel by its edges so that its oils squirt through the flame toward the sur-face of the drink. There should be a flash as the oils ignite and the aroma of the drink will be greatly enhanced. (Be careful not to hold the flame too close to the drink as this will leave a smoky film on the glass.) Finally wipe the zest round the rim of the glass.

▲

Flaming an orange zest.

ORDER TO FOLLOW

When making a cocktail, you should work in the order below.

1. Select glass and chill or heat if required
2. Prepare garnish if required
3. Add ingredients
4. Add ice (add last to minimise melt) if required
5. Mix (and strain or pour) or build if required
6. Add garnish if required
7. Consume or serve to another

LEMON / LIME WEDGES

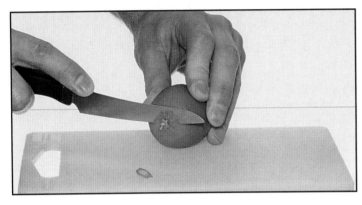

▲ Cutting lime wedges.

Wedges of lemons and limes are often required to squeeze into drinks or to use on the rim as a garnish. A wedge is an eighth segment of the fruit. Cut the 'knobs' from the top and bottom of the fruit. Slice the fruit in half lengthwise, then cut each half into four equal wedges lengthwise. A 'split' wedge of fruit refers to an incision in the fruit which allows it to be anchored on the glass rim.

SALT / SUGAR RIM

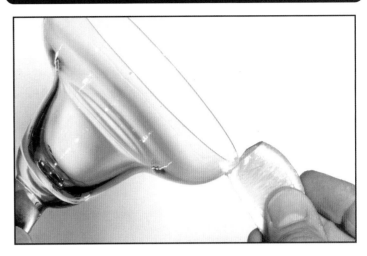

▲ Rimming a glass.

Some recipes call for the rim of the glass to be coated with salt, sugar or other ingredients such as desiccated coconut or chocolate. When using salt, moisten the rim of the glass by whipping a wedge of lime round the outside edge of the rim, then dip the outside edge into a saucer of salt. For sugar, chocolate etc., use an orange slice instead of a lime wedge or run the outside edge of the upturned glass over a sponge moist with water, then dip the outside edge into a saucer of sugar etc..

Whatever you are using to rim your glass should only end up on the outside of the glass so as not to contaminate the cocktail. If some of your garnish should become stuck to the inside edge, this may be whipped off using a fresh fruit wedge or paper towel.

Iodized table salt is too salty to use on the rim of a glass, so sea salt should be used instead. Both salt and sugar can be made finer by blending them in a clean, dry blender.

A professional piece of equipment with the unfortunate title of a 'rimmer' has three sections, one with a sponge for water or lime juice, one containing sugar and another containing salt. ■

A DAY AT THE BEACH

Glass: Collins
Method: Shake first three ingredients with ice and strain into ice-filled glass, then add grenadine.

1¹⁄₈	shot(s)	Malibu coconut rum liqueur
³⁄₄	shot(s)	Disaronno Originale amaretto
4	shot(s)	Freshly squeezed orange juice
¹⁄₄	shot(s)	Grenadine syrup

Comment: A sweet, long, fruity drink with coconut and almond.

ABBEY MARTINI UPDATED ●●●●◐○

Glass: Martini
Garnish: Flamed orange twist
Method: Shake all ingredients with ice and fine strain into chilled glass.

2	shot(s)	Plymouth gin
1	shot(s)	Cinzano Rosso (sweet) vermouth
1	shot(s)	Freshly squeezed orange juice
3	dashes	Angostura aromatic bitters

Origin: This classic (retro) cocktail is closely related to the better known Bronx.
Comment: A dry, orangey, herbal, gin laced concoction.

A.B.C. SHOT

Glass: Shot
Method: Layer by pouring ingredients in the following order.

¹⁄₂	shot(s)	Disaronno Originale amaretto
¹⁄₂	shot(s)	Baileys Irish cream liqueur
¹⁄₂	shot(s)	Rémy Martin Cognac

Comment: A stripy shot with almond, whiskey, cream and Cognac.

ABSINTHE SOUR

Glass: Martini
Garnish: Star anis
Method: Shake ingredients with ice and strain into glass.

1¹⁄₄	shot(s)	La Fée absinthe
1	shot(s)	Sugar (gomme) syrup
1	shot(s)	Freshly squeezed lemon juice
1	shot(s)	Egg white

Comment: A touch of the sours for absinthe lovers.

ABSINTHE WITHOUT LEAVE NEW ●●◐○○

Glass: Shot
Method: Layer in glass by carefully pouring ingredients in the following order.

³⁄₄	shot(s)	Pisang Ambon liqueur
³⁄₄	shot(s)	Baileys Irish Cream liqueur
¹⁄₂	shot(s)	La Fée Absinthe

Origin: Discovered in 2003 at Hush, London, England.
Comment: This green and brown stripy shot is easy to layer but not so easy to drink.

ABSOLUTELY FABULOUS UPDATED ●●●●○

Glass: Flute
Garnish: Strawberry on rim
Method: Shake vodka and cranberry juice with ice and strain into glass, then top up with Champagne.

1	shot(s)	Stolichnaya vodka
2	shot(s)	Cranberry juice
Top up with		Bollinger Champagne

Origin: Created in 1999 at Monte's Club, London, England, and named after the Absolutely Fabulous television series where Patsy consumed copious quantities of Stoli and Bolly – darlings.
Comment: Easy to quaff – Patsy would love it.

ACAPULCO

Glass: Collins
Method: Shake ingredients with ice and strain into ice-filled glass.

1	shot(s)	Sauza Hornitos Tequila
1	shot(s)	Mountgay Eclipse gold rum
1	shot(s)	Pressed grapefruit juice
2¹⁄₂	shot(s)	Pressed pineapple juice
¹⁄₄	shot(s)	Sugar (gomme) syrup

Comment: Innocuous-looking fruity mixture with a dry edge.

ACAPULCO DAIQUIRI NEW ●●●●○

Glass: Martini
Garnish: Lime wedge on rim
Method: Shake all ingredients with ice and fine strain into chilled glass.

1¹⁄₂	shot(s)	Havana Club light rum
¹⁄₂	shot(s)	Cointreau / triple sec
³⁄₄	shot(s)	Freshly squeezed lemon juice
³⁄₄	shot(s)	Rose's lime cordial
¹⁄₂	fresh	Egg white

Comment: A smooth, yet citrus-rich Daiquirí.

ADAM AND EVE

Glass: Rocks
Method: Half fill glass with ice, add sugar syrup, bitters and soda. Stir, add more ice and Bourbon, then float Galliano.

¹⁄₂	shot(s)	Sugar (gomme) syrup
4	dashes	Angostura aromatic bitters
3	shot(s)	Soda water
2	shot(s)	Buffalo Trace Bourbon
Float ¹⁄₄ shot		Galliano

Comment: Golden, herbal fizzy drink – not for the uninitiated, but good for Galliano fans.

ADIOS M-F SHOT

Glass: Shot
Method: Layer in glass by carefully pouring ingredients in the following order.

1	shot(s)	Kahlúa coffee liqueur
1	shot(s)	Sauza Hornitos Tequila

Comment: Lethal shot – surprisingly tasty with potent Tequila afterburn.

ADONIS UPDATED

●●●●●◐

Glass: Martini
Garnish: Orange twist
Method: Stir all ingredients with ice and strain into chilled glass.

3	shot(s)	Fino Sherry
1½	shot(s)	Cinzano Rosso vermouth
3	dashes	Fee Brothers Orange bitters

Origin: Thought to have been created in 1886 to celebrate the success of a Broadway musical.
Comment: Surprisingly delicate, dry, aromatic oldie.

AFFINITY UPDATED

●●●●○○

Glass: Martini
Garnish: Lemon twist
Method: Stir all ingredients with ice and strain into chilled glass.

2	shot(s)	The Famous Grouse Scotch whisky
1	shot(s)	Cinzano Rosso vermouth
1	shot(s)	Cinzano Extra Dry vermouth
3	dashes	Angostura aromatic bitters

AKA: Scotch Manhattan
Variant: Rob Roy & Violet Affinity
Comment: This classic (retro) cocktail may be something of an acquired taste for many modern drinkers.

AFTER EIGHT SHOT

Glass: Shot
Method: Shake ingredients with ice and strain into glass.

½	shot(s)	Absolut vodka
½	shot(s)	Bols Dark crème de cacao
½	shot(s)	Green crème de menthe

Comment: Sludge-green, sweet 'n' sticky with mint-choc flavours.

AFTER SIX SHOT

Glass: Shot
Method: Layer in glass by carefully pouring ingredients in the following order.

½	shot(s)	Kahlúa coffee liqueur
½	shot(s)	White crème de menthe
½	shot(s)	Baileys Irish cream liqueur

Comment: A layered, creamy, coffee and mint shot.

AFTERBURNER

Glass: Snifter
Method: Pour ingredients into glass, swirl to mix, flambé, then extinguish flame.

1	shot(s)	Peppermint schnapps
1	shot(s)	Kahlúa coffee liqueur
½	shot(s)	Wray & Nephew overproof rum

Comment: A surprisingly smooth and moreish drink.

AGENT ORANGE I

Glass: Rocks.
Method: Shake ingredients with ice and strain into ice-filled glass.

1	shot(s)	Absolut vodka
½	shot(s)	Grand Marnier
½	shot(s)	Cointreau / triple sec
2	shot(s)	Freshly squeezed orange juice

Comment: Fresh orange juice is good for you. This has all of the flavour, but few of the health benefits.

AGENT ORANGE II

Glass: Collins
Method: Shake ingredients with ice and strain into ice-filled glass.

½	shot(s)	Absolut vodka
½	shot(s)	Pusser's Navy rum
½	shot(s)	Plymouth gin
¼	shot(s)	Grenadine syrup
½	shot(s)	Pressed apple juice
½	shot(s)	Southern Comfort
½	shot(s)	Buffalo Trace Bourbon
½	shot(s)	Midori melon liqueur
5	shot(s)	Freshly squeezed orange juice

Comment: The apricot in Southern Comfort dominates this Bourbon based drink but as the name would suggest there's more than a hint of orange.

AGGRAVATION

Glass: Rocks
Garnish: Dust with nutmeg
Method: Shake with ice and strain into ice-filled glass.

1½	shot(s)	The Famous Grouse Scotch whisky
1	shot(s)	Kahlúa coffee liqueur
1	shot(s)	Double (heavy) cream
1	shot(s)	Milk

Comment: Bedtime milk has never been so sexy.

A.J.

Glass: Martini
Garnish: Apple wedge
Method: Shake ingredients with ice and strain into glass.

2	shot(s)	Calvados (or applejack brandy)
2	shot(s)	Pressed grapefruit juice
¼	shot(s)	Sugar (gomme) syrup

Comment: You'll either love or hate this, but if you like Calvados the former will apply!

ALABAMA FIZZ

Glass: Collins
Garnish: Mint sprig & lemon slice
Method: Shake all but soda water with ice and strain into ice-filled glass, then top up with soda water and stir.

2	shot(s)	Plymouth gin
1½	shot(s)	Freshly squeezed lemon juice
½	shot(s)	Sugar (gomme) syrup
Top up with		Soda water

Comment: This version of the classic Gin Fizz is a gin and tonic with bells on. You'll never ask for a straight G&T again!

25

ALABAMA SLAMMER # 1

Glass: Martini
Garnish: Split lemon wheel
Method: Shake ingredients with ice and strain into glass.

1	shot(s)	Absolut vodka
1	shot(s)	Southern Comfort
2	shot(s)	Freshly squeezed orange juice
1/4	shot(s)	Grenadine syrup

Comment: A medium sweet, red, fruity drink.

ALABAMA SLAMMER #2 UPDATED

●●●●◐○

Glass: Old-fashioned
Garnish: Peach wedge on rim
Method: Shake all ingredients with ice and strain into ice-filled glass.

1	shot(s)	Southern Comfort
1/2	shot(s)	Plymouth Sloe gin
1/2	shot(s)	Disaronno Originale amaretto
2 1/4	shot(s)	Freshly squeezed orange juice
1	shot(s)	Freshly squeezed lemon juice

Comment: Rich and quite sweet with a citrus bite.

ALAN'S APPLE BREEZE

●●●●●○

Glass: Collins
Garnish: Red apple wedge on rim
Method: Shake all ingredients with ice and strain into ice-filled glass.

2	shot(s)	Havana Club light rum
3/4	shot(s)	Bols Apricot brandy liqueur
2	shot(s)	Pressed apple juice
2	shot(s)	Cranberry juice
1/2	shot(s)	Freshly squeezed lime juice
1/2	shot(s)	Sugar (gomme) syrup

Origin: Created in 2002 by Alan Johnston at Metropolitan, Glasgow, Scotland.
Comment: A sweet, tangy version of the Apple Breeze.

ALASKA MARTINI

●●●●●○

Glass: Martini
Garnish: Orange Twist
Method: Shake all ingredients with ice and fine strain into chilled glass.

2 1/2	shot(s)	Plymouth gin
3/4	shot(s)	Yellow Chartreuse
1	shot(s)	Fino Sherry
1/8	shot(s)	Fee Brothers Orange bitters

AKA: Nome
Origin: Adapted from the Alaska in The Savoy Cocktail Book. The addition of dry sherry is recommended in David Embury's The Fine Art Of Mixing Drinks.
Comment: If you like gin and Chartreuse, you'll also love this strong and complex Martini.

ALESSANDRO

●●●●○○

Glass: Martini
Method: Shake all ingredients with ice and fine strain into chilled glass.

2	shot(s)	Opal Nera black sambuca
3/4	shot(s)	Plymouth gin
3/4	shot(s)	Double (heavy) cream
3/4	shot(s)	Milk

Comment: Hints of aniseed, elderflower and gin emerge from this grey, creamy drink.

ALEXANDER

Glass: Martini
Garnish: Dust with nutmeg
Method: Shake ingredients with ice and strain into glass.

1 1/2	shot(s)	Plymouth gin
1 1/2	shot(s)	Bols White crème de cacao
1 1/2	shot(s)	Double (heavy) cream

AKA: Gin Alexander or Princess Mary
Comment: A Prohibition favourite – white, smooth and nicer than you'd imagine.

ALEXANDER THE GREAT

Glass: Martini
Garnish: Coffee beans and chocolate sprinkle
Method: Shake ingredients with ice and strain into glass.

2	shot(s)	Absolut vodka
1	shot(s)	Kahlúa coffee liqueur
1	shot(s)	Bols White crème de cacao
1	shot(s)	Double (heavy) cream

Comment: A tasty combination of coffee, chocolate and cream, laced with vodka.

ALEXANDER'S BIG BROTHER

Glass: Martini
Garnish: Physalis
Method: Shake ingredients with ice and strain into glass.

1 1/2	shot(s)	Plymouth gin
3/4	shot(s)	Bols Blue curaçao
3/4	shot(s)	Double (heavy) cream
3/4	shot(s)	Milk

Comment: Creamy blue, should be your last choice on any cocktail menu.

ALEXANDER'S SISTER

Glass: Martini
Garnish: Mint leaf
Method: Shake ingredients with ice and strain into glass.

1 1/2	shot(s)	Plymouth gin
3/4	shot(s)	Green crème de menthe
3/4	shot(s)	Double (heavy) cream
3/4	shot(s)	Milk

Comment: A green minty thing for dairy lovers.

ALEXANDRA

Glass: Martini
Garnish: Three coffee beans
Method: Shake ingredients with ice and strain into glass.

2	shot(s)	Pusser's Navy rum
1	shot(s)	Kahlúa coffee liqueur
1	shot(s)	Double (heavy) cream

Comment: Surprisingly potent, despite the ladylike name.

ALFONSO I

Glass: Flute
Garnish: Twist of lemon
Method: Place sugar cube in glass and cover with bitters, then add Dubonnet and top up with Champagne.

1	cube	Sugar
4	drop	Angostura aromatic bitters
1/2	shot(s)	Dubonnet Red
Top up with		Piper-Heidsieck Brut Champagne

Origin: Named after the deposed Spanish king Alfonso XIII, who first tasted this drink while exiled in France.
Comment: Herbal variation on the classic Champagne Cocktail.

ALGONQUIN UPDATED

Glass: Old-fashioned
Garnish: Cherry on stick
Method: Shake ingredients with ice and strain into ice-filled glass.

2	shot(s)	Buffalo Trace Bourbon
1½	shot(s)	Cinzano Extra Dry vermouth
1½	shot(s)	Pressed pineapple juice
2	dashes	Péychaud's Bitters

Origin: One of several classic (retro) cocktails accredited to New York City's Algonquin Hotel.
Comment: Pineapple juice adds fruit and froth, while Péychaud's Bitters combine subtly with the Bourbon in this dry aromatic drink.

ALICE FROM DALLAS

Glass: Shot.
Method: Layer in glass by pouring ingredients carefully in the following order.

1/2	shot(s)	Kahlúa coffee liqueur
1/2	shot(s)	Grand Marnier
1/2	shot(s)	Sauza Hornitos Tequila

Comment: Coffee and orange spiked with Tequila.

ALICE IN WONDERLAND

Glass: Shot
Garnish: Lime wedge
Method: Layer in glass by carefully pouring ingredients in the following order.

| 1 | shot(s) | Sauza Hornitos Tequila |
| 1/2 | shot(s) | Grand Marnier |

Comment: Brings a whole new dimension to Tequila and orange.

ALL FALL DOWN

Glass: Shot
Method: Layer in glass by carefully pouring ingredients in the following order.

1/2	shot(s)	Sauza Hornitos Tequila
1/2	shot(s)	Pusser's Navy rum
1/2	shot(s)	Kahlúa coffee liqueur

Comment: Too many of these and you will.

ALL WHITE FRAPPÉ

Glass: Old-fashioned
Garnish: Lemon zest
Method: Blend all ingredients with 3/4 scoop crushed ice and serve with short straws.

1	shot(s)	Pernod anise
1	shot(s)	Bols White crème de cacao
1	shot(s)	Peppermint schnapps
1	shot(s)	Freshly squeezed lemon juice

Comment: Aniseed, chocolate, peppermint and lemon juice are an unlikely but tasty combination for summer afternoons.

AMARETTO SOUR

Glass: Old-fashioned
Garnish: Cherry & lemon slice
Method: Shake ingredients with ice and strain into ice-filled glass.

2	shot(s)	Disaronno Originale amaretto
1½	shot(s)	Freshly squeezed lemon juice
1/4	shot(s)	Sugar (gomme) syrup
1/2	shot(s)	Pasteurised egg white
4	dashes	Angostura aromatic bitters

Comment: Sweet 'n' sour – frothy with an almond buzz.

AMARO DOLCE

Glass: Rocks
Method: Muddle lime in glass to release the juices and oils in the skin of the lime. Pour rest of ingredients into glass, add crushed ice and stir. Serve with a straw.

1	whole	Lime cut into eighths
1	shot(s)	Stoli Razberi
1	shot(s)	Campari
1	shot(s)	Freshly squeezed lime juice
3/4	shot(s)	Sugar (gomme) syrup

Origin: Created in 2002 by Alex Kammerling, London, England.
Comment: Not to everyone's taste, this Caipirinha-like drink features that distinctive bitter Campari edge.

AMBER

Glass: Collins
Garnish: Apple chevron & nutmeg dust
Method: Muddle ginger in base of shaker. Add other ingredients, shake with ice and strain into glass filled with crushed ice.

2	nails	Fresh root ginger
1½	shot(s)	Zubrówka (Bison grass) vodka
4	shot(s)	Pressed apple juice
1/2	shot(s)	Ginger syrup
1/2	shot(s)	Apple schnapps liqueur

Origin: Created in 2001 by Douglas Ankrah for Akbar at the Red Fort, Soho, London, England.
Comment: A great combination of adult flavours in a long, thirst-quenching drink. Also great served up.

AMBROSIA

Glass: Flute
Method: Shake first four ingredients with ice and strain into glass, then top up with Champagne.

1	shot(s)	Rémy Martin Cognac
1	shot(s)	Calvados or Applejack Brandy
¼	shot(s)	Freshly squeezed lemon juice
¼	shot(s)	Cointreau / triple sec
Top up with		Champagne

Comment: Bubbly apples – very strong!

AMBROSIA'TINI

●●●●○○

Glass: Martini
Garnish: Dust with ground nutmeg
Method: Shake all ingredients with ice and fine strain into chilled glass.

¾	shot(s)	Rémy Martin Cognac
2	shot(s)	Warninks Advocaat
1	shot(s)	Cuarenta Y Tres (Licor 43)
½	shot(s)	Yellow Chartreuse

Origin: I created this drink and named it after the Greek for 'elixir of life, the food of the gods'. In Britain Ambrosia is a brand of custard, so advocaat seemed appropriate, while if there is a God, he/she/it surely drinks Chartreuse.
Comment: Easy-drinking but complex with a herbal edge.

AMERICAN BEAUTY **UPDATED**

●●●●○

Glass: Martini
Garnish: Float rose petal
Method: Shake all ingredients with ice and fine strain into chilled glass.

¾	shot(s)	Rémy Martin Cognac
¾	shot(s)	Cinzano Extra Dry vermouth
¾	shot(s)	Freshly squeezed orange juice
½	shot(s)	Tawny port
½	shot(s)	Sugar (gomme) syrup
¼	shot(s)	Grenadine syrup

Variant: Add 1/4 shot white crème de menthe
Comment: A complex cocktail that harnesses the flavours of Cognac, port and orange - a beauty.

AMERICANA

Glass: Flute
Garnish: Slice of peach
Method: Coat sugar cube with bitters and Bourbon, place in glass and top up with Champagne.

¼	shot(s)	Buffalo Trace Bourbon
1	cube	Sugar
1	dash	Angostura aromatic bitters
Top up with		Piper-Heidsieck Brut Champagne

Comment: The Wild West take on the classic Champagne Cocktail.

AMIGO SHOT

Glass: Shot
Garnish: Sprinkle with nutmeg
Method: Layer ingredients by carefully pouring in the following order.

½	shot(s)	Kahlúa coffee liqueur
½	shot(s)	Double (heavy) cream
½	shot(s)	Sauza Hornitos Tequila

Comment: Coffee and Tequila combine well in this smooth and creamy shot.

AMOUR MARIE

Glass: Collins
Method: Shake first three ingredients with ice and strain into ice-filled glass , then top up with soda water.

1½	shot(s)	Plymouth gin
2	shot(s)	Parfait Amour
1½	shot(s)	Cinzano Extra Dry vermouth
Top up with		Soda water (club soda)

Comment: A bittersweet long drink with a full-on violet flavour.

ANDALUCIA

Glass: Martini
Garnish: Lemon twist
Method: Stir ingredients with ice and strain into glass.

2	shot(s)	Tio Pepe Fino Sherry
1½	shot(s)	Spanish brandy
¾	shot(s)	Havana Club light rum

Comment: If you like sherry, you'll love this bone-dry cocktail. If you don't, don't drink it!

AÑEJO HIGHBALL

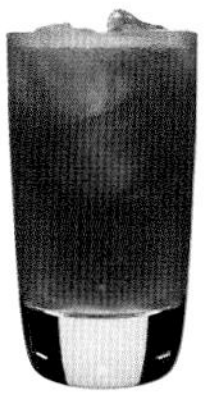

●●●●○○

Glass: Collins
Garnish: Orange slice
Method: Shake first four ingredients with ice and strain into ice-filled glass. Top up with ginger beer.

1½	shot(s)	Appleton Estate V/X aged rum
½	shot(s)	Orange curaçao
¼	shot(s)	Freshly squeezed lime juice
2	dashes	Angostura aromatic bitters
Top up with		Jamaican ginger beer

Origin: Created in 2002 by the famous New York bartender, Dale DeGroff. 'Añejo', which is the Spanish for 'old', refers to the aged rum used in the recipe.
Comment: Neither sweet nor overly alcoholic - simply tasty and refreshing.

ANGEL FACE MARTINI

Glass: Martini
Garnish: Peach or apricot slice on rim
Method: Shake all ingredients with ice and fine strain into chilled glass.

1	shot(s)	Plymouth gin
1	shot(s)	Calvados or Applejack brandy
1	shot(s)	Bols Apricot brandy
1/8	shot(s)	Sugar (gomme) syrup
1	shot(s)	Chilled water

Origin: Adapted from a recipe first published in The Savoy Cocktail Book in the 1950s.
Comment: A golden combination of gin, apple and apricot.

ANGEL'S DELIGHT UPDATED

Glass: Martini
Garnish: Strawberry on rim
Method: Shake all ingredients with ice and fine strain into chilled glass.

1	shot(s)	Cointreau / triple sec
1	shot(s)	Plymouth gin
1/2	shot(s)	Grenadine syrup
1	shot(s)	Double (heavy) cream
1	shot(s)	Milk

Comment: This drink shares its name with the popular British powdered dessert, Angel Delight. Like its namesake it's 'fluffy' and pink.

ANGEL'S HIP

Glass: Shot
Method: Layer in glass by carefully pouring ingredients in the following order.

3/4	shot(s)	Bénédictine D.O.M liqueur
3/4	shot(s)	Baileys Irish cream liqueur

Comment: A warming layered shot that slips down easily.

ANGEL'S RUSH

Glass: Shot
Garnish: Dust with nutmeg
Method: Layer in glass by carefully pouring ingredients in the following order.

3/4	shot(s)	Frangelico hazelnut liqueur
3/4	shot(s)	Double (heavy) cream

Comment: A nutty, creamy shot.

ANGERS ROSE

Glass: Martini
Garnish: Pineapple leaf
Method: Shake ingredients with ice and strain into glass.

1	shot(s)	Cointreau / triple sec
1	shot(s)	Buffalo Trace Bourbon
2	shot(s)	Pressed pineapple juice
1/4	shot(s)	Campari
1/2	fresh	Egg white

Comment: A relatively dry cocktail – orange, pineapple and Bourbon with Campari herbal notes.

AMERICANO

Glass: Collins
Garnish: Orange slice
Method: Pour Campari into ice-filled glass and add vermouth, then top up with soda and stir.

1 1/2	shot(s)	Campari
1 1/2	shot(s)	Cinzano Rosso vermouth
Top up with		Soda water (club soda)

Origin: First served in the 1860s in Gaspare Campari's bar in Milan. This was originally known as the 'Milano-Torino' as the original two base ingredients came from these two cities. It was not until Prohibition that the Italians noticed an influx of Americans who enjoyed the drink and, as a dubious compliment, dubbed the drink Americano.

Comment: A bitter, fizzy, long refreshing drink, which if you like Campari you'll love.

ANIS'TINI NEW

Glass: Martini
Garnish: Star anise
Method: Muddle star anise in base of shaker. Add other ingredients, shake with ice and fine strain into chilled glass.

2	air-dried	Star anises
1	shot(s)	Absolut vodka
3/4	shot(s)	Opal Bianca Sambuca
1/2	shot(s)	Pernod anis
1 1/2	shot(s)	Chilled water

Origin: Discovered in 2002 at Lot 61, New York City.
Comment: Specs of star anise are evident in this aniseedy Martini.

ANITA'S ATTITUDE ADJUSTER

Glass: Sling
Garnish: Split lemon wheel
Method: Shake first seven ingredients with ice and strain into ice-filled glass, then top up with sparkling wine and stir.

½	shot(s)	Cointreau / triple sec
½	shot(s)	Sauza Hornitos Tequila
½	shot(s)	Havana Club light rum
½	shot(s)	Plymouth gin
½	shot(s)	Absolut vodka
½	shot(s)	Freshly squeezed lime juice
¾	shot(s)	Sugar (gomme) syrup
Top up with		Piper-Heidsieck Brut Champagne

Comment: A refreshing combination of five different spirits with a hint of lime and a topping of sparkling wine.

ANTHONY'S FAVOURITE

Glass: Sling
Garnish: Redcurrants
Method: Pour the following ingredients into ice-filled glass in the order below. Don't stir!

1	shot(s)	Havana Club light rum
1	shot(s)	Pusser's Navy rum
1	shot(s)	Guava juice
2	shot(s)	Pressed pineapple juice
1	shot(s)	Freshly squeezed lime juice
1	shot(s)	Freshly squeezed lemon juice
Top up with		Freshly squeezed orange juice
½	shot(s)	Grenadine syrup

Comment: A long, tropical rum-laced cooler.

APACHE

Glass: Shot
Method: Layer in glass by carefully pouring in the following order.

½	shot(s)	Midori melon liqueur
¾	shot(s)	Kahlúa coffee liqueur
½	shot(s)	Baileys Irish cream liqueur

Comment: A brown (coffee), green (melon) and cream (whiskey cream) striped shot.

●●●●●○

APHRODISIAC

Glass: Collins
Garnish: Apple slice on rim
Method: Muddle ginger with vodka in base of shaker. Add other ingredients, shake with ice and fine strain into ice-filled glass.

3	fresh	Thumb-nail sized slices root ginger
2	shot(s)	Vanilla infused vodka
½	shot(s)	Green Chartreuse
2½	shot(s)	Pressed apple juice
2	shot(s)	Gavi (white wine)

Origin: Created in 2002 by Yannick Miseriaux at The Fifth Floor Bar, London, England.
Comment: As strong in flavour as it is high in alcohol.

APOTHECARY

Glass: Shot
Method: Stir ingredients with ice and strain into glass.

½	shot(s)	Punt É Mes
½	shot(s)	Fernet Branca
½	shot(s)	Green crème de menthe

Comment: An acquired taste – good luck acquiring it!

APPLE BRANDY SOUR

Glass: Martini
Garnish: Cherry & lemon slice
Method: Vigorously shake ingredients with ice and strain into glass.

2	shot(s)	Calvados (or applejack brandy)
1	shot(s)	Freshly squeezed lemon juice
¼	shot(s)	Sugar (gomme) syrup
½	fresh	Egg white

Comment: Sour by name and by nature.

APPLE BREEZE

Glass: Collins
Garnish: Apple wedge on rim
Method: Shake all ingredients with ice and fine strain into ice-filled glass.

2½	shot(s)	Absolut vodka
3	shot(s)	Pressed apple juice
2	shot(s)	Cranberry juice

Comment: A lot more interesting than the better known Sea Breeze.

●●●●○

APPLE & CRANBERRY PIE'TINI NEW

Glass: Martini
Garnish: Cinnamon dust
Method: Shake first four ingredients with ice and fine strain into chilled glass. Float cream on surface of drink by pouring over back of dessertspoon.

1½	shot(s)	Finlandia Cranberry vodka
¾	shot(s)	Apple Schnapps
1	shot(s)	Cranberry juice
½	shot(s)	Freshly squeezed lime juice
¾	shot(s)	Double (heavy) cream

Origin: I created this drink in 2003 for Finlandia.
Comment: Sip apple and cranberry through a creamy cinnamon layer.

APPLE & CUSTARD MARTINI

Glass: Martini
Garnish: Apple wedge on rim
Method: Shake all ingredients with ice and strain into glass.

2	shot(s)	Warninks Advocaat
1½	shot(s)	Calvados (or applejack brandy)
½	shot(s)	Sourz Sour Apple liqueur
¼	shot(s)	Vanilla syrup

Origin: I created this in 2002 after rediscovering Advocaat on a trip to Amsterdam.
Comment: Smooth and creamy, this tastes like its name.

●●●●◐○

APPLE & MELON MARTINI NEW

Glass: Martini
Garnish: Apple wedge on rim
Method: Shake all ingredients with ice and fine strain into chilled glass.

2	shot(s)	Absolut vodka
1	shot(s)	Sourz Sour Apple liqueur
1/2	shot(s)	Midori Melon liqueur
1/2	shot(s)	Freshly squeezed lime juice

Comment: The ubiquitous green apple Martini with extra colour and flavour thanks to a dash of melon liqueur.

APPLE & SPICE

Glass: Shot
Garnish: Sprinkle with cinnamon
Method: Layer in glass by carefully pouring ingredients in the following order.

3/4	shot(s)	Calvados (or applejack brandy)
3/4	shot(s)	Double (heavy) cream

Comment: Creamy apple shot.

●●●●●○

APPLE CART UPDATED

Glass: Martini
Garnish: Apple slice on rim
Method: Shake all ingredients with ice and fine strain into chilled glass.

2	shot(s)	Calvados (or applejack brandy)
3/4	shot(s)	Cointreau / triple sec
1/2	shot(s)	Freshly squeezed lemon juice
1/2	shot(s)	Sugar (gomme) syrup
1/2	shot(s)	Chilled water

AKA: Calvados Sidecar
Origin: This classic (retro) cocktail is an adaptation of the even older Sidecar.
Comment: A serious combination of apple with orange and sweet with sour.

APPLE COLADA

Glass: Hurricane
Garnish: Pineapple leaf
Method: Blend ingredients with crushed ice and serve.

3/4	shot(s)	Havana Club light rum
1 1/2	shot(s)	Apple schnapps
1	shot(s)	Cream of coconut
2	shot(s)	Double (heavy) cream
3	shot(s)	Pressed pineapple juice

Comment: The Piña Colada is back with added apple.

●●●●◐○

APPLE CRUMBLE MARTINI #1

Glass: Martini
Garnish: Apple wedge on rim
Method: Shake all ingredients with ice and fine strain into chilled glass.

2	shot(s)	The Famous Grouse Scotch Whisky
1/4	shot(s)	Teichenné butterscotch schnapps
1	shot(s)	Pressed apple juice
1/2	shot(s)	Freshly squeezed lemon juice
1/2	shot(s)	Sugar (gomme) syrup

Comment: That's the way the apple crumbles - in this case enhancing the flavour of the Scotch.

●●●●●○

APPLE CRUMBLE MARTINI #2

Glass: Martini
Garnish: Dust with ground cinnamon
Method: Shake all ingredients with ice and fine strain into chilled glass.

2	shot(s)	Tuaca liqueur
1/2	shot(s)	Freshly squeezed lemon juice
2	shot(s)	Pressed apple juice

Origin: Created in 2002 by Eion Richards at Bonds Bar, London, England.
Comment: Easy to make and equally easy to drink.

APPLE DAIQUIRÍ

Glass: Martini
Garnish: Split red apple wedge
Method: Vigorously shake ingredients with cubed ice and fine strain into chilled glass.

1 3/4	shot(s)	Havana Club light rum
3/4	shot(s)	Apple Schnapps
1/2	shot(s)	Cinnamon schnapps
1/2	shot(s)	Freshly squeezed lime juice
1/2	shot(s)	Sugar (gomme) syrup
1/2	shot(s)	Chilled water

Origin: I created this in 1999.
Comment: Sour apple and cinnamon.

●●●●●○

APPLE MANHATTAN UPDATED

Glass: Martini
Garnish: Apple slice on rim
Method: Shake all ingredients with ice and fine strain into chilled glass.

2	shot(s)	Buffalo Trace Bourbon
1 1/2	shot(s)	Apple Schnapps
1/2	shot(s)	Cinzano Rosso (sweet) vermouth

Origin: My take on a drink created by David Marsden at First on First in New York City and latterly popularised by Dale DeGroff. Traditionalists may want to stir this drink.
Comment: Rusty gold in colour, this is a flavoursome number for Bourbon lovers.

APPLE MARTINI

●●●●○

#1 (POPULAR US VERSION) UPDATED

Glass: Martini
Garnish: Float thin apple slice
Method: Shake all ingredients with ice and fine strain into chilled glass.

2	shot(s)	Absolut vodka
1½	shot(s)	Sourz Sour Apple liqueur
¼	shot(s)	Rose's lime cordial

AKA: Green Apple Martini
Variation: Toffee Apple Martini, Apple & Melon Martini and other Apple Martini versions.
Comment: A hugely popular drink across North America. Some bars add some sour mix in place of Rose's, others add a dash of fresh lime and sugar.

●●●●◐

#2 (DELUXE US VERSION) UPDATED

Glass: Martini
Garnish: Cherry in glass
Method: Shake all ingredients with ice and fine strain into chilled glass.

2	shot(s)	Absolut vodka
1	shot(s)	Sourz Sour Apple liqueur
½	shot(s)	Freshly squeezed lime juice
¼	shot(s)	Sugar (gomme) syrup
½	fresh	Egg white

AKA: Sour Apple Martini
Comment: Apple fortified with vodka and sexed up with a hint of orange and a lemon sour edge.

●●●●○

#3 (UK VERSION) NEW

Glass: Martini
Garnish: Apple wedge on rim
Method: Shake all ingredients with ice and fine strain into chilled glass.

2	shot(s)	Absolut vodka
¾	shot(s)	Apple Schnapps
2	shot(s)	Pressed apple juice

Comment: There are as many different recipes for this drink as there are varieties of apple and brands of apple liqueur. The best are great.

●●●●●○

APPLE OF MY EIRE

Glass: Martini
Garnish: Clove
Method: Muddle cloves and cinnamon in base of shaker, add Drambuie and continue to muddle. Add the rest of the ingredients and shake with ice. Strain into glass.

7	whole	Cloves
¼	spoon	Ground cinnamon
1	shot(s)	Drambuie
1	shot(s)	Passoã passion fruit liqueur
½	shot(s)	Grand Marnier
¾	shot(s)	Pressed apple juice
¾	shot(s)	Cranberry juice

Origin: Adapted from a recipe created by Elaine in 2002 at Living Room, Liverpool, England. The original uses a blend of apple purée with cloves and cinnamon.
Comment: Cinnamon and cloves combine with a veritable fruit basket to produce a drink reminiscent of cold mulled wine – very refreshing.

●●●●●◐

APPLE OF ONE'S EYE

Glass: Collins
Garnish: Apple wedge on rim
Method: Shake first three ingredients with ice and strain into ice-filled glass. Top up with ginger beer.

2	shot(s)	Rémy Martin Cognac
½	shot(s)	Freshly squeezed lime juice
3	shot(s)	Pressed apple juice
Top up with		Jamaican ginger beer

Comment: This spicy concoction is definitely something to cherish.

●●●●○○

APPLE PIE

Glass: Shot
Method: Layer by carefully pouring ingredients in the following order.

¾	shot(s)	After Shock Red
¾	shot(s)	Sourz Sour Apple liqueur
½	shot(s)	Baileys Irish Cream liqueur

Origin: Created in 2002 by Wayne Collins for Maxxium UK.
Comment: Looks innocent but packs a real flavour punch.

●●●●●○

APPLE PIE MARTINI

Glass: Martini
Garnish: Apple slice on rim
Method: Shake all ingredients with ice and fine strain into chilled glass.

1½	shot(s)	Zubrówka (Bison grass) vodka
½	shot(s)	Goldschläger cinnamon schnapps
2	shot(s)	Pressed apple juice
1	shot(s)	Cranberry juice

Origin: Created in 2000 by Alexia Pau Barrera at Sand Bar, Clapham, England.
Comment: There's a good hit of cinnamon in this apple pie.

APPLE PIE SHOT

Glass: Shot
Garnish: Dust with cinnamon, then add a dot of whipped cream.
Method: Shake ingredients with ice and strain into glass.

1	shot(s)	Apple schnapps
1/2	shot(s)	Frangelico hazelnut liqueur

Comment: Nuts, apple, cinnamon and cream – pudding, anyone?

APPLEISSIMO

●●●●●○

Glass: Collins
Garnish: Apple slice on rim
Method: Pour apple schnapps and apple juice into ice-filled glass. Stir anise and cranberry with ice and carefully strain into glass so as to layer over first two ingredients and serve with straws.

1½	shot(s)	Apple schnapps
3	shot(s)	Pressed apple juice
1½	shot(s)	Pernod anise
1½	shot(s)	Cranberry juice

Comment: A two layered drink. Stir the layers together with straws before drinking.

APPLESINTH UPDATED

●●●●○

Glass: Old-fashioned
Garnish: Apple wedge on rim
Method: Shake all ingredients with ice and strain into glass filled with crushed ice.

1	shot(s)	La Fée absinthe
1	shot(s)	Apple schnapps liqueur
2	shot(s)	Pressed apple juice
3/4	shot(s)	Freshly squeezed lime juice
1/2	shot(s)	Passion fruit syrup

Origin: Created in 1999 by Alex Kammerling, London, England.
Comment: Hints of apple and liquorice combine to make a very moreish cocktail.

APPLE SPRITZ NEW

●●●●○

Glass: Flute
Garnish: Peach or apple slice on rim
Method: Pour first two ingredients into glass and top up with Champagne.

3/4	shot(s)	Apple liqueur schnapps
1/4	shot(s)	Teichenné peach schnapps
Top up with		Piper-Heidsieck Brut Champagne

Origin: Discovered in 2003 at Paramount Hotel, New York City.
Comment: Sweet, fruity Champagne – oh yeah baby.

APPLE STRUDEL MARTINI

Glass: Martini
Garnish: Dust surface of drink with cinnamon
Method: Shake first five ingredients with ice and strain into glass, then float single cream.

1/2	shot(s)	Cinnamon schnapps
1	shot(s)	Apple schnapps Liqueur
1/2	shot(s)	Bols White crème de cacao
1/2	shot(s)	Bols Brown crème de cacao
1	shot(s)	Pressed apple juice
3/4	shot(s)	Double (heavy) cream

Variant: May also be served as a shot in a shot glass.
Origin: Created by Alex Kammerling in 1999.
Comment: Tastes just like mum's homemade apple pie with cream.

APPLE STRUDEL MARTINI #2

●●●●●◐

Glass: Martini
Garnish: Dust with cinnamon
Method: Shake all ingredients with ice and fine strain into chilled glass.

2	shot(s)	Stoli Vanil
2	shot(s)	Pressed apple juice
1/4	shot(s)	Apple schnapps liqueur

Comment: The flavour of this drink is just as described on the box.

APPLE SUNRISE

Glass: Collins
Method: Pour ingredients into ice-filled glass and stir.

1/2	shot(s)	Sisca Crème de cassis
2	shot(s)	Calvados or applejack brandy
4	shot(s)	Freshly squeezed orange juice

Created by: Charles Schumann of Munich in 1980.
Comment: A pleasing mix of fruits with the apple punch of Calvados.

APRICOT COCKTAIL

Glass: Martini
Garnish: Split lemon wheel
Method: Shake ingredients with ice and strain into glass.

1½	shot(s)	Plymouth gin
1½	shot(s)	Bols Apricot brandy liqueur
1/4	shot(s)	Grenadine syrup
4	dashes	Angostura aromatic bitters
1/2	shot(s)	Freshly squeezed lemon juice

Comment: This very red cocktail combines gin, apricot and lemon.

APRICOT COOLER

Glass: Collins
Garnish: Apricot peel spiral
Method: Shake all but soda with ice and strain into ice-filled glass, then top up with soda and stir.

2	shot(s)	Bols Apricot brandy liqueur
1	shot(s)	Freshly squeezed lime juice
½	shot(s)	Sugar (gomme) syrup
4	dashes	Angostura aromatic bitters
⅛	shot(s)	Grenadine syrup
Top up with		Soda water (club soda)

Comment: A little like liquid sherbet Dib Dab. Refreshing and drinkable.

APRICOT FIZZ

Glass: Collins
Garnish: Lemon wedge
Method: Shake first four ingredients with ice and strain into ice-filled glass, then top up with soda water.

1½	shot(s)	Bols Apricot brandy liqueur
1	shot(s)	Freshly squeezed orange juice
1¼	shot(s)	Freshly squeezed lime juice
¾	shot(s)	Sugar (gomme) syrup
Top up with		Soda water (club soda)

Comment: A low-alcohol, well-balanced, refreshing cocktail.

APRICOT LADY

Glass: Old-fashioned
Garnish: Lemon wedge & cherry on stick
Method: Shake ingredients with ice and strain into glass.

1½	shot(s)	Havana Club light rum
1	shot(s)	Bols Apricot brandy liqueur
1	shot(s)	Freshly squeezed lemon juice
½	fresh	Egg white
¼	shot(s)	Sugar (gomme) syrup

Comment: Like drinking fluffy marzipan.

APRICOT MANGO MARTINI

Glass: Martini
Garnish: Lemon twist
Method: Muddle mango in the base of a shaker. Add other ingredients, shake with ice and fine strain into glass.

1	handful	Fresh chopped mango
2	shot(s)	Plymouth gin
½	shot(s)	Bols Apricot brandy liqueur
¾	shot(s)	Freshly squeezed lemon juice
½	shot(s)	Sugar (gomme) syrup

Comment: A simple, great tasting variation on the fresh fruit Martini.

APRICOT STONE SOUR

Glass: Martini
Garnish: Apricot slice
Method: Shake ingredients with ice and strain into glass.

2	shot(s)	Bols Apricot brandy liqueur
½	shot(s)	Freshly squeezed orange juice
1	shot(s)	Freshly squeezed lime juice
¼	shot(s)	Sugar (gomme) syrup

Comment: The name says it all.

APRIL SHOWER

Glass: Martini
Garnish: Starfruit
Method: Shake ingredients with ice and strain into glass.

2	shot(s)	Freshly squeezed orange juice
½	shot(s)	Bénédictine D.O.M liqueur
1½	shot(s)	Rémy Martin Cognac

Comment: A medium dry, mustard coloured, Cognac based drink.

AQUARIUS

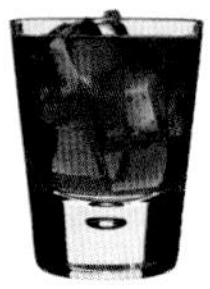

Glass: Rocks
Method: Shake ingredients with ice and strain into ice-filled glass.

2	shot(s)	The Famous Grouse Scotch whisky
1	shot(s)	Bols Cherry brandy liqueur
1½	shot(s)	Cranberry juice
¼	shot(s)	Sugar (gomme) syrup

Comment: The sweet cherry edge is balanced by the dryness of cranberry and Scotch.

ARCHANGEL

Glass: Collins
Garnish: Strawberry slice and basil leaf
Method: Shake ingredients with ice and strain into ice-filled glass.

1	shot(s)	Strawberry purée
3	shot(s)	Pressed pineapple juice
½	shot(s)	Pitú Cachaça
½	shot(s)	Wray & Nephew overproof rum
1	shot(s)	Teichenné Peach schnapps
4	fresh	Basil leaves

Origin: Made by Sean Finnegan at Mash & Air, Manchester in 1999. Joint winner of the Manchester Food & Drink Festival cocktail competition.
Comment: Fragrant, fruity, sweet, well-balanced – the basil adds an extra dimension to the Batida base.

ARCHIE RED

Glass: Martini
Garnish: Lemon shaving
Method: Shake ingredients with ice and strain into glass.

1	shot(s)	Teichenné Peach schnapps
1	shot(s)	Absolut vodka
½	shot(s)	Chambord black raspberry liqueur
½	shot(s)	Freshly squeezed lemon juice
3	drops	La Fée absinthe

Origin: Created by Chris Langan at Blue Bar Café.
Comment: Blackberry, peach with a touch of anis, laced with vodka. A little sweetie.

ARCHIE SLINGBACK

Glass: Sling
Garnish: Slice of peach
Method: Shake ingredients with ice and strain into glass.

2	shot(s)	Plymouth gin
1½	shot(s)	Peach purée
2	shot(s)	Pressed apple juice
1	shot(s)	Teichenné Peach schnapps
½	shot(s)	Freshly squeezed lime juice
¼	shot(s)	Sugar (gomme) syrup

Origin: Created by Jenifer at Match bar, London, England.
Comment: Refreshing, long, peach cocktail.

ARIZONA BREEZE

●●●●○○

Glass: Collins
Garnish: Grapefruit wedge on rim
Method: Shake ingredients with ice and strain into ice-filled glass.

2½	shot(s)	Plymouth gin
3	shot(s)	Cranberry juice
2	shot(s)	Pressed grapefruit juice
¼	shot(s)	Sugar (gomme) syrup

Comment: An aromatic variation on the Sea Breeze, combining gin, cranberry and grapefruit.

ARNAUD **UPDATED**

●●●●○

Glass: Martini
Garnish: Blackberry on rim
Method: Stir all ingredients with ice and strain into chilled glass.

1½	shot(s)	Plymouth gin
1½	shot(s)	Cinzano Extra Dry vermouth
1½	shot(s)	Sisca crème de cassis

Origin: A classic (retro) cocktail named after the pre-war stage actress Yvonne Arnaud.
Comment: An interesting balance of blackcurrant, vermouth and gin. Sweet palate and dry finish.

ARTLANTIC

Glass: Collins
Garnish: Orange slice & mint sprig
Method: Shake ingredients with ice and strain into ice-filled glass.

1	shot(s)	Spiced rum
½	shot(s)	Disaronno Originale amaretto
½	shot(s)	Bols Blue curaçao
½	shot(s)	Freshly squeezed lime juice
3	shot(s)	Pressed apple juice

Origin: Atlantic Bar & Grill, London, England.
Comment: This sea green cocktail tastes much better than it looks.

ASSISTED SUICIDE

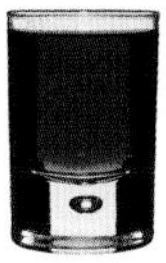

Glass: Shot
Method: Pour ingredients into glass in the following order.

1	shot(s)	Polish Pure Spirit
½	shot(s)	Jägermeister
Top up with		Cola

Comment: Killer! Polish Pure Spirit, at 79.9% alcohol (or nearly 160° Proof), is not for the faint-hearted. Surprisingly Jägermeister and cola combine well.

ASIAN PEAR MARTINI

●●●●○

Glass: Martini
Garnish: Pear slice on rim
Method: Shake all ingredients with ice and fine strain into glass.

2	shot(s)	Sake
¼	shot(s)	Xanté pear liqueur
½	shot(s)	Poire William eau de vie
1½	shot(s)	Freshly extracted pear juice
¼	shot(s)	Freshly squeezed lemon juice

Origin: I created this drink in 2002.
Comment: Sake and pear juice with something of a kick.

ATLANTIC BREEZE

Glass: Collins
Garnish: Orange slice
Method: Pour first four ingredients into ice-filled glass and stir, then float Galliano.

1½	shot(s)	Havana Club light rum
½	shot(s)	Bols Apricot brandy
2½	shot(s)	Pressed pineapple juice
½	shot(s)	Freshly squeezed lemon juice
¼	shot(s)	Galliano

Comment: A fruity, tropical cocktail finished with Galliano's herbal tones.

ATOMIC DOG

Glass: Collins
Method: Shake ingredients with ice and strain into glass.

1½	shot(s)	Havana Club light rum
¾	shot(s)	Midori melon liqueur
¾	shot(s)	Malibu coconut rum liqueur
3½	shot(s)	Pressed pineapple juice
¾	shot(s)	Freshly squeezed lemon juice

Comment: A long, refreshing drink with melon, coconut and pineapple juice.

ATTITUDE ADJUSTER

Glass: Hurricane
Garnish: 3 coffee beans
Method: Shake first three ingredients with ice and strain into ice-filled glass, then top up with cola and float orange and coffee liqueurs.

2	shot(s)	Plymouth gin
1	shot(s)	Cointreau / triple sec
1	shot(s)	Freshly squeezed lime juice
Top up with		Cola
¼	shot(s)	Grand Marnier
¼	shot(s)	Kahlúa coffee liqueur

Comment: I've simplified and tried to improve this somewhat dodgy but popular cocktail – but failed.

AUNTIE'S HOT XMAS PUNCH

●●●●●○

Glass: Toddy
Garnish: Cinnamon stick in glass
Method: Pour all ingredients into glass and stir. Microwave for a minute (vary time depending on your microwave), stir again and serve.

3/4	shot(s)	Freshly squeezed lemon juice
1½	shot(s)	Pedro Ximénez Sherry
2¼	shot(s)	Rémy Martin Cognac
3	shot(s)	Pressed apple juice
4	dashes	Péychaud's bitters

Origin: I created this drink to serve live on Christmas Eve 2002 during a broadcast on BBC radio. 'Auntie' is a nickname for the BBC and the drink uses the traditional punch proportions of 1 sour, 2 sweet, 3 strong and 4 weak.
Comment: A fruity seasonal warmer.

AUTUMN PUNCH

●●●●●○

Glass: Sling
Garnish: Physalis fruit on rim
Method: Cut passion fruit in half and scoop out flesh into shaker. Add vodka, passion fruit syrup, pear and lemon juice, shake with ice and strain into ice-filled glass. Top up with Champagne.

1	fresh	Passion fruit
2	shot(s)	Zubrówka (Bison grass) vodka
¼	shot(s)	Passion fruit syrup
1	shot(s)	Freshly extracted pear juice
½	shot(s)	Freshly squeezed lemon juice
Top up with		Piper-Heidsieck Brut Champagne

Origin: Created in 2001 by Max Warner at Baltic Bar, London, England.
Comment: Autumnal in colour with a wonderful meld of complementary flavours.

AUNT AGATHA

Glass: Rocks
Garnish: Orange slice
Method: Pour Navy rum into ice-filled glass, add orange juice and stir, then float bitters.

2	shot(s)	Pusser's Navy rum
3	shot(s)	Freshly squeezed orange juice
4	dashes	Angostura aromatic bitters

Origin: Aunt Agatha was the confused and dotty mother-in-law of Samantha in Bewitched!
Comment: Basic but a 'classic' style that tastes good.

AVALANCHE # 1

Glass: Collins
Garnish: Banana slice
Method: Blend ingredients with crushed ice and serve.

2	shot(s)	Bols Crème de banane
1	shot(s)	Bols White crème de cacao
½	shot(s)	Disaronno Originale Amaretto
2	shot(s)	Double (heavy) cream
½		Peeled banana

Origin: Created in Maudes Bar, New York City, 1979.
Comment: Creamy, rich and smooth. Fluffy but lovely.

AVALANCHE # 2

Glass: Shot
Method: Layer in glass by carefully pouring ingredients in the following order.

½	shot(s)	Southern Comfort
½	shot(s)	Kahlúa coffee liqueur
½	shot(s)	Bols White crème de cacao

Comment: Rich, smooth and sticky – looks great!

AVIATION UPDATED

●●●●●

Glass: Martini
Garnish: Lemon zest
Method: Shake all ingredients with ice and fine strain into chilled glass.

2½	shot(s)	Plymouth gin
1½	shot(s)	Freshly squeezed lemon juice
½	shot(s)	Maraschino liqueur
½	shot(s)	Sugar (gomme) syrup

Variation: Bee's Knees
Origin: A classic (retro) cocktail which enjoyed something of a revival in London around the Millennium.
Comment: This is a fantastic, tangy cocktail and dangerously easy to drink – too many of these and you really will be flying.

AWOL NEW

●●●●○

Glass: Shot
Method: Layer by carefully pouring ingredients into glass in the following order. Then flame drink and allow to burn for no more than 10 seconds before extinguishing flame and consuming.

¾	shot(s)	Midori melon liqueur
¾	shot(s)	Pressed pineapple juice
½	shot(s)	Absolut vodka
½	shot(s)	Wray & Nephew Overproof rum

Origin: Created in 1993 by Lane Zellman at Louis XVI Restaurant, St. Louis Hotel, New Orleans, USA.
Comment: A strong but surprisingly palatable shot.

AZURE MARTINI

Glass: Martini
Garnish: Apple slice
Method: Muddle ingredients in base of shaker, shake with ice and strain into glass.

½		Fresh chopped apple
2	shot(s)	Pitú Cachaça
½	shot(s)	Cinnamon schnapps
½	shot(s)	Freshly squeezed lime juice
¼	shot(s)	Freshly squeezed lemon juice
¼	shot(s)	Sugar (gomme) syrup

Origin: Ben Reed at the Met Bar, London, England.
Comment: Apple, cinnamon and sours with that Cachaça edge.

B & B | CLASSIC

Glass: Old-fashioned
Method: Pour ingredients into ice-filled glass and stir well.

2	shot(s)	Bénédictine D.O.M liqueur
2	shot(s)	Rémy Martin Cognac

Origin: Created in 1937 by a bartender at New York's famous 21 Club.
Comment: A classic drink of lasting character.

B-52 SHOT

Glass: Shot
Method: Layer in glass by carefully pouring ingredients in the following order.

1/2	shot(s)	Kahlúa coffee liqueur
1/2	shot(s)	Baileys Irish cream liqueur
1/2	shot(s)	Grand Marnier

Origin: Named after B-52 bombers in Vietnam.
Comment: Probably the best-known and most popular shot.

B-53 SHOT

Glass: Shot
Method: Layer in glass by carefully pouring ingredients in the following order.

1/2	shot(s)	Kahlúa coffee liqueur
1/2	shot(s)	Baileys Irish cream liqueur
1/2	shot(s)	Absolut vodka

Comment: Why settle for a 52 when you can have a 53?

B-54 SHOT

Glass: Shot
Method: Layer in glass by carefully pouring ingredients in the following order.

1/2	shot(s)	Disaronno Originale Amaretto
1/2	shot(s)	Kahlúa coffee liqueur
1/2	shot(s)	Baileys Irish cream liqueur

Comment: Layered and sticky – but nice.

B-55 SHOT

Glass: Shot
Method: Layer in glass by carefully pouring ingredients in the following order.

1/2	shot(s)	Kahlúa coffee liqueur
1/2	shot(s)	Baileys Irish cream liqueur
1/2	shot(s)	La Fée absinthe

Comment: The latest and scariest of the B-something range of layered shots.

B-52 FROZEN

Glass: Rocks
Garnish: Crumbled Cadbury's Flake bar
Method: Blend ingredients with one scoop of crushed ice.

1	shot(s)	Baileys Irish Cream liqueur
1	shot(s)	Grand Marnier
1	shot(s)	Kahlúa coffee liqueur

Comment: The classic shot blended with ice.

B. J. SHOT

Glass: Shot
Garnish: Thin layer of single cream
Method: Layer in glass, by pouring ingredients carefully in the following order. Instruct drinker to down in one without using hands.

1/2	shot(s)	Grand Marnier
1/3	shot(s)	Baileys Irish cream liqueur

Comment: You know what the letters stand for – tastes better!

BABY BLUE MARTINI

Glass: Martini
Garnish: Orange twist
Method: Shake all ingredients with ice and fine strain into chilled glass.

1	shot(s)	Plymouth gin
1	shot(s)	Bols Blue Curaçao
1	shot(s)	Squeezed pink grapefruit juice
1	shot(s)	Pressed pineapple juice

Comment: Turquoise blue, easy drinking and fairly sweet.

BABY WOO WOO

Glass: Shot
Garnish: Lime wedge
Method: Shake ingredients with ice and strain into glass.

1/2	shot(s)	Absolut vodka
1/2	shot(s)	Teichenné Peach schnapps
3/4	shot(s)	Cranberry juice

Comment: A very downable shot.

BABY GUINNESS UPDATED

Glass: Shot
Method: Layer in glass by carefully pouring ingredients in the following order.

1	shot(s)	Kahlúa coffee liqueur
1/2	shot(s)	Baileys Irish Cream liqueur

Comment: Looks like a miniature pint of Guinness stout.

BACARDI COCKTAIL

Glass: Martini
Garnish: Stemmed cherry
Method: Vigorously shake ingredients with crushed ice and strain into glass.

2¹/₂	shot (s)	Bacardi light rum
³/₄	shot (s)	Freshly squeezed lime juice
¹/₂	shot (s)	Grenadine syrup

Origin: In 1936, a bar in New York was found to be selling the classic Bacardi Cocktail – without including Bacardi rum. To protect their brand, Bacardi sued. During the court case, aiming to establish how unique Bacardi rum was, Henri Schueg, the third president of the Bacardi company, took the stand. He was asked, 'How is this Bacardi rum of yours made?' and replied, 'Oh! That is my secret!' Despite this, the courts recognised that Bacardi was a unique rum and ruled that a Bacardi Cocktail must be made with Bacardi.

Comment: This classic pink drink is a perfectly balanced combination of the flavour of rum, the sourness of lime juice and the sweetness of grenadine.

BAHAMA MAMA

Glass: Collins
Garnish: Pineapple wedge & cherry
Method: Shake all ingredients with ice and strain into ice-filled glass.

³/₄	shot(s)	Pusser's Navy rum
³/₄	shot(s)	Appleton Estate V/X aged rum
1	shot(s)	Malibu coconut rum liqueur
1³/₄	shot(s)	Freshly squeezed orange juice
2¹/₂	shot(s)	Pressed pineapple juice
3	dashes	Angostura aromatic bitters

Comment: A tropical, fruity number laced with flavoursome rum.

BAHAMAS DAIQUIRÍ

Glass: Martini
Garnish: Pineapple wedge on rim
Method: Shake all ingredients with ice and fine strain into chilled glass.

1¹/₂	shot(s)	Myers's Planter's Punch rum
³/₄	shot(s)	Malibu coconut rum liqueur
¹/₄	shot(s)	Kahlúa coffee liqueur
1¹/₂	shot(s)	Freshly extracted pineapple juice
¹/₂	shot(s)	Freshly squeezed lime juice

Origin: Adapted from the Bahamas Martini created in 2002 by Yannick Miseriaux at the Fifth Floor Bar, London, England.
Comment: Totally tropical with a sweet tangy edge.

BALALAIKA

Glass: Martini
Garnish: Orange slice
Method: Shake ingredients with ice and strain into glass.

1¹/₂	shot(s)	Absolut vodka
1¹/₂	shot(s)	Cointreau / triple sec
1¹/₂	shot(s)	Freshly squeezed lemon juice

Comment: Oranges and lemons say the bells of Saint Clements.

BALD EAGLE MARTINI

Glass: Martini
Garnish: Salt rim
Method: Shake all ingredients with ice and strain into glass.

2	shot(s)	Sauza Hornitos Tequila
1	shot(s)	Pink grapefruit juice
¹/₂	shot(s)	Cranberry juice
¹/₂	shot(s)	Freshly squeezed lime juice
¹/₂	shot(s)	Freshly squeezed lemon juice

Origin: Created for me in 2001 by Salvatore Calabrese at The Lanesborough Library Bar, London, England.
Comment: If you like Tequila and you like your drinks on the sour side this is for you.

BALD EAGLE

Glass: Shot
Method: Layer ingredients in glass by carefully pouring in the following order.

³/₄	shot(s)	Peppermint schnapps
³/₄	shot(s)	Sauza Hornitos Tequila

Comment: A strong and minty mouthwash.

BALI TRADER

Glass: Martini
Garnish: Banana chunk on rim
Method: Shake all ingredients with ice and fine strain into chilled glass.

2	shot(s)	Absolut vodka
1	shot(s)	Pisang Ambon green banana liqueur
1	shot(s)	Pressed pineapple juice

Comment: A tasty Caribbean combination of banana and pineapple.

BALLET RUSSE

Glass: Martini
Method: Shake ingredients with ice and strain into glass.

1	shot(s)	Absolut vodka
3/4	shot(s)	Sisca crème de cassis
1 3/4	shot(s)	Freshly squeezed lime juice
1 1/4	shot(s)	Sugar (gomme) syrup
1/4	shot(s)	Freshly squeezed lemon juice

Comment: Intense flavour and good length.

BALTIMORE EGG NOG

Glass: Collins
Garnish: Freshly grated nutmeg
Method: Shake all ingredients with ice and fine strain into ice-filled glass.

1 1/2	shot(s)	Rémy Martin Cognac
1 1/2	shot(s)	Madeira
1	shot(s)	Pusser's Navy rum
1	shot(s)	Double (heavy) cream
1	shot(s)	Milk
1	shot(s)	Sugar (gomme) syrup
1	fresh	Beaten egg

Comment: A flavoursome liquid meal.

BAMBOO

Glass: Martini
Garnish: Orange twist
Method: Stir ingredients with ice and strain into glass.

2	shot(s)	Fino Sherry
1/2	shot(s)	Cinzano Extra Dry vermouth
1	shot(s)	Cointreau / triple sec

Comment: Dry and refined - for sophisticated palates only.

BANANA BANSHEE

Glass: Collins
Garnish: Banana slice
Method: Blend ingredients with crushed ice and serve.

1 1/2	shot(s)	Bols Crème de banane
1 1/2	shot(s)	Bols White crème de cacao
1/2	shot(s)	Orange curaçao
1 1/2	shot(s)	Double (heavy) cream
1 1/2	shot(s)	Milk
1/2		Peeled banana

Comment: A very popular, long, creamy cocktail.

BANANA BOAT

Glass: Hurricane
Garnish: Split banana chunk
Method: Blend ingredients with crushed ice and serve.

1	shot(s)	Havana Club light rum
1	shot(s)	Bols Crème de banane
1	shot(s)	Bols White crème de cacao
1/2	fresh	Peeled banana
2	scoops	Vanilla ice cream

Comment: Rich and creamy - like a Banana Banshee with ice cream.

BANANA BOOMER

Glass: Martini
Garnish: Split banana chunk
Method: Shake ingredients with ice and strain into glass.

1	shot(s)	Bols Crème de banane
1/2	shot(s)	Bols Apricot brandy liqueur
1/2	shot(s)	Bols Cherry brandy liqueur
1	shot(s)	Freshly squeezed orange juice
1	shot(s)	Pressed pineapple juice

Comment: Bubble gum flavours for the child at heart.

BANANA BLISS

Glass: Martini
Garnish: Split banana chunk
Method: Stir ingredients with ice and strain into glass.

2	shot(s)	Bols Crème de banane
2	shot(s)	Rémy Martin Cognac

Comment: Crème de banane and Cognac go shockingly well together.

BANANA COLADA

Glass: Hurricane
Garnish: Split banana chunk
Method: Blend ingredients with crushed ice and serve.

1/2	shot(s)	Bols crème de banane
2	shot(s)	Mount Gay Gold rum
1/2	fresh	Peeled banana
1	shot(s)	Double (heavy) cream
1	shot(s)	Coco López cream of coconut
4	shot(s)	Pressed pineapple juice

Comment: A Piña Colada with gold rum and banana.

BANANA DAIQUIRÍ

Glass: Hurricane
Garnish: Split banana slice
Method: Blend ingredients with crushed ice and serve.

2	shot(s)	Havana Club light rum
1/2	shot(s)	Freshly squeezed lime juice
1/2	shot(s)	Bols crème de banane
1/2	fresh	Peeled banana

Comment: A tangy banana disco drink.

BANANA SPLIT

Glass: Hurricane
Garnish: Split banana chunk and strawberry
Method: Blend ingredients with crushed ice
and serve.

1	shot(s)	Bols Crème de banane
1	shot(s)	Bols Strawberry (fraise) liqueur
1	shot(s)	Bols Brown crème de cacao
1	fresh	Peeled banana
10	fresh	Fresh hulled strawberries
2	scoops	Vanilla ice cream

Comment: Short on alcohol, but very tasty.

BANANAS & CREAM

Glass: Collins
Garnish: Banana chunk on rim
Method: Blend all ingredients with crushed ice
and serve with straws.

2	shot(s)	Bols Crème de banane
1	shot(s)	Disaronno Originale amaretto
1	shot(s)	Baileys Irish cream liqueur
1	shot(s)	Double (heavy) cream
2	shot(s)	Milk

Comment: Banana and cream frappé with hints
of almond – one for a summer afternoon.

BANOFFEE MARTINI

Glass: Martini
Garnish: Dust with chocolate powder
Method: Muddle banana in base of shaker. Add
other ingredients, shake with ice and fine strain
into chilled glass.

1/4	fresh	Banana
1 1/2	shot(s)	Stoli Vanil
3/4	shot(s)	Teichenné butterscotch schnapps
3/4	shot(s)	Bols crème de banane
1	spoon	Maple syrup
1/2	shot(s)	Double (heavy) cream
1/2	shot(s)	Milk

Origin: Adapted from a recipe created in 2002
by Barry Wilson, Zinc Bar & Grill, Edinburgh,
Scotland.
Comment: Thick and rich, one for after the
cheese course.

BANSHEE

Glass: Shot
Method: Shake ingredients with ice and strain
into glass.

1/2	shot(s)	Bols Crème de banane
1/2	shot(s)	Bols White crème de cacao
1/2	shot(s)	Double (heavy) cream

Comment: Won't get you drunk quickly,
but might make you sick.

BARBARA

Glass: Martini
Garnish: Sprinkle ground nutmeg
Method: Shake ingredients with ice and strain
into glass.

2	shot(s)	Absolut vodka
1	shot(s)	Bols White crème de cacao
2	shot(s)	Double (heavy) cream

Comment: Quite neutral and subtle - nutmeg
works well.

BARBARY COAST HIGHBALL

Glass: Collins
Method: Shake first four ingredients with ice
and strain into ice-filled glass, then top up with
soda water and stir.

1	shot(s)	Buffalo Trace Bourbon
1	shot(s)	Bols Brown crème de cacao
1	shot(s)	Plymouth gin
1	shot(s)	Double (heavy) cream
Top up with		Soda water

Comment: Looks like a glass of weak tea -
Bourbon predominates.

BARBARY COAST MARTINI

Glass: Martini
Garnish: Dust with ground cinnamon
Method: Shake all ingredients with ice and fine
strain into chilled glass.

1 1/4	shot(s)	The Famous Grouse Scotch whisky
1 1/4	shot(s)	Plymouth gin
1 1/4	shot(s)	Bols White crème de cacao
1 1/4	shot(s)	Double (heavy) cream

Origin: Adapted from a 1947 edition of Trader
Vic's Bartender's Guide.
Comment: It may be creamy, but this is a
serious drink.

BARTENDER'S ROOT BEER

Glass: Collins
Garnish: Lime wedge on rim
Method: Pour first three ingredients into ice-
filled glass and top up with cola.

1	shot(s)	Galliano
1	shot(s)	Kahlúa Coffee liqueur
1/4	shot(s)	Freshly squeezed lime juice
Top up with		Cola

Comment: Not quite the root of all evil, but tasty
all the same.

BASIL BEAUTY NEW

Glass: Martini
Garnish: Pineapple wedge on rim
Method: Lightly muddle basil in base of shaker.
Cut passion fruit in half and scoop contents into
shaker. Add other ingredients, shake with ice
and fine strain into chilled glass.

4	fresh	Basil leaves
1	whole	Passion fruit
2	shot(s)	Absolut Citron
2	shot(s)	Pressed pineapple juice
1/4	shot(s)	Freshly squeezed lime juice
1/2	shot(s)	Coconut syrup

Origin: Created in 2003 by Wayne Collins for
Maxxium UK.
Comment: Pineapple, passion fruit, hints of
lime, basil and coconut all laced with citrus
vodka.

BASIL GRANDE

Glass: Martini
Garnish: Dust with black pepper & float basil leaf
Method: Muddle strawberries and basil leaves in shaker base. Add other ingredients, shake with ice and fine strain into glass.

4	fresh	Hulled strawberries
5	fresh	Basil leaves
1	shot(s)	Absolut vodka
1	shot(s)	Chambord black raspberry liqueur
1	shot(s)	Grand Marnier
3	shot(s)	Cranberry juice

Origin: Created in 2001 by Jamie Wilkinson at Living Room, Manchester, England.
Comment: Fruity, with interest courtesy of the basil and grind of pepper.

BAY BREEZE

Glass: Collins
Method: Shake ingredients with ice and strain into ice-filled glass.

2	shot(s)	Absolut vodka
4	shot(s)	Cranberry juice
2	shot(s)	Pressed pineapple juice

Comment: An easy-drinking version of the Seabreeze.

BAY CITY BOMBER

Glass: Sling
Method: Shake first ten ingredients with ice and strain into ice-filled glass, then float overproof rum.

1/2	shot(s)	Absolut vodka
1/2	shot(s)	Havana Club light rum
1/2	shot(s)	Sauza Hornitos Tequila
1/2	shot(s)	Plymouth gin
1/2	shot(s)	Cointreau / triple sec
1	shot(s)	Freshly squeezed orange juice
1	shot(s)	Pressed pineapple juice
1	shot(s)	Cranberry juice
3/4	shot(s)	Freshly squeezed lime juice
1/8	shot(s)	Sugar (gomme) syrup
Float		Wray & Nephew overproof rum

Comment: A strong but drinkable punch.

BAY OF PASSION

Glass: Collins
Garnish: Split cherry
Method: Shake ingredients with ice and strain into ice-filled glass.

1	shot(s)	Passoã passion fruit liqueur
1	shot(s)	Absolut vodka
4	shot(s)	Cranberry juice
2	shot(s)	Pressed pineapple juice

Comment: Variation on a Bay Breeze - fruity with a tropical tinge.

BATIDA ABACI

●●●●◐

UPDATED

Glass: Collins
Garnish: Pineapple wedge on rim
Method: Shake all ingredients with ice and strain into ice-filled glass.

2¼	shot(s)	Pitú Cachaça
3	shot(s)	Freshly extracted pineapple juice
1/2	shot(s)	Sugar (gomme) syrup
1/2	shot(s)	Freshly squeezed lemon juice

Variant: This drink is great made with just about any fruit. When made with strawberries it's called a 'Batida Morango', with passion fruit it becomes a 'Batida Maracuja' and with guava a 'Batida Goiaba'. It can also be served frozen: simply blend all ingredients with a 12oz scoop of crushed ice and an extra 1/4 shot of sugar syrup.
Origin: This is a traditional Brazilian working-man's drink.
Comment: Unfortunately, this excellent drink has not transferred as quickly from its native Brazil as the Caipirinha.

BAZOOKA

Glass: Shot
Method: Shake ingredients with ice and strain into glass.

3/4	shot(s)	Southern Comfort
1/2	shot(s)	Bols Crème de banane
1/8	shot(s)	Grenadine syrup
1/4	shot(s)	Double (heavy) cream

Comment: A sticky, bright pink shot.

BAZOOKA JOE

Glass: Shot
Method: Pour first two ingredients into glass, then float Irish cream on top of drink.

1/2	shot(s)	Bols Blue curaçao
1/2	shot(s)	Bols Crème de banane
1/2	shot(s)	Baileys Irish cream liqueur

Comment: Banana and orange topped with whiskey cream.

●●●●○○

BBC NEW

Glass: Martini
Garnish: Freshly grated nutmeg
Method: Shake all ingredients with ice and fine strain into chilled glass.

1¼	shot(s)	Rémy Martin Cognac
1	shot(s)	Bénédictine D.O.M. liqueur
3/4	shot(s)	Double (heavy) cream
3/4	shot(s)	Milk

Origin: Thought to have originated in the UK in the late 1970s and named, not after the British Broadcasting Company, but Brandy Bénédictine and Cream.
Comment: Brandy & Bénédictine (a classic combo) smoothed with cream. Drier than you might expect.

●●●●○○

BE-TON UPDATED

Glass: Collins
Garnish: Squeezed lime wedge in glass
Method: Pour Becherovka into ice-filled glass, then top up with tonic water and stir.

2	shot(s)	Becherovka (Carlsbad Becher)
Top up with		Tonic water

Origin: Becherovka (or Carlsbad Becher as it's sometimes known) is the Czech national liqueur. Matured in oak it contains cinnamon, cloves, nutmeg and other herbs.
Comment: This spicy drink is the Czech Republic's answer to the Gin 'n' Tonic.

●●●●●○

BEACH BLONDE UPDATED

Glass: Collins
Garnish: Banana slice on rim
Method: Blend all ingredients with a scoop of crushed ice and serve with straws.

1/2	fresh	Peeled banana
1	shot(s)	Wray & Nephew Overproof white rum
3	shot(s)	Warninks Advocaat
3	shot(s)	Freshly squeezed orange juice

Origin: Created in 2002 by Alex Kammerling for Warninks.
Comment: Fruity, creamy holiday drinking.

BEACH ICED TEA

Glass: Sling
Garnish: Lemon slice
Method: Shake first seven ingredients with ice and strain into ice-filled glass, then top up with cranberry and stir.

1/2	shot(s)	Havana Club light rum
1/2	shot(s)	Plymouth gin
1/2	shot(s)	Absolut vodka
1/2	shot(s)	Sauza Hornitos Tequila
1/2	shot(s)	Cointreau / triple sec
1	shot(s)	Freshly squeezed lemon juice
1/2	shot(s)	Sugar (gomme) syrup
Top up with		Cranberry juice

Comment: A Long Island Iced Tea with cranberry juice instead of cola.

BEACHCOMBER

Glass: Martini
Garnish: Split lime wedge
Method: Shake ingredients with ice and strain into glass.

2	shot(s)	Havana Club light rum
1/2	shot(s)	Cointreau / triple sec
1	shot(s)	Freshly squeezed lime juice
1/4	shot(s)	Maraschino liqueur

Comment: A kind of Daiquirí with added triple sec.

BEAM-ME-UP SCOTTY

Glass: Shot
Method: Layer in glass by carefully pouring ingredients in the following order.

1/2	shot(s)	Kahlúa coffee liqueur
1/2	shot(s)	Bols crème de banane
1/2	shot(s)	Baileys Irish cream liqueur

Comment: A layered shot with a taste reminiscent of banana flambée.

BEE'S KNEES MARTINI # 1

Glass: Martini
Garnish: Orange twist
Method: Shake ingredients with ice and strain into glass.

1¼	shot(s)	Havana Club light rum
1¼	shot(s)	Pusser's Navy rum
3/4	shot(s)	Runny honey
1	shot(s)	Freshly squeezed orange juice
1	shot(s)	Double (heavy) cream

Comment: Smooth and orangey to start, with a rum and honey finish.

BEE'S KNEES MARTINI # 2

Glass: Martini
Garnish: Orange wedge
Method: In base of shaker stir honey with gin until honey dissolves. Add lemon and orange juice, shake with ice and fine strain into chilled glass.

2	shot(s)	Plymouth gin
4	spoons	Runny honey
1	shot(s)	Freshly squeezed lemon juice
1	shot(s)	Freshly squeezed orange juice

Variation: Made with light rum in place of gin this drink becomes a 'Honeysuckle Martini'.
Origin: Adapted from a recipe in David Embury's 'The Fine Art Of Mixing Drinks'.
Comment: This honeyed citrus concoction really is the bee's knees.

BEE'S KNEES # 3

Glass: Rocks
Garnish: Orange twist
Method: Shake ingredients with ice and strain into ice-filled glass.

1	shot(s)	Havana Club light rum
1	shot(s)	Freshly squeezed orange juice
1/2	shot(s)	Rose's lime cordial
4	drops	Fee Brothers Orange bitters

Comment: A refreshing, orangey summertime drink.

BEJA FLOR

Glass: Martini
Garnish: Split banana chunk
Method: Shake ingredients vigorously with ice and strain into glass.

2	shot(s)	Pitú Cachaça
1 1/2	shot(s)	Cointreau / triple sec
1	shot(s)	Bols crème de banane
1/2	shot(s)	Freshly squeezed lemon juice

Comment: A strong but fruity number – serve ice cold.

BELLA DONNA DAIQUIRÍ NEW

Glass: Martini
Garnish: Cinnamon rim
Method: Shake all ingredients with ice and fine strain into chilled glass.

1 1/2	shot(s)	Gosling's Black Seal rum
1 1/2	shot(s)	Disaronno Originale amaretto
1/2	shot(s)	Freshly squeezed lemon juice
1/4	shot(s)	Sugar (gomme) syrup
1/2	shot(s)	Chilled water

Origin: Adapted from a drinks discovered in 2003 at Bellagio, Las Vegas, USA.
Comment: This was the hit cocktail for Sauce staff at the Bellagio after working at the Nightclub & Bar Beverage & Convention. Try one and see why.

BELLINI

UPDATED

Glass: Flute
Garnish: Peach slice on rim
Method: Shake first three ingredients with ice and strain into chilled glass. Top up with prosecco and stir.

1 1/2	shot(s)	Freshly extracted peach juice
1/4	shot(s)	Teichenné peach schnapps
1/4	shot(s)	Freshly squeezed lemon juice
Top up with		Prosecco

Variant: With Champagne instead of Prosecco.
Origin: Created in 1934 at Harry's Bar, Venice, by Commendatore Guiseppi Cipriani of the Venetian Cipriani hotel family and named after the 15th century painter Giovanni Bellini due to his use of glowing pinks in his paintings. Harry's Bar, on Saint Mark's Square in Venice was the Italian ex-pat hangout between the wars. Everyone from Ernest Hemingway to F. Scott Fitzgerald to Dorothy Parker dropped by. Even James Bond was a fan.
Comment: Prosecco is a dry Italian sparkling wine, with a distinctive strawy edge which combines well with the sweetness of the fruit.

BELLINI-TINI

Glass: Martini
Garnish: Peach wedge
Method: Shake ingredients with ice and strain into glass.

2	shot(s)	Absolut vodka
1/2	shot(s)	Teichenné Peach schnapps
1/2	shot(s)	Fresh white peach purée
4	drops	Peach bitters

Comment: Peachy, peachy, peachy! Based on the Bellini, funnily enough.

BENTLEY

Glass: Old-fashioned
Garnish: Split apple wedge
Method: Stir ingredients with ice and strain into glass.

1 1/2	shot(s)	Calvados or applejack brandy
1 1/2	shot(s)	Dubonnet Red

Comment: Background molasses and apples.

BERRY CAIPIRINHA NEW

●●●●●◑

Glass: Rocks
Method: Muddle lime and berries in base of glass. Add other ingredients and fill glass with crushed ice. Churn drink with barspoon and serve with short straws.

3/4	fresh	Lime cut into wedges
3	fresh	Raspberries
3	fresh	Blackberries
2	shot(s)	Pitú Cachaça
3/4	shot(s)	Sugar (gomme) syrup

Variant: Black 'N' Blue Caipirovska
Comment: A fruity version of the popular Brazilian drink.

BESSIE & JESSIE

Glass: Collins
Method: Shake first two ingredients with ice and strain into ice-filled glass, then float Advocaat.

2	shot(s)	The Famous Grouse Scotch whisky
6	shot(s)	Milk
Float		Warninks Advocaat

Comment: Malty, eggy milk.

BETWEEN THE SHEETS UPDATED

●●●●●◑

Glass: Martini
Garnish: Flamed orange twist
Method: Shake all ingredients with ice and fine strain into chilled glass.

1	shot(s)	Havana Club light rum
1	shot(s)	Rémy Martin Cognac
1/2	shot(s)	Cointreau / triple sec
3/4	shot(s)	Freshly squeezed lemon juice
1/2	shot(s)	Sugar (gomme) syrup
1/2	shot(s)	Chilled water

Origin: Created in the 1930s by Harry MacElhone, of Harry's New York Bar in Paris, and derived from the Sidecar.
Comment: When made correctly this is a beautifully balanced drink to rival even a Daiquirí.

BEVERLY HILLS ICED TEA

Glass: Collins
Garnish: Split lime wedge
Method: Shake first five ingredients with ice and strain into ice-filled glass, then top up with Champagne and lightly stir.

1	shot(s)	Plymouth gin
1	shot(s)	Absolut vodka
1	shot(s)	Cointreau / triple sec
1/2	shot(s)	Freshly squeezed lime juice
1/2	shot(s)	Sugar syrup
Top up with		Piper-Heidsieck Brut Champagne

Comment: Very strong and refreshing.

BIG APPLE MARTINI

●●●●◐○

Glass: Martini
Garnish: Apple wedge on rim
Method: Shake all ingredients with ice and fine strain into chilled glass.

2 1/2	shot(s)	Absolut vodka
1	shot(s)	Sourz Sour Apple liqueur
1	shot(s)	Apple schnapps liqueur

Origin: One of the most popular cocktails in New York City shortly after the Millennium.
Comment: There's no apple juice in this Martini, but it has an appealing light minty green hue. (See 'Apple Martini' for more suggestions.)

THE BIG EASY

●●●●●○

Glass: Collins
Garnish: Half orange wheel
Method: Shake first three ingredients with ice and strain into ice-filled glass. Top up with ginger ale.

1 3/4	shot(s)	Southern Comfort
3/4	shot(s)	Cointreau / triple sec
2	shot(s)	Freshly squeezed orange juice
Top up with		Ginger ale

Comment: Fruity and refreshing with a hint of spice.

BIKINI MARTINI

Glass: Martini
Garnish: Orange zest
Method: Squeeze lime wedge and drop into glass, then shake all ingredients with Ice and strain into glass.

1 1/2	shot(s)	Plymouth gin
1/2	shot(s)	Bols Blue curaçao
1	spoon	Teichenné Peach schnapps

Created by: Dick Bradsell for Agent Provocateur swimwear launch In London 1999.
Comment: A vivid blue combination of lime, orange and peach laced with gin.

BINGO

Glass: Collins
Method: Shake first four ingredients with ice and strain into ice-filled glass, then top up with soda water.

2	shot(s)	Absolut vodka
2	shot(s)	Mandarine Napoléon
2	shot(s)	Bols Apricot brandy
1	shot(s)	Freshly squeezed lemon juice
Top up with		Soda water (club soda)

Comment: Loadsa flavour - great long drink.

BIRD OF PARADISE

Glass: Martini
Method: Shake ingredients with ice and strain into glass.

1	shot(s)	Sauza Hornitos Tequila
1	shot(s)	Bols White crème de cacao
1/2	shot(s)	Disaronno Originale amaretto
2	shot(s)	Double (heavy) cream

Comment: A great way to drink Tequila.

BISHOP

Glass: Liqueur coffee
Garnish: Dust with nutmeg
Method: Place bar spoon in glass, add ingredients and stir.

4	shot(s)	Port
1	shot(s)	Freshly squeezed orange juice
1/2	shot(s)	Sugar syrup
Top up with		Boiling water

Origin: A variation on the 18th century Negus - reputedly a favourite of the writer Dr. Johnson.
Comment: Mulled wine without the spice.

BIT-O-HONEY

Glass: Shot
Method: Layer in glass by carefully pouring ingredients in the following order.

3/4	shot(s)	Teichenné butterscotch schnapps
3/4	shot(s)	Baileys Irish cream liqueur

Variant: Layered with butterscotch, then Bärenjäger honey liqueur and an Irish cream float.
Comment: A great tasting combination of butterscotch and Irish cream liqueur.

BITTEREST PILL

Glass: Shot
Method: Layer in glass by carefully pouring ingredients in the following order.

1/2	shot(s)	Absolut vodka
1/2	shot(s)	Campari
1/2	shot(s)	Passion fruit syrup

Created by: Alex Kammerling, London, England
Comment: The bitterness of Campari, toned down by passion fruit syrup.

BLACK BISON MARTINI #1

●●●●○

Glass: Martini
Garnish: Blackberry in drink
Method: Muddle blackberries in base of shaker. Add other ingredients, shake with ice and fine strain into chilled glass.

12 fresh		Blackberries
2	shot(s)	Zubrówka (Bison Grass) vodka
1/4	shot(s)	Sisca crème de cassis
1/4	shot(s)	Chambord black raspberry liqueur
1/2	shot(s)	Freshly squeezed lime juice
1/4	shot(s)	Sugar (gomme) syrup

Origin: Created in 2000 by Brian Duell at Ché, London, England.
Comment: A richly flavoured cocktail in which the distinctive taste of Zubrówka shines through.

BLACK BISON MARTINI #2

●●●●○

Glass: Martini
Garnish: Apple wedge
Method: Shake all ingredients with cubed ice and strain into glass.

1 1/2	shot(s)	Plymouth gin
1/2	shot(s)	Apple schnapps Liqueur
2	shot(s)	Pressed apple juice
1/4	shot(s)	Cinzano Extra Dry vermouth

Origin: Discovered in 2001 at Oxo Tower bar, London, England.
Comment: A dry, fragrant cocktail, which as the name suggests, also works well with Zubrowka vodka in place of gin.

BLACK BULL

Glass: Coupette
Garnish: Split lemon slice
Method: Pour ingredients into ice-filled glass and stir.

2	shot(s)	Osborne Veterano brandy
1	shot(s)	Freshly squeezed lemon juice
Top up with		Cola

Origin: Promoted by Osborne, the Spanish brandy producer.
Comment: A strange start but a pleasant finish.

BLACK DREAM

Glass: Shot
Method Layer in glass by carefully pouring ingredients in the following order.

1/2	shot(s)	Baileys Irish cream liqueur
1/2	shot(s)	Opal Nera black sambuca

Comment: Slippery Nipple with black sambuca.

●●●●● ◖

BLACK FOREST GATEAU MARTINI NEW

Glass: Martini
Garnish: Dust with cocoa powder
Method: Shake first four ingredients with ice and strain into chilled glass. Float cream on drink.

2	shot(s)	Absolut vodka
3/4	shot(s)	Chambord liqueur
3/4	shot(s)	Bols Strawberry (fraise) liqueur
1/4	shot(s)	Sisca crème de cassis
1	shot(s)	Double (heavy) cream

Origin: Created in 2002 at Hush, London, England.
Comment: Dessert by name and dessert by nature. Wonderfully moreish, naughty but very nice.

BLACK IRISH

Glass: Hurricane
Method: Blend ingredients with crushed ice and serve.

1	shot(s)	Absolut vodka
1	shot(s)	Baileys Irish cream liqueur
1	shot(s)	Kahlúa coffee liqueur
2	scoops	Vanilla ice cream

AKA: Frozen Black Irish
Comment: Like an alcoholic, frozen caffè latte.

BLACK JACK

Glass: Shot
Method: Layer in glass by carefully pouring ingredients in the following order.

1	shot(s)	Opal Nera black sambuca
1	shot(s)	Jack Daniel's Tennessee whiskey

Comment: Great - if you like sambuca!

BLACK MAGIC

Glass: Flute
Garnish: Split black grape
Method: Pour first two ingredients into glass and top up with sparkling wine.

2	shot(s)	Red grape juice
1/2	shot(s)	Grand Marnier
Top up with		Piper-Heidsieck Brut Champagne

Comment: Subtle and dry, though dependent on your red grape juice.

BLACK MARTINI

Glass: Martini
Garnish: Flamed lemon zest
Method: Stir ingredients with ice and strain into glass.

2	shot(s)	Absolut Kurant vodka
1	shot(s)	Chambord black raspberry liqueur

Comment: A stunningly simple but fantastic drink.

BLACK MUSSEL

Glass: Flute
Method: Pour first two ingredients into glass and top up with Champagne.

1	shot(s)	Bols Blue curaçao
1/2	shot(s)	Sisca crème de cassis
Top up with		Piper-Heidsieck Brut Champagne

Comment: Blue curaçao adds a hint of orange to a Kir Royale.

●●●●● ○

BLACK 'N' BLUE CAIPIROVSKA

Glass: Rocks
Method: Muddle berries in base of glass. Add other ingredients. Fill glass with crushed ice and churn (stir). Serve with two short straws.

6	fresh	Blackberries
10	fresh	Blueberries
2	shot(s)	Absolut vodka
1/2	shot(s)	Freshly squeezed lime juice
1/2	shot(s)	Sugar (gomme) syrup

Comment: A great fruity twist on the regular Caipirovska.

BLACK RUSSIAN

Glass: Rocks
Garnish: Maraschino cherry
Method: Stir ingredients with ice and strain into ice-filled glass.

2	shot(s)	Absolut vodka
1/2	shot(s)	Kahlúa coffee liqueur

Variants: 1/ Served straight-up in Martini glass. 2/ Topped with cola and served over ice in a Collins glass. 3/ Made into a White Russian.
Comment: Most popularly served with cola. With or without, this drink combines vodka and coffee liqueur.

●●●●○ ○

BLACK VELVET UPDATED

Glass: Flute
Garnish: Shamrock or mint leaf
Method: Pour ingredients into chilled glass.

2 1/2	shot(s)	Guinness stout
Top up with		Piper-Heidsieck Brut Champagne

Origin: Thought to have originated in 1861 at Brook's Club, London, after the death of Price Albert. Some attribute this drink's creation to the Shelbourne Hotel, Dublin, Ireland.

Comment: A fitting tipple for Saint Patrick's Day in honour of Ireland's patron saint, who's credited for banishing snakes from the island back in 441 AD.

THOSE DRINKS I'VE SAMPLED RECENTLY ARE GRADED AS FOLLOWS:

● DISGUSTING ●○ PRETTY AWFUL ●● BEST AVOIDED
●●○ DISAPPOINTING ●●● ACCEPTABLE ●●●○ GOOD
●●●● RECOMMENDED ●●●●○ HIGHLY RECOMMENDED
●●●●● OUTSTANDING / EXCEPTIONAL

BLACK & WHITE DAIQUIRI

●●●●●◐

Glass: Martini
Garnish: Blackberry in drink
Method: Muddle berries in base of shaker. Add other ingredients, shake with ice and fine strain into chilled glass.

12	fresh	Blackberries
2	shot(s)	Malibu coconut rum liqueur
1	shot(s)	Havana Club light rum
3/4	shot(s)	Bols Blackberry liqueur (crème de mûre)
1/2	shot(s)	Freshly squeezed lime juice
1/2	shot(s)	Chilled water

Origin: I named this drink after the blackberries and the white Malibu bottle.
Comment: Blackberries and coconut add depth to the classic Daiquiri.

BLACK WIDOW

Glass: Martini
Method: Shake ingredients with ice and strain into ice-filled glass.

1	shot(s)	Opal Nera black sambuca
1	shot(s)	Bols Strawberry (fraise) liqueur
1	shot(s)	Malibu coconut rum liqueur
1/2	shot(s)	Double (heavy) cream
1/2	shot(s)	Milk

Comment: Despite its sludgy colour, the flavours go well together.

BLACKBERRY MARTINI

Glass: Martini
Garnish: Single blackberry
Method: Stir ingredients with ice and strain into glass.

2	shot(s)	Absolut Kurant vodka
1	shot(s)	Bols Blackberry liqueur (crème de mûre)

Comment: Very strong but simply lovely.

BLACKTHORN ENGLISH UPDATED

●●●●○

Glass: Martini
Garnish: Flamed orange zest
Method: Shake all ingredients with ice and fine strain into chilled glass.

1 1/2	shot(s)	Plymouth Sloe gin
3/4	shot(s)	Plymouth gin
3/4	shot(s)	Cinzano Rosso (sweet) vermouth
3	dashes	Fee Brothers Orange bitters
1	shot(s)	Chilled water

Origin: Classic (retro) cocktail whose origins are unknown.
Comment: A dry, subtle rust-coloured Martini.

BLACKTHORN IRISH UPDATED

●●●●◐○

Glass: Martini
Garnish: Flamed lemon zest
Method: Shake all ingredients with ice and fine strain into chilled glass.

1 1/2	shot(s)	Irish whiskey
1	shot(s)	Cinzano Extra Dry vermouth
1/4	shot(s)	Pernod anise
4	dashes	Angostura aromatic bitters
1	shot(s)	Chilled water

Origin: Classic (retro) cocktail whose origins are unknown.
Comment: A dry and aromatic Martini with hints of anis. Some may prefer with the addition of half a shot of sugar syrup.

BLIMEY

●●●●●○

Glass: Rocks
Garnish: Lime wedge
Method: Muddle blackberries in glass. Fill glass with crushed ice, add other ingredients and stir.

8	fresh	Blackberries
2	shot(s)	Finlandia Lime vodka
1	shot(s)	Freshly squeezed lime juice
3/4	shot(s)	Sisca crème de cassis
1/8	shot(s)	Sugar (gomme) syrup

Origin: I created this drink in 2002 and Tarja Tuunanen, UK Finlandia brand manager, named it.
Comment: This blackberry and lime blend is both fruity and aptly named.

BLING! BLING!

●●●●●

Glass: Shot
Method: Muddle raspberries in base of shaker. Add vodka, lime and sugar, shake with ice and fine strain into glass. Top up with Champagne.

8	fresh	Raspberries
1/2	shot(s)	Absolut vodka
1/2	shot(s)	Freshly squeezed lime juice
1/2	shot(s)	Sugar (gomme) syrup
Top up with		Piper-Heidsieck Brut Champagne

Origin: Created in 2001 by Phillip Jeffrey at the GE Club, London, England.
Comment: An ostentatious little number.

BLOOD & SAND

Glass: Martini
Method: Shake ingredients with ice and strain into glass.

1	shot(s)	The Famous Grouse Scotch whisky
1	shot(s)	Bols Cherry brandy liqueur
1	shot(s)	Cinzano Rosso sweet vermouth
1	shot(s)	Freshly squeezed orange juice

Origin: Made for the premiere of the Rudolph Valentino film, Blood and Sand.
Comment: One of the best Scotch cocktails.

BLOODY MARY

(ORIGINAL 1933 RECIPE)

Glass: Old-fashioned
Garnish: Salt & pepper rim plus celery stick
Method: Shake all ingredients with ice and
strain into empty glass.

2	shot(s)	100-proof (50% alc./vol.) vodka
2	shot(s)	Thick pressed tomato juice
1/4	shot(s)	Freshly squeezed lemon juice
5	dashes	Worcestershire sauce
4	pinch	Salt
2	pinch	Black pepper
2	pinch	Cayenne pepper

Variant: Red Snapper
Origin: Created in 1920 by Fernand Petiot, at that time a young
bartender at Harry's New York Bar in Paris, a popular nightclub
boasting a distinguished clientele that included the likes of
Ernest Hemingway, George Gershwin and F. Scott Fitzgerald.
Contrary to popular belief the drink was not named after Queen
Mary the first, whose nickname was 'Bloody Mary' for her
persecution of Protestants in the 17th century; or even after the
silent-movie actress Mary Pickford. The drink was actually
named by one of Petiot's customers, entertainer Roy Barton, as
a homage to the Bucket of Blood nightclub in Chicago, where he
once performed. The first version contained just vodka and
tomato juice.
Petiot left Paris in 1925 for the US and found employment as
Assistant Manager at Canton City Club in Ohio where he married
a local girl named Ruth Johnson. In the early 1930s the couple
moved to New York City, where in 1933, Petiot was hired as a
bartender at the King Cole Bar in Manhattan's Hotel Saint Regis.
Here he mixed his drink for Serge Obolansky, the hotel's
President, who pronounced it "too flat". Petiot mixed him
another with added salt, pepper, lemon juice and
Worcestershire sauce and so gave birth to this classic drink.
Vincent Astor, who owned the hotel, found the name Bloody
Mary a little crude for his clientele and so the drink was officially
renamed the Red Snapper – although customers continued to
order Bloody Marys. (Nowadays a Red Snapper is a Bloody Mary
made with gin).
Petiot's rich and famous clientele helped spread the popularity
of the Bloody Mary which quickly gained a reputation as a
restorative to be consumed the morning after.
The celery stick garnish dates back to 1960 when a bartender at
the Ambassador Hotel in Chicago noticed a lady stirring her
drink with a celery stick.
Comment: Bloody Mary recipes are as personal as Martinis.
Variations on the theme use everything from sake to Tequila as a
base. Purists will only use Tabasco, Worcestershire sauce, salt
and lemon to spice up – but everything from oysters to V8 can
be added.
Comment: Fiery stuff. The modern version is more user friendly.

(MODERN RECIPE) UPDATED

Glass: Collins
Garnish: Salt & pepper rim plus celery stick
Method: Shake all ingredients with ice and
strain into ice-filled glass.

2	shot(s)	Absolut vodka
5	shot(s)	Fresh tomato juice
1/2	shot(s)	Freshly squeezed lemon juice
8	drops	Tabasco sauce
4	dashes	Worcestershire sauce
1/2	spoon	Horseradish sauce
1/2	shot(s)	Tawny Port
2	pinch	Celery salt
2	pinch	Black pepper

Variant: Peppered Mary
Comment: A fiery Mary with the heat fuelled by
horseradish. If you like to fight a hangover with
spice, this is for you.

BLOODHOUND

Glass: Collins
Garnish: Lime wedge
Method: Pour first two ingredients into ice-filled glass, then top up with grapefruit juice and stir.

2	shot(s)	Campari
1	shot(s)	Absolut vodka
Top up with		Pressed grapefruit juice

Comment: For refined and toughened palates.

BLOOD CLOT SHOT

Glass: Shot
Method: Pour rum into glass, then pour grenadine through the centre of rum. Finally float cream.

1½	shot(s)	Havana Club light rum
¼	shot(s)	Grenadine syrup
Float		Double (heavy) cream

Comment: Tastes better than it looks.

BLOODY BULL

Glass: Martini
Garnish: Salt and pepper rim
Method: Shake ingredients with ice and strain into glass.

1½	shot(s)	Sauza Hornitos Tequila
½	shot(s)	Freshly squeezed lemon juice
4	drop(s)	Worcestershire sauce
4	drop(s)	Tabasco sauce
1½	shot(s)	Tomato juice
1½	shot(s)	Canned beef consommé

Comment: A Bloody Mary with beef consommé giving the drink extra richness.

BLOODY JOSEPH

Glass: Collins
Garnish: Stick of celery
Method: Shake ingredients with ice and strain into ice-filled glass.

2	shot(s)	The Famous Grouse Scotch whisky
5	shot(s)	Tomato juice
¼	shot(s)	Freshly squeezed lemon juice
1	pinch	Celery salt
1	pinch	Black pepper
4	drops	Tabasco sauce
4	drops	Worcestershire sauce

Comment: A Bloody Mary with whisky – not one of the better variations on the classic.

BLOODY MARIA

Glass: Collins
Garnish: Salt and pepper rim, celery stick & split lime wedge
Method: Shake ingredients with ice and strain into ice-filled glass.

2	shot(s)	Sauza Hornitos Tequila
5	shot(s)	Tomato juice
¼	shot(s)	Freshly squeezed lemon juice
1	pinch	Celery salt
1	pinch	Black pepper
4	drops	Tabasco sauce
4	drops	Worcestershire sauce

Comment: Tequila adds a very interesting kick to the classic Bloody Mary - surprisingly good!

BLOODY MARY MIX (MAKES 5 LITRES)

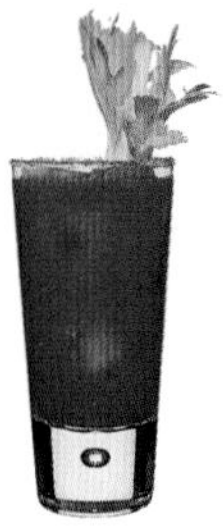

Method: First blanch fresh tomatoes (place in hot water for ten minutes, then in ice water for five). Remove skins from tomatoes and blend them, then strain purée to remove pips. Blend homemade tomato purée with the following ingredients and pour into a five litre container. Then add 3½ litres of tomato juice and mix well. Keep refrigerated and shake well before use - just add vodka for a Bloody Mary.

½	bottle	Tabasco sauce
1	bottle	Worcestershire sauce
2	spoons	Celery salt
1	spoon	Nutmeg
½	glass	Red wine
½	glass	Fino sherry
½	glass	Freshly squeezed lemon juice
½	glass	Freshly squeezed orange juice
2	spoons	Horseradish sauce
1	Zest	Orange
½	spoon	Black pepper

Note: Vine or plum tomatoes are best.
Created by: Jamie Terrell.
Comment: Well worth the effort if you're having a party.

BLOODY SHAME | VIRGIN

Glass: Collins
Garnish: Lemon wedge
Method: Shake ingredients with ice and strain into ice-filled glass.

4	shot(s)	Tomato juice
½	shot(s)	Freshly squeezed lemon juice
6	drops	Tabasco sauce
4	drops	Worcestershire sauce
1	pinch	Celery salt
1	pinch	Black pepper

AKA: Virgin Mary
Comment: A Bloody Mary with loadsa flavour and no booze - ideal if you're driving (or pregnant).

BLOW JOB

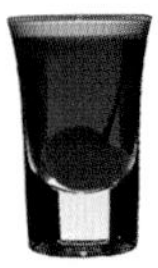

Glass: Shot
Garnish: Drop cherry into glass then float whipped cream
Method: Shake ingredients with ice and strain into glass.

½	shot(s)	Bols Crème de banane
½	shot(s)	Grand Marnier
½	shot(s)	Kahlúa coffee liqueur

Comment: Sugary shot.

BLUE ANGEL

Glass: Martini
Method: Shake ingredients with ice and strain into glass.

¾	shot(s)	Bols Blue curaçao
¾	shot(s)	Parfait Amour
¾	shot(s)	Rémy Martin Cognac
¾	shot(s)	Freshly squeezed lemon juice
¾	shot(s)	Double (heavy) cream

Comment: Blue and floral, with the violet flavours of Parfait Amour.

●●●○○

BLUE BIRD UPDATED

Glass: Martini
Garnish: Orange twist
Method: Shake all ingredients with ice and fine strain into chilled glass.

2	shot(s)	Plymouth gin
1	shot(s)	Bols Blue curaçao
3/4	shot(s)	Freshly squeezed lemon juice
1/4	shot(s)	Almond (orgeat) syrup

Origin: Thought to have been created in the late 1950s in Montmartre, Paris.
Comment: A blue rinsed, orange washed gin based 'tini' that benefits from being sweetened with almond rather than plain syrup.

BLUE BLAZER

Glass: Two rocks glasses
Method: Pour ingredients into rocks glass. Flambé the mixture and stir with a long handled bar spoon. Extinguish flame and strain into second rocks glass.

2	shot(s)	The Famous Grouse Scotch whisky
1/2	shot(s)	Hot water
1	spoon	Runny honey
4	twists	Lemon peel

Variant: This drink was originally mixed by pouring the ingredients from one metal mug to another while ignited.
Created by: 'Professor' Jerry Thomas, inventor of many famous cocktails in the 19th century. Thomas toured the world like a travelling showman, displaying this and other drinks.
Comment: Only attempt to make this the original way if you're very experienced or very stupid!

BLUE CHAMPAGNE

Glass: Flute
Method: Shake first four ingredients with ice and strain into glass, then top up with Champagne.

1	shot(s)	Absolut vodka
1/8	shot(s)	Cointreau / triple sec
1/4	shot(s)	Bols Blue curaçao
1/4	shot(s)	Freshly squeezed lemon juice
Top up with		Piper-Heidsieck Brut Champagne

Variant: With gin in place of vodka.
Comment: Dangerously easy to drink.

●●●●◐○

BLUE COSMO NEW

Glass: Martini
Garnish: Orange twist
Method: Shake all ingredients with ice and fine strain into chilled glass.

2	shot(s)	Absolut Citron vodka
3/4	shot(s)	Bols Blue curaçao
1 1/2	shot(s)	Ocean Spray White cranberry drink
1/4	shot(s)	Freshly squeezed lime juice

Variant: Purple Cosmo
Comment: This blue rinsed drink may have sales appeal but sadly is not quite as good as a traditional red Cosmo.

BLUE HAWAIIAN

Glass: Hurricane
Garnish: Spit pineapple wedge & cherry
Method: Blend ingredients with crushed ice and serve.

2	shot(s)	Havana Club light rum
1	shot(s)	Bols Blue curaçao
2	shot(s)	Cream of coconut
3	shot(s)	Pressed pineapple juice
1/4	shot(s)	Freshly squeezed lemon juice

Origin: Probably created by Don the Beachcomber in LA.
Comment: A blue Piña Colada.

BLUE HEAVEN

Glass: Collins
Garnish: Pineapple wedge & cherry
Method: Shake ingredients with ice and strain into ice-filled glass.

2	shot(s)	Havana Club light rum
1	shot(s)	Bols Blue curaçao
1/2	shot(s)	Disaronno Originale amaretto
1/2	shot(s)	Rose's lime cordial
4	shot(s)	Pressed pineapple juice

Comment: Orange liqueur shaken with amaretto, lime cordial and pineapple juice.

BLUE KAMIKAZE

Glass: Shot
Method: Shake ingredients with ice and strain into glass.

1/2	shot(s)	Absolut vodka
1/2	shot(s)	Bols Blue curaçao
1/2	shot(s)	Freshly squeezed lime juice

Comment: Tangy orange - but it's blue.

BLUE LADY

Glass: Martini
Method: Shake ingredients with ice and strain into glass.

1	shot(s)	Plymouth gin
2	shot(s)	Bols Blue curaçao
1	shot(s)	Freshly squeezed lemon juice
1/2	fresh	Egg white

Comment: Blue as in sexy, not blue rinse.

BLUE LAGOON

Glass: Collins
Method: Blend ingredients with crushed ice and serve.

1	shot(s)	Plymouth gin
1	shot(s)	Absolut vodka
1	shot(s)	Bols Blue curaçao
1	shot(s)	Freshly squeezed lime juice
1	shot(s)	Sugar (gomme) syrup

Variation: Vodka, blue curaçao and lemonade on the rocks.
Origin: Created in the 1960's by Andy MacElhone (son of Harry of Harry's Bar, Paris).
Comment: Better than the film – not hard!

BLUE MARGARITA UPDATED

●●●●◐○

Glass: Coupette
Garnish: Salt rim & lime wedge on rim
Method: Shake all ingredients with ice and fine strain into chilled glass.

2	shot(s)	Sauza Hornitos Tequila
1	shot(s)	Bols Blue Curaçao
1	shot(s)	Freshly squeezed lime juice
¼	shot(s)	Sugar (gomme) syrup

Variation: Blend with crushed ice.
Comment: As the name suggests, a Margarita only blue.

BLUE MONDAY NEW

●●●●○

Glass: Martini
Garnish: Orange twist
Method: Shake all ingredients with ice and fine strain into chilled glass.

1	shot(s)	Absolut Mandrin vodka
¼	shot(s)	Bols Blue Curaçao
2	shot(s)	Freshly squeezed lemon juice
1	shot(s)	Sugar (gomme) syrup

Origin: Created in 2003 by yours truly.
Comment: A citrus fresh Martini.

BLUE PASSION

Glass: Martini
Method: Shake ingredients with ice and strain into glass.

1	shot(s)	Havana Club light rum
1	shot(s)	Bols Blue curaçao
1¾	shot(s)	Freshly squeezed lime juice
1	shot(s)	Sugar (gomme) syrup

Comment: A great, tangy, moreish drink.

BLUE RASPBERRY MARTINI NEW

●●●●○

Glass: Martini
Garnish: Raspberries
Method: Shake all ingredients with ice and fine strain into chilled glass.

2	shot(s)	Stoli Razberi
½	shot(s)	Bols Blue Curaçao
¾	shot(s)	Freshly squeezed lime juice
½	shot(s)	Sugar (gomme) syrup
¾	shot(s)	Chilled water

Origin: Discovered in 2002 at The Sky Bar, Sunset Boulevard, Los Angeles, USA, where sour mix is used instead of fresh lime juice and sugar.
Comment: As turquoise-blue drinks go this one is surprisingly adult and tasty.

BLUE RIBAND

Glass: Martini
Garnish: Cherry dropped into glass
Method: Stir ingredients with ice and strain into glass.

2	shot(s)	Plymouth gin
1	shot(s)	Cointreau / triple sec
1	shot(s)	Bols Blue curaçao

Origin: The 'Blue Riband' was awarded to the liner that made the fastest Atlantic crossing - this cocktail is thought to have been created on one of these ships.
Comment: A killer Martini.

BLUE STAR

Glass: Martini
Garnish: Orange knot
Method: Shake ingredients with ice and strain into glass.

1½	shot(s)	Plymouth gin
¾	shot(s)	Cinzano Extra Dry vermouth
¾	shot(s)	Freshly squeezed orange juice
1½	shot(s)	Bols blue curaçao

Comment: Gin, orange and a kick.

BLUE WAVE

Glass: Hurricane
Garnish: Split pineapple leaf
Method: Shake ingredients with ice and strain into ice-filled glass.

1	shot(s)	Plymouth gin
1	shot(s)	Havana Club light rum
½	shot(s)	Bols Blue curaçao
3	shot(s)	Pressed pineapple juice
1¾	shot(s)	Freshly squeezed lime juice
¾	shot(s)	Sugar (gomme) syrup

Comment: Fruity, silly-looking holiday drink.

BLUEBERRY MARTINI

●●●●○

Glass: Martini
Garnish: Blueberries on stick
Method: Muddle blueberries in base of shaker. Add other ingredients, shake with ice and fine strain into chilled glass.

30	fresh	Blueberries
2	shot(s)	Absolut vodka
1	shot(s)	Blueberry liqueur (crème de myrtilles)
?	spoon	Sugar (gomme) syrup
¾	shot(s)	Chilled water

Comment: Rich blueberry fruit fortified with vodka.

BLUEBERRY PIE DAIQUIRÍ

●●●●○

Glass: Martini
Garnish: Float blueberries
Method: Muddle blueberries in base of shaker. Add other ingredients, shake with ice and fine strain into chilled glass.

20	fresh	Blueberries
1½	shot(s)	Havana Club light rum
1	shot(s)	Blueberry liqueur (crème de myrtilles)
¼	shot(s)	Freshly squeezed lime juice
¼	shot(s)	Vanilla sugar syrup
¾	shot(s)	Chilled water

Origin: I created this drink in December 2002.
Comment: If you like blueberry pie then give this liquid version a try.

THOSE DRINKS I'VE SAMPLED RECENTLY ARE GRADED AS FOLLOWS:

● DISGUSTING ●○ PRETTY AWFUL ●● BEST AVOIDED
●●○ DISAPPOINTING ●●● ACCEPTABLE ●●●◐ GOOD
●●●● RECOMMENDED ●●●●◐ HIGHLY RECOMMENDED
●●●●● OUTSTANDING / EXCEPTIONAL

BLUEBERRY TEA

Glass: Toddy
Garnish: Lemon wedge & cinnamon stick
Method: Pour first two ingredients into glass and top up with hot tea.

2/3	shot(s)	Disaronno Originale amaretto
2/3	shot(s)	Grand Marnier
Top up with		Hot tea

Comment: A toddy with a strange blueberry undertone.

BLUSH MARTINI

Glass: Martini
Garnish: Cinnamon powder sprinkled over flame
Method: Shake all ingredients with ice and strain into glass.

1	shot	Absolut vodka
3/4	shot(s)	Teichenné vanilla schnapps
1/2	shot(s)	Disaronno Originale amaretto
3/4	shot(s)	Milk
3/4	shot(s)	Double (heavy) cream
1/4	shot	Cranberry juice

Origin: Created by Colin William Crowden, Mashed Bar, Leicester, England.
Comment: Drier than it looks, but still one to follow the dessert trolley.

BLUSHIN' RUSSIAN

Glass: Martini
Method: Shake first four ingredients with ice and strain into glass, then float amaretto.

1	shot(s)	Absolut vodka
1	shot(s)	Kahlúa coffee liqueur
1	shot(s)	Double (heavy) cream
1	shot(s)	Milk
1/2	shot(s)	Disaronno Originale amaretto

Comment: White Russian with a marzipan topping.

BMW

Glass: Martini
Method: Shake ingredients with ice and strain into glass.

1	shot(s)	Baileys Irish cream liqueur
1 1/2	shot(s)	Malibu coconut rum liqueur
1/2	shot(s)	The Famous Grouse Scotch whisky
3/4	shot(s)	Double (heavy) cream
3/4	shot(s)	Milk

Comment: A silky smooth combination of coconut and cream, laced with whisky.

●●●●○

BOBBY BURNS

Glass: Martini
Garnish: Stemmed maraschino cherry in drink
Method: Shake all ingredients with ice and fine strain into chilled glass.

1 1/2	shot(s)	The Famous Grouse Scotch whisky
1 1/2	shot(s)	Cinzano Rosso (sweet) vermouth
1/4	shot(s)	Bénédictine D.O.M liqueur

Comment: Strictly speaking this drink should be stirred, but I prefer mine shaken so that's how it appears here.

BOHEMIAN ICED TEA

Glass: Old-fashioned
Method: Stir all ingredients with ice in a tea pot and serve In ice-filled glass.

1 1/2	shot(s)	Becherovka liqueur
1/2	shot(s)	Absolut Citron vodka
1/2	shot(s)	Krupnik honey vodka
1/2	shot(s)	Teichenné Peach schnapps
3	shot(s)	Chilled Earl Grey lemon tea

Origin: Created by Alex Kammerling at Detroit, London, England.
Comment: A fruity and refreshing drink with surprising flavours.

BOLSHOI PUNCH

Glass: Rocks
Method: Shake ingredients with ice and strain into ice-filled glass.

1	shot(s)	Havana Club light rum
1	shot(s)	Absolut vodka
1	shot(s)	Sisca crème de cassis
3/4	shot(s)	Freshly squeezed lime juice
1/2	shot(s)	Sugar syrup

Comment: Innocuous-seeming pink classic - easy to drink.

BOMBAY

Glass: Martini
Garnish: Orange peel knot
Method: Stir ingredients with ice and strain into glass.

2	shot(s)	Rémy Martin Cognac
1	shot(s)	Cinzano Extra Dry vermouth
1	shot(s)	Cinzano Rosso sweet vermouth
1/2	shot(s)	La Fée absinthe
1/2	shot(s)	Orange curaçao

Comment: One for those anis lovers out there.

●●●●○

BOMBER

Glass: Collins
Garnish: Lime squeeze
Method: Shake first three ingredients with ice and strain into ice-filled glass, then top up with ginger beer.

1	shot(s)	Havana Club Light Rum
1	shot(s)	Spiced rum
1	shot(s)	Freshly squeezed lime juice
Top up with		Ginger beer

Created by: The B. Bar crew at The Reading Festival, England 1998.
Comment: Cross between a Moscow Mule and a Cuba Libre.

BOOMERANG

Glass: Martini
Garnish: Split lemon wedge
Method: Shake ingredients with ice and strain into glass.

1½	shot(s)	Buffalo Trace Bourbon
1	shot(s)	Cinzano Extra Dry vermouth
1	shot(s)	Cinzano Rosso sweet vermouth
½	shot(s)	Freshly squeezed lemon juice
½	shot(s)	Sugar (gomme) syrup
4	dashes	Angostura aromatic bitters
4	drops	Maraschino liqueur

Comment: Manhattan with lemon juice.

BON BON MARTINI

Glass: Martini
Garnish: Lemon zest (or a Bon Bon)
Method: Shake all ingredients with cubed ice and strain into glass.

1	shot(s)	Stoli Vanil
½	shot(s)	Teichenné butterscotch schnapps
¾	shot(s)	Limoncello liqueur
¾	shot(s)	Freshly squeezed lemon juice
¼	shot(s)	Vanilla syrup
1	shot(s)	Chilled water

Origin: Discovered in 2001 at Lab Bar, London, England.
Comment: Relive your youth and the taste of those big round sweets in this Martini.

BORA BORA BREW | VIRGIN

Glass: Collins
Method: Pour ingredients into ice-filled glass and stir.

4	shot(s)	Pressed pineapple juice
½	shot(s)	Grenadine syrup
Top up with		Ginger ale

Comment: A great combination.

BOSOM CARESSER

Glass: Martini
Garnish: Orange peel knot
Method: Shake ingredients with ice and strain into glass.

2	shot(s)	Rémy Martin Cognac
½	shot(s)	Grand Marnier
½	shot(s)	Madeira
1	fresh	Egg yolk
⅛	shot(s)	Grenadine syrup

Comment: Smoothly alcoholic.

BOSSANOVA I

Glass: Collins
Garnish: Split lime wedge
Method: Shake ingredients with ice and strain into ice-filled glass.

2	shot(s)	Havana Club light rum
¾	shot(s)	Galliano
¾	shot(s)	Bols Apricot brandy Liqueur
4	shot(s)	Pressed apple juice
1	shot(s)	Freshly squeezed lime juice
½	shot(s)	Sugar (gomme) syrup

Comment: Apple juice with the added zing of rum, Galliano, apricot brandy and lime.

BOSSANOVA II

Glass: Collins
Method: Shake ingredients with ice and strain into ice-filled glass.

1½	shot(s)	Appleton Estate V/X aged rum
1½	shot(s)	Galliano
1	shot(s)	Bols Apricot brandy Liqueur
1½	shot(s)	Pressed pineapple juice
½	shot(s)	Freshly squeezed lemon juice
½	fresh	Egg white

Comment: Frothy with a subtle anis backgound.

BOSTON

Glass: Martini
Method: Shake ingredients with ice and strain into glass.

1½	shot(s)	Plymouth gin
1	shot(s)	Bols Apricot brandy Liqueur
1	shot(s)	Freshly squeezed lemon juice
½	shot(s)	Sugar (gomme) syrup
1	spoon	Grenadine syrup

Comment: Tangy fruit.

BOSTON FLIP

Glass: Wine goblet
Garnish: Dust with nutmeg
Method: Shake all the ingredients with ice and strain into glass.

2	shot(s)	Buffalo Trace Bourbon
2	shot(s)	Madeira
1	fresh	Egg yolk
¼	shot(s)	Sugar (gomme) syrup

Comment: With the addition of milk this cocktail would be similar to Egg Nog.

BOUNTY MARTINI

Glass: Martini
Method: Muddle ingredients in shaker can. Add ice, then shake and strain into glass.

1	shot(s)	Absolut vodka
1	shot(s)	Stoli Vanil
1 ½	shot(s)	Cream of coconut
¼	shot(s)	Sugar (gomme) syrup
6	dashes	Fee Brothers Orange bitters
3	fresh	Hulled strawberries

Origin: Created by Guillaume Jubien at The Light Bar, St Martins Hotel, London, England.
Comment: A liquid ice lolly - surprisingly subtle and rich.

BOSTON TEA PARTY

Glass: Collins
Method: Shake first nine ingredients with ice and strain into ice-filled glass. Top up with half orange juice and half cola. Serve with a straw using the straw to stir ingredients together.

½	shot(s)	Absolut vodka
½	shot(s)	The Famous Grouse Scotch whisky
½	shot(s)	Cinzano Extra Dry vermouth
½	shot(s)	Cointreau / triple sec
½	shot(s)	Pusser's Navy rum
½	shot(s)	Plymouth gin
½	shot(s)	Sauza Hornitos Tequila
1	shot(s)	Freshly squeezed lime juice
½	shot(s)	Sugar (gomme) syrup
Top up with		Half orange juice and half cola

Comment: It was a tax imposed by the British Crown on early US settlers that led to the Boston Tea Party and eventually the War of Independence. This long, refreshing cocktail doesn't taste like tea, but it does resemble the colour.

BOURBON BLUSH **NEW**

●●●●◑

Glass: Martini
Garnish: Strawberry on rim
Method: Muddle strawberries in base of shaker. Add other ingredients, shake with ice and fine strain into chilled glass.

3	fresh	Strawberries
2	shot(s)	Buffalo Trace Bourbon
¾	shot(s)	Bols Strawberry (fraise) liqueur
¼	shot(s)	Maple syrup

Origin: Created in 2003 by Simon King at MJU @ Millennium Hotel, London, England.
Comment: Strawberry and maple syrup combine brilliantly with Bourbon in this drink.

BOURBON MILK PUNCH

Glass: Martini
Garnish: Dust with nutmeg.
Method: Shake ingredients with ice and strain into glass.

1	shot(s)	Buffalo Trace Bourbon
2	shot(s)	Double (heavy) cream
1	shot(s)	Milk
½	shot(s)	Sugar (gomme) syrup
½	shot(s)	Galliano

Comment: A bedtime drink with the herbal edge of Galliano.

BOURBON COOKIE

●●●●○

Glass: Old-fashioned
Garnish: Cinnamon dust
Method: Shake all ingredients with ice and fine strain into ice-filled glass.

2	shot(s)	Buffalo Trace Bourbon
½	shot(s)	Double (heavy) cream
½	shot(s)	Milk
½	shot(s)	Mango or passion fruit syrup
½	shot(s)	Teichenné butterscotch schnapps

Origin: Created in 2002 by Andres Masso, London, England.
Comment: Looks tame but packs a flavoursome punch.

BOURBON SMASH

Glass: Collins
Garnish: Lime wheel on rim
Method: Muddle raspberries in base of shaker. Add other ingredients, shake with ice and strain into ice-filled glass.

12	fresh	Raspberries
4	fresh	Torn mint leaves
2¹/₂	shot(s)	Buffalo Trace Bourbon
3¹/₂	shot(s)	Cranberry juice
1	shot(s)	Freshly squeezed lime juice
¹/₂	shot(s)	Sugar (gomme) syrup
2	dashes	Angostura aromatic bitters

Comment: This refreshing long drink has a sharp edge that adds to its appeal.

BOURBONELLA

Glass: Martini
Garnish: Split stemmed cherry
Method: Stir ingredients with ice and strain into glass.

2	shot(s)	Buffalo Trace Bourbon
1	shot(s)	Cinzano Extra Dry vermouth
1	shot(s)	Orange curaçao
¹/₂	shot(s)	Grenadine syrup

Comment: If you like Bourbon, you'll like this.

BRADFORD UPDATED

Glass: Martini
Garnish: Olive on stick or lemon twist
Method: Shake all ingredients with ice and fine strain into chilled glass.

2¹/₂	shot(s)	Plymouth gin
¹/₂	shot(s)	Cinzano Extra Dry vermouth
3	dashes	Fee Brothers orange bitters (optional)

Origin: A Bradford is a Martini which is shaken rather than stirred. Like the Martini itself the origin of the Bradford is lost in time.
Comment: More approachable than a stirred Traditional Dry Martini and downright soft compared to a Naked Martini.

BRAIN SHOT

Glass: Shot
Method: Layer in glass by carefully pouring ingredients in the following order.

1	shot(s)	Southern Comfort
¹/₄	shot(s)	Cointreau / triple sec
¹/₄	shot(s)	Baileys Irish cream liqueur

Comment: A shot for the unimaginative.

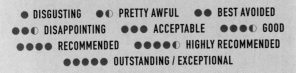
BRAMBLE

Glass: Old-fashioned
Garnish: Blackberry & lemon slice
Method: Fill glass with crushed ice, add gin, lemon juice and sugar syrup and stir. Top up with more crushed ice. Then lace drink with creme de mûre by slowly pouring over fresh ice. The mûre should make a pleasing 'bleeding' effect in the glass. Serve immediately with two short straws.

2	shot(s)	Plymouth gin
1¹/₂	shot(s)	Freshly squeezed lemon juice
¹/₂	shot(s)	Sugar syrup
¹/₂	shot(s)	Bols Blackberry (Crème de mûre) liqueur

Origin: Created in the mid-80s by Dick Bradsell at Fred's Club, Soho, London, England.

Comment: One of the best and most popular drinks created in the 1980s.

BRANDY ALEXANDER

Glass: Martini
Garnish: Sprinkle ground nutmeg
Method: Shake ingredients with ice and strain into glass.

1¹/₂	shot(s)	Rémy Martin Cognac
¹/₂	shot(s)	Bols Brown crème de cacao
¹/₂	shot(s)	Bols White crème de cacao
2	shot(s)	Double (heavy) cream

Comment: This classic blend of brandy and chocolate smoothed with cream is based on the original Alexander. Made with gin, this was a Prohibition favourite, as the cream, chocolate and nutmeg disguised the rough taste of homemade 'bathtub' gin. Creamy, subtle, spicy and rich.

BRAMBLETTE NEW

●●●●◐○

Glass: Martini
Garnish: Orange zest
Method: Shake all ingredients with ice and fine strain into chilled glass.

2	shot(s)	Plymouth gin
1	shot(s)	Violet liqueur
³/₄	shot(s)	Freshly squeezed lemon juice
¹/₄	shot(s)	Sugar (gomme) syrup

Comment: A grey/purple martini style drink with a floral gin laced palate.

BRANDY BLAZER

Glass: Snifter
Method: Pour ingredients into glass. Flambé the mixture and stir with a long handled bar spoon. Extinguish flame and strain into snifter glass.

2	shot(s)	Rémy Martin Cognac
¹/₂	shot(s)	Sugar (gomme) syrup
1	twist	Lemon peel
1	twist	Orange peel

Comment: A variation on 'Professor' Jerry Thomas' Blue Blazer, this is a fun and aromatic way to liven your winter nights.

BRANDY BUCK

●●●●○○

Glass: Collins
Garnish: Lemon wedge on rim
Method: Pour ingredients into ice-filled glass and stir.

2¹/₂	shot(s)	Rémy Martin Cognac
¹/₄	shot(s)	Freshly squeezed lemon juice
Top up with		Ginger ale

Comment: Lemon juice adds balance to the sweet ginger ale. Cognac provides the backbone.

BRANDY CRUSTA UPDATED

●●●●●○

Glass: Small Flute
Garnish: Sugar rim & whole spiral of lemon peel in glass
Method: Shake all ingredients with ice and fine strain into chilled glass.

2	shot(s)	Rémy Martin Cognac
¹/₂	shot(s)	Cointreau / triple sec
¹/₂	shot(s)	Maraschino liqueur
¹/₂	shot(s)	Freshly squeezed lemon juice
³/₄	shot(s)	Chilled water
4	dashes	Angostura aromatic bitters

Origin: Created in 1852 by Joseph Santina at Jewel of the South, Gravier Street, New Orleans, USA.
Comment: This old classic zings with fresh lemon and the sweetness of maraschino, which is beautifully balanced with the rich strong Cognac base.

BRANDY FIX

Glass: Rocks
Method: Shake ingredients with ice and strain into ice-filled glass.

1	shot(s)	Sugar (gomme) syrup
2	shot(s)	Freshly squeezed lemon juice
1/2	shot(s)	Bols Cherry brandy liqueur
1	shot(s)	Rémy Martin Cognac

Comment: Tart and tangy.

BRANDY FIZZ

Glass: Collins
Garnish: Split lemon wheel
Method: Shake first three ingredients with ice and strain into ice-filled glass, then top up with lemonade and stir.

2	shot(s)	Rémy Martin Cognac
1	shot(s)	Freshly squeezed lemon juice
1/2	shot(s)	Sugar (gomme) syrup
Top up with		Lemonade

Comment: A long, refreshing and tasty drink combining the vanilla flavour of Cognac with lemon.

BRANDY FLIP

Glass: Flute or wine goblet
Garnish: Sprinkle ground nutmeg
Method: Shake ingredients with ice and strain into glass.

2	shot(s)	Rémy Martin Cognac
1/2	shot(s)	Sugar (gomme) syrup
1	fesh	Egg yolk

Comment: A brandy drink for those with an iron stomach.

BRANDY GUMP

Glass: Martini
Garnish: Lemon sail
Method: Shake ingredients with ice and strain into glass.

2	shot(s)	Rémy Martin Cognac
2	shot(s)	Freshly squeezed lemon juice
1	shot(s)	Grenadine syrup
1/4	shot(s)	Sugar (gomme) syrup

Comment: A vivid colour. The taste almost hides the Cognac.

BRANDY MILK PUNCH

Glass: Collins
Garnish: Sprinkle ground nutmeg
Method: Shake ingredients with ice and strain into ice-filled glass.

2	shot(s)	Rémy Martin Cognac
4	shot(s)	Milk
1/4	shot(s)	Sugar (gomme) syrup

Comment: Milk brings out the vanilla in the Cognac – delicious. A traditional New Orleans hangover cure.

BRANDY SOUR

Glass: Old-fashioned
Garnish: Cherry
Method: Shake ingredients with ice and strain into glass.

2	shot(s)	Rémy Martin Cognac
1	shot(s)	Freshly squeezed lemon juice
1/3	shot(s)	Sugar (gomme) syrup
1/2	fresh	Egg white
4	drops	Angostura aromatic bitters

Comment: After the Whiskey Sour, this is the most requested sour.

BRAZEN MARTINI

Glass: Martini
Garnish: Frozen blueberries
Method: Stir ingredients with ice and strain into chilled glass.

| 3 | shot(s) | Zubrówka Bison vodka |
| 1/2 | shot(s) | Parfait Amour |

Comment: Not for the faint hearted – a great combination of strawy bison vodka with violet Parfait Amour.

BRAZILIAN BERRY

Glass: Rocks
Garnish: Mint sprig
Method: Muddle fruit in base of glass. Fill glass with crushed ice. Add other ingredients and stir.

4	fresh	Blackcurrants
3	fresh	Raspberries
1 1/2	shot(s)	Sauvignon Blanc wine
1	shot(s)	Pitú Cachaça
1	shot(s)	Sisca crème de cassis

Origin: Created in 2002 by Dan Spink at Browns, St Martin's Lane, London, England.
Comment: This drink combines Sauvignon Blanc, Cachaça and rich berry fruits.

BRAZILIAN COFFEE

Glass: Toddy
Method: Blend ingredients with crushed ice and serve.

1	shot(s)	Pitú Cachaça
1	shot(s)	Double (heavy) cream
1/2	shot(s)	Sugar (gomme) syrup
2	shot(s)	Illy coffee (cold)

Comment: Strong coffee and plenty of sugar are essential in this Brazilian number.

BRAZILIAN MONK

Glass: Hurricane
Method: Blend ingredients with crushed ice and serve.

1	shot(s)	Frangelico hazelnut liqueur
1	shot(s)	Kahlúa coffee liqueur
1	shot(s)	Bols Brown crème de cacao
3	scoops	Vanilla ice cream

Comment: Nutty and rich – serve alfresco.

BRONX

●●●●○○

UPDATED

Glass: Martini
Garnish: Cherry on rim
Method: Shake all ingredients with ice and fine strain into chilled glass.

1½	shot(s)	Plymouth gin
¾	shot(s)	Cinzano Extra Dry vermouth
¾	shot(s)	Cinzano Rosso sweet vermouth
1½	shot(s)	Freshly squeezed orange juice
2 dashes		Angostura aromatic bitters (optional)

Variant: 1/ Bloody Bronx – made with the juice of a blood orange. 2/ Golden Bronx – with the addition of an egg yolk. 3/ Silver Bronx - with the addition of egg white. Also see the Abby.
Origin: Created in 1906 by Johnny Solon, a bartender at New York's Waldorf-Astoria Hotel (the Empire State Building occupies the site today) and named after the newly opened Bronx Zoo. Reputed to be the first cocktail to use fruit juice.
Comment: A serious, dry, complex cocktail – less bitter than many of its era, but even with the modern formula above, still quite challenging to today's palate.

BREAKFAST AT TERRELL'S

Glass: Flute
Garnish: Kumquat half
Method: Shake ingredients with ice and strain into glass. Then top with champagne.

1½	shot(s)	Mandarine Napoléon
1½	shot(s)	Freshly squeezed orange juice
½	shot(s)	Double (heavy) cream
¼	shot(s)	Sugar (gomme) syrup
Top up with		Piper-Heidsieck Brut Champagne

Origin: Created by Jamie Terrell for Philip Holzberg at Vinexpo, Bordeaux, France, 1999.
Comment: An excellent drink served any time, but really tastes of breakfast.

BREAKFAST EGGNOG

Glass: Martini
Garnish: Sprinkle ground nutmeg
Method: Shake ingredients with ice and strain into glass.

2	shot(s)	Ruby Port
1	shot(s)	Bols White crème de cacao
1	shot(s)	Freshly squeezed lemon juice
¼	shot(s)	Mount Gay Eclipse gold rum
½	fresh	Egg white

Comment: Breakfast? The mind boggles.

BREAKFAST MARTINI

●●●●●○

Glass: Martini
Garnish: Slice of toast on rim
Method: Stir marmalade with gin in base of shaker until it dissolves. Add other ingredients, shake with ice and fine strain into chilled glass.

1	spoon	Orange marmalade (rindless)
1¾	shot(s)	Plymouth gin
¾	shot(s)	Cointreau / triple sec
¾	shot(s)	Freshly squeezed lemon juice
¾	shot(s)	Sugar (gomme) syrup

Origin: Created in the late 1990s by Salvatore Calabrese at the Library Bar, London, England, this is very similar to the Marmalade Cocktail created in the 1920s by Harry Craddock and published in The Savoy Cocktail Book.
Comment: The success or failure of this tangy drink is partly reliant on the quality of marmalade used.

THE BROADMOOR

●●●●●○

Glass: Martini
Garnish: Flamed orange twist
Method: Shake all ingredients with ice and fine strain into chilled glass.

2	shot(s)	The Famous Grouse Scotch
½	shot(s)	Green Chartreuse
½	shot(s)	Sugar (gomme) syrup
4	dashes	Fee Brothers Orange bitters

Origin: I discovered this fantastic drink in 2002 at Milk & Honey, London, England.
Comment: Beautifully simple and seriously complex.

BRUBAKER OLD-FASHIONED NEW

●●●●○

Glass: Old-fashioned
Garnish: Two lemon twists.
Method: Stir malt extract in glass with Scotch so as to dissolve malt extract. Add ice and one shot of Scotch and stir. Add rest of Scotch, sugar and Angostura and stir some more. Add more ice and keep stirring so that ice dilutes the drink.

2	spoons	Malt Extract (available in health-food shops)
2	shot(s)	The Famous Grouse Scotch whisky
¼	shot(s)	Sugar (gomme) syrup
3	dashes	Angostura aromatic bitters

Origin: Created in 2003 by Shelim Islam at the GE Club, London, England. Shelim named this drink after a horse in the sports section of a paper (which is also a film made in the seventies starring Robert Redford).
Comment: If you like Scotch you should try this extra malty dram. After all that stirring you'll deserve one.

BUBBLE GUM SHOT

Glass: Shot
Method: Shake ingredients with ice and strain into glass.

²/₃	shot(s)	Midori melon liqueur
¹/₂	shot(s)	Disaronno Originale amaretto
¹/₂	shot(s)	Double (heavy) cream

Comment: As the name suggests, this tastes a little like bubble gum.

THE BUCK

Glass: Collins
Method: Shake first three ingredients with ice and strain into ice-filled glass, then top up with ginger ale.

1¹/₂	shot(s)	Plymouth gin
1	shot(s)	Freshly squeezed lemon juice
¹/₂	shot(s)	Green crème de menthe
Top up with		Ginger ale

Comment: A long drink with subtle flavours of ginger, mint and lemon.

BUCK'S FIZZ

Glass: Flute
Method: Pour ingredients into chilled glass.

2	shot(s)	Freshly squeezed orange juice
Top up with		Piper-Heidsieck Brut Champagne

AKA: Mimosa
Origin: Created in 1921 by Mr McGarry, first bartender at the Buck's Club, London.
Comment: Not really a cocktail and not that challenging, but great at parties.

●●●●●○

BUENA VIDA

Glass: Old-fashioned
Garnish: Pineapple wedge on rim
Method: Shake all ingredients with ice and strain into glass filled with crushed ice.

2	shot(s)	Sauza Hornitos Tequila
1³/₄	shot(s)	Pink grapefruit juice
³/₄	shot(s)	Pressed pineapple juice
¹/₂	shot(s)	Vanilla syrup
3	dash(es)	Angostura aromatic bitters

Comment: The fruits combine brilliantly with the Tequila and spice comes courtesy of angostura.

●●●●◐○

BUG JUICE NEW

Glass: Martini
Garnish: Orange wheel in drink
Method: Shake all ingredients with ice and fine strain into chilled glass.

2	shot(s)	Absolut Mandrin vodka
1	shot(s)	Passoä passion fruit liqueur
3¹/₂	shot(s)	Pressed pineapple juice

Origin: Created in 2003 by yours truly.
Comment: Fortunately this drink is named after its orange colour rather than its orange, passion and pineapple taste.

BULLFROG

Glass: Rocks
Garnish: Split stemmed cherry
Method: Shake ingredients with ice and strain into ice-filled glass.

1	shot(s)	Absolut vodka
1	shot(s)	Green crème de menthe
1¹/₂	shot(s)	Double (heavy) cream
1¹/₂	shot(s)	Milk

Comment: Tastes like choc-mint ice cream.

BULLSHOT

Glass: Rocks
Method: Pour ingredients into ice-filled glass and stir. Instruct drinker to down in one.

1¹/₂	shot(s)	Absolut vodka
1	tblspn	Beef bouillon
4	drops	Tabasco sauce
4	drops	Worcestershire sauce
¹/₂	shot(s)	Freshly squeezed lime juice
1	pinch	Celery salt
1	pinch	Black pepper

Comment: Rather like a Bloody Bull. Allegedly a hangover cure.

BULL'S BLOOD

Glass: Martini
Method: Shake ingredients with ice and strain into glass.

¹/₂	shot(s)	Havana Club light rum
1	shot(s)	Rémy Martin Cognac
1	shot(s)	Orange curaçao
2¹/₂	shot(s)	Freshly squeezed orange juice

Comment: A good, dry, fruity cocktail - even if it isn't as red as it thinks it is.

BULLDOG

Glass: Collins
Method: Shake first three ingredients with ice and strain into ice-filled glass, then top up with cola.

1	shot(s)	Havana Club light rum
1	shot(s)	Kahlúa coffee liqueur
3	shot(s)	Double (heavy) cream
Top up with		Cola

Comment: Surprisingly nice, like a cola float.

●●●●◐○

BUMBLE BEE

Glass: Shot
Method: Layer by carefully pouring ingredients in the following order.

¹/₂	shot(s)	Kahlúa coffee liqueur
¹/₂	shot(s)	Opal Bianco Sambuca
¹/₂	shot(s)	Baileys Irish Cream liqueur

Comment: A B-52 with a liquorice kick.

BUONA SERA SHOT

Glass: Shot
Method: Pour ingredients into glass.

1/2	shot(s)	Kahlúa coffee liqueur
1/2	shot(s)	Disaronno Originale amaretto
1/2	shot(s)	Vanilla-infused Havana Club light rum

Comment: A good combination.

●●○○○

BURNING BUSH SHOT

Glass: Shot
Method: Pour ingredients into glass.

1	shot(s)	Sauza Hornitos Tequila
6	drops	Tabasco sauce

AKA: Prairie Dog, Prairie Fire
Comment: Hold onto your bowels!

●●●○○

BURNING RED

Glass: Collins
Method: Shake all ingredients with ice and strain into glass.

2	shot(s)	Plymouth gin
2	shot(s)	Rubicon guava juice
1/4	shot(s)	Grenadine syrup
1/4	shot(s)	Sisca crème de cassis
1/4	shot(s)	Bols Cherry brandy liqueur
3	dash(es)	Angostura Aromatic bitters
Top up with		Soda water

Origin: Created in 2001 by Antonio Miranda at 10 Rooms, London, England.
Comment: It may be red, but it's not particularly hot – would be more aptly named fruity red.

BURNT TOASTED ALMOND

Glass: Martini
Garnish: Sprinkle ground nutmeg
Method: Shake ingredients with ice and strain into glass.

1	shot(s)	Absolut vodka
1/2	shot(s)	Baileys Irish cream liqueur
1/2	shot(s)	Kahlúa coffee liqueur
1	shot(s)	Disaronno Originale amaretto
2	shot(s)	Double (heavy) cream

Comment: There's more than just almond to this beauty.

BUTTERFLY'S KISS NEW

●●●◐○

Glass: Martini
Garnish: Cinnamon stick
Method: Stir all ingredients with ice and strain into chilled glass.

2	shot(s)	Vanilla infused Absolut vodka
1	shot(s)	Frangelico hazelnut liqueur
1/2	shot(s)	Goldschläger cinnamon schnapps
1/2	shot(s)	Sugar (gomme) syrup
1/2	shot(s)	Chilled water

Origin: Adapted from a drink I discovered in 2003 at Bar Marmont, 8171 Sunset Boulevard, Hollywood, USA.
Comment: Golden coloured Martini style drink complete with the odd gold flake and a hazelnut cinnamon twang.

BUTTERSCOTCH DAIQUIRI

Glass: Martini
Method: Shake ingredients with ice and strain into glass.

2	shot(s)	Havana Club light rum
1	shot(s)	Teichenné butterscotch schnapps
1	shot(s)	Freshly squeezed lime juice
1/2	shot(s)	Sugar (gomme) syrup

Comment: Lime coloured and tastes, well, like butterscotch cut with lime.

●●●●○

BUTTERSCOTCH MARTINI

Glass: Martini
Garnish: Butterscotch sweet
Method: Shake all ingredients with ice and fine strain into chilled glass.

2	shot(s)	Mount Gay gold rum
3/4	shot(s)	Teichenné butterscotch schnapps
3/4	shot(s)	Bols White crème de cacao
1/8	shot(s)	Sugar (gomme) syrup
1/2	shot(s)	Chilled water

Comment: Sweet and suckable.

●●●●○

BUTTERSCOTCH DELIGHT

Glass: Shot
Method: Layer by carefully pouring ingredients in the following order.

3/4	shot(s)	Teichenné butterscotch schnapps
3/4	shot(s)	Baileys Irish Cream liqueur

Origin: The origin of this drink is unknown but it is very popular in the bars in and around Seattle, USA.
Comment: Sweet connotations!

BUZZARD'S BREATH

Glass: Hurricane
Garnish: Split pineapple wedge.
Method: Blend ingredients with crushed ice and serve.

2	shot(s)	Pitú Cachaça
2	shot(s)	Cream of coconut
2	shot(s)	Double (heavy) cream
5	shot(s)	Pressed pineapple juice

Comment: A Piña Colada made with Cachaça.

●●●●○

BYZANTINE

Glass: Collins
Garnish: Basil leaf
Method: Muddle basil in base of shaker. Add other ingredients apart from tonic water, shake with ice and strain into ice-filled glass. Top up with tonic water.

6	fresh	Basil leaves
1 1/2	shot(s)	Plymouth gin
1/2	shot(s)	Passion fruit syrup
2	shot(s)	Pressed pineapple juice
1/2	shot(s)	Lime & lemongrass cordial
Top up with		Tonic water

Origin: Created in 2001 by Douglas Ankrah for Akbar, Soho, London, England.
Comment: This fruity, herbal drink is even better made the way Douglas originally intended, with basil infused gin instead of muddled leaves.

C C KAZI

Glass: Martini
Method: Shake ingredients with ice and strain into glass.

1½	shot(s)	Sauza Hornitos Tequila
2	shot(s)	Cranberry juice
¼	shot(s)	Freshly squeezed lime juice
¼	shot(s)	Sugar (gomme) syrup

Comment: A dry and lively drink with Tequila coming through.

●●●●○

CABLE CAR NEW

Glass: Martini
Garnish: Lemon twist
Method: Shake all ingredients with ice and fine strain into chilled glass.

2	shot(s)	Spiced rum
1	shot(s)	Cointreau / triple sec
½	shot(s)	Freshly squeezed lemon juice
¼	shot(s)	Sugar (gomme) syrup
½	fresh	Egg white

Origin: Created by Tony-Abou-Ganim in 1996 at the Starlight Room, Sir Francis Drake Hotel in San Francisco. Positioned atop the hotel, the bar is passed by the Nob Hill cable cars, earning the bar the catch phrase 'Between the stars and the cable cars'.
Comment: Vanilla and spice from the rum interact with the orange liqueur in this balanced Daiquirí style drink.

CACHAÇA DAIQUIRÍ STRAIGHT UP

Glass: Martini
Method: Shake ingredients with ice and strain into glass.

2	shot(s)	Pitú Cachaça
½	shot(s)	Freshly squeezed lime juice
¼	shot(s)	Sugar (gomme) syrup
¾	shot(s)	Chilled water

Comment: Might be in a Martini glass but it tastes like a Caipirinha.

CACTUS BANGER

Glass: Martini
Method: Shake ingredients with ice and strain into glass.

1	shot(s)	Sauza Hornitos Tequila
1	shot(s)	Grand Marnier
3	shot(s)	Freshly squeezed orange juice
½	shot(s)	Freshly squeezed lime juice

Comment: A golden, sunny looking and sunny tasting drink.

●●●●◐○

CACTUS JACK UPDATED

Glass: Martini
Garnish: Pineapple leaf
Method: Shake all ingredients with ice and fine strain into chilled glass.

1	shot(s)	Sauza Hornitos Tequila
¾	shot(s)	Bols Blue Curaçao
1¼	shot(s)	Freshly squeezed orange juice
1	shot(s)	Pressed pineapple juice
½	shot(s)	Freshly squeezed lemon juice

Comment: Vivid in colour, this orange led, Tequila based drink has a balanced sweet and sourness.

CAFÉ GATES

Glass: Toddy
Garnish: Three coffee beans
Method: Place bar spoon in glass, add first three ingredients and top up with coffee, then float cream.

1	shot(s)	Grand Marnier
1	shot(s)	Kahlúa coffee liqueur
1	shot(s)	Bols Brown crème de cacao
Top up with		Filter coffee (hot)
Float		Lightly whipped cream

Comment: Chocolate orange with coffee and cream.

CAFÉ TOLEDO

Glass: Toddy
Method: Place bar spoon in glass, add first three ingredients and top up with coffee, then float cream.

1	shot(s)	Chocolate syrup
1	shot(s)	Baileys Irish Cream liqueur
1	shot(s)	Kahlúa coffee liqueur
Top up with		Filter coffee (hot)
Float		Lightly whipped cream

Comment: A rich, creamy, chocolate after dinner coffee.

●●●●○

CAIPIRISSIMA UPDATED

Glass: Rocks
Method: Muddle lime in base of glass. Add other ingredients and fill glass with crushed ice. Churn drink with barspoon and serve with short straws.

¾	fresh	Lime cut into wedges
2	shot(s)	Havana Club light rum
¾	shot(s)	Sugar (gomme) syrup

Comment: A Daiquirí style drink made like a Caipirinha to give that rustic edge.

●●●●○

CAIPIROVSKA / CAIPIROSCA UPDATED

Glass: Rocks
Method: Muddle lime in base of glass. Add other ingredients and fill glass with crushed ice. Churn drink with barspoon and serve with short straws.

¾	fresh	Lime cut into wedges
2	shot(s)	Absolut vodka
¾	shot(s)	Sugar (gomme) syrup

Comment: Lacks the character of a cachaça based Caipirinha.

CAIPIRINHA

●●●●●

UPDATED

Pronounced: Ki-Pee-Ree-Nya
Glass: Rocks
Method: Muddle lime in base of glass to release the juices and oils in its skin. Pour Cachaça and sugar into glass, add crushed ice and churn with barspoon. Serve with straws.

³/₄	fresh	**Lime cut into wedges**
2	shot(s)	**Pitú Cachaça**
³/₄	shot(s)	**Sugar (gomme) syrup**

Variant: Caipiruva, Caipirissima, Berry Caipirinha, Caipirovska and Black 'N' Blue Caipirovska.
Origin: Cachaça, a spirit distilled from sugar cane juice, is the national spirit of Brazil - and Brazilians consume an astonishing 2,000,000,000 litres of it a year. The Caipirinha is a traditional Brazilian cocktail, using sugar and green lemons known as 'limon subtil', which grow in the country. (Limes are the best substitute when these are not available.) The name means 'little countryside drink'. Caipirinhas and variations on the theme are staples in Cachaçerias, Brazilian bars which specialise in Cachaça.
Comment: There is much debate among bartenders as to whether granulated sugar or syrup should be used to make this drink. Those who favour granulated sugar argue that muddling with the abrasive sugar helps extract the oils from the lime's skin. Personally, I hate the crunch of sugar as inevitably not all the granulated sugar dissolves. Whether you should use brown or white sugar to make your syrup is another question! Either way, this is refreshing drink.

CAIPIRUVA NEW

Glass: Old-fashioned
Method: Muddle grapes in base of shaker. Add other ingredients, shake with ice and strain into glass filled with crushed ice.

10	fresh	**Seedless grapes**
2	shot(s)	**Pitú Cachaça**
³/₄	shot(s)	**Freshly squeezed lime juice**
³/₄	shot(s)	**Sugar (gomme) syrup**

Comment: A grape juice laced twist on the Caipirinha.

●●●○○

CAJUN MARTINI UPDATED

Glass: Martini
Garnish: Chilli pepper
Method: Stir vermouth with ice. Strain, discarding vermouth to leave only a coating on the ice. Pour pepper vodka into mixing glass, stir with coated ice and strain into chilled glass.

¹/₂	shot(s)	**Cinzano Extra Dry vermouth**
2¹/₂	shot(s)	**Absolut Peppar vodka**

Comment: A very hot vodka Martini. I dare you!

CALIFORNIA LEMONADE

Glass: Hurricane
Garnish: Split lemon wedge
Method: Shake ingredients with ice and strain into ice-filled glass.

1	shot(s)	**Absolut vodka**
1	shot(s)	**Plymouth gin**
1	shot(s)	**Rémy Martin Cognac**
³/₄	shot(s)	**Freshly squeezed lime juice**
³/₄	shot(s)	**Sugar (gomme) syrup**
¹/₄	shot(s)	**Fresh lemon juice**
2	shot(s)	**Freshly squeezed orange juice**
¹/₂	shot(s)	**Grenadine syrup**

Comment: Drinkable but pretty nondescript.

●●●●●●

CALL ME OLD-FASHIONED

Glass: Old-fashioned
Garnish: Orange peel twist
Method: Stir sugar syrup and Angostura with two ice cubes in a glass. Add one shot of Cognac and two more ice cubes. Stir some more and add another two ice cubes and another shot of Cognac. Stir lots more and add more ice if required.

2	shot(s)	**Rémy Martin Cognac**
¹/₄	shot(s)	**Sugar (gomme) syrup**
2	dash	**Angostura aromatic bitters**

Origin: Named by me in 2001.

Comment: An Old-Fashioned made with Cognac instead of whiskey – works well.

CAMERON'TINI

Glass: Martini
Garnish: Lemon twist
Method: Shake all ingredients with ice and fine strain into chilled glass.

1³/₄	shot(s)	The Famous Grouse Scotch whisky
1¹/₄	shot(s)	Freshly squeezed lemon juice
1¹/₄	shot(s)	Almond (orgeat) syrup
¹/₂	shot(s)	Chilled water

Origin: Adapted from a recipe in the 1947 edition of Trader Vic's Bartender's Guide.
Comment: Rich, honeyed and balanced, but most emphatically rich.

CAMOMILE & BLACKTHORN BREEZE

Glass: Collins
Garnish: Lemon wheel on rim
Method: Shake all ingredients with cubed ice and strain into ice-filled glass.

2	shot(s)	Finlandia Lime vodka
2	shot(s)	Lapponia Tyrni (blackthorn berry) liqueur
4	shot(s)	Cold camomile tea

Origin: I created this in 2002 after a trip to Finland with Finlandia vodka.
Comment: Adult, clean and subtle in flavour with a distinctive blackthorn bite.

CANARIE NEW

Glass: Collins (10oz / 290ml max)
Method: Pour pastis and lemon syrup into glass. Serve iced water separately in a small jug (known in France as a 'broc') so the customer can dilute to their own taste (I recommend five shots). Lastly, add ice to fill glass.

1	shot(s)	Ricard Pastis
¹/₂	shot(s)	Lemon (citron) syrup
Top up with		Chilled water

Origin: Very popular throughout France, this drink is fittingly named after the bird, typically bred for its bright yellow plumage.
Comment: The traditional French café drink with a twist of lemon sweetness.

CANARIES

Glass: Hurricane
Garnish: Pineapple leaf.
Method: Shake ingredients with ice and strain into ice-filled glass.

1	shot(s)	Havana Club light rum
1	shot(s)	Cointreau / triple sec
1	shot(s)	Bols Crème de banane
1	shot(s)	Bols Cherry brandy liqueur
3	shot(s)	Pressed pineapple juice
3	shot(s)	Freshly squeezed orange juice

Comment: A long, fruity drink fit for consumption on a tropical beach.

CAPE CODDER

UPDATED

Glass: Old-fashioned
Garnish: Redcurrants
Method: Shake all ingredients with ice and strain into ice-filled glass.

2	shot(s)	Absolut vodka
3	shot(s)	Cranberry juice
¹/₄	shot(s)	Freshly squeezed lime juice

Variation: Without lime juice this is a Cape Cod. Lengthened with soda this becomes the Cape Cod Cooler.
Origin: Named after the resort on the Massachusetts coast. This fish shaped piece of land is where some of the first Europeans settled in the US. Here they found cranberry bogs, the indigenous North American berry on which this drink is based. Provincetown, a small town on the northern tip of the Cape is often cited as the birthplace of the Cosmopolitan, another classic that shares the same three ingredients.
Comment: A dry and refreshing but not particularly interesting.

CANARY FLIP UPDATED

●●●●◐○

Glass: Martini
Garnish: Lemon zest
Method: Shake all ingredients with ice and fine strain into chilled glass.

2	shot(s)	Warninks Advocaat
2	shot(s)	Sauvignon Blanc wine
3/4	shot(s)	Freshly squeezed lemon juice

Origin: Created in 2002 by Alex Kammerling for Warninks.
Comment: A delightful balance of egg, brandy and wine.

CAPPUCCINO

Glass: Toddy
Method: Place bar spoon in glass, add first three ingredients, top up with coffee and float cream.

1	shot(s)	Disaronno Originale amaretto
1	shot(s)	Bols Brown crème de cacao
1	shot(s)	Rémy Martin Cognac
Top up with		Filter coffee (hot)
Float		Lightly whipped cream

Comment: Dark and rich with a strong nut flavour.

CARAMEL MANHATTAN

●●●●●◐

Glass: Martini
Garnish: Lemon twist & pineapple wedge on rim
Method: Shake all ingredients with ice and fine strain into chilled glass.

1½	shot(s)	Buffalo Trace Bourbon
1	shot(s)	Caramel liqueur
½	shot(s)	Cinzano Rosso (sweet) vermouth
1	shot(s)	Pressed pineapple juice

Origin: Adapted from a drink created in 2002 by Nick Strangeway, London, England.
Comment: Rich flavours combine harmoniously with the character of the Bourbon still evident.

CARAVAN NEW

●●●○○

Glass: Collins
Garnish: Cherries
Method: Pour ingredients into ice-filled glass. Stir and serve with straws.

3	shot(s)	Red wine (Shiraz)
½	shot(s)	Grand Marnier liqueur
Top up with		Cola

Origin: Popular in the French Alpine ski resorts.
Comment: A punch-like long drink.

CARDINAL PUNCH UPDATED

●●●◐○

Glass: Old-fashioned
Method: Pour cassis into ice-filled glass and top up with wine. Stir and serve with short straws.

1	shot(s)	Sisca crème de cassis
Top up with		Red wine (Shiraz)

Comment: One for those that like a particularly fruity red.

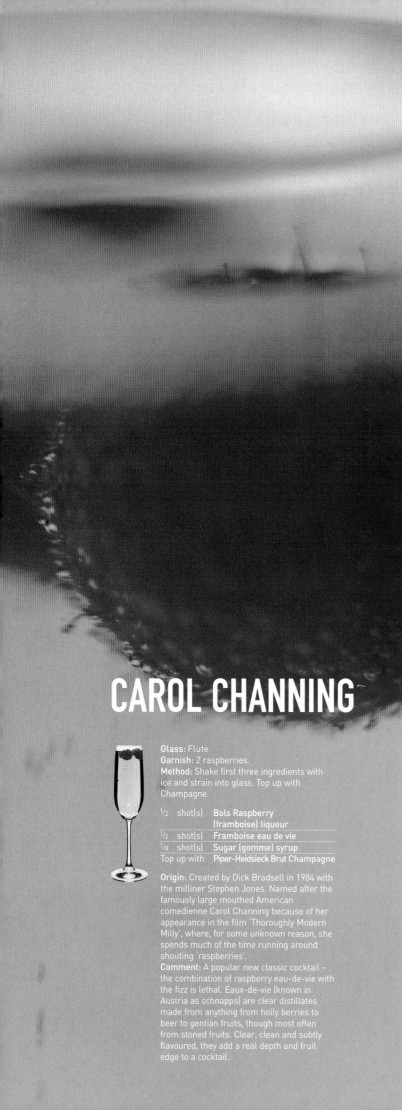

CAROL CHANNING

Glass: Flute
Garnish: 2 raspberries.
Method: Shake first three ingredients with ice and strain into glass. Top up with Champagne.

½	shot(s)	Bols Raspberry (framboise) liqueur
½	shot(s)	Framboise eau de vie
⅛	shot(s)	Sugar (gomme) syrup
Top up with		Piper-Heidsieck Brut Champagne

Origin: Created by Dick Bradsell in 1984 with the milliner Stephen Jones. Named after the famously large mouthed American comedienne Carol Channing because of her appearance in the film 'Thoroughly Modern Milly', where, for some unknown reason, she spends much of the time running around shouting 'raspberries'.
Comment: A popular new classic cocktail – the combination of raspberry eau-de-vie with the fizz is lethal. Eaux-de-vie (known in Austria as schnapps) are clear distillates made from anything from holly berries to beer to gentian fruits, though most often from stoned fruits. Clear, clean and subtly flavoured, they add a real depth and fruit edge to a cocktail.

CARIBBEAN BREEZE

●●●●○

Glass: Collins
Garnish: Pineapple wedge on rim
Method: Shake all ingredients with ice and strain into ice-filled glass.

1¼	shot(s)	Pusser's Navy rum
½	shot(s)	Bols Crème de banane
2½	shot(s)	Pressed pineapple juice
2	shot(s)	Cranberry juice
½	shot(s)	Rose's lime cordial

Comment: A long drink with bags of tangy fruit flavours.

CARIBBEAN CRUISE

●●●●○○

Glass: Collins
Garnish: Pineapple wedge on rim
Method: Shake ingredients with ice and strain into ice-filled glass.

1½	shot(s)	Havana Club light rum
1½	shot(s)	Malibu coconut rum liqueur
4	shot(s)	Pressed pineapple juice
1	spoon	Grenadine syrup

Comment: Long, frothy and fruity - one for the beach bar.

CARIBBEAN PIÑA COLADA

Glass: Hurricane
Garnish: Fresh mint & split pineapple wedge with cherry on stick.
Method: Blend ingredients with crushed ice and serve

2	shot(s)	Havana Club light rum
4	shot(s)	Pressed pineapple juice
½	shot(s)	Cream of coconut
4	dashes	Angostura aromatic bitters
1	pinch	Salt

Comment: Angostura and salt make this a less sticky Colada.

CARIBBEAN PUNCH

●●●●○

Glass: Collins
Method: Shake all ingredients with ice and strain into a glass filled with crushed ice.

2¼	shot(s)	Wray & Nephew overproof rum
½	shot(s)	Disaronno Originale amaretto
½	shot(s)	Malibu coconut rum liqueur
¼	shot(s)	Galliano
¼	shot(s)	Grenadine syrup
¾	shot(s)	Freshly squeezed lemon juice
3	shot(s)	Pressed pineapple juice

Comment: Red in colour and innocent looking, this flavoursome drink sure packs a punch.

CARPANO MARTINI

Glass: Martini
Garnish: Orange twist.
Method: Shake ingredients with ice and strain into glass.

1¼	shot(s)	Plymouth sloe gin
1	shot(s)	Punt E Mes
¼	shot(s)	Freshly squeezed lime juice
¼	shot(s)	Sugar (gomme) syrup

Origin: Created by David Myers at Titanic, London.
Comment: A strong tasting but well balanced and refreshing drink.

CARROT CAKE

●●●●◐○

Glass: Martini
Garnish: Cinnamon dust
Method: Shake all ingredients with ice and fine strain into chilled glass.

2	shot(s)	Baileys Irish Cream liqueur
¾	shot(s)	Goldschläger cinnamon schnapps
1½	shot(s)	Kahlúa coffee liqueur

Comment: Tastes nothing like carrot cake - surely that's a good thing.

CASABLANCA

Glass: Martini
Method: Shake ingredients with ice and strain into glass.

1	shot(s)	Absolut vodka
¼	shot(s)	Galliano
1¼	shot(s)	Warninks advocaat
¼	shot(s)	Freshly squeezed lemon juice
1¼	shot(s)	Freshly squeezed orange juice

Comment: Creamy, fruity, alcoholic custard. Different!

CASANOVA UPDATED

●●●●○

Glass: Martini
Garnish: Crumble Flake bar over drink
Method: Shake all ingredients with ice and fine strain into chilled glass.

1½	shot(s)	Buffalo Trace Bourbon
¾	shot(s)	Alvada Marsala
¾	shot(s)	Kahlúa coffee liqueur
¾	shot(s)	Double (heavy) cream
¾	shot(s)	Milk
⅛	shot(s)	Sugar (gomme) syrup

Comment: Rich, medium-sweet and creamy with a mocha coffee finish.

CASCADE MARTINI UPDATED

●●●●○

Glass: Martini
Garnish: Raspberries on stick
Method: Shake all ingredients with ice and fine strain into chilled glass.

8	fresh	Raspberries
1½	shot(s)	Stoli Razberi
2½	shot(s)	Cranberry juice
½	shot(s)	Freshly squeezed lemon juice
¼	shot(s)	Chambord black raspberry liqueur
¼	shot(s)	Vanilla syrup

Comment: Rich raspberry with hints of citrus and vanilla.

CASINO

Glass: Martini
Garnish: Split stemmed cherry
Method: Stir ingredients with ice and strain into glass.

2	shot(s)	Plymouth gin
½	shot(s)	Freshly squeezed lemon juice
½	shot(s)	Maraschino liqueur
4	dashes	Fee Brothers Orange bitters

Comment: Tart and flowery.

CHAMPAGNE COCKTAIL

●●●●◐○

UPDATED

Glass: Flute
Garnish: Orange peel twist
Method: Rub sugar cube with orange peel, then place in base of glass and soak with Angostura. Cover soaked cube with Cognac, then top up with Champagne.

1	cube	Brown sugar
3	dashes	Angostura aromatic bitters
1	shot(s)	Rémy Martin Cognac
Top up with		Piper-Heidsieck Brut Champagne

Origin: Said to have originated from a winning recipe by John Dougherty named Business Brace at the 1899 New York Cocktail competition.
Comment: A classic (retro) cocktail that gets sweeter as you reach the dissolving cube at the bottom.

CASSINI

Glass: Martini
Garnish: Stemmed cherry / redcurrants
Method: Shake ingredients with ice and strain into glass.

2	shot(s)	Absolut vodka
2½	shot(s)	Cranberry juice
½	shot(s)	Sisca crème de cassis

Origin: Created by me in 1998.
Comment: A simple but pleasant berry drink.

CASTRO

Glass: Martini
Method: Shake ingredients with ice and strain into glass.

1½	shot(s)	Appleton Estate V/X aged rum
¾	shot(s)	Calvados (or apple jack brandy)
1½	shot(s)	Freshly squeezed orange juice
¾	shot(s)	Freshly squeezed lime juice
¾	shot(s)	Rose's lime cordial
1/2	shot(s)	Sugar syrup

Comment: Named after the Cuban dictator who holds the record for the longest presidency of any country. The bearded wonder would approve of this rum based sweet and sour cocktail.

CAUSEWAY

Glass: Collins
Method: Shake first five ingredients with ice and strain into ice-filled glass, then top up with ginger ale.

2	shot(s)	Black Bush Irish whiskey
1	shot(s)	Drambuie liqueur
4	dashes	Angostura aromatic bitters
4	drops	Fee Brothers Orange bitters
¼	shot(s)	Freshly squeezed lemon juice
Top up with		Ginger ale

Origin: Created by David Myers at Titanic, London, England.
Comment: An aromatic whiskey drink.

CELERY MARTINI

Glass: Martini
Garnish: Salt rim and celery
Method: Muddle chopped celery in shaker can with sugar and vodka. Shake with ice and strain.

1	cup	Chopped celery
2	shot(s)	Absolut vodka
½	shot(s)	Sugar (gomme) syrup

Origin: Created by Andreas Tsanos at Momos, London, England in 2001.
Comment: I only usually like celery when loaded with blue cheese - but I love this Martini.

CHAM 69

Glass: Sling
Garnish: Blackberries, blueberries and raspberries.
Method: Shake ingredients with ice and strain into ice-filled glass.

1¹/₂	shot(s)	Chambord black raspberry liqueur
2	shot(s)	Absolut vodka
1¹/₄	shot(s)	Disaronno Originale amaretto
1¹/₂	shot(s)	Freshly squeezed lime juice
³/₄	shot(s)	Sugar (gomme) syrup
Top up with		Lemonade

Origin: Created by me in 1998.
Comment: A long, fruity combination of sweet and sour.

CHAMPAGNE COBBLER

Glass: Flute
Method: Pour first two ingredients into glass and top up with Champagne.

³/₄	shot(s)	Cointreau / triple sec
³/₄	shot(s)	Freshly squeezed lemon juice
Top up with		Piper-Heidsieck Brut Champagne

Comment: Citrus Champagne.

CHAMPAGNE CUP

Glass: Flute
Garnish: Stemmed maraschino cherry.
Method: Stir first three ingredients with ice and strain into glass, then top up with Champagne and lightly stir.

³/₄	shot(s)	Rémy Martin Cognac
¹/₂	shot(s)	Orange curaçao
¹/₄	shot(s)	Maraschino syrup
Top up with		Piper-Heidsieck Brut Champagne

Variant: More usually made in large quantities and served from a jug.

CHAMPAGNE DAISY

Glass: Flute
Garnish: Pomegranate wedge.
Method: Shake first three ingredients with ice and strain into glass, then top up with Champagne.

1	shot(s)	Yellow Chartreuse
¹/₈	shot(s)	Grenadine syrup
1	shot(s)	Freshly squeezed lemon juice
Top up with		Piper-Heidsieck Brut Champagne

Comment: If you like Chartreuse, you'll like this.

CHAMPAGNE PUNCH

Glass: Hurricane
Garnish: Pineapple leaf and mint
Method: Shake first seven ingredients with ice and strain into ice-filled glass, then top up with Champagne.

1¹/₂	shot(s)	Pusser's Navy rum
¹/₂	shot(s)	Rémy Martin Cognac
¹/₂	shot(s)	Orange curaçao
¹/₂	shot(s)	Maraschino liqueur
¹/₂	shot(s)	Freshly squeezed lemon juice
1	shot(s)	Sugar (gomme) syrup
3	shot(s)	Pressed pineapple juice
Top up with		Piper-Heidsieck Brut Champagne

Comment: Loads of flavour, very strong.

CHARLIE CHAPLIN

Glass: Martini
Method: Shake ingredients with ice and strain into glass.

1¹/₂	shot(s)	Plymouth sloe gin
1¹/₂	shot(s)	Bols Apricot brandy Liqueur
1¹/₂	shot(s)	Freshly squeezed lemon juice

Comment: Old school, fruity cocktail.

●●●●○

CHARLIE LYCHEE'TINI

Glass: Martini
Garnish: Whole lychee from tin in drink
Method: Stir all ingredients with ice and strain into chilled glass.

1	shot(s)	Tio Pepe Fino Sherry
1	shot(s)	ABA Pisco
1	shot(s)	Sake
1	shot(s)	Lychee syrup from tinned fruit
¹/₈	shot	Elderflower syrup

Origin: I created this drink in 2002 and named it for Charlie Rouse, who loves Sherry.
Comment: Subtle with an interesting salty edge, this tastes almost like a wine.

CHARTINI

Glass: Martini
Garnish: Split stemmed cherry on rim
Method: Stir ingredients with ice and strain into glass.

2¹/₂	shot(s)	Plymouth gin
1¹/₄	shot(s)	Green Chartreuse

Comment: A killer Martini with aromatic Chartreuse.

CHEEKY MONKEY

Glass: Martini
Method: Shake all ingredients with ice and strain into glass.

1	shot(s)	Absolut Citron vodka
1	shot(s)	Yellow Chartreuse
2	shot(s)	Freshly squeezed orange juice
1/2	shot(s)	Sugar (gomme) syrup
4	dashes	Fee Brothers Orange bitters

Origin: Adapted from a recipe created by Tony Conigliaro in 2001 at Isola, Knightsbridge, London, England.
Comment: Fire yellow in colour, this drink features the distinctive flavour of Chartreuse with a talented citrus supporting cast.

CHELSEA SIDECAR

Glass: Martini
Method: Shake ingredients with ice and strain into glass.

1 1/2	shot(s)	Plymouth gin
1 1/2	shot(s)	Cointreau / triple sec
1 1/4	shot(s)	Freshly squeezed lime juice
1	shot(s)	Sugar (gomme) syrup
1/4	shot(s)	Freshly squeezed lemon juice

Comment: Tasty and long.

CHERRUTE

Glass: Martini
Garnish: Cherry on rim
Method: Shake ingredients with ice and strain into glass.

2	shot(s)	Absolut vodka
1	shot(s)	Bols Cherry brandy liqueur
2	shot(s)	Pressed grapefruit juice

Comment: Sweet cherry brandy with the fruity acidity of grapefruit, laced with vodka.

CHERRY BLOSSOM

Glass: Martini
Garnish: Split lime wedge
Method: Shake ingredients with ice and strain into glass.

3/4	shot(s)	Bols Cherry brandy liqueur
3/4	shot(s)	Kirsch
1/2	shot(s)	Cointreau / triple sec
1 1/4	shot(s)	Freshly squeezed lemon juice
1/2	shot(s)	Sugar (gomme) syrup
1/4	shot(s)	Grenadine syrup

Comment: Bundles of flavour – tangy and moreish.

CHERRY DAIQUIRÍ

Glass: Martini
Garnish: Cherry on rim
Method: Muddle cherries in base of shaker. Add other ingredients, shake vigorously with ice and fine strain into chilled glass.

8	fresh	Stoned cherries
2	shot(s)	Vanilla infused Havana Club rum
1	shot(s)	Bols Cherry brandy liqueur
?	shot(s)	Maraschino syrup
1/2	shot(s)	Freshly squeezed lime juice
1/2	shot(s)	Chilled water

Origin: Created in 2003 by yours truly.
Comment: Cherry sweetness paired with Daiquiri sharpness.

CHERRY FIZZ

Glass: Collins
Garnish: Split lime wedge
Method: Shake first four ingredients with ice and strain into ice-filled glass, then top up with lemonade.

1 1/2	shot(s)	Bols Cherry brandy liqueur
2	shot(s)	Freshly squeezed orange juice
1	shot(s)	Freshly squeezed lime juice
1/2	shot(s)	Sugar (gomme) syrup
Top up with		Lemonade

Comment: Cherry dominates this citrus sparkler.

CHERRY & HAZELNUT DAIQUIRÍ

Glass: Martini
Garnish: Cherry on rim
Method: Shake all ingredients with ice and fine strain into chilled glass.

2	shot(s)	Havana Club light rum
3/4	shot(s)	Maraschino liqueur
1?	shot(s)	Frangelico hazelnut liqueur
1/2	shot(s)	Freshly squeezed lime juice
1/2	shot(s)	Chilled water

Origin: Adam Wyartt and I created this in 2003.
Comment: Nutty and surprisingly tangy.

CHERRY MARTINI

Glass: Martini
Garnish: Stemmed cherry
Method: Shake all ingredients with ice and strain into glass.

2	shot(s)	Wisniówka cherry vodka
3/4	shot(s)	Bols Cherry brandy liqueur
1	shot(s)	Freshly squeezed lemon juice
1/2	shot(s)	Sugar (gomme) syrup

Comment: A cocktail that does what it says on the box.

CHERRY MASH SOUR

Glass: Old-fashioned
Garnish: Lemon twist & cherry
Method: Shake all ingredients with ice and strain into ice-filled glass.

2	shot(s)	Jack Daniel's Tennessee whiskey
1/2	shot(s)	Bols Cherry brandy liqueur
3/4	shot(s)	Freshly squeezed lemon juice
1/2	shot(s)	Sugar (gomme) syrup

Origin: Created by Dale DeGroff when Beverage Manager at the Rainbow Room Promenade Bar, New York City.
Comment: The rich flavour of Tennessee whiskey soured with lemon and sweetened with cherry liqueur.

●●●●●◖

CHE'S REVOLUTION NEW

Glass: Martini
Garnish: Pineapple wedge on rim
Method: Muddle mint with rum in base of shaker. Add other ingredients, shake with ice and fine strain into chilled glass.

4	fresh	Mint leaves
2	shot(s)	Havana Club light rum
1/4	shot(s)	Maple syrup
2	shot(s)	Pressed pineapple juice

Origin: Created in 2003 by Ben Reed for the launch party of MJU Bar @ Millennium Hotel, London, England.
Comment: Complex and smooth with hints of maple syrup and mint amongst the pineapple and rum.

CHI-CHI

Glass: Hurricane
Garnish: Split pineapple wedge/mint
Method: Blend ingredients with crushed ice and serve.

2	shot(s)	Absolut vodka
6	shot(s)	Pressed pineapple juice
1	shot(s)	Double (heavy) cream
1	shot(s)	Cream of coconut

Comment: Piña Colada with vodka.

CHICAGO COFFEE

Glass: Snifter
Garnish: Sugar rim & dust with chocolate powder
Method: Blend first four ingredients with ice and leave in blender can. Sugar rim, pour Cognac into glass, flambé and swirl until the flame begins to caramelise the sugar on rim of glass. Then quickly add the contents of the blender and float cream.

1	shot(s)	Kahlúa coffee liqueur
1	shot(s)	Baileys Irish Cream liqueur
1	scoop	Vanilla ice cream
3	shot(s)	Filter coffee coffee (hot)
1 1/2	shot(s)	Rémy Martin Cognac
Float		Lightly whipped cream

Comment: Tricky to do, but great for dessert.

●●●●◖○

CHICLET DAIQUIRÍ

Glass: Martini
Garnish: Banana slice on rim
Method: Blend all ingredients with a 12oz scoop of crushed ice and serve in chilled glass.

2 1/2	shot(s)	Havana Club light rum
1/2	shot(s)	Bols Crème de banane
1/8	shot(s)	White crème de menthe
1/2	shot(s)	Freshly squeezed lime juice
1/4	shot(s)	Sugar (gomme) syrup

Origin: Often found on Cuban bar menus, this was created at La Floridita, Havana.
Comment: A wonderfully refreshing drink on a summer's day with surprisingly subtle flavours.

CHIHUAHUA MARTINI

Glass: Martini
Method: Shake ingredients with ice and strain into glass.

2	shot(s)	Sauza Hornitos Tequila
3	shot(s)	Pressed grapefruit juice
4	dashes	Angostura aromatic bitters

Comment: Tequila and grapefruit juice pepped up with Angostura.

CHILL BREEZE

Glass: Collins
Garnish: Split lime wheel
Method: Shake ingredients with ice and strain into ice-filled glass.

2	shot(s)	Passoã passion fruit liqueur
1	shot(s)	Absolut vodka
1	shot(s)	Bols Cherry brandy liqueur
4	shot(s)	Cranberry juice

Comment: Long, dry, passion and cherry – good!

●●●●○○

CHILL-OUT MARTINI

Glass: Martini
Garnish: Pineapple wedge on rim
Method: Shake all ingredients with ice and fine strain into chilled glass.

1 1/2	shot(s)	Absolut Mandrin vodka
1 1/2	shot(s)	Malibu coconut rum
1 1/2	shot(s)	Baileys Irish Cream liqueur
1 1/2	shot(s)	Freshly squeezed orange juice

Comment: Smooth, creamy sweet orange and surprisingly strong.

CHIMAYO

Glass: Martini
Method: Shake ingredients with ice and strain into glass.

2	shot(s)	Sauza Hornitos Tequila
1	shot(s)	Sisca crème de cassis
2	shot(s)	Pressed apple juice

Origin: Created by Adewale at the Arts Café, Leeds, England.
Comment: Simple and effective – apple juice and cassis take the 'bite' off the Tequila.

●●●●○

CHIN CHIN

Glass: Flute
Method: Shake first three ingredients with ice and strain into glass. Top up with Champagne.

2	shot(s)	The Famous Grouse Scotch whisky
1	shot(s)	Honey syrup
1	shot(s)	Pressed apple juice
Top up with		Piper-Heidsieck Brut Champagne

Origin: Created by Tony Conigliaro at Isola, Knightsbridge, London, England.
Comment: Golden honey in colour and also in flavour. An unusual and great tasting Champagne cocktail.

CHINA BEACH

Glass: Martini
Method: Stir ingredients with ice and strain into glass.

1	shot(s)	Canton Ginger liqueur
2	shot(s)	Cranberry juice
1	shot(s)	Absolut vodka

Comment: Dry and flavourful.

●●●●◐○

CHINA BLUE UPDATED

Glass: Collins
Garnish: Orange slice in drink
Method: Shake all ingredients with ice and strain into ice-filled glass.

1	shot(s)	Bols Blue Curaçao
1	shot(s)	Bols Lychee liqueur
4	shot(s)	Pressed grapefruit juice

Origin: Philip Duff tells me that he became aware of this drink in 1999 when I did the first Bols Academies in Japan and that it is well-known along the Pacific Rim.
Comment: Looks sweet, but due to generous splash of grapefruit is actually balanced and refreshing.

●●●●●○

CHINA BLUE MARTINI NEW

Glass: Martini
Garnish: Peeled lychee in drink
Method: Shake all ingredients with ice and fine strain into chilled glass.

1	shot(s)	Bols Blue Curaçao
1	shot(s)	Lychee liqueur
2	shot(s)	Pressed grapefruit juice
1/4	shot(s)	Freshly squeezed lemon juice

Origin: An almost inevitable short adaptation of the original long drink above.
Comment: This simple cocktail with its turquoise colour, tastes more adult and interesting than it looks.

CHINESE PASSION

Glass: Collins
Garnish: Orange slice in glass
Method: Shake ingredients with ice and strain into ice-filled glass.

1	shot(s)	Passoã passion fruit liqueur
1 1/2	shot(s)	Buffalo Trace Bourbon
1 1/2	shot(s)	Teichenné Peach schnapps
5	shot(s)	Freshly squeezed orange juice

Comment: Bizarrely, an element of Chinese flavour.

CHINESE COCKTAIL

Glass: Martini
Method: Shake ingredients with ice and strain into glass.

2	shot(s)	Mount Gay Eclipse gold rum
1/2	shot(s)	Orange curaçao
1/2	shot(s)	Maraschino liqueur
1/8	shot(s)	Grenadine syrup
6	dashes	Angostura aromatic bitters

Comment: This does not look or taste Chinese.

●●●●◐○

CHOC & NUT MARTINI

Glass: Martini
Garnish: Wipe rim with orange and dust with cocoa powder.
Method: Shake all ingredients with ice and fine strain into chilled glass.

2	shot(s)	Absolut vodka
1	shot(s)	Frangelico hazelnut liqueur
1	shot(s)	Bols White crème de cacao
1/4	shot(s)	Chilled water

Comment: Surprise, surprise - it's chocolate and hazelnut.

CHOCOLATE BISCUIT

Glass: Martini
Garnish: Chocolate powder
Method: Shake ingredients with ice and strain into glass.

1 1/2	shot(s)	Rémy Martin Cognac
1 1/2	shot(s)	Kahlúa coffee liqueur
1 1/2	shot(s)	Bols Brown crème de cacao

Origin: Created in 1999 by Gillian Stanfield at The Atlantic Bar & Grill, London, England.
Comment: Sweet and rich, with coffee and chocolate complementing the Cognac.

CHOCOLATE CHIP MINT COOKIE

Glass: Hurricane
Garnish: Chocolate powder rim
Method: Blend ingredients with crushed ice and serve.

4		Oreo cookies
1 1/2	shot(s)	Bols White crème de cacao
1 1/2	shot(s)	Green crème de menthe
3	scoops	Vanilla ice cream

Comment: Tastes just like the name suggests.

●●●●●○

CHOCOLATE MARTINI UPDATED

Glass: Martini
Garnish: White Cacao chocolate powder rim
Method: Shake all ingredients with ice and fine strain into chilled glass.

2	shot(s)	Absolut vodka
1	shot(s)	Bols White crème de cacao
1	shot(s)	Cinzano Extra Dry vermouth

Comment: Vodka and chocolate made more interesting with a hint of vermouth.

CHOCOLATE MONKEY

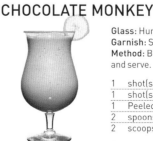

Glass: Hurricane
Garnish: Split banana slice
Method: Blend ingredients with crushed ice and serve.

1	shot(s)	Bols Crème de banane
1	shot(s)	Bols Brown crème de cacao
1	Peeled	Banana
2	spoons	Chocolate powder
2	scoops	Vanilla ice cream

Comment: The chocolate and banana go very well together.

A B C D E F G H I J K L M N O P Q R S T U V W X Y Z

CHOCOLATE 'N' CRANBERRY MARTINI NEW

●●●●○

Glass: Martini
Garnish: White cacao & cocoa powder rim
Method: Shake all ingredients with ice and fine strain into chilled, rimmed glass.

1	shot(s)	Finlandia Cranberry vodka
1	shot(s)	Stoli Vanil
1/2	shot(s)	Bols White crème de cacao
1	shot(s)	Cinzano Extra Dry vermouth
1	shot(s)	Cranberry juice

Origin: I created this drink in 2003 for Finlandia.
Comment: The chocolate rim makes this vanilla and cranberry vodka laced drink.

CHOCOLATE PUFF

●●●●○

Glass: Old-fashioned
Garnish: Crumbled Cadbury's Flake bar
Method: Shake all ingredients with ice and strain into glass.

1	shot(s)	Mount Gay Eclipse gold rum
1	shot(s)	Bols Brown crème de cacao
6	spoons	Natural yoghurt
2	zests	Fresh orange
1/4	shot(s)	Sugar (gomme) syrup

Origin: Created by Wayne Collins in 2002 for Maxxium UK.
Comment: Smooth as you like. The orange is surprisingly evident.

CICADA COCKTAIL

●●●◑○

Glass: Martini
Garnish: Grate fresh nutmeg
Method: Shake all ingredients with ice and fine strain into chilled glass.

2	shot(s)	Jack Daniel's Tennessee whiskey
1	shot(s)	Disaronno Originale amaretto
1/2	shot(s)	Double (heavy) cream
3/4	shot(s)	Sugar (gomme) syrup

Origin: Those familiar with the Grasshopper cocktail (named for its green colour) will understand why this one is called the Cicada (they're a bit browner).
Comment: Smoothed whisky with more than a hint of almond.

CIDER APPLE COOLER

●●●●○

Glass: Collins
Method: Shake all ingredients with ice and strain into ice-filled glass.

2	shot(s)	Calvados (or applejack brandy)
1	shot(s)	Apple schnapps liqueur
4 1/2	shot(s)	Pressed apple juice

Comment: Not unlike the taste of strong dry cider – only cider doesn't come this good.

CHOCOLATE MINT MARTINI

Glass: Martini
Garnish: Chocolate powder rim
Method: Stir ingredients with ice and strain into glass.

2	shot(s)	Absolut vodka
1/2	shot(s)	White crème de menthe
1	shot(s)	Bols White crème de cacao
1/2	shot(s)	Cinzano Extra Dry vermouth

Comment: Tastes of after dinner mints.

CIDER APPLE MARTINI UPDATED

●●●●○

Glass: Martini
Garnish: Apple wedge
Method: Shake all ingredients with ice and fine strain into chilled glass.

1½	shot(s)	Calvados or applejack brandy
¾	shot(s)	Apple schnapps
¾	shot(s)	Freshly squeezed lemon juice
1	shot(s)	Pressed apple juice
¼	shot(s)	Sugar (gomme) syrup

Origin: Created in 1998 by Jamie Terrell at Lab, London, England.
Comment: As the name suggests, rich cider flavours with a sharp finish.

CINNAMON DAIQUIRÍ

Glass: Martini
Garnish: Dust with cinnamon
Method: Shake all ingredients vigorously with ice and strain into glass.

2	shot(s)	Havana Club light rum
⅓	shot(s)	Cinnamon schnapps
1	shot(s)	Sugar (gomme) syrup
1	shot(s)	Freshly squeezed lime juice

Created by: Porik of Che, London, England in 1999.
Comment: A subtle spicy cinnamon taste with tangy length.

CITRUS CAIPIROVSKA NEW

●●●●○

Glass: Rocks
Method: Muddle lemon in base of glass. Add other ingredients and fill glass with crushed ice. Churn drink with barspoon and serve with short straws.

¾	fresh	Lemon cut into wedges
2	shot(s)	Absolut Citron
¾	shot(s)	Sugar (gomme) syrup

Comment: Superbly refreshing balance of sweet and citrus sourness.

CITRUS MARTINI

Glass: Martini
Garnish: Lemon peel twist
Method: Shake ingredients with ice and strain into glass.

2	shot(s)	Absolut Citron vodka
1	shot(s)	Cointreau / triple sec
1	shot(s)	Freshly squeezed lemon juice
½	shot(s)	Sugar (gomme) syrup

Comment: Made well this drink is great, made badly it sucks.

CLARIDGE

Glass: Martini
Garnish: Lemon peel twist
Method: Shake ingredients with ice and strain.

1½	shot(s)	Plymouth gin
1½	shot(s)	Cinzano Extra Dry vermouth
¾	shot(s)	Cointreau / triple sec
¾	shot(s)	Bols Apricot brandy Liqueur

Comment: Gin for the strength, Martini for dryness and liqueur to sweeten – an interesting combination.

CLASSIC

Glass: Martini
Garnish: Lemon peel twist
Method: Shake ingredients with ice and strain into glass.

1½	shot(s)	Rémy Martin Cognac
½	shot(s)	Freshly squeezed lemon juice
½	shot(s)	Orange curaçao
½	shot(s)	Maraschino liqueur
½	shot(s)	Sugar (gomme) syrup

Comment: A great brandy based fruity drink.

CLOCKWORK ORANGE

●●●●○

Glass: Collins
Garnish: Orange wheel in glass
Method: Shake all ingredients with ice and strain into ice-filled glass.

1½	shot(s)	Rémy Martin Cognac
1½	shot(s)	Grand Marnier
4	shot(s)	Freshly squeezed orange juice

Comment: Not as memorable as the film but a pleasant orange drink all the same.

CLOUD 9

Glass: Hurricane
Garnish: Chocolate rim
Method: Blend first four ingredients with lots of ice until slushy, pour in glass and float cream.

2	shot(s)	Baileys Irish cream liqueur
1	shot(s)	Chambord black raspberry liqueur
1	shot(s)	Disaronno Originale amaretto
3	scoops	Vanilla ice cream
Float		Lightly whipped cream

Comment: The black raspberry liqueur and amaretto give a deeper taste to what could be an obvious drink.

CLOVER LEAF MARTINI UPDATED

●●●●◑

Glass: Martini
Garnish: Clover/mint leaf
Method: Muddle raspberries in base of shaker. Add other ingredients, shake with ice and fine strain into chilled glass.

10	fresh	Raspberries
2½	shot(s)	Plymouth gin
¾	shot(s)	Freshly squeezed lemon juice
¼	shot(s)	Grenadine syrup
¼	shot(s)	Sugar (gomme) syrup
½	fresh	Egg white

Variation: Traditionally made with raspberry syrup with no grenadine or fresh raspberries.
AKA: Without the mint leaf garnish this drink is called a 'Clover Club'.
Origin: A classic (retro) cocktail that's thought to have been created at the Bellevue-Stratford Hotel in Philadelphia.
Comment: Carpet scaring red, this drink is fruity, strong and recommended. Muddle some mint with the raspberries to add interest.

CLUB COCKTAIL

●●●●○

Glass: Martini
Garnish: Stemmed maraschino cherry in drink
Method: Stir all ingredients with ice and strain into chilled glass.

2	shot(s)	Havana Club light rum
1/2	shot(s)	Cinzano Rosso (sweet) vermouth
1/2	shot(s)	Cinzano Extra Dry vermouth
1/2	shot(s)	Maraschino syrup
4	dashes	Angostura aromatic bitters
3/4	shot(s)	Chilled water

Origin: David Embury once wrote, "There are as many Club Cocktails as there are clubs." I based this one on a drink by that name served at Milk & Honey, London, England.
Comment: An aromatic, spirited classical cocktail.

COCO CABANA

●●●●◐○

Glass: Martini
Garnish: Split pineapple wedge
Method: Shake all ingredients with ice and fine strain into chilled glass.

1 1/2	shot(s)	Malibu coconut rum liqueur
1/2	shot(s)	Midori melon liqueur
2	shot(s)	Pressed pineapple juice
3/4	shot(s)	Double (heavy) cream
3/4	shot(s)	Milk

Comment: A sweet, creamy tropical number for Barry Manilow fans.

COCO NAUT

Glass: Rocks
Method: Blend all ingredients with crushed ice and serve.

2	shot(s)	Wray & Nephew overproof rum
2	shot(s)	Cream of coconut
1	shot(s)	Freshly squeezed lime juice

Comment: This snow-white drink is hardly innocent with a double shot of overproof rum nicely masked by sweet coconut.

COCOBANANA

Glass: Hurricane
Garnish: Split banana slice
Method: Blend ingredients with crushed ice and serve.

1	shot(s)	Disaronno Originale amaretto
1	shot(s)	Mount Gay Eclipse gold rum
2	shot(s)	Pressed pineapple juice
1 1/2	shot(s)	Cream of coconut
2	scoop	Vanilla ice cream
1		Peeled banana

Comment: A Piña Colada with amaretto, ice cream and banana.

COCONUT DAIQUIRÍ

●●●●○

Glass: Martini
Method: Shake all ingredients with ice and fine strain into chilled glass.

2	shot(s)	Havana Club light rum
1	shot(s)	Malibu coconut rum liqueur
1/2	shot(s)	Freshly squeezed lime juice
1/2	shot(s)	Coconut syrup
3/4	shot(s)	Chilled water

Variation: Blend with a 12oz scoop of crushed ice and a tad more coconut syrup.
Comment: That special Daiquirí flavour with a pleasing tropical touch.

COCONUT WATER

●●●●○

Glass: Martini
Method: Stir all ingredients with ice and fine strain into chilled glass.

2 1/4	shot(s)	Malibu coconut rum liqueur
1	shot(s)	Absolut vodka
1/8	shot(s)	Coconut syrup
1 1/4	shot(s)	Chilled water

Origin: Created by yours truly in 2003.
Comment: Have you ever drunk from a fresh coconut in the Caribbean? Well, this is the alcoholic equivalent.

COCUBA

Glass: Martini
Garnish: Wipe cream of coconut round rim and dip in dessicated coconut.
Method: Shake ingredients with ice and strain.

1 1/2	shot(s)	Havana Club light rum
1 1/2	shot(s)	Malibu coconut rum liqueur
1/2	shot(s)	Frangelico hazelnut liqueur
3/4	shot(s)	Bols White crème de cacao

Created by: Neil Berrie of the Atlantic Bar & Grill, London, England in 1998.
Comment: An interesting mix of flavours - nuts predominate.

COFFEE & VANILLA DAIQUIRÍ

●●●●○

Glass: Martini
Garnish: Float three coffee beans
Method: Shake all ingredients with ice and fine strain into chilled glass.

2	shot(s)	Vanilla infused Havana Club rum
1	shot(s)	Kahlúa coffee liqueur
1/2	shot(s)	Freshly squeezed lime juice
1/8	shot(s)	Sugar (gomme) syrup
3/4	shot(s)	Chilled water

Origin: Created in 2002 by yours truly.
Comment: Coffee, vanilla, sweetness and sourness all in harmony.

COLA DE MONO

Glass: Martini
Garnish: Dusting of ground cinnamon
Method: Muddle cinnamon stick and pisco in base of shaker. Add other ingredients, shake with ice and fine strain into a chilled glass.

1	inch	Cinnamon stick
2	shot(s)	ABA Pisco
1	shot(s)	Espresso coffee (cold)
1	shot(s)	Kahlúa Coffee liqueur

Origin: I based this on a Chilean drink traditionally consumed at Christmas, the name of which literally translates as 'Tail of Monkey'. The original uses milk and sugar instead of coffee liqueur.
Comment: Coffee and cinnamon – a drink to be savoured.

COLD COMFORT

Glass: Old-fashioned
Method: Shake all ingredients vigorously with ice and strain into ice filled glass.

2	shot(s)	Wray & Nephew Overproof rum
6	spoons	Runny honey
1	shot(s)	Freshly squeezed lime juice

Origin: I discovered this while in Jamaica in 2001.
Comment: Take at the first sign of a cold, and then retreat under your bedcovers. Repeat dose regularly while symptoms persist. Warning – do not take if currently being prescribed another form of medication.

COLLAR & CUFF NEW

Glass: Toddy
Method: Place bar spoon in glass, add ingredients and stir.

2	spoons	Runny honey
1	shot(s)	The Famous Grouse Scotch whisky
1	shot(s)	Ginger liqueur
1	shot(s)	Freshly squeezed lemon juice
Top up with		Boiling water

Origin: Created in 2003 by yours truly.
Comment: Warming both due to the hot water and also the flavour of ginger. One for a cold winter's night.

COLLECTION MARTINI

Glass: Martini
Garnish: Lime wedge
Method: Vigorously shake all ingredients with ice and strain into glass.

³/₄	shot(s)	Absolut vodka
³/₄	shot(s)	Absolut Citron vodka
³/₄	shot(s)	Bénédictine D.O.M liqueur
³/₄	shot(s)	Bols Blackberry liqueur (Crème de mûre)
¹/₂	shot(s)	Freshly squeezed lime juice

Origin: Originally created by Matthew Randall whilst at The Collection, London, England.
Comment: Honey, spice and vodka enhanced by blackberries. Very alcoholic edge.

COLLINS

●●●●○

UPDATED

Glass: Collins
Garnish: Orange (flag) wheel and cheery on stick
Method: Shake first three ingredients with ice and strain into ice-filled glass, then top up with soda.

2	shot(s)	Spirit (see variant)
1	shot(s)	Freshly squeezed lemon juice
¹/₂	shot(s)	Sugar (gomme) syrup
Top up with		Soda water

Variant: Tom Collins (with old Tom gin), John Collins (with London Dry gin), Sandy or Jock Collins (with Scotch whisky), Pierre Collins (with Cognac/brandy), Pedro Collins (with rum), Mike Collins (with Irish Whiskey), Colonel Collins (with Bourbon), Captain Collins (with Canadian whiskey), Joe Collins (with vodka), Jack Collins (with applejack), Pepito Collins (with Tequila) as well as the self-explanatory Vodka Collins and Raspberry Collins.
Origin: Said to have been created by John Collins, a bartender at Limmer's Hotel, Conduit Street, London around 1800. John must have been well travelled because it is also claimed that the drink was invented around the same time in New Jersey/New York by John Collins, an Irish immigrant who named the drink after his brother. Wherever the Collins was invented, it was originally made with Dutch Jenever. Since then other spirits have spawned an entire family of variants.
Comment: A refreshing combination of spirit, lemon and sugar.

COLONIAL ROT

Glass: Collins
Method: Shake first five ingredients with ice and strain into ice-filled glass, then top up with half soda and half lemonade.

1	shot(s)	La Fée absinthe
1	shot(s)	Absolut Citron vodka
1/2	shot(s)	Sugar (gomme) syrup
1/2	shot(s)	Freshly squeezed lime juice
5	fresh	Mint leaves
Top up with		Half soda and half lemonade

Comment: Anis, mint and lemon.

COLONEL T

Glass: Sling
Garnish: Pineapple leaf
Method: Shake ingredients with ice and strain into ice-filled glass.

2	shot(s)	Buffalo Trace Bourbon
1	shot(s)	Bols Apricot brandy Liqueur
4	shot(s)	Pressed pineapple juice

Comment: Mellow and long with pineapple, apricot and Bourbon.

COLORADO BULLDOG

Glass: Collins
Method: Shake first four ingredients with ice and strain into ice-filled glass, then top up with cola.

1	shot(s)	Absolut vodka
1	shot(s)	Kahlúa coffee liqueur
1	shot(s)	Double (heavy) cream
2	shot(s)	Milk
Top up with		Cola

Comment: This dog's bite is hidden by cream.

COLORADO MOTHER

Glass: Collins
Method: Shake first four ingredients with ice and strain into ice-filled glass, then top up with cola.

1	shot(s)	Sauza Hornitos Tequila
1	shot(s)	Kahlúa coffee liqueur
1 1/2	shot(s)	Double (heavy) cream
1 1/2	shot(s)	Milk
Top up with		Cola

Comment: More bite than a Colorado Bulldog.

CONGO BLUE

Glass: Martini
Garnish: Twist of lemon
Method: Shake ingredients with ice and strain into glass.

1 1/4	shot(s)	Zubrówka Bison vodka
1/2	shot(s)	Midori melon liqueur
1	shot(s)	Pressed apple juice
1/2	shot(s)	Bols Blackberry liqueur (Crème de mûre)
1/4	shot(s)	Freshly squeezed lemon juice

Origin: Created in 1999 by Marc Dietrich at Atlantic Bar & Grill, London.
Comment: Though this drink is green in colour Marc tells me it is named after the beauty of the Congo sunset.

COOL MARTINI

Glass: Martini
Method: Shake ingredients with ice and strain into glass.

2	shot(s)	Midori melon liqueur
1	shot(s)	Sauza Hornitos Tequila
2	shot(s)	Cranberry juice

Comment: Tastes nothing like the ingredients - which include melon, Tequila and cranberry juice. Try it and see if you taste toffee - whatever, it's enjoyable and complex.

●●●●● ◐

COOLMAN MARTINI NEW

Glass: Martini
Garnish: Orange twist
Method: Shake all ingredients with ice and fine strain into chilled glass.

1 3/4	shot(s)	Zubrówka Bison vodka
1/2	shot(s)	Cointreau / triple sec
2	shot(s)	Pressed apple juice
1/4	shot(s)	Freshly squeezed lemon juice

Origin: Created by Jack Coleman at The Library Bar, Lanesborough Hotel, London, England.
Comment: Fragrant and complex with integrated hints of apple and orange laced with grassy vodka.

●●●●● ○

COOL ORCHARD

Glass: Old-fashioned
Garnish: Pineapple leaf & cherry
Method: Muddle ginger in base of shaker. Add other ingredients, shake with ice and strain into glass.

2	nail(s)	Fresh ginger
1 1/2	shot(s)	Appleton Estate V/X aged rum
1/2	shot(s)	Ginger syrup
1/4	shot(s)	Almond syrup
1	shot(s)	Pressed pineapple juice
1/2	shot(s)	Teichenné vanilla schnapps
1/4	shot(s)	Freshly squeezed lime juice

Origin: Created in 2001 by Douglas Ankrah for Akbar, Soho, London, England.
Comment: An unusual line up of cocktail ingredients combine to make a great drink.

CORCOVADO

Glass: Collins
Method: Shake first three ingredients with ice and strain into ice-filled glass, then top up with lemonade.

1	shot(s)	Bols Blue curaçao
1	shot(s)	Sauza Hornitos Tequila
1	shot(s)	Drambuie liqueur
Top up with		Lemonade/7-up

Comment: This drink doesn't taste as bad as it looks.

COSMOPOLITAN

●●●●◐
#1 UPDATED

Glass: Martini
Garnish: Flamed orange twist
Method: Shake all ingredients with ice and fine strain into chilled glass.

1½	shot(s)	Absolut Citron vodka
1	shot(s)	Cointreau / triple sec
1¼	shot(s)	Cranberry juice
¼	shot(s)	Freshly squeezed lime juice
3	dashes	Fee Brothers orange bitters
½	spoon	Rose's lime cordial

AKA: Stealth Martini
Variants: Metropolitan, Grand Cosmopolitan & Rude Cosmopolitan, Cosmo Blanco, Blue Cosmo.
Origin: The Cosmopolitan appeared sometime in the 1980s - exactly where or who first created it is unknown. Many believe it originated on the gay scene of (variously) Massachusetts, Minnesota or San Francisco, although that theory seems mainly to herald from the drink's pink hue.
Although the Cosmo's originator is unkown, Dale DeGroff can rightly claim to have adjusted the recipe to the now familiar triple sec,freshlime juice, citrus vodka and cranberry juice. It is his recipe that first appeared in magazines, particularly in New York where he was working at the time. However, it is Sex And The City's Carrie Bradshaw who popularised the drink when the television character stopped sipping at Martinis and switched to the Cosmo.
Comment: The balance of citrus, berry fruit and sweetness is perfect. There are many recipes for the Cosmopolitan, although the core ingredients of vodka, cranberry, triple sec and lime remain the same.

●●●●○
2 (POPULAR VERSION) UPDATED

Glass: Martini
Garnish: Flamed orange twist
Method: Shake all ingredients with ice and fine strain into chilled glass.

2	shot(s)	Absolut vodka
¾	shot(s)	Cointreau / triple sec
1¼	shot(s)	Cranberry juice
¼	shot(s)	Freshly squeezed lime juice

Comment: A simple version of this modern day classic, but good all the same.

3

Glass: Martini
Garnish: Flamed orange twist
Method: Shake ingredients with ice and strain into glass.

1½	shot(s)	Absolut Citron vodka
¾	shot(s)	Cointreau / triple sec
1½	shot(s)	Cranberry juice
½	shot(s)	Freshly squeezed lime juice
½	shot(s)	Freshly squeezed lemon juice
½	shot(s)	Sugar (gomme) syrup
¼	shot(s)	Rose's lime cordial
2	dashes	Fee Brothers Orange bitters

Comment: The more complicated and most recent version of one of the most popular cocktails of the moment.

CORDLESS SCREWDRIVER

Glass: Shot
Garnish: Serve with sugar coated orange wedge
Method: Pour vodka and champagne into glass, serve and instruct drinker to down in one and then bite into orange wedge.

2	shot(s)	Absolut Mandrin vodka
Top up with		Piper-Heidsieck Brut Champagne

Comment: A slammer style drink for those looking for a fruity alternative to Tequila.

CORPSE REVIVER

Glass: Martini
Garnish: Orange twist
Method: Stir ingredients with ice and strain into glass.

1½	shot(s)	Rémy Martin Cognac
1	shot(s)	Calvados or applejack brandy
1	shot(s)	Cinzano Rosso vermouth

Origin: Created by Frank Meier, Ritz Bar, Paris.
Comment: Pick-me-up hangover cure – or possibly put-you-right-back-down!

●●●●○
COSMO BLANCO NEW

Glass: Martini
Garnish: Orange twist
Method: Shake all ingredients with ice and fine strain into chilled glass.

2	shot(s)	Absolut Citron vodka
¾	shot(s)	Cointreau / triple sec
1¼	shot(s)	Ocean Spray White cranberry drink
¼	shot(s)	Freshly squeezed lime juice

Origin: Emerged during 2002 in New York City.
Comment: Just what it says on the tin – a white Cosmopolitan.

●●●●◐
COSMOPOLITAN DELIGHT

Glass: Martini
Garnish: Flamed orange twist
Method: Shake all ingredients with ice and fine strain into chilled glass.

1½	shot(s)	Rémy Martin Cognac
½	shot(s)	Grand Marnier
1¼	shot(s)	Red wine
¾	shot(s)	Freshly squeezed lemon juice
¼	shot(s)	Almond (orgeat) syrup
¼	shot(s)	Sugar (gomme) syrup

Origin: Adapted from Dale DeGroff's book, 'The Craft of the Cocktail'. He credits the original recipe to a 1902 book by Charlie Paul.
Comment: No relation to the modern Cosmopolitan, this is a mellow, balanced blend of citrus, brandy and red wine.

COWBOY MARTINI

Glass: Martini
Garnish: Orange twist
Method: Shake ingredients vigorously with ice so that the ice breaks up the mint. Pour through a fine gauze strainer into a frosted glass.

3	shot(s)	Plymouth gin
1/2	shot(s)	Sugar (gomme) syrup
8		Fresh mint leaves
4	drops	Orange bitters (optional)

AKA: The Cooperstown Cocktail
Origin: Dick Bradsell, at Detroit, London in the early 90s - 'In the West, cowboys drink Martinis with mint in.'
Comment: If the balance of this drink is not correct it can taste awful.

COX'S DAIQUIRI

●●●●●

Glass: Martini
Garnish: Cox's apple ring (in memory of Jennings Cox)
Method: Shake all ingredients with ice and fine strain into chilled glass.

2 1/2	shot(s)	Vanilla infused Havana Club rum
1/2	shot(s)	Freshly squeezed lime juice
1/4	shot(s)	Vanilla sugar syrup
1	shot(s)	Freshly pressed pineapple juice

Origin: One of two cocktails with which I won 'The Best Daiquirí in London Competition' in 2002. It is named after Jennings Cox, the American mining engineer credited with first creating the Daiquiri.
Comment: Vanilla and pineapple bring out the sweetness of the rum against a citrus background.

CRANAPPLE BREEZE

●●●●◑○

Glass: Collins
Garnish: Lime wheel on rim
Method: Shake first five ingredients with ice and strain into ice-filled glass. Top up with ginger ale and stir.

1	shot(s)	Absolut Citron vodka
1	shot(s)	Cointreau / triple sec
1	shot(s)	Cranberry juice
1	shot(s)	Pressed apple juice
1/2	shot(s)	Freshly squeezed lime juice
Top up with		Ginger ale

Origin: Created in 2002 by Wayne Collins.
Comment: A refreshing cooler for a hot day by the pool.

CRANBERRY COOLER

Glass: Collins
Method: Shake ingredients with ice and strain into ice-filled glass.

2	shot(s)	Disaronno Originale amaretto
2	shot(s)	Cranberry juice
2	shot(s)	Freshly squeezed orange juice

Comment: Tastes shockingly good for such a simple mix.

CRANBERRY & MINT MARTINI NEW

●●●●○

Glass: Martini
Garnish: Float mint leaf
Method: Lightly muddle mint in base of shaker. Add other ingredients, shake with ice and fine strain into chilled glass.

8	fresh	Mint leaves
2	shot(s)	Finlandia Cranberry vodka
2	shot(s)	Cranberry juice
1/4	shot(s)	Grenadine syrup

Origin: Created by yours truly in 2003.
Comment: This little red number combines the dryness of cranberry, the sweetness of cherry and the fragrance of mint.

CRANBERRY MARTINI NEW

●●●◑○

Glass: Martini
Garnish: Redcurrants
Method: Shake all ingredients with ice and fine strain into chilled glass.

2	shot(s)	Finlandia Cranberry vodka
1/4	shot(s)	Cinzano Extra Dry vermouth
1/8	shot(s)	Campari
1 1/2	shot(s)	Cranberry juice
1/4	shot(s)	Sugar (gomme) syrup

Origin: I created this drink in 2003 for Finlandia.
Comment: Full on cranberry with that characteristic dry edge.

CRANBERRY SAUCE NEW

●●●●○

Glass: Martini
Garnish: Dried cranberries in base of glass
Method: Shake all ingredients with ice and fine strain into chilled glass.

2	shot(s)	Finlandia Cranberry vodka
2	shot(s)	Cranberry juice
1	shot(s)	Lapponia cranberry liqueur

Origin: Created in 2003 by yours truly for Finlandia.
Comment: Rich fruity flavour but with that customary dry cranberry finish.

CREAMSICLE UPDATED

●●●●◑○

Glass: Martini
Garnish: Orange zest
Method: Shake all ingredients with ice and fine strain into chilled glass.

1 1/2	shot(s)	Absolut Mandrin vodka
1	shot(s)	Grand Marnier
3/4	shot(s)	Double cream
3/4	shot(s)	Milk
1/4	shot(s)	Sugar (gomme) syrup

Origin: Adapted from a cocktail discovered in 1999 at Lot 61, New York City.
Comment: A milky orange number with a surprisingly pleasant taste.

CUBA LIBRE

Glass: Collins
Garnish: Split lime wedge
Method: Pour ingredients into ice-filled glass and stir.

2	shot(s)	Havana Club light rum
¹/₂	shot(s)	Freshly squeezed lime juice
Top up with		Cola

Origin: This classic mix was allegedly so named in the early 1890s when a group of off-duty American soldiers were gathered in a bar in old Havana drinking rum and the new soft drink, Coca Cola. The Captain raised his glass and sung out the battle cry that had inspired Cuba's victorious soldiers at war, Cuba Libre.
Nice though this story is, Coca Cola was not available in Havana in the early 90s.
The Cuba Libre peaked in popularity during the 1940s. During the war, all spirits production was turned to industrial alcohol - in the absence of whiskey and gin, Americans turned to rum. Some attribute the name to the popularity of the Andrews Sisters song, Cuba Libre.

Comment: Basically a rum and cola with a squeeze of lime – Cuba Libre sounds better though!

CREAMY BEE NEW

Glass: Martini
Garnish: Cinnamon rim & raspberry
Method: Shake all ingredients with ice and fine strain into chilled glass.

1¹/₂	shot(s)	Krupnik honey liqueur
¹/₂	shot(s)	Baileys Irish Cream liqueur
¹/₂	shot(s)	Chambord black raspberry liqueur
¹/₂	shot(s)	Frangelico hazelnut liqueur
¹/₄	shot(s)	Goldschläger cinnamon schnapps

Origin: Created in 2002 at Hush, London, England. Originally made with cinnamon syrup in place of Goldschläger.
Comment: Creamy cinnamon with hints of honey, nuts and berries.

CREAMY CREAMSICLE

Glass: Martini
Method: Shake ingredients with ice and strain into glass.

1¹/₂	shot(s)	Disaronno Originale amaretto
1	shot(s)	Freshly squeezed orange juice
1	shot(s)	Double (heavy) cream
1	shot(s)	Milk

Comment: The amaretto and orange juice work perfectly with the cream.

CREAM CAKE

Glass: Martini
Garnish: Crumbled Cadbury's Flake bar
Method: Shake all ingredients with ice and fine strain into chilled glass.

1?	shot(s)	Baileys Irish Cream liqueur
1¹/₄	shot(s)	Teichenné Peach schnapps
1¹/₄	shot(s)	Disaronno Originale amaretto
1	shot(s)	Double (heavy) cream

Comment: Creamy pleasure for the sweet of tooth.

CRÈME BRÛLÉE MARTINI NEW

Glass: Martini
Garnish: Cinnamon Dust
Method: Shake all ingredients with ice and fine strain into chilled glass.

2	shot(s)	Stoli Vanil
¹/₂	shot(s)	Cartron caramel liqueur
³/₄	shot(s)	Licor 43 (Cuarenta Y Tres) liqueur
1	shot(s)	Double (heavy) cream
¹/₂	fresh	Egg yolk

Origin: Adapted from a drink created in 2002 by Yannick Miseriaux at the Fifth Floor Bar, London, England.
Comment: OK so there's no crust courtesy of a broiler or blowtorch, but this does have egg yolk, caramel, vanilla, sugar and cream, and due to a cinnamon dusting even a brown top.

CRÈME DE CAFÉ

Glass: Rocks
Method: Shake ingredients with ice and strain into ice-filled glass.

1	shot(s)	Kahlúa coffee liqueur
3/4	shot(s)	Mount Gay Eclipse gold rum
3/4	shot(s)	Opal Bianca sambuca
1	shot(s)	Double (heavy) cream
1	shot(s)	Milk

Comment: Coffee predominates over the creaminess with hints of aniseed and rum.

CRIME OF PASSION SHOT

Glass: Shot
Method: Shake ingredients with ice and strain into glass.

1/2	shot(s)	Bols Cherry brandy liqueur
1	shot(s)	Passoã passion fruit liqueur
1/2	shot(s)	Absolut vodka

Comment: Passion, cherry and vodka - hardly criminal.

CROWN STAG

Glass: Rocks
Garnish: Slice of lemon
Method: Shake ingredients with ice and strain into ice-filled glass.

1	shot(s)	Absolut vodka
1	shot(s)	Chambord black raspberry liqueur
1	shot(s)	Jägermeister

Comment: Surprisingly workable combination.

CUBAN SPECIAL

Glass: Rocks
Method: Shake ingredients with ice and strain into ice-filled glass.

1½	shot(s)	Havana Club light rum
1	shot(s)	Cointreau / triple sec
2½	shot(s)	Pressed pineapple juice
1/2	shot(s)	Freshly squeezed lime juice

Comment: Not that special, but certainly ok.

CUBANITA

Glass: Collins
Garnish: Split lime wedge.
Method: Pour ingredients into glass filled with ice and stir.

2	shot(s)	Havana Club light rum
5	shot(s)	Tomato juice
1	pinch	Salt
1/4	shot(s)	Freshly squeezed lemon juice
5	drops	Worcester Sauce
5	drops	Tabasco

Comment: The Bloody Mary returns - this time with rum.

CUBAN MASTER

Glass: Collins
Method: Shake ingredients with ice and strain into glass.

1½	shot(s)	Havana Club light rum
1	shot(s)	Rémy Martin Cognac
2	shot(s)	Freshly squeezed orange juice
2	shot(s)	Pressed pineapple juice
1/2	shot(s)	Freshly squeezed lemon juice
1/2	shot(s)	Sugar (gomme) syrup

Origin: While in Cuba I was introduced to a master cantinero (bartender) who is famous on the island for winning cocktail competitions. When I met him, he was an old man and I was the worse for a day of discovering new drinks. He told me of a cocktail as shown above only his was blended and without sugar syrup (but to be honest my notes were so bad I can't be sure what he said). However, when I returned home I experimented with the remembered recipe to arrive at the above.

Comment: A long fruity medium dry cocktail based on rum and brandy – would make a good punch.

DAIQUIRÍ

NATURAL

Pronounced: Dye-Ker-Ree
Glass: Martini
Garnish: Lime wedge
Method: Shake all ingredients vigorously with crushed ice and strain through a fine strainer into glass, thus removing fine fragments of lime and ice.

2	shot(s)	Havana Club light rum (or aged)
1/2	shot(s)	Freshly squeezed lime juice
1/4	shot(s)	Sugar (gomme) syrup

Variant: Flavoured syrups may be substituted in place of sugar syrup. Alternatively the rum itself can be flavoured - see Vanilla Daiquirí. Or fresh fruit can be used. This cocktail is also often served frozen - see Frozen Daiquirí.

Variant: Ideally a Daiquirí should be shaken with crushed ice, which dilutes the mix. But if (like me) you're often too lazy to crush ice, the same effect is achieved by adding half a shot of chilled water and shaking with cubed ice.
Origin: Mr Jennings Cox, an American mining engineer who was working at a Cuban copper mine outside Santiago, created the Daiquirí in 1896.
A popular version of the story states that another engineer called Pagliuchi, the captain of a guerrilla group, was viewing mines in the region and met with Cox. During their meeting they set about making a drink from the ingredients Cox had: rum, lemons and sugar. The concoction was exquisite and Cox named the drink Daiquirí after the name of the mine, which in turn was named after the nearest town.
According to Cox's granddaughter, however, Cox ran out of gin when entertaining American guests. Wary of serving them straight rum, he added lime and sugar.
The Daiquirí seems to have come to America with US Admiral Lucius Johnson, who fought in the Spanish-American war. He introduced the drink to the Army & Navy Club in Washington DC - and in their Daiquirí Lounge, a plaque honours his place in cocktail history.
Comment: The classic proportions to a Daiquirí are 8 parts rum to 2 parts lime to 1 part sugar. A deliciously simple, clean, refreshing sour drink, this is a must-try

FROZEN

Glass: Martini
Method: Blend ingredients with crushed ice and serve.

2	shot(s)	Havana Club light rum
1/2	shot(s)	Freshly squeezed lime juice
1/4	shot(s)	Sugar (gomme) syrup
5	drops	Maraschino liqueur

Variant: With fruit.

Origin: Emilio González is said to have first adapted the natural Daiquirí into this frozen version at the Plaza Hotel in Cuba. However, it was in 1912 that Constantino Ribalaigua Vert of Havana's Floridita bar made this drink famous. The Floridita today is known as 'the cradle of the Daiquirí'.
Ernest Hemingway, the hard-drinking, Nobel prize-winning author, lived in Cuba for years, indulging his passions for fishing, shooting and boozing. In the 30s and the 40s he would often work his way through twelve of the Floridita's frozen Daiquirís - often doubles, called Papa Dobles in his honour. The Hemingway Daiquirí, which includes grapefruit, was created for him and continues to bear his name.
In 'Islands in the Stream', Hemingway's hero stares deep into his frozen Daiquirí, observing that 'it reminded him of the sea. The frappéd part of the drink was like the wake of a ship and the clear part was the way the water looked when the bow cut it when you were in shallow water over marl bottom. That was almost the exact colour.' His bar stool can still be seen at the Floridita today.
Comment: Great on a hot day, but the coldness masks a lot of the flavour found when this drink is served 'up' or natural.

CUCUMBER MARTINI

Glass: Martini
Garnish: Strip of cucumber
Method: Muddle cucumber in base of shaker. Add other ingredients, shake with ice and strain into glass.

2	inch	Peeled chopped cucumber
1	shot(s)	Zubrowka Bison vodka
1	shot(s)	Absolut vodka
1/2	shot(s)	Sugar (gomme) syrup

Origin: There are many different Cucumber Martini recipes; this is mine.
Comment: Cucumber has never tasted so good.

CUMBERSOME

Glass: Martini
Garnish: Physalis fruit
Method: Muddle cucumber in base of shaker. Add other ingredients, shake with ice and strain into a chilled Martini glass.

4	inch	Fresh chopped peeled cucumber
2	shot(s)	Plymouth Gin
1/2	shot(s)	Campari
1	shot(s)	Freshly squeezed orange juice
1/2	shot(s)	Sugar (gomme) syrup

Origin: Created in 2002 by Shelim Islam at the GE Club, London, England.
Comment: Interesting and fresh as you like with a pleasant bitterness.

CURDISH MARTINI

Glass: Martini
Garnish: Lemon zest
Method: Shake all ingredients with ice and strain into glass.

2	shot(s)	Plymouth gin
1/2	shot(s)	Sourz Sour Apple Liqueur
2/3	shot(s)	Freshly squeezed lime juice
2	spoons	Lemon curd

Origin: Created in 2001 by Tadgh Ryan at West Street, London, England.
Comment: Beautifully balanced with the tang of lemon curd.

CUSTARD TART

Glass: Shot
Garnish: Physalis fruit
Method: Muddle physalis fruits in base of shaker can. Add other ingredients, shake with ice and strain.

3	fresh	Physalis fruits
3/4	shot(s)	Havana Club light rum
1/2	shot(s)	Teichenné Peach Scnapps
1/3	shot(s)	Freshly squeezed lime juice
1/2	shot(s)	Warninks Advocaat

Origin: Created by Alex Kammerling in 2001.
Comment: Custardy, strangely enough.

DAMN-THE-WEATHER

Glass: Martini
Method: Shake ingredients with ice and strain into glass.

1	shot(s)	Plymouth gin
1/2	shot(s)	Cointreau / triple sec
1	shot(s)	Cinzano Rosso vermouth
2	shot(s)	Freshly squeezed orange juice

Comment: A slightly herbal orange flavour.

●●●●○

DAMSON IN DISTRESS NEW

Glass: Shot
Method: Shake all ingredients with ice and fine strain into chilled glass.

1½	shot(s)	Plymouth Damson gin
1/2	shot(s)	Disaronno Originale amaretto
1/4	shot(s)	Freshly squeezed lemon juice

Origin: Discovered in 2003 at Hush, London, England.
Comment: Damson and amaretto sharpened by lemon juice.

●●●●●

DARK DAIQUIRÍ

Glass: Martini
Garnish: Lime wedge on rim
Method: Shake ingredients vigorously with ice and strain into chilled glass.

1½	shot(s)	Appleton Estate V/X aged rum
1/2	shot(s)	Pusser's Navy rum
1/2	shot(s)	Freshly squeezed lime juice
1/2	shot(s)	Sugar (gomme) syrup
1	shot(s)	Chilled water

Comment: The fine sweet and sour balance of a great Daiquirí with hints of molasses.

●●●●○

DC MARTINI

Glass: Martini
Method: Stir all ingredients with ice and strain into glass.

2	shot(s)	Vanilla infused Appleton Estate V/X aged rum
1/4	shot(s)	Frangelico hazelnut liqueur
1/4	shot(s)	Bols White crème de cacao
1/4	shot(s)	Sugar (gomme) syrup
1/2	shot(s)	Chilled water

Origin: Discovered by the editor in 2000 at Teatro, London, England.
Comment: Vanilla, chocolate and a hint of nut. Add more sugar to taste.

DARK 'N' STORMY

●●●●○

UPDATED

Glass: Collins
Garnish: Lime wedge on rim
Method: Shake first three ingredients with ice and strain into ice-filled glass. Top up with ginger beer. Stir and serve with straws.

2	shot(s)	Gosling's Black Seal rum
1	shot(s)	Freshly squeezed lime juice
1/2	shot(s)	Sugar (gomme) syrup
Top up with		Ginger beer

Origin: The national drink of Bermuda, where ginger beer and Gosling's rum are produced.
Comment: This deliciously spicy drink is part of the Mule family - but is distinctive due to the strong flavour of the rum.

●●●●◐○

DEAD MAN'S MULE NEW

Glass: Collins
Garnish: Lime wedge on rim
Method: Shake first four ingredients with ice and strain into ice-filled glass. Top up with ginger beer.

³/₄	shot(s)	La Fée Absinthe
³/₄	shot(s)	Goldschläger cinnamon schnapps
³/₄	shot(s)	Almond (orgeat) syrup
¹/₂	shot(s)	Freshly squeezed lime juice
Top up with		Ginger beer

Origin: Discovered in 2003 at the Met Bar, London, England.
Comment: Strong in every respect. Big, full-on flavours of aniseed, cinnamon and ginger.

DEAN'S GATE

Glass: Martini
Garnish: Orange twist
Method: Shake ingredients with ice and strain into glass.

2	shot(s)	Havana Club light rum
1	shot(s)	Rose's lime cordial
1	shot(s)	Drambuie liqueur

Comment: Lime and Drambuie make an indescribable flavour.

DEATH BY CHOCOLATE | FROZEN

Glass: Hurricane
Garnish: Chocolate shavings.
Method: Blend ingredients with crushed ice and serve.

1	shot(s)	Absolut vodka
1¹/₂	shot(s)	Baileys Irish cream liqueur
1	shot(s)	Bols Brown crème de cacao
3	scoops	Chocolate ice cream

Comment: Unsophisticated but delicious.

●●◐○○○

DEATH IN THE AFTERNOON NEW

Glass: Flute
Garnish: Float rose petal
Method: Shake absinthe with ice (to chill and dilute) and strain into glass. Top up with Champagne.

1	shot(s)	La Fée Absinthe
Top up with		Piper-Heidsieck Brut Champagne

Origin: Unknown origin but emerged in London's bars in 2002.
Comment: Bravado dominates this drink.

DÉBUT D'ÉTÉ

Glass: Rocks
Garnish: Slice of lime & fresh cranberries
Method: Shake ingredients and strain into glass filled with crushed ice.

1¹/₂	shot(s)	Rémy Martin Cognac
1¹/₄	shot(s)	Maraschino liqueur
1	shot(s)	Cranberry juice
³/₄	shot(s)	Freshly squeezed lime juice
¹/₄	shot(s)	Passion syrup

Created by: Rodolphe Sorel at Match Bar, London, England in 2000.
Comment: A lengthy and flavoursome concoction.

DEEP SOUTH

Glass: Rocks
Method: Muddle ginger and lime with Clément Shrubb in glass. Then add crushed ice and orange juice and stir.

2	shot(s)	Clément Creole Shrubb
1	whole	Lime cut into segments
2	slices	Peeled fresh root ginger
Top up with		Freshly squeezed orange juice

Origin: Discovered at AKA Bar, London, England.
Comment: Citrussy with delicate orange and ginger flavours.

●●●●●◐

DELLA'TINI

Glass: Martini
Garnish: Pineapple wedge on rim
Method: Shake all ingredients with ice and fine strain into chilled glass.

2	shot(s)	Malibu coconut rum liqueur
³/₄	shot(s)	Madeira
¹/₂	shot(s)	Cuarenta Y Tres (Licor 43)
¹/₄	shot(s)	Freshly squeezed lemon juice
1	shot(s)	Chilled water

Origin: I created this drink and named it after a friend in Funchal, the home of Madeira.
Comment: The acidic, resinous flavours of Madeira balance the equally strong, but sweet flavoured liqueurs.

DEPTH BOMB

Glass: Rocks
Method: Shake ingredients with ice and strain into ice-filled glass.

1	shot(s)	Calvados or applejack brandy
1	shot(s)	Rémy Martin Cognac
³/₄	shot(s)	Freshly squeezed lime juice
¹/₂	shot(s)	Sugar (gomme) syrup
¹/₄	shot(s)	Grenadine syrup

Comment: The lime, sugar and grenadine bring the subtle apple of Calvados out.

●●◐○○○

DEPTH CHARGE

Glass: Boston & shot
Method: Three-quarter fill Boston glass with lager. Fill shot glass with vodka. Drop shot glass into lager and consume.

1	glass	Pilsner lager
1¹/₂	shot(s)	Absolut vodka

Comment: One way to ruin good beer.

DERBY DAIQUIRÍ

Glass: Martini
Method: Shake ingredients with ice and strain into glass.

2¹/₂	shot(s)	Havana Club light rum
¹/₂	shot(s)	Freshly squeezed lime juice
¹/₄	shot(s)	Sugar (gomme) syrup
1	shot(s)	Freshly squeezed orange juice

Comment: Good and dry.

DESERT COOLER

Glass: Collins
Method: Shake first three ingredients with ice and strain into ice-filled glass, then top up with ginger beer.

2	shot(s)	Plymouth gin
1/2	shot(s)	Bols Cherry brandy liqueur
1	shot(s)	Freshly squeezed orange juice
Top up with		Ginger beer

Comment: Sandy in colour - as its name suggests - with a refreshing bite.

DETOX SHOT

Glass: Shot
Garnish: Squeeze lime wedge on drink.
Method: Layer in glass by carefully pouring ingredients in the following order.

1/2	shot(s)	Teichenné Peach schnapps
1/2	shot(s)	Cranberry juice
1/2	shot(s)	Absolut vodka

Comment: Very hard to layer, but layered or shaken, a perfect mix.

DETROIT MARTINI

Glass: Martini
Garnish: Mint sprig
Method: Shake ingredients with ice and strain into glass.

2	shot(s)	Absolut vodka
6	fresh	Mint leaves
1/2	shot(s)	Sugar (gomme) syrup

Origin: Dick Bradsell - based on the Cowboy Martini.
Comment: You can also add a touch of lime – one of those drinks that comes out differently every time.

DEVIL'S MANHATTAN

Glass: Martini
Garnish: Lemon twist
Method: Stir ingredients with ice and strain into glass.

2	shot(s)	Buffalo Trace Bourbon
1	shot(s)	Southern Comfort
1	shot(s)	Cinzano Extra Dry vermouth
4	dashes	Angostura aromatic bitters

Comment: A Manhattan with a shot of Southern Comfort.

●●●●●◐

EL DIABLO

Glass: Collins
Garnish: Squeeze lime wedge and drop into drink
Method: Shake first four ingredients with ice and strain into ice-filled glass. Top up with ginger beer.

2	shot(s)	Sauza Hornitos Tequila
1	shot(s)	Sisca crème de cassis
1	shot(s)	Freshly squeezed lime juice
1/2	shot(s)	Sugar (gomme) syrup
Top up with		Ginger ale

Origin: Thought to have originated in California during the 1940s.
Comment: The name of this drink translates as 'The Devil' and it's devilishly good.

DIABLE ROUGE

Glass: Martini
Garnish: 3 blueberries
Method: Shake ingredients with ice and strain into glass.

2	shot(s)	Absolut vodka
2 1/2	shot(s)	Pressed pineapple juice
1/2	shot(s)	Sisca crème de cassis

Comment: Not quite as rouge as the name would suggest.

DIANA'S BITTER

Glass: Martini
Garnish: Split lime wedge
Method: Shake ingredients with ice and strain into glass.

2	shot(s)	Plymouth gin
1	shot(s)	Freshly squeezed lime juice
1	shot(s)	Sugar (gomme) syrup
1 1/2	shot(s)	Campari

Comment: A Campari lover's drink: bittersweet and strong.

●●●●●○

DIPLOMAT

Glass: Old-fashioned
Method: Stir all ingredients with ice and strain into ice-filled glass.

1 1/2	shot(s)	Cinzano Extra Dry vermouth
1 1/2	shot(s)	Punt E Mes
1 1/2	shot(s)	Maraschino liqueur

Comment: A golden sweet & sour drink, won't be to everyone's taste.

●●●●●○

DIRTY BANANA

Glass: Collins
Garnish: Banana slice
Method: Blend all ingredients with crushed ice.

1 1/2	shot(s)	Appleton Estate V/X aged rum
1	shot(s)	Kahlúa coffee liqueur
1	shot(s)	Bols Crème de banane
1	half	Peeled & chopped banana
1	shot(s)	Double (heavy) cream
1	shot(s)	Milk

Origin: This cocktail is hard to avoid when holidaying in Jamaica. It's not sophisticated, but it's very tasty.
Comment: Long, creamy and filling banana drink with a 'dirty' flavour and colour courtesy of coffee liqueur.

DIRTY MARTINI

Glass: Martini
Garnish: Olive
Method: Shake ingredients with ice and strain into glass.

2¹/₂	shot(s)	Plymouth gin
¹/₂	shot(s)	Brine from cocktail olives
¹/₈	shot(s)	Cinzano Extra Dry vermouth

Comment: A pleasant variation on the classic Dry Martini.

DIRTY SANCHEZ

●●●●●○

Glass: Collins
Garnish: Lime wheel on rim
Method: Shake all but ginger beer with ice. Strain into ice-filled glass and top up with ginger beer.

2	shot(s)	Sauza Hornitos Tequila
³/₄	shot(s)	Agavero Tequila liqueur
¹/₂	shot(s)	Chambord black raspberry liqueur
¹/₂	shot(s)	Freshly squeezed lime juice
Top up with		Jamaican Ginger beer

Origin: Created in 2001 by Phillip Jeffrey and Ian Baldwin at the GE Club, London, England.
Comment: A wonderfully refreshing and complex long summer drink.

DNA

Glass: Martini
Garnish: Twist of orange
Method: Shake ingredients with ice and strain into glass.

1¹/₂	shot(s)	Plymouth gin
³/₄	shot(s)	Bols Apricot brandy Liqueur
¹/₄	shot(s)	Sugar (gomme) syrup
1	shot(s)	Freshly squeezed lemon juice
4	dashes	Orange bitters (optional)

Created by: Emmanuel Audermatte at The Atlantic Bar & Grill, London in 1999.
Comment: Sharp and fruity.

DOLCE-AMARO

Glass: Martini
Method: Stir ingredients with ice and strain into glass.

1¹/₂	shot(s)	Campari
1¹/₂	shot(s)	Cinzano Bianco vermouth
³/₄	shot(s)	Disaronno Originale amaretto

Comment: The name translates as bittersweet.

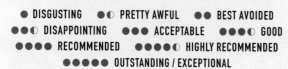

THOSE DRINKS I'VE SAMPLED RECENTLY ARE GRADED AS FOLLOWS:

● DISGUSTING ●● PRETTY AWFUL ●● BEST AVOIDED
●●●○ DISAPPOINTING ●●● ACCEPTABLE ●●●● GOOD
●●●● RECOMMENDED ●●●●○ HIGHLY RECOMMENDED
●●●●● OUTSTANDING / EXCEPTIONAL

DOLCE HAVANA

●●●●●○

Glass: Martini
Method: Shake all ingredients with ice and fine strain into chilled glass.

1¹/₄	shot(s)	Havana Club light rum
¹/₂	shot(s)	Campari
¹/₂	shot(s)	Cointreau / triple sec
1¹/₄	shot(s)	Freshly squeezed orange juice
1¹/₄	shot(s)	Freshly squeezed lime juice
¹/₈	shot(s)	Sugar (gomme) syrup

Origin: Created by Fabrizio Musorella in 2000 at the Library Bar, Lanesborough Hotel, London, England.
Comment: A melange of Mediterranean fruit.

DONNA'S CREAMY'TINI

●●●●◐○

Glass: Martini
Garnish: Cherry on rim
Method: Shake all ingredients with ice and fine strain into chilled glass.

1¹/₄	shot(s)	Disaronno Originale amaretto
1¹/₄	shot(s)	Bols Cherry brandy liqueur
1¹/₄	shot(s)	Bols Brown crème de cacao
1¹/₄	shot(s)	Double (heavy) cream

Origin: Adapted from a drink created in 2002 by Yannick Miseriaux at the Fifth Floor Bar, London, England.
Comment: A fine example of an alcoholic liquid pudding.

DORIAN GRAY UPDATED

●●●●○

Glass: Martini
Garnish: Orange twist
Method: Shake all ingredients with ice and fine strain into chilled glass.

1	shot(s)	Grand Marnier
1	shot(s)	Havana Club light rum
1¹/₂	shot(s)	Freshly squeezed orange juice
1¹/₂	shot(s)	Cranberry juice

Origin: Discovered in 1999 at One Aldwych, London, England.
Comment: Fresh and fruity – mandarin shines through.

DOUBLE VISION

Glass: Martini
Method: Shake ingredients with ice and strain into glass.

1	shot(s)	Absolut Citron vodka
1	shot(s)	Absolut Kurant vodka
4	dashes	Angostura aromatic bitters
1	shot(s)	Pressed apple juice
1	shot(s)	Freshly squeezed lime juice
¹/₂	shot(s)	Sugar (gomme) syrup

Comment: Well rounded and perfectly balanced.

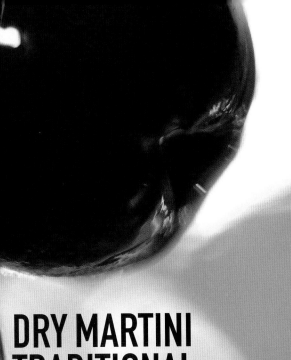

DRY MARTINI TRADITIONAL

●●●●●◐

UPDATED

Glass: Martini
Garnish: Olive on stick or lemon twist
Method: Stir vermouth with ice in a mixing glass and strain to discard excess vermouth, leaving only a coating on the ice. Pour gin into mixing glass containing coated ice, stir and strain into a chilled glass.

³/₄	shot(s)	Cinzano Extra Dry vermouth
2¹/₂	shot(s)	Plymouth gin
3	dashes	Fee Brothers Orange bitters (optional)

Variant: The proportion of gin to vermouth is a matter of taste, some say 7 to 1, others that one drop is sufficient. We recommend you ask the drinker how they would like their Martini, in the same manner you might ask how they have their steak. If the drinker orders a 'Sweet Martini' use sweet red vermouth rather than dry and use a cherry as garnish instead of an olive. A 'Wet Martini' is a Martini with extra vermouth - don't strain the vermouth out.
Variant: A 'Dickens' is a Martini without a twist, a 'Gibson' is Martini with an onion instead of an olive or a twist and a 'Franklin Martini', is named after Franklin Roosevelt and has two olives.
Origin: Although Martini vermouth is commonly used to make this recipe, the name is coincidental. It is said that this cocktail was invented in 1911 by a New York bartender called Martini di Arma di Taggia who was the head bartender at the fashionable Knickerbocker Hotel and that a French vermouth (Noilly Prat) was originally used with orange bitters.
Comment: If a Martini is shaken it becomes a 'Bradford'. Shaken Martinis taste very different due to further dilution and the air bubbles shaking introduces to the drink.

DOWNHILL RACER

Glass: Martini
Method: Shake ingredients with ice and strain into glass.

1	shot(s)	Disaronno Originale amaretto
1	shot(s)	Appleton Estate V/X aged rum
3	shot(s)	Pressed pineapple juice

Comment: A very easy drink to make – with good results.

●●●●●◐

DR ZEUS

Glass: Old-fashioned
Method: Fill glass with ice, add Fernet Branca, top up with water and leave to stand in glass. Separately muddle raisins in base of shaker, add other ingredients and shake vigorously with ice. Finally discard contents of glass and strain contents of shaker into the now Fernet Branca coated glass.

1	shot(s)	Fernet Branca
20		Raisins
2	shot(s)	Rémy Martin Cognac
¹/₄	shot(s)	Sugar (gomme) syrup
¹/₈	shot(s)	Kahlúa coffee liqueur
1	dash	Fee Brothers Orange bitters

Origin: Created by Adam Ennis in 2001 at Isola, Knightsbridge, London, England.
Comment: Not that far removed from a Sazerac cocktail, this is innovative and great tasting.

DRAGNET

Glass: Sling
Garnish: 3 red grapes.
Method: Shake all ingredients with ice and strain into ice-filled glass.

2	shot(s)	Pitú Cachaça
4	shot(s)	Red grape juice
1	shot(s)	Sugar (gomme) syrup

Comment: A dry, bizarre mix – try it!

DRAMATIC MARTINI

Glass: Martini
Garnish: Orange twist and dusting of nutmeg

2	shot(s)	Drambuie Cream
1	shot(s)	Tuaca liqueur
¹/₂	shot(s)	Mandarine Napoléon Liqueur
1	shot(s)	Milk

Comment: Orange, mandarin and the herbal notes of Tuaca.

DREAMSICLE

Glass: Martini
Method: Shake first three ingredients with ice and strain into glass, then float cream.

1¹/₂	shot(s)	Kahlúa coffee liqueur
³/₄	shot(s)	Cointreau / triple sec
1	shot(s)	Freshly squeezed orange juice
Float		Lightly whipped cream

Comment: The coffee and orange flavours are complemented by the cream.

●●●●◐○

DROWNED OUT

Glass: Collins
Garnish: Lime wedge on rim
Method: Pour ingredients into ice filled glass and stir.

2	shot(s)	Pernod anise
1	shot(s)	Freshly squeezed lime juice
Top up with		Ginger ale

Comment: Ginger combines with rather then drowns the aniseed.

DRY MARTINI NAKED NEW

●●●●○

Glass: Martini (frozen)
Garnish: Olive on stick or lemon twist
Method: Take glass from freezer and add vermouth. Swirl glass to coat inside with vermouth and then shake out excess. Take bottle of gin from the freezer and pour into glass.

¼	shot(s)	Cinzano Extra Dry vermouth
2½	shot(s)	Plymouth gin

Comment: The key to the success of this drink is for both the glass and gin to be freezing cold. Consume quickly whilst still cold. The temperature masks the strength of the alcohol – be warned.

DUCHARACHA

●●●●●

Glass: Collins
Garnish: Pineapple leaf
Method: Shake all ingredients with ice and strain into glass filled with crushed ice.

2	shot(s)	Sauza Hornitos Tequila
1¼	shot(s)	Rubicon passion fruit drink
3	shot(s)	Pressed apple juice
1	shot(s)	Agavero liqueur
½	shot(s)	Vanilla sugar syrup
½	shot(s)	Freshly squeezed lemon juice

Origin: Created in 2001 by Douglas Ankrah at Lab Bar, London, England.
Comment: Beautifully balanced – fruity with an almost herbal edge of Tequila.

DUTCH BREAKFAST MARTINI UPDATED

●●●●○

Glass: Martini
Garnish: Orange twist
Method: Shake all ingredients with ice and fine strain into chilled glass.

1½	shot(s)	Plymouth gin
1½	shot(s)	Warninks Advocaat
1	shot(s)	Freshly squeezed lemon juice
¼	shot(s)	Sugar (gomme) syrup
⅛	shot(s)	Galliano liqueur

Origin: Created in 2002 by Alex Kammerling for Warninks.
Comment: A tasty, aromatic, almost creamy alternative to a fry-up.

DUTCH COURAGE UPDATED

●●●●○

Glass: Collins
Garnish: Lemon wheel on rim
Method: Shake all ingredients with ice and strain into ice-filled glass.

1	shot(s)	Plymouth gin
1	shot(s)	Warninks Advocaat
1	shot(s)	Freshly squeezed lemon juice
5	shot(s)	Pressed apple juice

Origin: Created in 2002 by Alex Kammerling for Warninks.
Comment: A wonderful alternative to a traditional English lemonade on a summer afternoon.

DYEVITCHKA

Glass: Martini
Method: Shake ingredients with ice and strain into glass.

1	shot(s)	Absolut vodka
1	shot(s)	Cointreau / triple sec
¾	shot(s)	Freshly squeezed lime juice
¼	shot(s)	Sugar (gomme) syrup
2	shot(s)	Pressed pineapple juice

Comment: A medium sweet cocktail with loads of pineapple and a hint of orange liqueur, all laced with vodka.

EARL GREY FIZZ

●●●●○

Glass: Flute
Garnish: Lemon knot
Method: Shake first three ingredients with ice and strain into chilled glass. Top up with Champagne.

1	shot(s)	Zubrówka (Bison grass) vodka
½	shot(s)	Strong cold Earl Grey tea
¼	shot(s)	Sugar (gomme) syrup
Top up with		Piper-Heidsieck Brut Champagne

Origin: Created in 2002 by Henry Bessant at Lonsdale House, London, England.
Comment: Looks like a glass of Champagne but has a well judged little extra something.

EARL GREY MAR-TEA-NI

●●●●○

Glass: Martini
Garnish: Lemon zest
Method: Shake all ingredients with ice and fine strain into chilled glass.

2	shot(s)	Plymouth gin
1¼	shot(s)	Strong cold Earl Grey tea
¾	shot(s)	Freshly squeezed lemon juice
½	shot(s)	Sugar (gomme) syrup
½	fresh	Egg white

Origin: Created by Audrey Saunders at Bemelmans Bar at The Carlyle, New York City.
Comment: A fantastic and very English drink created by a New Yorker. The botanicals of gin combine wonderfully with the flavours and tannins of Earl Grey.

EAST INDIA COCKTAIL

●●●●○

Glass: Martini
Garnish: Flamed orange twist and dust with freshly grated nutmeg
Method: Shake all ingredients with ice and fine strain into chilled glass.

1½	shot(s)	Rémy Martin Cognac
1	shot(s)	Grand Marnier
2	shot(s)	Pressed pineapple juice
2	dashes	Angostura aromatic bitters

Origin: An old classic created by Frank Meier at the Ritz Bar, Paris. Dale DeGroff rightly claims creation of a very similar drink called a 'Millennium Cocktail'.
Comment: A rich but quite bitter short drink based on Cognac.

EAST INDIAN

Glass: Martini
Method: Stir ingredients with ice and strain into glass.

2	shot(s)	Fino Sherry
1½	shot(s)	Cinzano Extra Dry vermouth
½	shot(s)	Cinzano Bianco vermouth
⅛	shot(s)	Fee Brothers Orange bitters

Comment: Dry and pretty flat – like a lot of India.

EASTER MARTINI NEW

Glass: Martini
Garnish: Crumbled flake bar
Method: Break away outer shells of cardamom pods and muddle inner seeds in base of shaker. Add other ingredients, shake with ice and fine strain into chilled glass.

4	pods	Green cardamom
2	shot(s)	Absolut Vanilia vodka
1	shot(s)	Bols White crème de cacao
¼	shot(s)	Sugar (gomme) syrup
½	shot(s)	Chilled water
½	fresh	Egg white

Origin: Created in 2003 by Simon King at MJU Bar, Millennium Hotel, London, England.
Comment: A standard Chocolate Martini with extra interest thanks to the clever use of vanilla and cardamom. The egg was my own addition as it seemed appropriate for Easter.

EASY TIGER UPDATED

Glass: Martini
Garnish: Orange twist
Comment: Muddle ginger in base of shaker. Add honey and Tequila and stir so as to dissolve honey. Add other ingredients, shake with ice and fine strain into chilled glass.

2	slices	Fresh ginger (thumb nail sized)
2	spoons	Runny honey
2	shot(s)	Sauza Hornitos Tequila
1	shot(s)	Freshly squeezed lime juice
¾	shot(s)	Chilled water

Created by: Alex Kammerling in 1999.
Comment: Tangy, zesty with rich honey and ginger.

ECLIPSE NEW

Glass: Collins
Garnish: Mint leaf & raspberry
Method: Muddle raspberries in base of shaker. Add other ingredients, shake with ice and strain into glass filled with crushed ice. Serve with straws.

12	fresh	Raspberries
2	shot(s)	Jack Daniel's Tennessee whiskey
1	shot(s)	Chambord black raspberry liqueur
½	shot(s)	Freshly squeezed lime juice
2	shot(s)	Cranberry juice

Origin: Signature cocktail at the chain of Eclipse Bars, London, England.
Comment: A fruity summer cooler which I challenge anyone not to like.

EGG CUSTARD MARTINI

Glass: Martini
Garnish: Dust with freshly ground nutmeg
Method: Shake all ingredients with ice and fine strain into chilled glass.

2	shot(s)	Absolut vodka
1	shot(s)	Warninks Advocaat
½	shot(s)	Stoli Vanil
½	shot(s)	Buffalo Trace Bourbon
¼	shot(s)	Sugar (gomme) syrup

Origin: Created in 2002 by Alex Kammerling.
Comment: As custardy as the name would suggest but surprisingly potent.

EGGNOG

Glass: Collins
Garnish: Sprinkle ground nutmeg
Method: Shake ingredients with ice and strain into ice-filled glass.

2½	shot(s)	Dark spirit of your choice
½	shot(s)	Sugar (gomme) syrup
1	fresh	Egg
½	shot(s)	Double (heavy) cream
3	shot(s)	Milk

Comment: A lightly flavoured egg custard. Try it with Cognac or dark rum.

ELDERBUBBLE NEW

Glass: Flute
Garnish: Stick of cucumber & mint sprig
Method: Shake first three ingredients with ice and strain into chilled glass. Top up with Champagne.

1	shot(s)	Pölstar cucumber vodka
¾	shot(s)	Elderflower cordial
⅛	shot(s)	Freshly squeezed lemon juice
Top up with		Piper-Heidsieck Brut Champagne

Origin: Created in 2002 by Michael Mahe and popularised at Hush, London, England.
Comment: A refreshing summery Champagne cocktail.

ELDERFLOWER COLLINS

Glass: Collins
Garnish: Physalis on rim
Method: Shake first four ingredients with ice and strain into ice-filled glass. Top up with soda water (club soda).

2	shot(s)	Plymouth gin
½	shot(s)	Elderflower cordial
1	shot(s)	Freshly squeezed lemon juice
⅛	shot(s)	Sugar (gomme) syrup
Top up with		Soda water (club soda)

Comment: Just as it says on the lid – a Collins with a hint of elderflower.

ELDERFLOWER MARTINI NEW

●●●●○

Glass: Martini
Garnish: Float rose petal
Method: Shake all ingredients with ice and fine strain into chilled glass.

1½	shot(s)	Zubrówka (Bison) vodka
½	shot(s)	Cinzano Dry Vermouth
1½	shot(s)	Elderflower cordial

Comment: This veritable shrubbery is both floral and grassy with dry borders.

EMBASSY ROYAL

Glass: Martini
Garnish: Orange sail
Method: Shake ingredients with ice and strain into glass.

2	shot(s)	Buffalo Trace Bourbon
1	shot(s)	Drambuie liqueur
1	shot(s)	Cinzano Rosso sweet vermouth
1	shot(s)	Freshly squeezed orange juice

Comment: An aromatic, herbal concoction.

ELEGANTE MARGARITA

●●●●●

Glass: Coupette
Garnish: Lime wedge & salted rim (optional)
Method: Shake all ingredients with ice and strain into glass.

1½	shot(s)	Sauza Hornitos Tequila
½	shot(s)	Cointreau / triple sec
½	shot(s)	Rose's lime cordial
¾	shot(s)	Freshly squeezed lime juice
¾	shot(s)	Sugar (gomme) syrup

Origin: Created in 1999 by Robert Plotkin and Raymon Flores of BarMedia, USA.
Comment: One of the best Margarita recipes around. Richly endowed with flavour.

EMPEROR'S MEMOIRS

●●●●○

Glass: Collins
Garnish: Orange & lemon twists
Method: Shake all but ginger beer with ice and strain into ice-filled glass. Top up with ginger beer.

1	shot(s)	Plymouth gin
½	shot(s)	Punt E Mes
¼	shot(s)	Belvoir ginger cordial
¼	shot(s)	Freshly squeezed lemon juice
Top up with		Ginger beer

Origin: Created in 2001 by Douglas Ankrah for Akbar, Soho, London, England.
Comment: Not particularly alcoholic, but strong in a gingery, spicy way.

ELIXIR NEW

●●●●○

Glass: Collins
Garnish: Mint sprig
Method: Muddle mint in base of shaker. Add lime, sugar and Chartreuse, shake with ice and strain into ice-filled glass. Top up with soda, stir and serve with straws.

7	fresh	Mint leaves
1½	shot(s)	Green Chartreuse
1	shot(s)	Sugar (gomme) syrup
¾	shot(s)	Freshly squeezed lime juice
Top up with		Soda water (club soda)

Origin: Created in 2003 by Gian Franco Pola for Capannina in Cremona and Coconuts in Rimini, Italy.
Comment: A minty, herbal, refreshing summer drink.

ENGLISH MARTINI NEW

●●●●◑

Glass: Martini
Garnish: Rosemary
Method: Muddle rosemary in base of shaker. Add other ingredients, stir with ice and strain into chilled glass.

1	sprig	Rosemary
2½	shot(s)	Plymouth gin
¾	shot(s)	Elderflower cordial
½	shot(s)	Sugar (gomme) syrup

Origin: Adapted from a drink created in 2003 at MJU, Millennium Hotel, London, England.
Comment: Would be great served with roast lamb.

ELLE FOR LEATHER

●●●●◑

Glass: Collins
Garnish: Vanilla pod
Method: Shake first four ingredients with ice and strain into glass filled with crushed ice. Top up with Champagne.

1½	shot(s)	The Famous Grouse Scotch whisky
1	shot(s)	Teichenné vanilla schnapps
¼	shot(s)	Freshly squeezed lemon juice
⅛	shot(s)	Sugar (gomme) syrup
Top up with		Piper-Heidsieck Brut Champagne

Origin: Created in 2001 by Reece Clark at Hush Up, London, England.
Comment: A long, cool Champagne cocktail pepped up with Scotch whisky and vanilla schnapps. Easy drinking - yet adult.

ENVY UPDATED

●●●●○

Glass: Martini
Garnish: Star fruit on rim
Method: Shake all ingredients with ice and fine strain into chilled glass.

½	shot(s)	Absolut vodka
2	shot(s)	Midori melon liqueur
1	shot(s)	Teichenné peach schnapps
¾	shot(s)	Frangelico hazelnut liqueur
¼	shot(s)	Freshly squeezed lime juice

Comment: Green with ... melon and a hint of hazelnut. A tad on the sweet side.

ESCALATOR MARTINI

Glass: Martini
Garnish: Pear slice on rim
Method: Shake all ingredients with ice and fine strain into chilled glass.

1	shot(s)	Poire William eau de vie
1/2	shot(s)	Zubrówka (Bison grass) vodka
2	shot(s)	Pressed apple juice
1/8	shot(s)	Sugar (gomme) syrup

Origin: Created in 2002 by Kevin Connelly, England. It's called an escalator because the 'apples and pears', rhyming slang for 'stairs', are shaken.
Comment: This orchard-fresh concoction was originally made with Korte Palinka (Hungarian pear schnapps) - if using that or Poire William liqueur, little or no sugar is necessary.

ESPRESSO MARTINI

Glass: Martini
Garnish: Float 3 coffee beans
Method: Shake all ingredients with ice and strain into glass.

2	shot(s)	Absolut vodka
2	shot(s)	Espresso coffee (cold)
1/2	shot(s)	Kahlúa coffee liqueur
1/4	shot(s)	Sugar (gomme) syrup

Origin: A straight-up version of Dick Bradsell's Pharmaceutical Stimulant.
Comment: Forget the vodka Red Bull, this is the connoisseur's way of combining caffeine and vodka.

ESQUIRE MARTINI

Glass: Martini
Garnish: Blackberry
Method: Stir all ingredients with ice and strain into glass

1 1/2	shot(s)	Siwucha vodka
1 1/2	shot(s)	Stoli Razberi
1/2	shot(s)	Parfait Amour

Origin: Created by Dick Bradsell for Esquire Magazine.
Comment: One for hardened Martini drinkers.

E.T.

Glass: Shot
Method: Layer ingredients by carefully pouring in the following order.

1/2	shot(s)	Midori melon liqueur
1/2	shot(s)	Baileys Irish Cream liqueur
1/2	shot(s)	Absolut vodka

Comment: Fortified creamy melon.

EVITA

Glass: Martini
Method: Shake ingredients with ice and strain into glass.

1 1/4	shot(s)	Absolut vodka
3/4	shot(s)	Midori melon liqueur
2	shot(s)	Freshly squeezed orange juice
3/4	shot(s)	Freshly squeezed lime juice
1/4	shot(s)	Sugar (gomme) syrup

Comment: A tasty medium-sweet combination of melon, orange juice and lime.

EXOTIC PASSION

Glass: Collins
Garnish: Split strawberry
Method: Shake ingredients with ice and strain into ice-filled glass.

1	shot(s)	Passoã passion fruit liqueur
2	shot(s)	Absolut vodka
1	shot(s)	Bols Strawberry (fraise) liqueur
2	shot(s)	Pressed pineapple juice
2	shot(s)	Pressed grapefruit juice

Comment: Bittersweet flavour and quite floral.

EXTRADITION

Glass: Old-fashioned
Garnish: Strawberry on rim
Method: Muddle strawberries in base of shaker. Add other ingredients, shake with ice and fine strain into ice-filled glass.

3	fresh	Hulled strawberries
2	shot(s)	ABA Pisco
2	shot(s)	Pressed apple juice
3/4	shot(s)	Passion fruit syrup

Origin: Created in 2001 by Francis Timmons at Detroit, London, England.
Comment: A light fruity drink for a summer afternoon.

F-16 SHOT

Glass: Shot
Garnish: Split stemmed cherry on rim
Method: Layer in glass by pouring ingredients carefully in the following order.

1/2	shot(s)	Kahlúa coffee liqueur
1/2	shot(s)	Baileys Irish cream liqueur
1/2	shot(s)	Havana Club light rum

Comment: Named for the F-16 jet and closely related to the B-52.

FANCY DRINK

Glass: Sling
Garnish: Lemon slice & kumquat
Method: Shake first three ingredients with ice and strain into ice-filled glass. Top up with bitter lemon.

1	shot(s)	Grand Marnier
1	shot(s)	Havana Club light rum
2	shot(s)	Freshly squeezed grapefruit juice
Top up with		Bitter lemon

Comment: Tasty tart! Refreshingly sour.

FBI

Glass: Collins
Garnish: Crumbled Cadbury's Flake bar
Method: Blend all ingredients with two scoops of crushed ice and serve.

2	shot(s)	Absolut vodka
1	shot(s)	Baileys Irish Cream liqueur
1	shot(s)	Kahlúa coffee liqueur
3	scoops	Vanilla ice cream

Comment: Yummy alcoholic milkshake with coffee and whiskey cream.

LA FEUILLE MORTE NEW

●●●●◐○

Glass: Collins (10oz / 290ml max)
Method: Pour pastis, grenadine and mint syrup into glass. Serve iced water separately in a small jug (known in France as a 'broc') so the customer can dilute to their own taste (I recommend five shots). Lastly, add ice to fill glass.

1	shot(s)	Ricard
½	shot(s)	Grenadine syrup
½	shot(s)	Mint (menthe) syrup
Top up with		Chilled water

Origin: Pronounced 'Fueel-Mort', literally meaning 'the dead leaf' due to the drink's colour, this is a traditional French way to serve Ricard.
Comment: The traditional French café drink with a twist.

FIFTH AVENUE SHOT

Glass: Shot
Method: Layer ingredients in glass by carefully pouring in the following order.

½	shot(s)	Bols Brown crème de cacao
½	shot(s)	Bols Apricot brandy liqueur
½	shot(s)	Double (heavy) cream

Comment: Chocolate apricot and cream shot.

57 T-BIRD SHOT

●●●●●○

Glass: Shot
Method: Shake all ingredients with ice and strain into glass.

½	shot(s)	Absolut vodka
½	shot(s)	Grand Marnier
½	shot(s)	Disaronno Originale amaretto

Variations: With California Plates add 1/2 shot orange juice, with Cape Cod Plates add 1/2 shot cranberry juice, with Florida Plates add 1/2 shot grapefruit juice, with Hawaiian Plates add 1/2 shot pineapple juice.
Comment: '57 T-bird, or 1957 Ford Thunderbird to give it its full title, immortalised in the Beach Boys' song 'Fun Fun Fun', was the classic car for any 1950s teenager. Top down, radio up, girl next to you...

FINE-AND-DANDY

Glass: Martini
Method: Shake ingredients vigorously with ice and strain into glass.

2	shot(s)	Plymouth gin
¾	shot(s)	Cointreau / triple sec
1	shot(s)	Freshly squeezed lime juice
¾	shot(s)	Sugar (gomme) syrup
4	dashes	Angostura aromatic bitters

Comment: A white lady with lime juice.

FINITALY NEW

●●●●○

Glass: Martini
Garnish: Blueberry or raspberry on rim
Method: Shake all ingredients with ice and fine strain into chilled glass.

1½	shot(s)	Finlandia Cranberry vodka
½	shot(s)	Cinzano Rosso (sweet) vermouth
½	shot(s)	Chambord liqueur
1	shot(s)	Chilled water

Origin: Created by Michael Mahe at Hush, London, England.
Comment: A simple, berry led Martini.

FINNBERRY MARTINI

●●●●○

Glass: Martini
Garnish: Cranberries
Method: Shake all ingredients with ice and strain into glass.

2	shot(s)	Finlandia Cranberry vodka
2	shot(s)	Lingonberry or Cranberry juice
1	shot(s)	Lapponia Cloudberry liqueur

Origin: I created this in 2002 after a trip to Finland with Finlandia vodka.
Comment: This rich berry Martini can be varied by using other berry liqueurs in the Lapponia range – try using two with a half shot of each.

FIREBALL

Glass: Shot
Method: Shake ingredients with ice and strain into glass.

1	shot(s)	Cinnamon schnapps
4	drops	Tabasco sauce

Comment: A weird and spicy experience.

FISH HOUSE PUNCH

Glass: Collins
Garnish: Float lemon wheel
Method: Shake first six ingredients with ice and strain into ice-filled glass, then top up with soda water.

1	shot(s)	Rémy Martin Cognac
1	shot(s)	Peach brandy liqueur
1	shot(s)	Havana Club light rum
½	shot(s)	Strong cold tea
1½	shot(s)	Freshly squeezed lemon juice
½	shot(s)	Sugar (gomme) syrup
Top up with		Soda water (club soda)

Origin: Created at The Fishing and Social Club in Philadelphia in 1732.
Comment: A long, refreshing, mellow drink with citrus edge.

FJORD

Glass: Rocks
Method: Shake ingredients with ice and strain into ice-filled glass.

2	shot(s)	Linie Aquavit
½	shot(s)	Rémy Martin Cognac
1	shot(s)	Freshly squeezed orange juice
1	shot(s)	Freshly squeezed lime juice
½	shot(s)	Grenadine syrup

Comment: One of few aquavit based cocktails.

FLAMING HENRY

Glass: Shot
Method: Layer by carefully pouring ingredients in the order below. Finally ignite Bourbon - extinguish flame prior to drinking and beware of hot glass rim.

¹/₂	shot(s)	Disaronno Originale amaretto
¹/₂	shot(s)	Baileys Irish Cream liqueur
¹/₂	shot(s)	Buffalo Trace Bourbon

Origin: Created by Henry Smiff and friends in the South of France and popularised by one of their number, John Coe, the successful London drinks wholesaler.
Comment: Flaming good shot.

FLAMINGO #1 UPDATED

Glass: Martini
Garnish: Banana chunk on rim
Method: Shake all ingredients with ice and fine strain into chilled glass.

1	shot(s)	Buffalo Trace Bourbon
³/₄	shot(s)	Bols crème de banane
1¹/₂	shot(s)	Freshly squeezed orange juice
³/₄	shot(s)	Freshly squeezed lemon juice
¹/₂	fresh	Egg white

Comment: It's not pink but it has Bourbon, banana, orange and lemon smoothed with egg white.

FLAMINGO #2 NEW

Glass: Martini
Garnish: Starfruit
Method: Shake all ingredients with ice and fine strain into chilled glass.

2	shot(s)	Appleton Estate V/X aged rum
1¹/₂	shot(s)	Pressed pineapple juice
¹/₂	shot(s)	Freshly squeezed lime juice
¹/₂	shot(s)	Grenadine syrup

Origin Discovered in 2003 at Pravda, New York City.
Comment: Use less grenadine to reduce the sweetness and pink hue of this tasty frothy topped drink.

FLATLINER UPDATED

Glass: Shot
Method: Pour sambuca in chilled shot glass. Carefully pour Tequila so as to float on sambuca. Lastly drip pepper sauce onto drink. This will sink through Tequila to form an orange line on top of sambuca.

³/₄	shot(s)	Opal Bianca sambuca
³/₄	shot(s)	Sauza Hornitos Tequila
8	drops	Tabasco pepper sauce

Comment: A serious combination of sweetness, strength and heat. Looks great but tastes...

FLAMING FERRARI

A flaming drink to be downed in one and that requires an assistant to help the drinker consume the concoction.

Step 1.
Glass: Martini
Method: Layer ingredients in glass by carefully pouring in the following order.

¹/₂	shot(s)	Grenadine syrup
1	shot(s)	Galliano
1	shot(s)	Opal Nera black sambuca
1	shot(s)	Green Chartreuse

Step 2.
Glass: Two shot glasses.
Method: Pour each ingredient into its own shot glass.

1	shot	Grand Marnier
1	shot	Pusser's Navy rum

Step 3.
Method: Ignite the contents of the Martini glass. Give two long straws to the drinker and instruct them to drink the contents of the Martini glass in one gulp. As they do so, slowly pour the contents of the two shot glasses into the flaming Martini glass.

Comment: Not recommended if you want to remember the rest of the evening and please be careful – alcohol and fire is a dangerous mixture.

Variant: Flaming Lamborghini with coffee liqueur and blue curaçao in the shot glasses.

FLEUR ROUGE

Glass: Martini
Method: Shake ingredients with ice and strain into glass.

2	shot(s)	Fleur de Biére eau de vie
2¹⁄₂	shot(s)	Pressed apple juice
¹⁄₂	shot(s)	Sisca crème de cassis

Origin: I created this in 1998 after a trip to Burgundy's cassis region.
Comment: The flavour of the beer comes through with the mixture of cassis and apple juice.

THE FLIRT

Glass: Martini
Garnish: Lipstick on half of rim
Method: Shake all ingredients with ice and fine strain into chilled glass.

2	shot(s)	Sauza Hornitos Tequila
³⁄₄	shot(s)	Bols Apricot brandy liqueur
1	shot(s)	Freshly squeezed lime juice
1	shot(s)	Cranberry juice

Origin: Created in 2002 by Dick Bradsell at Lonsdale House, London, England.
Comment: A fruity drink to upset glass washers throughout the land.

●●●●●○

FLIRTINI

Glass: Martini
Garnish: Cherry on rim
Method: Shake first three ingredients with ice and fine strain into chilled Martini glass. Top up with Champagne.

³⁄₄	shot(s)	Absolut vodka
³⁄₄	shot(s)	Cointreau / triple sec
2	shot(s)	Pressed pineapple juice
Top up with		Piper-Heidsieck Brut Champagne

Origin: Adapted from a recipe by the famous New York bartender Dale DeGroff.
Comment: A flirtatious little number that slips down easily.

FLORIDA

Glass: Collins
Method: Shake ingredients with ice and strain into ice-filled glass.

1	shot(s)	Plymouth gin
¹⁄₂	shot(s)	Kirschwasser
¹⁄₂	shot(s)	Cointreau / triple sec
2	shot(s)	Freshly squeezed orange juice
¹⁄₂	shot(s)	Freshly squeezed lemon juice
¹⁄₄	shot(s)	Sugar (gomme) syrup

Comment: Aptly named – made even better with fresh orange juice.

FLORIDA DAIQUIRÍ

Glass: Martini
Method: Shake ingredients vigorously with crushed ice and strain into glass. If no crushed ice is available, use cubed ice and add ¹⁄₄ shot water to the recipe.

2	shot(s)	Havana Club light rum
¹⁄₂	shot(s)	Freshly squeezed lime juice
¹⁄₄	shot(s)	Sugar (gomme) syrup
¹⁄₄	shot(s)	Pressed grapefruit juice
¹⁄₈	shot(s)	Maraschino liqueur

Comment: The classic blend of rum, lime and sugar, but with the addition of a hint of grapefruit juice.

FLORIDA SLING

Glass: Sling
Garnish: Redcurrants
Method: Shake ingredients with ice and strain into ice-filled glass.

1¹⁄₂	shot(s)	Plymouth gin
¹⁄₄	shot(s)	Bols Cherry brandy liqueur
1¹⁄₂	shot(s)	Pressed pineapple juice
³⁄₄	shot(s)	Freshly squeezed lemon juice
¹⁄₂	shot(s)	Sugar (gomme) syrup
¹⁄₄	shot(s)	Grenadine syrup

Comment: Deep flavours, lasting finish.

●●●●●

FLORIDITA

Glass: Coupette
Garnish: Lime wedge & salted rim (optional)
Method: Shake all ingredients with ice and strain into glass.

1¹⁄₂	shot(s)	Sauza Hornitos Tequila
¹⁄₂	shot(s)	Cointreau / triple sec
¹⁄₂	shot(s)	Cranberry juice
¹⁄₄	shot(s)	Rose's lime cordial
1¹⁄₂	shot(s)	Pressed grapefruit juice
³⁄₄	shot(s)	Freshly squeezed lime juice
³⁄₄	shot(s)	Sugar (gomme) syrup

Origin: Created in 1999 by Robert Plotkin and Raymon Flores of BarMedia, USA.
Comment: A blush coloured Margarita-style drink with a well-matched amalgamation of flavours.

●●●●●

FLUTTER

Glass: Martini
Garnish: Orange twist
Method: Shake all ingredients with ice and fine strain into chilled glass.

2	shot(s)	Sauza Hornitos Tequila
1	shot(s)	Kahlúa coffee liqueur
1¹⁄₄	shot(s)	Pressed pineapple juice

Origin: Created in 2003 by Tony Conigliaro at Lonsdale House, London, England.
Comment: The three ingredients combine brilliantly.

●●●●●○

FLY LIKE A BUTTERFLY

Glass: Martini
Garnish: Orange twist
Method: Shake all ingredients with ice and fine strain into chilled glass.

1½	shot(s)	Cinzano Extra Dry vermouth
1½	shot(s)	Cinzano Rosso (sweet) vermouth
¾	shot(s)	Dubonnet red
¾	shot(s)	Freshly squeezed orange juice

Origin: My take on a classic called a 'Lovely Butterfly'.
Comment: This light, aromatic, sweet and sour beauty has a grown up quinine rich flavour but lacks the 'sting like a bee' finish.

FLYING DUTCHMAN MARTINI

Glass: Martini
Method: Pour Curaçao into glass and swirl around. Empty the glass then add Jenever and orange bitters.

½	shot(s)	Orange curaçao
3	shot(s)	Jenever
4	dashes	Fee Brothers Orange bitters

Comment: A Martini with more than a hint of orange.

FLYING GRASSHOPPER

Glass: Martini
Garnish: Chocolate powder rim & mint leaf.
Method: Shake ingredients with ice and strain.

1	shot(s)	Absolut vodka
¾	shot(s)	Bols White crème de cacao
¾	shot(s)	Green crème de menthe
1	shot(s)	Double (heavy) cream
1	shot(s)	Milk

Comment: A Grasshopper with vodka – tastes like a choc mint ice cream.

FLYING SCOTSMAN

Glass: Martini
Method: Stir ingredients with ice and strain into glass.

2	shot(s)	The Famous Grouse Scotch whisky
2	shot(s)	Cinzano Rosso sweet vermouth
¼	shot(s)	Sugar (gomme) syrup
4	dashes	Angostura aromatic bitters

Comment: A sweet but bitter and very interesting creation.

FOG CUTTER

Glass: Collins
Method: Shake first six ingredients with ice and strain into ice-filled glass, then float Sherry.

2	shot(s)	Havana Club light rum
1	shot(s)	Rémy Martin Cognac
½	shot(s)	Plymouth gin
1½	shot(s)	Freshly squeezed orange juice
1½	shot(s)	Freshly squeezed lemon juice
½	shot(s)	Orgeat (almond) syrup
½	shot(s)	Fino Sherry

Variant: With the addition of ¼ shot sugar syrup.
Comment: Looks like orange juice, but don't be fooled it's long, sour, fruity and strong.

FOG HORN

Glass: Rocks
Garnish: Split lime wedge
Method: Fill glass with ice, add gin and Rose's, then top up with ginger beer and stir.

2	shot(s)	Plymouth gin
½	shot(s)	Rose's lime cordial
Top up with		Ginger ale

Comment: Different! Almost flowery in taste with the spice of ginger beer.

●●●●●○

FORBIDDEN FRUITS

Glass: Collins
Garnish: Berries on stick
Method: Muddle berries in base of shaker can. Add other ingredients, shake with ice and strain into glass filled with crushed ice.

4	fresh	Blackberries
4	fresh	Blueberries
4	fresh	Strawberries
4	fresh	Raspberries
2	shot(s)	Plymouth gin
1	shot(s)	Fresh lime juice
½	shot(s)	Sugar (gomme) syrup
Top up with		Ginger Beer

Origin: Created in 2001 by Andres Masso at Lab Bar, London, England.
Comment: Long and fruity with something of a bite.

●●●●○○

FOREST BREEZE

Glass: Collins
Garnish: Blackberry & raspberry
Method: Muddle blackberries and raspberries in base of shaker. Add next five ingredients, shake with ice and strain into ice-filled glass. Top up with soda water (club soda).

6	fresh	Blackberries
6	fresh	Raspberries
2	shot(s)	Absolut vodka
½	shot(s)	Chambord black raspberry liqueur
½	shot(s)	Bols Blackberry liqueur (crème de mûre)
3	shot(s)	Cranberry juice
¼	shot(s)	Freshly squeezed lime juice
Top up with		Soda water (club soda)

Origin: Created in 2002 by Paul Mott at Waikiki, London, England.
Comment: The colour may scar your carpet but the fresh fruity flavour will please your taste buds.

FORTY-THREE DON JUAN

Glass: Martini
Garnish: Split orange wheel
Method: Shake ingredients with ice and strain into glass.

1	shot(s)	Cuarenta y Tres liqueur
1	shot(s)	Double (heavy) cream
2	shot(s)	Freshly squeezed orange juice
½	shot(s)	Rémy Martin Cognac

Comment: A lightly creamy but orange taste.

FORTY THREE OLE

Glass: Rocks
Method: Shake all ingredients with ice and strain into an ice-filled glass.

1	shot(s)	Cuarenta y Tres liqueur
2	shot(s)	Freshly squeezed orange juice
1	shot(s)	Rémy Martin Cognac

Comment: Smooth and very moreish.

FOSBURY FLIP

●●●●●◐

Glass: Collins
Garnish: Apricot slice on rim
Method: Shake all ingredients with ice and strain into ice-filled glass.

2	shot(s)	Appleton Estate V/X aged rum
1	shot(s)	Frangelico hazelnut liqueur
1	shot(s)	Bols Apricot brandy liqueur
2 1/2	shot(s)	Freshly squeezed orange juice
3/4	shot(s)	Freshly squeezed lime juice
1/8	shot(s)	Grenadine syrup
1	fresh	Egg yolk

Origin: Created in 2002 by Salvatore Calabrese at the Library Bar, Lanesborough Hotel, London, England, for Kirsten Fosbury.
Comment: This richly flavoured yellow, velvety drink is almost custardy in consistency.

FOUR W DAIQUIRI

●●●●●○

Glass: Martini
Garnish: Grapefruit wedge on rim
Method: Shake all ingredients with ice and fine strain into chilled glass.

2	shot(s)	Mount Gay Eclipse golden rum
1 1/2	shot(s)	Freshly squeezed grapefruit juice
3/4	shot(s)	Maple syrup
2	dashes	Angostura aromatic bitters
1/2	shot(s)	Chilled water

Origin: My version of an old drink created by Herb Smith and popularised by his friend Oscar at the Waldorf, New York City. The drink was named in honour of the Duke of Windsor and his bride, formerly Wallis Warfield Simpson. The four 'W's stand for Wallis Warfield Windsor Wallop.
Comment: The oomph of rum, the sourness of grapefruit and the richness of maple syrup aromatised by bitters.

FOURTH OF JULY

Glass: Martini
Garnish: Split stemmed cherry on rim
Method: Pour Bourbon and Galliano into warm glass, ignite and sprinkle cinnamon while flaming. Shake coffee liqueur, orange juice and cream with ice and strain into glass with Bourbon and Galliano.

1	shot(s)	Buffalo Trace Bourbon
1	shot(s)	Galliano
1	shot(s)	Kahlúa coffee liqueur
1	shot(s)	Freshly squeezed orange juice
1	shot(s)	Double (heavy) cream

Comment: A wonderfully rich and tasty after dinner drink.

FOURTH OF JULY

Glass: Shot
Method: Layer in glass by carefully pouring ingredients in the following order.

1/4	shot(s)	Grenadine syrup
1/2	shot(s)	Bols Blue curaçao
1/2	shot(s)	Absolut vodka

Comment: Looks cool... tastes less so!

FRAISE ROYALE

Glass: Flute
Garnish: Split strawberry
Method: Pour purée into flute and coat glass. Add Champagne and stir to mix fruit with Champagne. Finally add fraise liqueur.

2	shot(s)	Strawberry purée
Top up with		Piper-Heidsieck Brut Champagne
1/2	shot(s)	Bols Strawberry (fraise) liqueur

Comment: A fair way to enjoy Champagne and strawberries.

FRANKENJACK

Glass: Martini
Method: Shake ingredients with ice and strain into glass.

1	shot(s)	Plymouth gin
3/4	shot(s)	Cinzano Extra Dry vermouth
1/2	shot(s)	Bols Apricot brandy liqueur
1/4	shot(s)	Cointreau / triple sec

Comment: Dry and sophisticated.

FREDDY FUDPUCKER UPDATED

●●●●◐○

Glass: Collins
Garnish: Orange slice in glass
Method: Pour Tequila and orange juice into ice-filled glass and stir. Float Galliano.

2	shot(s)	Sauza Hornitos Tequila
4 1/2	shot(s)	Freshly squeezed orange juice
1/2	shot(s)	Galliano liqueur

Variant: Harvey Wallbanger
Comment: A Harvey Wallbanger for those that prefer to Tequila to vodka.

FRENCH 74

Glass: Flute
Garnish: Immerse cherry
Method: Shake the first three ingredients with ice and strain into glass, then top up with Champagne and lightly stir.

3/4	shot(s)	Absolut vodka
1/2	shot(s)	Freshly squeezed lemon juice
1/4	shot(s)	Sugar (gomme) syrup
Top up with		Piper-Heidsieck Brut Champagne

AKA: The Diamond Fizz
Comment: A classic mix of lemon juice, sugar and strength.

FRENCH 75

Glass: Flute
Garnish: Immerse cherry
Method: Shake first three ingredients with ice and strain into glass, then top up with Champagne and lightly stir.

³⁄₄	shot(s)	**Plymouth gin**
¹⁄₂	shot(s)	**Freshly squeezed lemon juice**
¹⁄₂	shot(s)	**Sugar (gomme) syrup**
Top up with		**Piper-Heidsieck Brut Champagne**

Origin: Thought to be created by Harry MacElhone of Harry's Bar, Paris in 1925 and named after the 75 field gun used by the French army during the First World War.
Comment: Fresh, clean, sophisticated - very drinkable and hasn't dated.

FRENCH 90

Glass: Flute
Garnish: Split lime wedge
Method: Shake first three ingredients with ice and strain into glass, then top up with Champagne and lightly stir.

1	shot(s)	**Rémy Martin Cognac**
¹⁄₂	shot(s)	**Freshly squeezed lime juice**
¹⁄₄	shot(s)	**Sugar (gomme) syrup**
Top up with		**Piper-Heidsieck Brut Champagne**

Comment: Not as good as a French 75.

FRENCH BISON-TINI

Glass: Martini
Garnish: Raspberries
Method: Shake ingredients with ice and strain into glass.

2	shot(s)	**Zubrówka Bison vodka**
2¹⁄₂	shot(s)	**Pressed pineapple juice**
¹⁄₂	shot(s)	**Chambord black raspberry liqueur**

Comment: A French Martini with the distinctive taste of Zubrówka.

FRENCH CONNECTION

Glass: Snifter
Method: Pour ingredients into glass, then swirl to mix.

1¹⁄₂	shot(s)	**Rémy Martin Cognac**
³⁄₄	shot(s)	**Disaronno Originale amaretto**

Comment: Strong nose with a complementary palate.

FRENCH KISS

Glass: Martini
Method: Shake ingredients with ice and strain into glass.

2	shot(s)	**Absolut vodka**
1¹⁄₂	shot(s)	**Bols Raspberry (framboise) liqueur**
³⁄₄	shot(s)	**Bols White crème de cacao**
³⁄₄	shot(s)	**Double (heavy) cream**

Comment: A well named lightly creamy and tasty drink.

FRENCH MARTINI #1

Glass: Martini
Method: Shake all ingredients with ice and fine strain into chilled glass.

2	shot(s)	**Absolut vodka**
2¹⁄₂	shot(s)	**Pressed pineapple juice**
¹⁄₂	shot(s)	**Chambord black raspberry liqueur**

Comment: Black raspberries and pineapple laced with vodka. Simple, delicious and very fruity.

FRENCH MARTINI # 2 UPDATED

●●●●○

Glass: Martini
Garnish: Three raspberries
Method: Shake all ingredients with ice and fine strain into chilled glass.

2½	shot(s)	Stoli Razberi
2	shot(s)	Pressed pineapple juice
¼	shot(s)	Chambord black raspberry liqueur

Comment: This yellow rather than pink French Martini is drier than the more common version also listed in this guide.

FRENCH MULE UPDATED

●●●●○

Glass: 12oz Collins
Garnish: Sprig of mint
Method: Shake first four ingredients with ice and strain into an ice-filled glass. Top up with ginger beer, stir and serve with straws.

2	shot(s)	Rémy Martin Cognac
1	shot(s)	Freshly squeezed lime juice
1	shot(s)	Sugar (gomme) syrup
4	dashes	Angostura aromatic bitters
Top up with		Ginger beer

Comment: This French answer to the vodka based Moscow Mule uses Cognac to make a spicy, long, refreshing drink.

FRENCH SPRING PUNCH

Glass: Sling
Garnish: Strawberry
Method: Pour ingredients into ice-filled glass.

1	shot(s)	Rémy Martin Cognac
¼	shot(s)	Bols Strawberry (fraise) liqueur
¼	shot(s)	Freshly squeezed lemon juice
¼	shot(s)	Sugar (gomme) syrup
Top up with		Piper-Heidsieck Brut Champagne

Origin: Created by Dick Bradsell & Rodolphe Sorel.
Comment: Not as popular as the Russian Spring Punch.

FRENCH TEAR

Glass: Martini
Method: Shake ingredients with ice and strain into glass.

1	shot(s)	Mandarine Napoléon
1	shot(s)	Spiced rum
2½	shot(s)	Pressed pineapple juice

Origin: Quo Vadis, London, England.
Comment: The spiced rum gets lost in the pineapple and mandarin, but this is still very drinkable.

FRESCA NOVA

Glass: Flute
Method: Shake first four ingredients with ice and strain into glass, top up with champagne.

1½	shot(s)	Grand Marnier
¾	shot(s)	Freshly squeezed orange juice
½	shot(s)	Sugar (gomme) syrup
1	shot(s)	Double (heavy) cream
Top up with		Piper-Heidsieck Brut Champagne

Origin: Created by Jamie Terrell for Philip Holzberg at Vinexpo 1999.
Comment: The Champagne soaks up the strong flavour of the Mandarine and leaves a dangerously consumable drink.

FRIAR TUCK

Glass: Martini
Garnish: Sprinkle ground nutmeg
Method: Shake ingredients with ice and strain into glass.

1	shot(s)	Frangelico hazelnut liqueur
1	shot(s)	Bols Brown crème de cacao
1	shot(s)	Double (heavy) cream
1	shot(s)	Milk

Variant: With Amaretto and ice cream.
Comment: Round, jolly and creamy with chocolate and hazelnut.

FRISKY BISON

Glass: Martini
Method: Shake ingredients with ice and strain into glass.

1½	shot(s)	Zubrówka Bison vodka
1	shot(s)	Sourz Apple Liqueur
1	shot(s)	Pressed apple juice
1	sprig	Mint
½	shot(s)	Freshly squeezed lime juice
¼	shot(s)	Sugar (gomme) syrup

Created by: Tony Kerr in 1999 at Mash & Air in Manchester, England.
Comment: A perfect balance of flavours, sweet 'n' sour freshness and depth.

FRISKY LEMONADE

●●●●○○

Glass: Collins
Garnish: Lime wedge squeezed & dropped into drink
Method: Pour ingredients into ice-filled glass and stir.

2	shot(s)	Finlandia Lime vodka
½	shot(s)	Cinzano Extra Dry vermouth
Top up with		Lemonade / Sprite / 7Up

Origin: Created by Aaron Rudd in 2002 at Home, London, England.
Comment: Reminiscent of alcoholic lemon barley water.

FRU FRU

Glass: Flute
Garnish: Split strawberry
Method: Shake first three ingredients with ice and strain into glass, then top up with Champagne.

1	shot(s)	Passoã passion fruit liqueur
1	shot(s)	Bols Strawberry (fraise) liqueur
1	shot(s)	Pressed grapefruit juice
Top up with		Piper-Heidsieck Brut Champagne

Comment: Dry bitterness of grapefruit complemented by passion fruit and strawberry.

⬤⬤⬤⬤⬤◗

FRUIT & NUT CHOCOLATE MARTINI

Glass: Martini
Garnish: Crumbled Cadbury's Flake bar
Method: Shake all ingredients with ice and fine strain into chilled glass.

1	shot(s)	Absolut Kurant vodka
1/2	shot(s)	Frangelico hazelnut liqueur
1/2	shot(s)	Bols White crème de cacao
1/2	shot(s)	Chambord black raspberry liqueur
1/2	shot(s)	Baileys Irish Cream liqueur
3/4	shot(s)	Double (heavy) cream
3/4	shot(s)	Milk

Comment: Naughty but nice – one for confectionery lovers.

FRUIT SALAD

Glass: Collins
Garnish: Orange slice
Method: Shake ingredients with ice and strain into ice-filled glass.

2	shot(s)	Absolut vodka
3/4	shot(s)	Bols crème de banane
4	shot(s)	Freshly squeezed orange juice
3/4	shot(s)	Galliano
1/4	shot(s)	Grenadine syrup

Comment: This variation on the Harvey Wallbanger tastes like Fruit Salad penny chews.

FRUIT SOUR

Glass: Rocks
Garnish: Lemon zest
Method: Shake ingredients with ice and strain into ice-filled glass.

1	shot(s)	Buffalo Trace Bourbon
1	shot(s)	Cointreau / triple sec
1	shot(s)	Freshly squeezed lemon juice
1/2	fresh	Egg white

Comment: Dry and slightly frothy.

⬤⬤⬤⬤⬤◯

FRUIT TREE DAIQUIRÍ

Glass: Martini
Garnish: Grapefruit or apricot wedge on rim
Method: Shake all ingredients with ice and fine strain into chilled glass.

2	shot(s)	Havana Club light rum
3/4	shot(s)	Bols Apricot brandy liqueur
?	shot(s)	Freshly squeezed grapefruit juice
3/4	shot(s)	Freshly squeezed lime juice
1/4	shot(s)	Maraschino syrup
1/2	shot(s)	Chilled water

Comment: A Papa Doble with apricot liqueur.

F. WILLY SHOT

Glass: Shot
Method: Shake ingredients with ice and strain into glass.

1/2	shot(s)	Absolut vodka
1/2	shot(s)	Havana Club light rum
1/2	shot(s)	Disaronno Originale amaretto
1/2	shot(s)	Cointreau / triple sec
1/4	shot(s)	Rose's lime cordial

Comment: Not as bad as it looks and sounds!

⬤⬤⬤⬤◯

FU MANCHU DAIQUIRI

Glass: Martini
Garnish: Pineapple wedge on rim
Method: Shake all ingredients with ice and fine strain into chilled glass.

2	shot(s)	Havana Club light rum
1	shot(s)	Freshly squeezed lime juice
1/2	shot(s)	Sugar (gomme) syrup
1/4	shot(s)	Cointreau / triple sec
1/4	shot(s)	White crème de menthe
3/4	shot(s)	Chilled water

Origin: Adapted from a recipe by David Embury.
Comment: A natural Daiquiri with a refreshing clean, citrussy, minty, edge.

FUNKY MONKEY

Glass: Collins
Garnish: Lime wedge
Method: Shake all ingredients with ice and strain into ice-filled glass, then top up with ginger beer and stir well.

1	shot(s)	Green Chartreuse
1	shot(s)	Galliano
1/2	shot(s)	Freshly squeezed lime juice
2	shot(s)	Freshly squeezed orange juice
Top up with		Ginger beer

Origin: Created in 1999 by Jamie Terrell.
Comment: The ginger compliments the strong Chartreuse and Galliano flavour.

⬤⬤⬤◗◯◯

FUZZY NAVEL UPDATED

Glass: Collins
Garnish: Lemon wheel in glass
Method: Shake ingredients with ice and strain into ice-filled glass.

2	shot(s)	Teichenné peach schnapps
5	shot(s)	Freshly squeezed orange juice

Variant: Hairy Naval with the addition of one shot vodka.
Origin: A not very well regarded but very well-known cocktail whose origins are unknown.
Comment: The hairy version is a slightly more interesting, dryer, less fluffy concoction. So why have a fluffy navel when you can have a hairy one?

GAL FRIDAY

Glass: Martini
Garnish: Split lemon wheel
Method: Shake ingredients with ice and strain into glass.

1	shot(s)	Cointreau / triple sec
1	shot(s)	Galliano
1	shot(s)	Freshly squeezed orange juice
1	shot(s)	Double (heavy) cream
1	shot(s)	Milk

Comment: Lightly flavoured – very pleasant and not sickly.

THE GAME BIRD

Glass: Flute
Garnish: Lemon twist
Method: Shake all ingredients but ginger ale with ice and strain into glass. Top up with ginger ale.

2	shot(s)	The Famous Grouse Scotch whisky
1	shot(s)	Sourz Sour Apple liqueur
1/2	shot(s)	Elderflower cordial
1/2	shot(s)	Freshly squeezed lemon juice
1/4	shot(s)	Sugar (gomme) syrup
Top up with		Ginger ale

Origin: Created by Wayne Collins in 2002.
Comment: Wayne created this cocktail to be made using Famous Grouse, hence the name. Like most of his creations this is delicious: fruity, spicy and well-balanced.

GATOR BITE NEW

Glass: Coupette
Garnish: Salt rim
Method: Shake all ingredients with ice and fine strain into chilled glass.

1	shot(s)	Green Chartreuse
1 1/2	shot(s)	Cointreau / triple sec
1	shot(s)	Freshly squeezed lime juice
3/4	shot(s)	Sugar (gomme) syrup

Comment: Looks like a Margarita, but instead of Tequila features the unique taste of Chartreuse. Yup it bites.

GEORGIA PEACH

Glass: Rocks
Garnish: Cranberries
Method: Shake ingredients with ice and strain into ice-filled glass.

1	shot(s)	Mount Gay Eclipse golden rum
1	shot(s)	Teichenné Peach schnapps
2 1/2	shot(s)	Cranberry juice

Comment: A fruity, peachy drink with a hint of rum.

GIMLET

Glass: Martini
Garnish: Split lime wedge or cherry
Method: Shake all ingredients with ice and fine strain into chilled glass.

2	shot(s)	Plymouth gin
1 3/4	shot(s)	Rose's lime cordial
1/2	shot(s)	Chilled water (optional)

Origin: In 1747, James Lind, a Scottish surgeon, discovered that consumption of citrus fruits helped prevent scurvy, one of the most common illnesses on board ship. (It is now understood that scurvy is caused by a Vitamin C deficiency and that it is the vitamins in citrus fruit which help ward off the condition.) Later, Lachlan Rose, the owner of a shipyard in Leith, solved the problem of how to keep citrus juice fresh for months on board ship. In 1867 he patented a process for preserving fruit using salts of sulphur. To give his new product wider appeal he sweetened the mixture, packaged it in an attractive bottle and named it 'Rose's Lime Cordial'.

Once the benefits of drinking lime juice became more broadly known, British sailors consumed so much of the stuff, often mixed with their daily ration of rum and water ('grog'), that they became affectionately known as 'Limeys'. Naval officers also had gin which they mixed to make Gimlets.

A 'gimlet' was originally the name of a small tool used to tap the barrels of spirits which were carried on British Navy ships: this could be the origin of the drink's name. Another story cites a naval doctor, Rear-Admiral Sir Thomas Desmond Gimlette (1857-1943), who is said to have mixed gin with lime 'to help the medicine go down'. This story is substantiated by a mention in his obituary in The Times, 6 October 1943.
Comment: Classically this drink is stirred rather than shaken. However, you chose to mix this, it is a simple blend of gin and sweet lime.

GE BLONDE

●●●●●●

Glass: Martini
Garnish: Apple wedge
Method: Shake all ingredients with ice and strain into glass.

1³/₄	shot(s)	The Famous Grouse Scotch whisky
1¹/₄	shot(s)	Sauvignon Blanc wine
1	shot(s)	Pressed apple juice
¹/₃	shot(s)	Sugar (gomme) syrup
¹/₄	shot(s)	Freshly squeezed lemon juice

Origin: A combined effort by the staff of London's GE Club in January 2002 and named by Linda, a waitress at the club who happens to be blonde. She claimed the name was inspired by the cocktail's straw colour.
Comment: The type of 'fresh' apple juice used and the brand of Scotch greatly affect the balance of this delicate drink. The Scotch used should be flavousome with subtle peat.

GIBSON MARTINI

Glass: Martini
Garnish: Two cocktail onions
Method: Stir vermouth with ice in a mixing glass. Strain, discarding vermouth, to leave only a coating on the ice. Pour gin into mixing glass containing coated ice and stir. Finally strain contents of mixing glass into glass.

¹/₂	shot(s)	Cinzano Extra Dry vermouth
2¹/₂	shot(s)	Plymouth gin

Origin: There are several stories as to this drink's origin. 1/ That it was named after the well-endowed Gibson Girls - hence the two onions.
2/ That it was invented in the 1940s for the American illustrator Charles Dana Gibson at The Player's Club in New York City and the onions represent the milky white breasts of the women he drew.
Variant: With vodka in place of gin.
Comment: A must-try for gin martini fans.

GIN AND IT

Glass: Rocks
Garnish: Squeeze orange wedge over drink and drop into drink.
Method: Pour ingredients into ice-filled glass and stir.

1¹/₂	shot(s)	Plymouth gin
1¹/₂	shot(s)	Cinzano Rosso vermouth

Origin: The name is short for 'Gin and Italian', a reference to the sweet vermouth which was traditionally Italian while French vermouth was dry.
Comment: An old school version of the classic Martini

GIN AND SIN

Glass: Martini
Garnish: Three blueberries on a stick
Method: Shake ingredients with ice and strain into glass.

1¹/₂	shot(s)	Plymouth gin
1	shot(s)	Freshly squeezed lemon juice
¹/₂	shot(s)	Sugar (gomme) syrup
¹/₂	shot(s)	Freshly squeezed orange juice
¹/₈	shot(s)	Grenadine syrup

Comment: Pleasant but lacking in personality.

GIN BUCK

Glass: Rocks
Garnish: Split lime wedge
Method: Add first two ingredients to ice-filled glass and stir, then top up with ginger ale.

2	shot(s)	Plymouth gin
1	shot(s)	Rose's lime cordial
Top up with		Ginger ale

AKA: Fog Horn
Comment: Long and refreshing - add fresh lime to taste.

GIN GARDEN MARTINI **UPDATED**

●●●●○

Glass: Martini
Garnish: Float cucumber slice
Method: Muddle cucumber in base of shaker. Add other ingredients, shake with ice and fine strain into chilled glass.

1	inch	Chopped peeled cucumber
2	shot(s)	Plymouth gin
1	shot(s)	Pressed apple juice
¹/₂	shot(s)	Elderflower cordial

Origin: Created in 2001 through a collaboration between Daniel Warner at Zander and Tobias Blazquez Garcia at Steam, London, England.
Comment: The archetypal English spirit, fruit and vegetable combo.

GIN-GER TOM

Glass: Collins
Garnish: Lime squeeze and mint sprig
Method: Pour ingredients into ice-filled glass and stir.

2	shot(s)	Plymouth gin
1	shot(s)	Ginger syrup
1	shot(s)	Freshly squeezed lime juice
¹/₄	shot(s)	Sugar (gomme) syrup
Top up with		Sparkling mineral water

Origin: Created by Jamie Terrell.
Comment: A Tom Collins with lime and ginger – very refreshing.

GIN FIX

Glass: Martini
Garnish: Lemon twist
Method: Shake ingredients with ice and strain into glass.

2	shot(s)	Plymouth gin
¹/₄	shot(s)	Cointreau / triple sec
1¹/₂	shot(s)	Pressed pineapple juice
¹/₂	shot(s)	Freshly squeezed lemon juice
¹/₄	shot(s)	Sugar (gomme) syrup

Comment: A slight pineapple taste with sweet and sour.

GIN FIZZ

Glass: 8oz (Collins)
Garnish: Slice of lemon & mint
Method: Shake first four ingredients with ice and strain into glass filled with crushed ice. Then top up with soda delivered from a siphon – bottled soda is fine in a Collins but a true Gin Fizz must be made using a soda siphon. Gently churn (stir) drink.

2	shot(s)	Plymouth gin
1	shot(s)	Freshly squeezed lemon juice
1/2	shot(s)	Sugar (gomme) syrup
1/2	fresh	Egg white
Top up with		Soda water (club soda)

Comment: With the addition of egg white this drink becomes a 'Silver Fizz'; with egg yolk it becomes a 'Golden Fizz'. This mid-19th century classic is based on the Collins family of cocktails and the Ramos Gin Fizz derives from it. Everyone has heard of this clean, fresh, long drink but few have actually tried it.

GIN GENIE

Glass: Collins
Garnish: Mint sprig
Method: Muddle mint in base of shaker. Add other ingredients, shake with ice and strain into glass filled with crushed ice.

8	fresh	Mint leaves
1 1/2	shot(s)	Plymouth gin
1	shot(s)	Freshly squeezed lemon juice
1	shot(s)	Plymouth sloe gin
1/2	shot(s)	Sugar (gomme) syrup

Origin: Created in 2002 by Wayne Collins for Maxxium UK.
Comment: A great, fruit-led long drink for gin-loving Bowie fans.

GIN RICKEY

Glass: Collins / Old Fashioned
Garnish: Immerse length of lemon peel in drink.
Method: Shake first three ingredients with ice and strain into ice-filled glass, then top up with soda water.

2	shot(s)	Plymouth gin
1	shot(s)	Freshly squeezed lime juice
1/2	shot(s)	Sugar (gomme) syrup
Top up with		Soda water (club soda)

Origin: Shoemaker's restaurant in Washington, circa 1900. Named after Colonel Jim Rickey, the customer for whom the barman created the first Rickey.
Comment: Basically a short Collins.

GIN SLING

Glass: Sling
Garnish: Split lemon wedge and cherry on a stick
Method: Shake first three ingredients with ice and strain into ice-filled glass, then top up with soda water.

1	shot(s)	Plymouth gin
2	shot(s)	Bols Cherry brandy liqueur
1	shot(s)	Freshly squeezed lemon juice
Top up with		Soda water (club soda)

Comment: Add sugar to taste.

GIN SOUR

Glass: Old-fashioned
Garnish: Lemon wedge on rim
Method: Shake all ingredients with ice and strain into empty chilled glass.

2	shot(s)	Plymouth gin
2	shot(s)	Freshly squeezed orange juice
1	shot(s)	Freshly squeezed lemon juice
1/2	shot(s)	Sugar (gomme) syrup
1/2	fresh	Egg white

Comment: Smooth and sour with the obligatory gin kick.

GINA

Glass: Sling
Garnish: Blueberries on a stick
Method: Shake first three ingredients with ice and strain into ice-filled glass, then top up with sparkling water.

1	shot(s)	Sisca crème de cassis
2	shot(s)	Plymouth gin
¹/₂	shot(s)	Freshly squeezed lemon juice
Top up with		Sparkling water

AKA: Cassis Collins
Comment: The lemon and blackcurrant bring out the botanicals in the gin.

GINGER COSMO NEW

●●●●○

Glass: Martini
Garnish: Slice of ginger on rim
Method: Shake all ingredients with ice and fine strain into chilled glass.

2	shot(s)	Absolut Citron vodka
³/₄	shot(s)	The King's Ginger Liqueur
1¹/₄	shot(s)	Cranberry juice
¹/₄	shot(s)	Freshly squeezed lime juice
¹/₈	shot(s)	Sugar (gomme) syrup

Origin: Emerged during 2002 in New York City.
Comment: Just what it says on the tin – your everyday Cosmo given new vitality courtesy of a hint of ginger spice.

GINGER NUT

●●●◐○

Glass: Collins
Garnish: Lemon wedge
Method: Pour ingredients into ice-filled glass and stir.

1¹/₂	shot(s)	Frangelico hazelnut liqueur
1¹/₂	shot(s)	Absolut Citron vodka
Top up with		Jamaican Ginger beer

Comment: A long refreshing meld of strong flavours.

GINGER ROGERS

●●●●○

Glass: Martini
Garnish: Vanilla sugar rim
Method: Cut a few slivers of ginger from root and muddle with Bourbon in base of shaker. Add other ingredients, shake with ice and fine strain into glass.

3	slices	Root ginger (thumb-nail sized)
1	shot(s)	Buffalo Trace Bourbon
¹/₂	shot(s)	Teichenné vanilla schnapps
¹/₂	shot(s)	Cinnamon schnapps
¹/₂	shot(s)	King's Ginger liqueur
¹/₂	shot(s)	Freshly squeezed lime juice
¹/₂	shot(s)	Ginger sugar syrup

Origin: Adapted from a recipe created in 2002 by Steve Dingley of Behind Bars, England.
Comment: A sipping drink for lovers of ginger. By the way, they say it's an aphrodisiac.

GINGER TOM NEW

●●●●○

Glass: Collins
Garnish: Orange (flag) wheel and cheery on stick
Method: Muddle ginger in base of shaker. Add other ingredients, shake with ice and strain into ice-filled glass. Top up with soda, stir and serve with straws.

2	fresh	Thumbnail slices ginger
2	shot(s)	Plymouth gin
1	shot(s)	Freshly squeezed lime juice
¹/₂	shot(s)	Sugar (gomme) syrup
Top up with		Soda water (club soda)

Origin: Discovered in 2003 at Shish, London, England.
Comment: A classic Tom (gin) Collins with a refreshing hint of spicy ginger.

GINGERBREAD MAN-DARINE MARTINI

Glass: Martini
Garnish: Orange peel spiral
Method: Shake ingredients with ice and strain into glass.

2	shot(s)	Mandarine Napoléon Liqueur
1	shot(s)	Ginger liqueur
1	shot(s)	Pressed apple juice
¹/₂	shot(s)	Freshly squeezed lime juice

Comment: Fruit and spice - very nice.

GINGERTINI

●●●●○

Glass: Martini
Method: Shake all ingredients with ice and fine strain into glass.

2	shot(s)	Plymouth gin
¹/₂	shot(s)	King's Ginger liqueur
¹/₄	shot(s)	Cinzano Extra Dry vermouth
¹/₄	shot(s)	Sugar (gomme) syrup
¹/₂	shot(s)	Chilled water

Origin: I created this in 2002.
Comment: A delicate Martini with a warming hint of ginger.

GIUSEPPE'S HABIT

●●●●○

Glass: Martini
Garnish: Star anise
Method: Spray the oils from two lemon twists into the cocktail shaker, wipe them around the rim of the glass and drop them into the shaker. Pour other ingredients into shaker, shake with ice and fine strain into glass.

2	twists	Lemon
1¹/₂	shot(s)	Galliano
³/₄	shot(s)	Frangelico hazelnut liqueur
³/₄	shot(s)	Cointreau / triple sec
1¹/₄	shot(s)	Pressed apple juice

Origin: Created in 2002 by Leon Stokes at Zinc Bar & Grill, Birmingham, England.
Comment: An intriguing drink that combines hazelnut, orange, apple, aniseed and peppermint.

GIVE ME A DIME

● ● ● ● ● ○

Glass: Martini
Garnish: Crumbled Cadbury's Flake bar
Method: Shake all ingredients with ice and fine strain into chilled glass.

1¹/₂	shot(s)	Bols White crème de cacao
1¹/₂	shot(s)	Teichenné Butterscotch schnapps
1¹/₂	shot(s)	Double (heavy) cream

Comment: Creamy, sweet and tasty.

GLASS TOWER

Glass: Collins
Method: Shake first five ingredients with ice and strain into ice-filled glass, then top up with soda and stir.

¹/₂	shot(s)	Absolut vodka
1	shot(s)	Teichenné Peach schnapps
¹/₂	shot(s)	Havana Club light rum
1	shot(s)	Cointreau / triple sec
¹/₂	shot(s)	Opal Bianca sambuca
Top up with		Soda water (club soda)

Comment: A heady combination of spirits and liqueurs.

GLOOM CHASER

Glass: Martini
Garnish: Blackberry
Method: Shake ingredients with ice and strain into glass.

1	shot(s)	Orange curaçao
1	shot(s)	Mandarine Napoléon Liqueur
1	shot(s)	Freshly squeezed lemon juice
¹/₂	shot(s)	Grenadine syrup

Comment: A happy coloured drink for happy people: heavy on the orange.

GLOOM LIFTER

Glass: Martini
Method: Shake ingredients with ice and strain into glass.

2	shot(s)	Irish whiskey
1	shot(s)	Freshly squeezed lime juice
¹/₂	shot(s)	Sugar (gomme) syrup
¹/₂	fresh	Egg white

Comment: A whiskey sour with lime juice.

GODCHILD

Glass: Rocks
Method: Pour ingredients into ice-filled glass and stir.

1¹/₂	shot(s)	Rémy Martin Cognac
1¹/₂	shot(s)	Disaronno Originale amaretto

Comment: A Godfather with brandy – simple but great.

GODFATHER

Glass: Rocks
Method: Shake ingredients with ice and strain into ice-filled glass.

2	shot(s)	The Famous Grouse Scotch whisky
1	shot(s)	Disaronno Originale amaretto

Variant: Based on vodka, this drink becomes a Godmother.
Comment: Easy to make, only two ingredients – how come it's so good?

GODFREY

● ● ● ● ● ○

Glass: Rocks
Garnish: Three blackberries on drink
Method: Muddle blackberries in base of shaker. Add other ingredients, shake with ice and fine strain into glass filled with crushed ice.

6	fresh	Blackberries
1¹/₂	shot(s)	Rémy Martin Cognac
¹/₂	shot(s)	Grand Marnier
¹/₄	shot(s)	Bols Blackberry (crème de mûre) liqueur
¹/₄	shot(s)	Freshly squeezed lemon juice
¹/₄	shot(s)	Sugar (gomme) syrup

Origin: Created by Salvatore Calabrese at the Library Bar, Lanesborough Hotel, London, England.
Comment: Well balanced with a rich blackberry flavour.

GOLD

Glass: Martini
Method: Shake ingredients with ice and strain into glass.

1¹/₂	shot(s)	The Famous Grouse Scotch whisky
1	shot(s)	Cointreau / triple sec
1	shot(s)	Bols crème de banane

Comment: The whisky cancels out the sweetness of the Cointreau.

GOLD MEMBER

● ● ● ● ● ○

Glass: Martini
Garnish: Apple wedge on rim
Method: Shake all ingredients with ice and fine strain into chilled glass.

³/₄	shot(s)	Goldschläger cinnamon schnapps
³/₄	shot(s)	Teichenné Butterscotch schnapps
³/₄	shot(s)	Apple schnapps
2¹/₄	shot(s)	Pressed apple juice

Origin: I can't remember whose menu I ripped this off from: the proportions listed here are my own. If this is your drink, drop me a line and I'll credit you.
Comment: Hints of cinnamon and apple – an interesting tipple, if a tad sweet.

GOLDEN BIRD

Glass: Martini
Garnish: Orange beak on rim
Method: Shake ingredients with ice and strain into glass.

1	shot(s)	Mandarine Napoléon Liqueur
1	shot(s)	Havana Club light rum
1/2	shot(s)	Bols Crème de banane
1	shot(s)	Pressed pineapple juice
1 1/2	shot(s)	Freshly squeezed orange juice

Comment: Fruity with the Mandarine predominating.

GOLDEN CADILLAC I

Glass: Martini
Garnish: Sprinkle ground nutmeg
Method: Shake ingredients with ice and strain into glass.

1	shot(s)	Bols White crème de cacao
1 1/2	shot(s)	Freshly squeezed orange juice
1	shot(s)	Double (heavy) cream
1/4	shot(s)	Galliano

Comment: A silky smooth but not very potent cocktail.

GOLDEN CADILLAC II

Glass: Martini
Method: Shake ingredients with ice and strain into glass.

1 1/4	shot(s)	Absolut vodka
1 1/4	shot(s)	Teichenné Peach schnapps
1/4	shot(s)	Galliano
1	shot(s)	Double (heavy) cream
1	shot(s)	Milk

Comment: Light and creamy with the merest hint of peach, herbs and spices.

GOLDEN DAWN MARTINI

Glass: Martini
Method: Shake first five ingredients with ice and fine strain into chilled glass. Carefully pour grenadine into center of drink so that it sinks to create sunrise effect.

1	shot(s)	Plymouth gin
1	shot(s)	Calvados or Applejack brandy
1	shot(s)	Bols Apricot brandy liqueur
1	shot(s)	Freshly squeezed orange juice
1/4	shot(s)	Sugar (gomme) syrup
1/4	shot(s)	Grenadine syrup

Origin: There are many different versions of this classic drink (David Embury's 'The Fine Art Of Mixing Drinks' lists three, none of which resemble the above) but this is my favourite.
Comment: Apple and apricot flavours dominate this aptly named strong drink that has a sweet ending.

GOLDEN DRAGON

Glass: Collins
Garnish: Green apple wedge on rim
Method: Shake all ingredients with ice and strain into ice-filled glass.

2	shot(s)	Sauza Hornitos Tequila
3/4	shot(s)	Pisang Ambon liqueur
2 1/4	shot(s)	Pressed apple juice
3/4	shot(s)	Passion fruit syrup
1 1/4	shot(s)	Freshly squeezed lime juice

Comment: If you like bright green drinks, you'll love this tangily tropical mix.

GOLDEN DREAM MARTINI

Glass: Martini
Garnish: Sponge biscuit on rim
Method: Shake all ingredients with ice and fine strain into glass.

1	shot(s)	Cointreau / triple sec
1	shot(s)	Galliano
2	shot(s)	Freshly squeezed orange juice
1	shot(s)	Double (heavy) cream

Comment: Tastes remarkably syllabub-like.

GOLDEN GIRL NEW

Glass: Martini glass
Garnish: Grated orange zest
Method: Shake all ingredients with ice and fine strain into chilled glass.

1 1/4	shot(s)	Appleton Estate V/X aged rum
1	shot(s)	Pressed pineapple juice
1	shot(s)	Tawny Port
1/2	shot(s)	Sugar (gomme) syrup
1	fresh	Egg

Origin: Created by Dale DeGroff, New York, USA. I've slightly increased the proportions of rum and port to Dale's original recipe.
Comment: This appropriately named velvety drink is something of a refined dessert in a glass.

GOLDEN RETRIEVER

Glass: Martini
Garnish: Orange twist
Method: Stir all ingredients with ice and strain into glass.

1	shot(s)	Havana Club light rum
1	shot(s)	Green Chartreuse
1	shot(s)	Licor 43
1 1/2	shot(s)	Chilled water

Origin: Created in 2002 by Dick Bradsell at Alfred's Bar, London, England.
Comment: The simple drinks are the best and this straw yellow cocktail subtly offers a myriad of flavours.

GOLDEN SCREW

Glass: Flute
Garnish: Physalis fruit
Method: Pour all ingredients into glass and then lightly stir.

¹/₂	shot(s)	Rémy Martin Cognac
¹/₂	shot(s)	Bols Apricot brandy liqueur
1	shot(s)	Freshly squeezed orange juice
Top up with		Piper-Heidsieck Brut champagne

Variant: With gin in place of brandy.
Comment: Midas' favourite fruity fizz.

GOLDEN SHOT

Glass: Shot
Method: Layer ingredients in glass by carefully pouring in the following order.

¹/₂	shot(s)	Drambuie
¹/₂	shot(s)	Baileys Irish cream liqueur
¹/₂	shot(s)	Absolut vodka

Comment: A strong shot that is not too sweet.

GOLDEN SLIPPER

Glass: Martini
Garnish: Apricot slice on rim
Method: Vigorously shake all ingredients with ice and fine strain into chilled glass.

1¹/₂	shot(s)	Yellow Chartreuse
1¹/₂	shot(s)	Bols Apricot brandy liqueur
1	fresh	Egg yolk

Comment: Rich in colour and equally rich in flavour. A dessert with a punch.

GOLF COCKTAIL

Glass: Martini
Method: Shake ingredients with ice and strain into glass.

2	shot(s)	Plymouth gin
1	shot(s)	Cinzano Extra Dry vermouth
4	dashes	Angostura aromatic bitters

Comment: A 'wet' Martini with Angostura.

GOOMBAY SMASH

Glass: Collins
Garnish: Lime peel
Method: Shake all ingredients with ice and strain into glass filled with crushed ice.

1¹/₂	shot(s)	Pusser's Navy rum
³/₄	shot(s)	Malibu coconut rum liqueur
3	shot(s)	Pressed pineapple juice
¹/₄	shot(s)	Freshly squeezed lime juice
¹/₄	shot(s)	Cointreau / triple sec
¹/₄	shot(s)	Sugar (gomme) syrup

Comment: Smashes are usually short drinks that include muddled mint. Whatever's in a name, this is bound to get you smashed.

GRAND MIMOSA

UPDATED

Glass: Flute
Garnish: Strawberry on rim
Method: Shake orange juice and Grand Marnier with ice and strain into chilled glass. Top up with Champagne.

1	shot(s)	Grand Marnier
2	shot(s)	Freshly squeezed orange juice
Top up with		Piper-Heidsieck Brut Champagne

Origin: The Mimosa was created in 1925 at the Ritz Hotel, Paris and named after the Mimosa plant - probably because of its trembling leaves, rather like the gentle fizz of this mixture. The Grand Mimosa as shown here benefits from the addition of Grand Marnier liqueur.
Comment: As its name suggests, the orange of Grand Marnier heavily influences this drink. Basically a Buck's Fizz with more of a kick.

GRAND COSMOPOLITAN

Glass: Martini
Garnish: Flamed orange twist
Method: Shake ingredients with ice and strain into glass.

1½	shot(s)	Absolut Citron vodka
¾	shot(s)	Grand Marnier
1½	shot(s)	Cranberry juice
½	shot(s)	Freshly squeezed lime juice
½	shot(s)	Freshly squeezed lemon juice
½	shot(s)	Sugar (gomme) syrup
¼	shot(s)	Rose's lime cordial
2	dashes	Fee Brothers Orange bitters

Comment: One of the more complicated and most recent versions of this modern classic. Heavily promoted by Grand Marnier and rightly so.

GRAND PASSION

Glass: Martini
Method: Cut passion fruits in half and scoop seeds and flesh into shaker. Add other ingredients, shake well with ice and fine strain into chilled glass.

2	fresh	Passion fruits
2	shot(s)	Havana Club light rum
1½	shot(s)	Rubicon Passion fruit drink
2	dashes	Angostura aromatic bitters
¼	shot(s)	Sugar (gomme) syrup

Comment: Are you lacking a little passion in your life? There's passion aplenty in this fruity little number.

GRANDE CHAMPAGNE COSMO

Glass: Martini
Garnish: Flamed orange twist
Method: Shake all ingredients with ice and fine strain into chilled glass.

2	shot(s)	Rémy Martin Cognac
¾	shot(s)	Grand Marnier
½	shot(s)	Freshly squeezed lemon juice
1	shot(s)	Cranberry juice

Comment: 'Grande Champagne' refers to the top Cru of the Cognac region (see 'Cognac' in Sauce Guide to Drink & Drinking).

GRANNY'S MARTINI

Glass: Martini
Garnish: Apple wheel on rim
Method: Shake all ingredients with ice and strain into glass.

1½	shot(s)	Havana Club light rum
¼	shot(s)	Cinnamon schnapps liqueur
½	shot(s)	Apple schnapps liqueur
2	shot(s)	Pressed apple juice

Comment: An apple Daiquiri with a hint of cinnamon – apple and cinnamon were made for each other.

GRAPE DELIGHT

Glass: Martini
Garnish: Grapes in drink
Method: Muddle grapes in base of shaker. Add rest of ingredients, shake with ice and strain into glass.

10	fresh	Seedless red grapes
1½	shot(s)	Plymouth gin
½	shot(s)	Plymouth sloe gin
⅓	shot(s)	Sugar (gomme) syrup
½	shot(s)	Freshly squeezed lime juice
4	dashes	Angostura aromatic bitters

Comment: The rust colour of this drink comes from the Angostura bitters, sloe gin and the muddled skins of red grapes. These combine to provide its delicate balanced flavour.

GRAPE EFFECT NEW

Glass: Martini
Garnish: Grapes on stick
Method: Muddle grapes in base of shaker. Add other ingredients, shake with ice and fine strain into chilled glass.

12	fresh	Green grapes
2	shot(s)	Havana Club light rum
½	shot(s)	Elderflower cordial

Comment: Delicately flavoured and heavily laced with rum.

GRAPE ESCAPE

Glass: Collins
Garnish: Mint sprig
Method: Muddle grapes and mint in base of shaker. Add Cognac and sugar, shake with ice and strain into glass filled with crushed ice. Top up with Champagne and stir. Serve with straws.

8	fresh	Green grapes
5	fresh	Mint leaves
2	shot(s)	Rémy Martin Cognac
½	shot(s)	Sugar (gomme) syrup
Top up with		Piper-Heidsieck Brut Champagne

Origin: Created in 2000 by Brian Lucas and Max Warner at Long Bar @ Sanderson, London, England.
Comment: A cracking drink – subtle and refreshing.

GRAPEFRUIT DAIQUIRI

Glass: Martini
Garnish: Cherry
Method: Shake ingredients with ice and strain into glass.

2	shot(s)	Appleton Estate V/X aged rum
1½	shot(s)	Pressed grapefruit juice
¾	shot(s)	Sugar (gomme) syrup / passion fruit syrup

Comment: The flavours of rum and grapefruit combine perfectly – clean and fresh.

GRAPPA MANHATTAN

Glass: Martini
Garnish: Stemmed cherry on rim
Method: Stir all ingredients with ice and strain into chilled glass.

2	shot(s)	Grappa de Moscato
1¹/₂	shot(s)	Cinzano Rosso (sweet) vermouth
¹/₄	shot(s)	Maraschino syrup
2	dashes	Angostura aromatic bitters

Comment: Now that quality grappa is more widely available more aromatic cocktails like this are bound to follow.

GRATEFUL DEAD

Glass: Sling
Garnish: Split lime wedge
Method: Shake first seven ingredients with ice and strain into ice-filled glass. Then top up with soda.

¹/₂	shot(s)	Absolut vodka
¹/₂	shot(s)	Plymouth gin
¹/₂	shot(s)	Havana Club light rum
¹/₂	shot(s)	Cointreau / triple sec
¹/₂	shot(s)	Midori melon liqueur
1	shot(s)	Freshly squeezed lime juice
¹/₂	shot(s)	Sugar (gomme) syrup
Top up with		Soda water (club soda)

Origin: LA Iced Tea with Midori in place of Chambord liqueur.
Comment: Don't be put off by the colour, this is actually quite pleasant.

GREAT MUGHAL MARTINI

Glass: Martini
Garnish: Lemon twist
Method: Muddle raisins in base of shaker. Add other ingredients, shake with ice and strain into glass.

20		Raisins
1¹/₂	shot(s)	Buffalo Trace Bourbon
¹/₄	shot(s)	Sugar (gomme) syrup
³/₄	shot(s)	Passion fruit syrup
¹/₄	shot(s)	Freshly squeezed lime juice
3	drops	Rosewater
1	shot(s)	Lime & lemongrass cordial

Origin: Created in 2001 by Douglas Ankrah for Red Fort, Soho, London, England.
Comment: Douglas' original recipe called for raisin infused Bourbon and we'd recommend you make this drink that way if time permits.

GREEK BUCK

Glass: Collins
Garnish: Lime wedge
Method: Shake first two ingredients with ice and strain into ice-filled glass. Top up with ginger beer and float ouzo.

2	shot(s)	Metaxa brandy
¹/₂	shot(s)	Freshly squeezed lemon juice
Top up with		Ginger beer
¹/₂	shot(s)	Ouzo

Comment: Great refreshing long drink, with or without the ouzo.

GREEN DINOSAUR

Glass: Collins
Method: Shake first seven ingredients with ice and strain into ice-filled glass, then float Midori.

³/₄	shot(s)	Sauza Hornitos Tequila
³/₄	shot(s)	Havana Club light rum
³/₄	shot(s)	Plymouth gin
³/₄	shot(s)	Absolut vodka
³/₄	shot(s)	Cointreau / triple sec
1¹/₂	shot(s)	Freshly squeezed lime juice
1	shot(s)	Sugar (gomme) syrup
¹/₂	shot(s)	Midori melon liqueur

Comment: In a similar vein to the Grateful Dead - quite good and very alcoholic, with a melon kick.

GREEN EYES

Glass: Martini
Garnish: Lime wedge on rim
Method: Shake ingredients with ice and strain into glass.

1¹/₂	shot(s)	Absolut vodka
¹/₂	shot(s)	Bols Blue curaçao
3	shot(s)	Freshly squeezed orange juice

Comment: A refreshing version of the classic Screwdriver.

GREEN FAIRY

Glass: Martini
Method: Vigorously shake all ingredients with ice and strain into glass.

1	shot(s)	La Fée absinthe
1	shot(s)	Freshly squeezed lemon juice
³/₄	shot(s)	Sugar (gomme) syrup
1	shot(s)	Chilled water
1	dash(es)	Angostura aromatic bitters
¹/₂	fresh	Egg white

Origin: Created by Dick Bradsell.
Comment: An Absinthe sour style drink served straight up.

GREEN FLY

Glass: Shot
Method: Layer ingredients in glass by pouring carefully in the following order.

¹/₂	shot(s)	Midori melon liqueur
¹/₂	shot(s)	Green Crème de menthe
¹/₂	shot(s)	Green Chartreuse

Origin: Created by Alex Turner at The Circus Bar, London, England.
Comment: A strong shot made up of three different layers of different green liqueurs.

GREEN HORNET

Glass: Shot
Method: Shake all ingredients with ice and strain into chilled glass.

³/₄	shot(s)	Absolut vodka
¹/₈	shot(s)	La Fée absinthe
³/₄	shot(s)	Pisang Ambon liqueur
¹/₂	shot(s)	Rose's lime cordial

Comment: A bright green, surprisingly palatable and balanced shot.

GREEN MAMBA

Glass: Rocks
Method: Shake ingredients with ice and strain into ice-filled glass.

1/2	shot(s)	Absolut vodka
1	shot(s)	Teichenné Peach schnapps
1	shot(s)	Bols Blue curaçao
2	shot(s)	Freshly squeezed orange juice

Comment: Orange and peach dominate this green drink.

GREEN MIST

Glass: Martini
Method: Shake ingredients with ice and strain into glass.

1 1/2	shot(s)	Galliano
1	shot(s)	Green Chartreuse
1	shot(s)	Cinzano Extra Dry vermouth

Comment: A drink not for the fainthearted. If you've got a cold this will kill or cure you.

●●●●●○

GREEN TEA MARTINI

Glass: Martini
Garnish: Banana chunk on rim
Method: Shake all ingredients with ice and fine strain into chilled glass.

2	shot(s)	Zubrówka (Bison grass) vodka
1/4	shot(s)	Pisang Ambon liqueur
1/8	shot(s)	Green crème de menthe
2	shot(s)	Pressed apple juice

Comment: It's green and, although it doesn't actually contain any tea, has something of the flavour of alcoholic peppermint tea.

●●●●●○

GRETA GARBO UPDATED

Glass: Martini
Garnish: Star Aniseed
Method: Shake all ingredients with ice and fine strain into chilled glass.

2	shot(s)	Havana Club light rum
1/4	shot(s)	Maraschino liqueur
1/2	shot(s)	Sugar (gomme) syrup
1	shot(s)	Freshly squeezed lime juice
1/2	spoon	Pernod anise

Comment: A most unusual daiquiri.

GUILLOTINE

Glass: Flute
Garnish: Blackberry, blueberry and pear slice
Method: Stir ingredients with ice and strain into glass.

1/2	shot(s)	Sisca Crème de cassis
1/2	shot(s)	Poire William eau de vie
Top up with		Piper-Heidsieck Brut Champagne

Comment: Add some life to your bubbly!

●●●●●○

GULF COAST SEX ON THE BEACH

Glass: Collins
Method: Shake all ingredients with ice and strain into ice-filled glass.

2	shot(s)	Havana Club light rum
1	shot(s)	Midori melon liqueur
1	shot(s)	Bols crème de banane
2	shot(s)	Pressed pineapple juice
2	shot(s)	Cranberry juice
1/4	shot(s)	Freshly squeezed lime juice

Origin: Created in 1997 by Roberto Canino and Wayne Collins at Navajo Joe, London, England.
Comment: Golden tan in colour and tropical in flavour, complete with frothy top.

GUYANAN RASPBERRY PUNCH

Glass: Collins
Garnish: Lime wedge & raspberries
Method: Shake ingredients with ice and strain.

2	shot(s)	Pusser's Navy rum
1	shot(s)	Bols Raspberry (framboise)
3	shot(s)	Cranberry juice
3/4	shot(s)	Freshly squeezed lime juice
4	dashes	Angostura aromatic bitters
1/4	shot(s)	Sugar (gomme) syrup

AKA: Mui Rico
Comment: Very similar to Trader Vic's Shinglestain: rum and berries.

●●●●●○

GYPSY MARTINI

Glass: Martini
Garnish: Rosemary
Method: Muddle rosemary and raisins in base of shaker. Add gin, sugar and water, shake with ice and strain into glass.

1	sprig	Fresh rosemary (remove stalk)
10		Raisins
2	shot(s)	Plymouth gin
1/2	shot(s)	Sugar (gomme) syrup
1	shot(s)	Chilled water

Origin: Adapted from a recipe created by Jason Fendick in 2002 for Steam, London, England.
Comment: Jason's original recipe called for raisin infused gin and we'd recommend you make this drink that way if time permits.

●●●●●○

HAIR OF THE DOG UPDATED

Glass: Martini
Garnish: Grate fresh nutmeg
Method: Stir honey with Scotch so as to dissolve honey. Add other ingredients, shake with ice and fine strain into chilled glass.

3	spoons	Runny honey
2	shot(s)	The Famous Grouse Scotch whisky
1	shot(s)	Double (heavy) cream
1	shot(s)	Milk

Origin: Traditionally drunk as a pick-me-up hangover cure.
Comment: This drink's name and reputation as a hangover cure may lead you to wrongly assume it tastes unpleasant. Honey, whisky and cream combine wonderfully.

HARVARD

Glass: Martini
Garnish: Lemon twist
Method: Stir ingredients with ice and strain into glass.

2	shot(s)	Rémy Martin Cognac
1	shot(s)	Cinzano Rosso vermouth
1/8	shot(s)	Sugar (gomme) syrup
8	dashes	Angostura aromatic bitters

Comment: An acquired taste of distinction.

HARVARD COOLER

Glass: Collins
Garnish: Lemon peel spiral
Method: Shake first three ingredients with ice and strain into ice-filled glass, then top up with soda and stir.

2	shot(s)	Calvados or applejack brandy
1	shot(s)	Freshly squeezed lime juice
1	shot(s)	Sugar (gomme) syrup
Top up with		Soda water (club soda)

Comment: Lime and sugar bring out the apples of the Calvados.

HARVEY WALLBANGER

Glass: Collins
Garnish: Orange slice in drink
Method: Pour vodka and orange into ice-filled glass and stir, then float Galliano on top of drink.

2	shot(s)	Absolut vodka
4	shot(s)	Freshly squeezed orange juice
3/4	shot(s)	Galliano

Origin: Harvey was a surfer at Manhattan Beach, California. His favourite drink was a Screwdriver with added Galliano. One day in the late 60s, while celebrating winning a surfing competition, he staggered from bar to bar, banging his surfboard on the walls and so a contemporary classic got its name.
Comment: It's a mystery how this rather unexciting drink became a classic.

HAVANA COBBLER

Glass: Rocks
Method: Shake first three ingredients with ice and strain into ice-filled glass, then carefully float Port on top of drink.

2	shot(s)	Havana Club light rum
1/4	shot(s)	Sugar (gomme) syrup
1/2	shot(s)	Ginger wine
1	shot(s)	Ruby Port

Comment: A harsh start leads to subtle ginger and a warming finish.

HAVANATHEONE NEW ●●●●●

Glass: Martini
Garnish: Mint leaf
Method: Lightly muddle mint in base of shaker. Add rum and honey and stir so as to dissolve honey. Add other ingredients, shake with ice and fine strain into chilled glass.

10	fresh	Mint leaves
2	shot(s)	Havana Club light rum
1	spoon	Runny honey
1/2	shot(s)	Freshly squeezed lime juice
1	shot(s)	Pressed apple juice

Origin: Discovered in 2003 at Hush, London, England.
Comment: A flavoursome Daiquirí featuring honey, apple and mint.

HAWAIIAN

Glass: Collins
Garnish: Split pineapple wedge
Method: Shake ingredients with ice and strain into ice-filled glass.

2	shot(s)	Malibu coconut rum liqueur
1/2	shot(s)	Cointreau / triple sec
1/2	shot(s)	Havana Club light rum
2	shot(s)	Freshly squeezed orange juice
2	shot(s)	Pressed pineapple juice
1	shot(s)	Freshly squeezed lime juice
1/2	shot(s)	Sugar (gomme) syrup
1	shot(s)	Cream of coconut

Comment: A great cocktail but not for Martini drinkers!

HAWAIIAN COSMOPOLITAN ●●●●●○

Glass: Martini
Garnish: Pineapple wedge on rim
Method: Shake all ingredients with ice and fine strain into chilled glass.

2	shot(s)	Absolut Citron vodka
1	shot(s)	Sourz Pineapple liqueur
1	shot(s)	Pressed apple juice
1/2	shot(s)	Freshly squeezed lime juice

Origin: Created in 2002 by Wayne Collins for Maxxium UK.
Comment: Fresh, tangy and distinctly tropical.

HAWAIIAN SEABREEZE

Glass: Collins
Garnish: Split pineapple wedge
Method: Shake ingredients with ice and strain into ice-filled glass.

2	shot(s)	Absolut vodka
4	shot(s)	Pressed pineapple juice
2	shot(s)	Cranberry juice

Variant: Easygoing relative of the Seabreeze - virtually a twin of the Bay Breeze.

HAZEL'ITO

Glass: Collins
Method: Muddle mint in base of glass. Add other ingredients, fill glass with crushed ice and churn drink with bar spoon to mix.

12	fresh	Mint leaves
2	shot(s)	Havana Club light rum
2	shot(s)	Frangelico hazelnut liqueur
1	shot(s)	Freshly squeezed lime juice
1/2	shot(s)	Sugar (gomme) syrup

Created: Created in January 2002 by Adam Wyartt.
Comment: Looks like a Mojito but has a nutty twang courtesy of Frangelico.

HAZELNUT MARTINI

Glass: Martini
Garnish: Chocolate powder rim
Method: Stir ingredients with ice and strain into glass.

1/2	shot(s)	Frangelico hazelnut liqueur
2	shot(s)	Absolut vodka
1/2	shot(s)	Bols White crème de cacao
3/4	shot(s)	Sugar (gomme) syrup
1/2	shot(s)	Chilled water

Comment: A hazelnut vodkatini with a hint of chocolate.

HAZY LAZY DAYS

Glass: Martini
Method: Shake ingredients with ice and strain into glass.

2	shot(s)	Sauza Hornitos Tequila
3	shot(s)	Pressed pineapple juice

Comment: One for the pineapple addict.

HEAD SHOT

Glass: Shot
Method: Pour ingredients into glass. Ignite and drink through straw while still flaming.

3/4	shot(s)	Opal Nera black sambuca
1/2	shot(s)	Green Chartreuse

Comment: Extremely dangerous!

HEAD STRONG

Glass: Martini
Method: Shake all ingredients vigorously with ice and strain into glass.

1 1/2	shot(s)	Plymouth gin
1 1/2	shot(s)	Cinzano Extra Dry vermouth
3/4	shot(s)	Cointreau / triple sec
3/4	shot(s)	Bols Apricot brandy liqueur
1/4	shot(s)	Teichenné Peach schnapps

Origin: I created this drink in 1999.
Comment: Like its colour, this cocktail will seriously cloud your judgement.

HEATHER JULEP

Glass: Collins
Garnish: Mint sprig
Method: Lightly muddle mint with Scotch in base of shaker. (Only the leaves should be used, as the stems are bitter. The leaves should be bruised, not crushed, as crushing releases bitter juices.) Place shaker and its contents in refrigerator with serving glass for at least two hours. Remove glass from refrigerator and half fill with crushed ice. Place Drambuie and sugar into shaker base with Scotch and mint. Shake with ice and strain into glass. Churn the drink with the crushed ice using a bar spoon. Top up the glass with more crushed ice so as to fill it and churn again. Serve with two long straws.

12	fresh	Mint leaves
2 1/2	shot(s)	The Famous Grouse Scotch
1/2	shot	Drambuie liqueur
3/4	shot(s)	Sugar (gomme) syrup

Origin: Adapted from a drink discovered in 2001 at Teatro, London, England.
Comment: This Scottish twist on the Bourbon based Mint Julep is well worth the time it takes to make.

HEDGEROW SLING

Glass: Sling
Garnish: Seasonal berries & lemon slice
Method: Shake first three ingredients with ice and strain into ice-filled glass, then top up with soda and pour crème de mûre on top.

2	shot(s)	Plymouth sloe gin
1	shot(s)	Freshly squeezed lemon juice
1/4	shot(s)	Sugar (gomme) syrup
1/2	shot(s)	Bols Blackberry (crème de mûre) liqueur
Top up with		Soda water

Origin: Created by Brian Duell at Detroit, London, England.
Comment: Citrus and berries with fizz and an alcoholic float.

HEMINGWAY

Glass: Flute
Garnish: Apple star
Method: Pour anis into chilled glass, then top up with Champagne.

1	shot(s)	Pernod anise
Top up with		Piper-Heidsieck Brut Champagne

Origin: Created at Cantineros' Club, the famous Cuban bar school.
Comment: One for Anis obsessives.

THOSE DRINKS I'VE SAMPLED RECENTLY ARE GRADED AS FOLLOWS:

● DISGUSTING ●○ PRETTY AWFUL ●● BEST AVOIDED
●●○ DISAPPOINTING ●●● ACCEPTABLE ●●●○ GOOD
●●●● RECOMMENDED ●●●●○ HIGHLY RECOMMENDED
●●●●● OUTSTANDING / EXCEPTIONAL

HEMINGWAY SPECIAL DAIQUIRI UPDATED

Glass: 10oz Martini (huge)
Garnish: Lime wedge on rim
Method: Shake all ingredients with ice and fine strain into chilled glass.

3¹/₂	shot(s)	Havana Club light rum
1	shot(s)	Freshly squeezed grapefruit juice
1	shot(s)	Maraschino liqueur
1	shot(s)	Freshly squeezed lime juice
¹/₂	shot(s)	Sugar (gomme) syrup

AKA: Papa Doble Daiquiri
Origin: Created by Constante Ribailagua, the legendary owner of La Floridita, Havana, Cuba for Ernest Hemingway when he one day wondered into the bar to use the toilet. When Hemingway tried the Floridita's standard frozen Daiquiri, he is quoted as saying, "That's good but I prefer it without sugar and with double rum" – so the Hemingway Special was born.
Comment: A true Hemingway Special (also known as a Papa Doble) should be served without the addition of sugar. However, Hemingway had something of a hardened palate - more delicate drinkers will prefer the recipe above.

HENRY III COFFEE

Glass: Toddy
Garnish: Three coffee beans
Method: Place bar spoon in glass, add ingredients and top up with coffee, then float cream.

¹/₂	shot(s)	Kahlúa coffee liqueur
¹/₂	shot(s)	Rémy Martin Cognac
¹/₂	shot(s)	Galliano
¹/₂	shot(s)	Mandarine Napoléon Liqueur
Top up with		Filter coffee (hot)
Float		Lightly whipped cream

Comment: Far more interesting than Irish coffee.

HIGH VOLTAGE

Glass: Old-fashioned
Garnish: Lime wedge
Method: Pour ingredients into ice-filled glass, then top up with soda and gently stir.

1¹/₂	shot(s)	The Famous Grouse Scotch whisky
1	shot(s)	Cointreau / triple sec
1	shot(s)	Freshly squeezed lime juice
Top up with		Soda water

Comment: A refreshing, whisky based drink – add sugar to taste.

HIGHLAND SLING

Glass: Sling
Garnish: Apple wedge on rim
Method: Shake all ingredients with ice and strain into ice-filled glass.

1¹/₂	shot(s)	The Famous Grouse Scotch whisky
¹/₂	shot(s)	Galliano
1	shot(s)	Cranberry juice
¹/₂	shot(s)	Bols Apricot brandy liqueur
2	shot(s)	Pressed apple juice

Comment: A surprisingly good combination of diverse flavours.

HILLARY'S HELL RAISER

Glass: Rocks
Garnish: Orange zest
Method: Shake ingredients with ice and strain into ice-filled glass.

2	shot(s)	Absolut vodka
1	shot(s)	Teichenné Peach schnapps
2¹/₂	shot(s)	Freshly squeezed orange juice
¹/₄	shot(s)	Grenadine syrup

Comment: A medium-sweet cocktail with orange juice, peach schnapps and a hint of pomegranate.

HOBSON'S CHOICE VIRGIN

Glass: Collins
Method: Shake ingredients with ice and strain into ice-filled glass.

2¹/₂	shot(s)	Freshly squeezed orange juice
2¹/₂	shot(s)	Pressed apple juice
1	shot(s)	Freshly squeezed lime juice
¹/₂	shot(s)	Cassis syrup

Comment: A good non-alcoholic cocktail.

HONG KONG FUEY

Glass: Collins
Garnish: Orange slice & lime slice
Method: Shake first eight ingredients with ice and strain into ice-filled glass. Then top-up with lemonade.

¹/₂	shot(s)	Absolut vodka
¹/₂	shot(s)	Plymouth gin
¹/₂	shot(s)	Havana Club light rum
¹/₂	shot(s)	Sauza Hornitos Tequila
¹/₂	shot(s)	Midori melon liqueur
¹/₄	shot(s)	Freshly squeezed lemon juice
¹/₄	shot(s)	Rose's lime cordial
²/₃	shot(s)	Green Chartreuse
Top up with		Lemonade

Origin: Brought to the UK from the USA by Mark Armstrong, this recipe comes from Dick Bradsell.
Comment: A long and slightly sticky drink.

HONEY BEE

Glass: Shot
Method: Pour ingredients into chilled glass.

¹/₂	shot(s)	Becherovka
¹/₂	shot(s)	Apple schnapps
¹/₂	shot(s)	Piper-Heidsieck Brut Champagne

Origin: Created in 1999 by Spike Marchant at Alphabet, London, England.
Comment: A spicy shot with flavours of honey and apple.

HONEY & MARMALADE DRAM'TINI

Glass: Martini
Garnish: Strips of orange peel

Method: Stir honey with Scotch in base of shaker until honey dissolves. Add lemon and orange juice, shake with ice and fine strain into chilled glass.

2	shot(s)	The Famous Grouse Scotch whisky
4	spoons	Runny honey
1	shot(s)	Freshly squeezed lemon juice
1	shot(s)	Freshly squeezed orange juice

Origin: I adapted this recipe from the Honeysuckle-Tini, which is also in this guide.
Comment: This citrussy drink seems to enrich and enhance the flavour of Scotch.

HONEY VODKA SOUR

Glass: Rocks
Garnish: Maraschino cherry
Method: Shake ingredients with ice and strain into glass.

2	shot(s)	Krupnik honey vodka
2	shot(s)	Fresh lemon juice
1	shot(s)	Sugar (gomme) syrup
1/2	fresh	Egg white
4	dashes	Angostura aromatic bitters

Comment: A vodka sour with true character.

HONEY – MUCH SWEETER THAN WINE

Glass: Martini
Method: Shake ingredients with ice and strain into glass.

2	shot(s)	Drambuie Cream liqueur
1/4	shot(s)	Frangelico hazelnut liqueur
1/2	shot(s)	Bols Brown crème de cacao
1 1/2	shot(s)	Milk
1/4	shot(s)	Honey syrup

Comment: Sweet by name and by nature.

HONEY WALL

Glass: Martini
Garnish: Flamed orange twist
Method: Stir all ingredients with ice and fine strain into chilled glass.

1 1/2	shot(s)	Appleton Estate V/X aged rum
1 1/2	shot(s)	Tuaca liqueur
1 1/2	shot(s)	Kikor chocolate liqueur

Origin: Created in 2002 by Dick Bradsell at Downstairs at Alfred, London, England.
Comment: Strong, rich and chocolatey.

HONEY BERRY SOUR

Glass: Old-fashioned
Method: Shake ingredients with ice and strain into ice-filled glass.

1 1/2	shot(s)	Krupnik honey vodka
3/4	shot(s)	Chambord black raspberry liqueur
1	shot(s)	Freshly squeezed lemon juice
1/4	shot(s)	Sugar (gomme) syrup
1/2	fresh	Egg white

Origin: Created by Tim Hallilaj.

Comment: A smooth and rounded creation with great length.
Krupnik is a traditional Polish liqueur, now generally categorised and marketed as a vodka. Poles have been drinking mead (a fermented honey drink) since time immemorial, and vodka since at least the 15th century. Krupnik is made from Polish vodka infused with honey and spices, and has a genuine honey flavour.

HONEYMOON MARTINI

Glass: Martini
Method: Shake ingredients with ice and strain into glass.

1¼	shot(s)	Bénédictine D.O.M liqueur
1¼	shot(s)	Calvados or Applejack brandy
1¼	shot(s)	Freshly squeezed lemon juice
¼	shot(s)	Orange curaçao

Comment: A romantic combination of apple, orange, lemon and herbs.

HONEYSUCKLE'TINI

Glass: Martini
Garnish: Mint leaf

Method: Stir honey with rum in base of shaker until honey dissolves. Add lemon and orange juice, shake with ice and fine strain into chilled glass.

2	shot(s)	Havana Club light rum
4	spoons	Runny honey
1	shot(s)	Freshly squeezed lemon juice
1	shot(s)	Freshly squeezed orange juice

Variation: Made with gin in place of rum this drink becomes the 'Bee's Knees Martini'.
Origin: Adapted from a recipe in David Embury's 'The Fine Art Of Mixing Drinks'.
Comment: Honey – I love it!

HONOLULU MARTINI

Glass: Martini
Method: Shake ingredients with ice and strain into glass.

2	shot(s)	Plymouth gin
½	shot(s)	Freshly squeezed orange juice
½	shot(s)	Pressed pineapple juice
¾	shot(s)	Freshly squeezed lime juice
½	shot(s)	Sugar (gomme) syrup

AKA: Honolulu with fruit
Comment: Refreshing and quite complex.

HOOPLA

Glass: Martini
Garnish: Split orange wheel
Method: Shake ingredients with ice and strain into glass.

1¼	shot(s)	Rémy Martin Cognac
1¼	shot(s)	Cointreau / triple sec
1¼	shot(s)	Cinzano Extra Dry vermouth
1¼	shot(s)	Freshly squeezed lemon juice

Comment: Sharp and dry with orange and brandy length.

HOT RUM PUNCH

Glass: Toddy
Garnish: Ground nutmeg
Method: Place bar spoon in glass add ingredients and stir.

1	shot(s)	Mount Gay Eclipse golden rum
1	shot(s)	Rémy Martin Cognac
½	shot(s)	Fino Sherry
¼	shot(s)	Sugar (gomme) syrup
1	shot(s)	Freshly squeezed lime juice
1	pinch	Ginger spice
Top up with		Boiling water

Origin: Punch was one of many rum-based drinks popular in the 18th century - including the toddy, the flip and the sling. American taverns at the time would serve punch cold at the bar, and warm it on request by dunking a red-hot iron in it. This version is said to have been a favourite drink of Mozart the composer.
Punch had existed in India for 1500 years before colonialists brought it back to Europe. The name derives from the Hindi word for five, 'panch', and refers to the five key ingredients: alcohol, citrus, sugar, water and spices. In India, it was made with Arrack (a local spirit).

Comment: A great winter warmer!

HOP TOAD NEW

Glass: Martini
Garnish: Apricot wedge on rim
Method: Shake all ingredients with ice and fine strain into a chilled glass.

1³/₄ shot(s)	Appleton Estate V/X aged rum
1 shot(s)	Bols Apricot brandy liqueur
1 shot(s)	Freshly squeezed lime juice
¹/₂ shot(s)	Sugar (gomme) syrup

Variation: Made with brandy this is sometimes known as a Bullfrog.
Origin: First published in Tom Bullock's Ideal Bartender, circa 1917.
Comment: Alcoholic apricot jam with a lovely twang of aged rum.

HORSE'S NECK WITH A KICK

Glass: Collins
Garnish: Peel rind of a large lemon in a spiral, place in glass with end hanging over rim.
Method: Place lemon spiral in glass and fill glass with ice. Pour in Bourbon and Angostura, then top up with ginger ale and stir.

2 shot(s)	Buffalo Trace Bourbon
4 dashes	Angostura aromatic bitters
Top up with	Ginger ale

Comment: A Horse's Neck without a kick is simply ginger ale and bitters.

HOT BUTTERED JACK

Glass: Toddy
Garnish: Grate nutmeg over drink
Method: Place butter and barspoon in glass. Half fill glass with boiling water and stir so as to dissolve butter. Add whisky and sugar, fill glass with boiling water and stir.

1 large	Knob (pat) salted butter
Half fill with	Boiling water
2 shot(s)	Jack Daniel's Tennessee whisky
³/₄ shot(s)	Sugar (gomme) syrup
Top up with	Boiling water

Comment: Warming and smooth – great on a cold day or just when you fancy a warning treat.

HOT BUTTERED RUM

Glass: Toddy
Garnish: Cinnamon stick and slice of lemon with cloves
Method: Place bar spoon in glass, add ingredients and stir.

3 spoons	Myers's Planters' Punch rum
¹/₂ shot(s)	Freshly squeezed lemon juice
¹/₂ shot(s)	Sugar (gomme) syrup
4 shot(s)	Pressed apple juice
¹/₄ spoon	Ground cinnamon
¹/₄ spoon	Ground nutmeg
1¹/₂ knob(s)	Unsalted butter
Top up with	Boiling water

Comment: Hot, spicy and aromatic.

HOT PASSION

Glass: Collins
Garnish: Split cherry on rim
Method: Shake ingredients with ice and strain into ice-filled glass.

1 shot(s)	Passoã passion fruit liqueur
1 shot(s)	Absolut vodka
3 shot(s)	Cranberry juice
3 shot(s)	Freshly squeezed orange juice

Comment: Tasty but slightly artificial version of a Madras.

HOT SHOT

Glass: Shot
Method: Pour Galliano into glass, then layer coffee and float cream.

³/₄ shot(s)	Galliano
³/₄ shot(s)	Espresso coffee (hot)
Float	Lightly whipped cream

Comment: Once big in Sweden.

HOT TODDY

Glass: Toddy
Garnish: Cinnamon stick
Method: Place bar spoon in glass, add ingredients and stir.

2 shot(s)	The Famous Grouse Scotch whisky
1 shot(s)	Sugar (gomme) syrup
3	Cloves
¹/₂ shot(s)	Freshly squeezed lemon juice
1 spoon	Runny honey
Top up with	Boiling water

Comment: Spicy, warming and great for when you're feeling down with a cold or flu.

HUNK MARTINI NEW

Glass: Martini
Garnish: Cherry in drink
Method: Shake all ingredients with ice and fine strain into chilled glass.

2 shot(s)	Absolut Vanilia
1³/₄ shot(s)	Pressed pineapple juice
¹/₂ shot(s)	Freshly squeezed lime juice
¹/₄ shot(s)	Sugar (gomme) syrup

Origin: The drink Carrie and co discovered in the summer of 2003. In this series the Sex And The City stars dropped Cosmopolitans in favour of Hunks – no change there then!
Comment: Pineapple and vanilla combine wonderfully. American readers may notice more than a passing resemblance to a Key Lime Pie served without the Graham Cracker rim.

HURRICANE UPDATED

●●●●○

Glass: Hurricane
Garnish: Pineapple wedge on rim
Method: Shake all ingredients with ice and strain into ice-filled glass.

1	shot(s)	Havana Club light rum
1	shot(s)	Pusser's Navy rum
1/2	shot(s)	Galliano liqueur
2	shot(s)	Freshly squeezed orange juice
2	shot(s)	Pressed pineapple juice
1	shot(s)	Passion fruit syrup
3/4	shot(s)	Freshly squeezed lime juice
3 dashes		Angostura aromatic bitters

Origin: Thought to have originated in 1939 at The Hurricane Bar, New York City but made famous by Pat O'Brien's in New Orleans. Some old cocktail books list a much earlier Hurricane made with Cognac, absinthe and vodka.
Comment: A fruit-packed, strong, tangy refreshing drink that relies on good the use of a flavoursome Naval rum.

HYDE & SEEK

Glass: Martini
Garnish: Orange slice in glass
Method: Shake ingredients with ice and strain into ice-filled glass.

2	shot(s)	Passoã passion fruit liqueur
1/2	shot(s)	Kahlúa coffee liqueur
1	shot(s)	Double (heavy) cream
1	shot(s)	Milk

Comment: Pink and fluffy.

IGNORANCE IS BLISS

Glass: Martini
Method: Shake ingredients with ice and strain into glass.

1	shot(s)	Absolut Citron vodka
1	shot(s)	Campari
1	shot(s)	Passion syrup
1	shot(s)	Pressed apple juice

Origin: Created by Alex Kammerling in 2000.
Comment: A balance of sweetness, flavour and bitterness.

IGUANA

Glass: Shot
Method: Shake ingredients with ice and strain into glass.

1/2	shot(s)	Absolut vodka
1/2	shot(s)	Sauza Hornitos Tequila
1/2	shot(s)	Kahlúa coffee liqueur

Comment: Coffee and Tequila's successful relationship is enhanced by the introduction of vodka.

IGUANA WANA

Glass: Rocks
Garnish: Orange slice
Method: Shake all ingredients with ice and strain into ice-filled glass.

3/4	shot(s)	Absolut vodka
1	shot(s)	Teichenné Peach schnapps
2 1/2	shot(s)	Freshly squeezed orange juice

Comment: Orange juice and peach schnapps, laced with vodka.

ILLUSION

●●●●○○

Glass: Collins
Garnish: Watermelon wedge on rim
Method: Shake all ingredients with ice and strain into ice-filled glass.

1 3/4	shot(s)	Absolut vodka
1	shot(s)	Cointreau / triple sec
1	shot(s)	Midori Melon liqueur
3	shot(s)	Freshly pressed pineapple juice

Comment: This medium-sweet, lime green drink is one for a summer's day by the pool.

IMPERIAL

Glass: Martini
Garnish: Green olive
Method: Stir ingredients with ice and strain into glass.

1 1/2	shot(s)	Plymouth gin
1 1/2	shot(s)	Cinzano Extra Dry vermouth
4	dashes	Angostura aromatic bitters
1/8	shot(s)	Maraschino liqueur

Comment: Very dry and refined – not for everyone.

INCOGNITO

●●●○○

Glass: Martini
Garnish: Apricot slice on rim
Method: Shake all ingredients with ice and fine strain into chilled glass.

1 1/2	shot(s)	Rémy Martin Cognac
1 1/2	shot(s)	Cinzano Extra Dry vermouth
1	shot(s)	Bols Apricot brandy liqueur
3	dashes	Angostura aromatic bitters

Comment: Dry with hints of sweet apricot – most unusual.

INK MARTINI NEW

●●●●○

Glass: Martini
Garnish: Orange twist
Method: Shake all ingredients with ice and fine strain into chilled glass.

1 1/4	shot(s)	Plymouth gin
1/2	shot(s)	Bols Blue Curaçao
1/2	shot(s)	Teichenné peach schnapps liqueur
2	shot(s)	Cranberry juice

Origin: Created in 2002 by Gentian Naci at Bar Epernay, Mailbox, Birmingham, England.
Comment: This simple, peachy-orange, appropriately named drink is surprisingly quaffable.

IN-MOTION-AL'TINI

Glass: Martini
Garnish: Lychee from tin in drink
Method: Stir all ingredients with ice and strain into chilled glass.

1	shot(s)	The Famous Grouse Scotch
1	shot(s)	Calvados or Applejack brandy
1	shot(s)	Lychee syrup from tinned fruit
1/2	shot(s)	Kwai Feh lychee liqueur
1/2	shot(s)	Ginger wine
1/2	shot(s)	Cinzano Rosso (sweet) vermouth

Origin: I created this drink in December 2002.
Comment: Follow the recipe carefully and make this for someone without the garnish and I defy them to name more than two of the six ingredients.

INTERNATIONAL INCIDENT

Glass: Martini
Method: Shake all ingredients with ice and fine strain into chilled glass.

3/4	shot(s)	Absolut vodka
3/4	shot(s)	Kahlúa coffee liqueur
3/4	shot(s)	Disaronno Originale amaretto
3/4	shot(s)	Frangelico hazelnut liqueur
1 1/2	shot(s)	Baileys Irish Cream liqueur

Comment: Rich and creamy.

INTIMATE

Glass: Martini
Garnish: Lemon peel twist & olive on stick.
Method: Shake ingredients with ice and strain into glass.

2	shot(s)	Absolut vodka
1/2	shot(s)	Cinzano Extra Dry vermouth
1	shot(s)	Bols Apricot brandy liqueur
4	dashes	Fee Brothers Orange bitters

Comment: Not too sweet.

IRISH ALEXANDER

Glass: Martini
Garnish: Crumbled Cadbury's Flake bar
Method: Shake all ingredients with ice and fine strain into chilled glass.

1 1/2	shot(s)	Baileys Irish Cream liqueur
1 1/2	shot(s)	Rémy Martin Cognac
1	shot(s)	Double (heavy) cream

Comment: Rich, thick, creamy and yummy.

IRISH CHARLIE

Glass: Shot
Method: Shake ingredients with ice and strain into glass.

3/4	shot(s)	Baileys Irish cream liqueur
3/4	shot(s)	White crème de menthe

Comment: The ingredients go surprisingly well together.

IRISH COFFEE

UPDATED

Glass: Toddy
Garnish: Three coffee beans.
Method: Place bar spoon in glass, add whiskey, then top up with coffee and stir. Float cream.

1	shot(s)	Irish whiskey
Top up with		Filter coffee (hot)
Float		Lightly whipped cream

AKA: Gaelic Coffee.

Tip: Heat the cream slightly and pour into the bowl of the spoon to get a better float.

Origin: Created in 1942 by Joe Sheridan, a bartender at Foynes Airport (near the present-day Shannon airport. In 1947, at the end of a trip to Ireland, an American journalist, Stan Delaphane, visited Joe Sheridan's bar and tried an Irish Coffee. Delaphane was so impressed that on returning home he passed the recipe on to the bartender at his local bar, the Buena Vista Café, in San Francisco. So the recipe spread and the drink became a classic.

Comment: Coffee with a whisky kick - a simple, but great idea.

IRISH CHOCOLATE ORANJ'TINI

Glass: Martini
Garnish: Crumbled Cadbury's Flake bar
Method: Shake all ingredients with ice and fine strain into chilled glass.

1½	shot(s)	Baileys Irish Cream liqueur
1½	shot(s)	Kahlúa coffee liqueur
1½	shot(s)	Grand Marnier

Comment: A B-52 served 'up'.

IRISH ESPRESSO'TINI

Glass: Martini
Garnish: Float three coffee beans
Method: Shake all ingredients with ice and fine strain into chilled glass.

2	shot(s)	Baileys Irish Cream liqueur
1¼	shot(s)	Vanilla infused Absolut vodka
1¼	shot(s)	Espresso coffee (cold)

Comment: Richly flavoured with a pleasingly bitter finish.

IRISH FLAG

Glass: Shot
Method: Layer in glass by carefully pouring each ingredient in the following order.

½	shot(s)	Grand Marnier
½	shot(s)	Green crème de menthe
½	shot(s)	Baileys Irish cream liqueur

Comment: Orange and mint smoothed with cream liqueur.

IRISH FRAPPE

Glass: Hurricane
Garnish: Float three coffee beans
Method: Blend all ingredients with two scoops of crushed ice and serve with straws.

3	shot(s)	Baileys Irish Cream liqueur
2	shot(s)	Espresso coffee (cold)
2	scoops	Coffee ice cream

Comment: A tasty frappé for evening consumption: coffee, cream and a hint of whiskey.

IRISH FORTY NINE COFFEE

Glass: Toddy
Garnish: Three coffee beans.
Method: Place bar spoon in glass, add Bailey's and Drambuie, then top up with coffee and float cream.

1	shot(s)	Baileys Irish cream liqueur
1	shot(s)	Drambuie
Top up with		Filter coffee (hot)
Float		Lightly whipped cream

Comment: Creamy, rich coffee.

IRISH LATTE

Glass: Toddy
Method: Pour ingredients into glass in the following order.

1	shot(s)	Hot Illy espresso coffee
1½	shot(s)	Baileys Irish Cream liqueur
Top up with		Steamed semi-skimmed foaming milk

Comment: A latte with extra interest and flavour courtesy of Irish cream liqueur.

IRISH MANHATTAN UPDATED

Glass: Martini
Garnish: Shamrock
Method: Stir all ingredients with ice and strain into chilled glass.

1½	shot(s)	Buffalo Trace Bourbon
1	shot(s)	Tuaca liqueur
½	shot(s)	Mandarine Napoléon liqueur
¼	shot(s)	Vanilla syrup
1	shot(s)	Chilled water

Origin: Adapted from a drink discovered in 2001 at Detroit, London, England.
Comment: There's nothing Irish about this drink, but it's good all the same.

ISLAND AFFAIR

Glass: Hurricane
Garnish: Starfruit
Method: Blend ingredients with ice and serve.

1	shot(s)	Midori melon liqueur
1	shot(s)	Cointreau / triple sec
1	shot(s)	Bols Blue curaçao
3	shot(s)	Mango juice
3	shot(s)	Freshly squeezed orange juice
1	shot(s)	Cream of coconut

Comment: Very tropical.

ISLAND BREEZE

Glass: Collins
Garnish: Grapefruit wedge on rim
Method: Shake all ingredients with ice and strain into ice-filled glass.

2	shot(s)	Malibu coconut rum liqueur
3	shot(s)	Cranberry juice
2	shot(s)	Freshly squeezed grapefruit juice

Origin: Named after the Twelve Islands Shipping Company – the Caribbean producers of Malibu.
Comment: Great balance of sweet and sour flavours.

ITALIAN COFFEE

Glass: Toddy
Garnish: Three coffee beans.
Method: Place bar spoon in glass, add amaretto and coffee liqueur, then top up with coffee and float cream.

1	shot(s)	Disaronno Originale amaretto
1/2	shot(s)	Kahlúa coffee liqueur
Top up with		Filter coffee (hot)
Float		Lightly whipped cream

Comment: One to remember!

ITALIAN COLADA

Glass: Collins
Method: Blend ingredients with crushed ice and pour into glass.

3/4	shot(s)	Rémy Martin Cognac
3/4	shot(s)	Havana Club light rum
1/4	shot(s)	Disaronno Originale amaretto
2	shot(s)	Pressed pineapple juice
1/2	shot(s)	Cream of coconut
1/2	shot(s)	Double (heavy) cream

Comment: Not overly sweet, but the cream and amaretto make it heavy.

ITALIAN JOB # 1

●●●●○

Glass: Collins
Method: Shake all ingredients apart from tonic with ice and strain into ice-filled glass. Top up with tonic water.

1	shot(s)	Monasterium liqueur
1	shot(s)	Campari
1	shot(s)	Mandarine Napoléon Liqueur
2	shot(s)	Pressed grapefruit juice
3/4	shot(s)	Freshly squeezed lemon juice
1/2	shot	Sugar (gomme) syrup
Top up with		Tonic water

Origin: Created by Tony Conigliaro in 2001 at Isola, Knightsbridge, London, England.
Comment: This orange coloured drink combines sweet and sour flavours in a most interesting and grown up way.

THE ITALIAN JOB #2 NEW

●●●●◐

Glass: Sling
Garnish: Orange peel twist
Method: Shake first three ingredients with ice and stain into glass filled with crushed ice. Top up with wine and serve with straws.

1	shot(s)	Tuaca liqueur
1	shot(s)	Disaronno Originale amaretto
1	shot(s)	Cranberry juice
Top up with		Red wine (Shiraz)

Origin: Discovered in 2002 at Rapscallion, Clapham, England.
Comment: Mix layers with straw prior to drinking for vanilled, almond fruity wine.

ITALIAN STINGER

Glass: Rocks
Method: Pour ingredients into ice-filled glass and stir.

1	shot(s)	Galliano
2	shot(s)	Italian brandy

Variant: With one shot of white crème de menthe in place of brandy.
Comment: For the hardcore.

ITALIAN SUN UPDATED

●●●●○

Glass: Martini
Garnish: Lemon twist
Method: Shake all ingredients with ice and fine strain into chilled glass.

2	shot(s)	Sauvignon Blanc or Pinot Grigio wine
1 1/2	shot(s)	Pallini Limoncello liqueur
3/4	shot(s)	Frangelico hazelnut liqueur
1/2	shot(s)	Freshly squeezed lemon juice

Origin: Created in 2002 by Dan Spink at Browns, St Martin's Lane, London, England.
Comment: Tastes reminiscent of a Bon Bon (a round, sugar coated, lemon flavoured sweet).

ITALIAN SURFER WITH A RUSSIAN ATTITUDE

Glass: Martini
Method: Shake ingredients with ice and strain into glass.

1 1/2	shot(s)	Absolut vodka
3/4	shot(s)	Disaronno Originale amaretto
3/4	shot(s)	Malibu coconut rum liqueur
1	shot(s)	Pressed pineapple juice
1	shot(s)	Cranberry juice

Variant: Served as a long drink, over ice in a Collins glass.
Comment: Tastes very similar to a Piña Colada – just a bit more sophisticated.

I.V.F. MARTINI

●●●●◐

Glass: Martini
Garnish: Float three coffee beans
Method: Shake first three ingredients with ice and strain into glass. Float cream on top.

1	shot(s)	La Fée absinthe
1	shot(s)	Kahlúa coffee liqueur
2	shot(s)	Espresso coffee (cold)
1	shot(s)	Double (heavy) cream

Origin: Created by Giovanni Burdi of abv Ltd, England.
Comment: IVF, or in vitro fertilisation, is when eggs are fertilised outside the womb in a test tube. After the woman has consumed copious amounts of fertility drugs, the fertilised eggs are then inserted back into the womb. What all this has to do with the name of a drink is anyone's guess.

JACK-IN-THE-BOX

Glass: Martini
Garnish: Small split pineapple wedge.
Method: Shake ingredients with ice and strain into glass.

2	shot(s)	Calvados (or applejack brandy)
2	shot(s)	Pressed pineapple juice
4	dashes	Angostura aromatic bitters
1/2	shot(s)	Sugar (gomme) syrup

Comment: Short and appley.

JACK PUNCH

Glass: Collins
Garnish: Pineapple wedge on rim
Method: Cut passion fruit in half and scoop seeds and flesh into shaker. Add other ingredients, shake with ice and strain into ice-filled glass.

1	fresh	Passion fruit
2	shot(s)	Jack Daniel's Tennessee whiskey
1/2	shot(s)	Cuarenta Y Tres (Licor 43)
2	shot(s)	Rubicon Passion fruit drink
2	shot(s)	Pressed pineapple juice
1/8	shot(s)	Sugar (gomme) syrup
4	dashes	Angostura aromatic bitters

Origin: Adapted from a recipe created in 2002 at Townhouse, London, England.
Comment: Vanilla hints in Jack Daniel's and Licor 43 combine to dominate this fruity long drink.

JACK ROSE NEW

Glass: Martini
Garnish: Sugar rim
Method: Shake all ingredients with ice and fine strain into chilled glass.

2	shot(s)	Calvados (or applejack brandy)
3/4	shot(s)	Grenadine syrup
3/4	shot(s)	Freshly squeezed lemon juice
3/4	shot(s)	Chilled water

Origin: Apparently named after the 1920s New York gangster.
Comment: Rose-coloured, tart and appley.

JACKIE O'S ROSE

Glass: Martini
Garnish: Sugar rim
Method: Shake ingredients with ice and strain into glass.

2	shot(s)	Havana Club light rum
1	shot(s)	Freshly squeezed lime juice
1/2	shot(s)	Sugar (gomme) syrup
1/2	shot(s)	Cointreau / triple sec

Comment: A Daiquirí with Cointreau - or a Margarita with rum. Nice balance of sweet and sour, anyway.

JACKTINI

Glass: Martini
Method: Shake all ingredients with ice and strain into glass.

1	shot(s)	Jack Daniel's Tennessee whiskey
1	shot(s)	Mandarine Napoléon
1³/4	shot(s)	Freshly squeezed lemon juice
1/2	shot(s)	Sugar (gomme) syrup

Comment: A citrus bite and a smooth Tennessee whisky draw enhanced with mandarine.

JACUZZI

Glass: Flute
Garnish: Peach slice
Method: Shake first three ingredients with ice and strain into glass, then top up with Champagne.

1	shot(s)	Teichenné Peach schnapps
1/2	shot(s)	Plymouth gin
1	shot(s)	Freshly squeezed orange juice
Top up with		Piper-Heidsieck Brut Champagne

Comment: Gin balances the sweetness of peach schnapps in this fruity Champagne cocktail.

JADED LADY

Glass: Martini
Method: Shake ingredients with ice and strain into glass.

1	shot(s)	Plymouth gin
1	shot(s)	Bols Blue curaçao
1	shot(s)	Warninks advocaat
1¹/2	shot(s)	Freshly squeezed orange juice

Comment: Thick and creamy with more than a hint of gin.

JALISCO NEW

Glass: Martini
Garnish: Two green grapes on stick on rim
Method: Muddle grapes in base of shaker. Add other ingredients, shake with ice and fine strain into chilled glass.

12	fresh	Green grapes
2¹/2	shot(s)	Sauza Hornitos Tequila
1/2	shot(s)	Sugar (gomme) syrup
3	dashes	Fee Brothers orange bitters

Origin: Created in 2003 by Shelim Islam at GE Club, London, England. Pronounced 'Hal-is-co', this cocktail takes its name from the Mexican state that is home to the town of Tequila and the spirit of the same name.
Comment: It's amazing just how well grapes combine with Tequila. Grape and lily (for that's what an agave is) – what a combination.

JAMAICAN MULE

Glass: Collins
Garnish: Squeeze lime and drop in glass.
Method: Pour ingredients into ice-filled glass and lightly stir.

2	shot(s)	Spiced rum
1/2	shot(s)	Freshly squeezed lime juice
1/2	shot(s)	Sugar (gomme) syrup
Top up with		Ginger beer

Comment: A long rum based drink with a spicy ginger taste.

JAMAICAN SUNSET

Glass: Collins
Method: Shake all ingredients with ice and strain into ice-filled glass.

1 1/2	shot(s)	Wray & Nephew overproof rum
2	shot(s)	Cranberry juice
4	shot(s)	Freshly squeezed orange juice

Comment: Made with vodka as a base this drink would be called a Madras. Rum adds both strength and flavour.

JA-MORA

Glass: Flute
Garnish: Float single raspberry.
Method: Shake first four ingredients with ice and strain into glass. Layer Champagne using barspoon to create a two layered drink.

1	shot(s)	Freshly squeezed orange juice
1	shot(s)	Pressed apple juice
1	shot(s)	Absolut vodka
1	shot(s)	Chambord black raspberry liqueur
Top up with		Piper-Heidsieck Brut Champagne

Origin: Created by Jamie Terrell and Andres Masso in 1998. Named after 'mora', the Spanish for raspberry. The 'j' and 'a' stand for the names of its two creators.
Comment: Very moreish with loads of flavour.

JAPANESE COCKTAIL **UPDATED**

Glass: Martini
Garnish: Lemon twist
Method: Shake all ingredients with ice and fine strain into chilled glass.

3	shot(s)	Rémy Martin Cognac
3/4	shot(s)	Almond (orgeat) syrup
3	dashes	Angostura aromatic bitters
1	shot(s)	Chilled water

Origin: A classic (retro) cocktail which features in Jerry Thomas' 1887 cocktail book.
Comment: Lightly sweetened and diluted Cognac flavoured and with almond and a hint of spice.

JAPANESE PEAR

Glass: Martini
Garnish: Pear slice on rim
Method: Shake all ingredients with ice and strain into glass.

1 1/2	shot(s)	Absolut vodka
1	shot(s)	Sake
1/2	shot(s)	Poire William eau de vie
1/4	shot(s)	Sugar (gomme) syrup

Origin: Adapted in 2002 from a recipe from Grand Pacific Blue Room, Sydney, Australia.
Comment: Originally made with Poire William liqueur, hence this version calls for a little sugar.

JAPANESE SLIPPER

Glass: Martini
Garnish: Sugar rim
Method: Shake ingredients with ice and strain into glass.

1 1/2	shot(s)	Sauza Hornitos Tequila
1 3/4	shot(s)	Midori melon liqueur
3/4	shot(s)	Freshly squeezed lime juice
1/2	shot(s)	Sugar (gomme) syrup

Comment: A vivid green combination of melon and tequila with a hint of lime.

JASMINE

Glass: Martini
Garnish: Lemon zest
Method: Shake all ingredients with ice and strain into glass.

1	shot(s)	Plymouth gin
1/2	shot(s)	Campari
1/2	shot(s)	Cointreau / triple sec
1	shot(s)	Freshly squeezed lemon juice
1/3	shot(s)	Sugar (gomme) syrup
1/2	shot(s)	Chilled water

Origin: Created by Alex Turner in 2001.
Comment: Delicate pinky colour with the distinctive flavour of Campari enhanced by lemon and orange.

JAYNE MANSFIELD

Glass: Flute
Garnish: Strawberry on rim
Method: Muddle strawberries in base of shaker. Add other ingredients, shake with ice and fine strain into glass.

4	fresh	Hulled strawberries
1	shot(s)	Havana Club light rum
1	shot(s)	Bols Strawberry (fraise) liqueur
1/4	shot(s)	Sugar (gomme) syrup
Top up with		Piper-Heidsieck Brut Champagne

Origin: Named after the Hollywood actress.
Comment: Champagne is made to go with strawberries.

JEAN-MARC

●●●●◖

NEW

Glass: Collins
Garnish: Mint sprig
Method: Muddle mint and ginger in base of shaker. Add other ingredients, shake with ice and fine strain into ice-filled glass. Top up with Appletiser, stir and serve with straws.

2	fresh	Thumb-nail sized slices ginger
4	fresh	Mint leaves
1½	shot(s)	Green Chartreuse
¼	shot(s)	Apple schnapps
Top up with		Appletiser

Origin: Created in 2003 by yours truly after judging a Chartreuse Cocktail competition in London and realising which flavours best combine with Chartreuse. Named after my friend the President Directeur General of Chartreuse.
Comment: Chartreuse combines well with apple, ginger and mint – they're all in this long, refreshing, summertime drink.

●●●●○

JELLY BELLY BEANY NEW

Glass: Martini
Garnish: Jelly Beans
Method: Shake all ingredients with ice and fine strain into chilled glass.

1½	shot(s)	Havana Club light rum
1	shot(s)	Teichenné peach schnapps
1	shot(s)	Malibu coconut rum liqueur
2	dashes	Fee Brothers orange bitters
½	shot(s)	Chilled water

Origin: Created in 2002 at Hush, London, England.
Comment: It's a sweetie but you're going to enjoy chewing on it.

●●●●○

JEREZ

Glass: Old-fashioned
Method: Stir all ingredients with ice and strain into ice-filled glass.

½	shot(s)	Tio Pepe Fino Sherry
½	shot(s)	Pedro Ximenez Sherry
1	shot(s)	Teichenné peach schnapps
1	shot(s)	Sauvignon Blanc wine
1	shot(s)	La Vielle Prune (prunelle)
1	dash	Angostura aromatic bitters

Origin: This drink heralds from one of the noble houses of Spain – well that's what the Sherry PR told me, anyway. I've changed the recipe slightly.
Comment: Sherry depth and stoned fruit flavours.

●●●●◖

JULEP MARTINI UPDATED

Glass: Martini
Garnish: Mint leaf
Method: Muddle mint in base of shaker. Add other ingredients, shake with ice and fine strain into chilled glass.

8	fresh	Mint leaves
2½	shot(s)	Buffalo Trace Bourbon
½	shot(s)	Sugar (gomme) syrup
¾	shot(s)	Chilled water

Origin: Adapted from a recipe created Dick Bradsell.
Comment: A short variation on the classic Julep: sweetened Bourbon and mint.

●●●●○

JUMPING JACK FLASH

Glass: Martini
Method: Shake all ingredients with ice and strain into glass.

1	shot(s)	Jack Daniel's Tennessee whiskey
1	shot(s)	Bols Crème de banane
½	shot(s)	Galliano
1	shot(s)	Freshly squeezed orange juice
1	shot(s)	Pressed pineapple juice

Comment: The Galliano complements the banana; both mix well with the fruit juices and the vanilla.

JUNE BUG

Glass: Hurricane
Garnish: Split pineapple wedge
Method: Shake ingredients with ice and strain into ice-filled glass.

1	shot(s)	Midori melon liqueur
1	shot(s)	Malibu coconut rum liqueur
1	shot(s)	Bols Crème de banane
4	shot(s)	Pressed pineapple juice
1	shot(s)	Freshly squeezed lime juice
1/2	shot(s)	Sugar (gomme) syrup

Comment: The lime juice counteracts the rest of the sweetness.

JUNGLE FIRE SLING

●●●○○

Glass: Sling
Method: Pour ingredients into ice-filled glass and stir with barspoon or straws.

1	shot(s)	Bols Cherry brandy liqueur
1/2	shot(s)	Parfait Amour
1/2	shot(s)	Bénédictine D.O.M. liqueur
1	shot(s)	Rémy Martin Cognac
Top up with		Ginger ale

Comment: Hardly the most refined of drinks, but it does have the refreshing zing of ginger with a soupçon of sticky fruit, herbs and Cognac in the background.

JUNGLE JUICE

Glass: Collins
Garnish: Orange slice
Method: Shake ingredients with ice and strain into ice-filled glass.

1	shot(s)	Absolut vodka
1	shot(s)	Havana Club light rum
1/2	shot(s)	Cointreau / triple sec
3/4	shot(s)	Freshly squeezed lime juice
1/4	shot(s)	Sugar (gomme) syrup
1	shot(s)	Cranberry juice
1	shot(s)	Freshly squeezed orange juice
1	shot(s)	Pressed pineapple juice

Comment: If this is what the juice of the jungle tastes like – I'm a monkey's uncle. OK, as fruity drinks go.

THE JUXTAPOSITION NEW

●●●●○

Glass: Martini
Garnish: Two pineapple wedges on rim
Method: Stir honey with vodka in base of shaker so as to dissolve honey. Add other ingredients, shake with ice and fine strain into chilled glass.

2	shot(s)	Finlandia Cranberry vodka
2	spoons	Runny honey
1	shot(s)	Pressed pineapple juice
3/4	shot(s)	Freshly squeezed lime juice
3	dashes	Angostura aromatic bitters

Origin: Adapted from a long drink created in 2003 by Michael Butt and Giles Looker of Soulshakers, England. The name means to place things side by side, hence the garnish.
Comment: Tangy and complex and smoothed by foaming pineapple.

K.G.B. # 1

Glass: Martini
Garnish: Lemon twist
Method: Shake ingredients with ice and strain into glass.

2	shot(s)	Plymouth gin
3/4	shot(s)	Kümmel
1/2	shot(s)	Bols Apricot brandy liqueur
1/2	shot(s)	Freshly squeezed lemon juice

Comment: A full flavoured drink.

K.G.B. # 2

Glass: Shot
Method: Layer in glass by pouring carefully in the following order.

1/2	shot(s)	Kahlúa coffee liqueur
1/2	shot(s)	Galliano
1/2	shot(s)	Rémy Martin Cognac

Comment: A stripy shot for Galliano lovers.

KAMIKAZE

●●●●○

Glass: Shot
Method: Shake all ingredients with ice and fine strain into chilled glass.

1	shot(s)	Sauza Hornitos Tequila
1/2	shot(s)	Cointreau / triple sec
1/2	shot(s)	Freshly squeezed lime juice

Comment: A bite-sized Margarita.

KAMANIWANALAYA

Glass: Collins
Method: Shake ingredients with ice and strain into glass.

1	shot(s)	Havana Club light rum
1	shot(s)	Pusser's Navy rum
1	shot(s)	Disaronno Originale amaretto
4	shot(s)	Pressed pineapple juice

Comment: Try saying the name after a few of these tropical pineapple mixtures.

KARAMEL SUTRA MARTINI NEW

●●●●○

Glass: Martini
Garnish: Fudge on rim
Method: Shake all ingredients with ice and fine strain into chilled glass.

1 1/4	shot(s)	Stoli Vanil
1 1/4	shot(s)	Tuaca liqueur
2	shot(s)	Dooley's toffee liqueur

Origin: Adapted from a drink discovered in 2003 at the Bellagio, Las Vegas, USA.
Comment: Creamy liquid confectionary that bites back.

KATINKA

Glass: Martini
Garnish: Split lime wedge
Method: Shake ingredients with ice and strain into glass.

1	shot(s)	Absolut vodka
1	shot(s)	Bols Apricot brandy liqueur
1	shot(s)	Freshly squeezed lime juice
1/2	shot(s)	Sugar (gomme) syrup

Comment: Tart and tasty.

KEE-WEE MARTINI

Glass: Martini
Garnish: Slice of kiwi on rim
Method: Cut kiwi fruit in half and scoop out flesh into juice extractor. Shake juice and other ingredients with ice and strain into chilled glass.

2	shot(s)	Freshly extracted kiwi juice
1 1/2	shot(s)	Plymouth gin
1/4	shot(s)	Freshly squeezed lemon juice
3/4	shot(s)	Sugar (gomme) syrup

Origin: My version of this ubiquitous drink.
Comment: The citrus hints in kiwi fruit combine brilliantly with those in the gin and fresh lemon juice.

KENTUCKY COLONEL NEW

Glass: Old-fashioned
Garnish: Peach slice & mint sprig
Method: Shake all ingredients with ice and strain into glass filled with crushed ice.

1 1/2	shot(s)	Buffalo Trace Bourbon
1/4	shot(s)	Southern Comfort
1/4	shot(s)	Cointreau / triple sec
1	shot(s)	Freshly extracted peach juice
1/2	shot(s)	Freshly squeezed lemon juice
1/2	shot(s)	Sugar (gomme) syrup

Origin: Created by Morgan Watson of Apartment, Belfast, Northern Ireland.
Comment: Peach and Bourbon with hints of orange and spice.

KENTUCKY DREAM

Glass: Old-fashioned
Garnish: Lemon twist
Method: Stir vanilla liqueur and Angostura bitters with two ice cubes in a glass. Add one shot of Bourbon and two more ice cubes. Stir some more and add another two ice cubes and another shot of Bourbon. Add last two ingredients, more ice cubes and stir lots more. The melting and stirring in of ice cubes is essential to the dilution and taste of the drink.

1/2	shot(s)	Teichenné vanilla schnapps
2	dashes	Angostura aromatic bitters
2	shot(s)	Buffalo Trace Bourbon
1/2	shot(s)	Bols Apricot brandy liqueur
1	shot(s)	Pressed apple juice

Origin: Created in 2002 by Wayne Collins for Maxxium UK.
Comment: Tames Bourbon in a dream-like way and adds hints of apricot, vanilla and apple.

KENTUCKY MAC

Glass: Rocks
Garnish: Mint sprig
Method: Shake ingredients vigorously with ice and strain into glass filled with crushed ice, then top up with apple juice float.

1 1/2	shot(s)	Buffalo Trace Bourbon
1	shot(s)	Ginger wine
2	nail(s)	Fresh root ginger
2	fresh	Mint leaves
Top up with		Pressed apple juice

Origin: Created by Jamie Terrell in 1999.
Comment: Spicy and smooth with lasting flavour.

KENTUCKY MUFFIN

Glass: Rocks
Method: Muddle blueberries in base of shaker. Add other ingredients, shake with ice and strain into glass filled with crushed ice. Stir well and serve with two straws.

12	fresh	Blueberries
2	shot(s)	Buffalo Trace Bourbon
1	shot(s)	Pressed apple juice
1/2	shot(s)	Freshly squeezed lime juice
1/2	shot(s)	Sugar (gomme) syrup

Origin: Created in 2000 at Mash, London, England.
Comment: Blueberries, lime and apple combine and are fortified with Bourbon.

KENTUCKY PEAR NEW

Glass: Martini
Garnish: Pear slice on rim
Method: Shake all ingredients with ice and fine strain into chilled glass.

1	shot(s)	Buffalo Trace Bourbon
1	shot(s)	Xanté pear & cognac liqueur
1	shot(s)	Freshly extracted pear juice
1	shot(s)	Pressed apple juice

Origin: Created in 2003 by Jes at The Cinnamon Club, London, England.
Comment: Pear, apple, vanilla and whiskey are happy bed partners in this richly flavoured drink.

KENTUCKY TEA

Glass: Collins
Method: Shake first four ingredients with ice and strain into ice-filled glass, then top up with ginger ale.

2	shot(s)	Buffalo Trace Bourbon
1	shot(s)	Cointreau / triple sec
1	shot(s)	Freshly squeezed lime juice
1/2	shot(s)	Sugar (gomme) syrup
Top up with		Ginger ale

Comment: Spicy whiskey and ginger.

KEY LIME

Glass: Coupette
Garnish: Split lime wedge
Method: Blend ingredients without ice and serve.

1	shot(s)	Stoli Vanil
1	shot(s)	Finlandia Lime vodka
1/2	shot(s)	Sugar (gomme) syrup
1/2	shot(s)	Rose's lime cordial
3	scoops	Vanilla ice cream

Comment: Tangy, smooth and rich! Alcoholic ice cream for the grown-up palate.

●●●●●○

KEY LIME PIE (ORIGINAL FORMULA) NEW

Glass: Martini
Garnish: Pie rim (wipe outside edge of rim with cream mix and dip into crunched up Graham Cracker or digestive biscuits).
Method: Shake first three ingredients with ice and strain into chilled rimmed glass. Shake cream and Licor 43 without ice so as to mix and whip. Float cream mix on surface of drink.

2	shot(s)	Malibu coconut rum liqueur
1	shot(s)	Cointreau / triple sec
1	shot(s)	Freshly squeezed lime juice
2	shot(s)	Double (heavy) cream
1/2	shot(s)	Licor 43 (Cuarenta Y Tres) liqueur

Origin: Created by Michael Walterhouse, owner of Dill & Prime, New York City.
Comment: This extremely rich drink is great when served as a dessert alternative.

●●●●●○

KEY LIME PIE (POPULAR FORMULA) NEW

Glass: Martini
Garnish: Pie rim (wipe outside edge of rim with lime cordial and dip into crunched up Graham Cracker or digestive biscuits).
Method: Shake all ingredients with ice and fine strain into chilled rimmed glass.

2	shot(s)	Stoli Vanil
1 3/4	shot(s)	Pressed pineapple juice
1/2	shot(s)	Freshly squeezed lime juice
1/4	shot(s)	Rose's lime cordial

Comment: Beautifully balance of pineapple, vanilla, sweet and sour.

●●●●◐○

KEY WEST COOLER NEW

Glass: Collins
Garnish: Lime wedge on rim
Method: Shake all ingredients with ice and strain into ice-filled glass.

1 1/2	shot(s)	Absolut vodka
1	shot(s)	Malibu coconut rum liqueur
2	shot(s)	Cranberry juice
2	shot(s)	Freshly squeezed orange juice

Comment: A coconut laced breeze that's perfectly suited to the poolside.

●●●●◐○

KILLER PUNCH UPDATED

Glass: Collins
Garnish: Lime wedge in drink
Method: Shake all ingredients with ice and strain into ice-filled glass.

1	shot(s)	Absolut vodka
1/2	shot(s)	Midori melon liqueur
1/2	shot(s)	Disaronno Originale amaretto
1/2	shot(s)	Freshly squeezed lime juice
4	shot(s)	Cranberry juice

Comment: Pretty soft, sweet and fruity as killers go.

●●●●○○

KIR UPDATED

Glass: Goblet
Method: Pour cassis into glass then top up with chilled wine.

3/4	shot(s)	Sisca Crème de cassis
Top up with		Dry white wine

Variation: Kir Royale
Origin: This drink takes its name from a colourful politician by the name of Canon Felix Kir, who in the early 1950s was the Mayor of Dijon, France. He used to serve an aperitif made with Crème de Cassis from Dijon and a local white wine called Bourgogne Aligoté at official receptions. This was a purely economic practice whose goal was to promote local products. The concoction quickly became known as Canon Kir's aperitif, then father Kir's aperitif and finally throughout the region as the 'Kir' aperitif.
Comment: Blackcurrant wine - clean, crisp and not too sweet.

KIR ROYALE

Glass: Flute
Method: Pour cassis into centre of glass and top up with Champagne.

1/2	shot(s)	Sisca crème de cassis
Top up with		Piper-Heidsieck Brut Champagne

Comment: Easy to make, easy to drink.

KISS ME BABY

Glass: Rocks
Method: Shake ingredients with ice and strain into ice-filled glass.

1 1/4	shot(s)	Teichenné Peach schnapps
1 1/4	shot(s)	Midori melon liqueur
1 1/4	shot(s)	Freshly squeezed orange juice
1 1/4	shot(s)	Cranberry juice

Comment: Four fruits combine perfectly in this light tropical concoction.

KNICKERBOCKER

Glass: Martini
Method: Stir ingredients with ice and strain into glass.

2	shot(s)	Plymouth gin
1/2	shot(s)	Cinzano Extra Dry vermouth
1/2	shot(s)	Cinzano Rosso vermouth

Origin: Thought to have been created at the Knickerbocker Hotel, New York.
Comment: Spicy and slightly medicinal.

KNICKER DROPPER GLORY

●●●●○○

Glass: Shot
Method: Shake all ingredients with ice and fine strain into chilled glass.

| 1 | shot(s) | Frangelico hazelnut liqueur |
| 1/2 | shot(s) | Freshly squeezed lemon juice |

Origin: Originally designed as a shot by Jason Fendick.
Comment: Nutty sweetness sharpened with lemon.

KOOL HAND LUKE

●●●●○○

Glass: Rocks
Method: Muddle lime in base of glass to release its juices. Pour rum and sugar syrup into glass, add crushed ice and stir well. Serve with straws.

1	fresh	Lime cut into eighths
2	shot(s)	Myers's Planters' Punch rum
1	shot(s)	Sugar (gomme) syrup
2	dashes	Angostura aromatic bitters

Comment: This looks like a Caipirinha and has a similar balance of sweet, sour and spirit. The bitters bring out the spice in the rum, which is every bit as pungent as Cachaça.

KRYPTONYTE

Glass: Martini
Method: Shake ingredients with ice and strain into glass.

1 1/2	shot(s)	Absolut vodka
1	shot(s)	Pisang Ambon
1/4	shot(s)	Mandarine Napoléon
2 1/2	shot(s)	Pressed pineapple juice

Created by: Jamie Terrell.
Comment: Spicily fruity - who needs Clark Kent?

KOI YELLOW NEW

●●●●○

Glass: Martini
Garnish: Float rose petal
Method: Shake all ingredients with ice and fine strain into chilled glass.

2	shot(s)	Stoli Razberi
1/2	shot(s)	Cointreau / triple sec
1	shot(s)	Freshly squeezed lemon juice
1/2	shot(s)	Sugar (gomme) syrup

Origin: The signature drink at Koi Restaurant, Los Angeles, USA.
Comment: Sherbet / raspberry Martini with a sweet and citrus sour finish.

THOSE DRINKS I'VE SAMPLED RECENTLY ARE GRADED AS FOLLOWS:

● DISGUSTING ●○ PRETTY AWFUL ●● BEST AVOIDED
●●○ DISAPPOINTING ●●● ACCEPTABLE ●●●○ GOOD
●●●● RECOMMENDED ●●●●○ HIGHLY RECOMMENDED
●●●●● OUTSTANDING / EXCEPTIONAL

KOOLAID UPDATED

●●●●○

Glass: Collins
Garnish: Lime wedge on rim
Method: Shake all ingredients with ice and strain into ice-filled glass.

1 1/2	shot(s)	Absolut vodka
3/4	shot(s)	Midori melon liqueur
3/4	shot(s)	Disaronno Originale amaretto
1/2	shot(s)	Freshly squeezed lime juice
2	shot(s)	Cranberry juice
1	shot(s)	Freshly squeezed orange juice

Origin: A drink with unknown origins that emerged and morphed during the 1990s.
Comment: Tangy liquid marzipan with hints of melon, cranberry and orange juice.

KRAKOW TEA NEW

●●●●○

Glass: Collins
Garnish: Mint sprig & lime wedge
Method: Shake all ingredients with ice and strain into ice-filled glass.

8	fresh	Mint leaves
2	shot(s)	Zubrówka (Bison grass) vodka
1	shot(s)	Strong cold camomile tea
4	shot(s)	Pressed apple juice
1/4	shot(s)	Freshly squeezed lime juice
1/4	shot(s)	Sugar (gomme) syrup

Origin: Created in 2002 by Domhnall Carlin at Apartment, Belfast, Northern Ireland.
Comment: Refreshing and floral with a citrus dry finish.

KURANT AFFAIR

●●●●○

Glass: Collins
Method: Shake all ingredients with ice and strain into ice-filled glass.

1 1/2	shot(s)	Absolut Kurant vodka
1 1/2	shot(s)	Absolut Citron vodka
5	shot(s)	Freshly pressed apple juice

Comment: Berry vodka and apple juice mask the citrus vodka's flavour in this tall, refreshing summery drink.

L.A. ICED TEA

Glass: Sling
Garnish: Split lime wedge
Method: Shake first seven ingredients with ice and strain into glass, then top up with soda water.

1/2	shot(s)	Absolut vodka
1/2	shot(s)	Plymouth gin
1/2	shot(s)	Havana Club light rum
1/2	shot(s)	Cointreau / triple sec
1/2	shot(s)	Midori melon liqueur
1	shot(s)	Freshly squeezed lime juice
1/2	shot(s)	Sugar (gomme) syrup
Top up with		Soda water (club soda)

Comment: The lasting flavour is that of the melon liqueur.

LABORATORY

Glass: Snifter
Method: Pour ingredients into chilled glass and serve.

3/4	shot(s)	Bols White crème de menthe
1/2	shot(s)	Freshly squeezed lime juice
1/2	bottle	Chilled pilsner lager

Origin: Discovered in 2002 at Lightship Ten, London, England.
Comment: Breath freshening lager.

LAGO COSMO NEW

Glass: Martini
Garnish: Flamed orange twist
Method: Shake all ingredients with ice and fine strain into chilled glass.

1 1/2	shot(s)	Finlandia Cranberry vodka
3/4	shot(s)	Cointreau / triple sec
1 3/4	shot(s)	Freshly squeezed orange juice
1/4	shot(s)	Freshly squeezed lime juice
1/2	shot(s)	Sugar (gomme) syrup

Origin: Discovered in 2003 at Nectar @ Bellagio, Las Vegas, USA.
Comment: A Cosmo with cranberry vodka in place of citrus vodka and orange juice in place of cranberry juice.

LANDSLIDE

Glass: Shot
Method: Layer ingredients in glass by carefully pouring ingredients in the following order.

1/2	shot(s)	Disaronno Originale amaretto
1/2	shot(s)	Bols Crème de banane
1/2	shot(s)	Baileys Irish cream liqueur

Comment: A sweet but pleasant combination of banana, almond and Irish cream.

LAS BRISAS

Glass: Hurricane
Garnish: Pineapple leaf
Method: Blend ingredients with crushed ice and serve.

2	shot(s)	Mount Gay Eclipse golden rum
2 1/2	shot(s)	Freshly squeezed orange juice
2 1/2	shot(s)	Pressed pineapple juice
1	shot(s)	Cream of coconut
1	shot(s)	Double (heavy) cream
1	shot(s)	Milk

Comment: A Piña Colada with orange juice and gold rum.

LAZARUS

Glass: Martini
Method: Shake ingredients with ice and strain into glass.

1	shot(s)	Absolut vodka
1	shot(s)	Kahlúa coffee liqueur
1/2	shot(s)	Rémy Martin Cognac
1	shot(s)	Espresso coffee (cold)

Origin: Created in 2000 by David Whitehead at Atrium, Leeds, England.
Comment: Strong alcohol and coffee.

THE LEGEND

Glass: Martini
Garnish: Split lime wedge
Method: Shake ingredients with ice and strain into glass.

2	shot(s)	Absolut vodka
1	shot(s)	Freshly squeezed lime juice
1/4	shot(s)	Sugar (gomme) syrup
1/4	shot(s)	Bols Blackberry (Crème de mûre) liqueur
4	drops	Fee Brother's Orange bitters

Origin: Created by Dick Bradsell for Karen Hampsen at Legends, London, England.
Comment: The Legend developed from a drink made with vodka, lime and mûre.

LEMON BEAT

Glass: Rocks
Garnish: Split lemon wheel
Method: Shake ingredients with ice and strain into ice-filled glass.

2	shot(s)	Pitú Cachaça
1	shot(s)	Freshly squeezed lemon juice
2	spoons	Clear runny honey

Comment: A simple but effective drink.

LEMON BUTTER COOKIE

Glass: Old-fashioned
Garnish: Lemon twist
Method: Shake all ingredients with ice and strain into glass filled with crushed ice.

3/4	shot(s)	Zubrówka (Bison grass) vodka
3/4	shot(s)	Absolut vodka
3/4	shot(s)	Krupnik honey liqueur
2	shot(s)	Pressed apple juice
1/2	shot(s)	Almond (orgeat) syrup
1/8	shot(s)	Freshly squeezed lemon juice

Origin: Created in 2002 by Mark 'Q-Ball' Linnie and Martin Oliver at The Mixing Tin, Leeds, England.
Comment: An appropriate name for a most unusually flavoured drink modelled on the Polish Martini.

LEMON CHIFFON PIE

Glass: Coupette
Garnish: Split lemon wheel
Method: Blend ingredients with crushed ice and serve.

1	shot(s)	Havana Club light rum
1	shot(s)	Bols White crème de cacao
1	shot(s)	Freshly squeezed lemon juice
2	scoops	Vanilla ice cream

Comment: Creamy and tangy – like a lemon pie.

LEMON DROP

Glass: Shot
Garnish: Sugar coated slice of lemon
Method: Shake all ingredients and fine strain into chilled glass.

1/2	shot(s)	Absolut vodka
1/2	shot(s)	Cointreau / triple sec
1/2	shot(s)	Freshly squeezed lemon juice

Comment: Lemon and orange combine to make a fresh tasting citrus shot.

LEMON LIME & BITTERS

Glass: Collins
Garnish: Lime wedge
Method: Squeeze lime wedges and drop into glass. Add Angostura bitters and fill glass with ice. Top up with lemonade and stir. Serve with straws.

4	fresh	Lime wedges
5	dashes	Angostura aromatic bitters
Top up with		Lemonade / Sprite / 7Up

AKA: LLB
Origin: First made and very popular in Australia.
Comment: If you're unlucky enough to be the driver, this refreshing long drink is a good almost no alcohol option.

LEMON MARTINI

Glass: Martini
Garnish: Orange twist dropped into drink
Method: Shake ingredients with ice and strain into glass.

1½	shot(s)	Absolut Citron vodka
1	shot(s)	Freshly squeezed lemon juice
¼	shot(s)	Sugar (gomme) syrup
¼	shot(s)	Cointreau / triple sec
½	spoon	Fee Brothers Orange bitters

Origin: Created by Dick Bradsell at Fred's, London, England, in the late 80s.
Comment: Orange undertones add citrus depth to the lemon explosion.

LEMON MERINGUE MARTINI

Glass: Martini
Garnish: Lemon twist
Method: Shake ingredients with ice and strain into glass.

2	shot(s)	Absolut Citron vodka
1	shot(s)	Drambuie Cream liqueur
1	shot(s)	Freshly squeezed lemon juice
1/4	shot(s)	Sugar (gomme) syrup

Origin: Created by Ben Reed, London, England, in 2000.
Comment: Smooth, rather than creamy, in consistency, this tastes of the most delicious lemon meringue you've ever experienced.

LEMON MERINGUE PIE'TINI NEW

Glass: Martini
Garnish: Pie rim (wipe outside edge of rim with cream mix and dip into crunched up Graham Cracker or digestive biscuits).
Method: Shake first three ingredients with ice and fine strain into chilled rimmed glass. Shake cream and Licor 43 without ice so as to mix and whip. Float cream mix by pouring over back of table spoon.

1	shot(s)	Pallini Limoncello
1	shot(s)	Sugar (gomme) syrup
1	shot(s)	Freshly squeezed lemon juice
2	shot(s)	Double (heavy) cream
½	shot(s)	Licor 43 (Cuarenta Y Tres) liqueur

Origin: Created by Michael Walterhouse at Dill & Prime, New York City.
Comment: Rich and syrupy base sipped through a vanilla cream topping.

LEMON MIMOSA

Glass: Flute
Garnish: Lemon zest
Method: Pour lemon juice into chilled glass and top up with Champagne.

| 1 | shot(s) | Freshly squeezed lemon juice |
| Top up with | | Piper-Heidsieck Brut Champagne |

Comment: Very sour – but some like it like that. Add sugar syrup to taste.

LEMONADE CLARET

Glass: Martini
Garnish: Float orange sail
Method: Shake ingredients with ice and strain into glass.

2½	shot(s)	Buffalo Trace Bourbon
1	shot(s)	Cinzano Rosso vermouth
½	shot(s)	Cinzano Extra Dry vermouth
½	shot(s)	Galliano
½	shot(s)	Campari

Comment: A rollercoaster of sweet, sour, bitterness and strength.

LEMONGRAD

Glass: Collins
Garnish: Lemon wedge squeezed over drink
Method: Pour all ingredients into ice-filled glass and lightly stir.

2	shot(s)	Absolut Citron vodka
1	shot(s)	Belvoir elderflower cordial
½	shot(s)	Freshly squeezed lemon juice
Top up with		Tonic water

Origin: Created in 2002 by Alex Kammerling, London, England.
Comment: A great summer afternoon drink. Fresh lemon with elderflower and quinine.

LIBERTY

Glass: Martini
Garnish: Apple peel
Method: Stir ingredients with ice and strain into glass.

2	shot(s)	Calvados (or applejack brandy)
2	shot(s)	Havana Club light rum
½	shot(s)	Freshly squeezed lime juice
1	shot(s)	Sugar (gomme) syrup

Comment: Apple and honey flavours.

LIQUORICE ALL SORT

Glass: Collins
Garnish: Liquorice Allsort sweet
Method: Shake first four ingredients with ice and strain into ice-filled glass. Then top up with lemonade.

1	shot(s)	Opal Nera black sambuca
1	shot(s)	Bols crème de banane
1	shot(s)	Bols Strawberry (fraise) liqueur
1	shot(s)	Bols Blue curaçao
Top up with		Lemonade / Sprite / 7-Up

Origin: George Bassett (1818-1886), a manufacturer of a variety of liquorice sweets, did not invent the Liquorice Allsort that carries his name. The famous sweet was invented 15 years after George died by one of Bassett's salesmen who accidentally dropped a tray of sweets that had been laid out in neat rows. They fell in a muddle and the Liquorice Allsort was born.
Comment: This aptly named semi-sweet drink has a strong licorice flavour with hints of fruit.

LIFE (LOVE IN THE FUTURE ECSTASY)

Glass: Rocks
Garnish: Mint Leaf
Method: Muddle mint with sugar in bottom of glass, add vodka and lime, then stir and fill glass with crushed ice. Lace with tea liqueur.

8	leaves	Fresh mint
1/4	shot(s)	Sugar (gomme) syrup
1 1/2	shot(s)	Absolut vodka
1/2	shot(s)	Freshly squeezed lime juice
3/4	shot(s)	Tea liqueur

Origin: Created by Jasper Eyears and Cairbry Hill in 1999, London, England.
Comment: Refreshing tea and mint.

LIGHT BREEZE

Glass: Collins
Garnish: Lemon wedge on rim
Method: Pour all ingredients into ice-filled glass and stir.

2	shot(s)	Pernod Anise
3	shot(s)	Cranberry juice
2	shot(s)	Freshly squeezed grapefruit juice

Origin: I created this in 2000 at the Light Bar, Shoreditch, London, England (hence the name).
Comment: A Seabreeze based on anise rather than vodka, with aniseed depth and sweetness.

LIGHTER BREEZE

Glass: Collins
Garnish: Apple wedge on rim
Method: Pour all ingredients into ice-filled glass and stir.

2	shot(s)	Pernod Anise
1/2	shot(s)	Elderflower cordial
3	shot(s)	Pressed apple juice
2	shot(s)	Cranberry juice

Comment: Long, fragrant and refreshing.

LENINADE

NEW

Glass: Martini
Garnish: Mint leaf
Method: Lightly muddle mint in base of shaker. Add next four ingredients, shake with ice and fine strain into chilled glass. Top up with 7-Up.

10	fresh	Mint leaves
2	shot(s)	Absolut Citron vodka
3/4	shot(s)	Freshly squeezed lemon juice
1/4	shot(s)	Sugar (gomme) syrup
1/8	shot(s)	Grenadine syrup
Top up with		7-Up

Variant: The same recipe works well as a long drink served in an ice-filled Collins glass.
Origin: Discovered in 2003 at Pravda, New York City.
Comment: Minty citrus with a great balance of sweet and sour.

LIME BREEZE

Glass: Collins
Garnish: Lime wedge on rim
Method: Pour ingredients into ice-filled glass and stir.

2	shot(s)	Finlandia Lime vodka
4	shot(s)	Cranberry juice
2	shot(s)	Pressed grapefruit juice

Comment: A lime driven Sea Breeze.

LIME SOUR

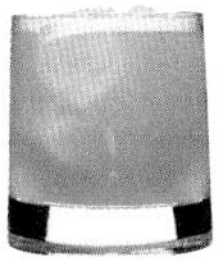

Glass: Old-fashioned
Garnish: Lime wedge on rim
Method: Shake all ingredients with ice and strain into ice-filled glass.

2	shot(s)	Finlandia Lime vodka
1¼	shot(s)	Freshly squeezed lime juice
¼	shot(s)	Sugar (gomme) syrup
½	fresh	Egg white

Comment: Fresh egg white gives this drink a wonderfully frothy top and smoothes the alcohol and the citrus tang of the lime juice.

LIMELITE

Glass: Collins
Garnish: Lime wedge
Method: Pour ingredients into ice-filled glass and stir.

2	shot(s)	Finlandia Lime vodka
½	shot(s)	Cointreau / triple sec
Top up with		Lemonade / Sprite / 7-up
½	shot(s)	Freshly squeezed lime juice

Comment: Long and refreshing – a great summertime tipple.

LIMEOSA

Glass: Flute
Method: Shake first two ingredients with ice and strain into glass. Top up with chilled Champagne and gently stir.

1	shot(s)	Finlandia Lime vodka
2	shot(s)	Freshly squeezed orange juice
Top up with		Piper-Heidsieck Brut Champagne

Comment: Why settle for a plain old Buck's Fizz when the drink can benefit from a shot of lime-flavoured vodka?

LIMERICK

Glass: Collins
Garnish: Lime wedge squeezed over drink
Method: Shake first three ingredients with ice and strain into ice-filled glass. Top up with soda water and lightly stir.

2	shot(s)	Finlandia Lime vodka
1	shot(s)	Freshly squeezed lime juice
½	shot(s)	Sugar (gomme) syrup
Top up with		Soda water

Origin: I created this twist on the classic Vodka Rickey in 2002.
Comment: Refreshing lime cooler.

LIMESTONE BREEZE

Glass: Collins
Garnish: Lime wedge on rim
Method: Pour ingredients into ice-filled glass and stir.

2	shot(s)	Finlandia Lime vodka
1	shot(s)	Disaronno Originale amaretto
4	shot(s)	Pressed apple juice

Origin: I created this in 2002 .
Comment: A richly flavoured, well-balanced long drink with a sweet edge.

LIMETINI

Glass: Martini
Garnish: Lime twist
Method: Shake all ingredients with ice and strain into glass.

2	shot(s)	Finlandia Lime vodka
½	shot(s)	Cointreau / triple sec
½	shot(s)	Freshly squeezed lime juice
½	shot(s)	Sugar (gomme) syrup
1		Chilled water

Variant: If you can find a bottle, try substituting a lime liqueur such as Monin Original for triple sec.
Comment: Opal coloured drink with a fresh, clean and sour flavour.

LIMEY COSMO

Glass: Martini
Garnish: Lime wedge on rim
Method: Shake all ingredients with ice and strain into glass.

1½	shot(s)	Finlandia Lime vodka
1	shot(s)	Cointreau / triple sec
1¼	shot(s)	Cranberry juice
¼	shot(s)	Freshly squeezed lime juice
½	shot(s)	Rose's lime cordial

Comment: If you like Cosmopolitans, you'll love this zesty alternative.

LIMEY MARTINI

Glass: Martini
Garnish: Lime twist
Method: Shake all ingredients with ice and strain into glass.

1¾	shot(s)	Finlandia Lime vodka
½	shot(s)	Freshly squeezed lime juice
½	shot(s)	Sugar (gomme) syrup
1	spoon	Rose's lime cordial
3	dash(es)	Angostura aromatic bitters
1	shot(s)	Chilled water

Origin: I created this and named it after the British naval tradition of mixing lime juice with spirits in an attempt to prevent scurvy. This practice gained British sailors the nickname 'limeys'. Angostura was also popular with sailors as it was said to ward off chronic stomach complaints.
Comment: A rust coloured drink with a delicate sour flavour.

LIMEY MULE

Glass: Collins
Garnish: Lime wedge squeezed & dropped in drink
Method: Pour ingredients into ice-filled glass and stir.

1³/₄	shot(s)	Finlandia Lime vodka
1	shot(s)	Freshly squeezed lime juice
¹/₂	shot(s)	Sugar (gomme) syrup
Top up with		Ginger ale

Comment: Made with plain vodka this drink is a Moscow Mule. This variant uses lime flavoured vodka.

LIMINAL SHOT

Glass: Shot
Method: Layer in glass by carefully pouring ingredients in the following order.

¹/₂	shot(s)	Grenadine syrup
¹/₂	shot(s)	Bols Blue curaçao
³/₄	shot(s)	Finlandia Lime vodka

Comment: This red, blue and white striped drink's name is defined as meaning: transitional, marginal, a boundary or a threshold – appropriate for a layered drink.

LIMITED LIABILITY

Glass: Old-fashioned
Method: Shake all ingredients with ice and strain into ice-filled glass.

2	shot(s)	Finlandia Lime vodka
³/₄	shot(s)	Freshly squeezed lime juice
1	shot(s)	Honey liqueur

Origin: I created this in 2002.
Comment: A sour and flavorsome short - honey and lime complement each other.

LIMNOLOGY

Glass: Martini
Garnish: Lime twist
Method: Stir ingredients with ice and strain into chilled glass.

2	shot(s)	Finlandia Lime vodka
1	shot(s)	Rose's lime cordial
1	shot(s)	Chilled water

Origin: A term for the study of the physical phenomena of lakes and other fresh waters – appropriate as it's based on Finlandia vodka, which is made using natural spring water so pure that it doesn't require any purification.
Comment: A vodka Gimlet made with lime flavoured vodka.

LIMOUSINE

Glass: Old-fashioned
Method: Pour ingredients into glass and stir

2	shot(s)	Finlandia Lime vodka
1	shot(s)	Honey liqueur
4	shot(s)	Hot camomile tea

Origin: I created this drink in 2002.
Comment: This hot drink is both warm in flavour and warming. In summer serve cold over ice.

LINSTEAD

Glass: Martini
Garnish: Float lemon twist
Method: Shake ingredients with ice and strain into glass.

2	shot(s)	The Famous Grouse Scotch whisky
2	shot(s)	Pressed pineapple juice
¹/₄	shot(s)	Sugar (gomme) syrup
¹/₂	spoon	Opal Bianca Sambuca

Comment: The pastis comes through first with the pineapple, leaving the Scotch till the end.

LIQUID LOVER

Glass: Martini
Method: Shake all ingredients with ice and strain into glass.
Garnish: Flamed lemon twist

1¹/₂	shot(s)	Zubrówka (Bison grass) vodka
³/₄	shot(s)	Parfait Amour
³/₄	shot(s)	Rose's lime cordial
¹/₂	shot(s)	Freshly squeezed lemon juice
1	shot(s)	Chilled water

Comment: A subtly flavoured, light lilac cocktail with a lovely clean bite.

LIQUORICE SHOT

Glass: Shot
Method: Shake all ingredients with ice and fine strain into chilled glass.

¹/₂	shot(s)	Absolut vodka
¹/₂	shot(s)	Opal Bianca sambuca
¹/₂	shot(s)	Sisca Crème de cassis

Comment: A shot for liquorice fans.

LOCH ALMOND

Glass: Collins
Garnish: Float Amaretti biscuit
Method: Pour ingredients into glass and stir.

1¹/₂	shot(s)	The Famous Grouse Scotch
1¹/₂	shot(s)	Disaronno Originale amaretto
Top up with		Ginger ale

Comment: If you think you don't like Scotch but like amaretto, try this spicy almond combination.

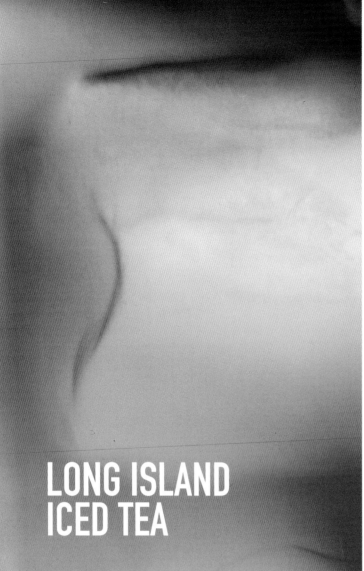

LONG ISLAND ICED TEA

Glass: Sling
Garnish: Split lemon wheel
Method: Shake first seven ingredients with ice and strain into ice-filled glass, then top up with cola and stir.

¹/₂	shot(s)	Havana Club light rum
¹/₂	shot(s)	Plymouth gin
¹/₂	shot(s)	Absolut vodka
¹/₂	shot(s)	Sauza Hornitos Tequila
¹/₂	shot(s)	Cointreau / triple sec
1	shot(s)	Freshly squeezed lime juice
¹/₂	shot(s)	Sugar (gomme) syrup
Top up with		Cola

Origin: A Prohibition drink, this was originally made with whatever spirit was available. The cocktail looks like iced tea - disguising its contents - hence the name. The 'loads of spirits with citrus and mixer' formula has spawned a host of variations - Anita's Attitude Adjuster, Long Beach Iced Tea, LA Iced Tea and New England Iced Tea to name just a few.
A student night/happy hour favourite, the connotations of heavy duty boozing have sent this drink downmarket. All the same, it remains a refreshing, easy-drinking classic - especially served correctly, without overdoing the cola.
Comment: A cooling, downable combination of five different spirits with a hint of lime and a splash of cola.

LOLA

Glass: Martini
Garnish: Orange twist dropped into drink
Method: Shake ingredients with ice and strain into glass.

1³/₄	shot(s)	Mount Gay Eclipse golden rum
³/₄	shot(s)	Mandarine Napoléon Liqueur
³/₄	shot(s)	Bols White crème de cacao
³/₄	shot(s)	Freshly squeezed orange juice
¹/₂	shot(s)	Double (heavy) cream

Origin: Created in 1999 by Jamie Terrell.
Comment: Strong with creamy orange.

LONELY BULL

Glass: Rocks
Garnish: Sprinkle ground nutmeg
Method: Shake ingredients with ice and strain into ice-filled glass.

1¹/₂	shot(s)	Sauza Hornitos Tequila
1¹/₂	shot(s)	Kahlúa coffee liqueur
2	shot(s)	Double (heavy) cream
2	shot(s)	Milk

Comment: Like a creamy iced coffee – yum.

LONG BEACH ICED TEA

Glass: Sling
Garnish: Split lemon wheel
Method: Shake first seven ingredients with ice and strain into ice-filled glass, then top up with cranberry juice.

¹/₂	shot(s)	Kahlúa coffee liqueur
¹/₂	shot(s)	Sauza Hornitos Tequila
¹/₂	shot(s)	Havana Club light rum
¹/₂	shot(s)	Plymouth gin
¹/₂	shot(s)	Absolut vodka
1¹/₂	shot(s)	Freshly squeezed lime juice
³/₄	shot(s)	Sugar (gomme) syrup
Top up with		Cranberry juice

Comment: Long Island with cranberry and coffee.

LONG ISLAND SPICED TEA

Glass: Collins
Method: Shake first seven ingredients with ice and strain into ice-filled glass. Top up with cola.

¹/₂	shot(s)	Spiced rum
¹/₂	shot(s)	Absolut vodka
¹/₂	shot(s)	Plymouth gin
¹/₂	shot(s)	Sauza Hornitos Tequila
¹/₂	shot(s)	Cointreau / triple sec
1	shot(s)	Freshly squeezed lime juice
¹/₂	shot(s)	Sugar (gomme) syrup
Top up with		Cola

Comment: A contemporary spicy twist on an American classic.

LORETTO LADY

Glass: Collins
Garnish: Mint sprig
Method: Pour ingredients into ice-filled glass and stir.

2	shot(s)	Buffalo Trace Bourbon
1	shot(s)	Cointreau / triple sec
Top up with		Ginger ale

Comment: A refreshing drink but lacks depth.

LORETTO LEMONADE

Glass: Collins
Garnish: Lemon and mint
Method: Shake first four ingredients with ice and strain into ice-filled glass, then top up with ginger beer.

1¹/₂	shot(s)	Maker's Mark Bourbon
¹/₂	shot(s)	Midori melon liqueur
¹/₂	shot(s)	Freshly squeezed lime juice
2¹/₂	shot(s)	Pressed apple juice
Top up with		Ginger beer

Origin: Created by Jamie Terrell and winner of 1997 Maker's Mark contest.
Comment: A complex and refreshing drink.

LOTUS MARTINI ●●●●●

Glass: Martini
Garnish: Mint leaf
Method: Muddle mint leaves with gin in base of shaker. Add other ingredients, shake with ice and strain into glass.

6	fresh	Fresh mint leaves
1³/₄	shot(s)	Plymouth gin
¹/₄	shot(s)	Grenadine syrup
¹/₄	shot(s)	Bols Blue curaçao
1¹/₂	shot(s)	Lychee juice from tinned fruit

Origin: Created in 2001 by Martin Walander at Match Bar, London, England.
Comment: This violet coloured drink may have an unlikely list of ingredients, but boy does it look and taste good.

LOUISIANA TRADE ●●●●○

Glass: Rocks
Garnish: Lime wedge squeezed and dropped into drink.
Method: Shake all ingredients with ice and strain into glass filled with crushed ice.

2	shots	Southern Comfort
¹/₂	shot(s)	Maple syrup
¹/₄	shot(s)	Sugar (gomme) syrup
1	shot(s)	Freshly squeezed lime juice

Origin: Created in 2001 by Mehdi Otmann at Zeta, London, England.
Comment: Peach and apricot with a limey freshness and a rich sweetness courtesy of the inclusion of maple syrup.

LOVE JUNK

Glass: Rocks
Garnish: Apple wedge
Method: Shake ingredients with ice and strain into ice-filled glass.

1	shot(s)	Absolut vodka
³/₄	shot(s)	Midori melon liqueur
³/₄	shot(s)	Teichenné Peach schnapps
3	shot(s)	Pressed apple juice

Comment: A light, crisp, refreshing blend of peach, melon and apple juice, laced with vodka and served over ice.

LOVED UP ●●●●○

Glass: Martini
Method: Shake all ingredients with ice and strain into glass.

1¹/₂	shot(s)	Sauza Hornitos Tequila
¹/₂	shot(s)	Cointreau / triple sec
¹/₂	shot(s)	Chambord black raspberry liqueur
¹/₂	shot(s)	Freshly squeezed lime juice
1	shot(s)	Freshly squeezed orange juice
¹/₄	shot(s)	Sugar (gomme) syrup

Origin: Adapted from a cocktail discovered in 2002 at the Merc Bar, New York, where the original name was listed as simply 'Love'.
Description: The flavour of Tequila predominates in this rusty coloured drink, which also features orange and black raspberry.

LUCKY LINDY NEW ●●●◑○

Glass: Collins
Garnish: Lemon wheel
Method: Stir honey with Bourbon in base of shaker so as to dissolve honey. Add lemon juice, shake with ice and strain into ice-filled glass. Top up with 7-Up.

3	spoon(s)	Runny honey
2	shot(s)	Buffalo Trace Bourbon
¹/₂	shot(s)	Freshly squeezed lemon juice
Top up with		7-Up

Origin: Adapted from a drink discovered in 2003 at The Grange Hall, New York City.
Comment: A long refreshing drink that combines whisky, citrus and honey – a long chilled hot toddy without the spice.

LUSH

Glass: Flute
Garnish: Raspberry in glass
Method: Pour vodka and Chambord into glass and gently stir while adding Champagne.

1	shot(s)	Absolut vodka
¹/₂	shot(s)	Chambord black raspberry liqueur
Top up with		Piper-Heidsieck Brut Champagne

Origin: Spike Marchant of Alphabet, London, England.
Comment: Why drink Champagne when you can drink it with raspberries and a kick?

LUX DAIQUIRÍ

Glass: Large Martini
Garnish: Maraschino cherry
Method: Blend all ingredients with one 12oz scoop of crushed ice and serve in chilled glass.

3	shot(s)	Havana Club light rum
3/4	shot(s)	Freshly squeezed lime juice
1/2	shot(s)	Luxardo maraschino liqueur
1/4	shot(s)	Sugar (gomme) syrup
1/4	shot(s)	Maraschino syrup

Origin: This was one of two cocktails with which I won a Havana Club Daiquiri competition in 2002. I named it after Girolamo Luxardo, creator of the now famous liqueur, 'Luxardo Maraschino'.
Comment: A classic frozen Daiquirí heavily laced with maraschino cherry.

LUXURY COCKTAIL

Glass: Martini
Method: Shake ingredients with ice and strain into glass.

1 3/4	shot(s)	Plymouth gin
3/4	shot(s)	Pimm's No.1
3/4	shot(s)	Bols Crème de banane
3/4	shot(s)	Cinzano Rosso sweet vermouth
1/4	shot(s)	Rose's lime cordial
4	dashes	Angostura aromatic bitters

Comment: Sticky bananas at the outset – then into bitter refined aftertaste.

LUXURY MOJITO

Glass: Collins
Garnish: Mint sprig
Method: Muddle mint in glass with sugar and lime juice. Fill glass with crushed ice and add rum and Angostura, then top up with Champagne and stir.

12	fresh	Mint leaves
1/4	shot(s)	Sugar (gomme) syrup
1	shot(s)	Freshly squeezed lime juice
2	shot(s)	Appleton Estate V/X aged rum
3	dashes	Angostura aromatic bitters
Top up with		Piper-Heidsieck Brut Champagne

Comment: A Mojito made with aged rum and topped with Champagne instead of soda water: deeper and more complex than the original.

LYCHEE & ROSE PETAL MARTINI

Glass: Martini
Garnish: Float rose petal
Method: Stir all ingredients with ice and strain into chilled glass.

1 1/2	shot(s)	Plymouth gin
1 1/2	shot(s)	Rose petal vodka liqueur
1 1/2	shot(s)	Lychee syrup from tinned fruit
2	dashes	Peychaud's bitters

Origin: Created in 2002 by Dick Bradsell for Opium, London, England.
Comment: Light pink in colour and wonderfully subtle in flavour.

LYCHEE MARTINI

Glass: Martini
Garnish: Whole lychee from tin in drink
Method: Stir all ingredients with ice and strain into chilled glass.

2	shot(s)	Absolut vodka
1/2	shot(s)	Lychee liqueur
2	shot(s)	Lychee syrup from tinned fruit

Origin: Rumoured to have been first made in 2001 at Clay, a Korean restaurant in New York City.
Comment: If you like lychee you'll like this delicate Martini.

LYNCHBURG LEMONADE UPDATED

Glass: Collins
Garnish: Lemon wheel in glass
Method: Shake first three ingredients with ice and strain into ice-filled glass, then top up with 7-Up.

1 1/2	shot(s)	Jack Daniel's Tennessee whiskey
1	shot(s)	Cointreau / triple sec
1	shot(s)	Freshly squeezed lemon juice
Top up with		7-Up

Variant: With three dashes Angostura bitters.
Origin: Created for the Jack Daniel's distillery in, yep, you guessed it, Lynchburg, Tennessee.
Comment: Tangy, light and very easy to drink, this benefits from sweet, flavoursome edge of Bourbon

MAC ORANGE'TINI

Glass: Martini
Garnish: Flamed orange twist
Method: Shake all ingredients with ice and fine strain into chilled glass.

2	shot(s)	The Famous Grouse Scotch whisky
3/4	shot(s)	Ginger wine
2	shot(s)	Freshly squeezed orange juice
4	dashes	Fee Brothers Orange bitters
1/2	spoon	Sugar (gomme) syrup

Comment: A Whisky Mac with orange topping off the ginger.

MAD MONK MILKSHAKE

Glass: Collins
Garnish: Tie cord around glass
Method: Shake ingredients with ice and strain into ice-filled glass.

2	shot(s)	Frangelico hazelnut liqueur
1	shot(s)	Baileys Irish cream liqueur
1/4	shot(s)	Kahlúa coffee liqueur
2	shot(s)	Double (heavy) cream
2	shot(s)	Milk

Comment: Long and creamy with hazelnut and coffee.
Variant: Blend instead of shaking and serve frozen.

MADAGASCAR SOUR

Glass: Martini
Garnish: Lime wedge on rim
Method: Shake ingredients with ice and strain into glass.

1 ¹/₂	shot(s)	Havana Club light rum
¹/₂	shot(s)	Vanilla liqueur
¹/₂	shot(s)	Vanilla sugar syrup
1	shot(s)	Freshly squeezed lime juice

Origin: Created at the Lab Bar, London, England.
Comment: A perfect balance of sweet and sour with the lime complementing the vanilla.

MADRAS UPDATED

●●●●◐○

Glass: Collins
Garnish: Orange wheel in glass
Method: Shake all ingredients with ice and strain into ice-filled glass.

2	shot(s)	Absolut vodka
3	shot(s)	Cranberry juice
2	shot(s)	Freshly squeezed orange juice

Comment: A Seabreeze but with orange juice in place of grapefruit juice, making it slightly sweeter.

MADROSKA UPDATED

●●●●○○

Glass: Collins
Garnish: Orange wheel in glass
Method: Shake all ingredients with ice and strain into ice-filled glass.

2	shot(s)	Absolut vodka
2¹/₂	shot(s)	Pressed apple juice
1¹/₂	shot(s)	Cranberry juice
1	shot(s)	Freshly squeezed orange juice

Origin: Created in 1998 by Jamie Terrell, London, England.
Comment: A Madras with more than a hint of apple juice.

MAE WEST MARTINI

●●●●●◐

Glass: Martini
Garnish: Melon wedge on rim
Method: Shake all ingredients with ice and fine strain into chilled glass.

2	shot(s)	Absolut vodka
¹/₂	shot(s)	Disaronno Originale amaretto
¹/₄	shot(s)	Midori melon liqueur
1¹/₂	shot(s)	Cranberry juice

Comment: A rosé coloured, semi-sweet concoction with a cherry-chocolate flavour.

MAGIC TRACE

Glass: Martini
Garnish: Lemon wedge on rim
Method: Shake ingredients with ice and strain into glass.

1	shot(s)	Buffalo Trace Bourbon
³/₄	shot(s)	Drambuie liqueur
¹/₄	shot(s)	Cinzano Extra Dry vermouth
1	shot(s)	Freshly squeezed orange juice
¹/₄	shot(s)	Freshly squeezed lemon juice
¹/₄	shot(s)	Sugar (gomme) syrup

Comment: Very drinkable mix of strong flavours.

MAI TAI

●●●●○
(ORIGINAL)

Glass: Old-fashioned
Garnish: Lime wedge (pineapple) & fresh mint
Method: Shake with ice and strain into a glass filled with crushed ice.

2	shot(s)	Appleton Estate V/X aged rum
1	shot(s)	Freshly squeezed lime juice
¹/₂	shot(s)	Orange curaçao
¹/₂	shot(s)	Orgeat (almond) syrup
¹/₄	shot(s)	Sugar (gomme) syrup

Origin: In 1934, Victor Jules Bergeron or Trader Vic as he became known, opened his first restaurant in Oakland, San Francisco. He served Polynesian food with a mix of Chinese, French and American dishes cooked in Chinese wood-fired ovens. As well as his distinctive food, Vic also became famous for the rum based cocktails he created, particularly the Mai Tai. He created the drink one evening in 1944 at his Oakland restaurant. He tested the drink on two friends, Ham and Carrie Guild from Tahiti. After the first sip, Carrie exclaimed, "Mai Tai - Roa Ae", which in Tahitian means 'Out of this world - the best!'. So Bergeron named his drink the Mai Tai. For the authentic Trader Vic Mai Tai, the chain's secretly formulated mix is available from www.tradervics.com - or visit Trader Vic's in the Hilton Hotel, Park Lane, London, England.

Comment: Originally Trader Vic made this drink using 17-year-old rum from Jamaica. Later, when supplies of this dwindled, he started using a combination of rums to achieve the desired flavour. Sheer demand in his chain of restaurants later necessitated the introduction of a pre-mixed Mai Tai mix. This original formula is basically a zoomed up Daiquiri – and works well.

●●●●○
(FULL-ON FORMULA)

Glass: Old-fashioned
Garnish: Mint sprig & lime wedge
Method: Shake first nine ingredients with ice and strain into glass filled with crushed ice. Float overproof Navy rum on drink.

1	shot(s)	Pusser's Navy rum
¹/₂	shot(s)	Myers's rum
¹/₂	shot(s)	Orange curaçao
¹/₂	shot(s)	Bols Apricot brandy liqueur
³/₄	shot(s)	Freshly squeezed lime juice
1	shot(s)	Orgeat (almond) syrup
1¹/₂	shot(s)	Pressed pineapple juice
¹/₂	shot(s)	Freshly squeezed orange juice
6	dashes	Angostura aromatic bitters
¹/₂	shot(s)	Woods 100 overproof navy rum

Comment: This drink breaks the golden rule – simple is beautiful. However, it's tasty and very dangerous, containing two ingredients that top 50% alcohol by volume.

●●●●○
(POPULAR VERSION)

Glass: Old-fashioned
Garnish: Mint sprig & lime wedge
Method: Shake ingredients with ice and strain into glass filled with crushed ice.

1	shot	Myers's Rum
1	shot(s)	Appleton Estate V/X aged rum
¹/₂	shot(s)	Orange curaçao
³/₄	shot(s)	Freshly squeezed lime juice
³/₄	shot(s)	Orgeat (almond) syrup
1	shot(s)	Pressed pineapple juice
6	dash(es)	Angostura aromatic bitters

Comment: Sweeter and without the bite of the original due to the introduction of pineapple juice.

MANHATTAN

DRY UPDATED

Glass: Martini
Garnish: Lemon twist
Method: Stir all ingredients with ice and strain into chilled glass.

2¹/₂	shot(s)	Buffalo Trace Bourbon
1	shot(s)	Cinzano Extra Dry vermouth
4	dashes	Angostura aromatic bitters

Variant: As for 'Manhattan Sweet'. Create an Oddball Manhattan by the addition of a few dashes of Chartreuse or blue curaçao.
Comment: A bone dry Manhattan for those with dry palates.

PERFECT UPDATED

Glass: Martini
Garnish: Twist of orange & cherry on stick
Method: Stir all ingredients with ice and strain into chilled glass.

2¹/₂	shot(s)	Buffalo Trace Bourbon
¹/₂	shot(s)	Cinzano Rosso (sweet) vermouth
¹/₂	shot(s)	Cinzano Extra Dry vermouth
4	dashes	Angostura aromatic bitters

Variant: As for 'Manhattan Sweet'.
Comment: The Manhattan version most popularly served – medium dry.

SWEET UPDATED

Glass: Martini
Garnish: Twist of orange & cherry on stick
Method: Stir ingredients with ice and strain into chilled glass.

2¹/₂	shot(s)	Buffalo Trace Bourbon
1	shot(s)	Cinzano Rosso (sweet) vermouth
1	spoon	Syrup from jar of maraschino cherries
4	dashes	Angostura aromatic bitters

Variant: Served over ice in an old-fashioned glass. Originally a rye drink, it is called a Rob Roy when Scotch is substituted, a Harvard when made with brandy (as in the Midwestern states of the US) or a Star Cocktail when made with applejack.
Origin: The Manhattan is said to have first been created at the Manhattan Club in New York City in 1874 for Lady Randolph Churchill, American mother of Winston. Some believe it was made to celebrate the successful gubernatorial campaign of Samuel Tilden. Still others claim it was invented by a man called Black who ran a saloon on Broadway.
Comment: I must confess to preferring my Manhattans served sweet, perfect at a push. The Manhattan is complex, challenging and moreish. Best of all, it's available in a style to suit every palate.

ISLAND

Glass: Martini
Garnish: Cherry on stick
Method: Stir ingredients with ice and strain into glass.

2	shot(s)	Rémy Martin Cognac
1	shot(s)	Cinzano Rosso vermouth
4	dashes	Angostura aromatic bitters
¹/₈	shot(s)	Maraschino syrup

Comment: A twist on the classic whiskey-based Manhattan.

MAIDEN'S PRAYER MARTINI

Glass: Martini
Garnish: Flamed orange twist
Method: Shake all ingredients with ice and fine strain into chilled glass.

1¹/₂	shot(s)	Plymouth gin
¹/₂	shot(s)	Cointreau / triple sec
1¹/₂	shot(s)	Freshly squeezed orange juice
³/₄	shot(s)	Freshly squeezed lemon juice

Origin: My adaptation of a classic recipe.
Comment: A Gin Sour with triple sec in place of sugar and without the smoothing properties of egg white. Some like it rough!

MAINBRACE

Glass: Martini
Garnish: Orange zest
Method: Shake all ingredients with ice and fine strain into chilled glass.

1¹/₂	shot(s)	Plymouth gin
1¹/₂	shot(s)	Cointreau / triple sec
1¹/₂	shot(s)	Freshly squeezed grapefruit juice

Comment: Full-on grapefruit laced with gin and a hint of orange. Tart finish.

MAGIC BUS

Glass: Martini
Method: Shake ingredients with ice and strain into glass.

1	shot(s)	Sauza Hornitos Tequila
1	shot(s)	Cointreau / triple sec
1¹/₂	shot(s)	Cranberry juice
1	shot(s)	Freshly squeezed orange juice

Comment: Combines the flavour of orange and cranberry laced with Tequila.

MAMBO

Glass: Collins
Garnish: Orange slice
Method: Shake ingredients with ice and strain into ice-filled glass.

1	shot(s)	Absolut vodka
1	shot(s)	Orange curaçao
1	shot(s)	Bols Apricot brandy liqueur
¹/₄	shot(s)	Campari
5	shot(s)	Freshly squeezed orange juice

Origin: Created by Nichole Colella.
Comment: A bitter orange, long, cooling drink.

MAN-BOUR-TINI UPDATED

Glass: Martini
Garnish: Orange twist
Method: Shake all ingredients with ice and fine strain into chilled glass.

1	shot(s)	Mandarine Napoléon liqueur
³/₄	shot(s)	Buffalo Trace Bourbon
¹/₂	shot(s)	Freshly squeezed lime juice
2	shot(s)	Cranberry juice
¹/₄	shot(s)	Sugar (gomme) syrup

Origin: Created in 1999 by yours truly.
Comment: A rounded, fruity Bourbon based drink with a mandarin and lime citrus sourness.

MANDARINE COLLINS

Glass: Collins
Garnish: Half orange slice
Method: Shake first three ingredients with ice and strain into ice-filled glass. Top up with soda.

1¹/₂	shot(s)	Plymouth gin
1	shot(s)	Mandarine Napoléon
1	shot(s)	Freshly squeezed lemon juice
Top up with		Soda water (club soda)

Comment: A tangy, long refreshing drink with an intense mandarin flavour.

MANDARINE SOUR

Glass: Old-fashioned
Method: Shake ingredients with ice and strain into ice-filled glass.

2	shot(s)	Mandarine Napoléon
1	shot(s)	Freshly squeezed lemon juice
¹/₄	shot(s)	Sugar (gomme) syrup
¹/₂	fresh	Egg white

Comment: Sour, but with a strong mandarin sweetness.

MANDARITO

Glass: Rocks
Method: Muddle lime wedges and mint leaves in the base of the glass. Add other ingredients and fill glass with crushed ice. Stir and serve with two short wide bore straws.

¹/₂	fresh	Lime cut into wedges
6	fresh	Mint leaves (or basil)
1¹/₂	shot(s)	Mandarine Napoléon
1	shot(s)	Absolut vodka
¹/₄	shot(s)	Sugar (gomme) syrup

Origin: A cocktail promoted by Mandarine Napoléon.
Comment: This drink works well with either mint, basil or with no added herbs at all. Adjust sugar content to suit palate.

MARGARITA FROZEN

Glass: Hurricane
Garnish: Salt rim & split lime wedge
Method: Blend ingredients with lots of crushed ice until slushy and serve.

2	shot(s)	Sauza Hornitos Tequila
1	shot(s)	Cointreau / triple sec
1	shot(s)	Freshly squeezed lime juice

Comment: A true classic - citrus freshness with the subtle agave of Tequila, served frozen with a biting salt rim.

MARGARITA ON-THE-ROCKS

Glass: Rocks
Garnish: Salt rim & split lime wedge.
Method: Shake ingredients with ice and strain into ice-filled glass.

2	shot(s)	Sauza Hornitos Tequila
1	shot(s)	Cointreau / triple sec
1	shot(s)	Freshly squeezed lime juice

Comment: Tangy citrus, Tequila and salt - this drink is better served straight-up or frozen.

MARGARITA STRAIGHT UP

UPDATED
●●●●◐

Glass: Coupette
Garnish: Salt rim & lime wedge
Method: Shake ingredients with ice and strain into chilled glass.

2	shot(s)	Sauza Hornitos Tequila
1	shot(s)	Cointreau / triple sec
1	shot(s)	Freshly squeezed lime juice

Variant: Margaritas made with premium Tequilas are sometimes referred to as 'Deluxe' or 'Cadillac' Margaritas.
Tip: For the perfect salt rim, liquidise sea salt to make it finer, then run a lime wedge around the outside edge of the glass before dipping the rim in salt.
Origin: There are countless versions of how the Margarita was invented - as so often, nobody really knows. It's not impossible that several people came up with the same drink at the same time and gave it the same name independently. These four versions are the most popular...
1/ In 1948 a socialite called Margaret Sames was hosting a party at her cliff side house in Acapulco, Mexico. Among her guests was Nicky Hilton of the famous hotel family (and one of Liz Taylor's many ex-husbands). Looking for something to pep up the party, Margaret began to experiment at the bar and created the first Margarita. She thought nothing of it until, when flying back from Acapulco airport, she saw a bar advertising 'Margarita's Drink', a cocktail with exactly the same ingredients as her own.
2/ Pancho Morales, a bartender from Juarez, Mexico, was asked to make a 'Magnolia' but couldn't remember the exact ingredients, so threw something together. Although it wasn't what the lady asked for, she loved it. Her name was Margarita.
3/ Carlos Herrera made the cocktail for a lady called Marjorie who didn't drink any spirit other than Tequila. He added Cointreau and lime and the unique salt rim which caught people's attention at the bar.
4/ Vernon Underwood was president of Young's Market Company, who in the 1930s had started distributing Cuervo Tequila. He went to Johnny Durlesser, head bartender of the Tail O' The Cock in LA, and asked him to create something amazing with his new spirit. He named it after his wife Margaret and hispanicised her name to Margarita.
5/ The drink could be named after 'Margarita Island' located in the Caribbean north of Venezuela, two-and-a-half hours from Miami. Margarita is the Spanish equivalent of the girl's name 'Margaret', and the Spanish word for daisy. With Tequila the main ingredient, a Spanish name was a must.
Comment: A refreshing, sour classic, with a perfect balance of citrus and agave. Rimming only half the glass with salt gives the drinker the option of enjoying the cocktail with or without salt.

MARGARITA IMPÉRIAL

Glass: Margarita
Garnish: Salt rim & split lime wedge
Method: Shake ingredients with ice and strain into glass.

2	shot(s)	Sauza Hornitos Tequila
1	shot(s)	Mandarine Napoléon
1	shot(s)	Freshly squeezed lime juice

Comment: The mandarin of Mandarine Napoléon dominates this drink.

MARGARITA - FRESH FRUIT UPDATED
●●●●○

Glass: Old-fashioned
Garnish: Chosen fruit
Method: Muddle chopped fruit with other ingredients in base of shaker, then shake with ice and strain into ice-filled glass.

1	cup	Chopped fruit of your choice
2	shot(s)	Sauza Hornitos Tequila
1	shot(s)	Cointreau / triple sec
1	shot(s)	Freshly squeezed lime juice
1/2	shot(s)	Sugar (gomme) syrup

Comment: The quantity of sugar syrup may need adjustment, depending on the ripeness of the fruit.

MARKEE

Glass: Martini
Garnish: Raspberry & mint leaf
Method: Shake ingredients with ice and strain into glass.

1 1/2	shot(s)	Buffalo Trace Bourbon
2	shot(s)	Cranberry juice
1/2	shot(s)	Chambord black raspberry liqueur
1/2	shot(s)	Freshly squeezed lemon juice
1/4	shot(s)	Sugar (gomme) syrup

Origin: Discovered at Match, London, England.
Comment: Raspberry and Bourbon combine perfectly in this short fruity drink.

MARTINEZ UPDATED
●●●●◐

Glass: Martini
Garnish: Orange twist
Method: Stir all ingredients with ice and strain into chilled glass.

2	shot(s)	Plymouth gin
1/2	shot(s)	Cinzano Rosso (sweet) vermouth
1/4	shot(s)	Cointreau / triple sec
1/4	shot(s)	Sugar (gomme) syrup
3	dashes	Fee Brothers Orange bitters (optional)

Origin: A variation on a nineteenth century drink, supposed to be a forerunner of the Martini. Originally this would have been made with a sweet style of gin known as 'Old Tom'.
Comment: The ingredients combine well and the flavours are well balanced. This medium dry Martini is somewhat more approachable than a modern Dry Martini.

MARTINI ROYALE **UPDATED**

●●●●○○

Glass: Martini
Garnish: Lemon twist
Method: Stir vodka and crème de cassis with ice and strain into chilled glass. Top up with Champagne.

1¹/₂ shot(s)	**Absolut vodka**
¹/₂ shot(s)	**Sisca crème de cassis**
Top up with	**Piper-Heidsieck Brut Champagne**

Origin: Created in 2001 by Dick Bradsell at Monte's, London, England.
Comment: The Kir Royale meets the vodkatini in this pink but powerful drink.

MARTINI THYME

●●●●●○

Glass: Martini
Garnish: Thread three green olives onto thyme sprig and place in drink
Method: Muddle thyme with vodka in base of shaker. Add other ingredients, shake with ice and fine strain into glass.

1	fistful	**Lemon thyme (remove stalks)**
1	shot(s)	**Plymouth gin**
³/₄	shot(s)	**Green Chartreuse**
¹/₄	shot(s)	**Sugar (gomme) syrup**

Origin: A combination of two very similar drinks, that both originally called for thyme infused gin. Purists will be relieved to read that both were originally stirred and not shaken. The first I discovered at The Lobby Bar (One Aldwych, London) and the other came from Tony Conigliaro at Isola London, England.
Comment: A wonderfully fresh herbal Martini with the distinctive taste of Chartreuse. You'll either love it or hate it.

MARY PICKFORD **UPDATED**

●●●●●○

Glass: Martini
Garnish: Cherry in drink
Method: Shake all ingredients with ice and fine strain into chilled glass.

2¹/₄ shot(s)	**Havana Club light rum**
1³/₄ shot(s)	**Pressed pineapple juice**
¹/₄ shot(s)	**Grenadine syrup**
¹/₈ shot(s)	**Maraschino liqueur**

Origin: Created during Prohibition at the Hotel Naciônal de Cuba, Havana for the silent movie star.
Comment: A pale pink cocktail which, when made correctly, has a perfect balance between the fruit flavours and the spirit of the rum.

MARY ROSE **UPDATED**

●●●●●○

Glass: Martini
Garnish: Lime twist (discard) & rosemary sprig.
Method: Muddle rosemary in base of shaker. Add other ingredients; shake with ice and fine strain into chilled glass.

1	sprig	**Fresh rosemary**
2	shot(s)	**Plymouth gin**
1	shot(s)	**Green Chartreuse**
¹/₂	shot(s)	**Sugar (gomme) syrup**
³/₄	shot(s)	**Chilled water**

Origin: Created in 1999 by Philip Jeffrey at the Great Eastern Hotel, London, England. Named after King Henry VIII's warship, which was sunk during an engagement with the French fleet in 1545, and now displayed in Portsmouth.
Comment: Herbal, herbal and herbal with a hint of spice.

THE MARTINI

The origin of the classic Martini is disputed and shrouded in mystery. Tens of books have been written about the original Martini, and it's a topic which can raise temperatures among drinks aficionados. Most agree that it was created some time around the turn of the last century.

When or wherever the Martini was actually invented, and however it acquired its name, for several decades the name was only applied to a drink containing gin and vermouth in varying proportions. Then came the Vodkatini to stretch the meaning of the name. But even then, if a drink didn't contain gin and/or vodka and vermouth it simply wasn't a Martini. Purists hold to this definition today.

Language and the meaning of words are changing faster than ever, and today pretty much any drink served in a V-shaped glass is popularly termed a Martini regardless of its contents. These contemporary non-traditional Martinis are sometimes referred to as Neo-martinis or Alternatinis and the pages of this guide are filled with such drinks.

Although you'll find exceptions in this guide (rules are made for breaking), I believe a drink should at least be based on gin or vodka to properly be termed a Martini. It may also contain all manner of fruits and liqueurs with not even a dash of vermouth - if it's served in a V-shaped glass with gin or vodka, it's still a Martini.

Even the name of the glass itself has changed. The old guard of bartending still insist on referring to this as a 'Cocktail Glass'. To my understanding that's now a generic term for glasses designed to hold cocktails, a term which also encompasses the likes of Hurricanes, Slings and Coupettes. Today a V-shaped glass is commonly recognised as a Martini glass.

For those seeking traditional Martinis based on gin and/or vodka with vermouth and without muddled fruit and suchlike, here are a few classic variations.

Dickens Martini – without a twist (see Dry Martini).
Dirty Martini – with the brine from an olive jar (see Dirty Martini).
Dry Martini (Traditional) – stirred with gin/vodka
Dry Martini (Naked) – frozen gin/vodka poured into a vermouth washed frozen glass.
Franklin Martini - named after Franklin Roosevelt and served with two olives.
Gibson Martini – with two onions instead of an olive or a twist.
Martinez – said to be the original Martini.
Vesper Martini – James Bond's Martini, made with gin and vodka.
Vodkatini – very dry vodka based Martini.
Wet Martini – heavy on the vermouth.

Please also see entries in this guide under Dry Martini (Traditional), Dry Martini (Naked), Dirty Martini, Martinez, Vesper Martini, Vodkatini and Wet Martini.

MAT THE RAT

Glass: Collins
Garnish: Lime wedge
Method: Shake all ingredients with ice and strain into ice-filled glass.

2	shot(s)	Spiced rum
1/2	shot(s)	Cointreau / triple sec
1 1/2	shot(s)	Freshly squeezed orange juice
1/2	shot(s)	Freshly squeezed lime juice
Top up with		Traditional lemonade

Origin: A popular drink in UK branches of TGI Friday's, where this drink was created.
Comment: Whether or not Mat was a rat, we shall never know. However, this drink that's named after him is long and thirst-quenching.

MATADOR

Glass: Collins
Garnish: Split pineapple wedge
Method: Shake ingredients with ice and strain into ice-filled glass.

2	shot(s)	Sauza Hornitos Tequila
3/4	shot(s)	Cointreau / triple sec
3/4	shot(s)	Freshly squeezed lime juice
5	shot(s)	Pressed pineapple juice

Comment: A long Margarita with pineapple juice. The lime and Tequila work wonders with the sweet pineapple.

MAURESQUE NEW

Glass: Collins (10oz / 290ml max)
Method: Pour pastis and almond syrup into glass. Serve iced water separately in a small jug (known in France as a 'broc') so the customer can dilute to their own taste (I recommend five shots). Lastly, add ice to fill glass.

1	shot(s)	Ricard pastis
1/2	shot(s)	Almond (orgeat) syrup
Top up with		Chilled water

Origin: Pronounced 'Mor-Esk', this drink is very popular in the South of France.
Comment: Long refreshing aniseed, liquorice and almond.

MAYAN UPDATED

Glass: Old-fashioned
Garnish: Coffee beans
Method: Shake all ingredients with ice and strain into ice-filled glass.

1 1/2	shot(s)	Sauza Hornitos Tequila
1/2	shot(s)	Kahlúa coffee liqueur
2 1/2	shot(s)	Pressed pineapple juice

Comment: Tequila, coffee and pineapple juice combine in this medium dry short drink.

MAYAN WHORE

Glass: Sling
Garnish: Split pineapple wedge
Method: Pour first three ingredients into ice-filled glass, then top up with soda. Do not stir. Serve with straw.

2	shot(s)	Sauza Hornitos Tequila
2 1/2	shot(s)	Pressed pineapple juice
1	shot(s)	Kahlúa coffee liqueur
Top up with		Soda water

Comment: An implausible ménage à trois: coffee, Tequila and pineapple, served long and fizzy.

MAYFAIR MARTINI

Glass: Martini
Garnish: Orange zest
Method: Shake all ingredients with ice and strain into glass.

1	shot(s)	Drambuie Cream liqueur
1	shot(s)	Absolut vodka
1	shot(s)	Freshly squeezed lime juice
2	shot(s)	Freshly squeezed orange juice

Origin: Created by Alex Kammerling in 2001.
Comment: Creamy yet light with a lovely orange citrus bite.

THE MAYFLOWER MARTINI

Glass: Martini
Garnish: Edible flower petal
Method: Shake all ingredients with ice and fine strain into chilled glass.

1 1/2	shot(s)	Plymouth gin
1/2	shot(s)	Bols Apricot brandy liqueur
1	shot(s)	Pressed apple juice
1/4	shot(s)	Elderflower cordial
1/2	shot(s)	Freshly squeezed lemon juice

Origin: Created in 2002 by Wayne Collins for Maxxium UK.
Comment: Fragrant balance of English fruits and flowers.

MC MARTINI

Glass: Martini
Garnish: Apple slice
Method: Cut passion fruit in half and scoop seeds and flesh into shaker. Add other ingredients, shake with ice and fine strain into chilled glass.

2	fresh	Passion fruit
1 3/4	shot(s)	Absolut vodka
1/2	shot(s)	Chambord black raspberry liqueur
1 1/2	shot(s)	Pressed apple juice

Origin: Created in 1999 by Timothy Schofield at Teatro, London, England, and named after Mark Cummings, a director of commercials.
Comment: The passion fruit gives this fruity drink an almost powdery consistency.

MEDICINAL SOLUTION UPDATED

●●●○○

Glass: Martini
Garnish: Three blueberries on a stick
Method: Shake all ingredients with ice and fine strain into chilled glass.

2	shot(s)	Absolut vodka
1	shot(s)	Parfait amour
1/2	shot(s)	Sugar (gomme) syrup
1	shot(s)	Double (heavy) cream

Comment: This fairly sweet and bizarre tasting drink is somehow reminiscent of medicine, but in a pleasant way.

MELON BALL

Glass: Shot
Method: Shake ingredients with ice and strain into glass.

1/2	shot(s)	Absolut vodka
1/2	shot(s)	Midori melon liqueur
3/4	shot(s)	Freshly squeezed orange juice

Comment: A vivid green combination of vodka, melon and orange.

MELON BREEZE

Glass: Collins
Method: Pour ingredients into glass and stir.

2	shot(s)	Melon vodka
3	shot(s)	Pressed grapefruit juice
3	shot(s)	Cranberry juice

Origin: Created at Lab, London, England, by Douglas Ankrah and Richard Hargroves.
Comment: Melon comes through first, leaving the grapefruit and dryness of cranberry in this interesting take on the Seabreeze.

MELON CHIQUITA PUNCH

Glass: Martini
Method: Shake ingredients with ice and strain into glass.

1 1/2	shot(s)	Midori melon liqueur
1 1/2	shot(s)	Bols Crème de banane
1	shot(s)	Pressed pineapple juice
1	shot(s)	Milk

Comment: Smooth, creamy melon with hints of pineapple and banana.

MELON COLLIE MARTINI NEW

●●●●○

Glass: Martini
Garnish: Crumbled Cadbury's Flake bar
Method: Shake all ingredients with ice and fine strain into chilled glass.

1/2	shot(s)	Havana Club light rum
1/2	shot(s)	Malibu coconut rum
3/4	shot(s)	Midori melon liqueur
1/4	shot(s)	Bols White crème de cacao
1	shot(s)	Double (heavy) cream
1	shot(s)	Milk

Origin: Created in 2003 by Simon King at MJU, Millennium Hotel, London, England.
Comment: Something of a holiday disco drink but tasty all the same.

MELON DAIQUIRÍ

●●●●○

Glass: Martini
Garnish: Melon slice on rim
Method: Muddle melon in base of shaker. Add other ingredients, shake with ice and fine strain into chilled glass.

2	cups	Diced honeydew melon
2	shot(s)	Havana Club light rum
1/2	shot(s)	Midori melon liqueur
1/2	shot(s)	Freshly squeezed lime juice
1/8	shot(s)	Sugar (gomme) syrup

Comment: A classic Daiquiri with the gentle touch of melon.

MELON MARGARITA UPDATED

●●●●○

Glass: Coupette
Garnish: Melon balls on stick
Method: Muddle melon in base of shaker. Add other ingredients; shake with ice and fine strain into chilled glass.

1	cup	Diced honeydew melon
2	shot(s)	Sauza Hornitos Tequila
1	shot(s)	Midori melon liqueur
1	shot(s)	Freshly squeezed lime juice

Comment: Looks like stagnant pond water but tastes fantastic.

MELON MARTINI

Glass: Martini
Garnish: Split lime wedge
Method: Shake ingredients with ice and strain into glass.

2 1/4	shot(s)	Absolut vodka
1	shot(s)	Midori melon liqueur
1/2	shot(s)	Freshly squeezed lime juice
1/4	shot(s)	Sugar (gomme) syrup

Comment: Bright green, lime and melon with more than a hint of vodka. Do it properly - have a fresh one.

MELON MARTINI (FRESH) UPDATED

●●●●◐

Glass: Martini
Garnish: Melon wedge on rim
Method: Muddle melon in base of shaker. Add other ingredients; shake with ice and fine strain into chilled glass.

1	cup	Diced gallia melon
2	shot(s)	Absolut vodka
1/4	shot(s)	Midori melon liqueur
1/4	shot(s)	Sugar (gomme) syrup

Origin: The fresh fruit Martini revolution took off in the late 80s in New York with London following a decade later.
Comment: Of all the fresh fruit Martinis, melon appears to be the most popular. Surprisingly clean and, well, fresh-tasting, it's amazing that such a subtle flavour as melon can come through so strongly and naturally.

METROPOLITAN

●●●●○

UPDATED

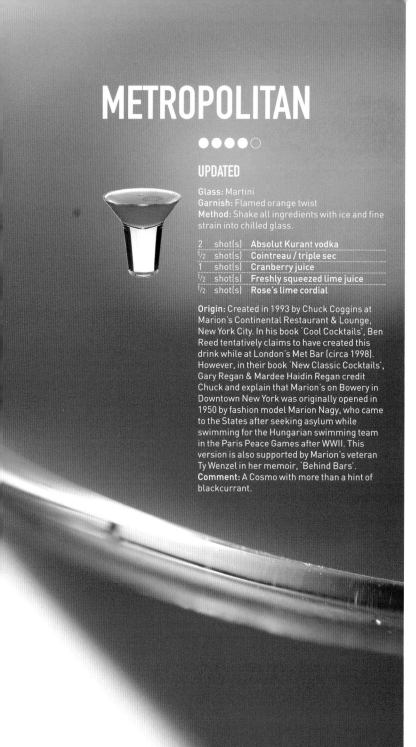

Glass: Martini
Garnish: Flamed orange twist
Method: Shake all ingredients with ice and fine strain into chilled glass.

2	shot(s)	Absolut Kurant vodka
1/2	shot(s)	Cointreau / triple sec
1	shot(s)	Cranberry juice
1/2	shot(s)	Freshly squeezed lime juice
1/2	shot(s)	Rose's lime cordial

Origin: Created in 1993 by Chuck Coggins at Marion's Continental Restaurant & Lounge, New York City. In his book 'Cool Cocktails', Ben Reed tentatively claims to have created this drink while at London's Met Bar (circa 1998). However, in their book 'New Classic Cocktails', Gary Regan & Mardee Haidin Regan credit Chuck and explain that Marion's on Bowery in Downtown New York was originally opened in 1950 by fashion model Marion Nagy, who came to the States after seeking asylum while swimming for the Hungarian swimming team in the Paris Peace Games after WWII. This version is also supported by Marion's veteran Ty Wenzel in her memoir, 'Behind Bars'.
Comment: A Cosmo with more than a hint of blackcurrant.

MELONCHOLY MARTINI

●●●●○

Glass: Martini
Method: Shake all ingredients with ice and strain into glass

1	shot(s)	Absolut vodka
1	shot(s)	Midori melon liqueur
1/2	shot(s)	Cointreau / triple sec
1/2	shot(s)	Malibu coconut rum liqueur
1	shot(s)	Pressed pineapple juice
3/4	shot(s)	Double (heavy) cream
1/4	shot(s)	Freshly squeezed lime juice

Origin: Created in 2002 by Daniel O'Brien at Ocean Bar, Edinburgh, Scotland.
Comment: A tad on the sweet side, but the flavours in this smooth, lime-green drink combine surprisingly well.

MELLOW MARTINI

Glass: Martini
Garnish: Fresh lychee on a stick
Method: Shake ingredients with ice and strain into glass.

1 1/2	shot(s)	Absolut vodka
3/4	shot(s)	Lychee liqueur
3/4	shot(s)	Bols Crème de bananes
2	shot(s)	Pressed pineapple juice

Comment: Fruity tropical flavour.

MERRY WIDOW

Glass: Martini
Garnish: Lemon zest twist
Method: Stir all ingredients with ice in mixing glass and strain.

1 1/2	shot(s)	Absolut vodka
1 1/2	shot(s)	Dubonnet red
1 1/2	shot(s)	Cinzano Extra Dry vermouth
1	dash	Fee Brothers Orange bitters

Comment: Strong and bitter.

MET MANHATTAN

Glass: Martini
Garnish: Orange twist
Method: Shake ingredients with ice and strain into glass.

2	shot(s)	Buffalo Trace Bourbon
1	shot(s)	Grand Marnier
3/4	shot(s)	Teichenné Butterscotch schnapps
1	dash	Fee Brothers Orange bitters

Origin: The Met Bar, Metropolitan Hotel, London, England

METROPOLIS

Glass: Flute
Garnish: Split strawberry and blackberry
Method: Pour first three ingredients into glass and top up with Champagne.

1	shot(s)	Absolut vodka
1/2	shot(s)	Bols Strawberry (fraise) liqueur
1/2	shot(s)	Strawberry purée
Top up with		Piper-Heidsieck Brut Champagne

Origin: Met Bar, Metropolitan Hotel, London, E$ngland.
Comment: The freshness and sweetness of strawberries enhances the Champagne's dryness.

MEXICAN MULE

Glass: Collins
Method: Shake ingredients with ice and strain into ice-filled glass.

1¹/₂	shot(s)	Sauza Hornitos Tequila
³/₄	shot(s)	Freshly squeezed lime juice
¹/₄	shot(s)	Sugar (gomme) syrup
Top up with		Ginger ale

Comment: A Tequila version of a Moscow Mule.

MEXICAN SURFER

Glass: Martini
Method: Shake ingredients with ice and strain into glass.

2	shot(s)	Sauza Hornitos Tequila
1¹/₂	shot(s)	Pressed pineapple juice
1¹/₂	shot(s)	Rose's lime cordial

Comment: A sweet and sour fruity cocktail with Tequila, pineapple and lime juice.

MEXICAN RUNNER FROZEN

Glass: Coupette
Garnish: Split strawberry
Method: Blend ingredients with crushed ice and serve.

1	shot(s)	Sauza Hornitos Tequila
1	shot(s)	Pusser's Navy rum
¹/₂	shot(s)	Bols Crème de banane
¹/₂	shot(s)	Sisca crème de cassis
1¹/₂	shot(s)	Freshly squeezed lime juice
¹/₂	shot(s)	Sugar (gomme) syrup
6-10 Fresh		Hulled strawberries

Comment: Fresh 'n' fruity with a sinister edge of rum and Tequila.

●●●●◗○

MEXICO CITY

Glass: Coupette
Garnish: Lime wedge on rim
Method: Shake all ingredients with ice and strain into glass.

1¹/₄	shot(s)	Sauza Hornitos Tequila
³/₄	shot(s)	Grand Marnier
¹/₂	shot(s)	Freshly squeezed lime juice
¹/₂	shot(s)	Cranberry juice
¹/₄	shot(s)	Sugar (gomme) syrup

Origin: Adapted from a cocktail discovered in 2002 at the Merc Bar, New York City.
Comment: This maroon coloured Margarita-style drink benefits from a hint of cranberry.

MIDNIGHT MINT

Glass: Martini
Garnish: Chocolate powder rim
Method: Shake ingredients with ice and strain into glass.

1¹/₂	shot(s)	Baileys Irish cream liqueur
³/₄	shot(s)	Bols White crème de cacao
³/₄	shot(s)	Green crème de menthe

Origin: Created by Jamie Terrell in 1997.
Comment: The colour may put you off, but this is a very creamy minty drink.

MIDNIGHT SNOWSTORM

Glass: Toddy
Method: Place bar spoon in glass and add crème de menthe, then top up with hot chocolate and float cream.

1¹/₂	shot(s)	Bols White crème de menthe
Top up with		Hot chocolate
Float		Lightly whipped cream

Comment: Like a molten After Eight.

●●●●○○

MILANESE

Glass: Old-fashioned
Garnish: Orange zest
Method: Shake all ingredients and strain into glass filled with ice.

1¹/₂	shot(s)	Campari
¹/₂	shot(s)	Galliano
1	shot(s)	Freshly squeezed lemon juice
¹/₃	shot(s)	Orgeat syrup

Origin: Created by Alex Turner in 2001, London, England.
Comment: Also works well served long and topped with soda.

MILANO

Glass: Martini
Garnish: Split cherry on rim
Method: Shake ingredients with ice and strain into glass.

1¹/₂	shot(s)	Plymouth gin
1¹/₂	shot(s)	Galliano
1¹/₂	shot(s)	Freshly squeezed lemon juice
³/₄	shot(s)	Sugar (gomme) syrup

Comment: A brief interlude with anis – then on to sour gin.

●●●●◗

MILK & HONEY MARTINI

Glass: Martini
Garnish: Grate fresh nutmeg over drink
Method: Stir Scotch with honey in base of shaker until honey dissolves. Add other ingredients, shake with ice and fine strain into chilled glass.

2	shot(s)	The Famous Grouse Scotch whisky
3	spoons	Runny honey
¹/₂	shot(s)	Honey liqueur
³/₄	shot(s)	Double (heavy) cream
³/₄	shot(s)	Milk

Origin: I created this in December 2002.
Comment: The rich flavour of Scotch is tamed by honey and cream.

MILK PUNCH

Glass: Collins
Method: Shake ingredients with ice and strain into ice-filled glass.

2	shot(s)	Buffalo Trace Bourbon
¹/₂	shot(s)	Sugar (gomme) syrup
2	shot(s)	Double (heavy) cream
2	shot(s)	Milk

Comment: The cream and sugar bring out the flavour of the whiskey.

MINT JULEP

Glass: Collins
Garnish: Mint sprig and slice of lemon
Method: Lightly muddle (only bruise) mint with Bourbon in base of shaker. (Crushing the leaves releases the bitter, inner juices. Discard stems, which are also bitter.) Place shaker and its contents in refrigerator with serving glass for at least two hours. Remove glass from refrigerator and half fill with crushed ice. Place sugar and Angostura into shaker base with Bourbon and mint. Shake with ice and strain into glass. Churn the drink with the crushed ice using a bar spoon. Top up the glass with more crushed ice so as to fill it and churn again. Serve with two long straws.

12	fresh	Mint leaves
2¹/₂	shot(s)	Buffalo Trace Bourbon
³/₄	shot(s)	Sugar (gomme) syrup
3	dashes	Angostura aromatic bitters

Variant: Substitute Bourbon with: rye whiskey, rum, gin, brandy or Calvados/applejack.

Variant: Float half a shot of aged rum on drink.

Origin: The name derives from the Arabic word 'julab', meaning rosewater and it has become the ultimate Deep South cocktail, famously served at the Kentucky Derby. The first known written reference is in 1803, when it could be made with rum, brandy or whiskey, but by 1900, whiskey had become the normal ingredient.
The Mint Julep reached Britain in 1837, thanks to the novelist Captain Frederick Marryat, who complained of being woken at 7am by a slave brandishing a Julep. He popularised it through his descriptions of American Fourth of July celebrations.

Comment: Serving this drink ice cold and giving the flavours in the mint time to marry with the Bourbon are key to the quality of the finished Julep. Hence, it's a drink that requires advanced planning.

MILKY MOJITO

●●●●○

Glass: Collins
Garnish: Mint spring
Method: Muddle mint in glass with sugar and lime juice. Fill glass with crushed ice and add anise, then top up with soda and stir.

10	fresh	Mint leaves
1	shot(s)	Freshly squeezed lime juice
³/₄	shot(s)	Sugar (gomme) syrup
2	shot(s)	Pernod anise
Top up with		Soda water (club soda)

Comment: A tasty anise alternative to a Mojito. The name refers to the opaque white colour the drink becomes after soda is added to the anise.

MILLIONAIRE'S DAIQUIRÍ NEW

●●●●○○

Glass: Martini
Garnish: Star fruit
Method: Shake all ingredients with ice and fine strain into chilled glass.

1³/₄	shot(s)	Havana Club light rum
³/₄	shot(s)	Plymouth sloe gin
³/₄	shot(s)	Bols Apricot brandy liqueur
³/₄	shot(s)	Freshly squeezed lime juice
¹/₄	shot(s)	Grenadine syrup

Origin: This heralds from a classic (retro) cocktail known simply as the Millionaire. Originally sloe gin was the main ingredient, but as David Embury once wrote, "Since the sloe gin, which is a liqueur, predominates in this drink, I do not regard it as a true cocktail." Thus the above is my modern formulation.
Comment: The colour of this cocktail, due to sloe liqueur and grenadine, belies a surprisingly dry finish.

MILLION DOLLAR NEW

●●●●○

Glass: Martini
Garnish: Physalis on rim
Method: Shake all ingredients with ice and fine strain into chilled glass.

2	shot(s)	Plymouth gin
³/₄	shot(s)	Pressed pineapple juice
³/₄	shot(s)	Cinzano Rosso (sweet) vermouth
¹/₈	shot(s)	Grenadine syrup
¹/₂	fresh	Egg white

Origin: A classic (retro) cocktail which can be found in all the old bar tomes. Thought to have been created around 1910 by Ngiam Tong Boon at Raffles Hotel, Singapore (he is more famous for creating the Singapore Sling).
Comment: To say this drink is a million dollar is an overstatement. It does, however, have a smooth, almost rosewater flavour.

THOSE DRINKS I'VE SAMPLED RECENTLY ARE GRADED AS FOLLOWS:

● DISGUSTING	●○ PRETTY AWFUL
●● BEST AVOIDED	●●○ DISAPPOINTING
●●● ACCEPTABLE	●●●○ GOOD
●●●● RECOMMENDED	●●●●○ HIGHLY RECOMMENDED
●●●●● OUTSTANDING / EXCEPTIONAL	

MILLY MARTINI NEW

●●●●○

Glass: Martini
Garnish: Pineapple wedge on rim
Method: Muddle basil in base of shaker. Add other ingredients; shake with ice and fine strain into chilled glass.

5	fresh	Basil leaves
2	shot(s)	Plymouth gin
2	shot(s)	Pressed pineapple juice
1/2	shot(s)	Sugar (gomme) syrup
2	dashes	Fee Brothers Orange bitters

Origin: Created in 2003 by Shelim Islam at the GE Club, London, England.
Comment: Gin and pineapple with a pleasing hint of basil.

MINT FIZZ

Glass: Collins
Method: Shake first four ingredients with ice and strain into ice-filled glass, then top up with soda and stir.

2	shot(s)	Plymouth gin
1	shot(s)	Freshly squeezed lime juice
1/4	shot(s)	White crème de menthe
1/2	shot(s)	Sugar (gomme) syrup
Top up with		Soda (club soda)

Comment: This drink is greatly improved if fresh mint is used.

MISS MARTINI

Glass: Martini
Garnish: Floating raspberry
Method: Shake ingredients with ice and strain into glass.

1 1/2	shot(s)	Absolut vodka
1/2	shot(s)	Chambord black raspberry liqueur
1/2	shot(s)	Raspberry purée
1/4	shot(s)	Double (heavy) cream
1/2	spoon	Sugar (gomme) syrup
1/2	spoon	Fee Brothers Orange bitters

Origin: Created in 1997 by Giovanni Burdi at Match Bar, London, England.
Comment: A gender-neutral drink.

MISS MONEYPENNY

●●●●◐○

Glass: Martini
Method: Shake all ingredients with ice and strain into glass.

1 1/2	shot(s)	Absolut vodka
3/4	shot(s)	Teichenné Peach schnapps Liqueur
3/4	shot(s)	Freshly squeezed lemon juice
1/4	shot(s)	Sugar (gomme) syrup
1	shot(s)	Chilled water

Comment: If you like peach schnapps, you'll love this cocktail which adds some punch to the liqueur.

MISSISSIPPI PUNCH

●●●●●

Glass: Collins
Method: Shake all ingredients with cubed ice and strain into a glass filled with crushed ice.

1 1/2	shot(s)	Sugar (gomme) syrup
3/4	shot(s)	Freshly squeezed lemon juice
1 1/2	shot(s)	Buffalo Trace Bourbon
3/4	shot(s)	Rémy Martin Cognac
3	shot(s)	Chilled water

Comment: A beautifully balanced concoction.

MISSISSIPPI SCHNAPPER UPDATED

●●●●◐○

Glass: Martini
Garnish: Flamed orange twist
Method: Shake all ingredients with ice and fine strain into chilled glass.

2	shot(s)	Jack Daniel's Tennessee whiskey
3/4	shot(s)	Teichenné Peach schnapps Liqueur
1/2	shot(s)	Cointreau / triple sec
1/4	shot(s)	Freshly squeezed lime juice
1/4	shot(s)	Sugar (gomme) syrup

Origin: Created in 1999 by Dan Cottle at Velvet, Manchester, England.
Comment: Orange predominates with peach sweetness balanced by whiskey and lime.

MISTER STU

Glass: Collins
Method: Shake all ingredients with ice and strain into glass.

1	shot(s)	Disaronno Originale Amaretto
1	shot(s)	Sauza Hornitos Tequila
1/2	shot(s)	Malibu coconut rum liqueur
3	shot(s)	Pressed pineapple juice
3	shot(s)	Freshly squeezed orange juice

Comment: A complex and deep cocktail.

MITCH MARTINI

Glass: Martini
Garnish: Lemon zest.
Method: Shake ingredients with ice and strain into glass.

1 1/2	shot(s)	Zubrówka Bison vodka
1 1/2	shot(s)	Pressed apple juice
1/2	shot(s)	Passion fruit syrup
1/4	shot(s)	Teichenné Peach schnapps Liqueur
1/2	shot(s)	Freshly squeezed lemon juice

Origin: Created in 1997 by Giovanni Burdi at the Match Bar, London EC1.
Comment: One of London's best contemporary classics, and a great example of the new Martinis - try it!

MOJITO

●●●●●

UPDATED

Glass: Collins
Garnish: Mint sprig
Method: Muddle mint in base of glass. Add rum, sugar and lime juice. Half fill glass with crushed ice and churn (stir) with bar spoon. Fill glass to brim with more crushed ice and churn some more. Top up with soda, stir and serve with straws.

12	fresh	Mint leaves
2	shot(s)	Havana Club light rum
1	shot(s)	Freshly squeezed lime juice
1/4	shot(s)	Sugar (gomme) syrup
Top up with		Soda water (club soda)

Variant: Add three dashes of Angostura aromatic bitters.
Variant: Muddle in fresh fruit e.g. raspberries.
Origin: Between the wars, and especially during Prohibition, Cuba had a thriving international bar culture. In fact, when Prohibition was announced, numerous companies outfitted ferries for the overnight booze cruise to the island. At the heart of this bar culture were their highly trained professional bartenders, many of them trained at the Association Cantineros Cuba - the legendary Havana bar school.
The Mojito was probably invented after Americans introduced the locals to the Mint Julep. Bodeguita del Medio is the bar usually credited as the first to make a Mojito.
Comment: When well made, this Cuban cousin of the Mint Julep is one of the world's greatest and most refreshing cocktails.

MOCHA MARTINI **UPDATED**

●●●●●

Glass: Martini
Garnish: Dust centre with cocoa powder
Method: Shake first four ingredients with ice and fine strain into chilled glass. Float just half a shot of cream in centre of drink.

1	shot(s)	Buffalo Trace Bourbon
1 1/2	shot(s)	Espresso coffee (cold)
1	shot(s)	Bailey's Irish cream liqueur
1	shot(s)	Bols Brown crème de cacao
1/2	shot(s)	Double (heavy) cream

Comment: Made with great espresso coffee, this drink is a superb, richly flavoured balance of sweet and bitter.

MOCHA MINT

Glass: Rocks
Method: Shake ingredients with ice and strain into ice-filled glass.

1	shot(s)	Kahlúa coffee liqueur
1	shot(s)	White crème de menthe
1	shot(s)	Bols White crème de cacao

Comment: Choccy coffee mint – as the name would suggest.

MOKSHA MARTINI

●●●●●

Glass: Martini
Garnish: Head of basil leaves
Method: Muddle basil and ginger in base of shaker. Add other ingredients, shake with ice and fine strain into glass.

3	fresh	Basil leaves
2	nail(s)	Fresh root ginger
1 1/2	shot(s)	Absolut vodka
1/2	shot(s)	Ginger syrup
1/2	shot(s)	Apple liqueur
3/4	shot(s)	Freshly squeezed lemon juice

Origin: Created in 2001 by Douglas Ankrah for Red Fort, London, England.
Comment: Moksha is a Hindu term for Salvation, referring to the release from worldly existence, final or eternal emancipation and the liberation of the soul from the recurring cycle of birth and death. The Hindus believe that the soul does not die with the body, but, after a while, is born again in some other form.

NEW	A DRINK NEW TO SAUCE GUIDES.
UPDATED	ENTRY CHANGED SINCE LAST VOLUME.
shot(s)	25ML MEASURE (UK) OR 1OZ (US). HOWEVER, IT DOESN'T REALLY MATTER WHAT MEASURE YOU USE AS A SHOT, SO LONG AS YOU USE THE SAME MEASURE OR FRACTIONS OF THAT MEASURE TO MEASURE ALL THE INGREDIENTS. THIS WILL ENSURE THE PROPORTIONS OF ONE INGREDIENT TO ANOTHER WILL BE AS THE RECIPE INTENDED.

MOLOTOV COCKTAIL

●●●●○○

Glass: Martini
Garnish: Lemon zest
Method: Shake all ingredients with ice and fine strain into chilled glass.

1½	shot(s)	Finlandia Lime vodka
1¼	shot(s)	Parfait Amour liqueur
½	shot(s)	Freshly squeezed lemon juice
½	shot(s)	Opal Nera black sambuca

Origin: I created this drink after a visit to the Rajamäki distillery, where Finlandia is bottled. At the start of the Second World War the plant was used to produce Molotov cocktails, inflammatory bombs with which the Finns put hundreds of Soviet tanks out of action.
I selected the ingredients to represent the four liquids used in the wartime weapon. Finlandia lime, which is clear, stands for alcohol, parfait amour shares the purple hue of paraffin, lemon juice represents gasoline and black sambuca replaces tar.
Comment: This inky cocktail combines sweet and sour with hints of liquorice and is as potent as its name suggests.

LA MOMIE NEW

●●●○○

Glass: Shot
Method: Pour Ricard into chilled glass and top up with chilled water.

½	shot(s)	Ricard pastis
Top up with		Chilled water

Origin: Pronounced 'Mom-Ee', this shot is very popular in the South of France.
Comment: A bite-sized aniseed tipple.

MOMISETTE UPDATED

●●●●○

Glass: Collins (10oz / 290ml max)
Method: Pour pastis and almond syrup into glass. Serve with bottle of sparkling water so the customer can dilute to their own taste (I recommend five shots). Lastly, add ice to fill glass.

1	shot(s)	Ricard pastis
¼	shot(s)	Almond (orgeat) syrup
Top up with		Sparkling mineral water

Origin: A traditional French drink, the name of which literally translates as 'tiny mummy'.
Comment: Complex balance of anis, almond and liquorice.

MOMO SPECIAL

●●●●○

Glass: Collins
Method: Muddle mint with vodka in base of shaker. Add lime juice and sugar, shake with ice and strain into ice-filled glass. Top up with soda and stir.

2	shot(s)	Absolut vodka
12	fresh	Mint leaves
½	shot(s)	Freshly squeezed lime juice
½	shot(s)	Sugar (gomme) syrup
Top up with		Soda water (club soda)

Origin: Created in 1998 by Simon Mainoo at Momo, London, England.
Comment: Light green in colour and minty in flavour. The flavour is much enriched by macerating the mint in the vodka some hours before making.

MONA LISA UPDATED

●●●●○

Glass: Collins
Garnish: Orange slice
Method: Shake first three ingredients with ice and strain into ice-filled glass. Top up with tonic water.

1	shot(s)	Green Chartreuse
3	shot(s)	Freshly squeezed orange juice
2	dashes	Angostura aromatic bitters
Top up with		Tonic water

Comment: Chartreuse fans will appreciate this drink, which is also an approachable way for novices to acquire a taste for the green stuff.

MONARCH MARTINI NEW

●●●●○

Glass: Martini
Garnish: Lemon twist
Method: Lightly muddle mint in base of shaker. Add other ingredients, shake with ice and fine strain into chilled glass.

7	fresh	Mint leaves
1½	shot(s)	Plymouth gin
½	shot(s)	Freshly squeezed lemon juice
¾	shot(s)	Elderflower cordial
½	shot(s)	Sugar (gomme) syrup
½	shot(s)	Chilled water

Origin: Created in 2003 by Douglas Ankrah at Townhouse, London, England. Doug's original recipe omitted water and included a dash of peach bitters.
Comment: Wonderfully floral and minty – worthy of a right royal drinker.

MONKEY GLAND # 1

●●●●○○

Glass: Martini
Method: Stir all ingredients with ice and strain into chilled glass.

2	shot(s)	Plymouth gin
¼	shot(s)	La Fée absinthe
2	shot(s)	Freshly squeezed orange juice
⅛	shot(s)	Grenadine syrup

Variant: Try substituting Bénédictine for absinthe.
Origin: Created by Harry MacElhone at his Harry's New York Bar in Paris in the 1920s. The Monkey Gland takes its name from the work of the Russian doctor Serge Voronoff, director of experimental surgery at the Laboratory of Physiology of the Collége de France, who attempted to delay the ageing process by transplanting monkey testicles into human beings.
Comment: This classic gin based drink is tastier than its name suggests.

MONKEY GLAND # 2

Glass: Rocks
Garnish: Orange wedge
Method: Stir ingredients with ice and strain into ice-filled glass.

2¼	shot(s)	Plymouth gin
2¼	shot(s)	Freshly squeezed orange juice
¼	shot(s)	Bénédictine D.O.M liqueur
¼	shot(s)	Grenadine syrup

Comment: Bad name for an OK cocktail.

MOSCOW MULE

Glass: Collins
Garnish: Mint sprig & lime squeeze
Method: Shake first four ingredients with ice and strain into an ice-filled glass. Top up with ginger beer and stir.

2	shot(s)	Absolut vodka
1	shot(s)	Freshly squeezed lime juice
1/2	shot(s)	Sugar (gomme) syrup
3	dashes	Angostura aromatic bitters
Top up with		Ginger beer

Origin: In 1941 Jack Martin of Heublein, then owner of Smirnoff vodka and Jack Morgan, the owner of Hollywood's Cock'n'Bull Saloon, met at the Chatham Bar in New York. The war had halted Smirnoff production and Martin was worried about Smirnoff's future. His friend Morgan was trying to market ginger beer. Nobody knows which of them came up with the idea of mixing the two and adding a dash of lime, but their new cocktail, the Moscow Mule, was the result.
"The name's a complete mystery. In Moscow there is no ginger beer, nor bitters, nor ice," observed the art dealer James Birch. Of course, the moniker could be attributed to the way the drink 'kicked like a mule'.
Smirnoff promoted this cocktail with the serving gimmick of a copper mug, and now promote a similar mix as a pre-mix in a copper-coloured bottle.

Comment: A long vodka based drink with spice provided by ginger beer and angostura.

●●●●●◑

MONKEY SHINE NEW

Glass: Martini
Garnish: Cinnamon rim
Method: Shake all ingredients with ice and fine strain into chilled glass.

1³/₄	shot(s)	Mount Gay gold rum
1	shot(s)	Malibu coconut rum liqueur
1¹/₂	shot(s)	Pressed pineapple juice

Origin: An adaptation of a drink discovered in 2003 at the Bellagio Resort & Casino, Las Vegas.
Comment: The sweet tropical fruitiness of this drink is set off by the spicy rim.

MONKEY WRENCH

Glass: Collins
Method: Pour rum into ice-filled glass, then top up with grapefruit juice and stir.

| 2 | shot(s) | Mount Gay Eclipse gold rum |
| Top up with | | Pressed grapefruit juice |

Comment: Simple but not unpleasant.

MONK'S CANDY BAR

Glass: Martini
Garnish: Sprinkle with nutmeg
Method: Shake ingredients with ice and strain into glass.

1¹/₂	shot(s)	Frangelico hazelnut liqueur
1	shot(s)	Teichenné Butterscotch schnapps
³/₄	shot(s)	Kahlúa coffee liqueur
1	shot(s)	Double (heavy) cream
1	shot(s)	Milk

Comment: Hazelnut, butterscotch and coffee mixed with milk and cream makes a cocktail reminiscent of a candy bar.

MONK'S HABIT

Glass: Collins
Garnish: Tie strip of orange rind and float on drink.
Method: Shake ingredients with ice and strain into glass.

1	shot(s)	Havana Club light rum
1/2	shot(s)	Cointreau / triple sec
1	shot(s)	Frangelico hazelnut liqueur
3¹/₂	shot(s)	Pressed pineapple juice
1/4	shot(s)	Grenadine syrup

Comment: Fruit and nut laced with rum.

THOSE DRINKS I'VE SAMPLED RECENTLY ARE GRADED AS FOLLOWS:

● DISGUSTING   ●◐ PRETTY AWFUL   ●● BEST AVOIDED
●●◐ DISAPPOINTING   ●●● ACCEPTABLE   ●●●◐ GOOD
●●●● RECOMMENDED   ●●●●◐ HIGHLY RECOMMENDED
●●●●● OUTSTANDING / EXCEPTIONAL

MONK'S ORCHARD

Glass: Old-fashioned
Garnish: Mint sprig & ground cinnamon
Method: Muddle mint leaves with gin in base of shaker. Add next four ingredients and shake with ice, then strain into glass filled with crushed ice and top up with tonic water.

6	fresh	Mint leaves
1	shot(s)	Plymouth gin
1	shot(s)	Pressed apple juice
1/2	shot(s)	Calvados (or applejack brandy)
1/4	shot(s)	Sugar (gomme) syrup
1/4	shot(s)	Frangelico hazelnut liqueur
Top up with		Tonic water

Origin: Created in 2001 by Steve Dingly at Toast Bar, London, England for the Tanqueray competition.
Comment: A well-balanced cocktail comprising a multitude of flavours - noticeably apple, nuts and mint.

MONTE CARLO

Glass: Collins
Garnish: Maraschino cherry in glass
Method: Shake first four ingredients with ice, strain into ice-filled glass and top up with soda.

1	shot(s)	Pernod anise
1	shot(s)	Maraschino liqueur
1	shot(s)	Freshly squeezed lime juice
1/4	shot(s)	Grenadine syrup
Top up with		Soda water (club soda)

Origin: An adaptation of a Martini style drink created in 2002 by Alex Turner, bar consultant, London, England.
Comment: A long, fragrant, almost floral summer cooler.

MONTGOMERY MARTINI

Glass: Martini
Garnish: Apple slice on rim
Method: Muddle ginger in base of shaker. Add honey and vodka and stir until honey dissolves. Add other ingredients, shake with ice and fine strain into chilled glass.

2	slices	root ginger (Thumb-nail sized)
1	spoon	Runny honey
1 1/2	shot(s)	Zubrówka (Bison Grass) vodka
1/2	shot(s)	Krupnik honey liqueur
2	shot(s)	Pressed Pineapple juice

Origin: Discovered at the ICA Bar, London, England.
Comment: Predominantly alcoholic pineapple with a hint of ginger and honey.

MONZA

Glass: Collins
Garnish: Slice of apple
Method: Shake all ingredients with ice and strain into ice-filled glass.

2	shot(s)	Absolut vodka
2	shot(s)	Campari
2	shot(s)	Pressed apple juice
2	shot(s)	Passion fruit juice
1/4	shot(s)	Sugar (gomme) syrup

Origin: A classic cocktail promoted by Campari.
Comment: If you like Campari you'll love this.

MORNING GLORY

Glass: Martini
Garnish: Lemon twist peel
Method: Shake ingredients with ice and strain into glass.

2	shot(s)	Rémy Martin Cognac
1	shot(s)	Orange curaçao
1	shot(s)	Freshly squeezed lemon juice
4	dashes	Angostura aromatic bitters
1/2	spoon	La Fée absinthe / pastis

Comment: Sophisticated and balanced.

MORNING GLORY FIZZ

Glass: Old-fashioned
Garnish: Lime wedge on rim
Method: Shake first six ingredients with ice and strain into ice-filled glass. Top up with soda water from a siphon.

1	shot(s)	The Famous Grouse Scotch whisky
1/4	shot(s)	La Fée absinthe
3/4	shot(s)	Freshly squeezed lime juice
3/4	shot(s)	Freshly squeezed lemon juice
1/4	shot(s)	Sugar (gomme) syrup
1/2	fresh	Egg white
Top up with		Soda water from a siphon

Comment: This classic sour and aromatic cocktail is traditionally thought of as a morning after pick-me-up but is great at any time.

MOSCOW LASSI

Glass: Collins
Garnish: Cucumber
Method: Muddle cucumber in base of shaker. Add other ingredients. Shake with ice and fine strain into ice-filled glass.

2	inch	Chopped cucumber
1	shot(s)	Mango purée
1 1/2	shot(s)	Absolut vodka
2	shot(s)	Pressed apple juice
3	spoon(s)	Greek yoghurt
1/2	shot(s)	Sugar (gomme) syrup

Origin: Created in 2001 by Jamie Stephenson at Gaucho Grill, Manchester, England.
Comment: You may have tried a Lassi at your local Indian restaurant, but I bet it didn't taste this good.

MOULIN ROUGE

Glass: Sling
Method: Shake brandy and pineapple juice with ice and strain into ice-filled glass, then top up with sparkling wine and stir.

1/2	shot(s)	Rémy Martin Cognac
4	shot(s)	Pressed pineapple juice
Top up with		Piper-Heidsieck Brut Champagne

Comment: Dry, but with a fruity freshness.

MOUNTAIN SIPPER

Glass: Old-fashioned
Garnish: Orange zest
Method: Shake all ingredients with ice and strain into ice-filled glass.

2	shot(s)	Jack Daniel's Tennessee whisky
1	shot(s)	Cointreau / triple sec
1	shot(s)	Cranberry juice
1	shot(s)	Pressed grapefruit juice
1/8	shot(s)	Sugar (gomme) syrup

Comment: Fruity citrus flavours balance the richness of the whiskey.

MRS ROBINSON

Glass: Old-fashioned
Garnish: Three raspberries
Method: Muddle raspberries in base of shaker. Add next four ingredients, shake with ice and strain into ice-filled glass. Top up with soda and stir.

8	fresh	Raspberries
2	shot(s)	Buffalo Trace Bourbon
1	shot(s)	Bols Raspberry (framboise) liqueur
1/4	shot(s)	Freshly squeezed lemon juice
1/4	shot(s)	Sugar (gomme) syrup
Top up with		Soda water (club soda)

Origin: Created in 2000 by Max Warner at Long Bar, Sanderson, London, England.
Comment: Rich raspberry fruit laced with Bourbon.

MUDDY WATER

Glass: Rocks
Garnish: Float 3 coffee beans
Method: Shake ingredients with ice and strain into ice-filled glass.

1	shot(s)	Absolut vodka
1	shot(s)	Kahlúa coffee liqueur
1	shot(s)	Baileys Irish Cream liqueur

Comment: Coffee and whiskey cream with added vodka.

MUDSLIDE

Glass: Hurricane
Garnish: Crumbled Cadbury's Flake bar
Method: Blend all ingredients with two scoops of crushed ice and serve.

1 1/2	shot(s)	Baileys Irish Cream liqueur
1 1/2	shot(s)	Kahlúa coffee liqueur
1 1/2	shot(s)	Absolut vodka
3	scoops	Vanilla ice cream

Comment: Simply scrumptious dessert drink with whiskey cream and coffee.

MULATA DAIQUIRI UPDATED

Glass: Martini
Garnish: Lime wedge on rim
Method: Shake all ingredients with ice and fine strain into chilled glass.

2	shot(s)	Appleton Estate V/X aged rum
1/2	shot(s)	Bols Brown crème de cacao
1/2	shot(s)	Freshly squeezed lime juice
1/4	shot(s)	Sugar (gomme) syrup

Comment: A classic Daiquirí with aged rum and a hint of chocolate.

MULLED WINE

Glass: Toddy
Garnish: Cinnamon stick
Method: Place bar spoon in glass, add ingredients and stir.

2	shot(s)	Red wine
1/2	shot(s)	Port
1/2	shot(s)	Freshly squeezed lemon juice
2		Cloves
1/2	spoon	Brown sugar
Top up with		Boiling water

Variant: Better if several servings are made at the same time - simmer ingredients in saucepan.
Comment: Warming, soothing and potent.

MYSTIQUE

Glass: Old-fashioned
Garnish: Orange twist & cherry
Method: Stir ingredients with ice and strain into ice-filled glass.

3/4	shot(s)	Drambuie
3/4	shot(s)	Teichenné peach schnapps liqueur
1/2	shot(s)	The Famous Grouse Scotch whisky
4	dashes	Fee Brothers Orange bitters
1/4	shot(s)	Maraschino syrup

Origin: Created by Greg Pearson at Mystique, Manchester, England in 1999. Joint winner of the Manchester Food & Drink Festival cocktail competition.
Comment: Peach combines brilliantly with the Drambuie and Scotch.

MYSTIQUE MARTINI

Glass: Martini
Garnish: Raspberries on stick
Method: Stir all ingredients with ice and fine strain into chilled glass.

2	shot(s)	The Famous Grouse Scotch whisky
1	shot(s)	Tuaca liqueur
3/4	shot(s)	Chambord black raspberry liqueur

Origin: Created in 2002 by Tim Halilaj, Albania.
Comment: Rust coloured and fruit charged.

MULE'S HIND LEG MARTINI

●●●●●

Glass: Martini
Garnish: Apricot slice on rim
Method: Shake all ingredients with ice and fine strain into chilled glass.

1	shot(s)	Plymouth gin
1	shot(s)	Bénédictine liqueur
1	shot(s)	Calvados (applejack brandy)
1	shot(s)	Maple syrup
1	shot(s)	Bols Apricot brandy liqueur

Origin: My version of a classic recipe.
Comment: Apricot and maple syrup dominate this medium sweet drink.

NARANJA DAIQUIRÍ

Glass: Martini
Garnish: Orange slice on rim
Method: Shake all ingredients with ice and fine strain into chilled glass.

1³/₄ shot(s)	Havana Club light rum
³/₄ shot(s)	Grand Marnier
1 shot(s)	Freshly squeezed orange juice
¹/₂ shot(s)	Freshly squeezed lime juice
¹/₈ shot(s)	Sugar (gomme) syrup

Comment: The Latino version of an orange Daiquiri.

NAVY GROG

Glass: Old-fashioned
Garnish: Lemon wedge
Method: Stir honey with rum in base of shaker until honey dissolves. Add lemon juice, water and bitters, shake with ice and fine strain into ice-filled glass.

1¹/₂ shot(s)	Pusser's Navy rum
3 spoons	Runny honey
¹/₄ shot(s)	Freshly squeezed lime juice
2¹/₂ shot(s)	Chilled water
2 dashes	Angostura aromatic bitters

Variation: Also great served hot. Simply strain into empty glass and microwave for about a minute, then garnish with a cinnamon stick.
Comment: Extremely drinkable honeyed cocktail.

NEGRONI

Glass: Old-fashioned / Collins
Garnish: Half orange slice
Method: Stir first three ingredients with ice and strain into glass, then top up with soda.

1 shot(s)	Plymouth gin
1 shot(s)	Campari
1 shot(s)	Cinzano Rosso vermouth
Top up with	Soda water (optional)

Origin: Named after Count Camillo Negroni from Florence who wanted an Americano 'with a bit more kick'.
Comment: Bitter and dry, but extremely refreshing and very tasty. Obviously a collins glass is used if you top up with soda water and an old-fashioned is used if you don't.

NEGUS

Glass: Toddy
Garnish: Sprinkle ground nutmeg
Method: Preheat glass and place bar spoon in glass, then add all ingredients and stir.

3 shot(s)	Port
1 shot(s)	Freshly squeezed lemon juice
¹/₂ shot(s)	Sugar (gomme) syrup
Top up with	Boiling Water

Variant: Bishop
Origin: Colonel Francis Negus was the M.P. for Ipswich from 1717 to 1732. He created this diluted version of the original Bishop.
Comment: A surprisingly tangy and refreshing hot drink.

NEOPOLITAN

Glass: Old-fashioned
Garnish: Three raspberries
Method: Shake first three ingredients with ice and strain into glass filled with crushed ice. Then float Chambord around glass to create marble effect.

2 shot(s)	Zubrówka (bison grass) vodka
1 shot(s)	Double (heavy) cream
¹/₂ shot(s)	Sugar (gomme) syrup
1 shot(s)	Chambord black raspberry liqueur

Created by: Jamie Terrell in 1997.
Comment: Full of flavour and interesting combinations.

NETHER REGION

Glass: Old-fashioned
Garnish: Squeezed lime wedge in drink
Method: Shake ingredients with ice and strain into ice-filled glass.

2 shot(s)	Absolut vodka
2 shot(s)	Rose's lime cordial

Origin: A very popular drink throughout the Netherlands where it's simply referred to as 'Vodka Lime'. There was even a TV series called Rozengeur en Wodka Lime (loosely translated, Rose Tinted Spectacles and Vodka Lime): this Dutch answer to 'Sex and the City' featured thirtysomething men and women drinking vodka with lime cordial. In the Netherlands this drink is almost always served unshaken in a long glass.
Comment: A simple but sharply pleasant adaptation of the Gimlet. Gimlets are best served 'up' and with gin, but this variation is perfectly drinkable. I apologise to any purists who may be upset by its inclusion.

NEVADA MARTINI

Glass: Martini
Garnish: Split lime wedge
Method: Shake ingredients with ice and strain into glass.

2 shot(s)	Pusser's Navy rum
1 shot(s)	Pressed grapefruit juice
³/₄ shot(s)	Freshly squeezed lime juice
³/₄ shot(s)	Sugar (gomme) syrup

Comment: Dark with bitter backnotes.

NEW ORLEANS PUNCH

Glass: Collins
Method: Shake all ingredients with cubed ice and strain into a glass filled with crushed ice.

1¹/₂ shot(s)	Buffalo Trace Bourbon
³/₄ shot(s)	Appleton Estate V/X aged rum
1¹/₂ shot(s)	Chambord black raspberry liqueur
³/₄ shot(s)	Freshly squeezed lemon juice
3 shot(s)	Cold black camomile tea

Comment: Raspberry is the predominant flavour in this long drink.

NEW YORKER

Glass: Martini
Garnish: Orange peel knot
Method: Shake ingredients with ice and strain into glass.

2	shot(s)	Buffalo Trace Bourbon
1	shot(s)	Freshly squeezed lemon juice
1/2	shot(s)	Grenadine syrup
1/2	shot(s)	Sugar (gomme) syrup

Comment: Simple and tasty.

NEWPORT CODEBREAKER

●●●●○

Glass: Collins
Method: Shake ingredients with ice and strain into ice-filled glass.

1	shot(s)	Sauza Hornitos Tequila
1	shot(s)	Pusser's Navy rum
1/2	shot(s)	Warninks Advocaat
1/2	shot(s)	Cream of coconut
4	shot(s)	Freshly squeezed orange juice

Origin: Adapted from a cocktail discovered in 1999 at Porter's Bar, Covent Garden, London.
Comment: This straw yellow drink is a most unusual mix of ingredients, but very tasty .

NIAGARA FALLS UPDATED

●●●●○

Glass: Flute
Garnish: Physalis
Method: Shake first four ingredients with ice and strain into glass. Top up with ginger ale, stir and serve with straws.

1	shot(s)	Absolut vodka
1	shot(s)	Grand Marnier
1/2	shot(s)	Freshly squeezed lemon juice
1/4	shot(s)	Sugar (gomme) syrup
Top up with		Ginger ale

Comment: Ginger ale and orange complement each other, fortified by vodka.

NICE PEAR-TINI

●●●●◐

Glass: Martini
Garnish: Pear slice on rim
Method: Shake all ingredients with ice and fine strain into chilled glass.

1	shot(s)	Rémy Martin Cognac
1/2	shot(s)	Xanté pear liqueur
1/2	shot(s)	Poire William eau de vie
2	shot(s)	Freshly extracted pear juice
1/4	shot(s)	Sugar (gomme) syrup

Origin: I created this in 2002.
Comment: Spirited, rich and fruity.

NIGHTMARE MARTINI

Glass: Martini
Garnish: Split cherry on rim
Method: Shake ingredients with ice and strain into glass.

1	shot(s)	Plymouth gin
1	shot(s)	Dubonnet Red
1/2	shot(s)	Bols cherry brandy liqueur
2	shot(s)	Freshly squeezed orange juice

Comment: Why this drink is called a nightmare I don't know – a very pleasant strong cherry flavour.

NINE-20-SEVEN

●●●●○

Glass: Flute
Method: Pour ingredients into chilled glass and lightly stir.

1/4	shot(s)	Stoli Vanil
1/4	shot(s)	Cuarenta Y Tres (Licor 43)
Top up with		Piper-Heidsieck Brut Champagne

Origin: Created in 2002 by Damian Caldwell at Home Bar, London, England. Damian was lost for a name for his new creation until a customer asked the time.
Comment: Champagne with a hint of vanilla.

NOBLE EUROPE

●●●●●

Glass: Old-fashioned
Garnish: Orange slice in glass
Method: Shake all ingredients with ice and strain into glass filled with crushed ice.

1 1/2	shot(s)	Tokaji Hungarian wine
1	shot(s)	Absolut vodka
1	shot(s)	Freshly squeezed orange juice
1	dash(es)	Vanilla essence

Origin: Created in 2002 by Dan Spink at Browns, St Martin's Lane, London, England.
Comment: A delicious cocktail that harnesses the rich, sweet flavours of Tokaji and delivers them in a very approachable drink. Also great served 'up'.

NOME NEW

●●●●○

Glass: Martini
Garnish: Mint leaf
Method: Stir all ingredients with ice and fine strain into chilled glass.

1 1/2	shot(s)	Plymouth gin
1 1/2	shot(s)	Tio Pepe Fino Sherry
1	shot(s)	Yellow Chartreuse

Origin: A classic (retro) cocktail whose origin is unknown.
Comment: This dyslexic gnome is dry and interesting.

NORTHERN LIGHTS NEW

●●●●○

Glass: Martini
Garnish: Star anise
Method: Shake all ingredients with ice and fine strain into chilled glass.

1 1/2	shot(s)	Zubrówka Bison vodka
3/4	shot(s)	Apple schnapps
1	shot(s)	Pressed apple juice
1/2	shot(s)	Freshly squeezed lime juice
1/2	shot(s)	Pernod anise
1/2	shot(s)	Sugar (gomme) syrup

Origin: Created in 2003 by Stewart Hudson at MJU Bar, Millennium Hotel, London, England.
Comment: Wonderfully refreshing apple and anise combo served up on a grassy vodka base.

NOVEMBER SEABREEZE VIRGIN

Glass: Collins
Method: Pour ingredients into ice-filled glass and stir.

3	shot(s)	Cranberry juice
3	shot(s)	Pressed apple juice
2	shot(s)	Freshly squeezed lime juice
Top up with		Soda water (club soda)

Comment: Sharp and dry.

●●●●◐○

NUTTY BERRY'TINI NEW

Glass: Martini
Garnish: Float mint leaf
Method: Shake all ingredients with ice and fine strain into chilled glass.

2	shot(s)	Finlandia cranberry vodka
1/2	shot(s)	Bols Cherry brandy liqueur
1/2	shot(s)	Frangelico hazelnut liqueur
1/4	shot(s)	Maraschino liqueur
1	shot(s)	Cranberry juice
1/2	shot(s)	Freshly squeezed lime juice

Origin: Created by yours truly in 2003.
Comment: Cranberry vodka and juice, sweetened with cherry liqueur, dried with lime juice and flavoured with hazelnut.

NUTTY BUDDY

Glass: Hurricane
Garnish: Chocolate shavings
Method: Blend ingredients with crushed ice and serve.

2	shot(s)	Frangelico hazelnut liqueur
1	shot(s)	Bols Brown crème de cacao
1/2	shot(s)	Chocolate syrup
3	scoops	Vanilla ice cream

Comment: Nuts, chocolate and vanilla... how can you go wrong?

●●●●○

NUTTY NASHVILLE

Glass: Martini
Garnish: Lemon twist
Method: Stir honey with Bourbon in base of shaker so as to dissolve honey. Add other ingredients, shake with ice and fine strain into chilled glass.

2 spoon(s)		Runny honey
2	shot(s)	Buffalo Trace Bourbon
1	shot(s)	Frangelico hazelnut liqueur
1	shot(s)	Krupnik honey liqueur

Origin: Created in 2001 by Jason Fendick at Rockwell, Trafalgar Hotel, London, England.
Comment: Bourbon and hazelnut smoothed and rounded by honey.

OH GOSH!

●●●●●

Glass: Martini
Garnish: Flamed lemon twist
Method: Shake all ingredients long and vigorously with cubed ice and strain into glass.

1	shot(s)	Havana Club light rum
1	shot(s)	Cointreau / triple sec
1/2	shot(s)	Freshly squeezed lime juice
1/4	shot(s)	Sugar (gomme) syrup
1/2	shot(s)	Chilled water

Origin: Created by Tony Conigliaro in 2001 at Isola, Knightsbridge, London, England. He named the drink after a customer who ordered a Daiquirí style drink with a difference – when the drink was served he took one sip and uttered "Oh gosh!".
Comment: A very subtle twist on a classic Daiquirí, but don't knock it until you've tried it as it harnesses citrus flavour from orange, lemon and lime - sublime.

NUTTY RUSSIAN

Glass: Rocks
Method: Shake ingredients with ice and strain into ice-filled glass.

1	shot(s)	Absolut vodka
1	shot(s)	Frangelico hazelnut liqueur
1	shot(s)	Kahlúa coffee liqueur

Comment: A Black Russian with Frangelico.

●●●●◐

NUTTY SUMMER MARTINI UPDATED

Glass: Martini
Garnish: Drop three dashes of Angostura onto surface of drink and stir around with a cocktail stick - essential to both the look and flavour.
Method: Shake all ingredients with ice and fine strain into chilled glass.

1¹/₂	shot(s)	Warninks Advocaat
³/₄	shot(s)	Disaronno Originale amaretto
³/₄	shot(s)	Malibu coconut rum liqueur
³/₄	shot(s)	Pressed pineapple juice
¹/₂	shot(s)	Double (heavy) cream

Origin: Created in 2001 by Daniel Spink at Hush Up, London, England.
Comment: This subtle, dessert style cocktail is packed with flavour. A superb after dinner tipple for summer.

●●●●◐○○

OATMEAL COOKIE

Glass: Shot
Method: Shake all ingredients with ice and fine strain into chilled glass.

¹/₂	shot(s)	Teichenné Butterscotch schnapps
¹/₄	shot(s)	Goldschläger cinnamon schnapps
³/₄	shot(s)	Baileys Irish Cream liqueur

Comment: A well balanced creamy shot with hints of butterscotch and cinnamon.

OIL SLICK

Glass: Shot
Method: Shake ingredients with ice and strain into glass.

| ³/₄ | shot(s) | Opal Nera black sambuca |
| ³/₄ | shot(s) | Baileys Irish cream liqueur |

Comment: Whiskey cream and liquorice.

OLD PAL

Glass: Martini
Garnish: Orange knot
Method: Stir ingredients with ice and strain into glass.

1¹/₄	shot(s)	Buffalo Trace Bourbon
1¹/₄	shot(s)	Cinzano Extra Dry vermouth
1¹/₄	shot(s)	Campari

Comment: Very dry, very bitter, very much an acquired taste.

OLD FASHIONED

●●●●●

UPDATED

Glass: Old-fashioned
Garnish: Orange (or lemon) twist
Method: Stir one shot of Bourbon with two ice cubes in a glass. Add sugar syrup and Angostura and two more ice cubes. Stir some more and add another two ice cubes and another shot of Bourbon. Stir lots more so as to melt ice and add more ice. The melting and stirring in of ice cubes is essential to the dilution and taste of the drink.

2¹/₂	shot(s)	Buffalo Trace Bourbon
¹/₂	shot(s)	Sugar (gomme) syrup
3	dashes	Angostura aromatic bitters

Variation: In the USA orange segments and even a maraschino cherry may sometimes be muddled in this drink: the practice probably originated during Prohibition as a means of disguising rough spirits. As Crosby Gaige wrote in his 1944 book, "Serious-minded persons omit fruit salad from Old Fashioneds."
Variant: Brubaker Old-fashioned, Call Me Old Fashioned.
Origin: Like the Martini, the glass this cocktail is served in has taken the name of the drink. The Old Fashioned is purported to have been created by an unnamed bartender at the Pendennis Club in Louisville, Kentucky, for a retired Colonel James E Pepper.
Comment: The Old Fashioned tames Bourbon, making it smooth and remarkably easy to drink.

ONION RING MARTINI

Glass: Martini
Garnish: Onion ring
Method: Muddle onion in base of shaker. Add other ingredients, shake with ice and strain into glass.

2	ring(s)	Fresh red onion
1	shot(s)	Sake
2	shot(s)	Plymouth gin
4	dashes	Fee Brothers Orange bitters
¹/₂	spoon	Sugar (gomme) syrup

Origin: Reputed to have been created at the Bamboo Bar, Bangkok, Thailand.
Comments: Certainly one of the most obscure Martini variations – drinkable, but leaves you with onion breath.

OPAL CAFÉ

Glass: Shot
Method: Shake first two ingredients with ice and strain into glass, then float cream.

¹/₂	shot(s)	Opal Nera black sambuca
¹/₂	shot(s)	Espresso coffee (cold)
	float	Double (heavy) cream

Comment: A good combination.

OPAL MARTINI

Glass: Martini
Garnish: Flamed orange twist
Method: Shake ingredients with ice and strain into glass.

2	shot(s)	Plymouth gin
1	shot(s)	Cointreau / triple sec
2	shot(s)	Freshly squeezed orange juice

Comment: Simple but effective.

OPENING SHOT

Glass: Rocks
Method: Shake ingredients with ice and strain into ice-filled glass.

1¹/₂	shot(s)	Buffalo Trace Bourbon
¹/₂	shot(s)	Cinzano Rosso vermouth
¹/₂	spoon	Grenadine syrup

Comment: A sweet Manattan-like drink on the rocks.

OPERA NEW

●●●●○

Glass: Martini
Garnish: Lemon twist
Method: Shake all ingredients with ice and fine strain into chilled glass.

2	shot(s)	Plymouth gin
2	shot(s)	Dubonnet Red
¹/₄	shot(s)	Maraschino liqueur
3	dashes	Fee Brothers Orange bitters

Origin: A classic (retro) cocktail.
Comment: Gin smoothed by sweet spicy red grape juice with a floral hint of maraschino.

ORANG-A-TANG

●●●○○

Glass: Sling
Method: Shake first five ingredients with ice and strain into ice-filled glass, then float rum.

1¹/₂	shot(s)	Absolut vodka
³/₄	shot(s)	Cointreau / triple sec
3	shot(s)	Freshly squeezed orange juice
³/₄	shot(s)	Freshly squeezed lime juice
¹/₂	spoon	Grenadine syrup
¹/₂	shot(s)	Mount Gay Eclipse gold rum

Variant: With dark rum float.
Comment: An appropriate name.

ORANGE BLOSSOM

Glass: Rocks
Method: Shake ingredients with ice and strain into ice-filled glass.

1¹/₂	shot(s)	Plymouth gin
1¹/₂	shot(s)	Freshly squeezed orange juice
¹/₂	shot(s)	Freshly squeezed lime juice
¹/₄	shot(s)	Orange curaçao
¹/₂	spoon	Grenadine syrup

Comment: Tastes like its namesake.

ORANGE CUSTARD MARTINI

●●●●○

Glass: Martini
Garnish: Orange zest
Method: Shake all ingredients with ice and strain into glass.

2	shot(s)	Warninks Advocaat
1	shot(s)	Tuaca liqueur
¹/₂	shot(s)	Grand Marnier
¹/₄	shot(s)	Vanilla syrup

Origin: I created this drink in 2002 after rediscovering Advocaat on a trip to Amsterdam.
Comment: Creamy and smooth with orange and vanilla and something of a kick.

ORANGE DAIQUIRI

●●●●●

Glass: Martini
Garnish: Orange twist
Method: Shake ingredients vigorously with crushed ice and strain into glass.

2	shot(s)	Clément Créole Shrubb liqueur
¹/₂	shot(s)	Freshly squeezed lime juice
¹/₄	shot(s)	Sugar (gomme) syrup

Origin: I conceived this cocktail in 1998, after visiting the (then) importers' offices of Créole Shrubb. I went with a bottle that evening to London's Met Bar where Ben Reed made the first Orange Daiquirí.
Comment: Orange with that Daiquirí tang.

ORANGE PASSION

Glass: Collins
Garnish: Orange slice in glass
Method: Shake ingredients with ice and strain into ice-filled glass.

2	shot(s)	Passoã passion fruit liqueur
1	shot(s)	Absolut vodka
6	shot(s)	Freshly squeezed orange juice

Comment: Orange and passion.

●●●●●◐

ORANJINIHA UPDATED

Glass: Collins
Garnish: Orange slice in glass
Method: Shake all ingredients with ice and strain into a glass filled with crushed ice.

2	shots	Absolut Mandrin vodka
3	shot(s)	Freshly squeezed orange juice
1	shot(s)	Freshly squeezed lemon juice
1	shot(s)	Sugar (gomme) syrup

Origin: Created in 2002 by Alex Kammerling, London, England.
Comment: This tall, richly flavoured orange drink makes a simple Screwdriver taste very sad.

●●●●●◖

ORCHARD BREEZE

Glass: Collins
Garnish: Apple slice on rim
Method: Shake all ingredients with ice and strain into ice-filled glass.

2	shot(s)	Absolut vodka
2¹⁄₂	shot(s)	Pressed apple juice
1¹⁄₂	shot(s)	Sauvignon Blanc wine
³⁄₄	shot(s)	Elderflower cordial
¹⁄₄	shot(s)	Freshly squeezed lime juice

Origin: Created in 2002 by Wayne Collins for Maxxium UK.
Comment: Refreshing, summery combination of white wine, apple, lime and elderflower laced with vodka.

ORIENTAL

Glass: Martini
Method: Shake ingredients with ice and strain into glass.

2	shot(s)	Buffalo Trace Bourbon
1	shot(s)	Cinzano Rosso vermouth
1	shot(s)	Bols White crème de cacao
1	shot(s)	Freshly squeezed lime juice
¹⁄₂	shot(s)	Sugar (gomme) syrup

Comment: Some very interesting things going on flavourwise.

OUZI

Glass: Shot
Method: Shake ingredients with ice and strain into glass.

³⁄₄	shot(s)	Absolut vodka
¹⁄₂	shot(s)	Ouzo
¹⁄₄	shot(s)	Sugar (gomme) syrup
¹⁄₄	shot(s)	Freshly squeezed lemon juice

Comment: Lemon and aniseed.

ORANGE MOJITO

●●●●●◐

UPDATED

Glass: Collins
Garnish: Mint sprig
Method: Lightly muddle mint in base of glass. Add other ingredients and half fill glass with crushed ice. Churn (stir) with bar spoon. Fill with crushed ice and churn some more. Top up with soda, stir and serve with straws.

8	fresh	Mint leaves
1¹⁄₂	shot(s)	Absolut Mandrin vodka
¹⁄₂	shot(s)	Mandarine Napoléon liqueur
¹⁄₂	shot(s)	Havana Club light rum
1	shot(s)	Freshly squeezed lime juice
¹⁄₂	shot(s)	Sugar (gomme) syrup
Top up with		Soda water (club soda)

Origin: Created in 2001 by Jamie MacDonald while working in Sydney, Australia.
Comment: Mint and orange combine to make a wonderfully fresh drink.

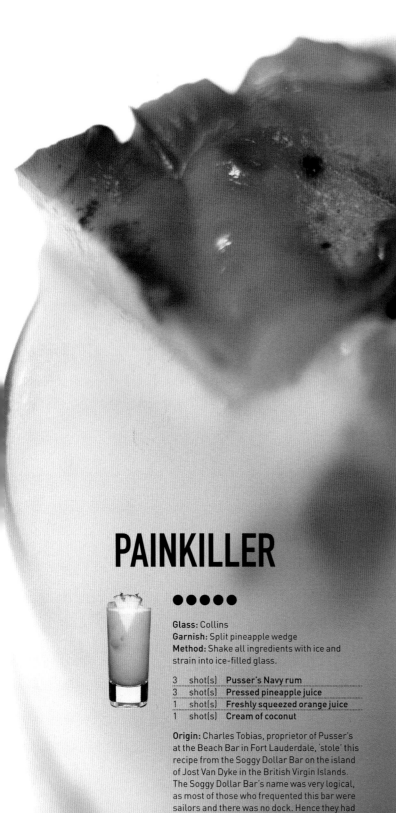

PAINKILLER

•••••

Glass: Collins
Garnish: Split pineapple wedge
Method: Shake all ingredients with ice and strain into ice-filled glass.

3	shot(s)	Pusser's Navy rum
3	shot(s)	Pressed pineapple juice
1	shot(s)	Freshly squeezed orange juice
1	shot(s)	Cream of coconut

Origin: Charles Tobias, proprietor of Pusser's at the Beach Bar in Fort Lauderdale, 'stole' this recipe from the Soggy Dollar Bar on the island of Jost Van Dyke in the British Virgin Islands. The Soggy Dollar Bar's name was very logical, as most of those who frequented this bar were sailors and there was no dock. Hence they had to swim ashore, and so would end up paying for drinks with wet dollars. Charles was one such sailor.
The Soggy Dollar was owned by an English woman, Daphne Henderson. Her Painkiller cocktail was locally famous, but she would not divulge the recipe. So Charles Tobias experimented and came up with this version, which he considers even better than the original.

Comment: A dark and smooth drink with lots of fruity flavours.

PAISLEY MARTINI

Glass: Martini
Garnish: Lemon twist
Method: Shake ingredients with ice and strain into glass.

3	shot(s)	Plymouth gin
3/4	shot(s)	Cinzano Extra Dry vermouth
1/4	shot(s)	The Famous Grouse Scotch whisky

Comment: Very dry and minimal in flavour.

PALE RIDER

•••••○○

Glass: Collins
Method: Shake ingredients with ice and strain into ice-filled glass.

2	shot(s)	Absolut Kurant vodka
1/2	shot(s)	Teichenné peach schnapps
2	shot(s)	Cranberry juice
1	shot(s)	Pressed pineapple juice
1	shot(s)	Freshly squeezed lime juice
3/4	shot(s)	Sugar (gomme) syrup

Origin: Created in 1997 by Wayne Collins at Navajo Joe, London, England.
Comment: A rollercoaster of flavours with a sweet fruity finish.

PALERMO UPDATED

•••••

Glass: Martini
Garnish: Vanilla pod if any
Method: Shake all ingredients with ice and fine strain into chilled glass.

1 1/2	shot(s)	Vanilla infused Havana Club light rum
1 1/4	shot(s)	Sauvignon Blanc wine
1 1/2	shot(s)	Pressed pineapple juice
1/4	shot(s)	Sugar (gomme) syrup

Origin: Adapted from a cocktail discovered in 2001 at Hotel du Vin, Bristol, England.
Comment: A relatively dry cocktail where the vanilla rum combines beautifully with the wine and the sweetness of the pineapple juice.

PALM SPRINGS

•••••○○

Glass: Collins
Garnish: Apple slice & mint sprig
Method: Shake all ingredients with ice and strain into glass filled with crushed ice.

4	fresh	Mint leaves
1	shot(s)	Passoã passion fruit liqueur
1	shot(s)	Mount Gay Eclipse gold rum
1/4	shot(s)	Freshly squeezed lime juice
1	shot(s)	Pressed apple juice
2	shot(s)	Cranberry juice

Comment: Sweet and aromatic.

PANADEER MARTINI

Glass: Martini
Garnish: Chocolate powder dust
Method: Shake all ingredients with ice and strain into glass.

1¹/₂	shot(s)	Havana Club light rum
¹/₂	shot(s)	Bols White crème de cacao
1	shot(s)	Milk
1	shot(s)	Double (heavy) cream
¹/₄	shot(s)	Grenadine syrup

Comment: A pink and fluffy, creamy Martini, but rather nice all the same.

PAPPY HONEYSUCKLE

Glass: Martini
Garnish: Physalis fruit
Method: Stir honey with whiskey in base of shaker so as to dissolve. Add other ingredients, shake with ice and fine strain into chilled glass.

1¹/₂	shot(s)	Black Bush Irish whiskey
2	spoons	Runny honey
1¹/₄	shot(s)	Sauvignon Blanc wine
1¹/₂	shot(s)	Pressed apple juice
¹/₂	shot(s)	Passion fruit syrup
¹/₄	shot(s)	Freshly squeezed lemon juice

Origin: Created in 2002 by Shelim Islam at the GE Club, London, England.
Comment: Fresh and fruity with honeyed sweetness.

PARADISE MARTINI

Glass: Martini
Garnish: Flamed orange zest
Method: Shake all ingredients with ice and fine strain into chilled glass.

2	shot(s)	Plymouth gin
³/₄	shot(s)	Bols Apricot brandy liqueur
1³/₄	shot(s)	Freshly squeezed orange juice
3	dashes	Fee Brothers Orange bitters (optional)

Origin: An old, old recipe that in recent times has been revitalized by Dale DeGroff.
Comment: Wonderfully fruity cocktail that when well made beautifully harnesses and balances its ingredients.

PARISIAN

Glass: Shot
Method: Layer in glass by pouring ingredients carefully in the following order.

¹/₂	shot(s)	Orange curaçao
¹/₂	shot(s)	Kirsch
¹/₂	shot(s)	Rémy Martin Cognac
¹/₂	shot(s)	Green Chartreuse

Comment: Sweet, bitter and weird.

PARK LANE MARTINI

Glass: Martini
Method: Shake ingredients with ice and strain into glass.

2	shot(s)	Plymouth gin
1	shot(s)	Bols Apricot brandy liqueur
1	shot(s)	Freshly squeezed orange juice
¹/₈	shot(s)	Grenadine syrup
¹/₂	fresh	Egg white

Comment: A frothy drink with lots of 'angles'.

PARMA VIOLET MARTINI

Glass: Martini
Garnish: Rose petal
Method: Shake all ingredients with ice and strain into glass.

1¹/₂	shot(s)	Absolut vodka
¹/₄	shot(s)	Teichenné peach schnapps
¹/₂	shot(s)	Freshly squeezed lemon juice
³/₄	shot(s)	Benoit Serres Liqueur de Violette
¹/₄	shot(s)	Sugar (gomme) syrup
4	dashes	Fee Brothers Orange bitters

Created by: Jamie Terrell at LAB, London, England in 2001.
Comment: As floral as the name would suggest.

PASSION FRUIT BATIDA

Glass: Old-fashioned
Method: Cut passion fruit in half and scoop seeds and flesh into shaker. Add other ingredients, shake with ice and pour without straining into glass.

1	fresh	Passion fruit
2¹/₄	shot(s)	Pitú Cachaça
2¹/₂	shot(s)	Rubicon Passion fruit drink
³/₄	shot(s)	Passion fruit syrup
¹/₂	shot(s)	Freshly squeezed lemon juice

Origin: A traditional drink from Brazil where it is known as a Batida Maracuja.
Variant: Serve blended with crushed ice (add ¹/₄ shot additional passion fruit syrup to the above recipe).
Comment: Refreshing and fruity.

PASSION FRUIT DAIQUIRI

Glass: Martini
Garnish: Physalis on rim
Method: Cut passion fruit in half and scoop seeds and flesh into shaker. Add other ingredients, shake with ice and fine strain into chilled glass.

2	fresh	Passion fruit
2	shot(s)	Havana Club light rum
¹/₂	shot(s)	Freshly squeezed lime juice
¹/₂	shot(s)	Passion fruit syrup
¹/₂	shot(s)	Chilled water

Origin: Formula by yours truly in 2002.
Comment: Get passionate with this intoxicating little beauty.

PASS-ON-THAT

Glass: Collins
Method: Shake ingredients with ice and strain into ice-filled glass.

1	shot(s)	Passoã passion fruit liqueur
1	shot(s)	Absolut vodka
3	shot(s)	Passion fruit juice
3	shot(s)	Cranberry juice

Comment: Passion fruit and berries.

PASSBOUR COOLER

Glass: Collins
Garnish: Orange slice in glass
Method: Shake ingredients with ice and strain into ice-filled glass.

1	shot(s)	Passoã passion fruit liqueur
1	shot(s)	Bols Cherry brandy liqueur
1	shot(s)	Buffalo Trace Bourbon
5	shot(s)	Cranberry juice

Comment: Interesting cherry and Bourbon flavours with subtle passion fruit in the background.

PASSION KILLER

Glass: Shot
Method: Layer ingredients by carefully pouring in the following order.

1/2	shot(s)	Midori melon liqueur
1/2	shot(s)	Passoã passion fruit liqueur
1/2	shot(s)	Sauza Hornitos Tequila

Comment: The tropical fruit liqueurs might well kill passion.

PASSION TIME

Glass: Martini
Method: Shake ingredients with ice and strain into glass.

1	shot(s)	Mandarine Napoléon
1	shot(s)	Plymouth gin
3	shot(s)	Passion fruit juice
1/3	shot(s)	Freshly squeezed lemon juice

Comment: Sweet and sour.

PASSOVER

Glass: Collins
Garnish: Orange slice in glass
Method: Shake ingredients with ice and strain into ice-filled glass.

2	shot(s)	Passoã passion fruit liqueur
1	shot(s)	Absolut vodka
6	shot(s)	Pressed grapefruit juice

Comment: Grapefruit complements the flavour of Passoã.

PAVLOVA SUPREME

Glass: Shot
Method: Layer in glass by carefully pouring ingredients in following order.

3/4	shot(s)	Chambord black raspberry liqueur
3/4	shot(s)	Absolut vodka (frozen)

Comment: Unimaginative but pleasant shot.

PEACH ALMOND SHAKE

Glass: Hurricane
Garnish: Split peach slice
Method: Blend ingredients with crushed ice and serve.

1	shot(s)	Teichenné peach schnapps
2	shot(s)	Disaronno Originale amaretto
1	Peeled	Sliced peach
2	scoops	Vanilla ice cream
1	shot(s)	Freshly squeezed lemon juice

Comment: Very sweet but with sourness too.

PEACH DAIQUIRI

⬤⬤⬤⬤◯

Glass: Martini
Garnish: Peach wedge on rim
Method: Shake all ingredients with ice and fine strain into chilled glass.

2	shot(s)	Havana Club light rum
1	shot(s)	Teichenné peach schnapps
1/2	shot(s)	Freshly squeezed lime juice
1/8	shot(s)	Sugar (gomme) syrup
1/2	shot(s)	Chilled water

Origin: My take on the Cuban Daiquiri de Melocoton.
Comment: Harder and drier than you'd expect.

PEACH DAIQUIRÍ FROZEN

Glass: Hurricane
Garnish: Split peach slice
Method: Blend ingredients with lots of ice until slushy and serve.

2	shot(s)	Havana Club light rum
1	shot(s)	Teichenné peach schnapps
1	shot(s)	Freshly squeezed lime juice
1/2	shot(s)	Sugar (gomme) syrup
1/2	peeled	Sliced peach

Comment: Very peachy - but not the most popular of the frozen fruit daiquirís.

PEACH MARGARITA FROZEN

Glass: Coupette
Garnish: Sugar rim & split peach wedge.
Method: Blend ingredients with lots of ice until slushy and serve.

1	shot(s)	Sauza Hornitos Tequila
1	shot(s)	Cointreau / triple sec
1	shot(s)	Teichenné peach schnapps
1	shot(s)	Freshly squeezed lime juice
1/4	shot(s)	Sugar (gomme) syrup
1/2	peeled	Sliced peach

Comment: A sweet and sour drink with peachyness.

PEACH MELBA MARTINI UPDATED ●●●●◐○

Glass: Martini
Garnish: Float flaked almonds
Method: Shake all ingredients with ice and fine strain into chilled glass.

1½	shot(s)	Stoli Vanil
¾	shot(s)	Teichenné Peach schnapps
¾	shot(s)	Chambord black raspberry liqueur
1	shot(s)	Double (heavy) cream
1	shot(s)	Milk

Origin: Melba is a name given to various dishes dedicated to Dame Nellie Melba, the famous 19th century Australian opera singer. Peach Melba was created in 1892 by the world famous chef Georges-Auguste Escoffier, who was the business partner of Cesar Ritz.
Comment: Not quite Peach Melba dessert, but rich and tasty all the same.

PEACHES AND CREAM

Glass: Sling
Garnish: Split peach wedge
Method: Blend ingredients with crushed ice and serve.

1	shot(s)	Peach brandy
1	shot(s)	Teichenné peach schnapps
½	peeled	Sliced peach
2	shot(s)	Double (heavy) cream
2	shot(s)	Milk

Comment: The sweetness of the schnapps is balanced against the cream – very smooth.

PEACHY KEEN

Glass: Hurricane
Garnish: Split peach wedge
Method: Blend ingredients with crushed ice and serve.

1	shot(s)	Havana Club light rum
½	shot(s)	Teichenné peach schnapps
3	shot(s)	Freshly squeezed orange juice
½	peeled	Sliced peach
2	scoops	Vanilla ice cream

Comment: Definitely peachy, but the orange saves the ice cream from cloying.

PEANUT BUTTER & JELLY SHOT

Glass: Shot
Method: Shake ingredients with ice and strain into glass.

½	shot(s)	Chambord black raspberry liqueur
½	shot(s)	Frangelico hazelnut liqueur
½	shot(s)	Baileys Irish cream liqueur

Comment: Does indeed taste like peanut butter and jelly (jam in the UK).

PEANUT 'N' MAPLE'TINI ●●●○○

Glass: Martini
Garnish: Float monkey nut
Method: Stir peanut butter and honey with vodka in base of shaker to dissolve. Add other ingredients, shake with ice and fine strain into chilled glass.

½	spoon	Smooth peanut butter
2½	shot(s)	Absolut vodka
1	shot(s)	Maple syrup
½	shot(s)	Bols crème de banane

Comment: You need to be a peanut butter freak to enjoy this rich concoction.

PEAR & CARDAMOM SIDECAR

Glass: Martini
Garnish: Pear slice on rim
Method: Break away outer shells of cardamom pods and muddle inner seeds in base of shaker. Add other ingredients, shake with ice and fine strain into glass.

7	pods	Green cardamom
1	shot(s)	Cointreau / triple sec
1	shot(s)	Xanté pear liqueur
1	shot(s)	Freshly squeezed lemon juice
1	shot(s)	Chilled water

Origin: Created in 2002 by Jason Scott at Oloroso, Edinburgh, Scotland.
Comment: A wonderful meld of aromatic ingredients.

PEAR & ELDERFLOWER MARTINI ●●●●●○

Glass: Martini
Garnish: Pear slice on rim
Method: Shake all ingredients with ice and fine strain into chilled glass.

2	shot(s)	Absolut vodka
2	shot(s)	Freshly extracted pear juice
½	shot(s)	Elderflower cordial

Origin: Created in 2001 by Angelo Vieira at St. Martins, London, England.
Comment: Pear and elderflower are a match made in St Martins Lane.

PEAR DROP MARTINI UPDATED ●●●●○

Glass: Martini
Garnish: Pear drop sweet in drink
Method: Shake all ingredients with ice and fine strain into chilled glass.

1¼	shot(s)	Xanté pear liqueur
1	shot(s)	Pallini Limoncello liqueur
1	shot(s)	Poire William eau de vie
1	shot(s)	Freshly extracted pear juice

Origin: Created in 2002 by yours truly.
Comment: Not as sticky as the sweet it takes its name from but full-on tangy pear.

PEAR SHAPED (DELUXE VERSION) NEW

Glass: Martini
Garnish: Pear slice on rim
Method: Cut passion fruit in half and scoop out flesh into base of shaker. Add other ingredients, shake with ice and fine strain into chilled glass.

1	fresh	Passion fruit
1½	shot(s)	The Famous Grouse Scotch whisky
1	shot(s)	Xanté pear & cognac liqueur
1	shot(s)	Freshly extracted pear juice
1	shot(s)	Pressed apple juice
¼	shot(s)	Freshly squeezed lime juice

Comment: Wonderful balance of flavours but pear predominates with a dry, yet floral finish.

PEAR SHAPED (POPULAR VERSION) NEW

Glass: Collins
Glass: Pear wedge on rim
Method: Shake all ingredients with ice and strain into ice-filled glass.

2	shot(s)	The Famous Grouse Scotch whisky
1	shot(s)	Xanté pear & cognac liqueur
3	shot(s)	Pressed apple juice
½	shot(s)	Freshly squeezed lime juice
¼	shot(s)	Vanilla sugar syrup

Origin: Adapted from a drink created in 2003 by Jamie Terrell at Dick's Bar, Atlantic, London, England.
Comment: Scotch, pear and apple combine wonderfully in this medium sweet long drink.

PEDRO COLLINS

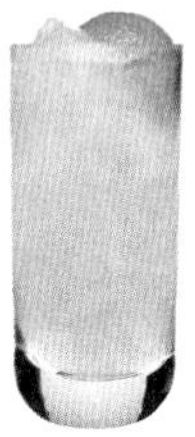

Glass: Collins
Garnish: Lime wedge
Method: Shake first three ingredients with ice and strain into ice-filled glass, then top up with soda.

2	shot(s)	Havana Club light rum
1	shot(s)	Freshly squeezed lemon juice
½	shot(s)	Sugar (gomme) syrup
Top up with		Soda water (club soda)

Comment: A Tom Collins made with rum.

PEPPER & VANILLA'TINI

Glass: Martini
Garnish: Strip yellow pepper
Method: Shake ingredients with ice and strain into chilled glass.

1	shot(s)	Vanilla infused Absolut vodka
¾	shot(s)	Pepper vodka
1	shot(s)	Cuarenta Y Tres (Licor 43)
¾	shot(s)	Tuaca liqueur
1	shot(s)	Freshly extracted yellow bell pepper juice

Origin: I created this in 2002.
Comment: Vanilla and pepper seem to complement each other in a kind of sweet and sour way.

PEPPERED MARY

Glass: Collins
Garnish: Peppered rim & cherry tomato
Method: Shake all ingredients with ice and fine strain into chilled glass.

2	shot(s)	Pepper vodka
2	shot(s)	Freshly extracted yellow bell pepper juice
2	shot(s)	Pressed tomato juice
½	shot(s)	Freshly squeezed lemon juice
7	drops	Tabasco Hot pepper sauce
1	spoon	Lee & Perrin's Worcestershire sauce

Origin: I created this drink in 2003.
Comment: Hot and sweet pepper spice this Bloody Mary.

PERFECT ALIBI

Glass: Collins
Garnish: Mint leaf & lime squeeze
Method: Muddle ginger in base of shaker. Add other ingredients, shake with ice and strain into ice-filled glass.

2	fresh	Thumb-nail sized slices ginger
½	shot(s)	Sugar (gomme) syrup
1½	shot(s)	Krupnik honey liqueur
½	shot(s)	Bärenjäger honey liqueur
3	shot(s)	Cold jasmine tea

Origin: Created in 2001 by Douglas Ankrah for Akbar, London, England.
Comment: A very unusual and pleasant mix of flavours. (Brew the tea fairly weak.)

PERFECT JOHN

Glass: Martini
Method: Shake ingredients with ice and strain into glass.

1	shot(s)	Absolut vodka
1	shot(s)	Cointreau / triple sec
3	shot(s)	Freshly squeezed orange juice
½	shot(s)	Galliano

Comment: A straight-up Harvey Wallbanger with Cointreau.

PERNOD & BLACK MARTINI

Glass: Martini
Garnish: Blackberry on rim
Method: Muddle blackberries in base of shaker. Add other ingredients, shake with ice and fine strain into chilled glass.

7	fresh	Blackberries
½	shot(s)	Pernod anise
1½	shot(s)	Absolut vodka
½	shot(s)	Bols Blackberry (crème de mûre) liqueur
1	shot(s)	Freshly squeezed lime juice
⅛	shot(s)	Vanilla sugar syrup
1	shot(s)	Chilled water

Origin: I created this in 2003.
Comment: Pernod enhances the rich tart flavours of blackberry.

PERROQUET NEW

Glass: Collins (10oz / 290ml max)
Method: Pour pastis and mint syrup into glass. Serve iced water separately in a small jug (known in France as a 'broc') so the customer can dilute to their own taste (I recommend five shots). Lastly, add ice to fill glass.

1	shot(s)	Ricard pastis
1/4	shot(s)	Green mint (menthe) syrup
Top up with		Chilled water

Origin: Very popular throughout France, this drink is named after the parrot due to the bird's brightly coloured plumage.
Comment: The traditional French café drink with a hint of sweet mint.

PERRY-TINI

Glass: Martini
Garnish: Pear slice on rim
Method: Shake first three ingredients with ice and fine strain into chilled glass. Top up with Champagne.

1	shot(s)	Poire William eaux de vie
1	shot(s)	Xanté pear liqueur
2	shot(s)	Freshly extracted pear juice
Top up with		Piper-Heidsieck Brut Champagne

Origin: Created in 2002 by yours truly.
Comment: Pear with a hint of sparkle.

PETER'S FRIENDS

Glass: Martini
Garnish: Raspberry and blueberry on stick
Method: Shake ingredients with ice and strain into the glass

2	shot(s)	The Famous Grouse Scotch whisky
1	shot(s)	Bols Blue curacao
1/4	shot(s)	Freshly squeezed lemon juice

Origin: Created in 2000 by David Whitehead at Atrium, Leeds, England.
Comment: The colour contrasts with the maltiness.

PHARMACEUTICAL STIMULANT

Glass: Rocks
Method: Shake ingredients with ice and strain into glass.

2	shot(s)	Absolut vodka
1/2	shot(s)	Kahlúa coffee liqueur
2	shot(s)	Espresso coffee (cold)
1/4	shot(s)	Sugar (gomme) syrup

Origin: Created by Dick Bradsell at The Pharmacy, London, England, in 1998.
Comment: Ten times better than a vodka-Red Bull: a real wake-up call.

PICCA MARTINI

Glass: Martini
Garnish: Split stemmed cherry on rim
Method: Shake ingredients with ice and strain into glass.

2	shot(s)	The Famous Grouse Scotch whisky
1	shot(s)	Galliano
1	shot(s)	Punt è Mes

Comment: Bittersweet whisky.

PICHUNCHO MARTINI

Glass: Martini
Garnish: Flamed orange twist
Method: Shake all ingredients with ice and fine strain into a chilled glass.

2 1/4	shot(s)	ABA Pisco
1 1/2	shot(s)	Cinzano Rosso (sweet) vermouth
1/4	shot(s)	Sugar (gomme) syrup

Origin: I based this Martini-style cocktail on Pichuncho, a traditional Chilean drink of pisco and vermouth served on the rocks.
Comment: This drink craves the best pisco and the best sweet vermouth. Find those and measure carefully and it's sublime. And, yes, it is better shaken than stirred.

PIERRE COLLINS

Glass: Collins
Method: Shake first three ingredients with ice and strain into ice-filled glass, then top up with soda.

2	shot(s)	Rémy Martin Cognac
1	shot(s)	Freshly squeezed lemon juice
1/2	shot(s)	Sugar (gomme) syrup
Top up with		Soda water (club soda)

Comment: Distinctive and tasty.

PILGRIM COCKTAIL

Glass: Martini
Garnish: Dust with grated nutmeg
Method: Shake all ingredients with ice and fine strain into chilled glass.

1 1/2	shot(s)	Mount Gay Eclipse gold rum
1/2	shot(s)	Grand Marnier
2 1/2	shot(s)	Freshly squeezed orange juice
3/4	shot(s)	Freshly squeezed lime juice
1/4	shot(s)	Berry Hill Pimento Allspice liqueur
3	dashes	Angostura aromatic bitters

Variation: Can also be served hot by simmering ingredients gently in a saucepan. Alternatively, mix as above, strain into an old fashioned glass then microwave for 40 seconds.
Comment: Whether you serve this hot or cold, it's a spicy winter drink.

PINA COLADA

●●●●◐

Glass: Hurricane
Garnish: Split pineapple wedge & cherry on stick
Method: Blend ingredients with crushed ice and serve.

2	shot(s)	Mount Gay Eclipse gold rum
3	shot(s)	Pressed pineapple juice
1	shot(s)	Cream of coconut
½	shot(s)	Double (heavy) cream

Variant: This is great with dark rum such as Myers's Planters' Punch rum.

Origin: Two Puerto Rican bartenders compete the ownership of this drink. Ramon Marrero Pérez claims to have first made it at the Caribe Hilton hotel in San Juan in 1954 using Coco López cream of coconut. But Don Ramon Patas Minyot says he created it at the (now-defunct) Barrachina Bar in 1963.

Comment: This is a truly wonderful creamy, fruity concoction, with a real depth of flavour and not half as sticky as the world would have you believe. But can you face the bar call?

PIMM'S CLASSIC

Glass: Collins
Garnish: Half slice of orange and lemon, a slice of cucumber, half a strawberry & a mint sprig.
Method: Pour ingredients into ice-filled glass and gently stir.

2	shot(s)	Pimms No.1 Cup
Top up with		Half lemonade and half ginger beer

Comment: Summer's not here until you've had one.

PIMM'S CUP

Glass: Collins
Garnish: Mint sprig
Method: Pour ingredients into ice-filled glass and stir.

2	shot(s)	Pimm's No.1 Cup
¼	shot(s)	Freshly squeezed lime juice
Top up with		Ginger ale

Comment: Not as good as the original – but still refreshing.

PINA COLADA MOCKTAIL VIRGIN

Glass: Hurricane
Garnish: Split pineapple wedge and leaf
Method: Blend ingredients with crushed ice and serve.

6	shot(s)	Pressed pineapple juice
2	shot(s)	Double (heavy) cream
2	shot(s)	Cream of coconut

AKA: Snow White
Comment: Tasty alcohol free cocktail.

PINEAPPLE & CARDAMOM DAIQUIRÍ

●●●●●◐

Glass: Martini
Garnish: Pineapple wedge on rim
Method: Break away outer shells of cardamom pods and muddle inner seeds in base of shaker. Add other ingredients, shake with ice and fine strain into chilled glass.

4	pods	Green cardamom
2	shot(s)	Havana Club light rum
1¾	shot(s)	Pressed pineapple juice
¼	shot(s)	Freshly squeezed lime juice
¼	shot(s)	Sugar (gomme) syrup

Origin: Adapted from Henry Bessant's Pineapple & Cardamom Martini.
Comment: One of the tastiest Daiquirís I've tried.

THOSE DRINKS I'VE SAMPLED RECENTLY ARE GRADED AS FOLLOWS:

● DISGUSTING ●◐ PRETTY AWFUL ●● BEST AVOIDED
●●◐ DISAPPOINTING ●●● ACCEPTABLE ●●●◐ GOOD
●●●● RECOMMENDED ●●●●◐ HIGHLY RECOMMENDED
●●●●● OUTSTANDING / EXCEPTIONAL

PINEAPPLE & CARDAMOM MARTINI

Glass: Martini
Garnish: Pineapple leaf on rim
Method: Break away outer shells of cardamom pods and muddle inner seeds with pineapple wedges in base of shaker. Add other ingredients, shake with ice and fine strain into chilled glass.

4	pods	Green cardamom
4	fresh	Pineapple wedges
2	shot(s)	Absolut vodka
2	shot(s)	Pressed pineapple juice
¼	shot(s)	Sugar (gomme) syrup

Origin: Created in 2002 by Henry Bessant at Lonsdale House, London, England.
Comment: This is about as good as it gets: a spectacular pairing of fruit and spice.

PINEAPPLE FIZZ

Glass: Collins
Method: Shake first four ingredients with ice and strain into ice-filled glass, then top up with soda water.

2	shot(s)	Mount Gay Eclipse gold rum
1½	shot(s)	Pressed pineapple juice
1	shot(s)	Freshly squeezed lime juice
½	shot(s)	Sugar (gomme) syrup
Top up with		Soda water (club soda)

Comment: Tasty and refreshing.

PINEAPPLE & GINGER MARTINI

Glass: Martini
Garnish: Pineapple wedge on rim
Method: Muddle ginger and pineapple in base of shaker. Add other ingredients, shake with ice and strain into glass.

2	fresh	Thumb-nail sized slices ginger
1	ring(s)	Chopped fresh pineapple
2	shot(s)	Absolut vodka
1	shot(s)	Pressed pineapple juice

Comment: Fresh and almost creamy, with a smooth rich pineapple flavour and subtle hints of vodka and ginger.

PINEAPPLE MARGARITA UPDATED

Glass: Coupette
Garnish: Split pineapple wedge
Method: Shake all ingredients with ice and fine strain into chilled glass.

2	shot(s)	Sauza Hornitos Tequila
¾	shot(s)	Cointreau / triple sec
1½	shot(s)	Pressed pineapple juice

Variant: Add half shot pineapple syrup, blend with crushed ice and serve frozen.
Comment: A Tequila Margarita with a pineapple fruit kick.

PINEAPPLE MOJITO NEW

Glass: Collins
Method: Lightly muddle mint in glass. Pour ingredients into glass and half fill with crushed ice. Churn drink with barspoon. Fill glass with crushed ice, stir again and serve with straws.

12	fresh	Mint leaves
2	shot(s)	Havana Club light rum
¾	shot(s)	Cuarenta Y Tres (Licor 43) liqueur
2	shot(s)	Pressed pineapple juice
1	shot(s)	Freshly squeezed lime juice

Origin: Discovered in 2003 at Apartment 195, London, England.
Comment: A fruity vanilla-ed twist on the classic Mojito.

PINK CADDY CONVERTIBLE

Glass: Martini & shot glass
Method: Shake first four ingredients with ice and fine strain into chilled glass. Serve Grand Marnier in a shot glass as an accompaniment to be sipped alternately with the cocktail.

1½	shot(s)	Sauza Hornitos Tequila
¾	shot(s)	Cointreau / triple sec
1½	shot(s)	Cranberry juice
½	shot(s)	Freshly squeezed lime juice
2	shot(s)	Grand Marnier

Origin: Created in 1994 by Wayne Collins at Bacchus Restaurant, Newport Beach, California. The liqueur on the side allows you to convert the flavour.
Comment: Without the liqueur served on the side this drink is quite sour.

PINK CHEVROLET

Glass: Flute
Garnish: Strawberry
Method: Pour strawberry liqueur into chilled glass and top up with Champagne.

1	shot(s)	Bols Strawberry (fraise) liqueur
Top up with		Piper-Heidsieck Brut Champagne

Comment: Strawberry Champagne – more fun with fresh strawberries.

NEW	A DRINK NEW TO SAUCE GUIDES.
UPDATED	ENTRY CHANGED SINCE LAST VOLUME.
shot(s)	25ML MEASURE (UK) OR 1OZ (US). HOWEVER, IT DOESN'T REALLY MATTER WHAT MEASURE YOU USE AS A SHOT, SO LONG AS YOU USE THE SAME MEASURE OR FRACTIONS OF THAT MEASURE TO MEASURE ALL THE INGREDIENTS. THIS WILL ENSURE THE PROPORTIONS OF ONE INGREDIENT TO ANOTHER WILL BE AS THE RECIPE INTENDED.

PINK GIN & TONIC

Glass: Collins
Garnish: Lime wedge
Method: Pour gin and Angostura into ice-filled glass, then top up with tonic water and stir.

2	shot(s)	Plymouth gin
4	dashes	Angostura aromatic bitters
Top up with		Tonic water

Origin: Gin was a big favourite in the Royal Navy – along with rum, which was served as a daily ration for the men right up until the 70s. It was mixed with various things to make health benefits more palatable – gin and lime (the gimlet) was supposed to be a remedy against scurvy.
Pink gin (without the tonic) was originally used against stomach upsets, with Angostura bitters considered medicinal. This version adds in another allegedly medicinal ingredient – tonic, which contains quinine so was prescribed (with gin) against malaria.

Comment: Basically a G&T with an extra pep of flavour from Angostura, this has a wider appeal than the Martini-like original Pink Gin.

PINK FLAMINGO

Glass: Collins
Garnish: Apple wheel
Method: Shake all ingredients with ice and fine strain into chilled glass.

2	shot(s)	Absolut Mandrin vodka
1	shot(s)	Sourz Sour Apple liqueur
1/2	shot(s)	Freshly squeezed lime juice
1	shot(s)	Cranberry juice

Origin: Created in 2002 by Wayne Collins for Maxxium UK.
Comment: Soapy and citrus flavoured – but in a nice way.

PINK FOREST

Glass: Martini
Garnish: Strawberry
Method: Shake ingredients with ice and strain into ice-filled glass.

2 1/2	shot(s)	Bols Strawberry (fraise) liqueur
1	shot(s)	Plymouth gin
1/2	shot(s)	Cointreau / triple sec
1/2	shot(s)	Double (heavy) cream

Comment: Strawberries and cream, heavily laced with gin and triple sec.

PINK HOUND

Glass: Martini
Method: Shake ingredients with ice and strain into glass.

1	shot(s)	Absolut vodka
1	shot(s)	Plymouth gin
3	shot(s)	Pink grapefruit juice

Comment: Dry, bitter and refreshing.

PINK LADY MARTINI

Glass: Martini
Garnish: Stemmed maraschino cherry on rim
Method: Shake all ingredients with ice and fine strain into chilled glass.

2 1/2	shot(s)	Plymouth gin
1	shot(s)	Calvados or Applejack brandy
1	shot(s)	Freshly squeezed lemon juice
1/2	shot(s)	Grenadine syrup
1/2	fresh	Egg white

Origin: A classic cocktail named after a successful 1912 stage play.
Comment: Despite the colour, this is sharp and alcoholic.

PINK LEMONADE

Glass: Hurricane
Garnish: Lemon slice and redcurrant stem
Method: Shake first six ingredients with ice and strain into ice-filled glass, then top up with Cranberry juice.

3/4	shot(s)	Plymouth gin
3/4	shot(s)	Sauza Hornitos Tequila
3/4	shot(s)	Havana Club light rum
3/4	shot(s)	Absolut vodka
2	shot(s)	Freshly squeezed lime juice
1	shot(s)	Sugar (gomme) syrup
Top up with		Cranberry juice

Comment: Very similar to a Long Beach Iced Tea – long and refreshing.

PINK PASSION

Glass: Martini
Garnish: Split cherry on rim
Method: Shake ingredients with ice and strain into glass.

3/4	shot(s)	Passoã passion fruit liqueur
3/4	shot(s)	Bols Cherry brandy liqueur
3/4	shot(s)	Buffalo Trace Bourbon
2	shot(s)	Cranberry juice
1/2	shot(s)	Coconut milk

Comment: Interesting and varied flavours.

PINK SIN MARTINI

Glass: Martini
Method: Shake all ingredients with cubed ice and fine strain into glass.

3/4	shot(s)	Cinnamon Schnapps
1	shot(s)	Bols White crème de cacao
1 1/2	shot(s)	Absolut vodka
1	shot(s)	Cranberry juice

Comment: While this drink looks a little like a Cosmo, the cinnamon and chocolate flavour is very different and far less subtle.

PINK TUTU

Glass: Rocks
Garnish: Orange slice
Method: Shake all ingredients with ice and strain into ice-filled glass.

1	shot(s)	Teichenné peach schnapps
1/2	shot(s)	Absolut vodka
1/2	shot(s)	Campari
2	shot(s)	Pressed grapefruit juice
1/4	shot(s)	Sugar (gomme) syrup

Origin: Created in 1999 by Dominique of Café Rouge, Leeds, England.
Comment: A cocktail that's both bitter and sweet. Originally served in a wine glass with a sugar rim. We prefer served as above or with crushed ice.

PISCO COLLINS

Glass: Collins
Method: Pour ingredients into ice-filled glass and stir.

1	shot(s)	ABA Pisco
3/4	shot(s)	Freshly squeezed lime juice
1/2	shot(s)	Sugar (gomme) syrup
Top up with		Soda (club soda)

Comment: Super refreshing.

PISCO KID

Glass: Old-fashioned
Garnish: Three raspberries
Method: Shake first five ingredients with ice and strain over crushed ice, then float crème de mûre on top.

1 1/2	shot(s)	ABA Pisco
3/4	shot(s)	Myers's Planters' Punch rum
1 1/2	shot(s)	Pressed pineapple juice
4	dashes	Fee Brothers Orange bitters
1/4	shot(s)	Sugar (gomme) syrup
3/4	shot(s)	Bols Crème de mûre (blackberry) liqueur

Origin: Created by Jamie Terrell to take first place in the Alto de Carmen cocktail competition in June 1999.
Comment: A tropical tasting and refreshingly smooth concoction.

PISCO NARANJA

Glass: Collins
Garnish: Orange wheel in drink
Method: Shake all ingredients with ice and strain into ice-filled glass.

2	shot(s)	ABA Pisco
4	shot(s)	Freshly squeezed orange juice
1	shot(s)	Grand Marnier

Origin: I based this recipe on the traditional Chilean combination of pisco and orange juice.
Comment: Aromatic brandy and orange juice pepped up and sweetened with a slug of Grand Marnier.

PISCO PUNCH

(DIFFORD'S FORMULA)

Glass: 12oz Collins
Garnish: Pineapple wedge on rim
Method: Muddle cloves with Pisco in base of shaker. Add all other ingredients except for Champagne, shake with ice and strain into ice-filled glass. Top up with Champagne.

4	dried	Cloves
2¼	shot(s)	ABA Pisco
1¾	shot(s)	Pressed pineapple juice
¼	shot(s)	Freshly squeezed orange juice
½	shot(s)	Freshly squeezed lemon juice
½	shot(s)	Sugar (gomme) syrup
Top up with		Piper-Heidsieck Brut Champagne

Origin: The creation of Pisco Punch is usually credited to Professor Jerry Burns and Duncan Nichol, of San Francisco's Bank Exchange. However, its origin could lie in the late 1800s, when the drink was served aboard steamships stopping in Chile en route to San Francisco. The following story of the Pisco Punch and the Bank Exchange comes from the 1973 edition of the California Historical Quarterly and Robert O'Brien's book, 'This Was San Francisco'. I'd like to thank a Sauce reader, Jon Derr, for bringing this to my attention and leading me to add my Pisco Punch formula to the many others already in existence.

The Bank Exchange was a ballroom that opened in 1854 and survived the earthquake and fire of 1906. Its popularity never waned and only Prohibition brought about its demise. Much of the Bank Exchange's notoriety was due to the Pisco Punch, so much so that the establishment gained the nickname 'Pisco John's' after one of its original owners.

The recipe was thought to have been carried to the grave by Duncan Nichol, the Scottish immigrant who owned the bar from the late 1870s until it closed. He had been given the recipe by its previous owners, Orrin Dorman and John Torrence. Nichol continued their tradition of absolute secrecy over the formula.

Comment: A tangy, balanced combination of rich flavours. The quality of Pisco used is crucial to the success of a Pisco Punch. This recipe is improved by using ¾ shot of the marinade prescribed in Alfredo Micheli's Pisco Punch or syrup from canned pineapple in place of the sugar syrup. If using the marinade drop one of the marinated pineapple wedges and cloves into the drink as the garnish.

(ALFREDO MICHELI'S FORMULA)

Glass: Goblet
Garnish: Pineapple wedge on rim
Method: Muddle orange and pineapple in base of shaker. Add Pisco and pineapple marinade, shake with ice and fine strain into ice-filled glass. Top up with no more than 2 shots of soda water.

2	fresh	Orange slices
3	marinaded	Pineapple wedges
2	shot(s)	ABA Pisco
¾	shot(s)	Pineapple marinade
Top up with		Soda water (club soda)

Recipe for marinade: Core and remove the rind from one ripe pineapple. Cut the pineapple into rings and then into wedges and place in deep container. Add 30 cloves and one litre of sugar syrup and marinate the pineapple and cloves for 24 hours.
Origin: Alfredo Micheli (who went by the nickname Mike) was employed at the Bank Exchange and spied on Duncan Nichol to learn how to make this legendary drink. After he believed he'd learnt the secret he left to start serving at a newly opened competitor to the Bank Exchange, Paoli's on Montgomery Street.
Comment: This subtly flavoured drink is justifiably legendary.

(LANES' FORMULA)

Glass: Collins
Garnish: Pineapple wedge
Method: Shake all ingredients and strain into a glass filled with crushed ice and stir.

3	shot(s)	ABA Pisco
½	shot(s)	Freshly squeezed lemon juice
½	shot(s)	Pressed pineapple juice
Top up with		Soda water (club soda)

Origin: This recipe is said to herald from John Lanes, the manager of the famous Bank Exchange in 1919.
Comment: The flavour of this cocktail is a tad flat and subdued. It is improved and opened by the use of a half shot of sugar syrup.

(MR PROSSER'S FORMULA)

Glass: Martini
Garnish: Grapes on rim
Method: Muddle grapes in base of shaker. Add other ingredients, shake with ice and fine strain into chilled glass.

20	fresh	White grapes
2½	shot(s)	ABA Pisco
1	shot(s)	Pressed pineapple juice
⅛	shot(s)	Le Fée Absinthe

Origin: Jack Koeppler, the bartender at the Buena Vista Café in San Francisco who's also famous for being the first bartender in America to serve Irish Coffee, was given this recipe by the son of its creator, a fellow San Franciscan by the name of Mr Prosser. I've adapted this recipe from his, which originally comprised:
2 shot(s) White grape juice, 2 shot(s) Pisco, 1 spoon pineapple juice and 1 spoon absinthe.
Comment: Aromatic take on the Pisco Punch.

PISCO SOUR

Glass: Old-fashioned
Method: Shake first four ingredients with ice and strain into glass. Apply three dashes of bitters to the frothy head of the drink.

2¹/₂	shot(s)	**ABA Pisco**
1	shot(s)	**Freshly squeezed lime juice**
1	shot(s)	**Sugar (gomme) syrup**
¹/₂	fresh	**Egg white**
3	dashes	**Angostura aromatic bitters**

Origin: The national drink of both Chile and Peru.
Comment: Traditionally this drink is blended with crushed ice, but I prefer it served straight-up in an old-fashioned glass – only be sure to drink it quickly while it's cold. A sublime drink which shows off the complexity of Pisco.

PISCOLA

Glass: Collins
Garnish: Lime wedge
Method: Pour pisco and bitters into ice-filled glass and top up with cola.

2¹/₂	shot(s)	**ABA Pisco**
3	dashes	**Angostura aromatic bitters**
Top up with		**Cola**

Origin: A popular long drink in its native Chile.
Comment: A 'brandy' and cola with a hint of angostura. Try it and see why the Chileans enjoy it.

PLAYA DEL MAR

Glass: Martini
Garnish: Pineapple wedge on rim
Method: Shake all ingredients with ice and fine strain into chilled glass.

1	shot(s)	**Sauza Hornitos Tequila**
¹/₂	shot(s)	**Cointreau / triple sec**
1¹/₂	shot(s)	**Cranberry juice**
1	shot(s)	**Pressed pineapple juice**
¹/₄	shot(s)	**Sugar (gomme) syrup**
¹/₂	shot(s)	**Freshly squeezed lime juice**

Origin: Created in 1997 by Wayne Collins at Navajo Joe, London, England.
Comment: A complex taste with a hint of Tequila.

PLAYMATE

Glass: Martini
Garnish: Orange peel twist
Method: Shake ingredients with ice and strain into glass.

1	shot(s)	**Bols Apricot brandy liqueur**
1	shot(s)	**Rémy Martin Cognac**
1	shot(s)	**Mandarine Napoléon**
1	shot(s)	**Freshly squeezed orange juice**
¹/₂	fresh	**Egg white**
4	dashes	**Angostura aromatic bitters**

Comment: Strong mandarin notes with a smooth aftertaste.

PLANTER'S PUNCH

Glass: Collins
Garnish: Slice of orange and mint sprig in glass.
Method: Shake all ingredients with cubed ice and strain into ice-filled glass.

1¹/₂	shot(s)	**Myers's Planters' Punch rum**
¹/₂	shot(s)	**Freshly squeezed lime juice**
1	shot(s)	**Sugar (gomme) syrup**
2	shot(s)	**Chilled water**
4	dash(es)	**Angostura aromatic bitters**

Origin: Invented in the late 19th century by the founder of Myers's rum, Fred L. Myers's. There are a number of different recipes including one on the back of each bottle of Myers's rum. The recipe shown above is known as the 'Old Plantation formula' using the classic rum punch proportions of 1 sour (lime), 2 sweet (sugar), 3 strong (rum) and 4 weak (water). There is also an American formula of 1 sweet, 2 sour, 3 weak and 4 strong. In David A. Embury's famous book 'The Fine Art of Mixing Drinks', he recommends 1 sweet, 2 sour, 3 strong and 4 weak.

Comment: A drink which harnesses the rich flavours of Myers's rum. Rum punches made to the above classic proportions with overproof rum should be served with crushed ice. However, Myers's has a more down to earth strength and so this punch is best served long with cubed ice.

PLAYMATE MARTINI

Glass: Martini
Garnish: Flamed orange twist
Method: Shake all ingredients with ice and strain into chilled glass.

1	shot(s)	Rémy Martin Cognac
1	shot(s)	Grand Marnier
1	shot(s)	Bols Apricot brandy liqueur
1	shot(s)	Freshly squeezed orange juice
¹/₂	fresh	Egg white
4	dashes	Angostura aromatic bitters

Comment: Smooth and easy drinking.

POINSETTIA

Glass: Flute
Garnish: Quarter slice of orange on rim
Method: Pour ingredients into glass and lightly stir with bar spoon.

¹/₂	shot(s)	Cointreau / triple sec
1	shot(s)	Cranberry juice
Top up with		Piper-Heidsieck Brut Champagne

Comment: Dry, zesty and fresh

POITINI

Glass: Flute
Garnish: Peach segment
Method: Stir poteen and peach schnapps with ice and strain into glass, then top up with chilled Champagne.

¹/₂	shot(s)	Poteen
¹/₂	shot(s)	Teichenné peach schnapps
Top up with		Piper-Heidsieck Brut Champagne

Comment: The peach schnapps almost gets lost under the Champagne and poteen (also spelt Poitin - hence the name).

POLISH MARTINI

Glass: Martini
Garnish: Lemon twist
Method: Stir ingredients with ice and strain into glass.

1	shot(s)	Zubrówka bison vodka
1	shot(s)	Krupnik honey liqueur
1	shot(s)	Absolut vodka
1	shot(s)	Pressed apple juice

Origin: Created by Dick Bradsell, for his (Polish) father-in-law, Victor Sarge.
Variant: Can also be made without the shot of plain vodka. i.e. equal parts Zubrówka, Krupnik and apple juice.
Comment: A round, smooth and extremely tasty Martini.

POLISH SPRING PUNCH

Glass: Sling
Garnish: Lemon slice and berries
Method: Pour ingredients into ice-filled glass and stir.

2	shot(s)	Absolut vodka
¹/₂	shot(s)	Chambord black raspberry liqueur
¹/₄	shot(s)	Bols Raspberry (framboise) liqueur
1	shot(s)	Freshly squeezed lemon juice
¹/₄	shot(s)	Sugar (gomme) syrup
Top up with		Piper-Heidsieck Brut Champagne

Origin: Created by Dick Bradsell.
Comment: Nothing very Polish about it, but it tastes good anyway.

POLLY'S SPECIAL

Glass: Martini
Garnish: Grapefruit wedge on rim
Method: Shake all ingredients with ice and fine strain into chilled glass.

1³/₄	shot(s)	The Famous Grouse Scotch whisky
1	shot(s)	Pressed grapefruit juice
1	shot(s)	Grand Marnier
¹/₄	shot(s)	Sugar (gomme) syrup

Origin: I adapted this recipe from a 1947 edition of Trader Vic's Bartender's Guide.
Comment: Sweet, sour, flavoursome and balanced – for grown-ups who like the taste of alcohol.

POMPANSKI MARTINI

Glass: Martini
Method: Shake all ingredients with ice and strain into glass.

1³/₄	shot(s)	Absolut vodka
¹/₂	shot(s)	Cointreau / triple sec
1¹/₂	shot(s)	Pressed grapefruit juice
¹/₄	shot(s)	Sugar (gomme) syrup
1	spoon	Cinzano Extra Dry vermouth

Comment: Dry and zesty with the sharp freshness of grapefruit and a hint of orange.

PONCHA

Glass: Collins
Garnish: Orange wedge on rim
Method: Pour aguardiente and honey into base of shaker and stir so as to dissolve honey. Add other ingredients, shake with ice and strain into ice filled glass.

2¹/₂	shot(s)	Aguardiente (Torres Aqua d'Or)
2	spoons	Runny honey
1	shot(s)	Freshly squeezed lemon juice
¹/₄	shot(s)	Sugar (gomme) syrup
1¹/₂	shot(s)	Freshly squeezed orange juice
1¹/₂	shot(s)	Pressed grapefruit juice

Origin: Every bar and bartender in Madeira mixes this traditional island drink differently - this is my take on it.
Comment: This citrus refresher is reputedly an excellent cold remedy.

PONTBERRY MARTINI

Glass: Martini
Method: Shake ingredients with ice and strain into glass.

1	shot(s)	**Absolut vodka**
3	spoons	**Bols Crème de mûre (blackberry) liqueur**
2	shot(s)	**Cranberry juice**

Origin: Created by Dick Bradsell in the late 90s for the opening of Pont Street Agent Provocateur.
Comment: A very light cocktail and easy drinking.

●●●●●◑

POOH'TINI

Glass: Martini
Method: Stir spoons of honey into vodka in base of shaker can. Add other ingredients, shake with ice and fine strain into glass.

1³/₄	spoon(s)	**Runny honey**
2	shot(s)	**Zubrówka (Bison grass) vodka**
¹/₂	shot(s)	**Krupnik honey liqueur**
1¹/₂	shot(s)	**Cold black camomile tea**

Origin: Adapted from a drink discovered in 1999 at Lot 61, New York City.
Comment: Honey, tea and Bison all meld well.

PORT WINE COCKTAIL

Glass: Martini
Garnish: Orange peel twist dropped into drink
Method: Stir ingredients with ice and strain into glass.

4	shot(s)	**Ruby Port**
1	shot(s)	**Rémy Martin Cognac**

Comment: Heavy but interesting.

EL PRESIDENTE I

Glass: Martini
Method: Shake ingredients with ice and strain into glass.

2¹/₂	shot(s)	**Havana Club light rum**
¹/₄	shot(s)	**Dubonnet Red**
¹/₃	shot(s)	**Grenadine syrup**

Comment: Lightly flavoured.

●●●●●○

PRICKLY PEAR MULE

Glass: Collins
Garnish: Pear slice on rim
Method: Shake all but ginger beer with ice and strain into ice-filled glass. Top up with ginger beer.

1¹/₄	shot(s)	**Xanté liqueur**
1¹/₄	shot(s)	**Poire William eau de vie**
3	shot(s)	**Freshly extracted pear juice**
¹/₄	shot(s)	**Freshly squeezed lemon juice**
2	dashes	**Angostura aromatic bitters**
Top up with		**Jamaican Ginger beer**

Origin: Created by yours truly in 2002.
Comment: Fill the glass with ice and go easy on the ginger beer which can predominate and overpower the subtle pear flavours.

PRAIRIE OYSTER

Glass: Coupette
Method: Being careful not to break the egg yolk, place it in the centre hollow of glass. Shake the rest of the ingredients with ice and strain over egg. Instruct drinker to down in one.

1	raw	**Egg yolk**
1	shot(s)	**Rémy Martin Cognac**
¹/₄	shot(s)	**Worcestershire sauce**
¹/₄	shot(s)	**Tomato juice**
6	drops	**Tabasco**
2	pinches	**Pepper**
2	pinches	**Salt**
¹/₂	spoon	**Malt vinegar**

Origin: Created by a sadist. Jeeves makes something similar for Bertie Wooster in a P.G. Wodehouse tale.

Comment: Pick-me-up hangover cure. Like many hangover cures, this works on the kill or... basis. Don't try this at home.

PRINCE CHARLES

Glass: Martini
Method: Shake ingredients with ice and strain into glass.

1½	shot(s)	Rémy Martin Cognac
1½	shot(s)	Drambuie liqueur
1½	shot(s)	Freshly squeezed lemon juice

Comment: Sour, but full of flavour.

PRINCETON

Glass: Martini
Garnish: Lemon twist
Method: Stir ingredients with ice and strain into glass.

3	shot(s)	Plymouth gin
1½	shot(s)	Ruby Port
4	dashes	Fee Brothers Orange bitters

Comment: Strong in flavour and alcohol content.

PRUNE FACE NEW

●●●●○

Glass: Old-fashioned
Garnish: Orange peel
Method: Pour Bourbon into glass with four ice cubes and stir until ice has at least half melted. Add other ingredients and additional ice and stir some more.

2	shot(s)	Buffalo Trace Bourbon
¾	shot(s)	Vielle de prune eau de vie
¼	shot(s)	Mandarin Napoleon liqueur
¼	shot(s)	Sugar (gomme) syrup

Origin: Created in 2002 by Daniel Warner at Zander, London, England and named after my friend's nickname for his stepmother.
Comment: Why muddle cherries into your Old Fashioned when you can add a hint of prune?

P.S. I LOVE YOU

●●●●○

Glass: Martini
Garnish: Crumbled Cadbury's Flake bar
Method: Shake all ingredients with ice and fine strain into chilled glass.

1¼	shot(s)	Baileys Irish Cream liqueur
1¼	shot(s)	DiSaronno Originale amaretto
¾	shot(s)	Mount Gay Eclipse gold rum
¾	shot(s)	Kahlúa coffee liqueur
1	shot(s)	Double (heavy) cream

Comment: And you'll love this creamy flavoursome drink.

PSYCHO TSUNAMI

Glass: Shot
Method: Layer ingredients by carefully pouring in the following order. The Tabasco will sink through the Tequila and sit on the layer of lime juice.

½	shot(s)	Bols Blue curaçao
½	shot(s)	Freshly squeezed lime juice
½	shot(s)	Sauza Hornitos Tequila (frozen)
2	dashes	Tabasco sauce

Comment: A great looking shot which leaves your mouth citrusy fresh. More fun than Listerine!
Origin: Created by Dick Bradsell and Wayne Collins at Tsunami, London, England.

PULP FICTION

●●●●○

Glass: Collins
Method: Shake all ingredients with ice and strain into ice filled glass. Top up with lemonade.

2	shot(s)	Pressed apple juice
2	shot(s)	Rémy Martin Cognac
1	shot(s)	Apple schnapps Liqueur
Top up with		Lemonade

Origin: Discovered in 2001 at Teatro, London, England.
Comment: Originally made with apple pulp, this drink has a zingy apple taste.

PURPLE COSMO NEW

●●●●◐

Glass: Martini
Garnish: Orange twist
Method: Stir all ingredients with ice and strain into chilled glass.

2	shot(s)	Absolut Citron vodka
¾	shot(s)	Parfait Amour
1½	shot(s)	Ocean Spray White cranberry drink
¼	shot(s)	Freshly squeezed lime juice

Variant: Blue Cosmo
Comment: If shaken this becomes more of a grey Cosmo. The flavour and colour of this drink make for an interesting twist on the standard Cosmo.

PURPLE FLIRT

Glass: Martini
Garnish: Redcurrants on rim
Method: Shake all ingredients with ice and strain into glass.

1½	shot(s)	Absolut vodka
¾	shot(s)	Opal Nera black sambuca
2	shot(s)	Cranberry juice

Comment: A dry, sambuca heavy Martini.

PURPLE HAZE

Glass: Large shot
Method: Shake first three ingredients with ice and strain into glass, then pour Chambord down the inside of the glass. This will fall to the bottom of the glass to form the purple haze.

1½	shot(s)	Absolut vodka
½	shot(s)	Freshly squeezed lime juice
¼	shot(s)	Sugar (gomme) syrup
⅛	shot(s)	Chambord black raspberry liqueur

Comment: A refined shot – subtly Chambordy.

PURPLE HOOTER

Glass: Rocks
Method: Shake ingredients with ice and strain into ice-filled glass.

2	shot(s)	Absolut vodka
1	shot(s)	Chambord black raspberry liqueur
½	shot(s)	Chilled water
1	shot(s)	Freshly squeezed lime juice
½	shot(s)	Sugar (gomme) syrup

Comment: Same ingredients as a Purple Haze shot, but bigger measurements!

PURPLE HOOTER #2

Glass: Shot
Method: Shake ingredients with ice and strain into glass.

1	shot(s)	Chambord black raspberry liqueur
1/2	shot(s)	Absolut vodka
1/4	shot(s)	Freshly squeezed lime juice

Comment: Almost chocolatey!

PURPLE PEAR MARTINI

●●●●●○

Glass: Martini
Garnish: Pear slice on rim
Method: Shake all ingredients with ice and fine strain into chilled glass.

2	shot(s)	Poire William eau de vie
2	shot(s)	Benoit Serres Liqueur de Violette
1/2	shot(s)	Sugar (gomme) syrup

Origin: I created this in 2002.
Comment: This floral drink suits its name.

PURR-FECT PUSSY MARTINI NEW

●●●●○

Glass: Martini
Garnish: Orange twist
Method: Stir all ingredients with ice and strain into chilled glass.

2	shot(s)	Absolut Vanilia vodka
1	shot(s)	Cinzano Extra dry vermouth
1	shot(s)	Cinzano Rosso (sweet) vermouth
4	dashes	Angostura aromatic bitters

Origin: I created this drink in 2003 after trying a very different cocktail also based on Tuaca made by Max at Ali-cats, Brighton, England. The name prompted me to make this twist on a classic Purr-fect Manhattan.
Comment: Aromatic and complex, spiced vanilla and orange.

PUSSYCAT

Glass: Rocks
Method: Shake ingredients with ice and strain into ice-filled glass.

1 1/2	shot(s)	Buffalo Trace Bourbon
1	shot(s)	Freshly squeezed lime juice
1/2	shot(s)	Sugar (gomme) syrup
2	shot(s)	Freshly squeezed orange juice
1/4	shot(s)	Grenadine syrup

Comment: Bourbon based with a fruity sourness.

PVC

Glass: Rocks
Garnish: Mint & squeeze of lime
Method: Shake ingredients with ice and strain into ice-filled glass.

1	shot(s)	Absolut Kurant vodka
1	shot(s)	Teichenné peach schnapps
1	shot(s)	Cranberry juice
3/4	shot(s)	Freshly squeezed lime juice
1/4	shot(s)	Sugar (gomme) syrup

Origin: Created in 1999 by Tory and Ade of Arts Café in Leeds, England.
Comment: A long Detox – sharp and dry but with great flavours.

QUADRUPLE ORANGE MARTINI

Glass: Martini
Garnish: Orange twist
Method: Shake all ingredients with ice and strain into glass.

1/2	shot(s)	Absolut Mandrin vodka
1	shot(s)	Grand Marnier liqueur
2	shot(s)	Freshly squeezed orange juice
1/4	shot(s)	Campari
1/2	fresh	Egg white

Origin: In 1998 I created a Triple Orange Martini using plain vodka. I renamed it with the advent of orange flavoured vodka, which peps up the orange notes.
Comment: Bags of orange flavour, toned down by Campari and softened by egg white.

QUARTERBACK NEW

●●●●○

Glass: Martini
Garnish: Orange knot
Method: Shake all ingredients with ice and fine strain into chilled glass.

1	shot(s)	Yellow Chartreuse
1	shot(s)	Cointreau / triple sec
1	shot(s)	Double (heavy) cream
1	shot(s)	Milk

Comment: This white, creamy drink has a flavoursome bite.

QUICK F.U.

Glass: Shot
Method: Layer in glass by carefully pouring in the following order.

3/4	shot(s)	Kahlúa coffee liqueur
1/2	shot(s)	Midori melon liqueur
1/2	shot(s)	Baileys Irish Cream liqueur

AKA: Apache Shot
Comment: A brown (coffee), green (melon) and cream (whiskey cream) layered shot.

RAMOS GIN FIZZ

●●●●●
(COMPLEX FORMULA) UPDATED

Glass: Old-fashioned
Garnish: Lime wedge on rim
Method: Shake all but soda with ice and strain into ice-filled glass. Top up with soda water from a siphon.

2½	shot(s)	Plymouth gin
¾	shot(s)	Milk
¾	shot(s)	Double (heavy) cream
½	shot(s)	Freshly squeezed lemon juice
½	shot(s)	Freshly squeezed lime juice
½	shot(s)	Sugar (gomme) syrup
½	spoon	Orange flower water (optional)
½	fresh	Egg white
Top up with		Soda water from siphon

Origin: Created in 1888 by Henry C. Ramos when he opened his Imperial Cabinet Bar in New Orleans. Ramos kept his recipe secret until the introduction of Prohibition when his bother Charles Henry Ramos published it in a full-page advertisement. Originally the drink was served without ice in a small, 8oz Collins-style glass.
Comment: Sherbety and moreish.

●●●●○
(SIMPLE FORMULA) NEW

Glass: Collins
Garnish: Lemon wedge
Method: Shake all but soda with ice and strain into ice-filled glass. Top up with soda.

2	shot(s)	Plymouth gin
¾	shot(s)	Freshly squeezed lemon juice
1½	shot(s)	Sugar (gomme) syrup
½	fresh	Egg white
Top up with		Soda water (from siphon)

Comment: Sweetened and smoothed gin with a hint of lemon.

RAGING BULL

Glass: Shot
Method: Combine coffee liqueur and Tequila in glass then float sambuca.

½	shot(s)	Kahlúa coffee liqueur
½	shot(s)	Sauza Hornitos Tequila
½	shot(s)	Opal Bianca white sambuca

Comment: Coffee and sambuca – always a good combination.

●●●●○
RANDY NEW

Glass: Old-fashioned
Garnish: Orange twist
Method: Stir ingredients with ice and strain into ice-filled glass.

1½	shot(s)	Rémy Martin Cognac
1½	shot(s)	Tawny Port
½	shot(s)	Grand Marnier liqueur
¼	shot(s)	Vanilla syrup

Origin: Created in 2003 by yours truly.
Comment: Named after the rhyming slang for port and brandy, the two base ingredients of this cocktail. Love interest comes courtesy of orange and vanilla.

●●●●○
RASPBERRY CAIPIRINHA NEW

Glass: Rocks
Method: Muddle lime and raspberries in base of glass. Add other ingredients and fill glass with crushed ice. Churn drink with barspoon and serve with short straws.

¾	fresh	Lime cut into wedges
8	fresh	Raspberries
2	shot(s)	Pitú Cachaça
¾	shot(s)	Sugar (gomme) syrup

Variant: Substitute other berries and fruits. Add raspberry liqueur in place of sugar. Base on rum in place of Cachaça to make a Raspberry Caipirissima.
Comment: A fruity twist on the popular Caipirinha.

●●●●○
RASPBERRY COLLINS UPDATED

Glass: Collins
Garnish: Three raspberries & lemon slice
Method: Muddle raspberries in base of shaker. Add next five ingredients, shake with ice and strain into an ice-filled glass. Top up with soda, stir and serve with straws.

10	fresh	Raspberries
2	shot(s)	Plymouth gin
1½	shot(s)	Freshly squeezed lemon juice
½	shot(s)	Bols Raspberry (framboise) liqueur
½	shot(s)	Sugar (gomme) syrup
3	dashes	Fee Brothers Orange bitters (optional)
Top up with		Soda water (club soda)

Variant: Raspberry Debonnaire
Origin: Created in 1999 by Cairbry Hill, London, England.
Comment: This fruity drink is the most popular modern adaptation of the classic Collins.

RASPBERRY DEBONNAIRE UPDATED

●●●●◐○

Glass: Collins
Garnish: Three raspberries & lemon slice
Method: Muddle raspberries in base of shaker. Add next five ingredients, shake with ice and strain into an ice-filled glass. Top up with soda, stir and serve with straws.

10	fresh	Raspberries
2	shot(s)	Absolut vodka
1½	shot(s)	Freshly squeezed lemon juice
½	shot(s)	Bols Raspberry (framboise) liqueur
½	shot(s)	Sugar (gomme) syrup
3	dashes	Fee Brothers Orange bitters (optional)
Top up with		Soda water (club soda)

Variant: Raspberry Collins
Comment: If based on gin rather than vodka it would be a Raspberry Collins.

RASPBERRY MARTINI #2 UPDATED

●●●●○

Glass: Martini
Garnish: Raspberries
Method: Muddle raspberries in base of shaker. Add other ingredients, shake with ice and fine strain into chilled glass.

12	fresh	Raspberries
2½	shot(s)	Absolut vodka
¾	shot(s)	Bols Raspberry (framboise) liqueur
¾	shot(s)	Sugar (gomme) syrup
4	dashes	Fee Brothers Orange bitters (optional)

Variant: Better made with vanilla vodka if you have it.
Origin: Created in 1997 by Dick Bradsell, London, England.
Comment: Rich raspberries fortified with vodka.

RASPBERRY LYNCHBURG UPDATED

●●●●◐○

Glass: Collins
Garnish: Raspberries on drink
Method: Shake first three ingredients with ice and strain into ice-filled glass. Top up with lemonade and drizzle Chambord around surface of drink. This will fall through the drink leaving coloured threads.

2	shot(s)	Jack Daniel's Tennessee whiskey
¾	shot(s)	Freshly squeezed lime juice
¼	shot(s)	Sugar (gomme) syrup
Top up with		Lemonade / Sprite / 7-Up
¾	shot(s)	Chambord black raspberry liqueur

Origin: Created in 1992 by Wayne Collins at Roadhouse, London, England.
Comment: This variation on a Lynchburg Lemonade has a complex sweet and sour flavour laced with whiskey.

RASPBERRY MOCHA'TINI NEW

●●●●○

Glass: Martini
Garnish: Three raspberries on stick
Method: Shake all ingredients with ice and fine strain into chilled glass.

1	shot(s)	Espresso coffee (cold)
1½	shot(s)	Stoli Razberi
¾	shot(s)	Bols Dark crème de cacao
¾	shot(s)	Bols Raspberry (framboise) liqueur

Origin: Discovered in 2002 at Lot 61, New York City.
Comment: Sweet chocolate and raspberry tempered by dry coffee and vodka.

RASPBERRY MARGARITA NEW

●●●●○

Glass: Coupette
Garnish: Lime wedge on rim
Method: Muddle raspberries in base of shaker. Add other ingredients, shake with ice and fine strain into chilled glass.

10	fresh	Raspberries
2	shot(s)	Sauza Hornitos Tequila
1	shot(s)	Cointreau / triple sec
1	shot(s)	Freshly squeezed lime juice
½	shot(s)	Sugar (gomme) syrup

Comment: Just that – a raspberry flavoured Margarita.

RASPBERRY MULE

●●●●○

Glass: Collins
Garnish: Lime wedge
Method: Muddle raspberries in base of a shaker. Add other ingredients apart from ginger beer, shake with ice and strain into ice-filled glass. Top up with ginger beer and stir.

12	fresh	Raspberries
2	shot(s)	Absolut vodka
1	shot(s)	Freshly squeezed lime juice
½	shot(s)	Sugar (gomme) syrup
Top up with		Ginger beer

Comment: The fruity alternative to a Moscow Mule.

RASPBERRY MARTINI # 1

●●●●○

Glass: Martini
Garnish: Float three raspberries
Method: Muddle raspberries in base of shaker. Add other ingredients, shake with ice and fine strain into chilled glass.

7	fresh	Raspberries
2	shot(s)	Plymouth Gin
1	shot(s)	Raspberry (framboise) liqueur
½	shot(s)	Sugar (gomme) syrup

Comment: Great raspberry flavour integrated with gin – not overly sweet.

NEW	A DRINK NEW TO SAUCE GUIDES.
UPDATED	ENTRY CHANGED SINCE LAST VOLUME.
shot(s)	25ML MEASURE (UK) OR 1OZ (US). HOWEVER, IT DOESN'T REALLY MATTER WHAT MEASURE YOU USE AS A SHOT, SO LONG AS YOU USE THE SAME MEASURE OR FRACTIONS OF THAT MEASURE TO MEASURE ALL THE INGREDIENTS. THIS WILL ENSURE THE PROPORTIONS OF ONE INGREDIENT TO ANOTHER WILL BE AS THE RECIPE INTENDED.

RASPBERRY SAKE'TINI

Glass: Martini
Garnish: Three fresh raspberries.
Method: Shake all ingredients with ice and fine strain into chilled glass.

1½	shot(s)	Sake
1½	shot(s)	Stoli Razberi
½	shot(s)	Sisca Crème de cassis
2	shot(s)	Pressed pineapple juice

Comment: Fruity with wafts of sake – not dissimilar to a French Martini in flavour.

RASPBERRY TART

Glass: Rocks
Garnish: Raspberry
Method: Blend ingredients with crushed ice and strain into glass.

8	fresh	Raspberries
1	shot(s)	Chambord black raspberry liqueur
1	shot(s)	Bols Raspberry (framboise) liqueur
1	scoop	Vanilla ice cream
1	shot(s)	Freshly squeezed lime juice

Comment: Creamy and rich but with a tart edge.

RASPBERRY WATKINS

Glass: Sling
Garnish: Three raspberries
Method: Shake first four ingredients with ice and strain into ice-filled glass, then top up with soda.

2	shot(s)	Absolut vodka
1	shot(s)	Chambord black raspberry liqueur
1	shot(s)	Rose's lime cordial
¼	shot(s)	Grenadine syrup
Top up with		Soda water (club soda)

Comment: A light, long fizzy and refreshing drink.

RAT PACK MANHATTAN

Glass: Martini
Garnish: Orange twist & cherry on stick
Method: Chill glass, add Grand Marnier, swirl to coat and then discard. Stir other ingredients with ice and fine strain into Grand Marnier coated glass.

1	shot(s)	Grand Marnier
1	shot(s)	Buffalo Trace Bourbon
½	shot(s)	Cinzano Rosso vermouth
½	shot(s)	Cinzano Extra Dry vermouth
4	dashes	Angostura aromatic bitters

Origin: Created in 2000 by Wayne Collins at High Holborn, London, England. Originally Wayne used different whiskies to represent each of the Rat Pack crooners. The wash of Grand Marnier was for Sammy Davis, the wild card of the bunch.
Comment: A twist on the classic Manhattan.

RATTLESNAKE

Glass: Shot
Method: Layer in glass by carefully pouring ingredients in the following order.

½	shot(s)	Kahlúa coffee liqueur
½	shot(s)	Bols White crème de cacao
½	shot(s)	Baileys Irish cream liqueur

Comment: A shot with a flavour reminiscent of a strong cappuccino.

RAY GUN

Glass: Flute
Garnish: Sliver of orange peel dropped into drink.
Method: Pour Chartreuse and blue curaçao into glass, then top up with Champagne.

½	shot(s)	Green Chartreuse
¾	shot(s)	Bols Blue curaçao
Top up with		Piper-Hiedsieck Brut Champagne

Comment: Not for the faint hearted.

RAZZITINI NEW

Glass: Martini
Garnish: Lemon twist / Raspberries on stick
Method: Shake first two ingredients with ice and fine strain into chilled glass. Top up with 7-Up.

2½	shot(s)	Absolut Citron vodka
¾	shot(s)	Chambord black raspberry liqueur
Top up with		7-Up

Origin: Discovered in 2003 at Paramount Hotel, New York City.
Comment: This citrus and raspberry Martini is a tad on the sweet side.

RAZZZZZBERRY MARTINI NEW

Glass: Martini
Garnish: Three raspberries on stick
Method: Shake all ingredients with ice and fine strain into chilled glass.

2	shot(s)	Stoli Vanil
½	shot(s)	Chambord black raspberry liqueur
2	shot(s)	Cranberry juice

Comment: Raspberry and vanilla with characteristic dry cranberry fruit.

REAL LEMONADE | VIRGIN

Glass: Collins
Garnish: Lemon wheel in glass
Method: Fill glass with ice, add ingredients and stir. Serve with straws.

2	shot(s)	Freshly squeezed lemon juice
1	shot(s)	Sugar (gomme) syrup
Top up with		Soda water (club soda)

Comment: The classic English summertime refresher.

REDBACK

Glass: Shot
Garnish: Split stemmed cherry on rim
Method: Pour sambuca into glass, then pour advocaat down the side of glass.

1	shot(s)	**Opal Nera black sambuca**
1/2	shot(s)	**Warninks Advocaat**

Comment: An impressive looking shot and a good taste too.

RED ANGEL

Glass: Martini
Method: Shake all ingredients with ice and strain into glass.

2	shot(s)	**Red wine**
1	shot(s)	**Grand Marnier**
1/4	shot(s)	**Maraschino liqueur**
1	shot(s)	**Chilled water**

Origin: Created in 2001 by Tony Conigliaro at Isola, Knightsbridge, London, England.
Comment: A subtly flavoured cocktail with a dry almost tannic edge.

THE RED ARMY ●●●●○

Glass: Rocks
Garnish: Two raspberries
Method: Muddle raspberries in base of shaker. Add other ingredients, shake with ice and strain into a glass filled with crushed ice.

12	fresh	**Raspberries**
2	shot(s)	**Stoli Razberi**
1	shot(s)	**Freshly squeezed lime juice**
3/4	shot(s)	**Sugar (gomme) syrup**
1/2	shot(s)	**Cointreau / triple sec**
1/2	shot(s)	**Bols Raspberry (framboise) liqueur**

Origin: Created in 2002 by Alex Kammerling, London, England.

RED EARL MARTINI

Glass: Martini
Garnish: Speared raspberries
Method: Muddle ginger with vodka in base of shaker. Add raspberries and muddle. Add other ingredients, shake with ice and fine strain into chilled glass.

2	slices	**Root ginger (thumb-nail sized)**
8	fresh	**Raspberries**
2	shot(s)	**Absolut vodka**
3/4	shot(s)	**Limoncello liqueur**
1/4	shot(s)	**Sugar (gomme) syrup**

Origin: Created by Salvatore Calabrese at the Library Bar, London, England for Charles Spencer, Diana's brother.
Comment: Fruity and spicy, with a kick.

RED EYED

Glass: Shot glass
Method: Pour frozen vodka into glass, pour cassis onto a bar spoon and carefully add to centre of vodka to form an eye.

1 1/2	shot(s)	**Absolut vodka**
1/4	shot(s)	**Sisca crème de cassis**

Comment: Vodka and blackcurrant - always a good combination.

RED HAZE ●●●●◐○

Glass: Collins
Method: Shake first three ingredients with ice and strain into ice-filled glass. Pour coffee liqueur around top of drink - this will fall to the base of the glass and create the haze.

2	shot(s)	**Malibu coconut rum liqueur**
1	shot(s)	**Pernod anise**
3	shot(s)	**Freshly squeezed grapefruit juice**
3/4	shot(s)	**Kahlúa coffee liqueur**

Origin: I created this drink in 2003 for Pernod.
Comment: Four very strong and distinctive flavours work together to tone each other down.

RED HOOKER UPDATED ●●●●◐○

Glass: Martini
Garnish: Peach slice on rim
Method: Shake all ingredients with ice and fine strain into chilled glass.

1	shot(s)	**Freshly extracted peach juice**
2	shot(s)	**Sauza Hornitos Tequila**
1	shot(s)	**Bols Raspberry (framboise) liqueur**
3/4	shot(s)	**Freshly squeezed lemon juice**
1/4	shot(s)	**Sugar (gomme) syrup**

Comment: An appropriately named red fruity drink with more than a hint of Tequila.

RED LION UPDATED ●●●●○

Glass: Martini
Garnish: Orange slice on rim
Method: Shake all ingredients with ice and fine strain into chilled glass.

1 1/4	shot(s)	**Plymouth gin**
1 1/4	shot(s)	**Grand Marnier**
1	shot(s)	**Freshly squeezed orange juice**
1	shot(s)	**Freshly squeezed lemon juice**
1/8	shot(s)	**Grenadine syrup**

Origin: My take on a classic cocktail created in the 1930s after Prohibition.
Comment: The colour of a summer's twilight with a rich tangy orange flavour.

RED MARAUDER ●●●●○

Glass: Martini
Garnish: Raspberries on cocktail stick rested on rim
Method: Shake all ingredients with ice and strain into glass.

2	shot(s)	**Rémy Martin Cognac**
2	shot(s)	**Cranberry juice**
1/2	shot(s)	**Chambord black raspberry liqueur**
1/4	shot(s)	**Freshly squeezed lime juice**

Origin: Originally created for Martell, long term sponsors of the Grand National, this cocktail is named after the horse that won in 2001.
Comment: This is a dry cocktail with a hint of raspberry and Cognac's distinctive flavour.

RED RUM MARTINI

●●●●●◐

Glass: Martini
Garnish: Redcurrants draped over rim
Method: Muddle redcurrants in base of shaker. Add other ingredients, shake with ice and fine strain into chilled glass.

2	dozen	**Fresh redcurrants**
2	shot(s)	**Appleton Estate V/X aged rum**
1/2	shot(s)	**Plymouth Sloe Gin**
1/2	shot(s)	**Freshly squeezed lemon juice**
1/2	shot(s)	**Vanilla sugar syrup**

Origin: Created by Jason Scott in 2002 at Oloroso, Edinburgh, Scotland. This cocktail, which is red and contains rum, is named after 'Red Rum', the only horse in the history of the Grand National to win the race three times (on the other two occasions he ran he came second). His last Grand National win was in 1977 at the age of 12 by a remarkable 25 lengths. He became a British hero, made an appearance on the BBC Sports Personality of the Year show and paraded right up until his death in 1995 at the age of 30.
Comment: A beautifully fruity, adult balance of bitter-sweet flavours.

RED MELON'TINI

●●●●◐

Glass: Martini
Garnish: Watermelon wedge on rim
Method: Muddle watermelon in base of shaker. Add other ingredients, shake with ice and fine strain into chilled glass.

2	cupfuls	**Diced watermelon**
2	shot(s)	**Pepper vodka**
1/4	shot(s)	**Sugar (gomme) syrup**
4	pinch	**Black pepper**

Origin: Discovered in 2002 at the Fifth Floor Bar, London, England.
Comment: Watermelon pepped up with vodka and the merest of peppery finishes.

RED NECK MARTINI

●●●●◐

Glass: Martini
Garnish: Orange twist
Method: Shake all ingredients with ice and fine strain into chilled glass.

2	shot(s)	**The Famous Grouse Scotch whisky**
1	shot(s)	**Dubonnet Red**
1	shot(s)	**Bols Cherry brandy liqueur**

Origin: Created by Sylvain Solignac in 2002 at Circus Bar, London, England.
Comment: Nicely balanced, aromatic and not too sweet – the flavour of the Scotch shines through.

RED PANTIES

Glass: Martini
Method: Shake ingredients with ice and strain into glass.

1 1/2	shot(s)	**Absolut vodka**
1	shot(s)	**Teichenné Peach schnapps**
2	shot(s)	**Freshly squeezed orange juice**
1/4	shot(s)	**Grenadine syrup**

Comment: It's not red and it's not pants - just a pleasant fruit Martini.

RED ROVER **UPDATED**

●●●●○

Glass: Old-fashioned
Garnish: Orange slice in glass
Method: Shake all ingredients with ice and strain into ice-filled glass.

3	shot(s)	**Red wine (Shiraz)**
1	shot(s)	**Pusser's Navy rum**
1/2	shot(s)	**Chambord black raspberry liqueur**

Comment: Carpet scaring red with the body of red wine but the flavours of a cocktail.

REEF JUICE

Glass: Collins
Garnish: Split pineapple wedge
Method: Shake all ingredients with ice and strain into ice-filled glass.

1¹/₂	shot(s)	Pusser's Navy rum
¹/₂	shot(s)	Absolut vodka
1	shot(s)	Bols crème de banane
¹/₂	shot(s)	Freshly squeezed lime juice
2	shot(s)	Pressed pineapple juice
¹/₂	shot(s)	Grenadine syrup

Origin: A recipe from Charles Tobias, proprietor of Pusser's at the Beach Bar in Fort Lauderdale. This one was a favourite of a friend who crashed his boat on the reef.
Comment: Tangy, fruity and moreish as well.

REGGAE RUM PUNCH

Glass: Collins
Garnish: Wedge of pineapple spiked with a maraschino cherry on rim
Method: Shake all ingredients with cubed ice and strain into a glass filled with crushed ice.

³/₄	shot(s)	Freshly squeezed lime juice
³/₄	shot(s)	Bols Strawberry (fraise) liqueur
1	shot(s)	Strawberry syrup
2	shot(s)	Wray & Nephew overproof rum
1¹/₂	shot(s)	Pressed pineapple juice
2¹/₂	shot(s)	Freshly squeezed orange juice

Origin: The most popular punch in Jamaica, where it is sold under different names with slightly varying ingredients. It always contains orange, pineapple and most importantly overproof rum.
Comment: A bright red drink with a frothy top. Jamaicans have a sweet tooth and they love their rum - this drink combines sweetness and strength with a generous amount of fruit. If you can't obtain strawberry syrup use grenadine as an alternative.

REMEMBER THE MAINE

Glass: Old-fashioned
Garnish: Stemmed cherry in drink
Method: Pour absinthe into ice-filled glass and top up with water. Separately, pour other ingredients into an ice-filled mixing glass and stir well. Discard absinthe, water and ice from glass. Finally strain contents of mixing glass into the now absinthe rinsed empty glass.

1	shot(s)	La Fée absinthe
Top up with		Chilled water
2	shot(s)	Buffalo Trace Bourbon
³/₄	shot(s)	Bols Cherry brandy liqueur
³/₄	shot(s)	Cinzano Rosso (sweet) vermouth

Origin: Created in 2001 by Jason Fendick at Rockwell, London, England.
Comment: A modern twist on the Sazerac.

RÉMY MARTINI

Glass: Martini
Method: Shake all ingredients with ice and strain into glass.

2	shot(s)	Rémy Martin Cognac
¹/₂	shot(s)	Cointreau / triple sec
¹/₄	shot(s)	Sugar (gomme) syrup
1¹/₂	shot(s)	Pressed pineapple juice
4	dashes	Angostura aromatic bitters

Comment: A fruity brandy drink.

RED SNAPPER

Glass: Martini
Garnish: Rim the glass with black pepper and celery salt, add cherry tomato on a stick
Method: Shake all ingredients with ice and fine strain into chilled glass.

2	shot(s)	Plymouth gin
2¹/₂	shot(s)	Pressed tomato juice
¹/₂	shot(s)	Freshly squeezed lemon juice
4	drops	Tabasco sauce
4	drops	Worcestershire sauce
¹/₄	shot(s)	Medium Sherry
1	pinch	Celery salt
1	pinch	Black pepper

Variant: Bloody Mary
Origin: Americans travelling through Europe during Prohibition often visited the famous Harry's New York Bar in Paris. Here they'd find the skilled French bartender Fernand Petiot, who in 1920 had created the Bloody Mary: then a plain mix of vodka and tomato juice. In 1925 he moved to the States and in 1933 became bartender at the King Cole Bar in Manhattan's St Regis Hotel. Here he mixed the drink for Serge Obolansky, the president of the hotel, who found it a bit flat: so Petiot added salt, pepper, lemon and Worcestershire sauce. Vincent Astor, who owned the hotel, found the name Bloody Mary a little crude for his clientele and so the drink was officially renamed the Red Snapper – although customers continued to order Bloody Marys. Nowadays a Red Snapper is a Bloody Mary made with gin.
Comment: Short and hard Bloody Mary, with the aromatic edge of gin.

RESOLUTE MARTINI

Glass: Martini
Garnish: Lemon zest
Method: Shake all ingredients with ice and fine strain into chilled glass.

2	shot(s)	Plymouth Gin
1	shot(s)	Freshly squeezed lemon juice
1	shot(s)	Bols Apricot brandy liqueur
1/4	shot(s)	Sugar (gomme) syrup

Comment: Simple but tasty with all three flavours working in harmony.

RHETT BUTLER

Glass: Old-fashioned
Garnish: Lime wedge
Method: Shake all ingredients with ice and fine strain into chilled glass.

1	shot(s)	Grand Marnier
1	shot(s)	Southern Comfort
2	shot(s)	Cranberry juice
1	shot(s)	Freshly squeezed lime juice

Comment: A simple and well-balanced classic drink.

RHUBARB & CUSTARD MARTINI

Glass: Martini
Garnish: Grate fresh nutmeg over drink
Method: Shake all ingredients with ice and fine strain into chilled glass.

1 1/2	shot(s)	Plymouth Gin
1 1/2	shot(s)	Warninks Advocaat
1 1/2	shot(s)	Syrup from tinned rhubarb

Origin: I created this drink in 2002. Rhubarb and Custard is a great British dessert and was a cult children's TV cartoon, featuring a dog named Rhubarb and a naughty fat pink cat named Custard. Like many British men, Rhubarb spends a lot of time in his garden shed.
Comment: As sharp, sweet, creamy and flavourful as the dessert it imitates.

RHUBARB & LEMONGRASS MARTINI

Glass: Martini
Garnish: Stick of lemongrass in drink
Method: Pour gin into base of shaker. Break up lemongrass and muddle with gin. Add rhubarb syrup, shake with ice and fine strain into chilled glass.

2 1/4	shot(s)	Plymouth gin
4	inches	Lemongrass
2 1/4	shot(s)	Syrup from tinned rhubarb

Origin: I based this drink on one found in Zuma, London, England.
Comment: Fragrant exotic lemon flavours combine with, well, rhubarb.

RITZ FIZZ

Glass: Flute
Garnish: Float rose petal
Method: Pour all ingredients into a chilled glass and lightly stir.

1/2	shot(s)	Bols Blue curaçao
1/2	shot(s)	Disaronno Originale amaretto
1/2	shot(s)	Freshly squeezed lemon juice
Top up with		Piper-Heidsieck Brut Champagne

Comment: The amaretto works well with Champagne.

THE RITZ COCKTAIL

Glass: Martini
Garnish: Maraschino cherry on rim
Method: Stir first four ingredients with ice and strain into chilled glass. Top up with Champagne and gently stir.

1	shot(s)	Rémy Martin Cognac
1/2	shot(s)	Cointreau / triple sec
1/4	shot(s)	Maraschino liqueur
1/4	shot(s)	Freshly squeezed lemon juice
Top up with		Piper-Heidsieck Brut Champagne

Comment: This combination of spirit, liqueurs, fruit and Champagne resembles the taste of alcoholic lemon tea.

RIVIERA BREEZE NEW

Glass: Old-fashioned
Garnish: Orange slice in glass
Method: Pour pastis and orange juice into glass and then fill with ice. Top up with ginger ale and stir.

1 1/2	shot(s)	Ricard pastis
2	shot(s)	Freshly squeezed orange juice
Top up with		Ginger ale

Origin: Created in 2003 by Roo Buckley at Café Lebowitz, New York City.
Comment: An aniseed rich summertime cooler.

ROAD RUNNER

Glass: Martini
Garnish: Sprinkle ground nutmeg over drink.
Method: Blend ingredients with crushed ice and serve.

2	shot(s)	Absolut vodka
1	shot(s)	Disaronno Originale amaretto
1	shot(s)	Cream of coconut
1	shot(s)	Double (heavy) cream

Comment: Rich and yummy!

●●●●○

ROB ROY UPDATED

Glass: Martini
Garnish: Cherry & orange twist (discard orange)
Method: Stir all ingredients with ice and strain into chilled glass.

2	shot(s)	Famous Grouse Scotch whisky
1	shot(s)	Cinzano Rosso (sweet) vermouth
2	dashes	Angostura aromatic bitters
1/8	shot(s)	Maraschino syrup (optional)

Variant: Affinity
Origin: A classic (retro) cocktail of unknown origins, but thought to have been created circa 1940 and named after a Broadway show.
Comment: A Sweet Manhattan made with Scotch in place of Bourbon. The dry, peaty whisky and bitters ensure it's not too sweet.

●●●●●○

ROBIN HOOD # 1

Glass: Martini
Garnish: Apple slice on rim
Method: Shake all ingredients with ice and fine strain into chilled glass.

1 1/4	shot(s)	Havana Club light rum
1 1/4	shot(s)	Sourz Sour Apple liqueur
1 1/4	shot(s)	Rose's lime cordial
1/4	shot(s)	Freshly squeezed lime juice

Origin: Created in 2002 by Tony Conigliaro at Lonsdale House, London, England, originally using green apple liqueur and Silver Dry rum.
Comment: Sharp and refreshing with a clean apple flavour.

ROBIN HOOD # 2

Glass: Rocks
Method: Pour first three ingredients into ice-filled glass, top up with bitter lemon and stir.

1	shot(s)	Bols Blue curaçao
1	shot(s)	Teichenné Peach schnapps
1	shot(s)	Rose's lime cordial
Top up with		Bitter lemon

Comment: Sharp and fruity.

●●●●○

ROBIN HOOD #3 NEW

Glass: Martini
Garnish: Float apple slice
Method: Shake all ingredients with ice and fine strain into chilled glass.

1 1/2	shot(s)	Havana Club light rum
1 1/2	shot(s)	Apple schnapps liqueur
1 1/2	shot(s)	Rose's lime cordial
1/8	shot(s)	Sugar (gomme) syrup

Origin: Created in 2003 by Tony Conigliaro at Detroit, London, England.
Comment: American readers may notice a similarity between this and the popular Apple Martini. Great balance and flavour for such a simple drink.

ROCKY MOUNTAIN ROOTBEER

Glass: Collins
Method: Fill glass with ice, add vodka and Galliano, then top up with cola and stir.

2	shot(s)	Absolut vodka
3/4	shot(s)	Galliano
Top up with		Cola

Comment: Aptly named.

ROLLS ROYCE MARTINI

Glass: Martini
Method: Shake ingredients with ice and strain into glass.

1 1/2	shot(s)	Plymouth gin
3/4	shot(s)	Cinzano Extra Dry vermouth
3/4	shot(s)	Cinzano Rosso vermouth
1/2	shot(s)	Bénédictine D.O.M liqueur

Comment: The name promises too much, but very smooth anyway.

●●●●○

ROMAN PUNCH

Glass: Collins
Method: Shake all ingredients with cubed ice and strain into glass filled with crushed ice.

1 1/2	shot(s)	Bénédictine D.O.M liqueur
3/4	shot(s)	Freshly squeezed lemon juice
1 1/2	shot(s)	Rémy Martin Cognac
3/4	shot(s)	Wray & Nephew overproof rum
3	shot(s)	Chilled water

Comment: Spirited and refreshing with Bénédictine herbal notes.

●●●●○

ROSARITA MARGARITA

Glass: Coupette
Garnish: Lime wedge & salted rim (optional)
Method: Shake all ingredients with ice and strain into glass.

1 1/2	shot(s)	Sauza Hornitos Tequila
3/4	shot(s)	Grand Marnier
1/2	shot(s)	Cranberry juice
1/2	shot(s)	Rose's lime cordial
3/4	shot(s)	Freshly squeezed lime juice
3/4	shot(s)	Sugar (gomme) syrup

Origin: Created in 1999 by Robert Plotkin and Raymon Flores of BarMedia, USA.
Comment: This peachy coloured Margarita is well balanced and flavoursome.

ROSE (ENGLISH)

Glass: Martini
Garnish: Rose petal or cherry
Method: Stir ingredients with ice and strain into glass.

1 1/2	shot(s)	Kirsch
3	shot(s)	Cinzano Extra Dry vermouth
1/2	shot(s)	Parfait Amour

Comment: A surprisingly interesting and well-balanced drink.

ROY ROGERS | VIRGIN

Glass: Collins
Method: Fill glass with ice, add grenadine and cola, and then stir.

¼	shot(s)	Grenadine syrup
Top up with		Cola

Comment: I wouldn't bother.

ROYAL CASSIS

Glass: Martini
Garnish: Split stemmed cherry
Method: Shake ingredients with ice and strain into glass.

3	shot(s)	Rémy Martin Cognac
1	shot(s)	Sisca crème de cassis

Origin: I created this drink in 1998 after a trip to Burgundy's cassis region.
Comment: Very simple, but the sweetness of the cassis complements the Cognac.

ROYAL PIMM'S

Glass: Flute
Garnish: 3 berries on a stick with cucumber peel
Method: Pour Pimm's into chilled glass and top up with Champagne.

1	shot(s)	Pimm's No.1 Cup
Top up with		Piper-Heidsieck Brut Champagne

Comment: Subtle and refreshing.

ROYAL SMILE

Glass: Martini
Garnish: Apple wedge on rim
Method: Shake ingredients with ice and strain into glass.

1½	shot(s)	Plymouth gin
1½	shot(s)	Calvados or applejack brandy
¼	shot(s)	Grenadine syrup
½	shot(s)	Freshly squeezed lemon juice
½	shot(s)	Sugar (gomme) syrup

Comment: Sharp and strong with an apple edge.

RUBY MARTINI

● ● ● ● ○

Glass: Martini
Garnish: Lemon wedge on rim
Method: Shake all ingredients with ice and fine strain into chilled glass.

1½	shot(s)	Absolut Citron vodka
1	shot(s)	Cointreau / triple sec
2	shot(s)	Squeezed pink grapefruit juice
¼	shot(s)	Sugar (gomme) syrup

Origin: Several appearances in episodes of the hit US TV series, Sex And The City, helped this drink become fashionable in 2002, particularly in New York City. It is thought to have originated at the Wave restaurant in Chicago's W Hotel.
Comment: A sour, citrus-led derivation of the Cosmopolitan.

R U BOBBY MOORE?

● ● ● ● ◑

Glass: Martini
Garnish: Apple wedge on rim
Method: Shake all ingredients with ice and fine strain into chilled glass.

1½	shot(s)	Zubrówka (bison grass) vodka
1	shot(s)	Sauvignon Blanc wine
1	shot(s)	The Famous Grouse Scotch whisky
1	shot(s)	Pressed apple juice
¼	shot(s)	Sugar (gomme) syrup

Origin: I created this drink in 2002 and named it after the rhyming slang for 'are you bloody sure?'. Bobby Moore was the 60s England football captain and West Ham United defender who regrettably died young in 1993. My dictionary of rhyming slang has an alternative definition of 'Bobby More' as meaning 'door' – well, not in East London it doesn't.
Comment: Scotch goes brilliantly with apple which also mixes well with Zubrówka. The addition of wine makes the whole combination interestingly different.

RUDE COSMOPOLITAN

●●●●●◑

Glass: Martini
Garnish: Flamed orange twist
Method: Shake all ingredients with ice and fine strain into chilled glass.

1½	shot(s)	Sauza Hornitos Tequila
1	shot(s)	Cointreau / triple sec
1	shot(s)	Cranberry juice
½	shot(s)	Freshly squeezed lime juice
¼	shot(s)	Rose's lime cordial
½	spoon	Orange bitters (optional)

AKA: Mexico City
Comment: Don't let the pink appearance of this Cosmopolitan (made with Tequila in place of vodka) fool you into thinking that this is a fluffy cocktail. It's in fact both serious and superb.

RUM & RAISIN ALEXANDRA NEW

●●●●○

Glass: Martini
Garnish: Three red grapes on stick
Method: Muddle grapes in base of shaker. Add other ingredients, shake with ice and fine strain into chilled glass.

7	fresh	Red grapes
1½	shot(s)	Appleton Estate V/X aged rum
½	shot(s)	Sisca crème de cassis
½	shot(s)	Double cream
½	shot(s)	Milk
¼	shot(s)	Sugar (gomme) syrup

Origin: Created in 2003 by Ian Morgan, England.
Comment: Forgo the ice cream and try this creamy, quaffable, alcoholic dessert.

RUM COBBLER

Glass: Collins
Method: Shake first four ingredients with ice and strain into ice-filled glass, then top up with soda and stir.

2	shot(s)	Pusser's Navy rum
1	shot(s)	Freshly squeezed lime juice
½	shot(s)	Sugar (gomme) syrup
¼	shot(s)	Grenadine syrup
Top up with		Soda water (club soda)

Comment: The Navy rum leaps out at you.

RUM FIX

Glass: Collins
Garnish: Orange slice
Method: Shake first four ingredients with ice and strain into glass, then top up with lemonade and stir.

2	shot(s)	Havana Club light rum
3	shot(s)	Freshly squeezed orange juice
1	shot(s)	Freshly squeezed lime juice
½	shot(s)	Sugar (gomme) syrup
Top up with		Lemonade

Comment: Easy to drink – refreshing too!

RUM PUNCH

●●●●●

Glass: Collins
Garnish: Lime wheel and cherry
Method: Shake all ingredients with cubed ice and strain into glass filled with crushed ice.

¾	shot(s)	Freshly squeezed lime juice (sour)
1½	shot(s)	Sugar (gomme) syrup (sweet)
2¼	shot(s)	Wray & Nephew overproof rum (strong)
3	shot(s)	Chilled water (weak)
4	dashes	Angostura aromatic bitters

Comment: The classic proportions of this drink (followed above) are 'one of sour, two of sweet, three of strong and four of weak' – referring to lime juice, sugar syrup, rum and water respectively. In Jamaica, the spiritual home of the Rum Punch, they like their rum overproof (over 57% alc./vol.). Hence, the strength of this drink demands a good shake and then serving with crushed ice to dilute and tame it.

RUM RICKEY

Glass: Old-fashioned
Garnish: Lime wedge on rim
Method: Shake first three ingredients with ice and strain into ice-filled glass. Top up with soda.

1¹/₂	shot(s)	Mount Gay Eclipse golden rum
¹/₂	shot(s)	Bols Apricot brandy liqueur
¹/₂	shot(s)	Freshly squeezed lime juice
Top up with		Soda water (club soda)

Comment: A refreshingly dry rum based drink with a hint of apricot.

RUM RUNNER

Glass: Hurricane
Method: Shake ingredients with ice and strain into ice-filled glass.

1	shot(s)	Pusser's Navy rum
¹/₂	shot(s)	Bols Blackberry (Crème de mûre) liqueur
1	shot(s)	Bols Crème de banane
1	shot(s)	Freshly squeezed lime juice
¹/₂	shot(s)	Sugar (gomme) syrup
¹/₂	shot(s)	Grenadine syrup
2	shot(s)	Pressed pineapple juice

Comment: Fruity, sharp and rounded.

RUM SOUR

Glass: Collins
Method: Shake ingredients with ice and strain into ice-filled glass.

2	shot(s)	Havana Club light rum
3	shot(s)	Freshly squeezed orange juice
1	shot(s)	Freshly squeezed lime juice
¹/₂	shot(s)	Sugar (gomme) syrup
¹/₂	fresh	Egg white

Comment: Zesty, good summer drinking.

RUSSIAN BRIDE NEW

Glass: Martini
Garnish: Dust with chocolate powder
Method: Shake all ingredients with ice and fine strain into chilled glass.

2	shot(s)	Stoli Vanil
³/₄	shot(s)	Kahlúa coffee liqueur
¹/₄	shot(s)	Bols White crème de cacao
¹/₂	shot(s)	Double (heavy) cream
¹/₂	shot(s)	Milk

Origin: Created in 2002 by Miranda Dickson A.K.A. the Vodka Princess at the UK's Revolution Vodka Bar chain where some 500,000 are sold each year.
Comment: A little on the sweet side for some but vanilla, coffee and chocolate smoothed with cream is a tasty combination.

RUSSIAN QUALUUDE SHOT

Glass: Shot
Method: Layer ingredients by carefully pouring into glass in the following order, then flambé.

¹/₂	shot(s)	Galliano
¹/₂	shot(s)	Green Chartreuse
¹/₂	shot(s)	Absolut vodka

RUSSIAN SPRING PUNCH UPDATED

Glass: Sling
Garnish: Lemon slice & berries
Method: Shake first four ingredients with ice and strain into glass filled with crushed ice. Top up with Champagne, stir and serve with straws.

2	shot(s)	Absolut vodka
¹/₂	shot(s)	Sisca crème de cassis
1	shot(s)	Freshly squeezed lemon juice
¹/₄	shot(s)	Sugar (gomme) syrup
Top up with		Piper-Heidsieck Brut Champagne

Variant: Polish Spring Punch
Origin: Created by Dick Bradsell, London, England.
Comment: Well balanced, complex and refreshing – one of the best drinks to emerge during the 1990s.

RUSTY NAIL

Glass: Old-fashioned
Garnish: Lemon zest
Method: Stir ingredients with ice and strain into ice-filled glass.

2	shot(s)	The Famous Grouse Scotch whisky
1	shot(s)	Drambuie liqueur

Comment: The classic drink combining Scotch and the heather-honey smoothness of Drambuie – simple but great.

RUSTY RETURN

Glass: Martini
Method: Shake all ingredients with ice and strain into glass.

1¹/₂	shot(s)	Drambuie Cream
³/₄	shot(s)	Chambord black raspberry liqueur
³/₄	shot(s)	Teichenné butterscotch schnapps
1	shot(s)	The Famous Grouse Scotch whisky

Origin: Created in 2000 by Sebastien Protat at Teatro, London, England.
Comment: A creamy, sweet after dinner tipple.

ST. CLEMENTINE

Glass: Shot
Method: Shake first three ingredients with ice and strain into glass, then top up with bitter lemon.

¹/₂	shot(s)	Grand Marnier
¹/₂	shot(s)	Cointreau / triple sec
¹/₄	shot(s)	Freshly squeezed lemon juice
¹/₂	shot(s)	Bitter lemon

Comment: Citrus–tastic!

SAIGON COOLER NEW

●●●●○

Glass: Collins
Garnish: Three raspberries
Method: Muddle raspberries in base of shaker. Add other ingredients, shake with ice and fine strain into ice-filled glass.

6	fresh	Raspberries
2	shot(s)	Plymouth gin
1/2	shot(s)	Chambord black raspberry liqueur
3 1/2	shot(s)	Cranberry juice
3/4	shot(s)	Freshly squeezed lime juice

Origin: Created at Bam-Bou, London, England.
Comment: Well balanced sweet 'n' sour with a rich fruity flavour.

SAIGON SLING

●●●●○

Glass: Sling
Method: Shake first seven ingredients and top up with ginger ale

1 1/2	shot(s)	Plymouth gin
3/4	shot(s)	Ginger & lemongrass cordial
1/2	shot(s)	Krupnik honey liqueur
3/4	shot(s)	Freshly squeezed lime juice
1	shot(s)	Pressed pineapple juice
1/4	shot(s)	Passoã passion fruit liqueur
2	dash(es)	Péychaud's bitters
Top up with		Ginger ale

Origin: Created in 2001 by Rodolphe Manor for a London bartenders competition.
Comment: A wonderful and adult fusion of flavours.

SAILOR'S COMFORT

●●●◑○

Glass: Old-fashioned
Garnish: Lime wedge
Method: Shake first four ingredients with ice and strain into ice-filled glass. Top up with soda water (club soda).

1	shot(s)	Plymouth Sloe Gin
1	shot(s)	Southern Comfort
1	shot(s)	Rose's lime cordial
4	dashes	Angostura aromatic bitters
Top up with		Soda water (club soda)

Origin: Discovered in 2002 at Lightship Ten, London, England.
Comment: Lime, peach and hints of berry make a light easy drink.

SAINT CLEMENTS | VIRGIN

Glass: Collins
Method: Pour ingredients into ice-filled glass and stir.

Half fill with	Freshly squeezed orange juice
Top up with	Bitter lemon

Comment: Slightly more interesting than orange juice.

SAINT MORITZ

Glass: Martini
Garnish: Raspberry and blueberry on a stick
Method: Shake ingredients with ice and strain into glass.

2	shot(s)	Chambord black raspberry liqueur
1 1/2	shot(s)	Double (heavy) cream
1 1/2	shot(s)	Milk

Comment: Creamy raspberries – yummy.

SAINT PATRICK'S DAY

●●●●○

Glass: Martini
Garnish: Shamrock or lime wedge
Method: Shake all ingredients with ice and fine strain into chilled glass.

1 1/2	shot(s)	Irish whiskey
1 1/2	shot(s)	Green Chartreuse
1	shot(s)	Green crème de menthe
4	dashes	Angostura aromatic bitters

Comment: Suitably green with a fresh breath minty herbal flavour.

SAINTLY BELL

Glass: Martini
Garnish: Float raspberry
Method: Shake ingredients with ice and strain into glass.

1	shot(s)	Chambord black raspberry liqueur
1	shot(s)	Baileys Irish Cream liqueur
1	shot(s)	Bols Brown crème de cacao
1	shot(s)	Double (heavy) cream
1	shot(s)	Milk

Created by: Carrie Bell at the Saint, London, England.
Comment: Chocolatey, rich raspberries and cream

SAIL AWAY

Glass: Martini
Method: Shake all ingredients vigorously with ice and strain into glass.

1	shot(s)	Midori melon liqueur
1	shot(s)	Teichenné Peach schnapps
2	shot(s)	Absolut vodka
3/4	shot(s)	Freshly squeezed lime juice

Comment: Fluorescent green - melon and peach fruit with a sharp citrus edge.

SAKE'POLITAN

●●●●○

Glass: Martini
Garnish: Flamed orange zest
Method: Shake all ingredients with ice and fine strain into chilled glass.

3 1/2	shot(s)	Sake
3/4	shot(s)	Cointreau / triple sec
3/4	shot(s)	Cranberry juice
1/4	shot(s)	Freshly squeezed lime juice

Comment: A Cosmo with more than a hint of sake.

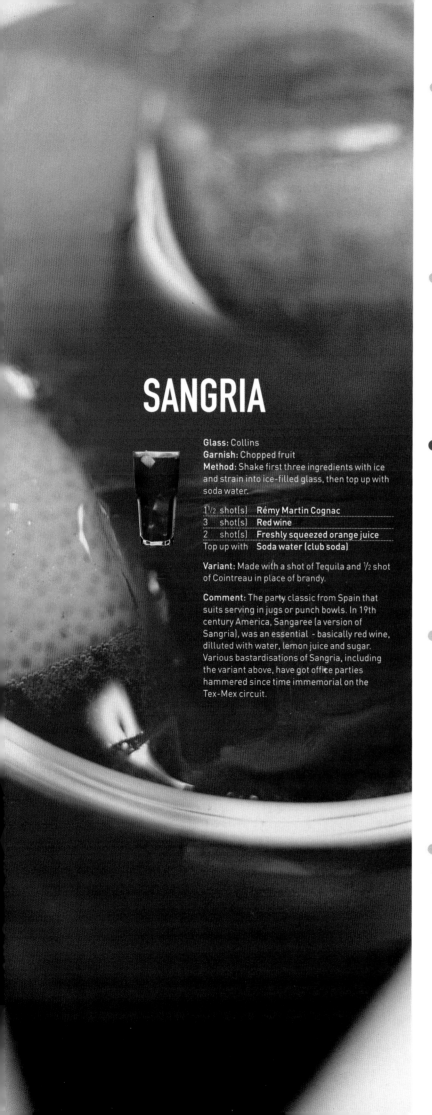

SANGRIA

Glass: Collins
Garnish: Chopped fruit
Method: Shake first three ingredients with ice and strain into ice-filled glass, then top up with soda water.

1¹/₂	shot(s)	**Rémy Martin Cognac**
3	shot(s)	**Red wine**
2	shot(s)	**Freshly squeezed orange juice**
Top up with		**Soda water (club soda)**

Variant: Made with a shot of Tequila and ¹/₂ shot of Cointreau in place of brandy.

Comment: The party classic from Spain that suits serving in jugs or punch bowls. In 19th century America, Sangaree (a version of Sangria), was an essential - basically red wine, dilluted with water, lemon juice and sugar. Various bastardisations of Sangria, including the variant above, have got office parties hammered since time immemorial on the Tex-Mex circuit.

SAKE-TINI

Glass: Martini
Garnish: Three thin slices of cucumber
Method: Stir all ingredients with ice and strain into chilled glass.

1	shot(s)	**Plymouth Gin**
2¹/₂	shot(s)	**Sake**
¹/₂	shot(s)	**Grand Marnier**

Comment: Sake adds the perfect aromatic edge to a vodka-tini.

SAKINI

Glass: Martini
Garnish: Olives on stick
Method: Stir ingredients with ice and strain into chilled glass.

1	shot(s)	**Sake**
2¹/₂	shot(s)	**Absolut vodka**

Comment: Very dry with the sake giving an almost wine-like delicacy.

SALTY DOG UPDATED

Glass: Martini
Garnish: Salt rim
Method: Shake all ingredients with ice and fine strain in chilled glass.

2	shot(s)	**Absolut vodka**
2¹/₄	shot(s)	**Pressed grapefruit juice**
¹/₈	shot(s)	**Maraschino liqueur** (optional)

Origin: Circa 1960s, creator unknown.
Comment: For a more interesting drink, try basing this classic on gin rather than vodka.

SALTECCA

Glass: Martini
Garnish: Lemon zest
Method: Stir all ingredients with ice and fine into chilled glass.

2	shot(s)	**Sauza Hornitos Tequila**
¹/₂	shot(s)	**Tio Pepe Fino Sherry**
¹/₈	shot(s)	**Brine from jar of salted capers**
¹/₈	shot(s)	**Sugar (gomme) syrup**
¹/₂	shot(s)	**Chilled water**

Comment: Reminiscent of salted water after boiling vegetables but you've got to try these things.

SALTY LYCHEE MARTINI

Glass: Martini
Garnish: Lychee from tin in drink
Method: Stir all ingredients with ice and strain into chilled glass.

2	shot(s)	**Tio Pepe Fino Sherry**
1	shot(s)	**Lanique Rose petal liqueur**
1	shot(s)	**Lychee syrup from tinned fruit**

Origin: I created this drink in 2002 after trying Dick Bradsell's Lychee & Rose Petal Martini (also in this guide).
Comment: Light pink in colour and wonderfully subtle in flavour with the salty tang of Fino sherry.

SAN FRANCISCO

Glass: Collins
Garnish: Split pineapple wedge
Method: Shake ingredients with ice and strain into ice-filled glass.

2	shot(s)	Absolut vodka
1	shot(s)	Cointreau / triple sec
1	shot(s)	Bols Crème de banane
2½	shot(s)	Freshly squeezed orange juice
2½	shot(s)	Pressed pineapple juice
¼	shot(s)	Grenadine syrup

Comment: Long, fruity drink laced with vodka.

●●●●○

SANDSTORM NEW

Glass: Collins
Garnish: Pineapple leaf
Method: Shake all ingredients with ice and strain into ice-filled glass.

1½	shot(s)	Plymouth gin
1	shot(s)	Grand Marnier Liqueur
½	shot(s)	Vanilla schnapps liqueur
1½	shot(s)	Pressed grapefruit juice
1½	shot(s)	Pressed pineapple juice
¼	shot(s)	Sugar (gomme) syrup
¼	shot(s)	Freshly squeezed lime juice
¼	shot(s)	Rose's lime cordial

Origin: Created in 2003 by James Cunningham at Zinc, Glasgow, Scotland and named for its cloudy yellow colour.
Comment: A long, fruity drink featuring well-balanced sweet and sourness.

LA SANG

Glass: Collins
Garnish: Chopped fruit
Method: Shake ingredients with ice and strain into ice-filled glass.

2	shot(s)	Rémy Martin Cognac
2½	shot(s)	Red wine (shiraz)
2	shot(s)	Freshly squeezed orange juice

Comment: French for 'The Blood' this cocktail is a twist on the classic Spanish Sangria, also meaning blood.

●●●●○

SANGRIA MARTINI NEW

Glass: Martini
Garnish: Quarter orange slice
Method: Shake all ingredients with ice and fine strain into chilled glass.

1	shot(s)	Red wine (Shiraz)
1	shot(s)	Freshly squeezed orange juice
1¾	shot(s)	Rémy Martin Cognac
½	shot(s)	Apple schnapps liqueur
½	shot(s)	Bols Raspberry (framboise) liqueur
½	shot(s)	Sugar (gomme) syrup

Origin: Created in 2003 by Angelo Vieira at Light Bar, St. Martins Hotel, London, England.
Comment: Brandy based and fruit laced – just like its namesake.

SANGRITA

Glass: Two shot glasses
Method: Shake ingredients with ice and strain into shot glass. Fill second shot glass with Tequila. Instruct drinker to down the Tequila first, followed by the sangrita chaser. (This may also be drunk by sipping the two drinks alternately.)

¾	shot(s)	Tomato juice
¾	shot(s)	Freshly squeezed orange juice
¼	shot(s)	Freshly squeezed lime juice
¼	spoon	Grenadine syrup
9	drops	Tabasco
1	pinch	Salt
1	pinch	Pepper

Comment: People often assume this spicy, non-alcoholic mixer is tomato-based like Bloody Mary mix. However, a true Sangrita is made with orange juice, lime juice, pomegranate juice and hot chilli sauce, which is what gives it a red colour. As pomegranate juice is not easily found, this recipe, unlike the true Mexican recipe, uses tomato juice.

SANTIAGO

Glass: Collins
Garnish: Lime slices
Method: Pour ingredients into ice-filled glass and stir.

1	shot(s)	Havana Club light rum
1	shot(s)	Spiced rum
4	dashes	Angostura aromatic bitters
½	shot(s)	Freshly squeezed lime juice
¼	shot(s)	Freshly squeezed orange juice
Top up with		Lemonade/7-up

Comment: Light, refreshing and slightly spicy.

SANTINI'S

Glass: Shot
Method: Layer in glass by carefully pouring ingredients in the following order.

½	shot(s)	Maraschino liqueur
½	shot(s)	Orange curaçao
½	shot(s)	Rémy Martin Cognac

Comment: Very sweet, flowery shot.

●●●●○

SATSUMA MARTINI

Glass: Martini
Garnish: Orange zest
Method: Shake all ingredients with ice and fine strain into chilled glass.

1½	shot(s)	Absolut Mandrin vodka
¾	shot(s)	Grand Marnier
2	shot(s)	Pressed apple juice
½	spoon	Fee Brothers Orange bitters

Origin: Discovered in 2002 at the Fifth Floor Bar, London, England.
Comment: Tastes like its namesake – hard to believe the dominant ingredient is apple.

SATURN MARTINI

Glass: Martini
Garnish: Grapes on stick
Method: Shake all ingredients with ice and strain into glass.

1	shot(s)	Absolut Citron vodka
6	fresh	Seedless white grapes
1/2	shot(s)	Honey syrup
1 1/2	shot(s)	Sauvignon Blanc wine
1	shot(s)	Chilled water

Origin: Created in 2001 by Tony Conigliaro at Isola, London, England.
Comment: Delicate, beautifully balanced and subtly flavoured – light and easy drinking. If you don't have honey syrup, this drink is as good made using plain sugar syrup.

SCARLETT O'HARA

Glass: Martini
Garnish: Cranberries
Method: Shake ingredients with ice and strain into glass.

2	shot(s)	Southern Comfort
1	shot(s)	Freshly squeezed lime juice
2	shot(s)	Cranberry juice

Origin: Created in 1939 and named after the heroine of Gone With The Wind, the Scarlett O'Hara is said by many to have put Southern Comfort on the proverbial drink map.
Comment: The tang of lime and the dryness of cranberry works perfectly with the apricot sweetness of Southern Comfort.

SCORPION

Glass: Martini
Method: Shake ingredients with ice and strain into glass.

1	shot(s)	Mount Gay Eclipse golden rum
1	shot(s)	Rémy Martin Cognac
1/2	shot(s)	Almond (orgeat) syrup
1 1/2	shot(s)	Freshly squeezed orange juice
2/3	shot(s)	Freshly squeezed lime juice
1/3	shot(s)	Sugar (gomme) syrup

Comment: Well balanced and complex.

SCORPION SLING

Glass: Sling
Garnish: Orange & mint
Method: Blend first six ingredients with crushed ice and pour into glass, then float a Daiquirí mix.

1	shot(s)	Mount Gay Eclipse golden rum
1	shot(s)	Rémy Martin Cognac
1/2	shot(s)	Almond (orgeat) syrup
1 1/2	shot(s)	Freshly squeezed orange juice
1	shot(s)	Freshly squeezed lemon juice
1/2	shot(s)	Sugar (gomme) syrup
1 1/2	shot(s)	Daiquirí float

Comment: The Daiquirí bit adds extra dimension – although it's a pain to make.

SAZERAC

●●●●●

UPDATED

Glass: Old-fashioned
Method: Fill glass with ice, pour in absinthe, top up with water and leave the mixture in the glass. Separately shake Bourbon, Cognac, sugar and bitters with ice. Finally discard contents of glass (absinthe, water and ice) and strain contents of shaker into empty absinthe-coated glass.

1	shot(s)	La Fée absinthe
Top up with		Chilled water
1	shot(s)	Buffalo Trace Bourbon
1	shot(s)	Rémy Martin Cognac
1/2	shot(s)	Sugar (gomme) syrup
3	dashes	Angostura aromatic bitters
3	dashes	Péychaud's bitters

Origin: This drink hails from the old days of New Orleans. At 13 Exchange Alley, John B. Schiller set up the Sazerac Coffee House – as he was the agent for Sazerac Cognacs, he made this cocktail originally with brandy. The Sazerac Company which developed from the Sazerac Coffee House now also markets Péychaud's bitters – an essential component of this drink and first made in 1793.
Comment: Don't be concerned about chucking expensive absinthe down the drain - its flavour will be very evident in the finished drink. Made correctly this is a delightfully interesting herbal classic.

SCOTCH BOUNTY MARTINI

Glass: Martini
Method: Shake ingredients with ice and strain into glass.

1	shot(s)	The Famous Grouse Scotch whisky
1	shot(s)	Bols White crème de cacao
1/2	shot(s)	Malibu Coconut rum
2	shot(s)	Freshly squeezed orange juice
1/8	shot(s)	Grenadine syrup

Comment: A medium-sweet combination of Scotch, coconut and orange.

SCOTCH MILK PUNCH

Glass: Martini
Method: Shake ingredients with ice and strain into glass.

2	shot(s)	The Famous Grouse Scotch whisky
1/2	shot(s)	Sugar (gomme) syrup
1	shot(s)	Double (heavy) cream
1	shot(s)	Milk

Comment: A creamy, malty affair – very good!

SCREAMING BANANA BANSHEE

Glass: Hurricane
Garnish: Banana slice
Method: Blend ingredients with crushed ice and serve.

1	shot(s)	Absolut vodka
3/4	shot(s)	Bols Crème de banane
3/4	shot(s)	Bols White crème de cacao
1 1/2	shot(s)	Double (heavy) cream
1 1/2	shot(s)	Milk
2	scoops	Vanilla ice cream

Comment: Choc, bananas and cream.

SCREWDRIVER

Glass: Collins
Garnish: Orange slice
Method: Pour vodka into ice-filled glass, then top up with orange juice and stir.

2	shot(s)	Absolut vodka
Top up with		Fresh orange juice

Origin: This cocktail first appeared in the 1950s in the Middle East. Parched US engineers working in the desert supposedly added orange juice to their vodka and stirred it with the nearest thing to hand, usually a screwdriver.

SEABREEZE (SIMPLE)

●●●●○○

Glass: Collins
Method: Shake all ingredients with ice and strain into ice-filled glass.

2	shot(s)	Absolut vodka
4	shot(s)	Cranberry juice
2	shot(s)	Pressed grapefruit juice

Origin: Thought to have originated in New York City and popularised during the mid 90s by Absolut.
Comment: Few bartenders shake this simple drink, instead simply pouring ingredients into the glass.

SEABREEZE (ADVANCED)

Glass: Collins
Method: Pour cranberry juice into ice-filled glass. Shake other ingredients with ice and strain into glass over cranberry juice.

4	shot(s)	Cranberry juice
2	shot(s)	Absolut vodka
1 1/2	shot(s)	Pressed grapefruit juice
1/2	shot(s)	Freshly squeezed lime juice

Comment: This layered version requires mixing with straws prior to drinking.

SERENDIPITY

●●●●○

Glass: Collins
Garnish: Slice of lemon
Method: Muddle blackberries in base of shaker. Add other ingredients, shake with ice and strain into glass filled with crushed ice.

6	fresh	Blackberries
1	shot(s)	Plymouth gin
1/2	shot(s)	Teichenné Vanilla schnapps
1/2	shot(s)	Sisca Crème de cassis
3	shot(s)	Cranberry juice
1/4	shot(s)	Freshly squeezed lemon juice
1/4	shot(s)	Sugar (gomme) syrup

Origin: Created in 2002 by Jamie Stephenson, Manchester, England.
Comment: This fruity vanilla drink is very red and very tasty.

SET THE JUICE LOOSE

Glass: Rocks
Method: Shake ingredients with ice and strain into ice-filled glass.

1	shot(s)	Bols Crème de banane
1	shot(s)	Bols Apricot brandy liqueur
1	shot(s)	Bols Cherry brandy liqueur
1 3/4	shot(s)	Freshly squeezed orange juice
1 3/4	shot(s)	Pressed pineapple juice

Comment: Don't be put off by the colour, this is a great medium sweet fruity cocktail.

SEX ON THE BEACH # 1

●●●●◑○

Glass: Rocks
Method: Shake ingredients with ice and strain into ice-filled glass.

1	shot(s)	Absolut vodka
1	shot(s)	Chambord black raspberry liqueur
1	shot(s)	Teichenné Peach schnapps
2 1/2	shot(s)	Pressed pineapple juice

Variant: With melon liqueur in place of peach schnapps.

Comment: Deliciously fun without sand in your privates. This drink is fruity flavoured with black raspberries, pineapple, peach and a vodka edge.

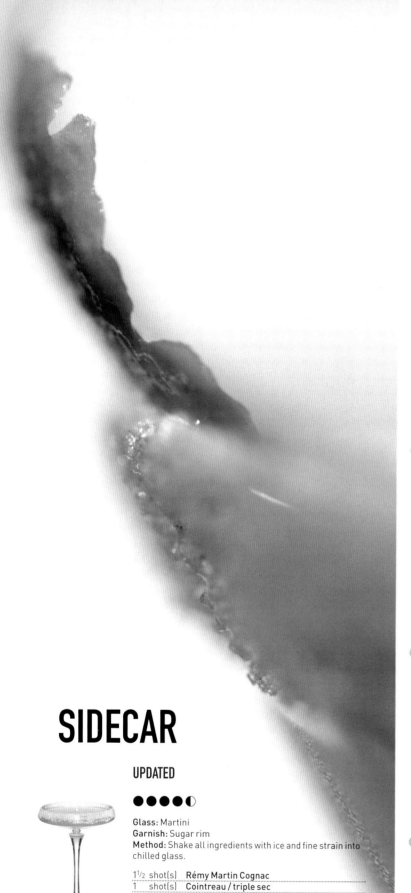

SIDECAR

UPDATED

●●●●◐

Glass: Martini
Garnish: Sugar rim
Method: Shake all ingredients with ice and fine strain into chilled glass.

1¹/₂	shot(s)	Rémy Martin Cognac
1	shot(s)	Cointreau / triple sec
1	shot(s)	Freshly squeezed lemon juice
³/₄	shot(s)	Chilled water

Variation: Apple Cart
Origin: Legend has it that this drink was created by Harry MacElhone at his Harry's New York Bar in Paris after the First World War and was named after an eccentric army captain who used to be chauffeur-driven to the bar in a motorcycle sidecar. However, in Harry's own book he credits the drink to MacGarry of Buck's Club, London.
Comment: This wonderful classic relies on the sugar rim to take the edge off the sourness of the drink. If serving without a sugared rim add a quarter shot of sugar syrup to compensate.

SEX ON THE BEACH # 2

Glass: Rocks
Method: Shake all ingredients with ice and strain into ice-filled glass.

1	shot(s)	Absolut vodka
1	shot(s)	Chambord black raspberry liqueur
1	shot(s)	Midori melon liqueur
2¹/₂	shot(s)	Pressed pineapple juice

Comment: Sweeter than most – but great flavours.

SEX ON THE BEACH # 3

Glass: Shot
Method: Layer in glass by carefully pouring ingredients in the following order.

¹/₂	shot(s)	Chambord black raspberry liqueur
¹/₂	shot(s)	Midori melon liqueur
¹/₂	shot(s)	Freshly squeezed lime juice
¹/₂	shot(s)	Pressed pineapple juice

Comment: A sweet and sour shot, combining raspberry, melon, lime and pineapple.

SEX ON THE SOFA

Glass: Rocks
Method: Shake all ingredients with ice and strain into ice-filled glass.

1¹/₂	shot(s)	Absolut vodka
³/₄	shot(s)	Teichenné Peach schnapps
1¹/₂	shot(s)	Freshly squeezed orange juice
1¹/₂	shot(s)	Cranberry juice

Comment: A medium sweet mix of peach, orange and cranberry, laced with vodka.

SHADY GROVE COOLER

Glass: Collins
Method: Shake first three ingredients with ice and strain into ice-filled glass, then top up with ginger ale and stir.

2	shot(s)	Plymouth gin
1	shot(s)	Freshly squeezed lime juice
¹/₂	shot(s)	Sugar (gomme) syrup
Top up with		Ginger ale

Comment: Long and refreshing.

SHAHAD MARTINI

Glass: Martini
Garnish: Lemon twist
Method: Shake all ingredients with ice and fine strain into glass.

1¹/₂	shot(s)	Date infused Appleton Estate V/X aged rum
1	shot(s)	Honey liqueur
¹/₂	shot(s)	Freshly squeezed lemon juice
¹/₄	shot(s)	Lemongrass & lime cordial

Origin: Created in 2001 by Douglas Ankrah for Akbar, Red Fort, London, England.
Comment: One of the many superb and very modern cocktails created by Douglas for Akbar using Indian flavours.

SHAMROCK EXPRESS

Glass: Old-fashioned
Method: Shake ingredients with ice and strain into ice-filled glass.

1¹/₂	shot(s)	Espresso coffee (cold)
³/₄	shot(s)	Teichenné Butterscotch schnapps
¹/₂	shot(s)	Absolut vodka
1	shot(s)	Baileys Irish cream liqueur
¹/₄	shot(s)	Sugar (gomme) syrup

Origin: Created in 1999 by Greg Pearson at Mystique, Manchester, England.
Comment: Strong coffee with the sweetness of butterscotch.

SHARK BITE

Glass: Hurricane
Garnish: Pineapple leaf
Method: Blend first three ingredients with crushed ice and pour into glass, then add grenadine. Do not stir before serving.

2	shot(s)	Pusser's Navy rum
3	shot(s)	Freshly squeezed orange juice
¹/₂	shot(s)	Freshly squeezed ime juice
¹/₂	shot(s)	Grenadine syrup

Created by: Paul Hunter.
Comment: Strong rum and orange juice flavours.

SHIRLEY TEMPLE | VIRGIN

Glass: Collins
Method: Add grenadine and ginger ale to ice-filled glass and stir.

¹/₄	shot(s)	Grenadine syrup
Top up with		Ginger ale

Comment: Improved with a squeeze of lemon. Not that exciting, though.

SHOWBIZ

Glass: Martini
Method: Shake ingredients with ice and strain into glass.

1³/₄	shot(s)	Absolut vodka
1	shot(s)	Sisca crème de cassis
1³/₄	shot(s)	Pressed grapefruit juice

Comment: A dry, tart combination of blackcurrant, grapefruit and vodka.

●●●●●○

SIDECAR NAMED DESIRE

Glass: Martini
Garnish: Sugar rim
Method: Vigorously shake all ingredients with ice and fine strain into chilled glass.

2	shot(s)	Rémy Martin Cognac
1	shot(s)	Sourz Sour Apple liqueur
1¹/₂	shot(s)	Freshly squeezed lemon juice
¹/₄	shot(s)	Sugar (gomme) syrup

Comment: Take a classic Sidecar and add some love interest – apple!

●●●●○

SIDEKICK NEW

Glass: Martini
Garnish: Quarter orange slice on rim
Method: Shake all ingredients with ice and fine strain into chilled glass.

2	shot(s)	Xanté pear & cognac liqueur
³/₄	shot(s)	Cointreau / triple sec
1	shot(s)	Freshly squeezed orange juice
¹/₂	shot(s)	Freshly squeezed lime juice

Origin: Adapted from a drink discovered in 2003 at the Temple Bar, New York City.
Comment: Rich pear and orange with a stabilising hint of sour lime.

SILENT THIRD

Glass: Martini
Method: Shake ingredients with ice and strain into glass.

1¹/₂	shot(s)	The Famous Grouse Scotch whisky
1¹/₂	shot(s)	Cointreau / triple sec
1¹/₂	shot(s)	Freshly squeezed lemon juice

Comment: A sour, sharp whisky drink.

SILK STOCKINGS

Glass: Flute
Garnish: Cinnamon rim
Method: Shake ingredients with ice and strain into glass.

1¹/₂	shot(s)	Sauza Hornitos Tequila
1	shot(s)	Bols White crème de cacao
³/₄	shot(s)	Double (heavy) cream
³/₄	shot(s)	Milk
¹/₄	shot(s)	Chambord black raspberry liqueur

Comment: An interesting combination of Tequila and Chambord.

●●●○○

SILVER BULLET MARTINI

Glass: Martini
Garnish: Lemon zest
Method: Shake all ingredients with ice and fine strain into chilled glass.

2	shot(s)	Plymouth gin
1	shot(s)	Opal Bianca sambuca
1	shot(s)	Freshly squeezed lemon juice
¹/₂	shot(s)	Sugar (gomme) syrup

Origin: A pre-1930s gin based drink that originally used Kümmel. Now more often based on vodka and made (as here) with sambuca.
Comment: A sweet but balanced combination of aniseed, gin and lemon.

SINGAPORE SLING

●●●●●

SINGAPORE SLING # 1

Glass: Sling
Garnish: Split lemon wheel
Method: Shake first seven ingredients with ice and strain into ice-filled glass, then top up with soda water and float cherry liqueur and grenadine.

2	shot(s)	Plymouth gin
3/4	shot(s)	Bols Cherry brandy liqueur
1/4	shot(s)	Bénédictine D.O.M liqueur
3/4	shot(s)	Freshly squeezed orange juice
3/4	shot(s)	Freshly squeezed lime juice
1/4	shot(s)	Rose's lime cordial
3	dashes	Angostura aromatic bitters
Top up with		Soda water (club soda)
1/4	shot(s)	Bols Cherry brandy liqueur
1/4	shot(s)	Grenadine syrup

Origin: Created by Ngiam Tong Boon at the Raffles Hotel, Singapore, using Cherry Heering and Bénédictine liqueur.
Raffle's Hotel, named for the colonial founder of Singapore, was the Near East's ex-pat central. Everyone from Noel Coward to the Prince of Siam to Ernest Hemingway stayed and drank there - W. Somerset Maugham would cruise for plot lines in the Palm Court bar outside. It still sticks out of modern-day Singapore like a vast colonial Christmas cake.

Comment: There are many versions of this drink – all star cherry liqueur. A complex mix of citrus and cherries.

●●●●○

SINGAPORE SLING # 2

Glass: Sling
Garnish: Split lemon wheel
Method: Shake first four ingredients with ice and strain into ice-filled glass, then top up with soda.

1	shot(s)	Plymouth gin
1	shot(s)	Bols Cherry brandy liqueur
1	shot(s)	Bénédictine D.O.M liqueur
4	dashes	Angostura aromatic bitters
Top up with		Soda water (club soda)

Comment: Said to be the original Singapore Sling recipe.

●●●●○

SINGAPORE SLING # 3

Glass: Sling
Garnish: Split lemon wedge
Method: Shake all ingredients with ice and strain into ice-filled glass.

1 1/2	shot(s)	Plymouth gin
1/4	shot(s)	Bénédictine D.O.M liqueur
1/2	shot(s)	Bols Cherry brandy liqueur
3	shot(s)	Pressed pineapple juice
1/2	shot(s)	Freshly squeezed lime juice
1/8	shot(s)	Grenadine syrup
2	dash(es)	Angostura aromatic bitters
Top up with		Soda water (club soda)

Comment: Yet another version of this classic - this one a modern interpretation.

SILVER FIZZ

Glass: Collins
Method: Shake first four ingredients with ice and strain into ice-filled glass, then top up with soda and stir.

2	shot(s)	Plymouth gin
1	shot(s)	Freshly squeezed lime juice
1/2	shot(s)	Sugar (gomme) syrup
1/2	fresh	Egg white
Top up with		Soda water (club soda)

Comment: Gin fizz with lime and egg white - very drinkable.

SIMPLE PIMM'S

Glass: Collins
Garnish: Chopped-up lemon slice & other fruits in drink.
Method: Pour ingredients into ice-filled glass and stir.

2	shot(s)	Pimm's No.1
6	shot(s)	Lemonade
Top up with		Ginger ale

Comment: The summer special.

SISCO KID

●●●●○○

Glass: Martini
Garnish: Float raspberry and blueberry
Method: Shake all ingredients with ice and fine strain into chilled glass.

1	shot(s)	Absolut vodka
1	shot(s)	Teichenné peach schnapps
1/2	shot(s)	Mango drink
1/2	shot(s)	Passion fruit drink
1/2	shot(s)	Freshly squeezed orange juice
1	shot(s)	Freshly squeezed lime juice

Origin: Created in 1991 by Wayne Collins at Bar Royal, London.
Comment: A tarty mix of tropical flavour.

SKI BREEZE

Glass: Collins
Method: Pour ingredients into ice-filled glass and stir.

2	shot(s)	Absolut Kurant vodka
3	shot(s)	Pressed apple juice
3	shot(s)	Ginger ale

Comment: Simple, understated and delicious.

SKYEDIVER

●●●●◐○

Glass: Martini
Garnish: Orange zest
Method: Shake all ingredients with ice and strain into glass.

1 3/4	shot(s)	Drambuie Cream liqueur
3/4	shot(s)	Mandarine Napoleon liqueur
3/4	shot(s)	Grand Marnier
1/2	shot(s)	Teichenné Butterscotch schnapps

Origin: Created in 2000 by Stefan Olafsson at Teatro, London, England.
Comment: A creamy orange after dinner cocktail.

●●●●○

SLEEPING BISON-TINI UPDATED

Glass: Martini
Garnish: Pear slice on rim
Method: Shake all ingredients with ice and fine strain into chilled glass.

1 1/2	shot(s)	Zubrówka (Bison grass) vodka
1/4	shot(s)	Bols Apricot brandy liqueur
1/4	shot(s)	Xanté liqueur
1	shot(s)	Freshly extracted pear juice
1	shot(s)	Pressed apple juice
1	shot(s)	Strong cold camomile tea

Comment: This lightly alcoholic drink features a wonderful meld of subtle flavours.

SLIPPERY NIPPER

Glass: Shot
Method: Layer in glass by carefully pouring ingredients in the following order.

1/4	shot(s)	Grenadine syrup
3/4	shot(s)	Opal Bianca white sambuca
3/4	shot(s)	Baileys Irish cream liqueur

Comment: The infamous red, clear and brown shot.

SLOE GIN FIZZ

Glass: Sling
Garnish: Lemon slice or cucumber slice
Method: Shake first five ingredients with ice and strain into ice-filled glass, then top up with soda water.

1	shot(s)	Plymouth gin
1	shot(s)	Plymouth sloe gin
1	shot(s)	Freshly squeezed lime juice
1/2	shot(s)	Sugar (gomme) syrup
1/2	fresh	Egg white
Top up with		Soda water (club soda)

Comment: A sour gin fizz with the dark richness of sloe gin.

SLOE MOTION

Glass: Flute
Garnish: Lemon zest & cucumber cross
Method: Pour sloe gin into glass and top up with Champagne.

3/4	shot(s)	Plymouth sloe gin
Top up with		Piper-Heidsieck Brut Champagne

Comment: A good complement to Champagne.

SLOE TEQUILA

Glass: Rocks
Method: Shake ingredients with ice and strain into ice-filled glass.

1	shot(s)	Plymouth sloe gin
1	shot(s)	Sauza Hornitos Tequila
1/2	shot(s)	Rose's lime cordial

Comment: A smooth combination.

SLOPPY JOE

Glass: Martini
Method: Shake ingredients with ice and strain into glass.

1	shot(s)	Havana Club light rum
1	shot(s)	Cinzano Extra Dry vermouth
1/4	shot(s)	Cointreau / triple sec
1	shot(s)	Freshly squeezed lime juice
1/2	shot(s)	Sugar (gomme) syrup
1/4	shot(s)	Grenadine syrup

Comment: Nicely balanced.

SLOW SCREW

Glass: Collins
Garnish: Orange slice
Method: Shake first two ingredients with ice and strain into ice-filled glass, then top up with orange juice.

1	shot(s)	Plymouth sloe gin
1	shot(s)	Absolut vodka
Top up with		Freshly squeezed orange juice

Comment: A Screwdriver with sloe gin.

SLOW COMFORTABLE SCREW

Glass: Collins
Method: Shake first three ingredients with ice and strain into ice-filled glass, then top up with orange juice.

1	shot(s)	Absolut vodka
1	shot(s)	Plymouth sloe gin
1	shot(s)	Southern Comfort
Top up with		Freshly squeezed orange juice

Comment: Who'd want a slow screw without some comfort?

SLOW COMFORTABLE SCREW AGAINST THE WALL

Glass: Collins
Method: Shake first three ingredients with ice and strain into ice-filled glass, then top up with Orange juice and float Galliano.

1	shot(s)	Absolut vodka
1	shot(s)	Plymouth sloe gin
1	shot(s)	Southern Comfort
Top up with		Freshly squeezed orange juice
1/2	shot(s)	Galliano

Comment: A slow comfortable screw with the aid of Galliano.

SLOW COMFORTABLE SCREW AGAINST THE WALL WITH A KISS

Glass: Collins
Method: Shake first three ingredients with ice and strain into ice-filled glass, then top up with orange juice and float Galliano and Amaretto.

1	shot(s)	Absolut vodka
1	shot(s)	Plymouth sloe gin
1	shot(s)	Southern Comfort
Top up with		Freshly squeezed orange juice
1/2	shot(s)	Galliano
1/2	shot(s)	Disaronno Originale amaretto

Comment: Much more complicated than its siblings – but still works!

SLOW SCREW, MILDLY COMFORTABLE, SLIGHTLY WILD

Glass: Hurricane
Garnish: Orange & cherry
Method: Shake first four ingredients with ice and strain into ice-filled glass, then add lemonade and top up with orange juice.

1	shot(s)	Plymouth sloe gin
1	shot(s)	Absolut vodka
3/4	shot(s)	Southern Comfort
3/4	shot(s)	Buffalo Trace Bourbon
2	shot(s)	Lemonade / 7-up
Top up with		Freshly squeezed orange juice

Comment: The use of Bourbon gives a wild touch!

SMARTINI

Glass: Martini
Garnish: Three Smarties in drink
Method: Shake all ingredients with ice and fine strain into chilled glass.

2	shot(s)	Absolut Citron vodka
1	shot(s)	Bols White crème de cacao
1/4	shot(s)	Sugar (gomme) syrup
3/4	shot(s)	Chilled water
4	dashes	Fee Brothers Orange bitters

Comment: Citrus with a crispy chocolate edge.

SMOKIE MARTINI

Glass: Martini
Method: Stir Scotch with ice in a mixing glass. Then strain, discarding Scotch to leave only a coating of Scotch on the ice. Pour gin into mixing glass containing coated ice and stir. Finally strain contents of mixing glass into glass.

1/2	shot(s)	The Famous Grouse Scotch whisky
2 1/2	shot(s)	Plymouth gin

Comment: A killer Martini for alcohol lovers.

SMOKY MARTINI

Glass: Martini
Garnish: Strips of orange zest in drink
Method: Stir ingredients with ice and strain into glass.

2	shot(s)	Plymouth gin
1	shot(s)	Plymouth sloe gin
1/4	shot(s)	Cinzano Extra dry vermouth
4	dashes	Fee Brothers Orange bitters

Origin: Created in 1997 by Giovanni Burdi at the Match Bar, London, England.
Comment: Dry and sophisticated with a distinctive 'smoke' – the basic Martini formula (gin plus vermouth) is enhanced with sloe gin and the traditional orange bitters variation.

SMOOTH & CREAMY'TINI

●●●●○

Glass: Martini
Garnish: Dust with grated nutmeg
Method: Shake all ingredients with ice and fine strain into chilled glass.

1¹/₂	shot(s)	Mount Gay Eclipse golden rum
1	shot(s)	Malibu coconut rum liqueur
¹/₄	shot(s)	Bols Crème de banane
³/₄	shot(s)	Double (heavy) cream
³/₄	shot(s)	Milk

Comment: Creamy and moreish.

SNAKEBITE

Glass: Collins
Method: Half fill glass with lager and then top up with cider and stir.

Half fill with	Lager
Top up with	Cider

Variant: There is a similarly named drink in rural Tennessee which has an actual snake's head marinating in the bottle.
Comment: Students' special – add blackcurrant for extra flavour (Snakebite and Black).

SNAP DRAGON

Glass: Martini
Garnish: Chocolate sprinkle
Method: Blend ingredients, including Brandy Snap biscuit, with crushed ice and serve.

1	shot(s)	Chambord black raspberry liqueur
1	shot(s)	Bols White crème de cacao
1	scoop	Vanilla ice cream
1		Brandy snap biscuit

Comment: Cream, chocolate and raspberries – lacks oomph and character.

SNOOD MURDEKIN

Glass: Shot
Method: Shake first three ingredients with ice and strain into glass, then float cream.

¹/₂	shot(s)	Absolut vodka
¹/₂	shot(s)	Chambord black raspberry liqueur
¹/₂	shot(s)	Kahlúa coffee liqueur
¹/₄	shot(s)	Double (heavy) cream

Origin: Created by Dick Bradsell at Detroit, London, England.
in the late 90s for Karin Wiklund, and named for the sad, flute-playing Moomin Troll. Then rapidly renamed after it didn't sell because nobody could pronounce it.
Comment: Moreish combination of coffee and raspberries.

SNOW FALL MARTINI NEW

●●●●○

Glass: Martini
Garnish: Vanilla pod
Method: Muddle vanilla pod in base of shaker. Add other ingredients, shake with ice and fine strain into chilled glass.

¹/₂	pod	Vanilla
2	shot(s)	Stoli Vanil
1¹/₄	shot(s)	Double (heavy) cream
1¹/₄	shot(s)	Milk
¹/₄	shot(s)	Sugar (gomme) syrup

Origin: Discovered in 2002 at Lot 61, New York City.
Comment: A very light alcoholic version of a vanilla milkshake.

SNOW ON EARTH

●●●○○

Glass: Shot
Method: Shake first three ingredients with ice and strain into glass. Carefully float cream on drink.

¹/₂	shot(s)	Kahlúa coffee liqueur
¹/₂	shot(s)	Chambord black raspberry liqueur
¹/₂	shot(s)	Krupnik honey liqueur
¹/₂	shot(s)	Double (heavy) cream

Comment: A sweet, flavoursome shot.

SNOWBALL

Glass: Collins
Method: Shake first three ingredients with ice and strain into ice filled glass. Top up with 7-Up and stir

2	shot(s)	Warninks Advocaat
¹/₂	shot(s)	Rose's lime cordial
¹/₂	shot(s)	Tio Pepe fino Sherry
Top up with		7-Up

Comment: The classic light, fluffy concoction for granny - try it, you may like it.

SNOWSHOE

Glass: Rocks
Method: Shake ingredients with ice and strain into ice-filled glass.

1¹/₂	shot(s)	Buffalo Trace Bourbon
1¹/₂	shot(s)	Peppermint schnapps

Comment: Stronger than Extra Strong mints!

SOPHISTICATED SAVAGE

Glass: Rocks
Garnish: Lime sugared rim
Method: Shake ingredients with ice and strain into ice-filled glass.

1	shot(s)	Tuaca liqueur
2	shot(s)	Pitú Cachaça
¹/₂	fresh	Egg white
¹/₂	shot(s)	Freshly squeezed lime juice
¹/₄	shot(s)	Sugar (gomme) syrup

Created by: Poul Jensen.
Comment: A sour drink with a horse kick leading into a smooth subtle finish.

SORREL RUM PUNCH

●●●●●◐

Glass: Collins
Method: Shake all ingredients with cubed ice and strain into glass filled with crushed glass.

³/₄	shot(s)	Freshly squeezed lime juice
1¹/₂	shot(s)	Sugar (gomme) syrup
2¹/₄	shot(s)	Wray & Nephew overproof rum
3	shot(s)	Sorrel ade

Origin: Another classic Jamaican drink based on overproof rum using the classic rum punch proportions of 'one of sour, two of sweet, three of strong and four of weak'. Sorrel (scientific name 'Hibiscus Sabdariffa') is a plant propagated for its red petals, which in Jamaica are used to make a refreshing drink. Known as 'sorrel ade', commercially produced brands such as 'Island Queen Red Velvet' can be purchased or you can buy dried sorrel and make your own.
Recipe: Homemade sorrel ade is made by soaking 140g of dried sorrel into 2.5 liters of water with 60g fresh ginger, half bar spoon of ground cloves and a dash or two of honey or brown sugar to taste. Bring this mixture to the boil then leave to cool and soak overnight. Strain and then keep refrigerated.
Comment: Sorrel ade looks a little like cranberry juice, and like cranberry juice has a bittersweet taste. This drink harnesses the flavour of sorrel ade and combines it with the traditional strength, flavour and bittersweetness of rum punch. Jamaica in a glass.

SOCIALITE

●●●●●○

Glass: Rocks
Method: Shake all ingredients with ice and strain into glass filled with crushed ice.

1	shot(s)	Freshly squeezed lemon juice
¹/₂	shot(s)	Vanilla sugar syrup
1	shot(s)	Grand Marnier
1	shot(s)	Stoli Vanil
1	shot(s)	Limoncello liqueur

Origin: Discovered in 2001 at Lab Bar, London, England.
Comment: Rich citrus with lashings of vanilla.

SOUR ITALIAN

Glass: Old-fashioned
Method: Shake ingredients with ice and strain into ice-filled glass.

2	shot(s)	Campari
³/₄	shot(s)	Galliano liqueur
¹/₃	shot(s)	Strega liqueur
2	shot(s)	Freshly squeezed lemon juice
¹/₄	shot(s)	Sugar (gomme) syrup

Origin: Created in 1999 by Tadgh Ryan, at Circus, London, England.

SOURPUSS MARTINI

●●●●○

Glass: Martini
Garnish: Physalis (Cape gooseberry) on rim
Method: Shake all ingredients with ice and fine strain into chilled glass.

1	shot(s)	Absolut Citron vodka
¹/₂	shot(s)	Midori melon liqueur
¹/₂	shot(s)	Sourz Sour Apple liqueur
2	shot(s)	Pressed apple juice

Origin: Created in 2001 by Colin 'Big Col' Crowden at Time, Leicester, England.
Comment: A lime-green, flavourful cocktail balancing sweet and sour.

SOUTH BEACH NEW

●●●●○

Glass: Martini
Garnish: Flamed orange twist
Method: Shake all ingredients with ice and fine strain into glass.

1	shot(s)	Campari
1	shot(s)	Disaronno Originale amaretto
2¹/₂	shot(s)	Freshly squeezed orange juice
¹/₄	shot(s)	Sugar (gomme) syrup

Origin: Created in 1992 by Dale DeGroff in New York City.
Comment: An unusual bitter-sweet combination with a strong orange and almond flavour.

SOUTH OF THE BORDER

Glass: Martini
Garnish: 3 coffee beans
Method: Shake ingredients with ice and strain into glass.

2	shot(s)	Sauza Hornitos Tequila
1¹/2	shot(s)	Kahlúa coffee liqueur
1	shot(s)	Freshly squeezed lime juice
¹/2	shot(s)	Sugar (gomme) syrup
¹/2	fresh	Egg white

Comment: A strange mix of lime and coffee – but it works!

SOUTH CHINA BREEZE

●●●●●○

Glass: Collins
Garnish: Half orange wheel
Method: Shake all ingredients with ice and strain into ice-filled glass.

2	shot(s)	Absolut Mandrin vodka
3	shot(s)	Pressed grapefruit juice
1¹/2	shot(s)	Lychee syrup from tinned fruit
4	dashes	Angostura aromatic bitters

Comment: Orange and grapefruit with an oriental influence by way of lychee.

SOUTH PACIFIC BREEZE

●●●●◐○

Glass: Collins
Garnish: Pineapple wedge on rim
Method: Pour gin and Galliano into an ice-filled glass. Top up with lemonade to just below the rim. Drizzle blue curaçao around top of drink (it should sink).

1¹/2	shot(s)	Plymouth gin
³/4	shot(s)	Galliano
Top up with		Lemonade / 7-Up / Sprite
³/4	shot(s)	Bols Blue Curaçao

Comment: Quite sweet but flavoursome – looks great.

SOUTHERN CIDER

●●●●○○

Glass: Martini
Garnish: Lime wedge
Method: Shake all ingredients with ice and strain into glass.

2	shot(s)	Southern Comfort
1	shot(s)	Freshly squeezed lime juice
1¹/2	shot(s)	Cranberry juice
¹/4	shot(s)	Sugar (gomme) syrup

Origin: Discovered at Opryland Hotel, Nashville, USA.
Comment: Strangely this cocktail does have a cidery taste.

SOUTHERN PEACH

Glass: Collins
Method: Shake ingredients with ice and strain into ice-filled glass.

1	shot(s)	Southern Comfort
1	shot(s)	Teichenné Peach schnapps
3	shot(s)	Cranberry juice
1	shot(s)	Freshly squeezed lime juice
¹/2	shot(s)	Sugar (gomme) syrup

Comment: Remarkably drinkable.

SOUTHERN PUNCH NEW

●●●●◐○

Glass: Collins
Garnish: Pineapple wedge on rim
Method: Shake all ingredients with ice and strain into ice-filled glass.

1¹/2	shot(s)	Southern Comfort
¹/2	shot(s)	Jack Daniel's Tennessee whiskey
2	shot(s)	Pressed pineapple juice
1	shot(s)	Freshly squeezed lemon juice
¹/2	shot(s)	Sugar (gomme) syrup
¹/2	shot(s)	Grenadine syrup

Comment: Tropical flavours with the warmth of the liquor trailed by a fresh lemon finish.

SOUTHERN TEA-KNEE

●●●●●

Glass: Martini
Garnish: Apricot slice on rim
Method: Shake all ingredients with ice and fine strain into chilled glass.

1	shot(s)	Southern Comfort
¹/2	shot(s)	Plymouth gin
¹/2	shot(s)	Bols Apricot brandy liqueur
¹/2	shot(s)	Bols Crème de banane
2	shot(s)	Strong cold Earl Grey tea

Origin: I created this in December 2002 while experimenting with Southern Comfort.
Comment: Sweet fruity flavours balanced by tannin bitterness in the tea.

SPARKLING PERRY

●●●●●○

Glass: Flute
Garnish: Pear slice on rim
Method: Pour ingredients into glass and lightly stir.

³/4	shot(s)	Poire William eau de vie
³/4	shot(s)	Xanté liqueur
1	shot(s)	Freshly extracted pear juice
Top up with		Piper-Heidsieck Brut Champagne

Origin: Created in December 2002 by yours truly.
Comment: Tastes like perry (pear cider) with bells on.

SPARKLY COSMO NEW

●●●●●◐

Glass: Flute
Garnish: Flamed orange twist
Method: Shake first four ingredients with ice and strain into chilled glass. Top up with Champagne.

1¹/4	shot(s)	Absolut Citron vodka
¹/2	shot(s)	Cointreau / triple sec
1	shot(s)	Cranberry juice
¹/8	shot(s)	Freshly squeezed lime juice
Top up with		Piper-Heidsieck Brut Champagne

Origin: Created in 2003 at Aura Kitchen & Bar, London, England.
Comment: The classic Cosmopolitan with a layer of fizz on top adding a biscuity complexity. Sex And The City meets Ab Fab.

SPICED CRANBERRY MARTINI NEW

Glass: Martini
Garnish: Cranberry juice & cinnamon rim
Method: Muddle cloves in base of shaker. Add other ingredients, shake with ice and fine strain into chilled glass.

7	dried	Cloves
1	shot(s)	Finlandia cranberry vodka
1	shot(s)	Pusser's Navy rum
2	shot(s)	Cranberry juice
1/2	shot(s)	Sugar (gomme) syrup

Origin: Created in 2003 by your truly for Finlandia.
Comment: The cloves add a festive note to this red, vaguely Martini styled drink.

SPICED PEAR NEW

Glass: Old-fashioned
Garnish: Pear slice
Method: Shake all ingredients with ice and strain into ice-filled glass.

1	shot(s)	Xanté pear & cognac liqueur
1	shot(s)	Morgan's spiced rum
1	shot(s)	Freshly extracted pear juice
1/2	shot(s)	Freshly squeezed lime juice
1/2	shot(s)	Sugar (gomme) syrup

Origin: Created in 2002 by James Stewart, Edinburgh, Scotland.
Comment: Just as it says on the tin – spiced pear. Ooh yeah!

SPICED SWIZZLE

Glass: Collins
Garnish: Lime wedge
Method: Shake first three ingredients with ice and strain into glass filled with crushed ice, then float amaretto.

2	shot(s)	Spiced rum
1	shot(s)	Freshly squeezed lime juice
1/4	shot(s)	Sugar (gomme) syrup
1/2	shot(s)	Disaronno Originale amaretto

Origin: Created by Douglas Ankrah of Lab, London, England.
Comment: Limy with spicy hints.

SPICY FINN NEW

Glass: Martini
Garnish: Blueberry or raspberry on rim
Method: Muddle ginger in base of shaker. Add other ingredients; shake with ice and fine strain into chilled glass.

3	slices	Root ginger (thumb nail sized)
2	shot(s)	Finlandia Cranberry vodka
1/2	shot(s)	Campari
1/2	shot(s)	Sugar (gomme) syrup
1	shot(s)	Chilled water

Origin: Created by Michael Mahe at Hush, London, England.
Comment: Cranberry vodka, Campari and ginger with a dash of gomme to sweeten things up.

SPICY ORANGE VEGY'TINI

Glass: Martini
Garnish: Chunk of carrot on rim
Method: Muddle coriander seeds in base of shaker. Add other ingredients, shake with ice and fine strain into chilled glass.

2	dozen	Coriander seeds
2	shot(s)	Plymouth gin
2 1/2	shot(s)	Freshly extracted carrot juice
1/4	shot(s)	Sugar (gomme) syrup
1	pinch	Black pepper
1	pinch	Salt

Origin: I created this drink in 2002.
Comment: Reminiscent of alcoholic carrot and coriander soup - almost a healthy option.

SPORRAN BREEZE

Glass: Collins
Garnish: Apple slice on rim
Method: Shake all ingredients with ice and strain into ice-filled glass.

2	shot(s)	The Famous Grouse Scotch whisky
1/2	shot(s)	Passion fruit syrup
4	shot(s)	Pressed apple juice

Origin: Phillip Jeffrey created this drink for me on 12 June 2002 at the GE Club, London, England. I take credit (if any's due) for the name.
Comment: As with all simple drinks, the quality and flavour of the three ingredients used greatly affects the end product – choose wisely and you'll have a deliciously fresh blend of malty fruit.

SPRITZER

Glass: Flute
Garnish: Lemon zest
Method: Pour wine in glass then top up with soda and stir. No ice!

3	shot(s)	Chilled dry white wine
Top up with		Chilled soda water (club soda)

Comment: The ultimate 'girlie' drink. Very refreshing if you can face the ridicule.

SPUTNIK

Glass: Martini
Method: Shake ingredients with ice and strain into glass.

1	shot(s)	Absolut vodka
1	shot(s)	Teichenné Peach schnapps
1 1/2	shot(s)	Freshly squeezed orange juice
1 1/2	shot(s)	Double (heavy) cream
1/2	fresh	Egg white

Comment: Creamy and fruity.

A B C D E F G H I J K L M N O P Q R **S** T U V W X Y Z

SPUTNIK # 2

Glass: Old-fashioned
Garnish: Orange wheel in drink
Method: Shake all ingredients with ice and strain into ice-filled glass.

1	shot(s)	Havana Club light rum
1	shot(s)	Rémy Martin Cognac
2	shot(s)	Freshly squeezed orange juice
1/2	shot(s)	Sugar (gomme) syrup

Origin: A cocktail served in underground clubs all over the former Eastern Block. It was originally made with cheap Cuban rum, Georgian brandy and tinned orange juice.
Comment: Orange, Cognac and rum combine wonderfully.

SQUASHED FROG

Glass: Shot
Method: Layer in glass by carefully pouring ingredients in the following order.

1/3	shot(s)	Grenadine syrup
1/3	shot(s)	Midori melon liqueur
1/3	shot(s)	Warninks Advocaat

Origin: A shot promoted by Midori.
Comment: Very sweet. However, the taste is not as offensive as the name might suggest.

STAIRS MARTINI

Glass: Martini
Garnish: Pear slice on rim
Method: Shake all ingredients with ice and fine strain into chilled glass.

2	shot(s)	Absolut vodka
1	shot(s)	Freshly extracted pear juice
1	shot(s)	Pressed apple juice
1/4	shot(s)	Freshly squeezed lemon juice
1/3	shot(s)	Sugar (gomme) syrup
4	dashes	Fee Brother's Orange bitters

Origin: Created in 2000 by Ian Baldwin at the GE Club, London, England.
Comment: In London's cockney rhyming slang 'apples and pears' means stairs. Hence, this is a very appropriately named and tasty cocktail.

STAR DAISY

Glass: Collins
Method: Shake first five ingredients with ice and strain into ice-filled glass, then top up with Soda water and stir.

2	shot(s)	Plymouth gin
1 1/2	shot(s)	Calvados or applejack brandy
1/2	shot(s)	Freshly squeezed lemon juice
1/4	shot(s)	Sugar (gomme) syrup
1/4	shot(s)	Grenadine syrup
Top up with		Soda water (club soda)

Comment: Hints of apple and spice.

STAR WARS

Glass: Martini
Method: Shake all ingredients with ice and strain into glass.

2	shot(s)	Rémy Martin Cognac
1/4	shot(s)	Pisang Ambon
1/4	shot(s)	Bols Blue curaçao
1/8	shot(s)	Freshly squeezed lemon juice
1	shot(s)	Pressed grapefruit juice
1/3	shot(s)	Sugar (gomme) syrup

Origin: Created in 2000 at Teatro, London, England.
Comment: Looks like swamp water, but tastes OK.

STEALTH SHOT

Glass: Shot
Method: Layer in glass by carefully pouring ingredients in the following order.

1/2	shot(s)	Kahlúa coffee liqueur
1/2	shot(s)	Tuaca liqueur
1/2	shot(s)	Baileys Irish cream liqueur

Origin: Created by Poul Jensen, at St. James', London, England.
Comment: Yep, it's another of the B-52 family, named after Stealth bombers.

STEEL BOTTOM

Glass: Collins
Method: Pour ingredients into glass.

1	shot(s)	Wray & Nephew overproof rum
Top up with		Red Stripe beer

Origin: A very popular drink in Jamaica.
Comment: For those that like their beer turbo charged.

STILETTO

Glass: Collins
Method: Shake all ingredients with ice and strain into an ice-filled glass.

2	shot(s)	Buffalo Trace Bourbon
1	shot(s)	Disaronno Originale amaretto
4	shot(s)	Cranberry juice
1/2	shot(s)	Freshly squeezed lime juice
1/4	shot(s)	Sugar (gomme) syrup

Comment: Long and fruity with a hint of Bourbon and almond.

STINGER UPDATED

Glass: Martini
Method: Shake all ingredients with ice and fine strain into chilled glass.

2	shot(s)	Rémy Martin Cognac
1	shot(s)	White crème de menthe
3/4	shot(s)	Chilled water

Variant: Can be made with other spirits in place of Cognac and may be served over ice or crushed ice in an old-fashioned glass.
Origin: In the classic film 'High Society', Bing Crosby explains to Grace Kelly how the Stinger gained its name: "It's a Stinger. It removes the sting."
Comment: This wonderful concoction must be served ice-cold and adequately diluted.

STONE & GRAVEL

Glass: Old Fashioned
Method: Pour ingredients into glass filled with crushed ice and stir.

1	shot(s)	Wray & Nephew overproof rum
3	shot(s)	Stones ginger wine

Origin: A very popular drink in Jamaica.
Comment: Simple, strong and surprisingly good.

STONED GROUSE

Glass: Old-fashioned
Garnish: Cube crystallised ginger
Method: Pour ingredients into glass filled with crushed ice and stir.

2	shot(s)	The Famous Grouse Scotch
2	shot(s)	Green ginger wine

Variation: Also great served simply on the rocks. (pictured)
Comment: The classic mix of Scotch and ginger cooled over crushed ice.

STONEY POINT MEADOW

Glass: Martini
Garnish: Lemon twist
Method: Shake all ingredients with ice and fine strain into chilled glass.

2¹/₂	shot(s)	Buffalo Trace Bourbon
³/₄	shot(s)	Elderflower cordial
³/₄	shot(s)	Vanilla sugar syrup
¹/₂	fresh	Egg white

Origin: Created in 2002 by Marie-Claire Rose at Blue Bar, Edinburgh, Scotland, and named after Albert Blanton, a nineteenth-century Bourbon distiller who built a house on his estate called Stoney Point Mansion.
Comment: Bourbon tamed and smoothed with vanilla and floral flavours.

STRASBERI SLING

Glass: Sling
Garnish: Mint sprig
Method: Shake all the ingredients with ice and strain into a glass.

1¹/₂	shot(s)	Stoli Razberi
1	shot(s)	Pimms no.1
¹/₂	shot(s)	Sugar (gomme) syrup
1	shot(s)	Freshly squeezed lime juice
4	shot(s)	Pressed apple juice

Origin: Created in 2002 by Alex Kammerling, London, England.
Comment: Raspberry and apple combine beautifully in this refreshing drink with its clean citrus tang.

STRAWBERRY DAIQUIRÍ

Glass: Martini
Garnish: Strawberry on rim
Method: Muddle strawberries in base of shaker. Add other ingredients, shake with ice and fine strain into chilled glass.

3	fresh	Hulled strawberries
2	shot(s)	Havana Club light rum
¹/₂	shot(s)	Freshly squeezed lime juice
¹/₂	shot(s)	Bols Strawberry (fraise) liqueur
¹/₄	shot(s)	Strawberry syrup
¹/₂	shot(s)	Chilled water

Origin: A popular drink in Cuba where it is known as a Fresca Daiquirí.
Comment: Makes strawberries and cream appear very dull.

THE STRAWBERRY ÉCLAIR

Glass: Shot
Method: Shake all ingredients with ice and fine strain into chilled glass.

¹/₂	shot(s)	Frangelico hazelnut liqueur
¹/₂	shot(s)	Bols Strawberry (fraise) liqueur
¹/₄	shot(s)	Freshly squeezed lime juice

Comment: This drink heralds from Australia where it is a popular shot.

STRAWBERRY FROZEN DAIQUIRÍ

Glass: Martini
Garnish: Split strawberry
Method: Blend ingredients with crushed ice and serve.

2	shot(s)	Havana Club light rum
1	shot(s)	Freshly squeezed lime juice
¹/₄	shot(s)	Strawberry syrup
6	Fresh	Strawberries

Comment: A delicious twist on a classic – Strawberry Mivvi for grown-ups.

STRAWBERRY FROZEN MARGARITA

Glass: Margarita
Garnish: Sugar rim & split strawberry.
Method: Blend ingredients with crushed ice and serve.

2	shot(s)	Freshly squeezed lime juice
1	shot(s)	Strawberry syrup
¹/₄	shot(s)	Freshly squeezed lemon juice
1	shot(s)	Sauza Hornitos Tequila
1	shot(s)	Cointreau / triple sec
1	shot(s)	Bols Strawberry (fraise) liqueur
12	Fresh	Strawberries

Comment: Better straight-up.

STRAWBERRY MINT

Glass: Hurricane
Garnish: Split strawberry & mint leaf.
Method: Blend ingredients with crushed ice and serve.

2	shot(s)	White crème de menthe
1	shot(s)	Bols Strawberry (fraise) liqueur
12	fresh	Strawberries
2	scoops	Vanilla ice cream

Comment: A creamy, strawberry cocktail with essence of mouthwash.

STRAWBERRY 'N' BALSAMIC'TINI ●●●●○

Glass: Martini
Garnish: Strawberry on rim
Method: Muddle strawberries in shaker base. Add other ingredients, shake with ice and fine strain into chilled glass.

4	fresh	Hulled strawberries
2	shot(s)	Absolut vodka
1/4	shot(s)	Balsamic vinegar
3/4	shot(s)	Bols Strawberry (fraise) liqueur

Origin: My version of a drink that became popular in London in 2002 and I believe originated in Che Bar.
Comment: The balsamic adds interest and depth to what would otherwise be an uninteresting drink.

STRAWBERRY PIÑA COLADA

Glass: Hurricane
Garnish: Split strawberry
Method: Blend ingredients with crushed ice and serve.

2	shot(s)	Havana Club light rum
1	shot(s)	Cream of coconut
1/2	shot(s)	Double (heavy) cream
1/2	shot(s)	Milk
12	Fresh	Strawberries
1	shot(s)	Strawberry syrup

Comment: Variations on the Piña Colada.

STRAWBERRY SHORTCAKE

Glass: Hurricane
Garnish: Split strawberry
Method: Blend first five ingredients with ice and pour into glass, then float cream.

1	shot(s)	Disaronno Originale amaretto
1	shot(s)	Bols White crème de cacao
12	Fresh	Strawberries
1	shot(s)	Strawberry syrup
2	scoops	Vanilla ice cream
Float		Lightly whipped cream

Comment: Excruciatingly sweet – but it does taste of strawberry shortcake.

STRUDEL MARTINI ●●●●◐

Glass: Martini
Garnish: Dust with cinnamon powder
Method: Shake ingredients with ice and strain into glass.

1 1/2	shot(s)	Absolut vodka
1/2	shot(s)	Pedro Ximénez Sherry
3/4	shot(s)	Pressed apple juice
1/2	shot(s)	Double (heavy) cream
1/2	shot(s)	Milk

Origin: Created in 2002 by Jason Borthwick, Tiles, Edinburgh, Scotland.
Comment: Still think Sherry is just for Granny?

STUPID CUPID

Glass: Martini
Method: Shake ingredients with ice and strain into glass.

2	shot(s)	Absolut Citron vodka
1/2	shot(s)	Plymouth sloe gin
1	shot(s)	Freshly squeezed lime juice
1/2	shot(s)	Sugar (gomme) syrup

Comment: Citrussy with subtle sloe gin.

SUITABLY FRANK

Glass: Shot
Method: Layer in glass by carefully pouring ingredients in the following order.

1/2	shot(s)	Bols Cherry brandy liqueur
1/2	shot(s)	Cuarenta Y Tres Liqueur (licor 43)
1/2	shot(s)	Absolut vodka

Comment: Frankly – it's good.

SUMMER BREEZE NEW ●●●●○

Glass: Collins
Garnish: Apple slice
Method: Shake all ingredients with ice and strain into ice-filled glass.

2	shot(s)	Absolut vodka
2	shot(s)	Cranberry juice
2	shot(s)	Pressed apple juice
1/2	shot(s)	Elderflower cordial
1/8	shot(s)	Freshly squeezed lime juice

Origin: Created in 2003 by Wayne Collins for Maxxium UK.
Comment: Cranberry, apple and elderflower fortified with vodka.

SUMMER MARTINI **NEW**

●●●●◐○

Glass: Martini
Garnish: Berries on a cocktail stick
Method: Muddle berries in base of shaker. Add other ingredients; shake with ice and fine strain into chilled glass.

3	fresh	Blackberries
3	fresh	Raspberries
3	fresh	Strawberries
1/2	shot(s)	Bols Blackberry (crème mûre) liqueur
1/2	shot	Bols Raspberry (framboise) liqueur
1/2	shot	Bols Strawberry (fraise) liqueur
2	shot(s)	Plymouth gin
3/4	shot(s)	Cinzano Extra Dry vermouth
2	dashes	Fee Brothers Orange bitters

Origin: Created in 2003 by Wayne Collins for Maxxium UK.
Comment: A drink which combines a trio of summer berries with the classic aromatic Martini.

SUMMER ROSE MARTINI **NEW**

●●●●○

Glass: Martini
Garnish: Red rose petal
Method: Stir first four ingredients with ice and strain into chilled glass. Pour grenadine into the centre of the drink. This should sink and settle to form a red layer in the base of the glass.

1 1/2	shot(s)	Absolut vodka
3/4	shot(s)	Bols White crème de cacao
1/2	shot(s)	Lychee liqueur
1/2	shot(s)	Grenadine syrup

Origin: Created in 2003 by Davide Lovison at Isola Bar, London, England.
Comment: This red and white layered drink could have been named War of the Roses. Unless you've a sweet tooth don't mix the factions – sip from the chocolate and lychee top and stop when you hit red.

SUMMER TIME MARTINI

Glass: Martini
Garnish: Kumquat
Method: Shake ingredients with ice and strain into glass.

1	shot(s)	Grand Marnier
1	shot(s)	Plymouth gin
2 1/2	shot(s)	Freshly squeezed orange juice
1/4	shot(s)	Grenadine syrup

Comment: Smooth as a summer's day.

SUNDOWNER MARTINI

●●●●◐○

Glass: Martini
Garnish: Flamed orange twist
Method: Shake all ingredients with ice and strain into chilled glass:

2	shot(s)	Rémy Martin Cognac
1/2	shot(s)	Grand Marnier
1 1/2	shot(s)	Freshly squeezed orange juice
1/4	shot(s)	Freshly squeezed lemon juice
1/4	shot(s)	Sugar (gomme) syrup

Origin: This cocktail is popular in South Africa where it is made with locally produced brandy and a local orange liqueur called Van der Hum.
Comment: Lacks complexity. In your face orange, but then again if you like orange...

SUNDOWNER # 2

●●●●●○

Glass: Old-fashioned
Garnish: Mint sprig
Method: Shake all ingredients with ice and strain into glass filled with crushed ice.

1 1/2	shot(s)	Southern Comfort
1/4	shot(s)	Cointreau / triple sec
1/2	shot(s)	Grand Marnier
2	shot(s)	Sauvignon Blanc wine
1/4	shot(s)	Sugar (gomme) syrup

Origin: Created in 2002 by Gary Regis at Bed Bar, London, England.
Comment: Subtle meld of summer and citrus flavours.

SUN KISSED VIRGIN

Glass: Sling
Garnish: Physalis
Method: Shake ingredients with ice and strain into ice-filled glass.

2	shot(s)	Freshly squeezed orange juice
2	shot(s)	Pressed pineapple juice
1	shot(s)	Freshly squeezed lime juice
3/4	shot(s)	Sugar (gomme) syrup
1/2	shot(s)	Almond (orgeat) syrup

Comment: A well-rounded soft drink.

SUNBURN

Glass: Martini
Garnish: Physalis
Method: Shake ingredients with ice and strain into glass.

1	shot(s)	Sauza Hornitos Tequila
1	shot(s)	Cointreau / triple sec
2 1/2	shot(s)	Cranberry juice

Comment: Pretty flat but drinkable.

SUNNY BREEZE

●●●●◐○

Glass: Collins
Garnish: Half orange wheel in drink
Method: Shake all ingredients with ice and strain into glass filled with crushed ice.

1 1/2	shot(s)	Pérnod anise
1/2	shot(s)	Cointreau / triple sec
1/2	shot(s)	Grand Marnier
3	shot(s)	Squeezed pink grapefruit juice

Origin: Created by yours truly in 2003 for Pernod.
Comment: A suitably named refreshing long drink with an adult dry edge and kick.

SUNSET STRIP

Glass: Collins
Method: Pour ingredients into ice-filled glass and stir.

1/2	shot(s)	Absolut vodka
1/2	shot(s)	Havana Club light rum
1/2	shot(s)	Plymouth gin
1/2	shot(s)	Sauza Hornitos Tequila
1/4	shot(s)	Grenadine syrup
Top up with		Pressed pineapple juice

Comment: Pineapple and spirits. Not stunning.

SUNSTROKE

Glass: Martini
Garnish: Physalis
Method: Shake ingredients with ice and strain into glass.

1	shot(s)	Absolut vodka
1	shot(s)	Cointreau / triple sec
2³/₄	shot(s)	Pressed grapefruit juice

Comment: OK, but there's more interesting things to do with grapefruit.

SUPERMINTY-CHOCOLATINI

●●●●◑○

Glass: Martini
Garnish: Chocolate powder rim
Method: Shake all ingredients with ice and fine strain into chilled glass.

2	shot(s)	Absolut vodka
1	shot(s)	Bols White crème de cacao
1	shot(s)	White crème de menthe

Comment: Obviously but nicely flavoured.

SWAMP WATER UPDATED

●●●●○

Glass: Collins
Garnish: Lime wedge & mint leaf
Method: Shake all ingredients with ice and strain into ice-filled glass.

1¹/₂	shot(s)	Green Chartreuse
4¹/₂	shot(s)	Pressed pineapple juice
¹/₂	shot(s)	Freshly squeezed lime juice

Comment: Long and refreshing - the herbal taste of Chartreuse combined with the fruitiness of pineapple.

SWEDISH BLUE MARTINI

Glass: Martini
Garnish: Orange peel twist
Method: Shake ingredients with ice and strain into glass.

1¹/₂	shot(s)	Absolut vodka
¹/₂	shot(s)	Bols Blue curaçao
¹/₂	shot(s)	Teichenné Peach schnapps liqueur
¹/₄	shot(s)	Freshly squeezed lime juice
¹/₄	shot(s)	Sugar (gomme) syrup
2	dashes	Fee Brothers Orange bitters

Origin: Timothy Schofield at Teatro, London, England.
Comment: A blue concoction with a sweet style.

SWEET LOUISE

Glass: Martini
Garnish: Blackberry
Method: Shake ingredients with ice and strain into glass.

1	shot(s)	Chambord black raspberry liqueur
1	shot(s)	Absolut Kurant vodka
1	shot(s)	Disaronno Originale amaretto
1	shot(s)	Passion fruit juice
¹/₄	shot(s)	Grenadine syrup
³/₄	shot(s)	Freshly squeezed lime juice.

Origin: Monte's Club, London.
Comment: Lots of contrasting flavours work very well together.

SWEET PASSION

Glass: Collins
Method: Shake ingredients with ice and strain into ice-filled glass.

1	shot(s)	Passoã passion fruit liqueur
1	shot(s)	Cointreau / triple sec
4	shot(s)	Pressed apple juice
¹/₂	shot(s)	Disaronno Originale amaretto
¹/₄	shot(s)	Maraschino liqueur

Comment: Sweet but very interesting and complex.

SWEET SCIENCE

Glass: Martini
Garnish: Orange slice
Method: Shake ingredients with ice and strain into glass.

1¹/₂	shot(s)	The Famous Grouse Scotch whisky
²/₃	shot(s)	Drambuie liqueur
1¹/₂	shot(s)	Freshly squeezed orange juice

Origin: Created by Charles Schumann of Munich, Germany.
Comment: A strong tasting whisky drink.

SWEET TART

Glass: Sling
Garnish: Sugar rim & redcurrants
Method: Shake ingredients with ice and strain into ice-filled glass. Top up with lemonade.

2	shot(s)	Absolut vodka
1¹/₂	shot(s)	Chambord black raspberry liqueur
1¹/₄	shot(s)	Disaronno Originale amaretto
1¹/₂	shot(s)	Freshly squeezed lime juice
³/₄	shot(s)	Sugar (gomme) syrup
Top up with		Lemonade

Comment: As the name suggests, a long fruity combination of sweet and sour.

NEW	A DRINK NEW TO SAUCE GUIDES.
UPDATED	ENTRY CHANGED SINCE LAST VOLUME.
shot(s)	25ML MEASURE (UK) OR 1OZ (US). HOWEVER, IT DOESN'T REALLY MATTER WHAT MEASURE YOU USE AS A SHOT, SO LONG AS YOU USE THE SAME MEASURE OR FRACTIONS OF THAT MEASURE TO MEASURE ALL THE INGREDIENTS. THIS WILL ENSURE THE PROPORTIONS OF ONE INGREDIENT TO ANOTHER WILL BE AS THE RECIPE INTENDED.

THOSE DRINKS I'VE SAMPLED RECENTLY ARE GRADED AS FOLLOWS:

● DISGUSTING ●◑ PRETTY AWFUL ●● BEST AVOIDED
●●◑ DISAPPOINTING ●●● ACCEPTABLE ●●●◑ GOOD
●●●● RECOMMENDED ●●●●◑ HIGHLY RECOMMENDED
●●●●● OUTSTANDING / EXCEPTIONAL

TNT

Glass: Martini
Garnish: Orange peel knot
Method: Stir ingredients with ice and strain into glass.

3	shot(s)	Rémy Martin Cognac
1½	shot(s)	Orange curaçao
4	dashes	Angostura aromatic bitters
½	spoon	La Fée absinthe

Comment: Strong and smooth.

TAINTED CHERRY

Glass: Martini
Garnish: Split cherry on rim
Method: Shake ingredients with ice and strain into glass.

1	shot(s)	Absolut vodka
1	shot(s)	Bols Cherry brandy liqueur
3	shot(s)	Freshly squeezed orange juice

Comment: Orange and cherry give an almost amaretto flavour.

TANGERINE

Glass: Collins
Method: Shake ingredients with ice and strain into ice-filled glass.

1	shot(s)	Absolut vodka
1	shot(s)	Disaronno Originale amaretto
1	shot(s)	Cointreau / triple sec
3	shot(s)	Freshly squeezed orange juice
½	shot(s)	Grenadine syrup

Comment: Oddly, this tastes of over-ripe tangerines.

TANGO MARTINI # 1

Glass: Martini
Method: Shake ingredients with ice and strain into glass.

1½	shot(s)	Plymouth gin
1	shot(s)	Cinzano Rosso vermouth
1	shot(s)	Cinzano Extra Dry vermouth
½	shot(s)	Orange curaçao
½	shot(s)	Freshly squeezed orange juice

Comment: A dry, bitter orange and gin cocktail.

NEW	A DRINK NEW TO SAUCE GUIDES.
UPDATED	ENTRY CHANGED SINCE LAST VOLUME.
shot(s)	25ML MEASURE (UK) OR 1OZ (US). HOWEVER, IT DOESN'T REALLY MATTER WHAT MEASURE YOU USE AS A SHOT, SO LONG AS YOU USE THE SAME MEASURE OR FRACTIONS OF THAT MEASURE TO MEASURE ALL THE INGREDIENTS. THIS WILL ENSURE THE PROPORTIONS OF ONE INGREDIENT TO ANOTHER WILL BE AS THE RECIPE INTENDED.

TANGO MARTINI # 2   NEW

●●●●●◐

Glass: Martini
Garnish: Orange twist
Method: Shake all ingredients with ice and fine strain into chilled glass.

1¾	shot(s)	Plymouth gin
¾	shot(s)	Passoã passion fruit liqueur
2	shot(s)	Pressed grapefruit juice
¼	shot(s)	Sugar (gomme) syrup

Origin: Adapted from a drink discovered in 2003 at the Bellagio, Las Vegas, USA.
Comment: Floral, delicate, sophisticated and balanced.

TANTRIS SIDECAR NEW

●●●●○

Glass: Martini
Garnish: Sugar rim
Method: Shake all ingredients with ice and fine strain into chilled glass.

1½	shot(s)	Calvados (or applejack brandy)
¼	shot(s)	Cointreau / triple sec
½	shot(s)	Green Chartreuse
¼	shot(s)	Freshly squeezed lemon juice
2	shot(s)	Pressed pineapple juice

Origin: Adapted from a drink created by Audrey Saunders, Bemelmans Bar at The Carlyle Hotel, New York City.
Comment: A Sidecar with extra interest courtesy of Chartreuse, pineapple and Calvados.

TARRABERRY'TINI NEW

●●●●○

Glass: Martini
Garnish: Tarragon sprig
Method: Muddle tarragon in base of shaker. Add other ingredients; shake with ice and fine strain into chilled glass.

1	fistful	Fresh tarragon
1½	shot(s)	Finlandia Cranberry vodka
¼	shot(s)	Pernod anise
2	shot(s)	Cranberry juice
¼	shot(s)	Freshly squeezed lemon juice

Origin: I created this drink in 2003 for Finlandia.
Comment: Cranberry with subtle hints of tarragon and lemon.

TARTE AUX POMMES CARRIBE

●●●●●◐

Glass: Collins
Garnish: Apple chevron
Method: Shake all ingredients with ice and strain into ice-filled glass.

1	shot(s)	Calvados (or applejack)
½	shot(s)	Sisca crème de cassis
¼	shot(s)	Cinnamon schnapps
4	shot(s)	Cranberry juice
4	dash(es)	Angostura aromatic bitters

Origin: Created in 2001 by Jamie Stephenson at The Lock, Manchester, England.
Comment: A cracking drink that's rich in flavour and well balanced.

TARTE TATIN MARTINI NEW

Glass: Martini
Garnish: Cinnamon dust
Method: Shake first three ingredients with ice and strain into chilled glass. Shake cream with ice and carefully pour so as to layer over drink.

2	shot(s)	Stoli Vanil
3/4	shot(s)	Apple schnapps
3/4	shot(s)	Cartron caramel liqueur
2 1/2	shot(s)	Double (heavy) cream

Origin: Created in 2003 by yours truly. Tatin is the name given to a tart of caramelised apples cooked under a pastry lid. The recipe was created at the beginning of the 20th century by the Tatin sisters at their hotel in Lamotte-Beuvron, France.
Comment: A creamy top hides a vanilla, apple and caramel combo.

TARTINI

Glass: Martini
Garnish: Raspberry
Method: Muddle raspberries in base of shaker. Add other ingredients, shake with ice and strain into ice-filled glass.

12	fresh	Raspberries
2	shot(s)	Stoli Razberi
1/2	shot(s)	Chambord black raspberry liqueur
1 1/2	shot(s)	Cranberry juice

Origin: Adapted from a cocktail I found at Soho Grand, New York City.
Comment: Rich raspberry flavour, well balanced with bite.

TEDDY BEAR'TINI NEW

Glass: Martini
Garnish: Pear slice
Method: Shake all ingredients with ice and fine strain into chilled glass.

1 1/2	shot(s)	Xanté pear & cognac liqueur
3/4	shot(s)	Apple schnapps
1 1/2	shot(s)	Pressed apple juice
1	pinch	Ground cinnamon

Origin: This drink was created in 2002 at The Borough, Edinburgh, Scotland. Originally named after a well-known cockney duo but renamed after the cockney rhyming slang for pear.
Comment: Beautifully balanced apple and pear with a hint of cinnamon spice.

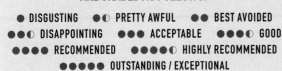

THOSE DRINKS I'VE SAMPLED RECENTLY ARE GRADED AS FOLLOWS:

● DISGUSTING ●●○ PRETTY AWFUL ●● BEST AVOIDED
●●●○ DISAPPOINTING ●●● ACCEPTABLE ●●●●○ GOOD
●●●● RECOMMENDED ●●●●○ HIGHLY RECOMMENDED
●●●●● OUTSTANDING / EXCEPTIONAL

TENNESSEE BERRY MULE NEW

Glass: Collins
Garnish: Three raspberries
Method: Muddle raspberries in base of shaker. Add whiskey, amaretto and cranberry juice, shake with ice and strain into ice-filled glass. Top up with ginger beer. Stir and serve with straws.

8	fresh	Raspberries
1 1/2	shot(s)	Jack Daniel's Tennessee whiskey
1	shot(s)	Disaronno Originale amaretto
1 1/2	shot(s)	Cranberry juice
1/2	shot(s)	Freshly squeezed lime juice
Top up with		Ginger beer

Origin: Adapted in 2003 from a recipe Alex Kammerling created for TGI Friday's UK. I named this drink partly for the ingredients and partly as a reference to Jack Daniel's proprietor (and nephew), Lemuel Motlow, who took up mule trading during Prohibition.
Comment: A berry rich cocktail laced with whiskey, flavoured with amaretto and topped with ginger beer.

TENNESSEE ICED TEA

Glass: Sling
Garnish: Lemon wedge on rim
Method: Shake first six ingredients with ice and strain into ice-filled glass. Top up with cola.

1	shot(s)	Jack Daniel's Tennessee whiskey
1/2	shot(s)	Havana Club light rum
1/2	shot(s)	Absolut vodka
1/2	shot(s)	Cointreau / triple sec
3/4	shot(s)	Freshly squeezed lemon juice
1/3	shot(s)	Sugar (gomme) syrup
Top up with		Cola

Comment: JD and coke with extra love interest courtesy of several other spirits and lemon juice.

TENNESSEE RUSH

Glass: Collins
Method: Shake ingredients with ice and strain into ice-filled glass.

2	shot(s)	Jack Daniel's Tennessee whiskey
1	shot(s)	Mandarine Napoléon
4	shot(s)	Cranberry juice
1	shot(s)	Freshly squeezed lime juice
1/4	shot(s)	Sugar (gomme) syrup

Comment: This ruby red cocktail is long, refreshing and not too sweet.

TEQUILA FIZZ

Glass: Sling
Garnish: Orange zest
Method: Shake first four ingredients with ice and strain into ice-filled glass. Top up with lemonade.

2	shot(s)	Sauza Hornitos Tequila
1 1/2	shot(s)	Freshly squeezed orange juice
1	shot(s)	Freshly squeezed lime juice
1/2	shot(s)	Sugar (gomme) syrup
Top up with		Lemonade / 7-Up

Comment: Refreshing with lingering lime.

TEQUILA SOUR

Glass: Collins
Garnish: Split lime wedge
Method: Shake first four ingredients with ice and strain into ice-filled glass, then top up with soda water.

2	shot(s)	Sauza Hornitos Tequila
1	shot(s)	Freshly squeezed orange juice
1	shot(s)	Freshly squeezed lime juice
1/2	shot(s)	Sugar (gomme) syrup
Top up with		Soda water (club soda)

Comment: Standard sour fizzed and fruited with orange juice and soda.

TEQUILA SUNRISE

Glass: Collins
Garnish: Orange wheel & cherry
Method: Pour Tequila and orange juice into a glass filled with ice and stir. Then pour grenadine in a circle around top of drink and allow to settle.

2	shot(s)	Sauza Hornitos Tequila
5	shot(s)	Freshly squeezed orange juice
1/2	shot(s)	Grenadine syrup

Comment: Everyone's heard of this drink, but those who have tried it will wonder why it's so famous.

TEQUILA SUNSET

Glass: Sling
Garnish: Sugar rim
Method: Shake ingredients with ice and strain into ice-filled glass.

2	shot(s)	Sauza Hornitos Tequila
2	shot(s)	Freshly squeezed lemon juice
1/2	shot(s)	Runny honey
1/2	shot(s)	Sugar (gomme) syrup

Comment: A good sweet and sour with subtle honey hints.

TEQUILA'TINI

Glass: Martini
Garnish: Lime twist
Method: Shake all ingredients with ice and fine strain into chilled glass.

2 1/2	shot(s)	Sauza Hornitos Tequila
1	shot(s)	Cinzano Extra Dry vermouth
3	dashes	Angostura aromatic bitters
1/2	shot(s)	Sugar (gomme) syrup

Comment: If you like Tequila and strong drinks – this is for you.

TESTAROSSA

Glass: Collins
Garnish: Orange wheel
Method: Pour ingredients into ice-filled glass and stir.

1 1/2	shot(s)	Campari
1 1/2	shot(s)	Absolut vodka
Top up with		Soda water (club soda)

Comment: A stronger Campari and soda.

TEQUILA SLAMMER

Glass: Large shot
Method: 1/ Pour Tequila into shot glass.
2/ Slowly top up with Champagne. 3/ Instruct drinker to hold and cover the top of the glass with the palm of their hand so as to grip glass and seal the contents inside. 4/ Instruct drinker to briskly pick glass up and slam down onto surface so as to make drink fizz then quickly gulp down drink in one while still fizzing.

1	shot (s)	Sauza Hornitos Tequila
1	shot (s)	Champagne

Variants: With cream soda or ginger ale. The original, with ginger ale, is a Hell's Angel drink – it needs no ice and can be carried in a bike bag.

Comment: Silly and potentially messy – but fun! The simplest slammer is a lick of salt, a shot of Tequila and then a bite of lemon (or lime). A Bermuda Slammer involves straight Tequila, a slice of lemon and salt, and a partner: one has to lick the salt off the other one's neck and bite the lemon (held between their partner's teeth) before downing a shot of Tequila.

TETANKA

●●●●●◐

Glass: Old Fashioned
Method: Shake all ingredients with ice and strain into ice-filled glass.

2	shot(s)	Zubrówka (bison grass) vodka
2¹/₂	shot(s)	Pressed apple juice

Origin: This drink hails from Poland and the name comes from the film 'Dances with Wolves'. Tetanka is a Native American word for buffalo and here refers to the bison grass flavoured vodka this cocktail is based on.
Comment: The taste of this excellent drink (which is equally good served straight-up) is a little reminiscent of Earl Grey tea.

TEXAS ICED TEA

●●●●●◐

Glass: Sling
Garnish: Lemon wedge on rim
Method: Shake all but cola with ice and strain into ice-filled glass. Top up with cola.

1	shot(s)	Sauza Hornitos Tequila
¹/₂	shot(s)	Havana Club light rum
¹/₂	shot(s)	Absolut vodka
¹/₂	shot(s)	Cointreau / triple sec
³/₄	shot(s)	Freshly squeezed lemon juice
¹/₃	shot(s)	Sugar (gomme) syrup
Top up with		Cola

Comment: Our favourite of the Iced Tea family of drinks. Tequila shines through.

THE THUNDERER

Glass: Martini
Method: Stir ingredients with ice and strain into glass.

2¹/₂	shot(s)	Absolut vodka
¹/₈	shot(s)	Parfait Amour liqueur
¹/₄	shot(s)	Sisca crème de cassis

Origin: The official drink of London's The Times newspaper, created by Dick Bradsell in 1981 for a competition. The Thunderer is the old nickname of The Times.
Comment: One for the Parfait Amour fan.

THOMAS BLOOD MARTINI

●●●●●○

Glass: Martini
Garnish: Apple wedge on rim
Method: Stir honey with vodka in base of shaker so as to dissolve. Add other ingredients, shake with ice and fine strain into chilled glass.

1	shot(s)	Absolut vodka
2	spoons	Runny honey
1	shot(s)	Krupnik honey liqueur
1	shot(s)	Apple schnapps liqueur
1	shot(s)	Freshly squeezed lemon juice

Comment: An appealing honey led mélange of sweet and sour.

THREE MILER

●●●●○

Glass: Martini
Garnish: Lemon twist
Method: Shake all ingredients with ice and fine strain into chilled glass.

1¹/₂	shot(s)	Rémy Martin Cognac
1¹/₂	shot(s)	Havana Club light rum
¹/₂	shot(s)	Freshly squeezed lemon juice
¹/₂	shot(s)	Grenadine syrup

Origin: Adapted from the Three Miller Cocktail in The Savoy Cocktail Book. Most other cocktail books spell it with one 'l' as I have here.
Comment: A seriously strong drink, both in terms of flavour and alcohol.

THREESOME NEW

●●●●○

Glass: Martini
Garnish: Pineapple wedge on rim
Method: Shake all ingredients with ice and fine strain into chilled glass.

1¹/₂	shot(s)	Calvados or Applejack brandy
1	shot(s)	Cointreau / triple sec
¹/₂	shot(s)	Pernod anise
1¹/₂	shot(s)	Pressed pineapple juice

Origin: Adapted from a drink discovered in 2002 at Circus Bar, London, England.
Comment: Why stop at three when you can have a foursome? An interesting meld of apple, orange, anise and pineapple.

THRILLER MARTINI

●●●●○

Glass: Martini
Garnish: Orange zest
Method: Shake all ingredients with ice and fine strain into chilled glass.

2¹/₂	shot(s)	The Famous Grouse Scotch whisky
³/₄	shot(s)	Ginger wine
³/₄	shot(s)	Freshly squeezed orange juice
¹/₈	shot(s)	Sugar (gomme) syrup

Comment: Spiced Scotch with a hint of orange.

THRILLER

Glass: Snifter
Method: Pour ingredients into glass and swirl to mix. Flambé, let burn for twenty seconds and then cover top of glass to extinguish flame.

¹/₂	shot(s)	Bols Strawberry (fraise) liqueur
¹/₂	shot(s)	Drambuie
¹/₂	shot(s)	Wray & Nephew overproof rum

Comment: Careful how you go!

THRILLER FROM VANILLA NEW

Glass: Martini
Garnish: Half vanilla pod
Method: Muddle vanilla in base of shaker. Add other ingredients; shake with ice and fine strain into chilled glass.

1/4	pod	Vanilla
3/4	shot(s)	Stoli Vanil
3/4	shot(s)	Plymouth gin
1/2	shot(s)	Cointreau / triple sec
2	shot(s)	Freshly squeezed orange juice

Origin: Discovered in 2003 at Oporto, Leeds, England.
Comment: Orange and creamy vanilla fortified with a hint of gin.

TI PUNCH

Glass: Rocks
Method: Place cut lime in glass and muddle. Add ice and other ingredients. Serve with teaspoon.

1	Whole	Lime cut into 8 wedges
3	shot(s)	Rhum Agricole
1	shot(s)	Sugar (gomme) syrup

Variant: Add a splash of chilled water
Origin: A popular drink in the French Islands of Martinique, Guadeloupe, Réunion and Maurice where it's often drunk straight down followed by a large glass of chilled water (called a 'Cras' in Martinique). It is in these islands, particularly Martinique that Rhum Agricole (a style of rum distilled only from sugar cane juice) is made (usually bottled at 50% alc/vol.).
Comment: This drink is usually served with a spoon and it's common for the bartender not to muddle the lime, but to leave the drinker to do this with the spoon provided.

TILT

Glass: Sling
Garnish: Pineapple leaf garnish
Method: Shake all ingredients with ice and strain into glass filled with crushed ice.

1 1/2	shot(s)	Pineapple vodka
1/2	shot(s)	Malibu Coconut rum liqueur
1 1/2	shot(s)	Pressed pineapple juice
1	shot(s)	Pink grapefruit juice
1/4	shot(s)	Vanilla sugar syrup
Top up with		Bitter lemon

Comment: Totally tropical taste.

TICK-TACK MARTINI

Glass: Martini
Garnish: Three Tic-Tac sweets
Method: Stir ingredients with ice and strain.

2	shot(s)	Absolut vodka
2/3	shot(s)	Opal Bianca white sambuca
1/3	shot(s)	White crème de menthe

Origin: Rodolphe Sorel in 1991 at Match EC1.
Comment: Strangely enough, tastes like a Tic-Tac mint.

TIGER'S MILK

Glass: Rocks
Garnish: Dust with cinnamon
Method: Shake ingredients with ice and strain into glass.

2	shot(s)	Calvados or apple jack brandy
2	shot(s)	Double (heavy) cream
2	shot(s)	Milk
1/4	shot(s)	Honey syrup

Comment: Creamy apple with a hint of honey and cinnamon.

TIRAMISU MARTINI

Glass: Martini
Garnish: Chocolate powder dust
Method: Shake all ingredients with ice and strain into glass.

1	shot(s)	Rémy Martin Cognac
1/2	shot(s)	Kahlúa coffee liqueur
1/2	shot(s)	Bols Brown crème de cacao
1/2	shot(s)	Double (heavy) cream
1/2	shot(s)	Milk
1	fresh	Egg yolk
1	spoon	Mascarpone

Origin: Created by Adam Ennis in 2001 at Isola, London, England.
Comment: The chef meets the bartender in this rich dessert cocktail.

TITIANI

Glass: Flute
Garnish: 2 black grapes
Method: Pour first two ingredients into glass and top up with Champagne, then stir.

2	shot(s)	Freshly squeezed juice of black concord grapes
1/8	shot(s)	Grenadine syrup
Top up with		Piper-Heidsieck Brut Champagne

Comment: Grapes complement the bubbly well.

TOAST & ORANGE MARTINI

Glass: Small Martini
Garnish: Flamed orange twist
Method: Shake all ingredients with ice and fine strain into chilled glass.

2	shot(s)	Buffalo Trace Bourbon
1	spoon	Orange marmalade
4	dashes	Péychaud's Bitters
1/8	shot(s)	Sugar (gomme) syrup

Comment: Bourbon with its edge rounded and enhanced by bitter orange and Péychaud's bitters.

TOASTED ALMOND

Glass: Martini
Garnish: Sprinkle dusting of chocolate powder on surface of drink.
Method: Shake ingredients with ice and strain into glass.

1	shot(s)	Disaronno Originale amaretto
1	shot(s)	Kahlúa coffee liqueur
1 1/2	shot(s)	Double (heavy) cream
1 1/2	shot(s)	Milk

Comment: Toasted!

TODDY MARTINI

Glass: Martini
Garnish: Lemon zest
Method: Shake all ingredients with ice and strain into glass.

1½	shot(s)	The Famous Grouse Scotch whisky
1	shot(s)	Honey liqueur
¾	shot(s)	Freshly squeezed lemon juice
½	shot(s)	Sugar (gomme) syrup

Origin: Created in 2001 by Jamie Terrell at LAB, London, England.
Comment: Ice cold but warming.

TOFFEE APPLE

●●●●●○

Glass: Sling
Garnish: Apple wedge on rim
Method: Shake all ingredients with ice and strain into ice-filled glass.

1	shot(s)	Calvados or Applejack brandy
2	shot(s)	Cartron Caramel liqueur
1	shot(s)	Apple schnapps
1	shot(s)	Freshly pressed apple juice
¼	shot(s)	Freshly squeezed lime juice

Origin: Created in 2002 by Nick Strangeway, London, England.
Comment: The taste is just as the name suggests – great!

TOFFEE APPLE MARTINI NEW

●●●●○

Glass: Martini
Garnish: Apple and fudge on rim
Method: Shake all ingredients with ice and fine strain into chilled glass.

1	shot(s)	Calvados or applejack brandy
1	shot(s)	Apple vodka
1½	shot(s)	Pressed apple juice
1	shot(s)	Clear toffee liqueur

Variant: If you're in the US try: 1 shot Laird's applejack, 1 shot Stoli Vanil, 1¼ shots clear toffee liqueur and 1 shot Pucker's Sour Apple liqueur.
Origin: Created in 2003 by yours truly.
Comment: This amber, liquid toffee apple is almost creamy on the palate.

TOKYO BLOODY MARY

Glass: Collins
Garnish: Stick of celery
Method: Shake ingredients with ice and strain into ice-filled glass.

2	shot(s)	Sake
4	shot(s)	Tomato juice
½	shot(s)	Freshly squeezed lemon juice
8	drops	Tabasco sauce
4	drops	Worcestershire sauce
4	drops	Medium Sherry
1	pinch	Celery salt
1	pinch	Black pepper

Comment: Sake works almost better than vodka! Add sugar to taste.

TOKYO ICED TEA

Glass: Sling
Garnish: Split lemon wheel
Method: Shake first seven ingredients with ice and strain into ice-filled glass, then top up with lemonade and stir.

½	shot(s)	Havana Club light rum
½	shot(s)	Plymouth gin
½	shot(s)	Absolut vodka
½	shot(s)	Sauza Hornitos Tequila
½	shot(s)	Cointreau / triple sec
1	shot(s)	Freshly squeezed lime juice
½	shot(s)	Midori melon liqueur
Top up with		Lemonade

Comment: With all these ingredients you'll be surprised how the half shot of melon liqueur shows through.

●●●●◑○

TOLLEYTOWN PUNCH

Glass: Collins
Garnish: Cranberries, orange and lemon slices
Method: Shake first four ingredients with ice and strain into ice-filled glass. Top up with ginger ale.

2	shot(s)	Jack Daniel's Tennessee whiskey
3	shot(s)	Cranberry juice
½	shot(s)	Pressed pineapple juice
½	shot(s)	Freshly squeezed orange juice
Top up with		Ginger ale

Origin: A drink promoted by Jack Daniel's. Tolleytown lies just down the road from Lynchburg.
Comment: A fruity long drink with a dry edge that also works well made in bulk and served from a punch bowl.

TOM COLLINS

Glass: Collins
Garnish: Lemon slice
Method: Shake first three ingredients with ice and strain into ice-filled glass, then top up with soda.

2	shot(s)	Plymouth gin
1	shot(s)	Freshly squeezed lemon juice
½	shot(s)	Sugar (gomme) syrup
Top up with		Soda water (club soda)

Variant: This cocktail is traditionally made using Old Tom gin which is now very difficult to source.
Comment: Clean, refreshing, ancient classic. As good in microfibres as it was in crinolines.

TOMAHAWK

Glass: Collins
Method: Shake ingredients with ice and strain into ice-filled glass.

1	shot(s)	Sauza Hornitos Tequila
1	shot(s)	Cointreau / triple sec
2	shot(s)	Cranberry juice
2	shot(s)	Pressed pineapple juice

Comment: Simple recipe, effective drink.

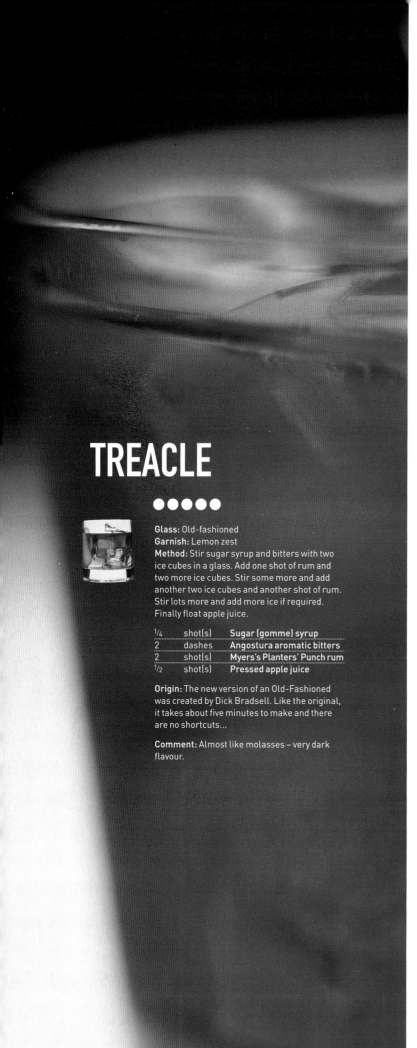

TREACLE

●●●●●

Glass: Old-fashioned
Garnish: Lemon zest
Method: Stir sugar syrup and bitters with two ice cubes in a glass. Add one shot of rum and two more ice cubes. Stir some more and add another two ice cubes and another shot of rum. Stir lots more and add more ice if required. Finally float apple juice.

1/4	shot(s)	**Sugar (gomme) syrup**
2	dashes	**Angostura aromatic bitters**
2	shot(s)	**Myers's Planters' Punch rum**
1/2	shot(s)	**Pressed apple juice**

Origin: The new version of an Old-Fashioned was created by Dick Bradsell. Like the original, it takes about five minutes to make and there are no shortcuts...

Comment: Almost like molasses – very dark flavour.

TOMATE NEW

Glass: Collins (10oz / 290ml max)
Method: Pour pastis and grenadine into glass. Serve iced water separately in a small jug (known in France as a 'broc') so the customer can dilute to their own taste (I recommend five shots). Lastly, add ice to fill glass.

1	shot(s)	**Ricard pastis**
1/4	shot(s)	**Grenadine syrup**
Top up with		**Chilled water**

Origin: Very popular throughout France. Pronounced 'Tom-Art', the name literally means 'tomato' and refers to the drink's colour.
Comment: The traditional aniseed and liquorice French café drink with a sweet hint of cherry.

TOOTIE FRUITY LIFESAVER

Glass: Collins
Method: Shake ingredients with ice and strain into ice-filled glass.

1	shot(s)	**Absolut vodka**
1 1/2	shot(s)	**Bols Crème de banane**
3/4	shot(s)	**Galliano**
2	shot(s)	**Cranberry juice**
2	shot(s)	**Pressed pineapple juice**
2	shot(s)	**Freshly squeezed orange juice**

Comment: Aptly named fruity drink.

TOP BANANA SHOT

Glass: Shot
Method: Layer ingredients by carefully pouring in the following order.

1/2	shot(s)	**Kahlúa coffee liqueur**
1/2	shot(s)	**Bols White crème de cacao**
1/2	shot(s)	**Bols Crème de banane**
1/2	shot(s)	**Absolut vodka**

Comment: Banana, chocolate and coffee.

TORPEDO

Glass: Martini
Garnish: Knot of orange peel
Method: Shake ingredients with ice and strain into glass.

2	shot(s)	**Rémy Martin Cognac**
1/4	shot(s)	**Orange curaçao**
1/8	shot(s)	**Freshly squeezed lemon juice**
1/4	shot(s)	**Sugar (gomme) syrup**
2	shot(s)	**Freshly squeezed orange juice**

Origin: Created at Teatro, London, England in 2000.
Comment: Perfectly balanced orange and brandy.

TOTAL RECALL

Glass: Collins
Garnish: Lime wedge
Method: Shake all ingredients and strain into ice-filled glass.

3/4	shot(s)	**Southern Comfort**
3/4	shot(s)	**Sauza Hornitos Tequila**
3/4	shot(s)	**Mount Gay Eclipse gold rum**
2	shot(s)	**Cranberry juice**
2	shot(s)	**Freshly squeezed orange juice**
3/4	shot(s)	**Freshly squeezed lime juice**

Comment: A long, burgundy coloured drink with a taste reminiscent of blood orange.

TRANSYLVANIAN MARTINI

Glass: Martini
Garnish: Pineapple wedge
Method: Shake ingredients with ice and strain into glass.

1¼	shot(s)	Passoã passion fruit liqueur
1¼	shot(s)	Absolut vodka
2½	shot(s)	Pressed pineapple juice

Origin: Created for the 1994 International Bartenders cocktail competition.
Comment: Sweet and dull.

TRE MARTINI

Glass: Martini
Garnish: Lemon twist
Method: Stir all ingredients with ice and strain into glass.

2	shot(s)	Havana Club light rum
⅓	shot(s)	Sugar (gomme) syrup
⅓	shot(s)	Chambord black raspberry liqueur
1	shot(s)	Freshly pressed apple juice

Origin: Created by Åsa Nevestveit, Sosho Match, London, England.
Comment: A simple, well balanced drink.

TRES COMPADRES MARGARITA

Glass: Coupette
Garnish: Lime wedge & salted rim (optional)
Method: Shake all ingredients with ice and strain into glass.

1¼	shot(s)	Sauza Hornitos Tequila
½	shot(s)	Cointreau / triple sec
½	shot(s)	Chambord black raspberry liqueur
½	shot(s)	Rose's lime cordial
¾	shot(s)	Freshly squeezed lime juice
¾	shot(s)	Freshly squeezed orange juice
¾	shot(s)	Pressed grapefruit juice

Origin: Created in 1999 by Robert Plotkin and Raymon Flores of BarMedia, USA.
Comment: A well balanced tasty twist on the standard Margarita.

TRIANGULAR MARTINI NEW

Glass: Martini
Garnish: Toblerone chocolate on rim
Method: Stir honey with vodka in base of shaker so as to dissolve honey. Add other ingredients; shake with ice and fine strain into chilled glass.

2	spoons	Runny honey
1½	shot(s)	Absolut Vanilia vodka
½	shot(s)	Disaronno Originale liqueur
1¼	shot(s)	Bols Brown crème de cacao
¾	shot(s)	Double (heavy) cream
½	fresh	Egg white

Origin: Created by yours truly in 2003. The famous triangular Toblerone chocolate bar was invented in 1908 by the Swiss chocolate maker Theodor Tobler and the name is a blend of Tobler with Torrone, the Italian word for honey-almond nougat, one of its main ingredients.
Comment: Nibble at the garnish as you sip honeyed, chocolate and almond flavoured liquid candy.

TRIBBBLE

Glass: Shot
Method: Layer ingredients by carefully pouring in the following order.

½	shot(s)	Teichenné butterscotch schnapps
½	shot(s)	Bols crème de banane
½	shot(s)	Baileys Irish Cream liqueur

Origin: A new drink created by the bartenders at TGI Friday's UK in 2002.
Comment: Named 'Tribbble' with three 'Bs' due to its three layers: butterscotch, banana and Baileys.

TRIFLE MARTINI

Glass: Martini
Garnish: Hundreds & thousands
Method: Shake ingredients with ice and strain into glass.

2	shot(s)	Absolut Kurant vodka
½	shot(s)	Chambord black raspberry liqueur
2	shot(s)	Drambuie Cream liqueur

Origin: Created by Ian Baldwin at GE Club, London, England.
Comment: A cocktail that tastes like its namesake.

TRIFLE'TINI

Glass: Martini
Garnish: Crumbled Cadbury's Flake bar
Method: Muddle raspberries and strawberries in base of shaker. Add other ingredients apart from cream, shake with ice and fine strain into chilled glass. Lightly whip cream and layer over drink.

10	fresh	Raspberries
2	fresh	Strawberries
2	shot(s)	Rémy Martin Cognac
¾	shot(s)	Disaronno Originale amaretto
½	shot(s)	Bols Strawberry (fraise) liqueur
1	shot(s)	Pedro Ximénez Sherry
1½	shot(s)	Double (heavy) cream

Origin: Created in 2000 by Ian Baldwin at the GE Club, London, England.
Comment: Very rich – looks and tastes like a trifle.

TRIPLE ORANGE MARTINI UPDATED

Glass: Martini
Garnish: Orange twist
Method: Shake all ingredients with ice and fine strain into chilled glass.

1	shot(s)	Absolut vodka
1	shot(s)	Grand Marnier
¼	shot(s)	Campari
2	shot(s)	Freshly squeezed orange juice
½	fresh	Egg white

Origin: I created this drink in 1998.
Variation: Best made with vanilla vodka, if you have some.
Comment: A trio of orange flavours. The bitter orange of Campari adds character and balance.

TROPICAL BLEND

Glass: Hurricane
Garnish: Passion fruit segment
Method: Blend ingredients with crushed ice and serve.

1	shot(s)	Midori melon liqueur
1	shot(s)	Bols Crème de banane
1	shot(s)	Mount Gay Eclipse gold rum
1/2	shot(s)	Cream of coconut
4	shot(s)	Pressed pineapple juice

Comment: Very sticky but has a good taste.

TROPICAL BREEZE

Glass: Collins
Garnish: Split cherry
Method: Shake ingredients with ice and strain into ice-filled glass.

2	shot(s)	Passoã passion fruit liqueur
1	shot(s)	Absolut vodka
4	shot(s)	Cranberry juice
2	shot(s)	Pressed grapefruit juice

Comment: A fruity version of the Seabreeze.

TROPICAL BREEZY'TINI ●●●●●○

Glass: Martini
Garnish: Pineapple wedge on rim
Method: Shake all ingredients with ice and fine strain into chilled glass.

2¼	shot(s)	Malibu coconut rum liqueur
1¼	shot(s)	Pressed pineapple juice
1¼	shot(s)	Cranberry juice

Origin: Created by yours truly in 2002.
Comment: A relatively low alcohol cocktail with bags of fruity flavour.

TROPICAL CAIPIRINHA NEW ●●●●●◐

Glass: Rocks
Garnish: Two squeezed lime wedges in drink
Method: Shake all ingredients with ice and strain into glass filled with crushed ice.

1	shot(s)	Pitú Cachaça
1	shot(s)	Malibu coconut rum liqueur
1	shot(s)	Pressed pineapple juice
1	shot(s)	Freshly squeezed lime juice
1/4	shot(s)	Sugar (gomme) syrup

Origin: Created by yours truly in 2003. (And yes, I know Caipirinhas are usually muddled.)
Comment: In drink circles, tropical usually spells sweet. This drink may have a 'tropical' flavour but it also boasts an adult sourness.

TROPICAL CREAM UPDATED ●●●●○

Glass: Martini
Garnish: Kiwi fruit on rim
Method: Shake all ingredients with ice and fine strain into chilled glass.

1/2	shot(s)	Havana Club light rum
1	shot(s)	Midori melon liqueur
1/2	shot(s)	Frangelico hazelnut liqueur
1/2	shot(s)	Teichenné peach schnapps
1/2	shot(s)	Malibu coconut rum liqueur
1	shot(s)	Freshly squeezed orange juice
1	shot(s)	Double (heavy) cream

Comment: A velvety, smooth, fruity cocktail.

TROPICAL DELIGHT

Glass: Hurricane
Garnish: Split banana chunk
Method: Blend ingredients with crushed ice and serve.

1	shot(s)	Mount Gay Eclipse gold rum
1	Peeled	Banana
1	shot(s)	Cream of coconut
3	shot(s)	Pressed pineapple juice
3	shot(s)	Freshly squeezed orange juice
2	scoops	Vanilla ice cream

Comment: Piña Colada with go faster stripes.

TROPICAL WINE COOLER

Glass: Collins
Method: Shake first six ingredients with ice and strain into ice-filled glass, top up with lemonade.

1	shot(s)	Disaronno Originale amaretto
1	shot(s)	Bols Cherry brandy liqueur
1½	shot(s)	Pressed pineapple juice
1½	shot(s)	Mango juice
1½	shot(s)	Passion fruit juice
1½	shot(s)	White wine
Top up with		Lemonade

Comment: Very complex and deep but well balanced flavours.

TURKISH COFFEE MARTINI ●●●●●○

Glass: Martini
Garnish: Float three coffee beans
Method: Break away outer shells of cardamom pods and muddle seeds in base of shaker. Add other ingredients, shake with ice and fine strain into glass.

10	pods	Green cardamom
2	shot(s)	Absolut vodka
2	shot(s)	Espresso coffee (cold)
1/2	shot(s)	Sugar (gomme) syrup

Origin: I created this drink in 2003.
Comment: Coffee is often made with cardamom in Arab countries. This drink harnesses the aromatic eucalyptus citrus flavour of cardamom coffee and adds a little vodka zing.

TURKISH DELIGHT NEW

●●●●○

Glass: Martini
Garnish: Turkish delight on rim
Method: Stir honey and vodka in base of shaker so as to dissolve honey. Add other ingredients; shake with ice and fine strain into chilled glass.

2	spoons	Runny honey
1	shot(s)	Absolut vodka
1	shot(s)	Absolut Vanilia vodka
1/2	shot(s)	Bols White crème de cacao
1/8	shot(s)	Rosewater
3/4	shot(s)	Chilled water
1/2	fresh	Egg white

Origin: Created by yours truly in 2003.
Comment: Rosewater, honey, chocolate and vanilla provide a distinctly Turkish Delight flavour - fortified with vodka.

TUTTI FRUTTI

Glass: Collins
Garnish: Split lime wedge
Method: Shake ingredients with ice and strain into ice-filled glass.

1	shot(s)	Passoã passion fruit liqueur
1	shot(s)	Midori melon liqueur
1	shot(s)	Sauza Hornitos Tequila
5	shot(s)	Cranberry juice

Comment: Berry drink with a tropical tinge.

TURQUOISE DAIQUIRÍ

Glass: Martini
Method: Shake ingredients with ice and strain into glass.

1	shot(s)	Matusalem Platino light rum
1/2	shot(s)	Cointreau / triple sec
1/2	shot(s)	Bols Blue curaçao
3/4	shot(s)	Freshly squeezed lime juice
1/4	shot(s)	Sugar (gomme) syrup
2	shot(s)	Pressed pineapple juice

Comment: Sweet and sour, fruity and refreshing.

TVR NEW

●●●◑○

Glass: Collins
Garnish: Lime wedge in drink
Method: Pour ingredients into ice-filled glass. Stir and serve with straws.

1	shot(s)	Sauza Hornitos Tequila
1	shot(s)	Absolut vodka
Top up with		Red Bull

Variant: Often served as a shot
Origin: A 90s drink named after its ingredients (Tequila, vodka and Red Bull), also the brand name of a British sports car.
Comment: While I find the smell of Red Bull reminiscent of perfumed puke, this is a popular drink and could taste worse.

TUXEDO MARTINI NEW

●●●●○

Glass: Martini
Garnish: Flamed orange twist
Method: Shake all ingredients with ice and fine strain into chilled glass.

2	shot(s)	Plymouth gin
1	shot(s)	Cinzano Dry vermouth
1/2	shot(s)	Tio Pepe Fino Sherry
1/8	shot(s)	Maraschino liqueur
1/8	shot(s)	La Fee Absinthe
3	dashes	Feé Brothers Orange bitters

Origin: I've come across two different versions of this classic (retro) cocktail. The one using Fino Sherry, gin and orange bitters appears to herald from the Tuxedo Club, Tuxedo Park, New York circa 1885. The other without Fino Sherry but with Maraschino, absinthe or Angostura or Peychaud's bitters appears to be an adaptation of an earlier drink called a Turf from the Ritz Hotel in Paris. This combination of both recipes is my own.

The Lorillards were wealthy tobacco magnates who owned country property in Tuxedo Park, just outside New York City. At a formal ball, held at the Tuxedo Club in October 1886, Griswold Lorillard and his friends sported the first dinner jackets while the other guests wore traditional white-tie and tails. Griswold named his tailless black jacket the Tuxedo after Tuxedo Park.
Comment: A very dry aromatic Martini to which the uninitiated may want to add a dash of sugar syrup.

20TH CENTURY MARTINI

Glass: Martini
Garnish: Split stemmed cherry on rim
Method: Shake ingredients with ice and strain into glass.

1 1/2	shot(s)	Plymouth gin
1	shot(s)	Cinzano Extra Dry vermouth
1	shot(s)	Bols White crème de cacao
3/4	shot(s)	Freshly squeezed lemon juice
1/4	shot(s)	Cherry syrup

Comment: Very simple, but this bizarre mix of sweet, sour, dryness and strength works well.

TWINKLE

●●●●○

Glass: Martini
Garnish: Lemon twist
Method: Shake first two ingredients with ice and fine strain into chilled glass. Top up with Prosecco (or Champagne).

3	shot(s)	Absolut vodka
3/4	shot(s)	Elderflower cordial
Top up with		Prosecco (or Piper-Heidsieck Brut Champagne)

Origin: Created in 2002 by Tony Conigliaro at Lonsdale House, London, England.
Comment: It's hard to believe this floral, dry, golden tipple contains three whole shots of vodka.

TWISTED SOBRIETY

Glass: Flute
Method: Shake first two ingredients with ice and fine strain into chilled glass. Top up with Champagne.

1	shot(s)	Rémy Martin Cognac
1	shot(s)	Poire William liqueur
Top up with		Piper-Heidsieck Brut Champagne

Comment: Fortified Champagne with a hint of pear.

TWO 'T' FRUITY MARTINI NEW

Glass: Martini
Garnish: Tooty Frooties
Method: Shake all ingredients with ice and fine strain into chilled glass.

2¹/₂	shot(s)	Absolut vodka
³/₄	shot(s)	Passion fruit syrup
3	dashes	Fee Brothers Orange bitters

Origin: Created in 2002 at Hush, London, England.
Comment: Simple is beautiful – this drink is both. The rawness of vodka is balanced with sweet passion fruit and hints of orange bitterness.

TYPHOON

Glass: Rocks
Method: Stir ingredients with ice and strain into ice-filled glass.

1	shot(s)	Plymouth gin
1	shot(s)	Opal Bianca white sambuca
¹/₂	shot(s)	Rose's lime cordial

Comment: Great for sambuca lovers.

UMBONGO

Glass: Collins
Garnish: Orange slice in glass
Method: Shake ingredients with ice and strain into ice-filled glass.

2	shot(s)	Passoã passion fruit liqueur
1	shot(s)	Absolut vodka
3	shot(s)	Passion fruit juice
3	shot(s)	Freshly squeezed orange juice

Comment: Palm trees, sandy beaches, blue sea...

UNCLE VANYA UPDATED

Glass: Martini
Garnish: Lime wedge on rim
Method: Shake all ingredients with ice and fine strain into chilled glass.

1³/₄	shot(s)	Absolut vodka
1	shot(s)	Bols Blackberry (crème de mûre) liqueur
1	shot(s)	Freshly squeezed lime juice
¹/₂	shot(s)	Sugar (gomme) syrup
¹/₂	fresh	Egg white

Origin: Named after Anton Chekhov's greatest play – a cheery tale of envy and despair. A popular drink in Britain's TGI Friday's bars, its origins are unknown.
Comment: Simple but great – smooth sweet 'n' sour blackcurrant, although possibly a tad on the sweet side for some.

UNIVERSAL SHOT

Glass: Shot
Method: Layer by pouring ingredients in the following order.

¹/₂	shot(s)	Midori melon liqueur
¹/₂	shot(s)	Pressed grapefruit juice
¹/₂	shot(s)	Absolut vodka

Comment: A shot combining vodka, melon and grapefruit. Also very nice shaken.

UPSIDE-DOWN RASPBERRY CHEESECAKE NEW

Glass: Martini
Garnish: Sprinkle crunched Graham Cracker or digestive biscuits
Method: First layer: Muddle raspberries in base of shaker. Add Chambord, shake and fine strain into centre of glass. Second layer: Grate lemon zest into shaker. Add rest of ingredients, shake with ice and strain into glass over a spoon so as to layer over raspberry base.

4	fresh	Raspberries
¹/₂	shot(s)	Chambord
next layer		
¹/₂	whole	Lemon grated zest
2	shot(s)	Absolut Vanilia
¹/₂	shot(s)	Bols Vanilla liqueur
¹/₂	shot(s)	Sugar (gomme) syrup
5	spoons	Mascarpone cheese
1	shot(s)	Double (heavy) cream

Origin: I created this in 2003 after adapting Wayne Collins' original cheesecake recipe.
Comment: Surprisingly, the biscuity top continues to float as you sip the vanilla cream layer right down to the point when you hit the raspberry topping – sorry, base.

URBAN OASIS NEW

Glass: Martini
Garnish: Orange twist
Method: Shake all ingredients with ice and fine strain into chilled glass.

1¹/₂	shot(s)	Absolut Mandrin
¹/₂	shot(s)	Absolut Kurant
¹/₄	shot(s)	Chambord black raspberry liqueur
2	shot(s)	Pressed pineapple juice

Origin: Discovered in 2003 at Paramount Hotel, New York City.
Comment: Alcoholic orange sherbet – how bad is that?

NEW	A DRINK NEW TO SAUCE GUIDES.
UPDATED	**ENTRY CHANGED SINCE LAST VOLUME.**
shot(s)	25ML MEASURE (UK) OR 1OZ (US). HOWEVER, IT DOESN'T REALLY MATTER WHAT MEASURE YOU USE AS A SHOT, SO LONG AS YOU USE THE SAME MEASURE OR FRACTIONS OF THAT MEASURE TO MEASURE ALL THE INGREDIENTS. THIS WILL ENSURE THE PROPORTIONS OF ONE INGREDIENT TO ANOTHER WILL BE AS THE RECIPE INTENDED.

U.S. MARTINI NEW

●●●●●○

Glass: Martini
Garnish: Vanilla pod
Method: Shake all ingredients with ice and fine strain into chilled glass.

1½	shot(s)	Vanilla infused Rémy Martin Cognac
1¼	shot(s)	Sauvignon Blanc wine
1½	shot(s)	Pressed pineapple juice
¼	shot(s)	Sugar (gomme) syrup

Origin: Adapted from the Palermo cocktail discovered in 2001 at Hotel du Vin, Bristol, England. I created this drink in 2003 and named it after Ugni and Sauvignon (two grape varieties: Ugni Blanc, the most common grape in Cognac, and Sauvignon Blanc, the grape used in the wine).
Comment: A relatively dry cocktail where the vanilla combines beautifully with the Cognac while the acidity of the wine balances the sweetness of the pineapple juice.

UTTERLY BUTTERLY

●●●●○○

Glass: Collins
Garnish: Apple wedge
Method: Stir peanut butter with vodka in base of shaker. Add other ingredients, shake with ice and fine strain into ice-filled glass.

1	spoon	Smooth Peanut butter
2	shot(s)	Absolut vodka
¼	shot(s)	Cinnamon schnapps
½	shot(s)	Malibu coconut rum liqueur
1½	shot(s)	Pressed apple juice
1½	shot(s)	Pressed pineapple juice
¾	shot(s)	Freshly squeezed lime juice

Comment: Yup, your eyes are not deceiving you and nor will your taste buds – it's made with peanut butter. Refreshingly different.

VACATION MARTINI NEW

●●●●○

Glass: Martini
Garnish: Orange wedge on rim
Method: Shake first four ingredients with ice and fine strain into chilled glass. Top up with 7-Up and then pour blue curaçao into centre of drink (it should sink to create a blue base).

1½	shot(s)	Havana Club light rum
½	shot(s)	Malibu coconut rum liqueur
½	shot(s)	Freshly squeezed lime juice
½	fresh	Egg white
Top up with		Chilled 7-Up
¼	shot(s)	Bols Blue Curacao

Origin: Discovered in 2003 at The Merc Bar, New York City.
Comment: A great looking, fairly sweet cocktail with subtle hints of coconut, lime, orange and rum.

THOSE DRINKS I'VE SAMPLED RECENTLY ARE GRADED AS FOLLOWS:

● DISGUSTING ●◐ PRETTY AWFUL ●● BEST AVOIDED
●●◐ DISAPPOINTING ●●● ACCEPTABLE ●●●◐ GOOD
●●●● RECOMMENDED ●●●●◐ HIGHLY RECOMMENDED
●●●●● OUTSTANDING / EXCEPTIONAL

VALENCIA

●●●●○

Glass: Flute
Garnish: ¼ orange wheel on rim
Method: Pour first three ingredients into chilled glass and top up with Champagne.

½	shot(s)	Bols Apricot brandy liqueur
¼	shot(s)	Freshly squeezed orange juice
4	dashes	Orange bitters (optional)
Top up with		Piper-Heidsieck Brut Champagne

Origin: Adapted from the Valencia Cocktail No.2 in The Savoy Cocktail Book. Sometimes also served as a Martini with gin in place of Champagne.
Comment: Floral and fruity – makes Bucks Fizz look a tad sad.

VALKYRIE NEW

●●●◐○

Pronounced 'val-keer-i'
Glass: Old-fashioned
Garnish: Large lemon twist
Method: Shake all ingredients with ice and strain into glass filled with crushed ice. Serve with straws.

2	shot(s)	Absolut Vanilia vodka
½	shot(s)	Freshly squeezed lemon juice
½	shot(s)	Vanilla sugar syrup

Origin: I created this drink in 2003 using a Daiquiri formula and the then newly available Absolut Vanilia. The name comes from Norse mythology and literally translates as 'chooser of the slain'.
Comment: This sipping drink has a rich vanilla, sweet 'n' sour flavour.

VAMPIRO

●●●●○

Glass: Old-fashioned
Garnish: Lime wedge on rim
Method: Shake all ingredients with ice and strain into ice-filled glass.

2	shot(s)	Sauza Hornitos Tequila
1	shot(s)	Pressed tomato juice
1	shot(s)	Freshly squeezed orange juice
½	shot(s)	Freshly squeezed lime juice
½	hot(s)	Grenadine syrup
8	drops	Hot pepper sauce
1	pinch	Celery salt
1	pinch	Freshly ground black pepper

Origin: The national drink of Mexico where it's usually made using pomegranate juice in place of tomato juice and without the grenadine.
Comment: Something of a supercharged Bloody Mary with Tequila and a hint of sweet grenadine.

VANDERBILT

Glass: Martini
Garnish: Cherry on stick & lemon twist
Method: Stir ingredients with ice and strain into glass.

2	shot(s)	Bols Cherry brandy liqueur
2	shot(s)	Rémy Martin Cognac
4	dashes	Angostura aromatic bitters
¼	shot(s)	Sugar (gomme) syrup

Comment: Heavy cherries.

VANILLA DAIQUIRI

●●●●●

Glass: Martini
Method: Shake ingredients with crushed ice and strain into glass.

2	shot(s)	**Havana Club light rum**
1/2	shot(s)	**Freshly squeezed lime juice**
1/4	shot(s)	**Sugar (gomme) syrup**

Tip: Flavour rum by slicing four vanilla pods down their length and placing in bottle. Replace cap and leave for at least a week, shaking periodically.

Tip: Ideally the ingredients should be shaken with crushed ice, which dilutes the mix. However, the same effect is achieved by adding 1/2 shot of chilled water.

Comment: Made with premium aged rum that has been flavoured with vanilla, this drink is even better. In 1999, Teatro in London put a Vanilla Daiquirí made with aged rum on their menu and christened it the 'VDQ' – short for Vanilla Dark Daiquirí.
A fantastic drink of flavour and balance. Made with aged rum it's even better!

●●●●◐○

VANILLA LAIKA NEW

Glass: Collins
Garnish: Berries
Method: Shake all ingredients with ice and strain into glass filled with crushed ice.

1 1/2	shot(s)	**Stoli Vanil**
3/4	shot(s)	**Bols Blackberry (Crème de mûre) liqueur**
1/4	shot(s)	**Freshly squeezed lemon juice**
3/4	shot(s)	**Sugar (gomme) syrup**
4	shot(s)	**Pressed apple juice**

Origin: Created by Jake Burger in 2002 at Townhouse, Leeds, England. Laika was a Russian dog and the first canine in space.
Comment: Vanilla berry fruit in a tall, refreshing drink.

●●●●●○

VANILIA SENSATION NEW

Glass: Martini
Garnish: Float apple slice
Method: Shake all ingredients with ice and fine strain into chilled glass.

2	shot(s)	**Absolut Vanilia vodka**
1	shot(s)	**Sourz Sour Apple liqueur**
1/2	shot(s)	**Cinzano Extra Dry vermouth**

Origin: A drink created in 2003 and promoted by Absolut.
Comment: A pleasing vanilla twist on an apple Martini.

●●●●○

VANILLA'TINI NEW

Glass: Martini
Garnish: Half vanilla pod
Method: Stir all ingredients with ice and strain into chilled glass.

2 1/2	shot(s)	**Absolut Vanilia vodka**
1/2	shot(s)	**Frangelico hazelnut liqueur**
1 1/2	shot(s)	**Chilled 7-Up**

Origin: Discovered in 2003 at Paramount Hotel, New York City.
Comment: Vanilla, hazelnut and a hint of creamy citrus in an interesting medium dry Martini.

●●●●◐○

VANITINI NEW

Glass: Martini
Garnish: Pineapple wedge on rim
Method: Shake all ingredients with ice and fine strain into chilled glass.

2	shot(s)	**Absolut Vanilia vodka**
2	shot(s)	**Sauvignon Blanc wine**
3/4	shot(s)	**Sourz Pineapple liqueur**
1/4	shot(s)	**Bols Blackberry (Crème de mûre) liqueur**

Origin: Created in 2003 by yours truly.
Comment: Vanilla and pineapple dried by the acidity of the wine; sweetened and flavoured by blackberry liqueur.

VAN'S THE MAN

Glass: Collins
Garnish: Lime squeeze
Method: Shake first three ingredients with ice and strain into ice-filled glass. Top up with Ginger beer.

1½	shot(s)	La Fée absinthe
1	shot(s)	Rose's lime cordial
1	shot(s)	Elderflower cordial
Top up with		Ginger beer

Origin: From a recipe created by Giovanni Burdi of abv Ltd, England.
Comment: Not named after the musician, but after Van Gogh who cut off one of his ears, reputedly as a direct result of over consumption of absinthe.

VANTE MARTINI NEW

Glass: Martini
Garnish: Orange twist
Method: Muddle cardamom in base of shaker. Add other ingredients; shake with ice and fine strain into chilled glass.

4	pods	Cardamom
1½	shot(s)	Absolut Vanilia vodka
1½	shot(s)	Sauvignon Blanc wine
1	shot(s)	Licor 43 (Cuaranta Y Tres) liqueur
¼	shot(s)	Pressed pineapple juice

Origin: Created in 2003 by yours truly.
Comment: An aromatic and complex Martini-style drink with a huge flavour.

VAVAVOOM

Glass: Flute
Method: Pour ingredients into chilled glass.

½	shot(s)	Freshly squeezed lemon juice
½	shot(s)	Cointreau / triple sec
½	shot(s)	Sugar (gomme) syrup
Top up with		Piper-Heidsieck Brut Champagne

Origin: Created in 2002 by Yannick Miseriaux at The Fifth Floor Bar, London, England and named after the Renault television advertisements.
Comment: Yannick's original recipe called for the ingredients to be marinated. This much simplified version still has vavavoom.

VELVET HAMMER

Glass: Martini
Garnish: Sprinkle ground nutmeg
Method: Shake ingredients with ice and strain into glass.

1	shot(s)	Cointreau / triple sec
1	shot(s)	Bols White crème de cacao
1	shot(s)	Double (heavy) cream
1	shot(s)	Milk
¼	shot(s)	Grenadine syrup

Variant: With apricot brandy and coffee liqueur in place of cacao and grenadine.
Comment: Lots of velvet, lacks hammers, though!

VELVET NAIL NEW

Glass: Old-fashioned
Method: Shake all ingredients with ice and strain into ice-filled glass.

2½	shot(s)	The Famous Grouse Scotch whisky
2	shot(s)	Drambuie Cream liqueur

Origin: Created in 2001 by Wayne Collins at High Holborn, London, England.
Comment: An adaptation of the classic Rusty Nail.

VELVET NUT

Glass: Martini
Method: Shake ingredients with ice and strain into glass.

1½	shot(s)	Disaronno Originale amaretto
¾	shot(s)	Bols White crème de cacao
1	shot(s)	Double (heavy) cream
1	shot(s)	Milk

Comment: Strong amaretto flavour.

VENETO

Glass: Martini
Method: Shake ingredients with ice and strain into glass.

1½	shot(s)	Remy Martin Cognac
¼	shot(s)	Opal Bianca white sambuca
¼	shot(s)	Freshly squeezed lemon juice
1	spoon	Sugar (gomme) syrup
½	fresh)	Egg white

Comment: Sweeter than sour.

VENETIAN SUNSET

Glass: Martini
Garnish: Cherry
Method: Shake ingredients with ice and strain into glass.

1½	shot(s)	Plymouth gin
1	shot(s)	Grand Marnier
1	shot(s)	Campari
1	shot(s)	Cinzano Extra Dry vermouth

Comment: A dry, bitter and orange-y affair.

VENUS IN FURS NEW

Glass: Collins
Garnish: Berries & lemon wheel in glass
Method: Shake all ingredients with ice and strain into ice-filled glass.

1	shot(s)	Absolut Kurant vodka
1	shot(s)	Absolut Citron vodka
4	shot(s)	Pressed apple juice
4	dashes	Angostura aromatic bitters

Origin: A cocktail which emerged in London's bars early in 2002.
Comment: Juicy flavours with a hint of spice make for a refreshing, quaffable drink.

VENUS MARTINI

Glass: Martini
Garnish: Raspberry in drink
Method: Muddle raspberries in base of shaker. Add other ingredients, shake with ice and fine strain into a chilled glass.

7	fresh	Raspberries
2	shot(s)	Plymouth Gin
1	shot(s)	Cointreau / triple sec
1/4	shot(s)	Sugar (gomme) syrup
4	dashes	Péychaud's Bitters (optional)

Comment: Raspberry with hints of bitter orange and gin – surprisingly dry.

VERDI MARTINI

Glass: Martini
Garnish: Lime wedge
Method: Shake all ingredients with ice and fine strain into chilled glass.

1 3/4	shot(s)	Stoli Razberi
1/2	shot(s)	Midori melon liqueur
1/2	shot(s)	Archers peach schnapps
1	shot(s)	Pressed pineapple juice
1	shot(s)	Pressed apple juice
1/4	shot(s)	Freshly squeezed lime juice

Origin: Adapted from a drink discovered in 2002 at the Fifth Floor Bar, London, England.
Comment: A melange of fruits combine in a gluggable short drink.

VERT'ICAL BREEZE

Glass: Collins
Method: Shake all ingredients with ice and strain into ice-filled glass.

1 1/2	shot(s)	La Fée absinthe
3	shot(s)	Cranberry juice
3	shot(s)	Pressed grapefruit juice

Comment: For those that don't speak French, 'vert' means green – the colour of absinthe. Vertical suggests take off – try it and see.

VIAGRA FALLS

Glass: Martini
Garnish: Flamed orange twist
Method: Shake all ingredients with ice and fine strain into chilled glass.

1	shot(s)	La Fée absinthe
1 3/4	shot(s)	Sourz Sour Apple liqueur
1 3/4	shot(s)	Chilled water
1/2	spoon	Fee Brothers Orange bitters

Origin: Created by Jack Leuwens, London, England.
Comment: Aniseed and apple – sure to get your pecker up.

VESPER MARTINI

Glass: Martini
Garnish: Lemon twist
Method: Vigorously shake ingredients with ice and fine strain into glass.

3	shot(s)	Plymouth gin
1	shot(s)	Absolut vodka
1/2	shot(s)	Cinzano Extra dry vermouth

Origin: This is the real James Bond 'shaken' Dry Martini from Fleming's book Casino Royale. In chapter seven, 007 explains to a Casino bartender exactly how he likes his Dry Martini mixed and served. When made, he compliments the bartender, but tells him it would be better made with a grain-based vodka. Bond also explains his Martini to Felix Leiter, the CIA man, saying, "This drink's my own invention. I'm going to patent it when I can think of a good name." Later in chapter eight, Bond meets the beautiful double agent Vesper Lynd. She explains why her parents named her Vesper and Bond asks if she'd mind if he named his favourite Martini after her.

Comment: Most bartenders advocate that a Martini should be stirred and not shaken, some citing the ridiculous argument that shaking will bruise the gin. The Vesper is always shaken, an action that aerates the drink, makes it colder and more dilute than simply stirring. It also gives the drink a slightly clouded appearance and can leave small shards of ice on the surface of the drink, but the use of a fine strainer removes these.

VIOLET AFFINITY NEW

Glass: Martini
Garnish: Lemon twist
Method: Stir all ingredients with ice and strain into chilled glass.

2	shot(s)	Benoit Serres Liqueur de Violette
1	shot(s)	Cinzano Rosso (sweet) vermouth
1	shot(s)	Cinzano Extra Dry vermouth

Origin: An adaptation of the classic (retro) Affinity.
Comment: Amazingly delicate and complex for such a simple drink.

VODKA BOATMAN

Glass: Martini
Method: Shake ingredients with ice and strain into glass.

1	shot(s)	Absolut vodka
1	shot(s)	Bols Cherry brandy liqueur
2	shot(s)	Freshly squeezed orange juice

Comment: Easy to make, easy to drink.

VODKA COLLINS

Glass: Collins
Method: Shake first three ingredients with ice and strain into ice-filled glass. Top up with soda.

2	shot(s)	Absolut vodka
1	shot(s)	Freshly squeezed lemon juice
1/2	shot(s)	Sugar (gomme) syrup
Top up with		Soda water (club soda)

AKA: Joe Collins
Comment: Tom Collins with vodka – dull as...

VODKA ESPRESSO

Glass: Rocks
Garnish: Three coffee beans
Method: Shake ingredients with ice and strain into glass.

2	shot(s)	Absolut vodka
1 1/2	shot(s)	Espresso coffee (cold)
1/4	shot(s)	Sugar (gomme) syrup
1/2	shot(s)	Kahlúa coffee liqueur

Origin: Created by Dick Bradsell at the Soho Brasserie in 1983.
Comment: A fantastic, simple and addictive bevvy.

VODKA RICKEY

Glass: Collins
Garnish: Lemon wheel
Method: Shake first three ingredients with ice and strain into ice-filled glass, then top up with soda.

2	shot(s)	Absolut vodka
1	shot(s)	Freshly squeezed lime juice
1/2	shot(s)	Sugar (gomme) syrup
Top up with		Soda water (club soda)

Comment: Classic sweet and sour.

VODKA SOUR

Glass: Snifter
Garnish: Lemon wheel & maraschino cherry on stick
Method: Shake all ingredients with ice and strain into ice-filled glass.

2	shot(s)	Absolut vodka
1	shot(s)	Freshly squeezed lemon juice
1/2	shot(s)	Sugar (gomme) syrup
4	dashes	Angostura aromatic bitters
1/2	fresh	Egg white

Comment: A great drink balancing sweet and sour, but both a Whiskey Sour and a Brandy Sour are better.

VODKA STINGER

Glass: Rocks
Method: Stir ingredients with ice and strain into ice-filled glass.

1 1/2	shot(s)	Absolut vodka
3/4	shot(s)	White crème de menthe

AKA: White spider
Comment: Fresh breath–tastic!

VODKATINI

Glass: Martini
Garnish: Lemon peel twist / olives
Method: Stir vermouth with ice in a mixing glass and strain to discard excess vermouth, leaving only a coating on the ice. Pour vodka into mixing glass containing coated ice, stir and strain.

1/2	shot(s)	Cinzano Extra Dry vermouth
2 1/2	shot(s)	Absolut vodka

Variant: Various flavours may be steeped in the vodka such as cardamom, fennel, ginger, lavender, mint and star anise.
Comment: If you must have a Martini made with vodka instead of gin, then be sure to add a little flavour as suggested above.

VOODOO

Glass: Collins
Garnish: Cinnamon sprinkled over a flame
Method: Shake and strain into an ice filled glass.

2	shot(s)	Appleton Estate V/X aged rum
1	shot(s)	Cinzano Rosso vermouth
4	shot(s)	Pressed apple juice
1	shot(s)	Freshly squeezed lime juice
1	shot(s)	Sugar (gomme) syrup

Origin: Created in 2002 by Alex Kammerling, London, England.
Comment: The rich flavour of the aged rum marries well with apple and lime juice.

WALNUT MARTINI

Glass: Martini
Method: Shake ingredients with ice and strain into glass.

2	shot(s)	Absolut vodka
1	shot(s)	Benoit Serres walnut liqueur
1	shot(s)	Tuaca liqueur

Comment: Nutty but nice.

WANDERING MINSTREL SHOT

Glass: Shot
Method: Shake ingredients with ice and strain into glass.

1/2	shot(s)	Absolut vodka
1/2	shot(s)	Rémy Martin Cognac
1/2	shot(s)	White crème de menthe
1/2	shot(s)	Kahlúa coffee liqueur

Comment: A minty, coffee kick!

WARD EIGHT

Glass: Martini
Method: Shake ingredients with ice and strain into glass.

2	shot(s)	Buffalo Trace Bourbon
1	shot(s)	Freshly squeezed lemon juice
1/2	shot(s)	Sugar (gomme) syrup
1/4	shot(s)	Grenadine syrup
1/4	shot(s)	Freshly squeezed orange juice

AKA: Scottish Guard's Cocktail
Origin: Ward Eight is an old political designation of New York - an Irish area - and it was famed for its corruption.
Comment: Flavoursome and lingering Bourbon based cocktail.

WARSAW

Glass: Martini
Method: Stir ingredients with ice and strain into glass.

2	shot(s)	Absolut vodka
1	shot(s)	Wiśniówka cherry vodka
1/2	shot(s)	Cointreau / triple sec
4	dashes	Angostura aromatic bitters

Comment: Subtle cherry notes with orange.

NEW	A DRINK NEW TO SAUCE GUIDES.
UPDATED	ENTRY CHANGED SINCE LAST VOLUME.
shot(s)	25ML MEASURE (UK) OR 1OZ (US). HOWEVER, IT DOESN'T REALLY MATTER WHAT MEASURE YOU USE AS A SHOT, SO LONG AS YOU USE THE SAME MEASURE OR FRACTIONS OF THAT MEASURE TO MEASURE ALL THE INGREDIENTS. THIS WILL ENSURE THE PROPORTIONS OF ONE INGREDIENT TO ANOTHER WILL BE AS THE RECIPE INTENDED.

WARSAW COOLER NEW

●●●●◐

Glass: Collins
Garnish: Mint sprig & orange zest
Method: Stir honey with Zubrówka in base of shaker so as to dissolve honey. Add other ingredients, shake with ice and strain into ice-filled glass.

2	spoons	Runny honey
1 1/2	shot(s)	Zubrówka (Bison) vodka
1/2	shot(s)	Spiced rum
1/4	shot(s)	Cointreau / triple sec
1/2	shot(s)	Sugar (gomme) syrup
3/4	shot(s)	Freshly squeezed lemon juice
2	shot(s)	Pressed apple juice

Origin: Created in 2002 by Morgan Watson of Apartment, Belfast, Northern Ireland.
Comment: Orange, honey, apple and spice laced with flavoured Polish vodka.

WATERMELON & BASIL MARTINI UPDATED

●●●●◐

Glass: Martini
Garnish: Watermelon wedge on rim
Method: Muddle melon in base of shaker. Add other ingredients; shake with ice and fine strain into chilled glass.

1 1/2	cup(s)	Diced ripe watermelon
7	fresh	Torn basil leaves
2	shot(s)	Plymouth gin
1/2	shot(s)	Sugar (gomme) syrup

Comment: Refreshing watermelon with interesting herbal hints from the basil and gin.

WATERMELON & BASIL SMASH UPDATED

●●●●○

Glass: Collins
Garnish: Watermelon wedge on rim
Method: Muddle melon in base of shaker. Add next three ingredients, shake with ice and strain into ice-filled glass. Top up with ginger ale.

2	cupfuls	Diced ripe watermelon
8	fresh	Torn basil leaves
2	shot(s)	Sauza Hornitos Tequila
3/4	shot(s)	Pallini Limoncello liqueur
Top up with		Jamaican Ginger beer

Comment: Sweet and sour, long and refreshing with subtle hints of basil, ginger and tequila amongst the fruit.

WATERMELON COSMO NEW

●●●●◐

Glass: Martini
Garnish: Watermelon wedge on rim
Method: Muddle watermelon in base of shaker. Add other ingredients, shake with ice and fine strain into chilled glass.

3/4	cupful	Diced ripe watermelon
1	shot(s)	Absolut Citron vodka
1	shot(s)	Melon vodka
3/4	shot(s)	Freshly squeezed lime juice
3/4	shot(s)	Cranberry juice
1/2	shot(s)	Midori melon liqueur
1/8	shot(s)	Rose's lime cordial
4	dashes	Fee Brothers Orange bitters

Origin: Created in 2003 by Eric Fossard at Cecconi's, London, England.
Comment: Looks like a standard Cosmo with a frothy top but is far more complex.

WATERMELON MARTINI UPDATED

●●●●○

Glass: Martini
Garnish: Watermelon wedge on rim
Method: Muddle watermelon in base of shaker. Add other ingredients, shake with ice and fine strain into chilled glass.

1½	cupfuls	Diced ripe watermelon
2	shot(s)	Absolut vodka
½	shot(s)	Sugar (gomme) syrup

Comment: So fruity, you can almost convince yourself this is a health drink! Simple yet beautiful.

WEDDING CAKE

Glass: Hurricane
Garnish: Chocolate chunks
Method: Blend ingredients with crushed ice and serve.

2	shot(s)	Havana Club light rum
1	shot(s)	Disaronno Originale amaretto
1	shot(s)	Double (heavy) cream
1	shot(s)	Milk
3	shot(s)	Pressed pineapple juice
1	shot(s)	Cream of coconut

Comment: Creamy coco – and nuts.

WEEPING JESUS

●●●●◐○

Glass: Rocks
Method: Shake first three ingredients with ice and strain into glass filled with crushed ice. Top up with lemonade.

1	shot(s)	La Fée absinthe
1	shot(s)	Teichenné Peach schnapps
1	shot(s)	Grenadine syrup
Top up with		Lemonade / 7-Up

Origin: Created in 2002 by Andy Jones at Yates, London, England.
Comment: This bright red cocktail makes the strong aniseed flavours of absinthe approachable.

WET MARTINI

●●●●●◐

Glass: Martini
Garnish: Olive or twist?
Method: Stir all ingredients with ice and strain into chilled glass.

3	shot(s)	Plymouth Gin
1½	shot(s)	Cinzano Extra Dry vermouth.

Origin: A generous measure of vermouth to three of gin, hence the name 'Wet' Martini.
Comment: Reputed to be a favourite of HRH Prince Charles.

WHAT THE HELL

Glass: Martini
Garnish: Half kumquat
Method: Shake ingredients with ice and strain into glass.

2	shot(s)	Plymouth gin
1	shot(s)	Bols Apricot brandy liqueur
1	shot(s)	Cinzano Extra Dry vermouth
½	shot(s)	Freshly squeezed lime juice
½	shot(s)	Sugar (gomme) syrup

Comment: Gin and dry apricots.

WHISKEY COBBLER

Glass: Rocks
Garnish: Lemon slice & mint sprig
Method: Stir ingredients with ice and strain into ice-filled glass.

2	shot(s)	The Famous Grouse Scotch whisky
½	shot(s)	Orange curaçao
½	shot(s)	Rémy Martin Cognac

Comment: Hardcore drink - but great bouquet and sophistication.

WHISKEY MARTINI

Glass: Martini
Garnish: Cherry on stick
Method: Stir ingredients with ice and strain into glass.

3	shot(s)	Buffalo Trace Bourbon
1	shot(s)	Orange curaçao
4	dashes	Angostura aromatic bitters

Comment: Two of these and you're history. Nice while it lasts, though.

WHISKEY COLLINS

Glass: Collins
Garnish: Lemon slice
Method: Shake first four ingredients with ice and strain into ice-filled glass, then top up with soda water.

2	shot(s)	Buffalo Trace Bourbon
¾	shot(s)	Freshly squeezed lemon juice
½	shot(s)	Sugar (gomme) syrup
3	dashes	Angostura aromatic bitters
Top up with		Soda water (club soda)

Comment: Another variation on the classic Tom.

WHISKY FIZZ

Glass: Collins
Method: Shake first four ingredients with ice and strain into ice-filled glass, then top up with soda.

2	shot(s)	The Famous Grouse Scotch whisky
1	shot(s)	Freshly squeezed lime juice
½	shot(s)	Sugar (gomme) syrup
2	shot(s)	Freshly squeezed orange juice
Top up with		Soda water (club soda)

Comment: Nice mix of whisky and citrus.

WHISKY MAC

Glass: Rocks
Method: Pour ingredients into ice-filled glass and stir.

2	shot(s)	The Famous Grouse Scotch whisky
1½	shot(s)	Ginger wine

Comment: An old classic, but it still works.

WHISKEY SOUR

●●●●○

Glass: Old-fashioned
Garnish: Cherry & lemon slice sail

2	shot(s)	Buffalo Trace Bourbon
³/₄	shot(s)	Freshly squeezed lemon juice
1	shot(s)	Sugar (gomme) syrup
¹/₂	fresh	Egg white
4	dashes	Angostura aromatic bitters

Comment: This recipe follows the classic sour proportions: three quarter part of the sour ingredient (lemon juice), one part of the sweet ingredient (sugar syrup) and two parts of the strong ingredient (whiskey) (3:4:8). I actually prefer mine sourer with 1 shot lemon juice and ¹/₂ shot sugar (4:2:8). You might want to experiment to find your preferred balance.

WHITE BULL

Glass: Martini
Garnish: Coffee beans
Method: Shake ingredients with ice and strain into glass.

1	shot(s)	Sauza Hornitos Tequila
1	shot(s)	Kahlúa coffee liqueur
1¹/₂	shot(s)	Double (heavy) cream
1¹/₂	shot(s)	Milk

Comment: The taste of Tequila is hardly recognisable.

WHITE CADILLAC

Glass: Martini
Garnish: Knot of orange peel
Method: Blend ingredients with crushed ice and serve.

1¹/₂	shot(s)	Cointreau / triple sec
³/₄	shot(s)	Galliano
1	shot(s)	Double (heavy) cream
1	shot(s)	Milk

Comment: Creamy and distinctive tasting - thanks to herbs and orange.

WHITE ELEPHANT

Glass: Martini
Garnish: Chocolate sprinkle
Method: Shake ingredients with ice and strain into glass.

2	shot(s)	Absolut vodka
1	shot(s)	Bols White crème de cacao
1	shot(s)	Double (heavy) cream
1	shot(s)	Milk

AKA: White Beach
Comment: Smooth and creamy.

WHITE HOUND

Glass: Martini
Method: Shake ingredients with ice and strain into glass.

³/₄	shot(s)	Absolut vodka
³/₄	shot(s)	Plymouth gin
2¹/₂	shot(s)	Pink grapefruit juice
¹/₄	shot(s)	Sugar (gomme) syrup

Comment: A refined balance of flavours.

WHITE KNIGHT

Glass: Martini
Method: Shake ingredients with ice and strain into glass.

1	shot(s)	The Famous Grouse Scotch whisky
1	shot(s)	Kahlúa coffee liqueur
1	shot(s)	Drambuie
1	shot(s)	Double (heavy) cream
1	shot(s)	Milk

Comment: A strong, dry, creamy, flavoursome cocktail with Scotch, coffee and Drambuie.

WHITE LADY UPDATED

●●●●●◐

Glass: Martini
Garnish: Lemon twist
Method: Shake all ingredients with ice and fine strain into chilled glass.

2	shot(s)	Plymouth gin
1	shot(s)	Cointreau / triple sec
1	shot(s)	Freshly squeezed lemon juice
1/4	shot(s)	Sugar (gomme) syrup
1/2	fresh	Egg white

Origin: Created in 1919 by Harry MacElhone at Ciro's Club, London, England.
Comment: A simple but lovely classic drink with a sour edge.

WHITE LILY

Glass: Martini
Method: Stir ingredients with ice and strain into glass.

1 1/2	shot(s)	Plymouth gin
1 1/2	shot(s)	Cointreau / triple sec
1 1/2	shot(s)	Matusalem Platino rum
1/8	shot(s)	La Fée absinthe

Comment: The Pastis gives a pleasant aftertaste.

WHITE MONKEY

Glass: Hurricane
Garnish: Pineapple leaf
Method: Blend first four ingredients with crushed ice and pour into glass, then float crème de banane.

1 1/2	shot(s)	Pusser's Navy rum
1 1/2	shot(s)	Havana Club light rum
4	shot(s)	Pressed pineapple juice
1	shot(s)	Cream of coconut
1/2	shot(s)	Bols crème de banane

Comment: A rich but flavoursome drink – shorter is better.

WHITE RUSSIAN

Glass: Rocks
Method: Shake all ingredients with ice and strain into ice-filled glass.

1 1/2	shot(s)	Absolut vodka
1/2	shot(s)	Kahlúa coffee liqueur
3/4	shot(s)	Double (heavy) cream
3/4	shot(s)	Milk

Comment: A Black Russian smoothed with cream.

WHITE SATIN

Glass: Martini
Method: Shake ingredients with ice and strain into glass.

1 1/2	shot(s)	Galliano
1 1/2	shot(s)	Kahlúa coffee liqueur
1/2	shot(s)	Double (heavy) cream
1	shot(s)	Milk

Comment: Smoother than a cashmere codpiece!

WHITE STINGER

●

Glass: Rocks
Method: Shake ingredients with ice and strain into ice-filled glass.

2	shot(s)	Absolut vodka
1/2	shot(s)	White crème de menthe
1/2	shot(s)	Bols White crème de cacao

Comment: Liquid After Eights.

WIBBLE

Glass: Martini
Garnish: Sprayed lemon twist
Method: Shake ingredients with ice and strain into glass.

1	shot(s)	Plymouth gin
1	shot(s)	Plymouth sloe gin
1	shot(s)	Pressed grapefruit juice
1	spoon	Freshly squeezed lemon juice
1	spoon	Sugar (gomme) syrup
1	spoon	Bols Blackberry (Crème de mûre) liqueur

Origin: Created by Dick Bradsell at The Player, London, in 1999.

Comment: As Dick says, 'It may make you wobble, but it won't make you fall down.' Complex and balanced

WIDOW'S KISS NEW

●●●●○

Glass: Martini
Garnish: Mint leaf
Method: Shake all ingredients with ice and fine strain into chilled glass.

3/4	shot(s)	Calvados or applejack brandy
3/4	shot(s)	Bénédictine D.O.M. liqueur
3/4	shot(s)	Green Chartreuse liqueur
1 1/2	shot(s)	Chilled water
1/8	shot(s)	Sugar (gomme) syrup
2	dashes	Angostura aromatic bitters

Origin: Adapted from a drink discovered in 2003 at Rex Cinema, London, England.
Comment: Herbal with hints of apple, mint and eucalyptus.

WILD HONEY

●●●●◐○

Glass: Martini
Method: Shake all ingredients with ice and fine strain into glass.

1 1/2	shot(s)	The Famous Grouse Scotch whisky
3/4	shot(s)	Stoli vanil
1	shot(s)	Drambuie liqueur
1/2	shot(s)	Galliano liqueur
1/2	shot(s)	Double (heavy) cream
1/2	shot(s)	Milk

Origin: Created in 2001 by James Price at Bar Red, London, England.
Comment: A serious after dinner whisky and honey, creamy cocktail.

WILD PROMENADE MARTINI

Glass: Martini
Garnish: Float 3 raspberries
Method: Muddle cucumber and raspberries in base of shaker. Add other ingredients, shake with ice and fine strain into ice-filled glass.

2	inch	Chopped cucumber
5	fresh	Raspberries
1¹/₂	shot(s)	Absolut vodka
¹/₂	shot(s)	Stoli Razberi vodka
¹/₂	shot(s)	Bols Raspberry (framboise) liqueur
¹/₄	shot(s)	Sugar (gomme) syrup

Origin: Created in 2002 by Mehdi Otmann at The Player, London, England.
Comment: Rich raspberry with green hints of cucumber.

WIMBLEDON MARTINI

Glass: Martini
Garnish: Strawberry on rim
Method: Shake all ingredients with ice and fine strain into chilled glass.

6	fresh	Hulled strawberries
1¹/₂	shot(s)	Havana Club light rum
1¹/₂	shot(s)	Bols Strawberry (fraise) liqueur
¹/₄	shot(s)	Sugar (gomme) syrup
1	shot(s)	Double (heavy) cream

Comment: Takes some getting through the strainer, but when you do it's simply strawberries and cream.

WINDY MILLER

Glass: Collins
Garnish: Thin slices of lemon
Method: Shake ingredients with ice and strain into glass filled with crushed ice. Top up with lemonade.

1	shot(s)	Absolut Citron vodka
1	shot(s)	Mandarine Napoléon
¹/₂	shot(s)	La Fée absinthe
Top up with		Lemonade / 7-Up

Origin: Discovered in 2000 by the editor at Teatro, London, England.
Comment: Do you remember Trumpton and Camberwick Green? If not, you're too young to be drinking cocktails. If you do, then sing between sips, 'Pugh, Pugh, Barney McGrew Cuthbert Dibble Grubb.'

WINE COOLER

Glass: Collins
Method: Pour first three ingredients into ice-filled glass, top up with soda and lightly stir.

¹/₂	shot(s)	Freshly squeezed lemon juice
¹/₂	shot(s)	Freshly squeezed orange juice
4	shot(s)	Dry white wine
Top up with		Soda water (club soda)

Comment: Very refreshing but you may want to add sugar.

WINK

Glass: Old-fashioned
Garnish: Wink as you serve
Method: Pour absinthe into ice-filled glass, top up with chilled water and leave to stand. Shake other ingredients with ice. Discard contents of absinthe, water and ice-filled glass. Strain contents of shaker into empty (absinthe washed) glass.

¹/₂	shot(s)	La Fée absinthe
2	shot(s)	Plymouth gin
¹/₂	shot(s)	Sugar (gomme) syrup
¹/₄	shot(s)	Cointreau / triple sec
2	dashes	Péychaud's Bitters
¹/₂	shot(s)	Chilled water

Origin: Created in 2002 by Tony Conigliaro at Lonsdale House, London, England.
Comment: A pink rinsed drink with a wonderfully aromatic flavour.

WINTER MARTINI

Glass: Martini
Garnish: Apple slice
Method: Vigorously shake all ingredients with ice and fine strain into chilled glass.

2¹/₂	shot(s)	Rémy Martin Cognac
1	shot(s)	Sourz Sour Apple liqueur
¹/₂	shot(s)	Sugar (gomme) syrup

Origin: Merc Bar, New York City.
Comment: A simple and Calvados-like drink.

WONKY MARTINI NEW

Glass: Martini
Garnish: Orange twist
Method: Stir all ingredients with ice and strain into chilled glass.

1¹/₂	shot(s)	Absolut Vanilia vodka
1¹/₂	shot(s)	Tuaca Liqueur
1¹/₂	shot(s)	Cinzano Rosso (sweet) vermouth
3	dashes	Fee Brothers Orange bitters

Origin: Created in 2003 by yours truly.
Comment: The strength of a traditional Martini invigorated with more than a hint of orange and vanilla.

WOO WOO

Glass: Rocks
Garnish: Split lime wedge
Method: Shake ingredients with ice and strain into ice-filled glass.

1	shot(s)	Teichenné Peach schnapps
1	shot(s)	Absolut vodka
3¹/₂	shot(s)	Cranberry juice

Comment: Fruity, dry cranberry laced with vodka and peach.

XANTHIA COCKTAIL

Glass: Martini
Method: Shake ingredients with ice and strain into glass.

1½	shot(s)	Plymouth gin
1½	shot(s)	Yellow Chartreuse
1½	shot(s)	Bols Cherry brandy liqueur

Comment: Distinctive but not a starter drink.

YANKEE-DUTCH

Glass: Martini
Garnish: Orange peel twist
Method: Shake ingredients with ice and strain into glass.

1	shot(s)	Buffalo Trace Bourbon
1	shot(s)	Absolut vodka
1	shot(s)	Bols Cherry brandy liqueur
1	shot(s)	Cointreau / triple sec

Comment: Complex combination.

YELLOW BELLY MARTINI

Glass: Martini
Garnish: Lemon twist
Method: Shake ingredients with ice and strain into glass.

1	shot(s)	Cytrynówka lemon vodka
1	shot(s)	Freshly squeezed lemon juice
1	shot(s)	Lemoncello lemon liqueur
¼	shot(s)	Sugar (gomme) syrup

Comment: Lemon, lemon, lemon. Nice, though...

YELLOW BIRD MARTINI

Glass: Martini
Garnish: Split banana slice
Method: Shake first six ingredients with ice and strain into glass, then float Galliano.

1½	shot(s)	Mount Gay Eclipse gold rum
½	shot(s)	Bols Crème de banane
¼	shot(s)	Bols Apricot brandy liqueur
2	shot(s)	Pressed pineapple juice
½	shot(s)	Freshly squeezed lime juice
½	shot(s)	Sugar (gomme) syrup
¼	shot(s)	Galliano liqueur

Comment: A sweet and sour cocktail with four different fruits, rum and a splash of Galliano.

●●●●○○

YELLOW FEVER MARTINI

Glass: Martini
Garnish: Pineapple wedge on rim
Method: Shake all ingredients with ice and fine strain into chilled glass.

2½	shot(s)	Absolut vodka
½	shot(s)	Galliano liqueur
1½	shot(s)	Pressed pineapple juice
½	shot(s)	Freshly squeezed lime juice
⅛	shot(s)	Sugar (gomme) syrup

Comment: Fortified pineapple with a subtle cooling hint of peppermint.

YELLOW MONKEY MARTINI

Glass: Martini
Garnish: 2 physalis fruits on stick
Method: Shake ingredients with ice and strain into glass.

½	shot(s)	Havana Club light rum
1	shot(s)	Galliano liqueur
1	shot(s)	Bols White crème de cacao
½	shot(s)	Bols Crème de banane
1	shot(s)	Double (heavy) cream
1	shot(s)	Milk

Comment: Not dissimilar to a banana milkshake.

●●●●○○

YELLOW PARROT

Glass: Martini
Garnish: Orange twist
Method: Stir all ingredients with ice and strain into chilled glass.

1	shot(s)	Pernod anise
1	shot(s)	Yellow Chartreuse
1	shot(s)	Bols Apricot brandy liqueur
1	shot(s)	Chilled water

Origin: Created in 1935 by Albert Coleman at The Stork Club, New York City.
Comment: This drink may lack subtlety but the aniseed flavour combines well with the other ingredients.

YULE LUVIT

Glass: Shot
Garnish: Sprinkle nutmeg
Method: Layer in glass by carefully pouring ingredients in the following order.

¾	shot(s)	Buffalo Trace Bourbon
¾	shot(s)	Frangelico hazelnut liqueur

Comment: Actually, you'll find it strongly nutty and sweet.

YUM

Glass: Collins
Method: Shake ingredients with ice and strain into ice-filled glass

1½	shot(s)	Mandarine Napoléon liqueur
½	shot(s)	Teichenné Peach schnapps
1	shot(s)	Freshly squeezed lemon juice
¼	shot(s)	Sugar (gomme) syrup
¼	shot(s)	Chambord black raspberry liqueur
3	shot(s)	Pressed apple juice

Comment: Apt name – yummy!

ZABAGLIONE MARTINI

Glass: Martini
Method: Shake all ingredients with ice and fine strain into chilled glass.

1½	shot(s)	Warninks Advocaat
½	shot(s)	Rémy Martin Cognac
1	shot(s)	Marsala
¾	shot(s)	Freshly squeezed lemon juice
1	fresh	Egg yolk

Origin: I created this drink in 2003 after the classic Italian dessert, which incidentally derives its name from the Neapolitan dialect word 'Zapillare', meaning 'to foam'.
Comment: Lacks the fluffiness of the dessert but shares the same sweet rich lemon, fortified wine and egg flavour.

ZAKUSKI MARTINI

Glass: Martini
Garnish: Lemon zest/cucumber peel
Method: Muddle cucumber in base of shaker. Add other ingredients, shake with ice and fine strain into glass.

1	inch	Peeled cucumber chopped
2	shot(s)	Absolut Citron vodka
½	shot(s)	Freshly squeezed lemon juice
⅓	shot(s)	Sugar (gomme) syrup
½	shot(s)	Cointreau / triple sec

Origin: Created in 2002 by Alex Kammerling, London, England.
Comment: Appropriately named after the Russian snack.

ZAZA NEW

Glass: Martini
Garnish: Orange or lemon peel twist
Method: Stirred

1½	shot(s)	Plymouth gin
1½	shot(s)	Dubonnet Red
½	shot(s)	Chilled water
3	dashes	Angostura aromatic bitters

AKA: Dubonnet Cocktail
Variation: Substitute sloe gin or Fino Sherry in place of gin.
Origin: This classic (retro) cocktail was created for and named after Zsa Zsa Gabor.
Comment: One of those drinks where dilution is key. Appreciation requires a palate that takes pleasure from gin's botanical flavours mixed with spicy red wine.

NEW	A DRINK NEW TO SAUCE GUIDES.
UPDATED	ENTRY CHANGED SINCE LAST VOLUME.
shot(s)	25ML MEASURE (UK) OR 1OZ (US). HOWEVER, IT DOESN'T REALLY MATTER WHAT MEASURE YOU USE AS A SHOT, SO LONG AS YOU USE THE SAME MEASURE OR FRACTIONS OF THAT MEASURE TO MEASURE ALL THE INGREDIENTS. THIS WILL ENSURE THE PROPORTIONS OF ONE INGREDIENT TO ANOTHER WILL BE AS THE RECIPE INTENDED.

ZELDA MARTINI

Glass: Martini
Garnish: Mint sprig
Method: Lightly muddle mint leaves in base of shaker. Add other ingredients, shake with ice and fine strain into chilled glass.

5	fresh	Mint leaves
2	shot(s)	Zubrówka (bison grass) vodka
1	shot(s)	Freshly squeezed lime juice
1	shot(s)	Almond (orgeat) syrup
½	shot(s)	Chilled water

Origin: Created in May 2002 by Phillip Jeffrey at the GE Club, London, England. He made it first for a friend called Zelda – and the name really wouldn't have worked if she'd been called Tracy.
Comment: Bison grass vodka combines brilliantly with mint and almond.

ZESTY

Glass: Old-fashioned
Method: Vigorously shake all ingredients with ice and strain into glass filled with crushed ice.

2	shot(s)	Frangelico hazelnut liqueur
½	shot(s)	Freshly squeezed lime juice

Comment: Citrus fresh with a nutty touch.

ZEUS MARTINI

Glass: Martini
Garnish: Float 3 coffee beans
Method: Pour Fernet Branca into frozen glass, swirl round and discard. Muddle raisins with Cognac in base of shaker. Add rest of ingredients to shaker, shake with ice and fine strain into glass.

1	shot(s)	Fernet Branca
25		Raisins
2	shot(s)	Rémy Martin Cognac
¼	shot(s)	Maple syrup
1	barspoon	Kahlúa coffee liqueur
1½	shot(s)	Chilled water

Origin: I adapted this from Dr Zeus (also in this guide), a cocktail created by Adam Ennis in 2001 at Isola, London, England.
Comment: Very rich in flavour, but delightfully so.

ZHIVAGO MARTINI

Glass: Martini
Garnish: Apple slice in rim
Method: Shake all ingredients with ice and fine strain into chilled glass.

1½	shot(s)	Stoli Vanil
½	shot(s)	Buffalo Trace Bourbon
½	shot(s)	Sourz Sour Apple liqueur
1	shot(s)	Freshly squeezed lime juice
¾	shot(s)	Sugar (gomme) syrup

Origin: Created in 2002 by Alex Kammerling.
Comment: Perfectly balanced sweet and sour – sweet apple, vanilla and Bourbon balanced by lime juice.

ZINGY GINGER MARTINI

Glass: Martini
Garnish: Lemon twist
Method: Vigorously shake all ingredients with ice and strain into glass.

2¹/₂	shot(s)	Absolut Citron vodka
¹/₃	shot(s)	Freshly squeezed lemon juice
¹/₃	shot(s)	Belvoir organic ginger cordial
³/₄	shot(s)	Chilled water

Origin: Created in 2001 by Reece Clark at Hush Up, London, England.
Comment: It sure is both zingy and gingery.

ZIPPERHEAD

Glass: Sling
Garnish: Blackberry, raspberry and blackcurrant
Method: Shake first two ingredients with ice and strain into ice-filled glass, then top up with lemonade.

1	shot(s)	Chambord black raspberry liqueur
2	shot(s)	Absolut vodka
Top up with		Lemonade / 7-Up

Comment: Fizzy raspberries.

ZOOM UPDATED

●●●●◐

Glass: Martini
Method: Shake ingredients with ice and strain into glass.

2¹/₂	shot(s)	Rémy Martin Cognac
3	spoon	Runny honey
1	shot(s)	Double (heavy) cream
1	shot(s)	Milk

Variant: Base on other spirits such as gin, rum or whiskey. **Variant:** Add ¹/₄ shot of crème de cacao for a chocolate finish.
Origin: A classics (retro) drink, the origins of which are lost in time.
Comment: Cognac smoothed with honey and softened with milk & cream.

ZUB-WAY UPDATED

●●●●◐○

Glass: Collins
Garnish: Three raspberries
Method: Muddle raspberries and watermelon in base of shaker. Add other ingredients; shake with ice and strain into ice-filled glass.

12	fresh	Raspberries
2	cups	Diced watermelon
2¹/₂	shot(s)	Zubrówka (Bison grass) vodka
¹/₂	shot(s)	Sugar (gomme) syrup

Origin: Created by Jamie Terrell in 1999.
Comment: Few ingredients, but loads of flavour.

ZUBROWKA NO. 6

Glass: Collins
Garnish: Cucumber, mint & seasonal fruits
Method: Pour first three ingredients into ice-filled glass, top up with lemonade.

1¹/₂	shot(s)	Zubrówka (Bison grass) vodka
1	shot(s)	Pimms No.6 Vodka Cup
1	shot(s)	Passion fruit purée
Top up with		Lemonade / 7-Up

Origin: Created by Jamie Terrell in 1999.
Comment: Pimms with passion.

ZOMBIE

●●●●○

UPDATED

Glass: Hurricane
Garnish: Pineapple wedge
Method: Shake first nine ingredients with ice and strain into glass filled with crushed ice. Float overproof rum on surface of drink.

³/₄	shot(s)	Havana Club light rum
³/₄	shot(s)	Pusser's Navy rum
³/₄	shot(s)	Mount Gay Eclipse gold rum
¹/₂	shot(s)	Bols apricot brandy
¹/₂	shot(s)	Grand Marnier liqueur
2¹/₂	shot(s)	Freshly squeezed orange juice
2¹/₂	shot(s)	Pressed pineapple juice
1	shot(s)	Freshly squeezed lime juice
¹/₂	shot(s)	Grenadine syrup
¹/₂	shot(s)	Wray & Nephew overproof rum

Origin: The name Zombie comes from the West African Congo word for a snake god used in voodoo – later a force which reanimates the dead (as in Night of the Living Zombies). This cocktail is thought to have been created by Don the Beachcomber at his Beachcomber restaurant in Hollywood. Charles H Baker claimed that a man named Christopher Clark invented a Zombie cocktail in 1935 after returning from Haiti. Joseph Lanza claims that a Zombie cocktail debuted at the 1939 World's Fair in Flushing, New York. Whatever the truth of the matter, this derives from Don the Beachcomber's recipe.
In his book 'The Fine Art of Mixing Drinks, David Embury describes the Zombie as the "grandfather of all pixies, and great-uncle to the gremlins".
Comment: A heady mix of four different rums with pineapple, orange, lime and grenadine. Trader Vic's menu describes this drink as "a real dirty stinker", but then Don and Vic were rivals.

ABA PISCO®

Pisco is the national drink of Chile. ABA Pisco is distilled using small copper pot stills from wine fermented from 100% Alexandria, a very aromatic Muscat grape. Pisco ABA is aged in oak barrels for three months and, unusually, is charcoal filtered to produce a smooth crystal clear spirit.

ABA Pisco is made by the Aguirre family using methods passed from father to son over generations living in the Elqui Valley. The family's property lies in the heart of this valley, an area recognised as producing the best grapes for Pisco production. Their distillery is called Fundo San Juan El Arenal, a name that means 'like a place of sand', referring to the local soil, which with the all year round sun and cool Andean evenings is crucial for producing grapes of the quality required for ABA Pisco.

ABA Pisco has a surprisingly smooth palate for a 40% spirit. This clear Pisco is also unexpectedly honeyed and delicately flavoured with hints of violet, rose, orange zest, jasmine and toasted cinnamon bagel.

Web: www.DrinksDispensary.com **Producer:** ABA LTDA., Santiago, Chile. **UK distributor:** Coe Vintners, Ilford, Essex. **Tel:** 020 8551 4966. **Email:** enquiries@coevintners.com

RECOMMENDED INGREDIENTS

In this, the fourth UK edition of Sauce Guide to Cocktails, I'd once again like to extend my thanks to the sponsoring brands that have helped make this publication possible. They were invited to do so due to the quality of their products and the support they've given to cocktail culture. For these reasons we are pleased to be listing them by name in our recipes, thus providing you with a better idea of the best ingredients to use in each drink. Believe me, the quality of ingredients used dramatically affects the finished cocktail.

In days gone by, and unfortunately still in some less quality driven venues, cocktails were made using unbranded / cheaper spirits, flavourless juices and pre-mixes. Happily, the best bars now strive to make the finest cocktails possible and recognise the need for fresh juices and quality ingredients, a fact evidenced by the plethora of premium drinks now displayed on many back-bar shelves. Follows a selection of such brands and their history, trivia and, above all, the best 12 recipes in this guide using each product.

For further information on spirits, liqueurs and fortified wines, please refer to Sauce Guide to Drink & Drinking. This covers categories ranging from absinthe to whiskey, with information on how they're made and how to serve them. It also lists the key brands within each category, their history and includes qualitative tasting notes and grades.

Cheers!
Simon Difford

ABSOLUT CITRON® VODKA

Absolut had long established itself as the original premium fashionable vodka when Absolut Citron was launched. It was an immediate hit, particularly in New York City where it was widely used in the popular Cosmopolitan cocktail. Absolut Citron is of course made using Absolut vodka, every drop of which originates from one source - Åhus, Sweden. Absolut is distilled not once, twice or ten times, but continuously. This is flavoured with extracts of mandarin, orange, lemon, lime and grapefruit.

Absolut Citron has a clean taste of freshly squeezed lemon juice with hints of lemon zest and lemon meringue. Underlying this is the wheatiness of pure grain vodka and a taste reminiscent of Schweppes Bitter Lemon. 40% alc./vol. (80°proof)

Web: www.absolut.com **Producer:** Swedish Wine & Spirits Corporation, Stockholm, Sweden.
UK distributor: Maxxium UK Ltd, Stirling. **Tel:** 01786 430 500.
Email: enquiries@maxxium.com

ABSOLUT KURANT® VODKA

Absolut Kurant comes in the familiar Absolut bottle which artists from Warhol onwards have made iconic. Only the purple livery distinguishes it from the rest of the range. It is of course based on Swedish Absolut vodka and is flavoured with natural extracts of blackcurrant. Blackcurrant, a distant cousin of the grape, is a fragrant dark berry which grows on shrubs that grow up to six feet high.

Absolut Kurant has a distinct character of blackcurrant. A hint of tartness and sweetness is added to the wheaty vodka. 40% alc./vol. (80°proof)

Web: www.absolut.com
Producer: Swedish Wine & Spirits Corporation, Stockholm, Sweden.
UK distributor: Maxxium UK Ltd, Stirling.
Tel: 01786 430 500.
Email: enquiries@maxxium.com

ABSOLUT MANDRIN® VODKA

Absolut Mandrin is easily recognisable due to its clever punt, painted orange to mimic the fruit. Amazingly the first 100,000 bottles produced had to be hand painted. If you have one unopened, keep it – they are collectors pieces. First launched in the US in July 2000, Absolut Mandrin is flavoured with mandarin and orange extracts. In keeping with all Absolut vodkas only natural ingredients are used.

Lightly sharp with hints of mandarin, orange squash, rich orange liqueur and a smidgen of aniseed. Perfumed orange squash finish. 40% alc./vol. (80°proof)

Web: www.absolut.com **Producer:** Swedish Wine & Spirits Corporation, Stockholm, Sweden.
UK distributor: Maxxium UK Ltd, Stirling. **Tel:** 01786 430 500.
Email: enquiries@maxxium.com

ABSOLUT VANILIA®

This, the latest of the Absolut family of flavours, was launched in the USA, Absolut's main market, early in 2003.

The Swedes have something of a reputation for design and Absolut's subtle variations on their iconic bottle seem to get better with every release. With its silver-white almost space-like bottle, Absolut Vanilia does not disappoint and presents a striking image on any back bar.

Absolut Vanilia is flavoured with vanilla from Madagascar and is much less sweet and more complex than other vanilla vodkas, with no added sugar. Pleasing peppery vodka notes precede hints of butterscotch, white and dark chocolate. Absolut Vanilia adds a wonderful vanilla, almost confectionery flavour to cocktails.

Web: www.absolut.com **Producer:** Swedish Wine & Spirits Corporation, Stockholm, Sweden.
UK distributor: Maxxium UK Ltd, Stirling. **Tel:** 01786 430 500.
Email: enquiries@maxxium.com

ABSOLUT® VODKA

In 1879, Lars Olsson Smith introduced a vodka called 'Absolut rent bränvin,' which translates as 'Absolutely pure vodka'. After Lars Olsson's death the brand enjoyed little success under the ownership of the Swedish state liquor monopoly. Then in 1979, the brand's centenary, the bottle was redesigned in the style of an old Swedish medicine bottle. The name 'Absolute Pure Vodka' was shortened to Absolut (the original Swedish spelling). The slogan 'Country of Sweden' was added, as was the silver medallion with an image of Lars Olsson Smith. These changes made it a major hit. Absolut is produced in the small southern Swedish town of Åhus using winter wheat from the Skåne region of southern Sweden. Unlike many other vodkas, Absolut does not require or undergo any charcoal filtration or any other form of chemical filtration.

Lightly peppery hints with light bready and malty notes, a slight hint of dried fruit and a caramelised sweetness. Absolut is probably more identified with cocktails than any other vodka brand. 40% alc./vol. (80°proof)

Web: www.absolutvodka.com **Producer:** Swedish Wine & Spirits Corporation, Stockholm, Sweden. **UK distributor:** Maxxium UK Ltd, Stirling, Scotland. **Tel:** 01786 430 500 **Email:** enquiries@maxxium.com

ANGOSTURA AROMATIC BITTERS®

These famous bitters were first made in 1824 by the German Surgeon-General of a military hospital in the town of Angostura, Venezuela, to help treat stomach disorders and indigestion. In 1875, due to unrest in Venezuela, production was moved to Trinidad. It was here that the laid-back Caribbean attitude affected Angostura's packaging. One day a new batch of labels was ordered and a simple mistake led to them being too big for the bottles. The error was spotted in time but everyone thought somebody else would deal with the problem. No one did, so they simply stuck the labels on the bottles intending to fix the next batch. No one quite got round to it and the oversized label became a trademark of the brand.

One of the smallest bottles on any bar, but packed with flavour. Turkish coffee, jasmine, dried mint, fruit poached with cloves and cinnamon, cherry with orange and lemon zest – a dash of Angostura adds that little something to bring cocktails to life. 44.7% alc./vol. (89.4°proof)

Web. www.in-the-spirit.co.uk **Producer:** Angostura Ltd, Laventille, Port of Spain, Trinidad, W. Indies. **UK distributor:** First Drinks Brands, Western Docks, Southampton. **Tel:** 02380 312 000 **Email:** enquires@first-drinks-brands.co.uk

APPLETON ESTATE V/X® JAMAICA RUM

Appleton Estate V/X Jamaica Rum is the flagship brand of the Appleton Estate Jamaica Rum family. This full-bodied, medium sweet rum is a perfect example of the famous estate rums for which Appleton is renowned.

An exceptional blend of several rums of varying ages with an average age of between five and ten years, Appleton Estate V/X Jamaica rum boasts a warm golden colour, a rich aroma and flavourful taste.

Smooth and mellow, Appleton Estate V/X Jamaica Rum can be enjoyed in sophisticated rum cocktails, blended long drinks with your favourite mixer.

40% alc./vol. (80°proof)

Web: www.rum.co.uk
Producer: J.Wray & Nephew Ltd, Kingston, Jamaica.
UK distributor: J. Wray & Nephew (UK) Ltd, 3rd Floor, 52-54 Southwark Street, London, SE1 1UN.
Tel: 020 7378 8858
Email: info@rum.co.uk

BAILEYS® IRISH CREAM LIQUEUR

Baileys is a unique blend of ingredients using Irish whiskey, fresh cream, and the finest spirits. The result is a warm sensuous experience which is enjoyed by 14 million consumers in the UK, making it one of the best-known spirit drinks of modern times. Baileys is only produced at a plant in Dublin which receives daily deliveries of fresh Irish cream from its herd of 40,000 cows. The complex and indulgent flavours of Baileys can add great depth to food and cocktail recipes. This versatile drink is most often paired with coffee and desserts for great everyday treats. Baileys appeals to all the senses, especially taste, which creates its sensual uniqueness, leaving people everywhere agreeing that nothing else is quite the same. If serving neat, serve chilled over ice. Enjoy!

Baileys is a complex blend of flavours and impacts and has a creamy, smooth and original palate whilst retaining control. Its flavour profile includes dark chocolate, espresso hints and a touch of nuttiness. 17% alc./vol.(34° proof)

Web: www.baileys.com **Producer:** R&A Bailey, Dublin, Ireland.
UK distributor: Diageo, Lakeside Drive, London.
Tel: 020 8965 7700 **Email:** info@diageouk.com

BÉNÉDICTINE D.O.M.® LIQUEUR

Bénédictine is believed to have been first formulated in 1510 by Dom Bernardo Vincelli, a Bénédictine monk at the Abbey of Fécamp, as an elixir. The Abbey was destroyed during the French Revolution but in 1863 a local merchant, Alexandre Le Grand, found the recipe and reformulated it to create Bénédictine. The initials D.O.M. on the label stand for Deo Optimo Maximo, which means 'To God, most good, most great'.

Bénédictine is based on 27 different herbs and spices including hyssop, aloe, cinnamon, génépi, cloves, nutmeg, myrrh, pine, tea, thyme, vanilla and honey, along with saffron to give the amber hue. Four different preparations are produced from these herbs, three by distillation and one by maceration. These are aged independently before being blended and left to marry and further age. The whole process takes some two years.

Bénédictine has a silky palate with honeyed, lightly spiced notes of saffron, ginger, cloves and some citrus zestiness, plus a hint of coffee and fudge.

Web: www.benedictine.fr **Producer:** Distillerie Bénédictine SA (Bacardi-Martini), Fécamp, Normandy, France.
UK distributor: First Drinks Brands, Southampton.
Tel: 02380 312 000 **Email:** enquiries@first-drinks-brands.co.uk

BOLS® APRICOT BRANDY

Apricot Brandy is sometimes also known as 'apry'. It is a liqueur produced by infusing apricots in selected Cognacs and flavouring with various herbs to bring out the best flavour and aroma of the apricots. Enriched with a hint of almond, this amber coloured liqueur is one of Bols most popular liqueurs.

With a mild aroma of juicy apricots this distinctively flavoured liqueur is suited to being used in a variety of different cocktails. The light clean taste features apricot with a hint of Cognac and almond. 24% alc./vol. (48°proof)

web: www.bols.com
Producer: Bols Royal Distilleries, Zoetermeer, The Netherlands.
UK distributor: Maxxium UK Ltd, Stirling, Scotland.
Tel: 01786 430 500
Email: enquiries@maxxium.com

BOLS® BLACKBERRY LIQUEUR

The Latin words 'Semper Idem' inscribed on the coat of arms of the Bols family literally translate as 'always the same'. For the distillers at Bols this motto represents their goal to produce liqueurs of a consistently high quality. It is to that end that they apply their years of experience and knowledge.

Some cocktail recipe books state 'crème de mûre' instead of 'blackberry liqueur'. This comes from 'mûre', the French for blackberry, and 'crème' from the French phrase 'crème de la crème', meaning 'best of the best'. In such cases you can use Bols Blackberry liqueur which is made from the finest fresh blackberries.

The intense blackberry flavour of this rich liqueur adds a concentrated fruit flavour to cocktails and can be used to boost the flavour when using fresh fruit in a drink.

Web: www.bols.com Producer: Bols Royal Distilleries, Zoetermeer, The Netherlands. UK distributor: Maxxium UK Ltd, Stirling, Scotland.
Tel: 01786 430 500 Email: enquiries@maxxium.com

BOLS BLUE® CURAÇAO

This vivid blue curaçao liqueur is probably the best known of the Bols range. Part of Remy Cointreau, Bols Royal Distilleries originated from a firm started in 1575 by a Dutchman called Lucas Bols. Prevented from distilling within the city walls due to the fire risk, Lucas distilled from a wooden shed outside Amsterdam. Today Bols is one of the largest liqueur producers in the world.
Bols Blue is distilled from a blend of predominantly natural products from around the world – herbs, sweet red oranges, the characteristically flavourful bitter Curaçao oranges and the rare Kinnow oranges. This gives Bols Blue a fresh, yet complex orange scent and taste.

Bols Blue is frequently used by bartenders due to its distinctive deep blue colour and taste which features orange squash and zest with a hint of spice. 21% alc./vol. (42°proof)

Web: www.bols.com Producer: Bols Royal Distilleries, Zoetermeer, The Netherlands. UK distributor: Maxxium UK Ltd, Stirling, Scotland.
Tel: 01786 430 500 Email: enquiries@maxxium.com

BOLS® CHERRY BRANDY LIQUEUR

This richly flavoured liqueur is made from the juice of ripe, dark red cherries. Crushing the kernels while pressing the cherries enhances almond notes in the cherry juice and is very evident in the finished liqueur. Extracts of various carefully selected herbs and spices such as cinnamon and cloves produce a well-balanced liqueur.
With its luscious cherry flavour and hints of almond and spice, this traditional liqueur is a versatile mixer.
24% alc./vol. (48°proof)

Web: www.bols.com
Producer: Bols Royal Distilleries, Zoetermeer, The Netherlands.
UK distributor: Maxxium UK Ltd, Stirling, Scotland.
Tel: 01786 430 500
Email: enquiries@maxxium.com

BOLS® CREME DE BANANE

The French term 'crème de' indicates that one particular flavour predominates in the liqueur; it does not imply that the liqueur contains cream. Many fruit liqueurs are described as 'crème de' followed by the name of a fruit. This refers to the liqueur's quality, as in the phrase 'crème de la crème'. Therefore crème de banane is a banana flavoured liqueur made by infusion and maceration of the fruit in neutral spirit.
Bols Crème de Banane is a yellow liqueur with the flavour of sun-ripened bananas, enhanced with a touch of soft vanilla and a hint of almond. Extracts of various carefully selected herbs and spices give this well-balanced liqueur its special taste.

Like many of the liqueurs in the Bols range, Crème de Bananes is extremely mixable and is found in a plethora of cocktails that use its exotic ripe banana flavour.
17% alc./vol. (34°proof)

Web: www.bols.com **Producer:** Bols Royal Distilleries, Zoetermeer, The Netherlands. **UK distributor:** Maxxium UK Ltd, Stirling, Scotland.
Tel: 01786 430 500 **Email:** enquiries@maxxium.com

BOLS® BROWN CRÈME DE CACAO

The finest roasted cacao beans are used to prepare Bols Brown crème de cacao. The cacao seeds are first broken open and then percolated. Various herbs are added to give the liqueur its own distinctive flavour. Please note that 'brown crème de cacao' liqueurs are sometimes alternatively named 'dark crème de cacao'.

Bols Crème de Cacao is perfect for adding a rich chocolate flavour to any cocktail. Choose between the lighter, more delicately flavoured white or this rich dark version.
24% alc./vol. (48°proof)

Web: www.bols.com
Producer: Bols Royal Distilleries, Zoetermeer, The Netherlands.
UK distributor: Maxxium UK Ltd, Stirling, Scotland.
Tel: 01786 430 500
Email: enquiries@maxxium.com

BOLS® RASPBERRY LIQUEUR

The French word for raspberry is 'framboise', so it is common to find cocktail recipe books referring to 'crème de framboise' for a raspberry liqueur. Bols Raspberry liqueur was introduced this year to answer the needs of modern bartenders for a quality liqueur based on the berry fruit most often used in their drinks.

Interestingly, the raspberry is related to the rose and its intense flavour lends itself to use in cocktails. To use raspberries as a cocktail ingredient, either purée the fruit in a blender or muddle them in the base of the shaker (or the glass the cocktail is to be served in). To further enhance the flavour add a splash of Bols Raspberry liqueur.

This liqueur delivers a rich raspberry flavour. The sugar content is well balanced to bring out and enhance the natural flavours of the fruit.

Web: www.bols.com **Producer:** Bols Royal Distilleries, Zoetermeer, The Netherlands.
UK distributor: Maxxium UK Ltd, Stirling, Scotland.
Tel: 01786 430 500 **Email:** enquiries@maxxium.com

BOLS® STRAWBERRY LIQUEUR

Bols are one of the largest and oldest producers of fine spirits and liqueurs in the world. Some of them even go back to the year 1575. However, this strawberry liqueur is a relatively new addition to the Bols range. It is a distillate of refreshing citrus fruit and real strawberry juice. The French word for strawberry is 'fraise' and cocktail recipes often call for the use of crème de fraise, or strawberry liqueur. Bols Strawberry liqueur is ideal for use in any recipe which calls for crème de fraise.

This liqueur has a rich ripe strawberry flavour with light hints of citrus fruit. It is great served chilled, in a cocktail, over strawberries or in a fruit salad. 17% alc./vol. (34°proof)

Web: www.bols.com
Producer: Bols Royal Distilleries, Zoetermeer, The Netherlands.
UK distributor: Maxxium UK Ltd, Stirling, Scotland.
Tel: 01786 430 500
Email: enquiries@maxxium.com

BOLS® WHITE CRÈME DE CACAO

A number of recipes require the chocolate flavour of crème de cacao but without the dark brown colour. In order to give this liqueur the taste without the dark colour, Bols extract the flavour of the finest roasted cacao beans by means of distillation instead of percolation. This process also gives Bols White crème de cacao a lighter flavour than Bols Brown crème de cacao. Bols Crème de Cacao is perfect for adding a rich chocolate flavour to any cocktail. Choose between this lighter, more delicately flavoured white or the rich dark version.
24% alc./vol. (48°proof)

Web: www.bols.com
Producer: Bols Royal Distilleries, Zoetermeer, The Netherlands.
UK distributor: Maxxium UK Ltd, Stirling, Scotland.
Tel: 01786 430 500
Email: enquiries@maxxium.com

BUFFALO TRACE® BOURBON

For thousands of years wild buffalo carved their way across the wilderness of America, leaving huge paths in their wake. Early pioneers used these paths, or traces as they were later known, on their adventure westward to discover new lands. The largest of these traces, the Great Buffalo Trace, is situated north of the Kentucky River and it is here, where the trace crossed the river, that a settlement was established and distillation commenced in 1787. In 1857 a modern distillery was built on the site, the first to incorporate steam power and today, on this same site, stands Buffalo Trace Distillery, a family owned business producing over 25 different American whiskeys.

Buffalo Trace Kentucky Straight Bourbon Whiskey, the flagship whiskey of the distillery is made in batches of just 20-25 barrels using Indiana corn, rye and malted barley. It is laid down to age for 9-11 years, slowly maturing and developing the characteristics of a superb bourbon.

Jim Murray describes Buffalo Trace as 'one of the world's great whiskeys'. It has a light palate with well-integrated flavours including vanilla, ginger, clove, chocolate, espresso coffee, mint, aniseed and honey. 45% alc/vol.(90°proof)

Web: www.buffalotrace.com **Producer:** Buffalo Trace Distillery, Frankfort, Kentucky, USA. **UK distributor:** InSpirit Brands, London. **Tel:** 020 7377 9457 **Email:** info@inspiritbrands.com

CAMPARI®

Renowned for its distinctive, bitter-sweet taste and vivid red colour, Campari was created in 1860 by Gaspare Campari from a secret recipe of herbs, plants and fruit which remains unchanged to this day.

Available in over 190 countries world-wide, Campari reflects a world of passion, prestige and transgression.

Campari may be enjoyed at whatever time of day and a few fundamentals of preparation should always be rigorously followed for it to be appreciated at its fullest:

•Campari must always be served chilled to enhance its balanced taste.

•The bottle must be kept from direct sunlight and heat, ideally in a refrigerator.

•Campari must never be served with lemon but can be garnished with a slice or peel of orange.

To fully appreciate the unique taste of Campari as a long drink – why not try lime cordial & tonic, orange or grapefruit juice – always serve a 50ml measure.

Campari can also be enjoyed in a variety of exciting cocktails.

Web: www.campari.com **Producer:** Campari SpA, Milan, Italy. **UK distributor:** FIOR Brands Ltd, Stirling, Scotland. **Tel:** 01786 406 360 **Email:** info@fiorbrands.co.uk

CHAMBORD® BLACK RASPBERRY LIQUEUR

Chambord Liqueur Royale de France, to use its full name, is believed to have been created in the time of Louis XIV, when hunting parties visited Chambord, the largest chateau in the French Loire Valley. It is a rich Framboise-style liqueur made from small black raspberries and herbs combined with honey and high quality neutral alcohol. Chambord is very popular in the United States where it is often mixed as a Kir-like drink with Champagne. Its distinctive orb shaped bottle is easily recognised and is a 'must stock' in most cocktail bars. Although there are other raspberry liqueurs, it is Chambord that graces our shelves and those of some of the world's most noted cocktail bars.

Chambord's rich flavour is ideally suited to a variety of cocktail recipes and has a taste that includes: raspberry fool, blackcurrant jam, cherry jam, honeyed vanilla, sloe and damson with a hint of raisins and stewed prunes. 16.5% alc./vol. (33°proof)

Web: www.chambordonline.com **Producer:** Chambord et Cie, Chambord, France. **UK distributor:** Malcolm Cowen Ltd, London. **Tel:** 020 8965 1937. **Email:**info@cowen.co.uk

CHARTREUSE VERTE® (GREEN)

Chartreuse was formulated in 1764 by Brother Antoine, a monk in a silent Carthusian order, when he completed the task of combining 130 different herbs from around the world with health giving and aromatic properties to create the 'Herbal Elixir Of The Grand Chartreuse'. The monks lived off the proceeds of selling the elixir, which quickly gained a reputation for its flavour and curing properties.

Today monks of the same Carthusian order still make Chartreuse to the same recipe of entirely natural ingredients. Chartreuse's vivid colour comes only from the plants used in its production, a process involving four distillations, three macerations and maturing in oak casks, many of which are more than 100 years old.

The challenging and distinctive flavour of Chartreuse is one you either like, hate or grow to adore. Dominant flavours in this complex liqueur include: lemon, mint, aniseed, ginger and apple – and these are the flavours with which it's best mixed. 55% alc./vol (110°proof)

Web. www.chartreuse.fr **Producer:** Chartreuse Diffusion, Voiron, France. **UK distributor:** John E Fells & Sons, Berkhamsted. **Tel:** 01442 870 900 **Email:** info@fells.co.uk

CINZANO® EXTRA DRY VERMOUTH

Over 250 years and world recognition have made Cinzano a cult beverage for today's root conscious consumer. Remarkably rich in culture, full of historical soul yet still as contemporary on the lips of the world's youth as it was 200 years ago. Graceful, moody, ambitious, intellectual, low key but by no means passive, Cinzano makes a very modern statement not to be taken lightly. All the richness of Italian culture with a delightful modern twist. From the vineyards surrounding Turin to the chic lounge-bars of Manhattan or Tokyo, Cinzano the 'original' Vermouth with universal appeal has been adopted by connoisseurs across the globe.

Created in 1757 in Italy according to a traditional method that is still used today, Cinzano Extra Dry is a unique blend of selected high quality wines, herbs and spices appreciated worldwide for its delicate bouquet and sophisticated crispy taste.

Enjoy Cinzano Extra Dry neat over ice, in creative cocktails or as a refreshing long drink with one of your favourite mixers such as lemonade, tonic or soda water.

Web: www.campari.com **Producer:** Francesco Cinzano & C.ia S.p.A – Milano-Italy. **UK distributor:** Fior Brands Ltd, Stirling, Scotland. **Tel:** 01786 406 360 **Email:** info@fiorbrands.co.uk

CINZANO® ROSSO VERMOUTH

1757. In the back of their herbal store, Giovanni Giacomo Cinzano and his partner Carlo Stefano created a vermouth that was to become famous for its delicate and complex bouquet. Turin – the herbal epicentre at the time – had given birth to a wine enriched with herbs from the local hillsides. Graceful, refined and poetic, this was and still is one of the most successful reflections of Italian culture. This ambitious and desirable drink, which conjures up scenes of the romantic Italian lifestyle, has gained world popularity, and is today a true statement of timeless authenticity and originality.

Made according to a traditional method that is still used today, Cinzano Rosso is a sweet red vermouth made with a unique blend of selected high quality wines and 35 herbs and spices.

Cinzano Rosso has a rich, round and sweetly aromatic flavour and can be drunk as a traditional aperitif or used as an ingredient of classic or modern cocktails.

Web: www.campari.com **Producer:** Francesco Cinzano & C.ia S.p.A – Milano-Italy. **UK distributor:** Fior Brands Ltd, Stirling, Scotland. **Tel:** 01786 406 360 **Email:** info@fiorbrands.co.uk

COINTREAU®

The distilling firm of Cointreau was started in 1849 by two brothers, Adolphe and Edouard-Jean Cointreau, who were confectioners in Angers. The liqueur we know today was created by Edouard Cointreau, the son of Edouard-Jean, and first marketed in the 1870s. Cointreau should not be confused with other liqueurs labelled mere 'triple secs'. This term is a confusing one as it means 'triple dry' and they tend to be very sweet. Where cocktail recipes call for the use of triple sec, we recommend Cointreau, which is made with the peel of bitter oranges from the Caribbean, sweet orange peel from Spain, neutral alcohol, sugar and water. A versatile cocktail ingredient, Cointreau can also be served straight over ice or mixed with fruit juices, tonic or lemonade.

The mainstay of many classic recipes, Cointreau has a luscious, ripe taste featuring bitter orange, zesty, citrus hints, a splash of orange juice and a hint of spice. 40% alc./vol. (80°proof)

Web: www.cointreau.com **Producer:** Remy Cointreau, Angers, France. **UK distributor:** Maxxium UK Ltd, Stirling, Scotland. **Tel:** 01786 430 500 **Email:** enquiries@maxxium.com

DISARONNO ORIGINALE® AMARETTO

Disaronno is said to have been first created in 1525 by a beautiful young woman for Bernardino Luini, an artist from Leonardo da Vinci's school. Luini used her as a model for his portrait of the Madonna, during which time they fell in love. The portrait can still be viewed in the Chapel of Santa Maria delle Grazie, in Saronno. As a token of her love the model presented the artist with a bottle of her home made liqueur which is now known as Amaretto, and remains unchanged to this day. Disaronno is the original and remains the biggest selling Amaretto with more than 70% of the worldwide market and a gold medal at the IWSC and a trophy for best International Liqueur 2003. It is an essential feature of any well stocked bar.

The rich flavours found in Disaronno include marzipan, macaroon, Madeira, Battenberg cake and vanilla. It also has lemon zestyness, almond, apricot and nutty kernel hinds that help retain its wonderful balance. 28% abv./vol. (56°proof)

Web: www.disaronno.com or www.in-the-spirit.co.uk **Producer:** Illva Saronno Spa, Saronno, Italy. **UK distributor:** First Drinks Brands, Western Docks, Southampton. **Tel:** 02380 312 000 **Email:** enquires@first-drinks-brands.co.uk

THE FAMOUS GROUSE® SCOTCH

Matthew Gloag, a retailer in Perth, developed his blend of Scotch to appeal to the growing numbers of sporting gentlemen travelling to the North East Highlands to participate in hunting, shooting and fishing. During 1896, he chose the fitting name 'Grouse Brand' and his daughter sketched the Red Grouse label that became its trademark. The popularity the new whisky enjoyed meant that people soon referred it as The Famous Grouse. The Famous Grouse is based on malts such as The Macallan and Highland Park which are married with grain whiskies in oak casks for six months prior to bottling. Because Grouse is married at a lower strength than most other whiskies it does not require heavy filtration prior to bottling. This helps retain flavour and fatty acids which help give a smooth mouthfeel to the whisky.

The Famous Grouse is Scotland's best selling whisky. It is malty, peaty, yet light with flavours of bitter chocolate, cocoa, toffee apple, fruit cake and subtle Sherry. 40% alc./vol. (80°proof)

Web: www.famousgrouse.com **Producer:** Highland Distillers Plc, West Kinfauns, Perth, Scotland. **UK distributor:** Maxxium Brands, Stirling. **Tel:** 01786 430 500. **Email:** enquiries@maxxium.com

FINLANDIA® CRANBERRY VODKA

Finland is famous not only for its 600,000 saunas but also for its pollution free countryside. Finns are justly proud of their clean, uncontaminated and sparsely populated country and it's this natural purity that lies at the heart of the Finlandia brand. Finlandia is made from Finnish six-row barley using continuous stills. The water used is taken from a natural spring, which is so clean that no purification is required. This purity of water and distillation also negates the need to charcoal filter the finished vodka, a practice common in other brands.

Launched in the autumn of 1994, Finlandia Cranberry vodka is based on Finlandia's clean tasting vodka. Originally red coloured to emphasise its flavour and distinguish it from the original vodka, in 2002 new contemporary packaging was introduced and with it came a colourless cranberry vodka with a much improved flavour.

Cranberry is one of the most used juices in cocktail making and so it follows that cranberry flavoured vodka is a very versatile mixer. Complex cranberry flavour with hints of peach and honeyed cherries. 40% alc./vol. (80°proof)

Web: www.finlandia-vodka.com **Producer:** Primalco Ltd, Helsinki, Finland. **UK distributor:** Bacardi-Martini Ltd **Tel:** 02380 635 252 **Email:** see finlandia-vodka.com

FINLANDIA® LIME VODKA

Finlandia vodka has something of a reputation for its clean flavour. This neutral base spirit is flavoured with essential lime oils to produce Finlandia Lime vodka.

The white reindeer prominently shown on the bottle originate from a Finnish legend about a beautiful young girl transformed into a fearsome white reindeer by a spell. The girl's boyfriend receives a fatal wound trying to kill the reindeer but his blood breaks the spell and the reindeer becomes a girl again. The couple are said to have fallen into eternal sleep. Thus many Finns believe it is lucky to see the sun, the moon and a white reindeer at once.

Finlandia lime has a perky lime/lemon zest flavour with hints of lemon sherbet, lemon drops, barley notes and some vodka spice. Being crystal clear adds to its versatility as a mixer. 40% alc./vol. (80°proof)

Web. www.finlandia-vodka.com **Producer:** Primalco Ltd, Helsinki, Finland. **UK distributor:** Bacardi-Martini Ltd. **Tel:** 02380 635 252 **Email:** see finlandia-vodka.com

FRANGELICO® HAZELNUT LIQUEUR

This Italian liqueur is produced from berries, herbs and hazelnuts. It is said to be named after a monk named Fra Angelico who lived as a hermit in the Piedmont area in the 17th century. His knowledge and understanding of nature inspired him to produce many fine foods and unique drinks, including the drink that bears his name. Frangelico uses the region's wild hazelnuts infused with herbs and berries. The brand was officially launched in the USA in 1978 and is now the world's third largest selling Italian liqueur. Frangelico is instantly recognisable by its eye-catching monk-shaped bottle and rope tie.

Frangelico has a rich and balanced flavour, now essential to many popular cocktails. The taste is complex, and as well as the obvious hazelnut, includes cheesecake base, butter and hints of espresso, citrus and vanilla. 24% alc./vol. (48°proof)

Web: www.frangelico.com **Producer:** Barbero 1981 S.p.A. (Cantrell & Cochrane), Canale D'Alba, Italy. **UK distributor:** Inspirit Brands, London. **Tel:** 020 7377 9457 **Email:** Info@inspiritbrands.com

GALLIANO®

Galliano is a vibrant, golden, vanilla flavoured liqueur from Italy, easily recognised by its distinctive, tall fluted bottle, inspired by Roman columns. Invented in 1896, Galliano is made from over 30 ingredients including star anise, lavender, ginger and vanilla.

A noted cocktail ingredient, Galliano's signature drink is the Harvey Wallbanger. Apparently, Harvey was a surfer at Manhattan Beach, California, and his favourite drink was a Screwdriver with added Galliano. One day in the late 60s, while celebrating winning a surfing competition, he staggered from bar to bar, banging his surf board on the walls and so the cocktail was born. The versatility of Galliano ensures that it can be enjoyed in cocktails as a long drink and works particularly well as a hot shot with coffee and cream.

The lovely smell of Galliano is reminiscent of a pack of Tic-Tac sweets, while its smooth vanilla taste is complimented by peppermint and spicy with cinnamon, ginger, nutmeg and citrus. 30% alc./vol. (60°proof)

Web: www.galliano.com Producer: Remy Cointreau, Angers, France.
UK distributor: Maxxium UK Ltd, Stirling, Scotland.
Tel: 01786 430 500 Email: enquiries@maxxium.com

GRAND MARNIER® CORDON ROUGE

Grand Marnier is one of the best known and most widely sold premium liqueurs in the world. With a Cognac base, its unique flavour and aroma come from the maceration and distillation of natural, tropical orange peels.

Founded in 1827 by Jean Baptiste Lapostolle, Grand Marnier is still a family-run business today and continues to use traditional production methods and the original Grand Marnier recipe.

Despite its traditional credentials and heritage, Grand Marnier is also recognised as an international, classic brand which enjoys a large and loyal worldwide following, particularly in the United States where cocktail culture began. Following that trend, Grand Marnier has become an essential ingredient for flavoursome, stylish mixed drinks across the increasingly popular cocktail bar scene in the UK.

It is silky rich with a zesty, juicy flavour, good underlying bite of bitter orange and hints of marmalade and Cognac richness at the edges, making it the perfect cocktail partner. A highly mixable spirit, Grand Marnier enhances and adds depth and complexity to premium cocktails and long drinks.

A superb cocktail ingredient which features in many classic and contemporary recipes. 40% alcohol / vol. 80 proof.

Web: www.grand-marnier.com
Producer: Marnier-Lapostolle (Société des Produits), Paris, France
UK Distributor: Fior Brands Ltd Tel: 01786 406 360

HAVANA CLUB® 3YO RUM

Founded in 1878 by Don Jose Arechabala, Havana Club is the best-known brand of Cuban rum and became popular during the late 20s and 30s when many Americans flocked to Cuba to party in Havana. The brand is synonymous with such legendary bars as La Bodeguita del Medio and El Floridita in Havana. It forms the basis of world-famous cocktails such as the Mojito and Daiquiri and has been enjoyed by such luminaries as Ernest Hemingway, Ava Gardner, Sophia Loren, Gary Cooper and Spencer Tracy. It truly embodies the 'Spirit of Cuba'.

Havana Club rum is produced in two Cuban distilleries, one at Santa Cruz del Norte, east of Havana, and the other at Santa Clara. It is distilled using a two column continuous method from Cuban molasses and then aged for three years in ex-Bourbon casks which are recharged prior to each filling. Rich and elegant, with demerara and muscovado sugar balanced by spicy citrus and pineapple freshness, hints of gingerbread, butterscotch and underlying oak. 40% alc./vol. (80°proof)

Web: www.havana-club.com **Producer:** Corporacion Cuba Ron SA, Ciudad de la Habana, Cuba. **UK distributor:** Pernod Ricard UK, Hounslow, Middlesex. **Tel:** 020 8538 4000

JACK DANIEL'S® TENNESSEE WHISKEY

The legendary 'J.D.' or 'Jack' is the creation of Jasper Newton (Jack) Daniel. Jack bought his first still in 1863 at the age of 13 (or thereabouts - although it's accepted that Jack was born in September, his exact birth date is unknown). Jack died on 8th October 1911, aged 61, from an infection that resulted from breaking a toe kicking his safe in a fit of temper. He left the distillery to his nephew, Lemuel Motlow, and Lem's name still features as 'proprietor' on the bottom of the label.
Jack Daniel's is a Tennessee whiskey, not a Bourbon. After distillation, the spirit which will become Jack Daniel's is dripped through ten feet of densely packed hard sugar maple charcoal. The 'charcoal mellowed' spirit is then aged in new white charred oak barrels for over four years before being reduced to bottling strength using cave spring water.

This charcoal mellowed whiskey has buttery corn on the cob notes with vanilla, gingerbread and caffè latte flavours. 40% alc./vol. (80°proof)

Web: www.jackdaniels.com **Producer:** Jack Daniel Distillery (Brown-Forman), Lynchburg, Tennessee, USA. **UK distributor:** Bacardi-Martini, Southampton. **Tel:** 02380 318 288

LA FÉE® ABSINTHE

La Fée is made in Paris to a 19th century recipe containing wormwood (Artemisia absinthium) and flavoured with anise, hyssop and other aromatic herbs. It was launched in 2000 by the team responsible for importing the first absinthe into the UK since the outbreak of World War I.

A mark of this brand's authenticity is its endorsement by Marie-Claude Delahaye, writer of many respected books on absinthe and founder of the Absinthe Museum in France. The museum is situated in Auvers-sur-Oise, the village famous for its painters where Vincent van Gogh and his brother, Theo, are buried.

As should be the case in a traditional French absinthe, La Fée turns cloudy with the addition of water. La Fée's bottle is as distinctive as its contents with its label dominated by an illustration of an eye.

La Fée has the flavour profile of a traditional French absinthe. It has clean, fresh and rounded aniseed flavours and well-balanced liquorice, mint, lemon, angelica and rootier notes. 68% alc./vol. (136°proof)

Web: www.eAbsinthe.com **Producer:** Produced in Paris, France for Green Utopia Ltd.
UK Distributor: BBH Spirits, Bayford, Hertfordshire.
Tel: 01992 511 445 **Email:** trade@eAbsinthe.com

MALIBU® COCONUT RUM LIQUEUR

Malibu Caribbean White Rum with Coconut is produced using a special blend of Barbadian white rum. Distilled from the finest molasses, at the West Indies Rum Distillery (est. 1893), the spirit is matured in American oak barrels for between one and two years then blended with sugar and coconut to produce the distinctively flavoured drink we know as Malibu.

First produced in 1980, the instantly recognisable white bottle with its pair of palm trees in front of a setting sun is a must stock for practically every bar. Over the last 23 years, a staggering 300 million bottles of Malibu have been sold worldwide.

Malibu has a subtle balanced coconut flavour with hints of Madeira cake. It is an extremely versatile cocktail ingredient and is also great simply served long with cranberry juice.
21% alc./vol. (42°proof)

Web: www.malibu-rum.com **Producer:** Twelve Islands Shipping Co. Ltd, Brighton, Black Rock, Barbados.
UK distributor: Allied Domecq, Spirits & Wine (UK) Ltd, Horsham, West Sussex , RH12 1ST **Tel:** 01403 222 600
Email: mailbox@balance-spirits.com

MIDORI® MELON LIQUEUR

Midori is flavoured with extracts of honeydew melons and can rightly claim to be the original melon liqueur. Midori's vibrant green colour, light melon taste and great versatility has ensured its demand in bars worldwide. Launched in 1978 in New York's famed Studio 54 nightclub, Midori was shaken within sight of the cast of Saturday Night Fever. That same year, Midori won first prize in the U.S. Bartenders Guild Annual Championship.

The name 'Midori' is Japanese for green and it is owned by Suntory, Japan's leading producer and distributor of alcoholic beverages. Despite its Japanese owner and name, Midori is made in Mexico where there is a plentiful supply of melon-ripening sunshine.

Midori is one of the most noted modern day cocktail ingredients due to its vibrant colour and flavour, being: juicy, luscious, lightly syrupy while retaining freshness, with honeyed melon and a hint of green apple. 20% alc./vol. (40°proof)

Web: www.midoriworld.com **Producer:** Suntory Limited, Japan. **UK distributor:** FIOR Brands Ltd, Stirling, Scotland. **Tel:** 01786 406 360 **Email:** info@fiorbrands.co.uk

MOUNT GAY ECLIPSE® GOLDEN RUM

Mount Gay is believed to be the oldest rum brand name. The distillery has origins dating back to at least 1703 (some say 1663), which makes it the oldest rum distillery in the world. The Mount Gay Rum Estate lies on a ridge in the north-ernmost parish of Barbados (St. Lucy). Originally called Mount Gilboa, the estate was renamed in 1801 to honor the death of Sir John Gay Alleyne, the longstanding manager of the estate (a Mount Alleyne already existed at the time).

Mount Gay rums are distilled from molasses using both continuous, fractional distillation and traditional copper pot stills. These two different distillates are blended together with Barbadian underground spring water before being aged in American white oak barrels which have previously been used to age Bourbon.

Eclipse is a light-bodied rum particularly suited to mixing. Its elegant palate includes cooked fruit, citrus zest, gingerbread, caramel sauce, vanilla custard with hints of butter-scotch garnish. 40% alc./vol. (80°proof)

Web: www.mountgay.com **Producer:** Mount Gay Distilleries Ltd, Exmouth Gap, Brandons St-Michael, Barbados. **UK distributor:** Maxxium UK Ltd, Stirling, Scotland. **Tel:** 01786 430 500 **Email:** enquiries@maxxium.com

OPAL BIANCA® SAMBUCA

In 1999, some ten years after launching his very successful Opal Nera black Sambuca, Alessandro Francoli set out to create the ultimate clear Sambuca. The result - Opal Bianca - is made using the finest natural ingredients including star anise, green anise, elder-berries, elderflowers and lemon peel. It possesses an exceptional smoothness. The modern bottle, designed to compliment the existing packaging of Opal Nera, reflects the fact that this is not just another traditional clear Italian sambuca.

Opal Bianca has a rich aniseed and black liquorice flavour with hints of spicy elderberry and fresh citrus.
38% alc./vol. (76°proof)

Web: www.opalnera.com Producer: Fratelli Francoli S.p.A., Ghemme, Corso Romagnano, Italy. UK distributor: Inspirit Brands, London. Tel: 020 7377 9457
Email: info@inspiritbrands.com

OPAL NERA® BLACK SAMBUCA

In 1989 Alessandro Francoli was on his honeymoon in America, when he took time out to present his company's traditional Italian grappa and Sambucas to a potential buyer. He noticed the interest the buyer showed in a coffee Sambuca, and this dark liqueur set Alessandro thinking. He experimented with different flavours combined with traditional Sambuca and created Opal Nera, a black coloured Sambuca with a hint of lemon. The unique colouring of Opal Nera comes from the rich, purple-blackness of elderber-ries, a key ingredient in all Sambucas, macerating the skins of which lends Opal its seductive and unmistakable colour.

Opal Nera Sambuca is a favourite with many bartenders due to its colour and flavour which includes: aniseed, soft black liquorice, light spice of elderberry and lemon zest. 40% alc./vol. (80°proof)

Web: www.opalnera.com Producer: Fratelli Francoli S.p.A., Ghemme, Corso Romagnano, Italy. UK distributor: Inspirit Brands, London. Tel: 020 7377 9457
Email: info@inspiritbrands.com

PASSOA® PASSION FRUIT LIQUEUR

The passion fruit was first discovered in South America, during the colonisation by Spanish missionaries in the 1500s. They first noticed the amazing flowers of the fruit in the jungle. Nobody knows exactly why it became known as the passion fruit. Was it because the crown-like flower reminded people of the thornbush of Christ's Passion? Or because of its supposed qualities as an aphrodisiac? Passoā is a passion fruit flavoured liqueur launched in the Netherlands in 1986 and is now the second biggest liqueur brand in Holland and the third biggest in Belgium. The matt black Passoā bottle features a brightly coloured tropical motif of palm trees suggesting its tropical fruit taste. While Passoā is widely used in cocktails, it is also great served over ice with two thirds orange or grapefruit juice.

Passoā is a superbly versatile mixer with a flavour profile that boasts balanced passion fruit and grapefruit with hints of cherries and a honeyed, citrus garnish. 20% alc./vol. (40°proof)

Web: www.passoa.com **Producer:** Cointreau, Angers, France. **UK distributor:** Maxxium UK Ltd, Stirling, Scotland. **Tel:** 01786 430 500 **Email:** enquiries@maxxium.com

PERNOD®

Pernod's story starts in 1789 when Dr Pierre Ordinaire prescribed his pain relieving and special reviving 'absinthe elixir' in Switzerland. Ten years later, Major Dubied bought the formula and set up an absinthe factory in Couvet, Switzerland with son-in-law, Henri-Louis Pernod. In 1805, Henri-Louis Pernod established Pernod Fils in Pontarlier, France. The authentic absinthe, the original Pernod was created from a recipe that included 'artemisia absinthium': the plant of absinthe. Pernod quickly gained fame as THE absinthe of Parisian café society. But a prohibitionist propaganda movement sprang up and a massive press campaign blamed absinthe abuse as the cause of socially unacceptable behaviour, insanity, tuberculosis and even murder, eventually leading to a ministerial decree banning it on 7th January 1915. Pernod Fils was forced to close. But by 1920, anise liquors were legalised again, albeit in a more sober form and in its new form Pernod remained popular as ever. The Pernod we enjoy today is an historic blend of 14 herbs including star anise, fennel, mint and coriander.

Serve : One Pernod to five parts mixer. Pernod is served best long with cranberry juice, apple juice or with bitter lemon. 40% alc.vol. (80° proof)

Web: www.pernod.net **Producer:** Pernod Entreprise (Pernod Ricard Group), France. **UK Distributor:** Pernod Ricard UK, Hounslow TW3 1HY. **Tel:** 020 8538 4000

PIPER-HEIDSIECK CUVÉE BRUT®

The Champagne house of Piper-Heidsieck takes its name from its founder, Florens-Louis Heidsieck, who originally moved to Reims to be a cloth merchant but instead discovered his love for wine-making. He started making his own Champagne in 1780 and founded his own house five years later when he had already become an expert at his art, so much so that he was granted the honour of personally presenting his wine to Queen Marie-Antoinette.

Piper-Heidsieck harvest and separately vinify wines from fifty carefully selected vineyards, known as crus. It is this technique which enables Piper-Heidsieck cuvée brut to develop its delicious aromas and flavour. This exceptionally well balanced Champagne is fresh and lively, with light aromas of citrus fruit, apple, pear and spring flowers.

Piper-Heidsieck adds a certain joie de vivre to any cocktail and so in keeping with this we recommend serving in luxurious flutes to enhance the aroma and preserve the wine's sparkle.

Web: www.piper-heidsieck.com **Producer:** Champagne Piper-Heidsieck, Reims, France. **UK distributor:** Maxxium UK Ltd, Stirling. **Tel:** 01786 430 500 **Email:** enquiries@maxxium.com

PLYMOUTH GIN®

Since 1793, Plymouth Gin has been handcrafted in England's oldest working gin distillery - Black Friars in Plymouth. It is still bottled at the unique strength of 41.2% ABV, and is based on a recipe that is over 200 years old. Plymouth Gin, which can only be produced in Plymouth, differs from London gins due to the use of only sweet botanicals. This unique blend of botanicals combine with soft Dartmoor water to result in a wonderfully aromatic and smooth gin. Plymouth has been used by bartenders in cocktails since 1896, when it was first mixed in the original Dry Martini, and is favoured by many top bartenders due to its fresh juniper, lemony bite with deeper liquorice notes.

41.2% alc./vol. (82.4° proof)

Web: www.plymouthgin.com
Producer: Coates & Co Ltd, Plymouth.
UK distributor: Maxxium UK Ltd, Stirling, Scotland.
Tel: 01786 430 500
Email: enquiries@maxxium.com

PLYMOUTH SLOE® GIN LIQUEUR

The making of fruit liqueurs is a long tradition in the British countryside and Plymouth Gin keeps true to a unique 1883 recipe. The sloe berries are slowly and gently steeped in Plymouth Gin, soft Darmoor water and a further secret ingredient. It is an unhurried process and is bottled only when the Head Distiller decides the perfect flavour has been reached. The result is an entirely natural product with no added flavourings or colourings.

This richly flavoured liqueur is initially dry but opens with smooth sweet juicy cherry, raspberry, lightly jammy notes and a complimentary mixture of figs, cloves, set honey and stewed fruits.
26% alc./vol. (52°proof)

Producer: Coates & Co (Plymouth) Ltd, Black Friars Distillery, Plymouth, England. **UK distributor:** Maxxium UK, Stirling. **Tel:** 01786 430 500. **Email:** enquiries@maxxium.com

PUSSER'S® NAVY RUM

The name 'Pusser' comes from the slang pronunciation of purser, the officer in charge of rum rations on board ship. For more than 300 years the British Navy issued a daily 'tot' of Pusser's rum, with a double issue before battle. This tradition, which started in Jamaica in 1665, was finally broken on 31st July 1970, a day now known as 'Black Tot Day'. After the Navy abolished the traditional daily 'tot' of rum, in 1979 the Admiralty approved the re-blending of Pusser's rum by Charles Tobias in the British Virgin Islands to the original Admiralty specifications. A significant donation from the sale of each bottle accrues to the benefit of The Royal Navy Sailor's Fund which was established to compensate the sailors for their lost tot.

In our opinion, the best Navy rum, delivering a rich medley of flavours: molasses, treacle, vanilla, cinnamon, nutmeg, sticky toffee pudding, espresso and creamy tiramisu with subtle hints of oak. 54.5% alc./vol. (109°proof)

Web. www.pussers.com **Producer:** Pusser's Rum, Tortola, British Virgin Isles. **UK distributor:** Malcolm Cowen Ltd, London. **Tel:** 020 8965 1937. **Email:** info@cowen.co.uk

RÉMY MARTIN GRAND CRU® COGNAC

When Rémy Martin founded his company in 1724 he was already an experienced producer of Cognac. He set out to make the Cognacs that carried his name amongst the finest. This tradition is still pursued at Rémy Martin with all the company's blends being made exclusively from Cognacs using grapes from only the two premiers crus, Grande and Petite Champagne. The wine is double distilled on the lees in small stills and aged in small oak casks from the nearby Limousin forest.

Rémy Martin V.S.O.P., a blend of 45% Petite Champagne and 55% Grande Champagne, is also the world's best selling V.S.O.P. with annual sales of 1.5 million cases, while Rémy Martin V.S. Grand Cru is one of the few to be made solely using grapes from the Petite Champagne region.

Rémy Martin is an ideal Cognac to use in cocktails whether you choose the V.S. or V.S.O.P. Both feature lots of rich, ripe, fruit and vanilla with tasting notes including fruitcake and stewed fruit.
40% alc./vol. (80°proof)

Web: www.remy.com **Distiller:** Rémy Martin & Co SA, Cognac, France. **UK distributor:** Maxxium UK Ltd, Stirling, Scotland. **Tel:** 01786 430 500 **Email:** enquiries@maxxium.com

SAUZA® HORNITOS® TEQUILA

Sauza Hornitos Tequila is produced by a company founded by Don Cenobio Sauza in 1873 and built by three successive generations of the Sauza family. Sauza was the first Tequila to be internationally exported and remains a dominant brand in Tequila, Mexico. Unlike many of its competitors, Sauza Hornitos is made using 100% agave spirit, evidenced in the rich agave flavours found on its palate. It is classified a 'Reposado Tequila', indicating that it has benefited from a period of resting in oak and unusually, the production process involves baking the agave rather than steaming, giving this Tequila a slightly smoky flavour. Fittingly, the name 'Hornitos' means 'little ovens'.

The elegant and subtle but animated flavour of Sauza Hornitos is well suited to cocktails. Careful tasting reveals muscovado and marzipan, balanced by light, dry earthy, herby, grassy agave, cinnamon, ripe citrus and gingerbread. 38% alc./vol. (76°proof)

Web: www.sauzatequila.com **Producer:** Tequila Sauza, S.A. de C.V., Guadalajara, Jalisco, Mexico. **UK distributor:** Allied Domecq, Spirits & Wine (UK) Ltd, Horsham, West Sussex, RH12 1ST **Tel:** 01403 222 600 **Email:** mailbox@balance-spirits.com

SISCA® CREME DE CASSIS

At the beginning of the 50s the Mayor of Dijon, France, was Canon Felix Kir, a colourful politician. At official receptions he used to serve an aperitif made with Sisca Crème de Cassis from Dijon and a local white wine called Bourgogne Aligoté. Very quickly the drink became known as Canon Kir's aperitif, then Father Kir's aperitif and finally throughout the region as the 'Kir' aperitif.
The director of Lejay Lagoute, producers of Sisca Crème de Cassis, approached Canon Kir for authorisation to use his name. On 20th November 1951, the Canon gave the company rights to use his name for an advert for cassis and in March 1952, Lejay Lagoute registered the brand name of 'Kir'. So when making a Kir it would seem fitting to use Sisca.

Sisca Crème de Cassis is a richly flavoured blackcurrant liqueur that captures the fruit's freshness, making it ideally suited to use in a wide variety of cocktails, including the Cannon's namesake. 15% alc./vol. (30°proof)

Web: www.cassis.com **Producer:** Lejay Lagoute, Dijon, France.
UK distributor: Malcolm Cowen Ltd, London. **Tel:** 020 8965 1937
Email: info@cowen.co.uk

SOURZ SOUR APPLE® LIQUEUR

The combination of sweet and sour is one of the most popular in cooking and is key to many of the best and most classic cocktails. In these citrus fruit is balanced by sugar, whether as syrup or in a liqueur. However, it was only in the late nineties when the innovative Sourz Sour Apple liqueur was launched that this classic balance of flavours could be found on the bar shelf. Sourz Sour Apple has a refreshing, mouth puckering sweet and sour rich apple flavour. Its bright lime green colour and modern bell-shaped bottle are as audacious as its flavour. Sourz is also available in peach, pineapple and Tropical Blue flavours.

Sourz Sour Apple tastes of fresh, rich, ripe cooking apples with a clean citrus acidity and hints of marzipan, cinnamon, baked apples and a touch of honey. 15% alc./vol. (30°proof)

Producer: Munson Shaw Co, Deerfield, Illinois, USA. **UK distributor:** Maxxium UK Ltd, Stirling, Scotland. **Tel:** 01786 430 500 **Email:** enquiries@maxxium.com

SOUTHERN COMFORT®

Southern Comfort is over a hundred years old. In the 1860s New Orleans saloons commonly served harsh tasting American whiskey straight from the barrel. M.W. Heron, a local bar owner on Bourbon Street, experimented to soften his, producing the famous Southern Comfort recipe, which is said to consist of more than 100 secret ingredients and was originally served straight from the barrel. The scene on every bottle of Southern Comfort is entitled 'Home on the Mississippi' and was created in 1874 by Nathaniel Currier and James Ives, generally regarded as the finest lithographers of the 19th century. It depicts the Woodland Plantation, which was originally built as a sugar cane plantation and mill in 1834 and remains the last of the great plantation houses on the West Bank of the Mississippi River.

Southern Comfort's unique flavour includes hints of crème caramel, crème brûlé, banana milkshake, orange marmalade, lemon zest and honey. 35% alc./vol. (70°proof)

Web: www.southerncomfort.com **Producer:** Brown-Forman Beverages UK, St Louis, Missouri, USA. **UK distributor:** Bacardi-Martini, Southampton. **Tel:** 02380 318 084
Email: trade_enquiries@bacardi.com

STOLI RAZBERI®

Launched in the 1950s, Stolichnaya is made using winter wheat and glacial water. 'Stoli', as it is fondly known, is double distilled and filtered through charcoal made from young silver birch trees and pure quartz sand. The name comes from the Russian word 'Stolitsa' meaning 'capital'.

Stoli Razberi is made by blending Stolichnaya vodka with natural essence of raspberry to create a spirit that captures the natural flavours of the fruit while maintaining Stolichnaya's character.

Whilst Stoli Razberi has a rich raspberry flavour, the taste is complex with hints of boiled sweets, raspberry jam, cherries and vanilla milkshake. Its finish is dry with lasting cherry and raspberry notes.
37.5% alc./vol. (75°proof)

Web: www.stoli.com or www.in-the-spirit.co.uk
UK distributor: First Drinks Brands, Southampton.
Tel: 023 80 312000,
Email: contact@first-drinks-brands.co.uk

STOLI VANIL®

Launched in 1996, Stoli Vanil is one of the range of flavoured vodkas from Stolichnaya Genuine Russian vodka, the world's best selling brand of vodka. Amazingly Stolichnaya is refined twice, then filtered through quartz, Siberian birch charcoal and then quartz again. Natural extracts of Madagascan and Indonesian vanilla pods are blended with this pure but characterful vodka to produce Stoli Vanil.

Mixologists love using Stoli Vanil due to its richly, almost cream soda, vanilla-ed flavour which makes it extremely mixable with a wide range of other spirits, liqueurs and fruit juices.

37.5% alc./vol. (75°proof)

Web: www.stoli.com or www.in-the-spirit.co.uk
UK distributor: First Drinks Brands, Southampton.
Tel: 02380 312 000
Email: contact@first-drinks-brands.co.uk

TEICHENNÉ® BUTTERSCOTCH SCHNAPPS

A family owned distiller and liqueur producer, the Teichenné firm was founded in 1956 when Juan Teichenné Senaux launched his distillery in the small town of L'Arboç (40 miles south of Barcelona). Born in France, Mr. Teichenné had moved to Spain as part of the French wine industry's search for new production sources. In those early days, production was very small, concentrating on 'handmade' brandies and liqueurs for sale locally in the Penedès Region. Expansion did not start until the 70s, when Joan Teichenné Canals took over the business after his father's death. In the 80s Teichenné led the Spanish boom in liqueur schnapps.
These fruit liqueurs also opened doors to international markets which have grown significantly ever since. In the UK, Teichenné is most noted for its distinctive butterscotch schnapps, as well as peach and numerous other flavours.

Since its arrival in the UK in 1996, bartenders have raved over this flavoursome schnapps liqueur. Rich butterscotch and fudge with a hint of cinnamon, baked apple and nutmeg. 20% alc./vol. (40°proof)

Web: www.teichenne.com **Producer:** Teichenné S.A., Tarragona, Spain. **UK distributor:** Inspirit Brands, London. **Tel:** 020 7377 9457
Email: info@inspiritbrands.com

TEICHENNÉ® PEACH SCHNAPPS

In the eighties, when schnapps were just beginning to emerge as a new category of liqueur, Juan Teichenné led the way and Teichenné Peach Schnapps was one of the Spanish producer's original flavours. This fresh and approachable liqueur was quickly picked up by the world's bartenders and peach schnapps became a key ingredient in many contemporary classic cocktails.

While Teichenné have since developed their schnapps range to include a plethora of excellent new flavours, Teichenné Peach Schnapps remains one of the bestselling, illustrating its quality and mixability.

Teichenné Peach Schnapps has a rich nose of ripe peach skin and peach kernel, giving it a soft, succulent flavour which lightens on the palate.
20% alc./vol. (40° proof)

Web: www.teichenne.com Producer: Teichenné S.A., Tarragona, Spain. UK distributor: InSpirit Brands, London. Tel: 020 7377 9457
Email: info@inspiritbrands.com

WRAY & NEPHEW® WHITE OVERPROOF RUM

Wray & Nephew is the world's top selling, award winning, high strength rum. Any spirit equal to or over 57% alc/vol is termed "overproof". This unaged white rum is one such example.

Made by J Wray & Nephew, the oldest distilling company in Jamaica, this brand is more than just a rum, it is an intrinsic part of Jamaica's culture, heritage and tradition. Wray & Nephew is a staple in every Jamaican household where it is used as part of medicine, ritual and everyday living and accounts for over 90% of all rum consumed on the island.

Wray & Nephew has a wonderful, fruity natural aroma with a rich molasses top note and hints of pineapple, banana, orange and coconut. Although the product is strong, when used correctly the brand's complex bouquet and delivery of unique flavour characteristics make it an excellent base for cocktails and a must in punches.
63% alc./vol. (126° proof)

Web: www.rum.co.uk Producer: J. Wray & Nephew Ltd, Kingston, Jamaica. UK distributor: J. Wray & Nephew (UK) Ltd, 3rd Floor, 52-54 Southwark Street, London, SE1-1UN Tel: 020 7378 8858
Email. info@rum.co.uk

XANTÉ® LIQUEUR

Pronounced 'zant-tay', this liqueur is based on Cognac and flavoured with natural pear essence. Launched at the end of 1995, Xanté is a modern liqueur not only in its presentation, but in its not being overly sweet, only containing 170 grams of sugar per litre. It was created by Richard Heinrich, the fourth generation of distillers and blenders at Maison Heinrich, a family firm established in 1894. Originally from Alsace, the Heinrich family moved to Belgium where they re-established their business and reputation for blending fine liqueurs. In 1997 the V&S Group (the owners of Absolut vodka) acquired rights to the brand and formula, allowing Xanté to be launched in other markets besides Scandinavia where it has already proved hugely successful.

Xanté is rich in flavour with hints of perfumed pear (almost pear marmalade) and spice, particularly cinnamon, fortified with Cognac. A beautiful balance of flavours with just enough sugar – not a sweetie. 38% alc./vol. (76°proof)

Web: www.xante.info **Producer:** The Xanté Company (V&S Group), Stockholm, Sweden. **UK distributor:** Fuel Brands Ltd, Stirling, Scotland. **Tel:** 01786 451 168. **Email:** g.shon@fuelbrands.co.uk

ZUBROWKA® (BISON GRASS) VODKA

Pronounced 'Zhu-bruff-ka', this Polish vodka is flavoured with Hierochloe Odorata grass, a blade of which is immersed in each bottle, giving the vodka a translucent greenish colour and a subtle flavour. The area where this grass grows in the Bialowieza Forest is the habitat of wild Polish Bison – so, although the bison don't eat this variety of grass, the vodka has the nickname 'Bison vodka'. The Hierochloe Odorata grass is harvested by hand in early summer when its flavour is best, then dried, cut to size and bound in bunches for delivery to the Bialystok distillery. The vodka is forced through the grass to impart the aromatic flavour to the vodka in a similar method to the way espresso coffee machines force water through coffee.

Herby, grassy with flavours of citrus, vanilla, lavender, tobacco, cold jasmine tea, caffè latte and hints of dry chocolate/vanilla. This subtle and delicately flavoured vodka is extremely mixable. 40% alc./vol. (80°proof)

Producer: Polmos Bialystok, Bialystok, Poland. **UK distributor:** Marblehead Brand Development, Glasgow, Scotland. **Tel:** 0141 955 9091 **Email:** information@marblehead.uk.com

PITCHER COCKTAILS

Turning long drinks designed for serving over ice in a Collins glass into a pitcher (jug) cocktail is easy. Simply measure how many Collins glasses of water it takes to fill your pitcher and multiply the glass recipe by that number.

Cocktails where the original recipe requires shaking should be made by simply pouring the ingredients into a pitcher and then stirring with ice. I also recommend filling your glasses with fresh ice prior to pouring from the pitcher so if possible use a pitcher with a lip that retains the ice while pouring. Cocktails served in this manner are the perfect accompaniment to summer barbeques or at parties. The following cocktails are ideally suited to being served in pitchers.

ESSENTIALS

WITH THE TEN SPIRITS AND LIQUEURS ILLUSTRATED ON THE INSIDE BACK COVER OF THIS GUIDE, A FEW MIXERS, SOME FRESH FRUIT AND A HANDFUL OF KITCHEN BASICS YOU CAN MAKE ALL 200 COCKTAILS ON THE OPPOSITE PAGE - THE RECIPES FOR WHICH CAN BE FOUND IN THIS GUIDE. LEAVE THE FLAP OPEN WHILE TURNING TO THE RECIPE.

ESSENTIAL SPIRITS & LIQUEURS

| ABSOLUT VODKA | PLYMOUTH GIN | HAVANA CLUB LIGHT RUM | SAUZA HORNITOS TEQUILA | COINTREAU | KAHLUA COFFEE LIQUEUR | GRAND MARNIER | CINZANO DRY VERMOUTH | CINZANO ROSSO VERMOUTH | BOLS APRICOT BRANDY LIQUEUR |

ESSENTIAL JUICES & MIXERS

| CRANBERRY JUICE | ORANGE JUICE | PRESSED APPLE JUICE | GRAPEFRUIT JUICE | PINEAPPLE JUICE | SODA WATER | COLA | GINGER ALE / GINGER BEER | BITTER LEMON | TONIC WATER |

FRIDGE & LARDER ESSENTIALS

| SUGAR (GOMME) SYRUP | GRENADINE SYRUP | LIME CORDIAL | ANGUSTORA AROMATIC BITTERS | PIPER-HEIDSIECK BRUT CHAMPAGNE | FRESH LIMES |

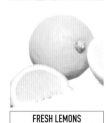     

| FRESH LEMONS | FRESH MINT | FRESH RASPBERRIES | MARASCHINO CHERRIES | VANILLA PODS | DOUBLE CREAM |

 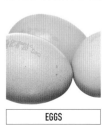    

| MILK | EGGS | SUGAR CUBES | RUNNY HONEY | FILTER & ESPRESSO COFFEE | EARL GREY TEA |

NOT FORGETTING... ICE - THE MOST IMPORTANT COCKTAIL INGREDIENT